NEW PERSPECTIVES ON THE 'CIVIL WARS' IN MEDIEVAL SCANDINAVIA

COMPARATIVE PERSPECTIVES ON MEDIEVAL HISTORY

VOLUME 1

General Editors
Hans Jacob Orning, *Universitetet i Oslo*
Grzegorz Pac, *Uniwersytet Warszawski*
Louisa Taylor, *University of the Highlands and Islands*

Editorial Board
Jenny Benham, *University of Cardiff*
Nora Berend, *University of Cambridge*
Warren C. Brown, *California Institute of Technology*
Michael Borgolte, *Humboldt-Universität zu Berlin*
Wojtek Jezierski, *Göteborgs universitet*
Chris Wickham, *University of Oxford*

New Perspectives on the 'Civil Wars' in Medieval Scandinavia

Edited by
HANS JACOB ORNING, KIM ESMARK, AND
JÓN VIÐAR SIGURÐSSON

BREPOLS

British Library Cataloguing in Publication Data
A catalogue record for this book is available from the British Library.

© 2024, Brepols Publishers n.v., Turnhout, Belgium.

All rights reserved. No part of this publication may be reproduced, stored in a retrieval system, or transmitted, in any form or by any means, electronic, mechanical, photocopying, recording, or otherwise without the prior permission of the publisher.

D/2024/0095/64
ISBN 978-2-503-60150-2
eISBN 978-2-503-60151-9
DOI 10.1484/M.CPMH-EB.5.130773

Printed in the EU on acid-free paper.

Table of Contents

List of Illustrations — 7

Acknowledgements — 9

1. Network Dynamics, Conflict as Context, and Internal War. Outline of a Scandinavian Medieval Case for Comparison
Kim ESMARK, Hans Jacob ORNING, and Jón Viðar SIGURÐSSON — 11

Part I
Case Studies

Introduction to Part One
Kim ESMARK, Hans Jacob ORNING, and Jón Viðar SIGURÐSSON — 37

2. Networks and *flokkar*. The Civil Wars in Norway c. 1134–1163
Jón Viðar SIGURÐSSON — 41

3. Messy Conflict. Socio-political Competition and War in Denmark c. 1128–1137
Kim ESMARK — 97

4. Constant Crisis in Norway, 1202–1208
Hans Jacob ORNING — 165

Part II
Thematic Analyses

Introduction to Part Two
Jenny BENHAM, Lars HERMANSON, and Bjørn POULSEN — 215

5. Spatial Practices in the Twelfth and Early Thirteenth Century Scandinavian Power Game
Bjørn Poulsen   217

6. The Memory of Margrethe. Noblewomen as Power Agents in Multi-Party Conflicts c. 1120–1170
Lars Hermanson   265

7. Peacemaking and Negotiations in High Medieval Scandinavia
Jenny Benham   309

Part III
European Comparisons

Introduction to Part Three
Gerd Althoff, Warren C. Brown, and Stephen D. White   343

8. Political Networks in Conflict. A German Perspective
Gerd Althoff   345

9. War Stories. Re-Thinking Rebellion in Anglo-Norman and Angevin England, 1066 to 1217
Stephen D. White   371

10. Scandinavia in Medieval Europe
Warren C. Brown   413

Index   429

List of Illustrations

Jón Viðar Sigurðsson

| Figure 2.1. | Genealogical tree of Magnus Barefoot. | 62 |
| Figure 2.2. | The Snorrunga family. | 67 |

Kim Esmark

Figure 3.1.	Main regions and localities mentioned in the text.	100
Figure 3.2.	Key political actors discussed in the text.	111
Figure 3.3.	The double marriage alliance of 1131/33.	134
Figure 3.4.	King Niels' marriage with Ulvhild, c. 1130.	141

Hans Jacob Orning

| Figure 4.1. | Scandinavia in the Civil War period. | 168 |

Bjørn Poulsen

| Figure 5.1. | Scandinavia in the Civil War period. | 220 |

Lars Hermanson

Figure 6.1.	Genealogical tree of Stenkil.	273
Figure 6.2.	Ingrid Ragvaldsdatter's family.	279
Figure 6.3.	Genealogical tree of Sverker the Elder.	287

Acknowledgements

This book is the product of the research project *The Civil Wars in Medieval Scandinavia in a Comparative Perspective* at the Center for Advanced Studies (CAS) in Oslo in 2017–18. The grant from CAS made it possible to assemble a group of scholars in an old villa in the centre of Oslo, cut off from ordinary obligations, devoting our time fully to research. It has taken time to finish this book, but the main bulk of work was done in spring 2018, when the contributors to this book stayed for all or most of the time in Oslo. Kim, Jón Viðar and Hans Jacob have led the book project. Jenny Benham, Gerd Althoff, Stephen D. White, Bjørn Poulsen, and Lars Hermanson were visiting scholars for one to six months.

We would like to thank CAS for providing an ideal environment and an extremely friendly atmosphere for doing this project. We also thank the scholars who were present in the first phase of the project in autumn 2017 — Henrik Vigh, Frederik Rosen, Ebrahim Afsah, Øyvind Østerud and Helle Vogt, who were vital for developing the theoretical framework that we have applied in this book (see *Medieval and Modern Civil Wars*, ed. by Jón Viðar Sigurðsson and Hans Jacob Orning (Leiden: Brill 2021)). We are also grateful to the Research Council of Norway for funding a project with a related topic, where Max Naderer, Hilde Nysether, and Louisa Taylor were important contributors in recruitment positions.

Huge thanks to Lars Kjær — the peer reviewer who at his own request turned unanonymous — and gave very useful response from a sceptic's viewpoint, and to Brepols' shepherd Chris Wickham for impressive feedback on everything from details to bigger issues. Our home departments — the Department of Archaeology, Conservation and History at the University of Oslo and the Department for Communication and Arts at the University of Roskilde — have been inspiring and supportive working places all along. Brepols, with Rosie Bonté and Maria Whelan, has, as usual been a most valuable sparring partner for finalizing this book. Jonas Adrian Kvarø Lønne drew the maps and figures, Kate Gilbert and Sarah Thomas proofread the text, and Victoria Ciobanu Austveg made the index — a huge thanks to all.

Oslo, 14 February 2024
Hans Jacob Orning, Kim Esmark, and Jón Viðar Sigurðsson

KIM ESMARK, HANS JACOB ORNING, AND
JÓN VIÐAR SIGURÐSSON

1. Network Dynamics, Conflict as Context, and Internal War

Outline of a Scandinavian Medieval Case for Comparison

In the twelfth and thirteenth centuries the still loosely organized Scandinavian kingdoms of Denmark, Norway, and Sweden experienced prolonged periods of violent succession dispute and armed factional struggle. In all three realms rival members of royal networks fought each other for the throne(s), backed up by shifting constellations of lay and ecclesiastical magnates, semi-professionalized warbands, rural and urban communities, and allies abroad. In the course of the fighting, kingships were temporarily divided, re-organized or subjected to joint rule among competing contenders. The 'civil wars', as modern historians have commonly termed these conflicts,[1] commenced almost simultaneously across Scandinavia in the years around 1130. In Norway and Sweden, the struggles continued with varying intensity until the middle of the thirteenth century, whereas in Denmark they were ended in 1157 only to erupt again in 1241.

---

1 Equivalent terms used in Scandinavian historiography: dynastic struggles, dynastic strife, dynastic civil wars, throne disputes, kings' wars, internal struggles.

> **Kim Esmark** • (kesmark@ruc.dk) is associate professor in the Department of Communication and Arts, University of Roskilde.
>
> **Hans Jacob Orning** • (h.j.orning@iakh.uio.no) is professor of medieval history in the Department of Archaeology, Conservation, and History, University of Oslo.
>
> **Jón Viðar Sigurðsson** • (j.v.sigurdsson@iakh.uio.no) is professor of medieval history in the Department of Archaeology, Conservation, and History, University of Oslo.

New Perspectives on the 'Civil Wars' in Medieval Scandinavia, ed. by Hans Jacob Orning, Kim Esmark, and Jón Viðar Sigurðsson, Comparative Perspectives on Medieval History, 1 (Turnhout: Brepols, 2024), pp. 11–34

This book is about the Scandinavian high medieval 'civil wars'.[2] What we present is not a comprehensive, chronologically ordered rehearsal of the general political or military history of events, which has already been treated extensively by generations of Danish, Norwegian, and Swedish historians. Rather, the purpose of our work may be described as exploratory. What we attempt to do is identify and traverse new interpretive paths in an otherwise well-trodden historical territory by applying comparative and interdisciplinary tools in a mixture of case studies and thematic analyses.

Throughout the nineteenth and deep into the twentieth century most Scandinavian medieval historians have tended (much like their colleagues in wider Europe) to describe and explain internal conflicts and wars within a predominantly *national* and implicitly *state-centred* politico-constitutional framework.[3] The 'civil wars' have been approached as basically internal conflicts, only marginally influenced by neighbouring polities or powers. This is despite the fact that royal and aristocratic networks were widely connected across borders (through kinship, marriage, and friendship) and appear to have strategized from the point of view of dynastic rather than proto-national concerns.[4] It is also the case that the Scandinavian 'civil wars' display many micro-structural similarities (differences notwithstanding) to, say, the wars of Stephen's reign in England and the internal struggles in the kingdom of Germany during the investiture conflict.

As for the state-centred framework, the 'civil war period' has commonly been regarded as a critically disruptive, but historically necessary stage in the transition from Viking realm to Christian kingdom, from decentralized 'feuding society' to institutionalized authority and organized government.[5] By thus inscribing the civil war period in a grand narrative of incipient state formation and nation-building (informed, implicitly, by neo-Hobbesian pessimist anthropology), the wars have often been classified and understood backwards through the analytical camera lens of teleological state idealism.[6]

---

2 On the difficult concept of 'civil war', see Sambanis, 'What is Civil War?'; Armitage, *Civil Wars*; Jón Viðar Sigurðsson and Orning, 'Introduction'.

3 This is obviously a generalizing picture, and it is beyond the scope or purpose of this chapter to provide an exhaustive overview of the massive historiography on the subject, but see for some influential examples Arup, *Danmarks historie*; Koch, *Kongemagt og kirke*; Fenger, *Kirker bygges alle vegne*; Holmsen, *Norges historie*; Helle, *Norge blir en stat*; Lunden, *Norge under Sverreætten*; Helle (ed.), *The Cambridge History of Scandinavia I. Prehistory to 1520*; Bagge, *From Viking Stronghold to Christian Kingdom*.

4 For commendable highlighting of the inter-Nordic aspect, though, see for instance Lind, 'De russiske ægteskaber'; Sawyer, 'The "Civil Wars" Revisited'; Esmark and others (eds), *Nordic Elites II*.

5 See footnote 3.

6 For critical discussion of these issues in a wider comparative and theoretical perspective, see Comaroff, 'Reflections'; Sahlins, *The Western Illusion*; Cheyette, 'The Invention of the State'; Bourdieu, 'Rethinking the State'.

In the present volume we take a different approach. The book evolves out of a larger collaborative, interdisciplinary research project on medieval and modern 'civil wars', in which Scandinavian medievalists worked closely with experts in English, French, and German medieval conflict, as well as with anthropologists and political scientists studying civil war in contemporary settings.[7] By thus building on comparative discussions of internal war in wider medieval Europe as well as modern intrastate conflict, we seek to escape some of the limitations of inherited historiographical frameworks. Most of us were already working together in various constellations on related projects on disputing practices and social elites in medieval Scandinavia. Many of the basic assumptions about power, conflict, culture, and socio-political action which inform the present book's analyses thus reach back to and indeed build on these earlier studies.[8] We are not reporting on a completed investigation, however, and the ambition is not to claim a well-rounded synthesis. Borrowing a formulation from anthropologist John Comaroff's reflection (in the first volume to appear from the project, *Medieval and Modern Civil Wars. A Comparative Perspective*) on comparison as methodological strategy, this book is more readily described as an attempt to 'trouble old truisms and call for fresh perspectives'.[9]

In essence, what we aim to do is *set up a case for comparison*: by explicating a specific Scandinavian experience in the light of comparative insights, we hope to include Denmark, Norway, and Sweden in the general discussion of medieval 'civil war' and to stimulate reflections on differences and similarities between the Northern world and wider Europe in the Middle Ages, both in this volume itself and elsewhere.

In terms of methodology, we build our case by focusing on the *practical workings* and underlying *socio-political dynamics* of political competition and armed struggle in twelfth and early thirteenth century Scandinavia: What sort of conflicts were these so-called 'civil wars'? Who was fighting and for what? What kind of social structures — dynastic marriage bonds, networks of family, friends, and followers, regional law communities, etc. — provided the framework for political and military action? Which types of resources were employed and competed for? How was aggression framed and justified in the face of public opinion? Who

---

7 See Acknowledgements. Publications emerging from the project so far include: Jón Viðar Sigurðsson and Orning (eds), *Medieval and Modern Civil Wars*; Orning and Østerud, *Krig uten stat*; and *Collegium Medievale*, 32.2 (2019), special issue.
8 Jón Viðar Sigurðsson, *Chieftains and Power in the Icelandic Commonwealth*; Orning and others (eds), *Gaver, ritualer, konflikter*; Esmark and others (eds), *Disputing Strategies*; Jezierski and others (eds), *Rituals, Performatives, and Political Order*; Poulsen and others (eds), *Nordic Elites I*; Esmark and others (eds), *Nordic Elites II*; Jezierski and others (eds), *Nordic Elites III*.
9 Comaroff, 'Reflections', p. 280.

profited from violent strife and who suffered? How did topography and infrastructure shape the processes of war? Which forces and mechanisms triggered and/or contained conflict? How did hostilities interrelate across the borders between kingdoms? How did alliance formation, mediation, peacemaking, and actual warfare play out, viewed from the perspective of the actors involved, and how did it affect the world in which it took place?

In the book we approach these multifarious questions from different angles, moving from extended case-studies of selected phases of the 'civil wars' (Part One), through thematically organized analyses of particular sub-topics (Part Two), to positioning the Scandinavian experience in a wider European comparative framework (Part Three). In the course of our work we have necessarily drawn on a wide range of empirical data, theories, concepts and analytical takes, emerging from the project's joint comparisons of various historical settings, from medieval European kingdoms through post-cold war 'new wars' to civil war in modern day Guinea-Bissau and Afghanistan.[10] From these interdisciplinary and cross-historical explorations we have collected a box of assorted analytical tools and heuristics to *think about power and internal conflict in regnal polities without centralized government*. Two specific overarching conceptions in particular crystallized as a sort of 'common ground' for the present book's investigations: *network dynamics* and *conflict as context*.

Network Dynamics

The main thesis underlying our work concerns the fundamental issue of what the 'civil wars' were all about. Rather than seeking to explain internal political conflict by reference to political 'parties' sharing opposing 'ideologies' or by ascribing agency and purpose to reified institutions and groups like 'the Crown', 'the Church' or 'the aristocracy' (as former historiographical paradigms would have it), we start from the assumption that the medieval Scandinavian 'game of thrones' was basically played out between competing networks and factions of landowning magnates.[11] What was at stake was the distribution of power, rank, and resources among the social elites. Competition centred on gaining access to and maintaining hold of various *points of accumulation*: landed estates, bishoprics, royal and

---

10 See in particular the contributions and literature references in Jón Viðar Sigurðsson and Orning (eds), *Medieval and Modern Civil Wars*.
11 The idea of opposing political ideals as a cause of the Danish medieval civil wars, which is normally associated with the early twentieth century 'Weibull thesis', has recently been revived in a new vigorous form by Lars Kjær, who proposes to 'pay much more attention to the stated principles of political actors' rather than search for 'material interests of the competing kin-networks' (Kjær, 'Political Conflict'). The present book obviously pursues the very approach denounced by Kjær.

ecclesiastical offices, military strongholds, lordships of towns, earldoms and other regional commands, positions as head of important families, etc. — as well as the royal throne itself, of course.[12] Some such accumulation points might look like genuine *officia* in centrally ordered hierarchies, but are better conceived of in this context as semi-autonomous patrimonially controlled entities: the big man does not owe his rank to his office as earl or bishop; he is earl or bishop because he is a big man and thus tends to administer his office in accordance with his political, not his institutional, status.

One indispensable asset in the competition was the capacity to establish and maintain networks of kinsmen, friends, patrons, and followers, who could be mobilized in case of need and called upon to provide local/regional presence and support.[13] Moreover, successful participation in this type of power game required a tactical and strategic sense for 'investing' cleverly in multiple loyalties, for anticipating moves of rival factions, and for adjusting to turns and conjunctures in the political field at large: who is currently on the rise, whose star is fading? *Network dynamics* thus constituted the defining feature of the conflicts we study. The structures of political contest and conflict were fundamentally rooted in ever-shifting configurations of elite networks, based on personal bonds and perceived mutual interests. In a sense power politics quite simply *was* networking. To operate in this space, therefore, political agents (kings, lay and ecclesiastical magnates, clerical communities, townsmen, etc.) needed first to possess *social power*, defined by A.-J. Bijsterveld as 'the ability to establish and control social networks of mutually obliging relations through social mechanisms' (gift exchange, marriage, dispute settlement, etc.).[14]

The *patrimonial* character of social power and network politics contained an important 'fractal aspect'. Through bonds with powerful patrons, lesser men achieved the capacity to provide patronage to dependants of their own. The creation and mobilization of networks thus potentially reached down into the wider fabric of society, the social strata of householders, guildsmen, local law communities, etc., and worked through interactions along both vertical and horizontal axes. From a king-centred perspective such conditions might appear as signs of blurred and disrupted lines of authority and command. However, the patrimonial logic should be

---

12 The notion of accumulation point borrowed from Orning and others, 'Constant Crisis', p. 14.
13 On these types of social bonds in a specifically Scandinavian high medieval context, see Jón Viðar Sigurðsson, *Viking Friendship*; Esmark and others, 'Kith and Kin'; Hermanson and others, 'Lords and Followers'; Hermanson and others, 'Friends and Allies'.
14 Bijsterveld, 'Memoria and Nobility Research', pp. 211–30. Bijsterveld developed his notion of social power in a discussion of historical sociologist Michael Mann's typology of power sources and its relevance in a medieval context. See for a practical application of the concept, Esmark, 'Social Power and Conversion of Capital', pp. 283–303.

acknowledged as a structuring principle in itself (an issue where political scientists often have overlooked the insights of Max Weber).[15]

But what about kings and kingship, then? Did not most if not all of the medieval Scandinavian 'civil wars' revolve around royal succession disputes? Although the wealth and prestige of Scandinavian monarchies in our period never compared to those of, say, England, France, or Germany, the powers exercised by Danish, Norwegian and even Swedish kings were evidently important — hence constantly competed for. The royal throne constituted a key point for accumulation and distribution of all types of power and legitimacy, while royal courts worked as focus points for political interaction and dispute between aristocratic factions. But Scandinavian kings of the civil war period did not yet possess the sort of sacred aura that (theoretically, at least) would come to place rulers of later times above society and the quarrels of lesser men, and they did not assume an autonomous, directive role vis à vis society. Whatever rudimentary administration kings might lean on, it 'existed alongside that of the nobility, rather than above it'.[16] In short, royal power was embedded within the social system and its norms and workings, not abstracted from it. The fact that all Scandinavian royal families intermarried systematically not only with other royal or princely houses, but also with important aristocratic kindreds both home and abroad, is but one expression of this condition.

Magnate networks and factions usually operated politically by associating themselves with a leading figure within the royal kindred, a potential prospect for the throne, whom they supported against claims from rival pretenders. Whichever member of the royal family aimed to win kingship, on the other hand, was destined to rely on the backing of one or more of these groups of magnates.[17] Struggles for the crowns of Denmark, Norway or Sweden were therefore driven by aristocratic networks as much as by kings and members of royal kindreds. Such struggles might assume genuine 'transregnal' character. Around 1200, for instance, the Swedish throne was disputed by two factions. On one side stood King Sverker, son of former Swedish king Karl Sverkerson (killed 1167). Sverker had been installed as ruler in 1196 by the mighty Earl Birger Brosa, whose daughter Sverker then married. Besides the Swedish earl, Sverker's run for the crown also received support from his former father-in-law, the Danish magnate Ebbe Sunesen and his brothers, all powerful war leaders. The opposite

---

15 Jón Viðar Sigurðsson, *Viking Friendship*; Jón Viðar Sigurðsson and Vigh, 'Who is the Enemy? Multipolar Micropolitics'.
16 Line, *Kingship and State Formation*, p. 472.
17 The observation that twelfth century kings of Sweden 'were forced to make alliances with powerful noble families', because they 'had little effective power outside the region where their own inherited lands lay' (Line, *Kingship and State Formation*, p. 473), applies (in various forms) to the other Scandinavian realms as well.

coalition congealed around four sons of another previous Swedish ruler, King Knut Eriksson (d. 1195), who enjoyed the military backing of the 'Birkibeinar', a Norwegian warband (*flokkr*), which already for decades had been fighting for the crown of Norway.

At least in this sense, then, power structures in the Scandinavian region do seem to have shared many basic traits with those found in other, better-described European realms of the early and central Middle Ages: rather than emanating from one specific royal or king-centred source political power was 'claimed and negotiated through the collective action of a series of overlapping and interleaving groups on a hierarchy of public stages'.[18] Attributes normally associated with 'the king' (or 'the state') were diffused and shared in complex ways among numerous groups and individuals throughout society and across individual polities. Infrastructure and communication logistics, moreover, necessarily made the distribution of power polycentric and any attempt by kings to 'rule' effectively remained dependent on local powerholders. Like Germany at around the same time the Scandinavian kingdoms were in effect 'polycentric realms'.[19] In this decentralized world there was no routinized penetration of society by agents or organs distinct from it. In short, kings of Denmark, Norway, and Sweden essentially deployed *the same powers* as other magnates in their realms, albeit on a larger scale.[20] They were 'lord-kings', not public governors.[21] To analyse internal war from the particular and particularistic viewpoint of kingship consequently distorts the picture. At its worst, the historian ends up participating in the odd kind of un-scientific 'tendency to ruler-worship' rightly criticized by Timothy Reuter.[22]

What about contemporary *ideals* of monarchy, then, which surely served to elevate the office of king? These were, as emphasized by Björn

---

18 Innes, *State and Society*, p. 140.
19 Reuter, 'The Medieval German Sonderweg?', p. 190.
20 See for a European comparative contextualization of these issues, Davies, 'The Medieval State'.
21 The term is borrowed from Bisson, *The Crisis*, p. 9, and passim. In his kaleidoscopic survey of the exercise of power in eleventh and twelfth century Europe Bisson does not discuss Scandinavia, and his gloomy vision of a post-Carolingian world submerged in violence and disruption until the uneasy emergence, from *c.* 1200 onwards, of centralized 'government', does not square with the present book's basic assumptions and arguments about power and order. The Scandinavian 'civil wars' were not local examples of Bisson's crisis (see also Riches, 'Review'). However, Bisson's description of monarchs such as King Henry I of England and many others, whom traditional institutional history used to hail as early state builders, seems in many ways to match the kings of the Nordic realms in the same period: rather than conceiving of kingship as an office in the service of higher societal goals, these rulers first of all focused on maintaining personal power, cultivating loyalties in those with whom they shared the proceeds of their lordship, and disciplining the unfaithful or trying to do so.
22 Reuter, 'The Medieval German Sonderweg?', p. 204.

Weiler in a sweeping comparative study which also incorporates Scandinavian evidence, surely 'no mere ornaments'. Values and expectations possessed real 'normative force'.[23] But the shared conception that kings should be pious, just, equitable, warlike, etc. was also abstract, flexible, and subject to interpretation and negotiation, especially in situations of succession strife or heated competition for the throne. Thus, opposing parties easily agreed on norms, but when evaluating the actions and character of a specific ruler or royal claimant, purpose and interest often made them arrive at contradictory conclusions. If ideals, according to Weiler, were 'foundational', they were also *functional*, something (to borrow a phrase of Stephen D. White's) with which rulers and magnates *did* (or tried to do) things.[24]

Returning to the logic of network dynamics, it needs stressing that when we talk about 'networks' and 'factions', we are not hinting at permanent, clearly-delimited groups, but fluctuating, intersecting socio-political formations. The competition between these formations is best understood as a sort of 'multipolar micropolitics'. Most people of the upper social strata in high medieval Scandinavia would be associated with several overlapping networks and criss-crossing groups. They would be subjects of both a king and one or more aristocratic lords; they would share bonds of blood and friendship with several groups and individuals; if sufficiently powerful they would lead their own band of armed retainers and shine as patrons of private churches, *Hausklöster* or town communities; through marriage, their family network would sometimes extend into those of kindreds from other kingdoms; they would probably also share some kind of local or regional affiliation focused on the community of the assembly, etc. In other words, most would potentially have loyalties to and experience the pressures from many sides at the same time. In situations of escalating tension, individuals and groups would have to evaluate the options available and the strength of particular bonds and obligations. Often, dilemmas easily arose. Bonds linking high ranking princes and magnates across distant realms and regions possibly worked somewhat differently in this respect than the face-to-face ties of smaller networks focused around a local patron or assembly. For the big men, multiple loyalties made it difficult to count

---

23 Weiler, *Paths to Kingship*, p. 410. See, in this vein, also Kjær, 'Political Conflict'.
24 White, *Re-Thinking Kinship and Feudalism*, p. xii (paraphrasing Bourdieu, *Outline*, p. 35). Contrary to assumptions held by much classic Scandinavian historiography, nobles, therefore, did not *automatically* oppose attempts to strengthen royal power. As argued for the case of Sweden (but applying to Norway and Denmark as well), 'magnate networks' might cooperate with kings in centralizing authority and building new institutions, if their position allowed them to profit from it, but 'they also hindered the process when it endangered their own access to the wealth of the kingdom, in other words, their participation in controlling those resources' (Line, *Kingship and State Formation*, p. 150).

on their followers — and necessary for them to take account of these followers' interests and counsel.

Sometimes those taking part in armed conflict would have to confront opponents whom they would otherwise regard, under different circumstances, as friends, allies, or even kinsmen. In many cases enemies would go into battle knowing that sooner or later they would probably have to live together again as friends. An army would lay siege to a town, while already planning to establish bonds with the townsmen afterwards. We need not succumb to functionalism to see that in practice such overlaps often had the effect of restraining the extent and nature of violence. Individuals caught in the middle could hardly support one friend or family member against other friends or relatives, but rather had to intercede and try to establish peace between them.[25]

To some extent adversaries in dynastic wars might also find themselves united by common class interests. This, too, probably worked to contain the level of aggression and the extent of plundering and destruction, and to minimize the kind of 'radical othering' that usually is a precondition for warfare aimed at outright destruction or annihilation of the opponent. In this context the issue of whether recruitment of mercenaries or lower-class warriors from outside established elite networks may have made internal warfare more uncompromising deserves attention.[26]

A further implication of the structure of overlapping groups was the recurrent switching of allegiances. Defection, retraction of faith, and the fractionalization of groups were common features of these conflicts, though concealed or at least covered by polyphonic discourses on loyalty, betrayal, honour, shame, reciprocity, and obligation. Efforts to shape perceptions and memories of what went on in the power game were therefore an integral part of the game itself. Nobody could play as they wished without bothering about norms and conventions. Strategies, actions, and aspirations would receive instant evaluation by all involved as well as observers and bystanders and therefore had to be framed, as far as possible, in the guise of collectively approved values and outlooks. Our written sources — sagas, histories, legends, skaldic poetry, charters, etc. — were all important tools in such interpretative struggles.[27]

Often overlapping bonds, fractionalization, and side-switching made it difficult to circumscribe the borders or front lines of a given conflict: who precisely was fighting whom at a particular moment and who or

---

25 Jón Viðar Sigurðsson, *Viking Friendship*; Jón Viðar Sigurðsson and Vigh, 'Who is the Enemy? Multipolar Micropolitics'.
26 Jón Viðar Sigurðsson, *Viking Friendship*; Jón Viðar Sigurðsson and Vigh, 'Who is the Enemy? Multipolar Micropolitics'.
27 For discussions of these issues, see Jezierski and others (eds), *Nordic Elites III*; Esmark, 'Spinning the Revolt'; Esmark, 'Just Rituals'.

what exactly did they think they were fighting for? One conflict or war, furthermore, easily provoked or spilled over into other conflicts or wars, thereby complicating the question of when struggles actually had begun and when or how they could be considered concluded.[28] This leads us to the second main guiding idea underlying our work, that of conflict as context.

Conflict as Context

In Scandinavian historiography 'civil wars' are usually assumed to have had a fairly clear beginning and end. In Denmark the years of internal strife started off on 7 January 1131 when King Niels' son Magnus killed his cousin and rival Knud Lavard, and was brought to a close at the battle of Grathe Moor 23 October 1157. In Norway the civil war period opened in 1134 with the battle of Färlev and ended 24 May 1240, when King Skule Bardsson was killed. In Sweden exact chronologies are harder to establish, but whether one chooses the 1130s or the 1150s as a starting point, the period of successive dynastic wars between the Erik and the Sverker families lasted until King Valdemar Birgersson's ascent to the throne in 1250. Within these chronological frames of internal unrest, a qualitatively distinct sociopolitical condition, characterized by unusual violence and disruption, supposedly predominated. The fact that only a minority of Scandinavian kings during the period died a natural death — most were either murdered, killed in battle, or driven into exile — is often taken as the most patent expression of this condition. This picture of a distinct 'civil war condition', objectively demarcated in essence and in time from previous and subsequent periods of relative peace and stability, seems to echo the views of certain medieval clerical authors. A Danish chronicler writing c. 1140 blamed the outbreak of hostilities in 1131 on the Devil, who 'sowed such great discord among the Danes that ever since Christianity took root in Denmark there has been no greater tribulation for the clergy and the people'.[29] Around 1180 the Norwegian cleric Theodoricus Monachus, who cited Lucan's *De Bello civili*, chose to end his history of Norway with the death of King Sigurd the Crusader in 1130, because he did not wish to write about the dark ages that followed:

> [I] am of the strong opinion that it would be unseemly to put on record for our descendants crimes, murders, perjuries, parricides, desecrations

---

28 Jón Viðar Sigurðsson, *Viking Friendship*; Jón Viðar Sigurðsson and Vigh, 'Who is the Enemy? Multipolar Micropolitics'.
29 'Chronicon Roskildensis', p. 26, 'tantam discordiam inter Danos seminauit, quod, ex quo Christianitas in Dania inleuit, maior tribulacio cleri et plebis non est facta'.

of sanctuaries, disdain for God, pillaging of the clergy as much as the entire populace, abductions of women, and all the other atrocities which would take too long to list. These have flowed abundantly as though into one gutter since the death of this King Sigurd.[30]

Clerical authors obviously had their reasons, both ideological and in terms of institutional interest, for strongly condemning armed struggles that involved the throne — the prime protector of the Church — and for doing so in such an alarmist and even dystopian tone.[31] On closer inspection, however, to make clear-cut distinctions between 'war' and 'peace' in medieval Scandinavian society still seems somewhat arbitrary and perhaps artificial. Conflict and competition — occasionally armed and violent — did not represent a momentary external disruption of the social system. It was, rather, ingrained permanently in its very core as a driver of fundamental processes of group-formation and power distribution. In essence, *conflict was context*. It framed politics and social life rather than undermining it, and one of the aims of our study is to uncover and understand this 'ordered disorder of conflict'. Decentralized power structures made tension and strife ubiquitous even in times of 'peace'. Vengeance and violent self-help were seen as perfectly legitimate ways of addressing wrongdoings; within the social elites even revolts against royal authority might be regarded not as anomalies but as legitimate consequences of prevailing norms and structures.[32] In the thought-provoking words of Danish historian Michael Kræmmer, on life during the dynastic wars in mid twelfth century Denmark:

> The war was part of daily life, its presence did not prevent people from taking care of the daily chores. The occasional loss of relatives no doubt caused sorrow, but it was also an inevitable part of life. To understand the relation to war and feuding in this period, one may compare with the relation to traffic in our own time. Every day it costs two human lives in Denmark alone [as well as numerous injuries, ed.], which is

---

30 *Theodoricus*, pp. 126–27, 'indignum ualde judicantes memorie posterorum tradere scelera, homicidia, periuria, parricidia, sanctorum locorum contaminationes, Dei contemptum, non minus religiosorum depredationes quam totius plebis, mulierum captiuationes et ceteras abominationes, quas longum est enumerare. Que ita exuberauerunt quasi in unam sentinam post mortem predicti regis Siwardi'.
31 This perspective has been particularly well developed in relation to the kingdom of Denmark in Breengaard, *Muren om Israels hus*. In a European historiographical context the question of how modern historians should read contemporary clerical laments about violence and disorder was also at the core of the classic debate in the 1990s on *la mutation de l'an mil*. Among the many interventions in the debate see in particular Barthélemy, 'La mutation féodale'; Bisson, 'The "Feudal" Revolution'; White, 'Debate: The "Feudal Revolution"'; Wickham, 'Debate: The "Feudal Revolution"'.
32 Cf. Breengaard, *Muren om Israels hus*, p. 330.

a worry to all, but no one contests that traffic is a necessary part of existence.[33]

Because conflict within the elite always involved wider networks, it worked 'constructively' (in a sociological sense) to test, confirm, or transform social bonds and group coherence, and to adjust status and hierarchies in the power field. Conflict, in this sense, was 'productive of sociopolitical forms'.[34] It was an 'endemic, recursive, perennial phenomenon, present even when absent'.[35] When exactly the routine quarrels and ongoing disputes between members of royal and aristocratic families and factions should be classified as something modern historians would see as regular 'civil war' is not always clear and is perhaps a matter of perspective and definition. Often, moreover, the dynastic integration of elite groups across the borders of the Scandinavian realms, and neighbouring kingdoms and principalities served to spread or integrate conflicts, while making any categorical distinction between 'internal' and 'external' war difficult to sustain.

'Peace' in Scandinavian medieval society thus did not exclude the constant and lurking presence of conflict and may be seen as a situation in which war is a state of latency rather than alterity. 'War', on the other hand, did not necessarily introduce a fundamental break or rupture, but is better conceived of as a political modality embedded in the social or societal environment, whether in *presentia* or *potentia*. This condition can be described as a state of *constant crisis*, where tension and strife were never wholly absent, but rather permanently oscillating between intensification/escalation and de-intensification/de-escalation.[36] As strategies and mechanisms of political contest were basically the same — on a structural level — in periods of nominal consensus and peace and in periods of conflict and war, it is not helpful to take the existence of such distinctions as an implicit analytical premise. To take but one concrete example: when

---

33 Kræmmer, *Den hvide klan*, p. 42.
34 Comaroff, 'Reflections', p. 285. See for a classic formulation of this idea, Simmel, 'Der Streit', and, for an equally classic application in medieval dispute studies, Geary, 'Living with Conflict'.
35 Comaroff, 'Reflections', p. 283.
36 The idea of conceiving of crisis not as a momentary interruption or turning point of 'normal' life, but as a durable circumstance — a 'terrain of action and meaning rather than an aberration' — is borrowed from anthropology, where it serves as analytic optic into ethnographic investigation of structurally violated, marginalized, and poor people around the world, who experience crisis not as episodic traumas, but as an endemic condition of fragmentation, suffering and decline (Vigh, 'Crisis and Chronicity'). In our context the notion of constant crisis does not necessarily signal dislocation and decay, but primarily serves to underline the temporal pervasiveness or 'normality' of tension, pressure and potential conflict within the socio-political system. The term may thus be read as 'synonym for the immanence of conflict to political society' (Comaroff, 'Reflections', p. 282).

Danish historians have agreed to identify a distinct 'civil war period' between 1131 and 1157, they risk underestimating the level of tension that existed both before and after that time frame. Although the lack of contemporary narratives make events before 1131 less well documented, and the growth of royal ideology and formalization of power relations during the supposedly constructive 'age of the Valdemars' in 1157–1241 tend to distract attention from the continued rumblings of factional strife that easily could have escalated into full-scale internal war, conflict in reality remained the context of political competition even outside the chronological window of regular 'civil war'.[37]

Certain factors might aggravate pressure and trigger crisis. The unexpected death of a key figure (or other 'genealogical accidents'), for instance, might invite inheritance or succession dispute and put network coherences at stake. That applied in particular to the death of a king. When a ruler died his network threatened to fall apart, and it was the task of his successor to establish a new royal network. In the case of several candidates to the throne, who all strove to rebuild a new social power base, competition was intensified, and tension easily grew.[38]

Disproportionate accumulations of wealth or influence by one particular faction might also challenge power balances and force other groups to take countermeasures; the inability of a king to satisfy the expectations of his adherents (honours, gifts, benefits) might make them turn away and start backing a potential rival; failed military exploits against neighbouring powers might undermine the reputation and charisma of a ruler, and make followers who profited from plunder search for a more successful war leader. Balances in the power field might also be disturbed by economic transformations such as the introduction of new sources of tribute and revenue, the privileging of certain regions through growth of towns and marketplaces, the systematic accumulation of land by ecclesiastical institutions, etc.

However, decentralized power structures also worked to contain and constrain conflict. To operate politically in a relatively horizontal, multipolar power landscape, actors were incited, if not forced, to negotiate, discuss, and compromise. Hardly any lord, group, or faction could afford to avoid consultation, hardly anybody could have it entirely their way, as the only

---

37 In Denmark Valdemar's victory in 1157 was supposedly followed by two generations of internal 'peace'. Yet, this 'peace' was sustained by brutally crushing every hint of opposition, by distributing gifts and benefits to supporting factions, and by carefully balancing competing aristocratic networks. In other words: the socio-political mechanisms of 'peace' were basically the same as those employed during times of 'war'. Cf. also Gelting, *Roskildekrøniken*, pp. 77–78.

38 Cf. Bagge, 'The Structure of Political Factions', p. 303: 'Life and death in the royal family and the number of heirs to the throne to some extent determined whether or not there was to be an internal struggle'.

way to gain and extend control was to associate with others by sharing control. Monopolizing or polarizing decision-making processes easily led alliances to break up or to become weakened by centrifugal tendencies.[39] This logic applied even to supposedly 'strong kings', who very much operated according to the logic of 'rule by consensus'.[40] Contrary, perhaps, to common-sense assumptions, unrivalled rulership did not necessarily promote social stability. Kings who faced no opposition tended to concentrate power and pursue their own interests, and *that* easily became a source of conflict. Rather than building their position by the monopolization of power, 'strong kings' were exactly those who succeeded in building alliances, integrating potential enemies, balancing competing networks against each other, and honouring the norms and expectations among magnates and the warrior class at large.[41] In that sense, power was always political.[42] Shared class interests within the elite probably also worked to mitigate conflict and stimulate consensus.

In other words, antagonism remained embedded in a sort of 'objective complicity', an underlying consensus about the preconditions, rules, and aims of conflict.[43] The contest for power was a kind of 'infinite game': while allowing for the occasional odd transgression, 'players' (kings, magnates, aristocratic factions) under normal circumstances only rarely attempted to outdo the others completely. After all, one's enemies today might turn out to be one's friends tomorrow.[44]

Strategies of cooperation and competition thus frequently overlapped. In an important recent comparative volume on power and rivalry across all of Europe from the early to the high Middle Ages, such processes are labelled *coopétition*.[45] The term itself is a neologism borrowed from management studies and serves as a heuristic for analysing strategies developed by Frankish, English, Italian, Iberian, Byzantine, etc., elites in the medieval game of power. Many of the recurrent observations in this rich panoramic study seem to pertain to the Scandinavian case, as we see it:

---

39 Jón Viðar Sigurðsson, *Viking Friendship*.
40 Schneidmüller, 'Rule by Consensus'.
41 Orning, 'Conflict and Social (Dis)Order', pp. 62–66.
42 This obviously diverges from the views of Bisson, who sees power in 'lord-kingships' (that is, regnal polities without proto-institutionalized 'government') as 'social-relational', 'personal', 'ceremonious' and 'affective' — which it was — but also as inherently 'unpolitical' (Bisson, *The Crisis*, p. 494, see also pp. 19, 77, 99, 161, 435). For the conception, closer to the approach of this book, that all social relations of power are necessarily 'political', see Miller, *Humiliation*; White, 'The Politics of Fidelity'; White, 'The Politics of Anger'; White, 'The Politics of Gift-exchange'.
43 Hölkeskamp, *Reconstructing*, p. 105; Bourdieu, *Sociology in Question*, p. 73.
44 Carse, *Finite and Infinite Games*.
45 Le Jan and others, *Coopétition*. See in particular pp. 9–20 (introduction by Régine Le Jan), pp. 383–90 (conclusion by Chris Wickham), and pp. 321–33 (contribution by Lucie Malbos on allies and competitors in late eleventh century Norway).

to participate in the game players had to recognize each other as partners; collaboration with competitors was strongly dependent on trust, which therefore became a key component in the structuring of order and hierarchy; players might prefer to neutralize rivals rather than destroy them, and often strove to maintain the status quo rather than running the risk of one party gaining advantage over others. The degree and intensity of *coopétition* necessarily depended on context and was temporary by nature. Sometimes competition might overshadow cooperation, sometimes it might be the other way round. *Coopétition* also did not preclude that competition *could* get out of control and into vengeance mode. Occasionally things *did* 'run amok', but *stasis* (in the form of repeated local crises and disturbances) at least generally tended to promote *homeostasis*, global balance, by counteracting major concentrations of power. In practice, political actors at all levels availed themselves of a wide cultural repertoire of ritual and discursive means to dampen conflict, to bridge competing claims, and to designing (albeit often temporary) settlements that could be perceived (or at least represented) as fair, balanced, and honourable to all parties.

The dynamics of a decentralized political game of balances or constant crisis where various groups keep one another in check through shifting constellations of rivalry and alliance have been analysed thoroughly in modern contexts by anthropologist and social scientists. As historians have been aware of for some time, these detailed and well documented studies are helpful when trying to make sense of the more sporadic and fragmented reports of internal war in medieval chronicles and sagas. According to recurrent observations in such studies alliance formation tends to follow a logic of segmentary opposition. Socio-political units alternate between fusion and fission, integration and splitting.[46] On the one hand, actors will seek to join up with the strongest group of allies, the faction most likely to win. On the other hand, however, units will also strive to maximize gain, and if they end up on the winning side, but as a minority within a large coalition, they might prefer to break out and join forces with a weaker faction instead. As summed up by Sverre Bagge:

> The larger the majority of a faction, the better chances of winning, but the least to gain from victory for each participant, and vice versa. In the long run, these opposing considerations will lead to factions of approximately equal numbers and strength, or, if one faction wins a complete victory, it will split later on. Usually, awareness of these consequences of total victory and fear that the opposing faction, if risking to lose, might encourage defections by offering one of the

---

46 Evans-Pritchard, *The Nuer*.

defectors the leadership of their faction, will ensure a certain balance between the struggling factions.[47]

While these game-based principles were first articulated by anthropologists in contexts of acephalous political systems studied in the 1930s, '40s and '50s,[48] the same mechanisms are also described in investigations of more recent civil war theatres. Political scientist Fotini Christia, for instance, in her exploration of alliance formation in 'multiparty conflicts' in contemporary Afghanistan, has shown how participants operate according to the same strategic concerns. 'While they desire to be on the winning side, commitment problems make them wary of winning the war as a weaker alliance partner'.[49] Hence, winning alliances will break up and result in the re-establishment of a power balance between different fractions and the continuation of conflict. Sustained, vehement interference from external actors and faltering attempts to consolidate a centralized state power — in this respect Afghanistan is probably more like medieval Scandinavia than mid-twentieth century Nuer or Swat — does not alter the fusion-fission game.[50]

What all this boils down to, then, is that while risk and instability was built into socio-political structures, and while the potentially destructive force of war should evidently not be denied altogether (and certainly *did* cause alarm among some contemporaries), the presence and persistence of tensions were not signs of malfunction or 'system crisis', but very much *the way things worked*. That is why we in this book try to think of the medieval Scandinavian 'civil wars' in terms of network dynamics, conflict as context, constant crisis, multiparty conflict, etc. and to avoid the trap of inadvertently applying what Fredric L. Cheyette once pointedly labelled the unconscious 'controlling image of the state',[51] i.e. the inclination to approach the problem of internal war from the unspoken theoretical assumption that socio-political order *necessarily* depends on the existence of central coercive government and state monopoly on violence.

A brief closing word on sources and methodology. Compared to texts available for the usually better documented regions around Europe, the source material for Scandinavian medieval history necessarily appears meagre. Charters and diplomas, which, elsewhere, have provided a key bulk of evidence in the historiography of medieval power and dispute, were introduced rather late in the Nordic realms. On Danish soil, the earliest known charter was issued in 1085, in Norway and Sweden charters

---

47 Bagge, 'The Structure of the Political Factions', p. 303.
48 Evans-Prichard, *The Nuer*; Barth, *Political Leadership*; Barth, 'Segmentary Opposition'.
49 Christia, *Alliance Formation*, p. 7.
50 For a fuller exposition and comparison between modern Afghanistan and medieval Norway, see Orning and Østerud, *Krig uten stat*, pp. 76–100.
51 Cheyette, 'The Invention of the State'.

did not appear until the second half of the twelfth century, and during the whole period dealt with here, charters were only produced and transmitted in fairly limited numbers.[52] These sources therefore feature less prominently in many of the book's chapters than readers accustomed to the richness of English, French, German, or Iberian archival records might expect. In contrast, Old Norse sagas and Latin chronicles, histories and saints' lives constitute a reasonably rewarding corpus of narrative evidence. Composed or compiled from the early twelfth century onwards these texts lend themselves well to analyses of networking and war-making, power struggles and legitimation. There is an inevitable imbalance here: sagas and chronicles primarily focus on the history of Denmark and Norway — the earliest Swedish history only dates from the fourteenth century.[53] However, the integration of socio-political networks across borders in the period under discussion in this book means that texts relating to Danish and Norwegian matters necessarily also incorporate some information about persons and events in Sweden. Narratives (supplemented by annalistic records, law books, charters, lists of kings, and archaeology) thus provide the main source material for almost all the studies in the volume and will be introduced and discussed in context in the individual chapters.[54]

---

[52] *Diplomatarium Danicum*, the exhaustive, multi-volume edition of Danish medieval charters counts *c.* 420 entries from the twelfth century, and this includes all regular charters or diplomas issued in Denmark, every single reference to lost documents, every single papal letter sent to Denmark, and every single record found in European archives that happen to mention a Danish individual or placename. *Diplomatarium Norwegium* likewise contains fewer than 150 entries from before 1200, and that again includes foreign documents sent to or containing information on Norway (Helle, *Norge blir en stat*, pp. 19–20). For the Swedish *Diplomatarium Suecanum* the number of charters and charter-like records is even smaller (Gunnar Karlsson (ed.), *Kilderne*; <https://sok.riksarkivet.se/sdhk>). The style of Scandinavian charters varies, but generally they are quite formulaic with only rare examples of the extensive narrations often found in charter records from other parts of Europe.

[53] The conversion to Christianity, and thus the introduction to literacy, happened later in Sweden than in Denmark and Norway, wherefore the written source material for the history of Sweden before 1250 are generally discouragingly meagre (instructive overview in Line, *Kingship and State Formation*, pp. xiv–xv).

[54] Despite the poor source evidence, it is certainly possible to think about power and networks in Sweden along the lines suggested in this book. In his study of royal power and state building in Sweden 1130–1290, richly informed by comparative literature, Philip Line thus concludes that while common cultural norms held society together, 'the survival of a king was also dependent on his own network of friends and kinship alliances. These could be extensive in a system of bilateral kinship. The limited evidence at our disposal indicates that the internal wars and rebellions of twelfth- and thirteenth-century Sweden resulted largely from conflict between such networks, whose leading personalities sought to avoid being marginalized in the decision making process, in other words, excluded from the king's counsel, or possibly from the kingship itself, if any of their number had a claim to it.' (Line, *Kingship and State Formation*, pp. 477–78).

In regard to methodology, any attempt to substitute an analysis of competing-factions-in-a-multipolar-power-field for conventional historiographic focus on kings, as we propose to do, necessarily implies a challenge: How do we write a network-oriented history of conflict without adopting kingship as both the focal point and the 'camera eye', while having to rely almost entirely on sources — whether that be chronicles, sagas, charters, saints' lives, annals, or law books — that predominantly were produced at royal courts or within the circles associated with royal power? How is it possible to map relations between magnates, whose names often remain unknown, and how do we capture the push and pull of interacting networks, that narrators and scribes (bar a few exceptions) normally left hidden in the dark? While the present volume does not pretend to dissolve this meta-problematic, it does at least present various ways to deal with it, centring on the comparative heuristic approach, the conscious construction of an alternative analytical framework and an endeavour to 'turn the lens'.

Works Cited

Primary Sources

Theodoricus Monachus, *De antiquitate regum Norwagiensium. On the Old Norwegian Kings*, ed. by Egil Kraggerud (Oslo: Novus, 2018)

Secondary Studies

Armitage, David, *Civil Wars: A History of Ideas* (New Haven: Yale University Press, 2017)

Arup, Erik, *Danmarks historie, vol. 1: Land og folk til 1282* (Copenhagen: H. Hagerups Forlag, 1925)

Bagge, Sverre, *From Viking Stronghold to Christian Kingdom: State Formation in Norway, c. 900–1350* (Copenhagen: Museum Tusculanum Press, 2012)

——, 'The Structure of the Political Factions in the Internal Struggles of the Scandinavian Countries during the High Middle Ages', *Scandinavian Journal of History*, 24 (1986), 299–320

Barth, Fredrik, *Political Leadership among Swat Pathans* (London: Berg Publishers, 1965)

——, 'Segmentary Opposition and the Theory of Games: A Study of Pathan Organization', *Journal of the Royal Anthropological Institute*, 89.1 (1959), 5–21

Barthélemy, Dominique, 'La mutation féodale a-t-elle eu lieu?', *Annales*, 3 (1992), 767–77

Bijsterveld, Arnoud-Jan, 'Memoria and Nobility Research in the Netherlands', in *Verortete Herrschaft*, ed. by Jens Lieven, Bert Thissen, and Ronald Wientjes (Bielefeld, 2014), pp. 211–32

Bisson, Thomas, *The Crisis of the Twelfth Century. Power, Lordship, and the Origins of European Government* (Princeton and Oxford: Princeton University Press, 2009)

——, 'The "Feudal" Revolution', *Past and Present*, 142 (1994), 6–42

Bourdieu, Pierre, *Outline of a Theory of Practice* (Cambridge: Cambridge University Press, 1977)

——, 'Rethinking the State: Genesis and Structure of the Bureaucratic Field', trans. by Loic J. D. Wacquant and Samar Farage, *Sociological Theory*, 12.1 (1994), 1–18

——, *Sociology in Question*, trans. by Richard Nice (London: Sage Publications, 1993)

Breengaard, Carsten, *Muren om Israels hus: regnum og sacerdotium i Danmark 1050–1170* (Copenhagen: C. E. G. Gad, 1982)

Carse, James, *Finite and Infinite Games* (New York: The Free Press, 1987)

Charles-Edwards, Thomas, *Early Christian Ireland* (Cambridge: Cambridge University Press, 2000)

Cheyette, Fredric L., 'The Invention of the State', in *The Walter Prescott Webb Memorial Lectures. Essays on Medieval Civilization*, ed. by Bede Karl Lachner and Kenneth Roy Philp (Austin: University of Texas, 1978), pp. 143–78

Christia, Fotini, *Alliance Formation in Civil Wars* (Cambridge: Cambridge University Press, 2012)

Chronicon Roskildensis. in *Scriptores minores historiae Danicæ: Medii ævi*, ed. by Martin Cl. Gertz (Copenhagen: C. E. G. Gad, 1917–1920), vol. 2: 1–33

Collegium Medievale, 32.2 (2019), special issue: *Conflicts in Medieval Scandinavia*

Collier, Paul, and Nicholas Sambanis, *Understanding Civil War: Evidence and Analysis* (Washington, DC: The World Bank, 2005)

Comaroff, John, 'Reflections of the Political Theology of Conflict: From Medieval Scandinavia to the Global Future', in *Medieval and Modern Civil Wars. A Comparative Perspective*, ed. by Jón Viðar Sigurðsson and Hans Jacob Orning (Leiden: Brill, 2021), pp. 279–308

Davies, Rees, 'The Medieval State: The Tyranny of a Concept?', *Journal of Historical Sociology*, 16.2 (2003), 280–300

Esmark, Kim, 'Just Rituals: Masquerade, Manipulation, and Officializing Strategies in Saxo's Gesta Danorum', in *Rituals, Performatives, and Political Order in Northern Europe, c. 650–1350*, ed. by Wojtek Jezierski, Lars Hermanson, Hans Jacob Orning, and Thomas Småberg (Turnhout: Brepols, 2015), pp. 237–68

——, 'Social Power and Conversion of Capital', in *Nordic Elites in Transformation, c. 1050–1250, vol. II: Social Networks*, ed. by Kim Esmark, Lars Hermanson, and Hans Jacob Orning (New York: Routledge, 2020), pp. 285–303

——, 'Spinning the Revolt. The Assassination and Sanctification of an 11th-Century Danish King', in *Rebellion and Resistance*, ed. by Henrik Jensen (Pisa: Edizioni Plus, 2009), pp. 15–32

Esmark, Kim, Jón Viðar Sigurðsson, and Helle Vogt, 'Kith and Kin: Ties of Blood and Marriage', in *Nordic Elites in Transformation, c. 1050–1250, vol. II: Social Networks*, ed. by Kim Esmark, Lars Hermanson, and Hans Jacob Orning (New York: Routledge, 2020), pp. 11–32

Esmark, Kim, Lars Hermanson, and Hans Jacob Orning (eds), *Nordic Elites in Transformation, c. 1050–1250, vol. II: Social Networks* (New York: Routledge, 2020)

Esmark, Kim, Lars Hermanson, Hans Jacob Orning, and Helle Vogt (eds), *Disputing Strategies in Medieval Scandinavia* (Leiden: Brill, 2013)

Evans-Prichard, E. E., *The Nuer: A Description of the Modes of Livelihood and Political Institutions of a Nilotic People* (New York: Oxford University Press, 1969)

Fenger, Ole, *Kirker bygges alle vegne: 1050–1250*, 2nd edn (Copenhagen: Gyldendals Bogklubber, 2002)

Geary, Patrick J., 'Living with Conflict in Stateless France: A Typology of Conflict Management Mechanisms, 1050–1200', in *Living with the Dead in the Middle Ages* (New York: Cornell University Press, 1994), pp. 125–60

Gelting, Michael H., *Roskildekrøniken*. 2nd edn (Højbjerg: Wormianum, 2002)
Gunnar, Karlsson (ed.), *Kilderne til den tidlige middelalders historie. Rapporter til den 20 nordiske historikerkongress* (Reykjavík: Sagnfræðistofnum Háskóla Íslands, 1987)
Helle, Knut (ed.), *The Cambridge History of Scandinavia I. Prehistory to 1520* (Cambridge: Cambridge University Press, 2003)
——, *Norge blir en stat 1130–1319* (Bergen: Universitetsforlaget, 1974)
Hermanson, Lars, and Hans Jacob Orning, 'Friends and Allies: Networks of Horizontal Bonds', in *Nordic Elites in Transformation. C. 1050–1250, vol. II: Social Networks*, ed. by Kim Esmark, Lars Hermanson, and Hans Jacob Orning (New York and London: Routledge, 2020), pp. 54–75
——, 'Lords and Followers: Patron-Client Relationships', in *Nordic Elites in Transformation, c. 1050–1250, vol. II: Social Networks*, ed. by Kim Esmark, Lars Hermanson, and Hans Jacob Orning (New York and London: Routledge, 2020), pp. 33–53
Hölkeskamp, Karl-J., *Reconstructing the Roman Republic: An Ancient Political Culture and Modern Research*, trans. by Henry Heitmann-Gordon (Princeton: Princeton University Press, 2010)
Holmsen, Andreas, *Norges historie. Fra de eldste tider til 1660* (Oslo: Universitetsforlaget, 1977 [1938])
Innes, Matthew, *State and Society in the Early Middle Ages: The Middle Rhine valley, 400–1000*, Cambridge Studies in Medieval life and Thought, 4th ser. (Cambridge: Cambridge University Press, 2000)
Jezierski, Wojtek, Kim Esmark, Hans Jacob Orning, and Jón Viðar Sigurðsson (eds), *Nordic Elites in Transformation, c. 1050–1250, vol. III: Legitimacy and Glory* (New York: Routledge, 2021)
Jezierski, Wojtek, Lars Hermanson, Hans Jacob Orning, and Thomas Småberg (eds), *Rituals, Performatives, and Political Order in Northern Europe, c. 650–1350* (Turnhout: Brepols, 2015)
Jón Viðar Sigurðsson, *Chieftains and Power in the Icelandic Commonwealth*, trans. by Jean Lundskær-Nielsen, The Viking Collection, 12 (Odense: Odense University Press, 1999)
——, *Viking Friendship. The Social Bond in Iceland and Norway, c. 900–1300* (Ithaca: Cornell University Press, 2017)
Jón Viðar Sigurðsson and Hans Jacob Orning (eds), *Medieval and Modern Civil Wars. A Comparative Perspective* (Leiden: Brill, 2021)
——, 'Introduction', in *Medieval and Modern Civil Wars. A Comparative Perspective*, ed. by Jón Viðar Sigurðsson and Hans Jacob Orning (Leiden: Brill, 2021), pp. ix–xxiii
Jón Viðar Sigurðsson and Henrik Vigh, 'Who is the Enemy? Multipolar Micropolitics', in *Medieval and Modern Civil Wars. A Comparative Perspective*, ed. by Hans Jacob Orning and Jón Viðar Sigurðsson (Leiden: Brill, 2021), pp. 34–61

Kjær, Lars, 'Political Conflict and Political Ideas in Twelfth-Century Denmark', *Viking and Medieval Scandinavia*, 13 (2017), 61–100

Koch, Hal, *Kongemagt og kirke – 1060–1241* (Copenhagen: Politiken, 1963)

Kræmmer, Michael, *Den hvide klan. Absalon, hans slægt og hans tid* (Copenhagen: Spektrum, 1999)

Le Jan, Régine, Geneviève Bührer-Thierry, and Stefano Gasparri (eds), *Coopétition. Rivaliser, coopérer dans les sociétés du Haut Moyen Âge (500–1100)* (Turnhout: Brepols, 2018)

Lind, John H., 'De russiske ægteskaber: Dynasti- og alliancepolitik i 1130'ernes danske borgerkrig', *Historisk Tidsskrift* (D), 92 (1992), 225–63

Line, Philip, *Kingship and State Formation in Sweden, 1130–1290* (Leiden: Brill, 2007)

Lunden, Kåre, *Norge under Sverreætten, 1177–1319. Høymiddelalder* (Oslo: Cappelen, 1976)

Miller, William Ian, *Humiliation and Other Essays on Honor, Social Discomfort, and Violence* (New York: Cornell University Press, 1993)

Orning, Hans Jacob, 'Conflict and Social (Dis)Order in Norway', in *Disputing Strategies in Medieval Scandinavia*, ed. by Kim Esmark, Lars Hermanson, Hans Jacob Orning, and Helle Vogt (Leiden: Brill, 2013), pp. 45–82

——, and Øyvind Østerud, *Krig uten stat. Hva har de nye krigene og middelalderkrigene felles?* (Oslo: Dreyers forlag, 2020)

——, and Henrik Vigh, 'Constant Crisis', in *Medieval and Modern Civil Wars. A Comparative Perspective*, ed. by Hans Jacob Orning and Jón Viðar Sigurðsson (Leiden: Brill, 2021), pp. 1–33

——, Kim Esmark, and Lars Hermanson (eds), *Gaver, ritualer, konflikter. Et rettsantropologisk perspektiv på nordisk middelalderhistorie* (Oslo: Unipub, 2010)

Poulsen, Bjørn, Helle Vogt, and Jón Viðar Sigurðsson (eds), *Nordic Elites in Transformation, c. 1050–1250, vol. 1: Material Resources* (New York: Routledge, 2019)

Reuter, Timoth, 'The Medieval German Sonderweg? The Empire and its Rulers in the High Middle Ages', in *Kings and Kingship in Medieval Europe*, ed. by Anne Duggan (London: The College, 1993), pp. 179–211

Riches, Theo, 'Review of The Crisis of the Twelfth Century', <https://reviews.history.ac.uk/review/754> [accessed 16 March 2023]

Sahlins, Marshall, *The Western Illusion of Human Nature* (Chicago: Paradigm, 2008)

Sambanis, Nicholas, 'What is Civil War? Conceptual and Empirical Complexities of an Operational Definition', *The Journal of Conflict Resolution*, 48.6 (2004), 814–58

Sawyer, Birgit, 'The "Civil Wars" Revisited', *Historisk Tidsskrift* (N), 82.1 (2003), 43–73

Schneidmüller, Bernd, 'Rule by Consensus. Forms and Concepts of Political Order in the European Middle Ages', *The Medieval History Journal*, 16 (2013), 449–71

Simmel, Georg, 'Der Streit', in *Soziologie. Untersuchungen über die Formen der Vergesellschaftung* (Leipzig: Duncker & Humblot, 1908)

Vigh, Henrik, 'Crisis and Chronicity: Anthropological Perspectives on Continuous Conflict and Decline', *Ethnos*, 73.1 (2008), 5–24

Weiler, Björn, *Paths to Kingship in Medieval Latin Europe, c. 950–1200* (Cambridge: Cambridge University Press, 2021)

White, Stephen D., 'Debate: The "Feudal Revolution" (Comment 2)', *Past and Present*, 152 (1996), 205–23

——, 'The Politics of Anger in Medieval France', in *Anger's Past: The Social Uses of an Emotion in the Middle Ages*, ed. by Barbara Rosenwein (Cornell: Cornell University Press, 1998), pp. 127–52

——, 'The Politics of Fidelity: Hugh of Lusignan and William of Aquitaine', in *Georges Duby: L'Écriture de l'Histoire*, ed. by Claudie Duhamel-Amado and Guy Lobrichon (Brussels: De Boeck Université, 1996), pp. 223–30

——, 'The Politics of Gift-Exchange. Or, Feudalism Revisited', in *Medieval Transformations: Texts, Power, and Gifts Revisited*, ed. by Esther Cohen and Mayke de Jong (Leiden: Brill, 2000), pp. 169–88

——, *Re-thinking Kinship and Feudalism* (Aldershot: Ashgate, 2005).

Wickham, Chris, 'Debate: The "Feudal Revolution" (Comment 4)', *Past and Present*, 155 (1997), 196–208

Part I

Case Studies

KIM ESMARK, HANS JACOB ORNING, AND
JÓN VIÐAR SIGURÐSSON

Introduction to Part One

The first section of this volume consists of three chapters dedicated to extended case studies of selected phases, important moments, and significant patterns of action during the long 'civil war period' in Scandinavia. All three studies take their analytical key from the model outlined in Chapter 1. They explore the processes of internal war by tracing the workings of socio-political networks in various contexts of permanent competition or 'constant crisis'.

In Chapter 2, entitled 'Networks and *flokkar*: The civil wars in Norway c. 1130–1163', Jón Viðar Sigurðsson addresses the importance of royal networks. Analysing the Norwegian kings' friends, relatives, foster families, courts and private armies in the years 1130–1139, he argues that one reason why the rivalry between King Magnus the Blind and his co-ruler Harald Gille escalated into armed warfare in 1134 was that the overlaps between the two kings' networks were too weak to maintain peaceful competition. Jón Viðar Sigurðsson then moves forward to the years 1157–1163 to discuss the organization of the *flokkr*, a troop of semi-professionalized warriors, usually 300–500 men strong, and the reasons why this particular unit developed into a key tool in Norwegian power politics around this time. For instance, *flokkar* now became main 'producers of kings', encroaching, as it were, on the public assemblies' traditional right to elect the ruler. In fact, as Jón Viðar Sigurðsson shows, a *flokkr* was instrumental in the landmark events of 1163, which brought Magnus Erlingsson — himself not a king's son — to power. Magnus' takeover signalled a turning point in the Norwegian power game, as it abandoned the ideal and traditional practice of joint rulership in favour of the European model of one realm, one king. The coup, however, only triggered renewed struggles, which would continue for decades to come.

In Chapter 3 by Kim Esmark, attention is turned towards the kingdom of Denmark. A political murder within the Danish royal family in 1131 unleashed a revenge war, which fast developed into a major three-year struggle for the throne between rival pretenders and competing aristocratic networks. It is argued that the conflict was inherently 'messy', e.g. polydimensional, driven and influenced by multiple parties home and abroad, fought for various purposes, and marked by side-switching, regional segmentation, and cross-border intervention and alliance formation.

Analysing, furthermore, structures and axes of tension in the power field in the years leading up to the murder in 1131, which triggered the war, the chapter argues that the armed conflict merely intensified already-existing dynamics of socio-political competition. The sudden escalation into large-scale war was merely the result of an unforeseeable coincidence of a series of contextual factors — genealogical, economic, and socio-political. Looking into the movements in the war's immediate aftermath, it is finally argued that the same competitive dynamics continued to play out after the formal end of the war in 1134. For all their efforts to assert a new balance of power, those on the winning side of the war were overtaken by the same tensions and factional rivalries that structured the power field throughout the period.

Chapter 4, written by Hans Jacob Orning, then takes us back to Norway and to what is usually regarded as one of the most intense periods of 'civil war', the years from 1202 to 1208. Through a close reading of *Bǫglunga sǫgur* and its detailed accounts of political and military strategies, he demonstrates that the conflict was not limited to the struggle between the two rival factions or *flokkar* commonly known as Birkibeinar and Baglar, but also operated within these groups as well as across them. Within the leading strata of both Birkibeinar and Baglar there tended to be rivalry for influence where normally no single actor was able to dominate the decision process. Bonds of kinship and friendship often crossed group boundaries, and so did communities among warriors and among the leading elites on each side. Hence, the formation and cohesion of groups was less pronounced and less solid than has been presumed by previous scholarship. In the same vein it is argued that although war was never a pleasant experience for those exposed to it, the actual impact of armed hostilities on local communities (geographically dispersed and mostly seeking to avoid being implicated altogether) was probably less substantial than commonly assumed. An overarching conclusion in the chapter is that the prevalence of conflict — both between groups and within and across the borders of these same groups — needs to be understood as a state of 'constant crisis', a condition where tension and strife remain an intrinsic part of the socio-political order, not external or indeed contrary to it.

The three case-studies are precisely that: case-studies. They do not intend to provide a comprehensive history of the civil war period, and, as the reader will note, there is also no separate chapter dealing with a specific Swedish case. The very limited source evidence for Sweden (discussed in the opening chapter of this book) simply does not allow the kind of close-up, micro-political analysis of networks in action pursued here. The little we do know about Swedish magnates and networks in the twelfth and thirteenth centuries mainly stems from Danish and Norwegian sources. Sweden therefore primarily appears in contexts, where these magnates and networks interacted with rulers and groups from Denmark and Norway.

Geography and settlement patterns obviously provided different conditions for 'civil war' in mountainous Norway, intensely farmed Denmark, and woodland Sweden — a fact that will be further explored in Part Two. With regard to networks and permanence of conflict, however, the many similarities between Norway and Denmark and between different phases of the Norwegian 'civil wars' (including these wars' Swedish dimension) are clearly discernible. Other comparable patterns are worth pointing to. Firstly, none of the struggles studied in the three chapters seem to have been driven by ideological motivations, religious antagonisms, or anything similar. These conflicts were fights among elite groups for wealth and power, e.g., for control of resources and for influence in decision-making processes. Religious ideas and discourses, for instance, might occasionally be mobilized as part of legitimation strategies, and surely motivated certain actors and actions, but the Scandinavian dynastic wars basically played out between groups that for all practical purposes shared the same political ambitions and socio-cultural norms. Claims to power and legitimacy were articulated by opposing parties within the same shared register of ideals and values. Royal thrones were strived for by rival pretenders and their friends and followers simply because they constituted the most important points of accumulation and distribution of material and symbolic sources of power in society.[1] Also, although labelled 'internal' by both contemporary and modern historiography, the wars analysed in the three case studies all connected directly to each other and they involved and were shaped in decisive ways by actors across the Scandinavian realms. Struggles for the Danish and the Norwegian crown repeatedly became interwoven and, as shown in all three chapters, rulers and elite groups in the kingdom of Sweden were entangled as well. In fact, this supra-national dimension of the wars extended even beyond the Scandinavian realms. To understand what these 'civil wars' were all about, then, we clearly need to consider the role played by personal networks and alliances stretching across what we anachronistically think of as national political borders and — in a wider sense — the boundaries between the Northern world and Central Europe.

---

1 Cf. the discussion of the objectives of rebels against the throne in thirteenth century Sweden in Philip Line, *Kingship and State Formation in Sweden, 1130–1290* (Leiden: Brill, 2007), p. 146: 'All those who rebelled were arguably threatened with exclusion from, or diminution of influence in, the king's ruling circle. This provides a more plausible explanation for their actions than any kind of ideological standpoint, since the battle for influence around the throne was an underlying cause of struggles among the high nobility in every kingdom of medieval Europe. By contrast, there is little evidence for long-term political programmes'.

JÓN VIÐAR SIGURÐSSON

2. Networks and *flokkar*

The Civil Wars in Norway c. 1134–1163

In around 1125, Hallkell Huk, who was a *lendr maðr* (a person who held land in exchange for military and administrative service) of King Sigurd the Crusader sailed to the Hebrides.[1] There he met Harald Gille, a young man from Ireland, who claimed to be the son of King Magnus Barefoot. King Magnus had conducted military campaigns in the Irish Sea region in 1098, 1099, and 1102. Hallkell brought Harald Gille and his mother to Norway, and to prove his paternity, Harald Gille underwent an ordeal (*skírsla*). The condition was that he would not claim the throne as long as King Sigurd the Crusader or his son Magnus (later nicknamed the Blind) were alive. These conditions were confirmed with an 'oath' (*svardagar*). After Harald successfully passed the ordeal, Sigurd the Crusader accepted his half-brother into the family.[2]

King Sigurd the Crusader passed away on 26 March 1130. After his death, Harald Gille and his friends held an assembly in Tønsberg and declared Harald king over 'half' the country, claiming that the oaths he had given to Sigurd the Crusader were made under duress.[3] Harald Gille and Magnus the Blind ruled jointly for a few years, but their relationship deteriorated, leading to a battle in 1134 in Fyrileiv, which Harald Gille lost. He fled to Denmark but returned the following year to capture Magnus in Bergen, where Magnus was mutilated, blinded, and castrated before being allowed to live in a monastery. In 1136, Sigurd Slembe, another son

---

1 *Orkneyinga saga*, p. 130.
2 *Heimskringla III*, p. 266. Cf. *Morkinskinna II*, pp. 142, 147–48, 152; *Ágrip*, pp. 50–51, 320–21; *GD*, 13.11.3. Orkneyinga saga has a slightly different version of these events (*Orkneyinga saga*, pp. 130–31).
3 *Heimskringla III*, pp. 278–79; *Orkneyinga saga*, pp. 140–41; *Ágrip*, pp. 51, 321.

> **Jón Viðar Sigurðsson** (j.v.sigurdsson@iakh.uio.no) is professor of medieval history in the Department of Archaeology, Conservation, and History, University of Oslo.

New Perspectives on the 'Civil Wars' in Medieval Scandinavia, ed. by Hans Jacob Orning, Kim Esmark, and Jón Viðar Sigurðsson, Comparative Perspectives on Medieval History, 1 (Turnhout: Brepols, 2024), pp. 41–96

of King Magnus Barefoot, killed Harald Gille in Bergen.[4] Harald Gille's two young sons, Sigurd Mouth and Inge Hunchback, were placed on the throne by *lendir menn*. In 1139, in a battle between the sons of Harald Gille and their supporters on the one side and Magnus the Blind and Sigurd Slembe on the other, Magnus the Blind was killed, and Sigurd Slembe captured and tortured to death. In 1142 Oystein Haraldsson, another son of Harald Gille, was fetched from Scotland and placed on the throne. The three half-brothers ruled together until a dispute broke out in the mid-1150s, leading to Sigurd Mouth's and Oystein Haraldsson's deaths. In 1157, King Sigurd Mouth's son Hakon the Broad-Shouldered was proclaimed king. He then killed Inge Hunchback in battle in 1161. The following year, Hakon was killed in battle by Inge's supporters, who had placed the infant Magnus Erlingsson, a son of Sigurd the Crusader's daughter, on the throne. In 1163 Magnus was crowned king in the first coronation ceremony of its kind in Scandinavia.

Scholars who study Norwegian medieval history, as well as medieval writers, agree that the civil wars began with the battle between Harald Gille and Magnus the Blind in 1134.[5] However, the early years of the civil wars have not received much attention in the scholarly debate, as they are typically viewed as a prelude to the more intense phase of the wars, which occurred between approximately 1177 and 1227 (see Chapter 4).[6] When historians explain the reasons for the outbreak of civil wars in medieval Norway, they have focused on the 'deeper' roots of these conflicts, such as the economic crisis, the influence of the Church, and the Danish kings.[7]

---

4 *Heimskringla III*, p. 297.
5 Snorre Sturluson, the author of *Heimskringla*, stresses that Sigurd the Crusader's 'time' (*ǫld*) was good for his people: there was both 'prosperity and peace' (*ár ok friðr*) (*Heimskringla III*, p. 277). This is the last time that Snorre Sturluson characterizes the reign of a Norwegian king in such a positive way, because a few years after Sigurd's death the civil wars broke out. It was therefore impossible for Snorre Sturluson, and the other saga authors, to describe the reigns of kings during the years 1134–1240 as good for the people. *Ágrip* (*Ágrip*, pp. 49–50) stresses that Sigurd's reign was good, regarding both 'harvests and many other beneficial things (*ár of margfalda aðra gœsku*)'. Theodoricus monachus states that a few years after King Sigurd's death the kingdom fell into decay (*Theodoricus*, pp. 126–27). In *Profectio Danorum in Hierosolymam*, also known as *Historia de profectione Danorum in Hierosolymam* from c. 1200 it is stated that when the world comes closer to its end, people will rise against people, kingdom against kingdom, children will stop respecting their parents, and respect for people and the elderly will diminish (*Scriptores minores historiæ*, pp. 460–61). Saxo Grammaticus in his *Gesta Danorum* claims that the descendants of Harald Gille were the main causes of the civil wars in Norway (GD, 13.11.3. Cf. GD, 14.29.1).
6 See for example: Holmsen, *Norges historie. Fra de eldste tider til 1660*; Gunnes, *Kongens ære*; Helle, *Norge blir en stat*; Helle, *Under kirke og kongemakt*; Moseng and others, *Norsk historie I*; Krag, *Norges historie*; Bagge, *From Viking Stronghold*; Jón Viðar Sigurðsson and Riisøy, *Norsk historie 800–1536*; Orning, 'Borgerkrig og statsutvikling'.
7 Helle, *Under kirke og kongemakt*, p. 19; Helle, *Norge blir en stat*, pp. 38–41.

In this chapter we will try to rectify this lack of interest in the outbreak of the civil wars, and also take an approach, which has mostly been ignored by Norwegian scholars, of examining the royal networks and the *flokkr* (plural *flokkar*, a group of warriors usually under the leadership of a king and his closest advisers, that became after 1161 the main feature of the civil wars) and its organization.[8] In the first part of this chapter, which focuses on the years 1130–1139, we will examine the royal networks, the king's friends (*vinir*), relatives (*frændr*), foster families, retinue of men who owed fealty and service to the king (*hirð*), and troops (*lið*). Then, we will move on to the years 1157–1163 and discuss the organization of the *flokkr* and why it became a crucial aspect in the power struggle during that period.

The most important sources for the history of Norway during the years c. 1130–1160 are the sagas; *Fagrskinna*, *Morkinskinna*, and *Heimskringla*. *Fagrskinna* and *Morkinskinna* were composed around 1220, and *Heimskringla* a few years later, c. 1230.[9] One important source for the events which took place after 1130 is *Hryggjarstykki*, a lost saga which both *Morkinskinna* and *Heimskringla* use as a source. In *Heimskringla* Snorre Sturluson notes that Eirik Oddsson had written a book, *Hryggjarstykki*, about Harald Gille and his two sons, and about Magnus the Blind and Sigurd Slembe right up until their deaths in 1139. Snorre then adds that Eirik was an intelligent man and that he had lived in Norway for a long period of time and had talked to trustworthy men who had seen or heard about the events when composing his book.[10] Snorre Sturluson is thus stressing that he has information from a source contemporary with the disputes during the years 1134–1139. Nothing is known about Eirik Oddsson other than that he was an Icelander, and that he probably wrote his narrative around 1150.[11] That Eirik's saga was produced such a short period of time after the

---

8 In the discussion about the outbreak of the civil wars, the royal networks are not considered. See, for example, Bjørgo, 'Samkongedøme kontra einekongedøme', pp. 1–33; Blom, *Samkongedømme – enekongedømme*, pp. 1–10; Helle, *Norge blir en stat*, pp. 12–21, 37–73; Bagge, 'Samkongedømme og enekongedømme', pp. 239–74; Bagge, 'Borgerkrig og statsutvikling', pp. 145–97; Bagge, 'Borgerkrig og statsutvikling – svar til Hans Jacob Orning', pp. 91–110; Orning, 'Borgerkrig og statsutvikling', pp. 193–216; Orning, 'Hvorfor vant kongene?', pp. 285–92. For the discussion of the *flokkr* see for example Bagge, 'Borgerkrig og statsutvikling', pp. 145–97 and Bagge, *From Viking Stronghold*, pp. 42–53.
9 For an overview of the debate, see, for example, Andersson, 'Kings' Sagas (Konungasögur)'; Andersson, *The Sagas of Norwegian Kings (1130–1265)*, and the introductions to the edition of these sagas in the *Íslenzk fornrit* series (*Heimskringla III*; *Ágrip*; *Morkinskinna I–II*).
10 *Heimskringla III*, pp. 318–19. The author of *Morkinskinna* also underlines this (*Morkinskinna II*, p. 185).
11 Bjarni Guðnason, *Fyrsta sagan*; Andersson, 'Kings' Sagas (Konungasögur)', p. 214.

events took place strengthens the credibility of the aforementioned sagas,[12] especially with regard to the friendship and family ties between the main saga figures. Even though the gap between the events and their recording is short, there are a number of source problems that must be taken into consideration. These will be addressed throughout the chapter.

The Royal Networks: Friends and Family

In the political landscape of medieval Norway, the death of a king or the ascent of a new one usually marked a turning point in power dynamics, this because the incoming king would typically restructure the former ruler's network. Sigurd the Crusader had been the sole king of Norway since 1123, having from 1103 ruled together with his brothers Olav (1099–1115) and Oystein (1088–1123), and it is likely that his network included most of the country's most prestigious families. While Sigurd's reign (*ǫld*) is generally praised in *Heimskringla*, other accounts such as *Morkinskinna* and *Ágrip* paint a less flattering picture, describing the king as hot-tempered and even resorting to publicly beating his queen.[13] It is therefore likely that Sigurd the Crusader's uncontrolled behaviour affected how he treated his friends, which could have weakened their trust in him. Additionally, there were probably lords who were not part of the royal network and were therefore searching for an opportunity to gain favour, waiting for a new king to take the throne.

For kings and lords, politics revolved around creating and maintaining networks. Kings needed to make friends, which we will discuss later in the chapter. Friendship was an agreement between two individuals with reciprocal duties established through support, gifts, and feasting. There were two main types of friendship: vertical friendship between lords and householders, and horizontal friendship between two lords or lords and kings. Loyalty was highly important in vertical friendships; lords protected their friends and received support in return. In horizontal friendships, loyalty was less important; kings and lords changed their friends according to their political goals. Friendship ties had to be renewed regularly, mainly through organizing feasts and giving gifts. Wealth and generosity were, therefore, the keys to power.[14]

---

12 For a discussion of the source problems regarding the sagas, see for example Bagge, 'Mellom kildekritikk og historisk antropologi', pp. 173–212; Helle, 'Den primitivistiske vendingen', pp. 571–609; Helle, 'Hvor står den historiske', pp. 50–86; Ghosh, *Kings' Sagas and Norwegian History*.
13 *Morkinskinna II*, pp. 139–47; *Ágrip*, pp. 49–50.
14 Jón Viðar Sigurðsson, *Viking Friendship*, pp. 11–71.

After it was confirmed that Harald Gille was the son of a king and the half-brother of Sigurd the Crusader, the latter granted him a share of the royal revenues.[15] Without this support, Harald Gille, who arrived in Norway with no wealth, would not have been able to form alliances and establish friendships. As an independent lord, he became a significant player in the power game and a potential contender for the throne. Many lords sought to become his friends in order to strengthen their own positions, even those who were already part of the royal network.[16] This allowed them to maintain their existing ties while also forming new ones with the emerging power player.

Nothing is known about Magnus the Blind's network in the years before the death of his father Sigurd the Crusader. It is, however, likely that Magnus the Blind, as a king's son and future king, had some economic resources at his disposal. Before Harald Gille's arrival on the political scene and his acceptance as a king's son, Magnus the Blind's position was undisputable: he was the future king. It is therefore likely that all the lords complied with his wishes; otherwise, they ran the risk of being excluded from his future royal network. This, however, changed after Harald Gille's ordeal. King Sigurd the Crusader, who had ruled jointly with his brothers Olav Magnusson (d. 1115) and Oystein Magnusson (d. 1123), was not convinced that Harald Gille would keep his oath to wait for the death of Magnus, and therefore tried to strengthen his son's position by asking that the people of the land swear an oath that only Magnus should be king after him, which they duly did.[17]

When Sigurd the Crusader died in Oslo in 1130, his son Magnus the Blind was with him. The townspeople, in accordance with the oath they had given the late king, accepted Magnus the Blind as their king, and many men became his *handgengnir menn* (liegemen, vassals) and *lendr menn*.[18] This means that Magnus the Blind established his royal network immediately after his father had passed away. *Handgengnir menn* and *lendir menn* usually came from the leading families and outranked all other *hirð*-men, which will be discussed below, with the exception of members of the royal family, dukes, and earls. The office of *lendr maðr* was not 'hereditary, although there was a certain tendency for men of the same

---

15 Morkinskinna narrates that King Sigurd put Harald in his group (*sveit*) among his cupbearers (*skutilsveinar*) (*Morkinskinna II*, p. 144).
16 *Heimskringla III*, p. 278. Individuals who probably belonged to Harald's network at this stage include Kristrod, Harald's half-brother on his mother's side (*Heimskringla III*, pp. 281–82; *Ágrip*, p. 322), Rognvald Kali Kolsson, who became jarl over Orkney, Ingemar Sveinsson, Tjostolv Alason, and Solmund Sigurdsson (*Orkneyinga saga*, pp. 130–31, 141). *Heimskringla* mentions that Torkel's foster father Sumarlidason had accompanied Harald when he came to Norway and was a close friend of his (*Heimskringla III*, pp. 298–99).
17 *Heimskringla III*, pp. 266, 278–79.
18 *Heimskringla III*, p. 278.

families to be appointed'.[19] Making a person a *lendr maðr* and giving him a royal farm (or several) to administrate was a form of gift, and thus the foundation of a friendship. In return, the king could claim the support of the new *lendr maðr*. The Norwegian nobility's economic resources were limited; they needed access to royal resources, particularly the royal farms, in order to maintain their social position. The kings might allow their friends to manage royal farms and to keep the income. These farms were the king's property; such an allocation was therefore only possible for the duration of the king's reign, or as long as the king permitted it. For this reason, the kings could use the allocation of these farms to pressure the lords. It was also crucial for the kings to establish ties with members of the social elite, because of their local networks and strong positions in society.

As already mentioned, Harald Gille and his friends were in Tønsberg when they learned that Sigurd the Crusader had died. They immediately gathered an assembly, where Harald Gille was made king over 'half' of the country. He could therefore claim half of the royal incomes in the country; taxes, fines, and rent from the royal properties. At the assembly it was also explicitly stated that the oaths Harald Gille had made to Sigurd the Crusader had been extracted from him under duress.[20]

Harald Gille instantly started to establish a royal network when he became king. The first step was to build himself a *hirð*, a retinue of men who owed fealty and service to the king.[21] The *hirð* was a crucial element in the royal network and the most important tool for the kings in order to exercise their power during the period c. 900–1300. It was divided into two parts: the men who dined at the king's table, and those who lived on their farms. After having served the king for a period, the *hirð*-men were allowed to travel back to their homes. At that time, they were often given one or more demesne farms from the king, and they could act as his representative agents in that area. Early in the eleventh century, the *hirð* was divided into *hirð*-men and *gestir* (guests). The difference between these groups was that the *hirð*-men usually came from distinguished families and were used

---

19 Bagge, *From Viking Stronghold*, p. 53.
20 *Heimskringla III*, pp. 278–79. *Ágrip* claims that Harald did not remember the oaths he had made (*Ágrip*, p. 51). *Fagrskinna* is more in line with *Heimskringla* (*Ágrip*, p. 321). *GD*, 14.1.3. *Orkneyinga saga* narrates that Rognvald Kali Kalason from Orkney, Harald's *frændi* (kin, though we do not know how they were related) helped him in 1134. He was the son of Kali Kolason from Agder, and Gunnhildr, the sister of St Magnus of Orkney. King Sigurd the Crusader gave him the name Rognvald when he made him joint jarl of Orkney. He was killed in Caithness in 1158 (*Orkneyinga saga*, pp. 140–41).
21 For a discussion about the structure of the *hirð*, see Helle, *Norge blir en stat*, pp. 200–14; Lunden, *Norge under Sverreætten*, pp. 416–20; Andersen, *Samlingen av Norge*, pp. 134–35, 289–94; Bagge, *Mennesket i middelalderens Norge*, pp. 182–90; Ersland and Holm, *Krigsmakt og kongemakt*, pp. 31–63.

for non-violent missions in times of peace, while the *gestir* were of lower rank and acted as some sort of police force.

Harald thus appointed *lendir menn*, but nothing is known about who they were. However, it is likely that some of them were lords that he had already established friendships with when he entered the country. Finally, there were the *lið* who gathered around him. Who these men were is unclear, as is why they were not included in the *hirð*. Most probably, the *lið* was the king's private army, which he could use in battles and disputes against other kings and claimants to the throne. The kings, as will be discussed below, could not raise the *leiðangr* in these kinds of disputes. The *leiðangr* was the 'official' army of the kingdom, a naval organization under the leadership of the king, and was mainly used to defend the realm or attack other kingdoms. Norway's householders provided the ships, the crew, the weapons, and bore the cost.[22] The main difference between the *lið* and *leiðangr* was thus that 'the leader of a *lið* was expected to pay his men for their service, to provide food, clothes and arms for them during the campaign, and to reward them afterwards with gold, silver and other precious things; the *leding* (*leiðang*), on the other hand, fought at its own expense (with no expectation of reward than a chance to loot), and was expected to bring its own arms and provisions [...]'.[23]

Thus, a few weeks after King Sigurd the Crusader's death, there were two kings in the country and two royal networks. At this stage men who most likely had friendships with both kings moved between them. This group of people is referred to in the sagas as *beggja vinir* (friends of both) and could therefore not support one friend in a dispute against another. Instead, they had to mediate.[24] Magnus the Blind's forces were weaker than those of Harald Gille, and so he was pressed to accept him as co-regent. However, he kept the ships, the tableware and things of value, and all the money his father had possessed. *Heimskringla* then adds that he was 'less pleased' (*unði* [...] *verr*) with his share.[25] It is likely that the largest part of Magnus the Blind's royal network had also belonged to his father. After Harald Gille became king, Magnus the Blind lost control over half of the royal income. He could therefore not keep up all the friendship obligations of his father; for this reason, the royal network he had partly inherited must have started to fall apart almost immediately after he became king.

---

22 Bjørkvik, 'Leidang', cols 432–42; Ersland and Holm, *Krigsmakt og kongemakt*, pp. 42–63.
23 Lund, 'The Armies of Swein Forkbeard and Cnut, "leding or lið?"', p. 106.
24 Jón Viðar Sigurðsson, *Viking Friendship*, pp. 27–28, 56, 82.
25 *Heimskringla III*, pp. 278–79. In *Ágrip* it is written that Sigurd's *hirð* was divided into two parts (*Ágrip*, p. 51), but *Fagrskinna*, as *Heimskringla*, states that each of the kings had their own *hirð* (*Ágrip*, pp. 321–22).

The *orrusta* at Fyrileiv

Royal property, as well as the population, was unevenly spread throughout the country, and there were no royal residence(s) permanently inhabited by the kings.[26] The partition of the country between Harald Gille and Magnus the Blind was therefore not an option. A king travelled around the country, largely receiving his incomes in the form of *veizla*,[27] provisions for himself and his men in the local region. When there were several kings, they usually travelled in different parts of the country, probably according to some prearranged pattern, occasionally meeting for eating, drinking, and discussion.[28]

The kings had to carry out several tasks jointly, and therefore they met in the most important cities in the realm — Trondheim, Bergen and Oslo. There were other tasks which they were able to fulfil individually. Giving the householders amendments (*réttarbætr*) was one of the responsibilities the kings had to do together. In the winter of 1133–1134 both Harald Gille and Magnus the Blind were in Trondheim, and it is likely that they provided the householders with amendments at the time.[29] During the winter, the kings invited each other to banquets, but nevertheless tension grew between their *lið*.[30] In the spring both kings travelled to the eastern part of the country. Magnus the Blind, who was in charge of his father's fleet, sailed there. On his way to Viken, he mobilized his friends in order to attack Harald Gille.[31]

Harald Gille, who lacked ships, travelled the inland route from Trondheim to Viken. When he learned about the activities of Magnus the Blind, he started mobilizing troops. *Heimskringla* states that wherever the kings then travelled, they attacked each other's farms (*bú*) and killed the men who were in charge.[32] The *bú* were most likely royal farms. When the royal income was divided between the two kings, the royal farms, as mentioned, were split equally between them, and they appointed trusted men to run them.

---

26 Bjørkvik, *Krongodset i mellomalderen*, pp. 201–31. Bjørkvik, *Det norske krongodset i mellomalderen*. Bjørkvik and Holmsen, *Kven åtte jorda i den gamle leiglendingstida?*
27 *Veizla*, or guesting, during the Viking Age and the Middle Ages signified free hospitality for the king and his entourage in the district where they were travelling. It was the householders in the area who had to provide food and drink for the king (Norseng, Veitsle).
28 Bagge, *From Viking Stronghold*, pp. 40–41. Cf. Blom, *Samkongedømme – enekongedømme*, pp. 6–7.
29 Blom, *Samkongedømme – enekongedømme*, p. 8.
30 The sagas often use the term *ǫfund* (envy/jealousy) to underline this tension (*Heimskringla III*, p. 306).
31 *Heimskringla III*, pp. 279–80.
32 *Heimskringla III*, p. 280. *Ágrip*, p. 322.

The kings usually did not plunder householders' farms or kill them, due to the friendships the kings had with all of the householders in the country. In the first paragraph of *Gulathing law*, from around 1160, it is stated that the king should be the householders' friend, they his friend, and God a friend to them all.[33] The loyalty between the kings and their subjects was thus based on friendship with clear mutual obligations. The kings should protect the householders, and in return, they should assist the kings in defending the country. When there were two or more kings jointly ruling, the householders were subjects to both or all of them. It was therefore difficult for the kings to plunder the householders, although this did occur occasionally.

The battle between the kings took place at Fyrileiv in 1134. At its start, Magnus the Blind had a force of around 7000 men, while Harald Gille only had *c.* 2000 men.[34] This battle is always considered to be the onset of the civil wars in Norway.[35] For the first time in more than a century, two kings were engaged in a violent struggle for the crown. The famous Stiklestad battle had taken place in 1030; it had been followed three years later by another, this time between Svend Alfivason and Tryggve Olavsson. There were around ten battles between kings during the period between *c.* 930 and *c.* 1030.[36] In the civil war period from 1130 to 1240, by contrast, approximately thirty battles were fought in Norway, as discussed in Chapter 5.[37] These numbers are based on confrontations that the sagas label as *orrusta* (battle). Other words for battles are *fundr* (meeting) and *bardagi* (encounter). The difference between *bardagi*, *fundr*, and *orrusta* was that *orrusta* was only used to describe confrontations involving kings.[38]

---

33 *Den eldre Gulatingslova*, p. 1; Jón Viðar Sigurðsson, *Viking Friendship*, pp. 48–50; Jón Viðar Sigurðsson, 'The Royal Ideology in Norway', forthcoming.
34 *Heimskringla III*, p. 280; *Ágrip*, p. 322; *Orkneyinga saga*, p. 141. Among Harald's men were Kristrod, his brother, Earl Rognvald Kali Kolsson, who became jarl over Orkney, Ingemar Sveinsson af Aski, Tjostolv Alason and Solmund Sigurdsson. Kristrod and Ingimar died in the battle (*Orkneyinga saga*, p. 141).
35 See for example Bagge, *Society and Politics*, p. 33; Bagge, *From Viking Stronghold*, p. 42; Birgit Sawyer, 'The "Civil Wars" Revisited', p. 48; Helle (ed.), *The Cambridge History of Scandinavia I*, p. 371; Orning, 'Borgerkrig og statsutvikling', p. 203.
36 *Heimskringla I*, pp. 173–75 (954, Avaldsnes), 178–80 (955, Rastarkalv), 186–92 (961, Fitjar), 208 ('orrostur' between earl Hakon Sigurdsson and the sons of Gunnhild), 221 (963, death of Erling Eiriksson), 243–47 (Sunnmøre, Sogn), 279–86 (986, Hjørungavåg); *Heimskringla II*, pp. 362–85 (1030, Stiklestad), 413 (1033, Soknasund).
37 1134 Fyrileiv, 1135 Bergen, 1137 Minne, 1137 Krókaskógur, 1139 Holmengrå, *c.* 1150 Leikberg, 1155 Bergen, 1161 Ekeberg, 1161 Tønsberg, 1161 Oslo, 1162 Sekken, 1163 Re, 1167 Overfallet på Rydjøkul, 1167 Stange, Viken 'nǫkkurar orrostur' (*Heimskringla III*, p. 411), 1177 Re, 1178 Hatthammeren, 1178 Hørte bro, 1179 Kalvskinnet, 1180 Ilevollene, 1181 Bergen, 1184 Fimreite, 1194 Florvåg, 1206 Nidaros, 1206 Bergen, 1207 Tønsberg, 1222 Ekornholmen, 1227 Vingir, 1227 Vorma, 1240 Låke, 1240 Oslo (April).
38 Jón Viðar Sigurðsson and Henrik Vigh, 'Who Is the Enemy?', p. 52.

According to *Heimskringla*, Harald Gille lost more than sixty *hirðmenn* in the battle, and we can assume that Magnus the Blind also lost some men. Thus, we can guess that approximately 100 men died in the battle. Although the sagas provide little information about the number of men killed in battles in Norway, the scant information available suggests that the number of men killed was rarely higher than this, except for the battle at Fimreite in 1184, which was the deadliest battle ever fought in Norway, where more than 2000 men died.[39] The discussion about the size of the population in Norway is problematic; it is most likely that around 300–350,000 people lived there in the middle of the twelfth century.[40] Therefore, it is difficult to claim, based on these numbers (excluding the battle at Fimreite), that the battle in Fyrileiv and other battles during the civil war period were particularly destructive.

Even though the battle of Fyrileiv was not especially deadly, it was, as mentioned, the first battle (*orrusta*) in the country for more than a century. There was often great tension between kings who ruled jointly during the period 1033–1134, but they did not fight for the throne. Sometimes the problem was 'solved' by the unexpected natural death of a king, but usually the royal networks with their multitude of overlaps prevented outbreaks of war. So why did the royal networks not manage to maintain the peace in 1134? There were probably two main reasons for this; firstly, King Magnus the Blind was not interested in sharing his position with Harald Gille, and secondly the overlaps between the two royal networks were not strong enough to prevent a battle between the two kings.

Medieval historians frequently refer to Max Gluckman and his idea of 'the peace in the feud'.[41] A person caught in a dispute between his relatives cannot support one kinsman against another and will thus try to establish peace between them. 'It is the strength of these "cross-linkages" joining two potentially hostile groups that prevents an outbreak of violence'.[42] Obviously, there was a difference between close and distant kinship, but when it comes to Norway with its small population and the frequent intermarriages between the social elites which had occurred for centuries, the overlaps of kinship must have been extensive. However, as I have

---

39 *Heimskringla III*, p. 282; *Ágrip*, p. 322; *Sverris saga*, p. 145. The primary reason for the high casualty rate was due to the nature of the engagement as a sea battle.
40 Helle, *Under kirke og kongemakt*, pp. 88–90. The size of the population in Norway around c. 1300 was probably around 450, 000. It seems that the population in Western Europe tripled in the years from 1000 to 1340 (Russell, 'Population in Europe 500–1500', p. 36; Cipolla, *Before the Industrial Revolution*, p. 3). If we use these numbers to calculate the population of Norway, it would have been approximately 300, 000 around the year 1150.
41 Gluckman, 'The Peace in the Feud', pp. 1–14.
42 Lambert, *Introduction*, pp. 6–7; Hyams, *Rancor and Reconciliation in Medieval England*, pp. 14–16.

argued in a number of publications, kinship ties in Norway were weaker than friendship ties, and they, also with a multitude of overlaps, even more so than kinship managed to maintain the 'peace in the feud'.[43]

The Danish Kings and Conflicts in Norway

Magnus the Blind controlled the whole country after the battle in Fyrileiv. When the king and his advisers discussed the future strategy against Harald Gille, the advisers wanted to keep the *flokkr* in Viken in order to be able to defend the country when Harald Gille came back. However, Magnus the Blind rejected this idea, let his troops disband, and sailed north to Bergen.[44]

After having lost the battle, Harald Gille went to the Danish king Erik the Unforgettable (1134–1137) for help.[45] They had 'sworn oaths of brotherhood',[46] so Erik was obliged to support Harald Gille. To make sure Harald Gille could continue his fight for the throne in Norway, Erik gave him Halland for revenue and passage (*veizlu ok yfirferð*), and *Knýtlinga saga* adds that the two kings parted in friendship (*vináttu*).[47]

Edward N. Luttwak argues in the article 'Give War a Chance' that the involvement of external actors in wars only prolonged them.[48] This description is aimed at the situation after the Second World War, but is equally applicable to the situation in Norway in the years from 1130 to 1240. The main reason why the civil wars in Norway lasted for more than a century is the Danish kings' involvement.[49] The Danish kings dominated

---

43 Jón Viðar Sigurðsson, *Viking Friendship*, pp. 58–89.
44 *Heimskringla III*, p. 282; *Ágrip*, p. 322; GD, 14.1.5.
45 Erik the Unforgettable was an illegitimate son of King Erik the Good (r. 1095–1103), and had fought his uncle King Niels, who had reigned after Erik's father, for the throne (*Ágrip*, p. 322).
46 *Heimskringla III*, p. 282; *Fagrskinna* (*Ágrip*, p. 322); *Orkneyinga saga*, p. 142. *Knýtlinga saga* (*Danakonunga sögur*, p. 264). Snorre writes that Erik and Harald previously had become sworn brothers. Saxo confirms that Erik helped Harald with an army. Saxo recorded that Erik decided to help Harald because Magnus had sent his wife, Erik's niece, away (GD, 14.1.5). Snorre also notes that the kin of the wife showed him ill will which, it is reasonable to assume, refers to Erik's support of Magnus' opponent Harald (*Heimskringla III*, p. 279).
47 *Danakonunga sögur*, p. 265.
48 Luttwak, *Give War a Chance*, p. 36.
49 Helle, *Norge blir en stat*, pp. 69–72. In the year 1170 Erling skakke was granted Viken as a fief (*lén*) from the Danish King Valdemar (*Heimskringla III*, p. 406); Bagge, *From Viking Stronghold*, p. 49. *Fagrskinna* writes that King Valdemar the Victorious forbade people in Viken from making 'trading voyages to Denmark. He also banned the bringing of corn and other things which they found profitable to Norway. But the people of Viken could not do without the Danish market. Many asked Erling to make peace with the king of the Danes by some means'. 'Eptir þetta bannaði Danakonungr Vikverjum kaupferð til Danmarkar. Svá ok bannaði hann at flytja korn í Noreg eða aðra þá hluti, sem þeim væri þurftuligir. En Vikverjar

politics in Scandinavia during the Viking Age (c. 800–1050). Their realm stretched from Schleswig-Holstein in Northern Germany, across Jutland, Zealand, over Scania in Sweden, and on to Lindesnes in Vest-Agder in Norway. Thus, they had lordship over the areas on either side of Øresund and the *Jótlandshaf*, the modern-day Skagerrak, and Kattegat. These areas were not only the most geographically central in Scandinavia, but they were also the most densely populated.

In 1042, the Norwegian king Magnus the Good became the king of Denmark. In 1036, he and the Danish king Hardeknud had come to an agreement to avoid a battle between them. They agreed that if one of them died without leaving a son, the other should inherit their territories and subjects. When Hardeknud died in 1042, Magnus the Good became the king of Denmark, turning the relationship between Denmark and Norway upside-down. The following year, he led the defence of Denmark against the Wends, a Slavic people, in a famous battle at Lyrskoghede. However, shortly after this, Svend Estridsen, son of Knud the Great's sister Estrid, claimed the throne of Denmark, which immediately led to conflict with Magnus. In 1047, shortly before his death, Magnus bequeathed the Danish throne to Svend and the Norwegian throne to Harald Hardruler, including Viken, which stretches from the Göta älv to Lindesnes.[50]

In the years up to 1241 the Danish kings tried to regain their influence in Norway, especially in Viken, which, as mentioned, had been under their control during the Viking Age. It was not until the death of Denmark's King Valdemar the Victorious on 28 March 1241 that the Norwegian realm came to be outside of 'the Danish force field' (danske kraftfeltet).[51] There were two main ways in which the Danish kings could exert their influence. The first and most common way was to provide aid for the Norwegian kings and pretenders to the throne, many of whom also had strong family ties to the Danish kings. The second was by attacking Viken.

Harald Gille, after the meeting with Erik the Unforgettable, travelled from Zealand, where he had met the Danish king, to Halland, where troops joined him, and further on to Konghelle.[52] Erik's gift made it possible for Harald Gille to use the Danish royal resources in Halland to build up a new fighting force — it also stopped Harald Gille's troops from plundering Halland. Before the two kings departed, Erik the Unforgettable gave Harald Gille 'eight unrigged warships', an appropriate gift for a king.[53]

---

megu ekki missa Danmarkar kaupstefnu. Báðu margir Erling, at hann skyldi gøra frið við Danakonung með nǫkkuru móti'. *Ágrip*, p. 355.

50 *Heimskringla III*, pp. 12–13; Jón Viðar Sigurðsson, *Viking Friendship*, pp. 9–44.
51 Bjørgo, Rian, and Kaartvedt, *Makt og avmakt: 800–1536*, p. 43.
52 *Heimskringla III*, p. 282; *Ágrip*, p. 322; *Danakonunga sögur*, p. 265.
53 Erik the Unforgettable had been King Sigurd the Crusader's friend. When Korskirken (the Cross Church) in Konghelle was consecrated, a church Sigurd ordered to be erected, Erik the Unforgettable sent a 'shrine' to him (*Heimskringla III*, p. 276.) Cf. *GD*, 14.1.8; Jón Viðar

When Harald Gille and his troops came to Konghelle in Båhuslen, the *lendir menn* of King Magnus the Blind and the townspeople rallied troops to fight him. This also shows that Magnus the Blind expected an attack and thought that the local people would be sufficiently able to defend the realm. However, he was not prepared for the tactic Harald Gille used. The king sent men to meet the army and requested that he not be prevented from taking what was rightfully his. The householders accepted his claim, abandoned their muster, and submitted to the king. Then Harald Gille gave *lén* (fiefs) and *veizlr* (revenues) to *lendir menn*, and amendments to those householders who supported him (*er í lið snerust með honum*).[54] The amendments were probably tax reductions, however, they were only valid for the duration of his reign, such amendments were therefore an important tool for kings to gain householders' friendship and support.[55] It is likely that all of these *lendir menn* had previously supported Magnus the Blind, and that they shifted their alliance on the condition that they were allowed to keep their *veizlr*. It was common in political struggles to switch sides like this. The *lendir menn*, and the social elite in general, were first and foremost concerned with their own power and social position, and they would therefore always support the most generous king; 'success depended on patronage' as David Crouch has so correctly formulated it.[56]

After Haraldr Gille had presented gifts to both the *lendir menn* and householders, a sizable crowd gathered around him. He travelled around Viken and gave *góðr friðr* (good peace) to all men except those who supported King Magnus the Blind; these people, probably those running the royal farms, were robbed or killed.[57] What *góðr friðr* refers to is unclear, but it most likely indicates the absence of plundering. It is important to underline the ideological aspect of this episode. According to the sagas, only kings could establish *friðr*. Lords, as well as kings, could only make a *sátt* (agreement). This fits well with the general pattern the sagas use to underline the (ideological) differences between kings, earls, and lords.[58]

Sigurðsson, *Viking Friendship*, pp. 53–54. King Sigurd and the Danish King Niels had also been friends and had travelled jointly in the so-called expedition into Kalmar in Sweden in 1123 or 1124 (Jensen, 'Korstog mod de hedenske svenskere', pp. 151–76).

54 *Heimskringla III*, p. 283. Harald is the only king during the period 1050–1170 to give *lén* to *lendir menn*. That he divided this part of his realm into *lén*, is in accordance with his strategy to let his friends share the administration with him.

55 Hamre, 'Retterbot', cols 108–10; Jón Viðar Sigurðsson, *Viking Friendship*, pp. 48–49, 61.

56 Crouch, *The Birth of Nobility*, p. 41.

57 *Heimskringla III*, p. 283. *Ágrip*, p. 322.

58 Jón Viðar Sigurðsson, 'Kings, Earls and Chieftains', p. 73; Jón Viðar Sigurðsson, *Viking Friendship*, pp. 90–106; Bagge, *Society and Politics*, pp. 146–51; Bagge, *Mennesket i middelalderens Norge*, pp. 52–53; Ármann Jakobsson, *Í leit að konungi. Konungsmynd íslenskra konungasagna*, pp. 96–106.

Kings, Counsel, and Gifts

After taking control of Viken, Harald Gille rallied a large army before sailing to Bergen. Magnus the Blind, who had been informed about the events, asked for advice from the lords who were with him. Sigurd Sigurdsson, one of the king's best advisers, attempted to give him some counsel, but the king rejected all of his advice. Sigurd Sigurdsson therefore left Bergen. Magnus the Blind's unwillingness to listen to his friends can also clearly be seen in the events after his victory in 1134. His closest friends and advisers suggested, as mentioned earlier, that he should keep the *flokkr* gathered in Viken and wait for Harald Gille. Magnus the Blind, however, rejected this and allowed his men to go back to their farms, and sailed back to Bergen himself. The sagas stress that he was *einráðr*, wanting to rule alone.[59]

Harald Gille, however, was open to advice (*ráðþægr*) and let his friends 'make decisions (*ráða með sér*) with him on anything they wanted. All this brought him friendship and praise'.[60] Norwegian historians have almost unanimously interpreted this as a weakness,[61] but in light of Sigurd the Crusader's regime and the fact that Harald Gille was a newcomer in the power game who lacked a social network, this was a good strategy. It afforded him support from the majority of the most influential men in the country, created a consensus and trust between them, and ensured loyalty to him.

The phrase 'ráða með sér' is used three times in *Heimskringla*. The first one is in *Óláfs saga helga*, when the Swedish king quarrels with the householders about his alliance with Olav Haraldsson; he states that he, like earlier kings, will let the farmers have their say in everything they wanted.[62] The second occasion is the above-mentioned portrayal of Harald Gille, and the final one is the description of his son, King Inge, in which he was said to be 'cheerful of speech and pleasant with his friends, generous with wealth, mostly letting leading men make decisions about the government with him'.[63]

That the kings let their friends rule with them did not mean that all the kings' friends were equally important. This can clearly be seen among King Inge Hunchback's friends. Gregorius Dagsson was his closest friend and came to be in charge (*forstjóri*) of ruling the land (*landráð*) together

---

59 *Heimskringla III*, p. 282; *Ágrip*, pp. 323–24.
60 *Heimskringla III*, p. 278, 'ráða með sér í ǫllu er þeir vildu. Slíkt allt dró honum til vinsælda og orðlofs'; *Morkinskinna II*, p. 175.
61 Arstad, 'En undersøkelse av Harald Gilles ettermæle', pp. 435–45. Arstad gives a good overview of the debate about Harald Gille in this article.
62 *Heimskringla II*, p. 116, 'láta bœndr ráða með sér ǫllu því, er þeir vildu'.
63 *Heimskringla III*, p. 331, 'blíðmæltr ok dæll vinum sínum, ǫrr af fé ok lét mjǫg hǫfðingja ráða með sér landráðum' Cf. *Heimskringla I*, pp. 151, 170; *Heimskringla II*, p. 169; *Eddukvæði II*, p. 279. Cf. *Jómsvíkinga saga*, p. 6.

with the king. Inge therefore allowed him to take what he wished from his own possessions.[64] The kings' group of friends was not homogenous, and obviously, the most powerful were usually the most influential.[65]

Another important difference between the two kings was their generosity — Magnus the Blind was supposedly greedy, while Harald Gille, on the other hand, gave his friends great gifts.[66] His lavishness is stressed in other sagas than the kings' sagas. *Hungrvaka*, the saga about the first bishops in Iceland, for example emphasizes that he was 'open-handed and generous with his friends' (*ǫrr ok stórlyndr við vini sína*).[67] In 1135, when he met the Icelandic bishop Magnus Einarsson in Sarpsborg, Harald Gille gave him a cup which weighed eight marks; afterwards it was made into a chalice in Skálholt cathedral.[68] Harald Gille's generosity resulted in most of the men in Norway wanting to become his friend.

Harald Gille arrived in Bergen on the eve of Yule and, out of respect for the holiday, postponed the planned attack on Magnus the Blind.[69] This gave Magnus the opportunity to prepare the city's defences. Among other things, Magnus set up a ballista on Holmen, and iron chains were placed across the bay from the royal palace. According to *Heimskringla*, no more than three days were kept sacred.[70] *Gulathing law* states that Yule should be respected,[71] and *Gammelnorsk homiliebok* claims that those who do so will gain a place in heaven, while those who disobey it will endure torture (*pinsl*) in the otherworld and battles (*bardaga*) in this one.[72] Harald Gille respected Yule and waited until 7 January to attack Bergen. He attacked with a force of nine hundred men, many of whom had joined him during the Yule celebrations, so his respect also contained a tactical element.[73]

Before the battle began, Harald Gille made a vow to St Olav that, in return for victory, he would build a church for him in the town at his own expense.[74] King Olav Haraldsson had been killed in the Battle of Stiklestad in the year 1030, and the following year he began to be venerated as a saint. His cult grew rapidly, and in the years to come, he became the most important saint in Scandinavia. By promising to build a church for St Olav, Harald Gille was again trying to establish a friendship. The saints, in the

---

64 *Heimskringla III*, p. 330.
65 For a discussion on the importance of consensus see Schneidmüller, *Konsensuale Herrschaft*, pp. 53–87; Patzold, *Konsens und Konkurrenz*, pp. 75–103.
66 *Heimskringla III*, pp. 278, 282; *Ágrip*, pp. 323–24.
67 *Biskupa sögur II*, p. 29; *GD*, 14.1.5.
68 *Biskupa sögur II*, p. 29.
69 *Heimskringla III*, p. 285; *Ágrip*, p. 324.
70 *Heimskringla III*, pp. 285–86.
71 *Den eldre Gulatingslova*, p. 18.
72 *Gammelnorsk homiliebok*, p. 35.
73 *Heimskringla III*, p. 286.
74 *Heimskringla III*, p. 286.

Old Norse sources, are often referred to as 'God's friends' (*guðs vinir*), and by establishing friendships with them, one hoped for the support of God, thus because the saints were intermediary between the people and God.[75] A church dedicated to Olav was indeed erected after the battle, emphasizing the friendship between Harald and St Olav.

Harald Gille, as mentioned above, attacked Bergen on the last day of Yule with a force of nine hundred men. Magnus the Blind, however, had only the men of Bergen to fight for him, and when the battle started, they ran back into their houses. The confrontation was quickly brought to an end, and Magnus the Blind was captured.[76] Harald Gille and his counsellors then conducted a meeting about the fate of Magnus the Blind; their conclusion was that he should be deprived of the throne in such a way that he thereafter could never call himself king. He was then given over to the king's slaves and mutilated (*meiddr*); his eyes were poked out, one leg cut off, and finally he was castrated. After this act of mutilation, he was sent to a monastery in Trondheim.[77] There are very few narratives about mutilation in the sagas.[78] Magnus the Blind is the first and only Norwegian king that was *meiddr*. In the power game in Europe, mutilation like this was a very rarely used method for removing a king from the throne.[79] However, as we shall see below, Magnus the Blind did return.

Killing a king was not an option for Harald Gille and his advisers (*ráðuneyti*), but the assassination of a bishop was. After Magnus the Blind had been captured, Harald Gille and his men started to look for the private treasures of Sigurd the Crusader, the ones Magnus the Blind had possession of when his father died. Bishop Reinald in Stavanger, an Englishman and a close friend of Magnus the Blind, was thought to have knowledge about where these treasures had been hidden. However, he denied any knowledge about them, he was therefore fined fifteen gold marks. The bishop rejected to pay, said that he did not wish to impoverish his bishopric and would rather risk his life. He was then hanged, and *Heimskringla* adds that this deed was spoken 'very ill of' (*mjǫk lastat*).[80]

---

75 Jón Viðar Sigurðsson, *Viking Friendship*, pp. 86–102.
76 *Heimskringla III*, pp. 285–86; *Orkneyinga saga*, p. 142; *Fagrskinna* (*Ágrip*, pp. 324–25) says Harald attacked with 1100 men. Saxo Grammaticus says that the Danish king sent military support to Harald before he attacked Bergen (*GD*, 14.1.8).
77 *Heimskringla III*, p. 287; *Ágrip*, pp. 324, 326; *Morkinskinna II*, p. 162; *GD*, 14.1.8.
78 Kari Ellen Gade lists three episodes of mutilation in *Heimskringla*, one of which was the mutilation of King Magnus, two in *Orkneyinga saga*, four entries in annals for Orkney, Man, and the Hebrides for the years 1095, 1154, 1198, and 1223 (Gade, '1235 Órækja meiddr ok heill gǫrr', pp. 123–25). Cf. Lawing, 'Perspectives on Disfigurement in Medieval Iceland'.
79 Skinner, *Living with Disfigurement in Early Medieval Europe*, p. 14. Cf. McManus, 'Good-Looking and Irresistible', pp. 58–64; Duindam, *Dynasties*, p. 61.
80 *Heimskringla III*, pp. 287–88. The killing of Reinald is also condemned by *Morkinskinna* (*Morkinskinna II*, p. 162).

When explaining the kings' successes and failures the sagas point to their personal abilities.[81] In *Heimskringla* Magnus the Blind is described in the following way: he was 'more handsome (*fríðari*)' than any other man in the country. He was 'a proud-minded and stern person, a man of great ability, and his father's popularity was what most ensured him the friendship of the common people. He was a great drinker, greedy, hostile and difficult to deal with'.[82] *Morkinskinna* stresses that he also was cruel (*grimmr*).[83] Harald Gille, however, in clear contrast to Magnus the Blind, had all the right personal qualities to become a successful king. He 'was affable, cheerful, playful, humble, generous, so that he spared nothing for his friends, open to advice, so that he let others make decisions with him on anything they wanted. All this brought him friendship and praise. Many men of the ruling class then came to be on good terms with him no less than with Magnus'.[84] *Morkinskinna* underlines that he was not a clever man (*ekki vitr maðr*), but not as *grimmr* as Magnus the Blind.[85]

The difference between the two kings was great. Harald Gille was generous and let his friends rule alongside him, while Magnus the Blind was his complete opposite — greedy and wanting to rule alone. Magnus the Blind's network collapsed after his victory in 1134, mainly because of his lack of generosity and unwillingness to follow his friends' advice. Harald Gille, however, followed the rules of the game, gave great gifts, and accepted that his friends ruled with him. After becoming the sole king of Norway, Harald Gille granted reconciliation to all men who requested it and took many men into his service who had previously been allied with Magnus the Blind. He also let the most important of them foster his sons, a topic we will return to.

Kings with and without Networks

The next chapter in this saga started when Sigurd Slembe entered the scene. He came to Bergen in 1136, where he claimed to be a son of King Magnus Barefoot. He said he had performed a positive ordeal in front of

---

81 Bagge, *Society and Politics*, pp. 146–91; Jón Viðar Sigurðsson, 'The Appearance and Personal Abilities', pp. 95–109; Jón Viðar Sigurðsson, 'Kings, Earls and Chieftains', pp. 69–108.
82 *Heimskringla III*, p. 278, 'Hann var maðr skapstór ok grimmr, atgervimaðr vas hann mikill en vinsæld fǫðr hans heimti hann mest til alþýðu vináttu. Hann var drykkjumaðr mikill, fégjarn, óþýðr ok ódæll'.
83 *Morkinskinna II*, p. 174.
84 *Heimskringla III*, p. 278, 'Haraldr gilli var maðr léttlátr, kátr, leikinn, lítillátr, ǫrr svá at hann sparði ekki við vini sína, ráðþægr, svá at hann lét aðra ráða með sér ǫllu því, er vildu. Slíkt allt dró honum til vinsælda ok orðlofs. Þýddusk þá hann margir ríkismenn engum mun síður en Magnús'.
85 *Morkinskinna II*, p. 174.

five bishops in Denmark to prove this. He therefore asked Harald Gille to accept kinship with him.[86] After consultation with his friends, the king brought charges against Sigurd Slembe for being present at the killing of Torkel Sumarlidason, a man who had accompanied Harald Gille when he came to Norway and was a close friend. It was thus decided that Sigurd Slembe should be killed. However, Sigurd managed to escape, and then stayed in Bergen plotting to kill king Harald Gille. Some of the men who supported him were Harald Gille's *hirðmenn* and *herbergismenn* (members of his household), who had previously been King Magnus the Blind's *hirðmenn*. Two of them gained information about where the king was sleeping, and passed it on to Sigurd Slembe, who then went with some of his men and killed him.[87] The morning after in the harbour of Bergen, Sigurd Slembe announced the killing of the king to the townspeople and asked them to accept him as their king. However, they refused and judged Sigurd Slembe and his men to be outlaws, forcing them to sail away from Bergen.[88]

After the killing of Harald Gille, his *lendir menn*, *hirð*, and queen sent a fast-sailing ship to Trøndelag to inform the people there about the murder, and to inform them that Sigurd Mouth, King Harald Gille's son who was fostered by Sada-Gyrd Bardsson, should be made king. Ottar Birting, Peter Sauda-Ulfsson, the brothers Guttorm Asolfsson of Rein and Ottar Balle, and a large number of other leading men in Trøndelag supported this decision. But Harald Gille's queen Ingrid travelled east to Viken where Inge, her son with Harald Gille, was fostered by Amund, the son of Gyrd Law-Bersason. When she arrived in Viken, the Borgarthing was summoned instantly, and the two-year-old Inge Hunchback was made king. Amund and Tjostolv Alason and many other powerful men supported him. Then *Heimskringla* adds 'nearly all the people now switched their allegiance to the brothers, most of all because their father was said to be saintly, and the land was sworn to them with the stipulation that it should submit to no other person as long as any of the sons of King Harald were alive'.[89]

After being driven out of Bergen, Sigurd Slembe sailed to Nordhordaland and held an assembly with the householders. They submitted to him and gave him the title of king. He then travelled to Sogn and held an assembly with the householders there; they also accepted him as king. After

---

86 Sigurd Slembe was ordained as a dean, and before he claimed kingship in Norway, he had travelled widely. to the Holy Land, Scotland, Orkney, Denmark and even Iceland (*Heimskringla III*, pp. 297–98; *Morkinskinna II*, pp. 168–75; *Orkneyinga saga*, pp. 115–17).
87 *Heimskringla III*, pp. 298–301; *Morkinskinna II*, pp. 162–63, 172, 176; *Ágrip*, pp. 327–29.
88 *Heimskringla III*, p. 301; *Morkinskinna II*, pp. 175–79; *Ágrip*, pp. 328–29; *GD*, 14.29.2.
89 *Heimskringla III*, p. 303 'Ok snerist undir þá bræðr nálega allr lýðr ok allra helst fyrir þess sakar at faðir þeirra vas kallaðr heilagr ok var þeim svo land svarit at undir engan mann annan skyldi ganga meðan nokkur þeirra lifði sona Haralds konungs'. *Morkinskinna II*, pp. 178–79; *Ágrip*, p. 329.

this he sailed north to Fjordane. When Sigurd Slembe came to Nordmøre, however, influential men (*ráðamenn*) in the new royal networks had sent letters and tokens to the householders so they had already switched their allegiance (*hlýðni*) to the sons of Harald Gille. Sigurd Slembe was, therefore, not accepted as their king. Because of this, he and his men decided to sail to Trøndelag. He had sent men there beforehand with messages to his friends and to former friends of Magnus the Blind. When Sigurd Slembe arrived in Trøndelag, the common people (*lýðr allr*) did not give him permission to enter the royal palace. He then sailed to the monastery where Magnus the Blind was and took him against the wishes of the monks — for Magnus the Blind had taken the vow to become a monk. *Heimskringla* adds that many people said he had left of his own free will. When this became known, Bjorn Egilsson, Gunnar of Gimsar, Halldor Sigurdsson, Aslak Hakonsson and the brothers Benedikt and Eirik, from King Magnus the Blind's former *hirð*, and several other men, joined him and Sigurd Slembe.[90]

King Magnus the Blind's re-entrance onto the political scene opened up opportunities for many of his former friends, and men who were not included in the royal networks of Sigurd Mouth and Inge Hunchback. Magnus the Blind's network had fallen apart after he was removed from the throne, and it looks like most of his influential friends were included in the network of Harald Gille and after his death, the networks of his sons. *Heimskringla* narrates, as mentioned previously, that after Harald Gille became the sole king he took many men into his service who had previously been allied with Magnus the Blind. However, men like Gunnar of Gimsar, Aslak Hakonsson, Bjorn Egilsson, the brothers Eirik and Benedikt and Halldor Sigurdsson did not reconcile with Harald Gille. They probably belonged to a less influential part of the social elite.[91]

Soon after Sigurd Slembe and Magnus the Blind had established their alliance, Sigurd Slembe travelled to the Irish Sea. Magnus the Blind, however, went to Oppland to recruit troops.[92] This was a deliberate strategy; Magnus the Blind was to gather forces in Norway, while Sigurd Slembe left the country. He was, after all, an outlaw, and had only been accepted as a king in a very small part of the country. Magnus the Blind was facing a significant problem too, however; he did not have access to the royal revenues, which obviously made it difficult for him to build a royal network and fighting force. The reason Magnus the Blind travelled to Oppland must have been that he had friends there who were willing to support him and to help him to recruit men to his *lið*, both from Norway and Sweden. These

---

90 *Heimskringla III*, pp. 302, 304; *Morkinskinna II*, pp. 178, 180; *Ágrip*, pp. 330, 331; *GD*, 14.29.2.
91 *Heimskringla III*, pp. 296, 304; *Morkinskinna II*, pp. 162–63, 180.
92 *Heimskringla III*, p. 304; *Morkinskinna II*, p. 180.

Oppland lords were counting on Magnus the Blind to give them control over some of the royal farms when he became king again. The situation was identical for the *lið* fighting for Magnus the Blind; those who joined were to be rewarded *after* his victory. In short, the men fighting for Magnus the Blind were willing to fight for him in the hope of gaining benefits in the future.

When Magnus the Blind left Oppland in the summer of 1137, he had gathered a large force. In a battle with King Inge Hunchback at Minne, Magnus the Blind lost and many of his men, including Halldor Sigurdsson, Bjorn Egilsson, and Gunnar of Gimsar were killed. After the battle, Magnus fled to Götaland in Sweden. There he managed to convince Earl Karl Sunesson,[93] who was married to Brigida, Harald Gille's daughter, to attack Norway. When Tjostolv Alason and Amund Gyrdsson learned this, they gathered troops and fought Karl and drove him out of the kingdom.[94] It is not mentioned whether Magnus the Blind and his men participated in this battle.

Magnus the Blind then made his way to Denmark where he met the Danish king Erik the Unforgettable, the former blood-brother of Harald Gille. Magnus the Blind convinced him that if he came with his army to Norway, no one would dare fight against him. Eirik summoned his levy and, according to *Heimskringla*, sailed with six hundred ships to Norway. Magnus the Blind and his men joined him on this expedition. The attack was a great failure, which weakened the friendship between King Erik the Unforgettable and Magnus the Blind and his men.[95]

Sigurd Slembe, who most likely had been kept informed about the developments, reappeared on the scene at this time. It was not possible for Magnus the Blind to gain any support in Norway. He did not have access to the royal resources, and Sigurd Slembe came back from the Irish Sea region without any wealth. In order to build up a *lið* which they could use to fight for the throne in Norway, they needed resources. They therefore came up with a new tactic, which is best described as guerrilla warfare (or plundering in Viking style). They looted lords who belonged to the royal networks, and they raided ships sailing in and out of the Oslo fjord, on the Göta älv, and in the Baltic Sea. This pillaging went on for two years.[96] In the autumn of 1139 Sigurd Slembe and Magnus the Blind sailed from Aalborg to Norway with thirty ships, which included both

---

93 In Morkinskinna his surname is Sørkvisson (*Morkinskinna II*, p. 182).
94 *Heimskringla III*, pp. 304–06, 332; *Morkinskinna II*, pp. 181–83; *Ágrip*, p. 331.
95 *Heimskringla III*, pp. 282, 307–08; *Morkinskinna II*, pp. 183–84; *Ágrip*, pp. 331–32; *Danakonunga sögur*, pp. 266–67, 332–33.
96 *Heimskringla III*, pp. 309–20; *Morkinskinna II*, pp. 185–210; *Fagrskinna* (*Ágrip*, pp. 332–34) only very briefly mention these events, but the essence is the same.

Danish and Norwegian troops.[97] To fight them the *lendir menn* of both Inge Hunchback and Sigurd Mouth joined forces, and the armies met at Holmengrå. After the first onslaught, the Danes fled with eighteen ships. Magnus the Blind and many Norwegians were killed, and Sigurd Slembe was captured, tortured, and killed.

Magnus Barefoot: A King without a Family

The discussion so far has focused on royal networks, and especially the kings' friends. However, there was another element present in all networks; the *frændr* (relatives). What role did they play in royal networks? The short answer to this question is that their influence was almost nonexistent. This becomes particularly evident if we look at the relatives of King Magnus Barefoot (r. 1093–1103 – see Fig. 2.1).

The kinship system in Scandinavia was bilateral, which means that a person could trace their kin through both the paternal and the maternal line. Only children of the same two parents had an identical kin-group. Their parents, as well as their grandparents, had their own and so forth. The overlaps between these ties were extensive and created a continuous network of family relations. *Frændi* (kinsman), *frændkona* (kinswoman), and *frændsemi* are the most commons term to describe family relationships. According to the *Gulathing law*, kinship was limited to the third degree, that is, an individual and their sons, daughters, father, mother, son's sons, son's daughters, daughter's sons, daughter's daughters, maternal and paternal grandparents, brothers, sisters, nephews, nieces, male and female cousins, aunts, and uncles. In some instances, the *frændi* term is used to distinguish between more distantly related individuals, but in these cases kings or lords were one of the parties involved. Despite this bilateral feature, the Scandinavian kinship system had clear patrilineal tendencies. Only sons could carry on the family legacy. However, the female link was also important, especially for the lords.[98]

If we now analyse Fig. 2.1 and start by discussing the support King Magnus Barefoot could expect from his *frændr* (uncles and cousins) on his father's side, it is obvious that there was not much help to be had. King Magnus Barefoot's uncle Magnus died in 1069, after ruling for only three

---

97 Skyum-Nielsen, *Kvinde og slave*, p. 137.
98 *Den eldre Gulatingslova*, §§ 24, 25, 26, 32, 114, 165, 167, 168; *Grágás II*, pp. 59–60; *Grágás III*, 'frændsemi'; *Sverris saga*, p. 152; Hansen, 'Ætten' i de eldste', pp. 23–55; Hansen, 'Slektskap', pp. 104–32. Mundal, 'Kvinnesynet og forståinga av biologisk arv', pp. 153–70. Jón Viðar Sigurðsson, *Viking Friendship*, p. 22. The Norse family pattern is similar to the one we find elsewhere in Europe, the male line being more important than the female line (Bouchard, 'Those of my blood'; Drell, *Kinship and Conquest*; Crouch, *The Birth of Nobility*).

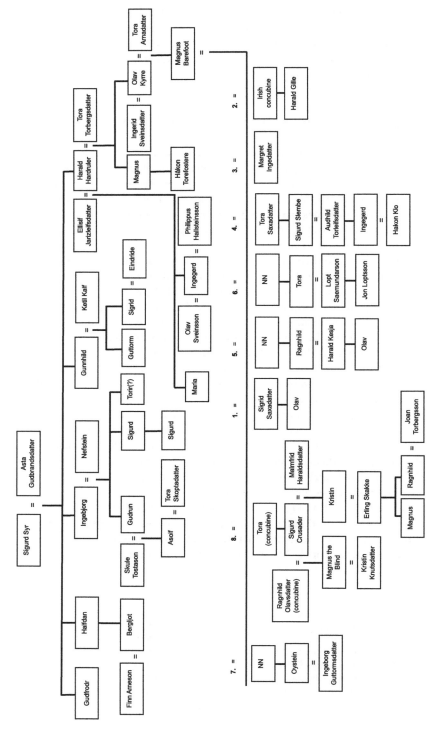

Figure 2.1. Genealogical tree of Magnus Barefoot. Figure by author.

years. His son Hakon Magnusson foster-son-of-Thorir (r. 1093–1095) became king in the same year as Magnus Barefoot, and for two years they ruled jointly, during which there was great tension between them. In short, the king's brothers, uncles, and cousins on their father's side were usually individuals they were competing against or ruling together with. This is in clear opposition to the lords' families where there was a stronger bond of loyalty between brothers, uncles, and cousins, and where they were usually not competing for the same positions but fighting to maintain the family honour.[99] It was an important 'fact of life in the middle ages that your kinsfolk were more likely to be your patrons and protectors and were more likely to advance you than anyone else'.[100]

The kings' daughters, as daughters of lords, were married to powerful local magnates in Norway or both kings and magnates in Sweden and Denmark, in order to establish or maintain friendships. These in-laws (*mágar*), especially those in Norway, could be useful for the kings. King Harald Hardruler's (Harald Sigurdsson) first wife was Ellisif Jarizleifsdatter. They had two daughters together, Maria, who died young, and Ingegerd.[101] The latter became queen of Denmark when her husband Oluf Hunger was elected king in 1086. She had one daughter with him. Ingegerd's second marriage, to a nephew of the Swedish king, was childless. We can also see this pattern when we look at Harald Gille's daughters. Brigida was first married to the Swedish king Inge Hallsteinsson.[102] When he died, she was married off to Earl Karl Sunesson, and when he passed away, she married the Swedish king Magnus Henriksson. Finally, Brigida was married to Earl Birger Brosa. Harald Gille's second daughter was Maria, and she was married to Simon Skalp, a son of Hallkell Huk, the man who brought Harald Gille to Norway. Harald Gille's third daughter, Margrethe, was married to Simon's brother Jon Hallkelsson.[103]

Brigida was born around 1130 and died after 1202. Assuming that she was married for the first time around 1145, it would mean that this occurred when her brothers were kings. Such alliances were common in Scandinavian politics. However, it is important to stress that we never hear of a king in one country supporting a king who was a relative by marriage in another country by sending soldiers. Conversely, friendship between kings, as we saw in the case of Harald Gille in 1134 when he travelled to Denmark, was important in order to have a place of shelter and for getting support to establish new fighting forces if necessary. Obviously, the

---

99 Miller, *Bloodtaking and Peacemaking*, p. 155; Jón Viðar Sigurðsson, *Chieftains and Power*, pp. 143–44; Jón Viðar Sigurðsson, *Viking Friendship*, p. 105.
100 Crouch, *The Birth of Nobility*, pp. 141, 144–45.
101 *Heimskringla III*, Ættaskrár. Niðjar Haralds Hárfagra, 2. framh.
102 It is unlikely that this is correct, King Inge died around 1130; Helle, 'Brigida Haraldsdatter'.
103 *Heimskringla III*, pp. 331–32.

symbol effect of these friendship ties was significant. It is also important to note that two of Harald Gille's daughters were married to the sons of the man who brought him to Norway. Hallkell Huk was a powerful lord; however, these marriages must have strengthened his sons' positions. At the same time, the sons of Hallkell Huk, with their networks, were now in-laws (*mágar*) to the kings of Norway and as such they could not support one against the other in a dispute; instead, they were forced to mediate. However, let us return to Magnus Barefoot and this time examine his mother's family.

The kings' mothers were usually, in clear contrast to most of the mothers of the local lords or kings in Europe, of low birth. This not only underlined the 'male dynastic line',[104] but also that the kings could not expect any support from their mothers' side of the family. In a dialogue between Magnus the Good (r. 1035–1047), the son of St Olav Haraldsson, and his mother, he complains about his mother's social position, and thus indirectly about her family: 'Many people owe a great deal to their fathers, and none more than I in most matters, but he did not choose a good mother for me'. She said: 'You should not accuse him regarding this account because he has made a lesser choice, but you should rather honour me more for the father I found for you'.[105]

Magnus Barefoot's mother was Tora Joansdatter. Nothing is known about her or her family.[106] She later married Brynjolv Ulfaldi Halldorsson on Vettaland in Bohuslän, who was one of the most powerful men in Viken.[107] This does not imply that Tora was from a noble family; as a king's mother and grandmother of many kings she was very attractive in the power game.

Magnus Barefoot had seven children with seven different women: Oystein Magnusson, Sigurd the Crusader, Olav Magnusson, Harald Gille, Sigurd Slembe, Ragnhild, and Tora. Nothing is known about the background of five of their mothers; there were three Jane Does, Tora *frilla* (concubine), and an Irish *frilla*.[108] The only other detail we know is that

---

104 Duindam, 'Dynasties', p. 63. Roger of Howden (d. 1201), in his annals, finds it strange that all kings' sons in Norway, even those born out of wedlock to a woman of low social status, could become kings (*Chronica magistri Rogeri de Houedene Volume 3*, p. 271).

105 *Morkinskinna I*, p. 166, 'Margir eigu sínum feðrum gott at launa ok eigi annarr maðr betra en ek um flesta hlutina, en vánt valði hann mér þo móðernit'. Hon segir. 'Ekki áttu honum þat at sǫk at gefa, því at velja mætti hann þat enn miðr, en meira áttu þat at virða við mik hvé ek valða þér fǫðurinn'.

106 *Heimskringla III*, p. 208. In Fagrskinna (*Ágrip*, p. 301) and Morkinskinna (*Morkinskinna II*, p. 9) she is said to be the daughter of Arne Lagi, and the king's *frilla*.

107 Krag, 'Magnus 3. Olavsson Berrføtt'.

108 *Orkneyinga saga* states that Harald's mother's family was from both the Hebrides and Ireland (*Orkneyinga saga*, pp. 130–31).

Oystein's mother was of low rank (*móðerni lítit*).[109] Sigrid was the king's concubine; her father was Saxi, a noble (*gǫfgr*) man in Trondheim. Magnus Barefoot later had a son with her sister Tora.[110] Whether Tora was a concubine like her sister is unknown, but it is likely. These relationships were entered into with the consent of the girls' families. Concubinage was advantageous for all parties involved. The girls secured their position in society, and the families of the concubines gained extra protection and greater access to royal resources. If a son was born who later became king, it would increase the family's honour. If the concubine was a daughter of a powerful lord, the kings could secure loyal support from powerful local actors.[111]

'Hazards of demography' was always a problem for the dynastic power. Kings had to produce royals to maintain authority, and one way to solve that issue was through 'polygynous reproduction'.[112] Kings of Norway were promiscuous, as the sagas so clearly show. One of the best examples is a story about Magnus Barefoot's grandchild, Sigurd Mouth. When Sigurd Mouth with his following was attending *veizlr* in Viken, he rode past a farm owned by a powerful man named Simon. As the king was riding through the farm, he heard beautiful singing coming from inside one of the buildings. He rode up to it and saw a woman standing there singing while she was grinding grain. Her name was Tora, a servant woman on the farm. The king then dismounted his horse, went inside to the woman and lay with her. Even though we can reasonably doubt this story, there is no reason to question that the kings had affairs with many girls, and some of them became pregnant.[113]

It was a challenge for the kings' advisers and entrusted men (*trúnaðarmenn*) to have an overview over all their affairs and children, and sometimes they actually kept information about the kings' children from them.[114] When a new unknown king's son or daughter came on the scene, their *frændsemi* had to be accepted. This can clearly be seen in Harald Gille and Sigurd Slembe's ordeals, and in an episode from 1163 when King Magnus Erlingsson and his kinsmen acknowledged the *frændsemi* of the most powerful Icelandic chieftains (*goði*) Jon Loptsson. He was a son of Tora, an otherwise unknown daughter of Magnus Barefoot, and the Icelandic

---

109 *Heimskringla III*, p. 229.
110 *Heimskringla III*, pp. 229, 297.
111 Cf. Auður Magnúsdóttir, *Frillor och fruar*, pp. 47–97.
112 Duindam, 'Dynasties', p. 61. Jan Rüdiger argues that polygamy was a 'sozialsemantisches Kommunikationssystem' and 'die politische Kultur strukturierendes Handlungsmuster' (Rüdiger, *Der König und seine Frauen*, p. 383; Rüdiger, *All the King's Women*).
113 *Heimskringla III*, pp. 325–26. Sigurd Mouth also had a child with Kristin Sigurdardottir, daughter of King Sigurd the Crusader, his cousin (*Heimskringla III*, p. 410).
114 *Morkinskinna II*, p. 168.

goði Lopt Sæmundarson.[115] After Tora's *frændsemi* had been accepted, all the children and grandchildren of Jon Loptsson could not only claim royal ancestry, but also *frændsemi* with all the kings in Norway during the years c. 1160–1200. It is also important to stress that Jon Loptsson came from the most powerful family in Iceland, and for Erling Skakke, King Magnus' father and the ruler of Norway at this time, it was essential to gain as much support for his son as possible, as we will discuss below. It is highly unlikely that a poor householder would have been treated in the same way as Jon Loptsson.

Magnus Barefoot was married only once, to the Swedish princess Margrethe Ingesdatter, nicknamed *friðkolla* (peace-girl), in 1101 (see Chapters 3 and 6). They had no children.[116] For the kings, such weddings were first and foremost about establishing political alliances, not producing heirs. This is in clear contrast to Frankish queens, where 'failure' in the 'production of sons' resulted in divorce.[117]

An important difference between the kings' families and the lords' families before the middle of the thirteenth century is the family-creation process. Due to the scarcity of sources, this process cannot be studied in Norway. Let us therefore go to Iceland where we have much better sources, and look at the case of the Snorrunga (Fig. 2.2).

Torstein was a chieftain (*goði*) in Iceland. His son Torgrim died young, but left behind a son, Snorre *goði*. He was one of the most influential chieftains in Iceland around the year 1000 and became the ancestor of an entire family line named after him, the Snorrunga family. The family included Snorre, his children, and his only grandson, Ljotr. Ljotr had no sons and the Snorrunga family therefore 'died out' after only three generations. Halldor was the most favoured of Snorre's sons and therefore became chieftain after him. He had no sons, but two daughters: Gudrun and Torkatla. The former was married to Kjartan, and together they had the son Torvald, who became the ancestor of the Vatnsfirdingar family. Torkatla was married to Gunnlaug. They had a daughter, Tordis, who married Gils Snorrason. Their son was Hvamm-Sturla, the ancestor of the Sturlunga family, which dominated Icelandic politics up to c. 1280.[118]

As Sturlungr to Sturlungar underlines, the process of creating new family lines was continually taking place in Iceland. If this was true for Norway too, which is likely, it is in clear contrast to the situation in the royal family, where due to the superiority of the male dynastic line, it is problematic to talk about the royal family in the same way as lords'

---

115 *Heimskringla III*, p. 395; *Sturlunga saga I*, p. 51.
116 Norseng, 'Margrete Fredkulla'. She was later married to King Niels Svendsson (d. 1134) in Denmark.
117 Stafford, *Queens, Concubines and Dowagers*, p. 86.
118 Jón Viðar Sigurðsson, 'Forholdet mellom frender', pp. 315–16.

NETWORKS AND *FLOKKAR* 67

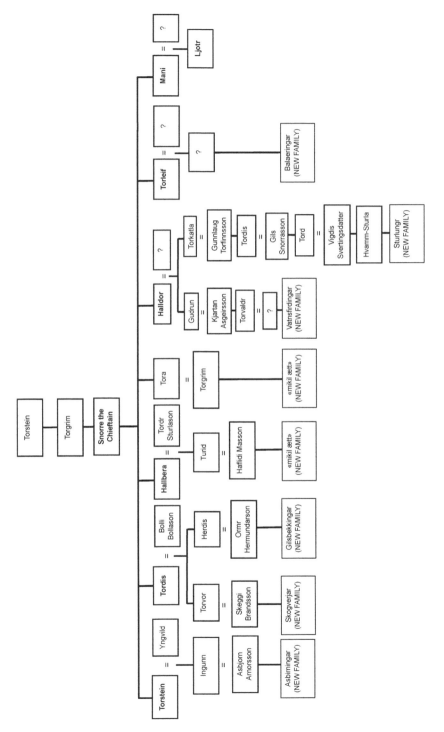

Figure 2.2. The Snorrunga family. Figure by author.

families. The kings belonged to a royal line (*stirps regia*), where only the father's line mattered.[119] Even though only chieftain's sons could maintain the family, the mother's family was of great significance because of the support it provided. Members or claimed members of the same line sat on the throne of Norway from 870 to 1319; the main reason was 'polygynous reproduction', which was accepted up to the middle of the thirteenth century. At this time a new law of succession was introduced, which said that only the king's oldest legitimate son should inherit the title. At the same time the kings started to marry their children off to children of other royal houses. Therefore, it is not until the second half of the thirteenth century that we can talk about a proper Norwegian royal family.

Fosterage

Most kings in the period c. 900–1180 let noble families foster their sons.[120] By allowing noblemen, many of whom had promising sons who expected to take over their father's position, foster the kings' sons (daughters were almost never fostered),[121] the kings were both giving their sons a family and building them a power base at the same time. The future kings could use their foster families' networks. Fostering was also beneficial for the foster families, not only did it increase their social status, but more importantly these ties gave the families better access to royal revenues.

---

119 Cf. Green, *Language and History in the Early Germanic World*, p. 131; Canning, *A History of Medieval Political Thought*, p. 22; Sundqvist, *An Arena for Higher Powers*, p. 8.
120 For example: Hakon Magnusson, first fostered by Sveinki Steinarsson in Viken, then by Torir Tordarson in Steig in Gudbrandsdalen (*Morkinskinna I*, p. 325; *Morkinskinna II*, pp. 16–17; *Heimskringla III*, p. 210). Magnus the Blind was fostered by Vidkun Jonsson in Bjarkøy in Hålogland (*Heimskringla III*, p. 258). Inge Haraldsson was fostered in Viken (*Morkinskinna II*, p. 177). His foster father was Amund Gyrdsson Law-Bersason (*Morkinskinna II*, p. 184; *Heimskringla III*, p. 303). Sigurd Mouth Haraldsson was fostered in Trondheim (*Morkinskinna II*, p. 177) by Sada-Gyrd Bardsson (*Heimskringla III*, pp. 303, 313). Magnus Haraldsson was fostered by Kyrpinga-Orm (*Heimskringla III*, p. 321). Sigurd Slembe was fostered by the priest Albrikt (*Morkinskinna II*, p. 168). Sigurd Sigurdsson was fostered by Markús in Skog (*Heimskringla III*, p. 384). Cf. *Morkinskinna I*, p. 326; *Morkinskinna II*, pp. 168, 225, 237; *Heimskringla III*, pp. 288, 342, 347, 348, 350, 360, 366, 390, 407. [F]óstbrœðralag ok fullkomit vinfengi; *Morkinskinna II*, p. 36; *Ágrip*, pp. 290–91. *Heimskringla* states that Magnus Barefoot grew up in the king's *hirð* (*Heimskringla III*, p. 208).
121 This contrasts with Ireland where both sexes were fostered 'up to a marriageable age — fourteen years for the girls, seventeen years for the boys — in strict conformity with the social status of their parents' (Amory, 'The Historical Worth of *Rígsþula*', p. 10)'. Cf. Mitchell, *Family Life in the Middle Ages*, p. 42.

Fosterage was a familiar institution in medieval Scandinavia.[122] It was a 'method of childrearing whereby adults, other than the biological parents, undertook to raise a child for a particular period of time'.[123] Fosterage was an important element of alliance-building; it helped to establish strong ties of loyalty between families. It was 'therefore a useful diplomatic tool within the network of chiefs and kings' — it was a kind of 'peace-weaving'.[124] Education was at 'the core' of the fosterage tradition in Ireland.[125] It is likely that this would also have been the case in Scandinavia. We do not have any information about what the kings' sons in Norway were taught, but they were most likely trained in *íþróttir* (athletics); such as the skaldic art, riding, swimming, skiing, shooting, rowing, playing the harp, playing chess, and writing in runes.[126]

An important consequence of fosterlings was to create strong emotional ties that formed 'the heart of those alliances'.[127] These can, for example, be seen in Saxo Grammaticus' description of the ties between King Valdemar and his foster brother, Absalon, Archbishop of Lund.[128] *Heimskringla* also stresses this indirectly when it records that Magnus the Blind stayed with his foster father Vidkun Jonsson in Bjarkøy in Hålogaland during the winter of 1138–1139, when he was being pursued by the kings of Norway.[129]

The importance of fosterage can also clearly be seen in how Harald Gille used fosterage to establish friendships with most of the important Norwegian lords. Three of his four sons were fostered by the leading men in the country: Sigurd Mouth by Sada-Gyrd Bardsson in Trondheim,[130] Inge in Viken by Amund Gyrdsson,[131] and finally Magnus by

---

122 Amory, 'The Historical Worth of *Rígsþula*', p. 10. It was also common in Ireland (Amory, 'The Historical Worth of *Rígsþula*', p. 10; Duffy, MacShamhráin, and Moynes, *Medieval Ireland: An Encyclopedia*, pp. 79–81, 183; O'Donnell, 'The Affect of Fosterage in Medieval Ireland'.
123 Duffy, MacShamhráin, and Moynes, *Medieval Ireland: An Encyclopedia*, p. 79.
124 Pollington, *The Mead-Hall Community*, pp. 21–22. Cf. Duffy, MacShamhráin, and Moynes, *Medieval Ireland: An Encyclopedia*, p. 183; Bagge, *Society and Politics*, pp. 83, 120, 134, 216; Miller, *Bloodtaking and Peacemaking*, pp. 122–24, 171–74; Nygård, 'Ok óksu allir upp heima þar'; Parkes, *Fosterage, Kinship, and Legend*, pp. 587–615; Mitchell, *Family Life in the Middle Ages*, p. 42.
125 Duffy, MacShamhráin, and Moynes, *Medieval Ireland: An Encyclopedia*, pp. 80, 183; Mitchell, *Family Life in the Middle Ages*, pp. 42, 157.
126 *Morkinskinna I*, p. 116; *Orkneyinga saga*, p. 130; *Heimskringla I*, p. 333; Sundqvist, 'Asarnas idrotter och religion', pp. 122–38.
127 O'Donnell, 'The Affect of Fosterage in Medieval Ireland', p. 87.
128 *GD*, 14.17.3.
129 *Heimskringla III*, p. 258.
130 According to Fagrskinna (*Ágrip*, p. 331).
131 *Heimskringla III*, pp. 302, 313. Cf. *Heimskringla III*, pp. 342 (foster brother), 348 (foster brother), 366, 384, 390, 407.

Kyrpinga-Orm. Magnus was made king after his father's death but died of sickness soon afterwards.[132]

Shortly after the death of King Harald Gille, the leading men in the realm decided that they should foster the brothers Sigurd Mouth and Inge Hunchback jointly, and that the brothers should have the same *hirð*. According to *Heimskringla*, Sigurd Mouth and Inge Hunchback had six foster fathers (*fóstrneyti*), who also acted as their advisers (*ráðuneyti*). When listing the foster fathers, *Heimskringla* first mentioned Sada-Gyrd Bardsson, then Amund Gyrdsson, the two 'original' foster fathers. Then Tjostolv Alason is mentioned; he was one of the lords in Viken who supported Inge's claim to the throne. Ottar Birting is the fourth lord listed; he was one of the lords who supported the decision to accept Sigurd Mouth as king. He, as also discussed in Chapter 6, later married Ingrid, Harald Gille's queen. Finally *Heimskringla* mentioned Ogmund Sviptir and Ogmund Dengir.[133] Ogmund Dengir was a son of Kyrpinga-Orm from Støle in Sunnhordland, one of the most influential men in the country, and who had fostered the brother of the two kings, Magnus.[134] We don't have any information about Ogmund Sviptir, though it is tempting to suggest that he also could have been a local lord from the western part of Norway, like Ogmund Dengir.[135] If this was the case then Sada-Gyrd and Ottar Birting came from Trøndelag, Amund and Tjostolv from Viken, and Ogmund Dengir and Ogmund Sviptir from the western part of Norway. The three 'pairs' of foster fathers thus represented the three main political regions in the country Viken, the western, and the central-northern part of Norway — thus preventing any rivalry between the regions.

When Sigurd Mouth and Inge Hunchback had been kings for six years, Oystein, another son of Harald Gille, came to Norway from Scotland. Arne Saebjarnarson, Thorleifr Brynjolvsson, and Kolbein Hruga had travelled west across the sea to collect the boy and brought him to Trondheim, where he was made king over one third of the realm. Oystein's two half-brothers, Sigurd Mouth and Inge, were at that time in the east of the country. After Oystein was made king, messengers travelled between him and his half-brothers, and they came to the agreement that they should rule the country together.[136] We know nothing about the ties between their two *hirðir*, but they are likely to have been strong, especially given the

---

132 *Heimskringla III*, p. 321.
133 *Heimskringla III*, pp. 303, 322, 330. Cf. *Morkinskinna II*, pp. 179, 221, 225. Peter Ulfsson, Guttorm in Rein, and Ottar Balle were also lords who had supported King Sigurd Mouth (*Morkinskinna II*, 179). *Fagrskinna* also mentioned Peter *birðarsveinn* who we know nothing about (*Ágrip*, pp. 331, 373).
134 *Heimskringla III*, pp. 321, 330; Norseng, 'Erling Skakke'.
135 *Heimskringla III*, p. 314; *Morkinskinna II*, pp. 199, 200.
136 *Heimskringla III*, p. 321.

family ties between them, as all the leading men in both *hirðir* belonged to the country's social elite.

According to *Heimskringla*, there was good (*góðr*) peace in Norway when Sigurd Mouth and Inge Hunchback were young.[137] This was because of the concord between their advisers. When the foster fathers died, Sigurd Mouth and Inge Hunchback divided their *hirð*[138] and as such there were three *hirðir* in the country. King Oystein Haraldsson had his own *hirð*, as he was a full-grown man.[139] Tension grew between Inge on one side, and Oystein and Sigurd Mouth on the other. In 1155 Sigurd Mouth was killed and Oystein Haraldsson followed two years later. In 1157, Sigurd Mouth's son Hakon the Broad-Shouldered was proclaimed king. He killed Inge Hunchback in a battle in 1161, and the year after Hakon the Broad-Shouldered was killed in battle by Inge's previous supporters, who had put the infant Magnus Erlingsson, a son of Sigurd the Crusader's daughter, on the throne.

Michael Mann has argued that all societies are made up of 'multiple overlapping and intersecting sociospatial networks of power'.[140] This is certainly the case for Norway in the twelfth century. It was through their networks that kings, and local lords exercised their power. The political game revolved around creating, maintaining, and enlarging networks: you especially needed to make friends (*vinir*). The most powerful leaders had the highest number of friends, and here the kings' networks stand out. Their networks usually included foreign rulers, local lords and their networks, householders, and the *hirð*, and it was friendship with the king that held the network together.[141]

The networks we are looking at in Norway in the twelfth century, and basically during the entire period *c.* 800–1250, are, however, different in two ways from the networks social scientists have studied in our contemporary societies. Firstly, the mutual obligations within networks in the Middle Age were stronger — we are not willing to die for our friends. Secondly, one also had to support the friends of a friend.[142] Even though there are some significant differences between medieval and contemporary networks, we can apply the approaches and the terminology which social

---

137 *Heimskringla III*, p. 330; *Morkinskinna II*, p. 221.
138 *Morkinskinna II*, p. 221.
139 *Morkinskinna II*, p. 225.
140 Mann, *The Sources of Social Power: Vol. 1*, p. 1.
141 Jón Viðar Sigurðsson, *Viking Friendship*, pp. 11–71. Cf. MacCarron and Kenna, 'Viking Sagas: Six Degrees of Icelandic Separation', pp. 12–17; MacCarron and Kenna, 'Network Analysis of the Íslendinga sögur', pp. 1–9; Jesch, *The Viking Diaspora*, pp. 163–82; Shepard, 'Networks', pp. 116–57.
142 Jón Viðar Sigurðsson, *Viking Friendship*, pp. 37–125.

scientists have developed in their study of contemporary networks to our medieval case-studies.[143]

Interaction in a network is largely a case of what is being exchanged. The necessary 'currency' in the networks we have studied has been support, protection, and gifts. However, let us not forget a key aspect: information. In all networks, there were people with peripheral positions, but there is no reason to underestimate their importance, not least when it came to maintaining the flow of information to the person(s) in the middle. The political landscape could change radically overnight, for example by a king or lord's death. Information was therefore crucial. In addition to being informed through one's networks, trading places, assemblies, meetings, and religious gatherings were inescapable arenas for gathering intelligence and passing it on.[144] This is why the Norwegian kings stayed in the cities so frequently.

Individuals in these networks had different tasks or roles; and the power they possessed, that is, their ability to influence decisions taken, depended on their relationship with the centre of the networks. The kings and lords surrounded themselves with councillors, and the royal advisers were, in many cases, lords. In this way they were part of the king's network at the same time as each of them also had their own networks. One person could possess several roles within the same network: for example, that of adviser, friend, kinsman, and *hirðmaðr*.

We do not have detailed information about the relationship between the members in different types of networks. However, we can assume that contacts between members of a lord's network were probably more frequent than members of a king's network. Whereas the kings' networks included members from all around the country, and even people beyond the borders of the realm, making contact difficult, the members of the smaller lords' networks most likely met each other regularly through attendance at the local assembly. This made the mobilization of the smaller networks quicker, which in some cases proved to be just as important as the actual size of the network.

In the article 'A Network Theory of Power', Manuel Castells discusses different types of networks and their power in societies where power is 'exercised through networks'. He claims that there are four different forms of power:

---

143 Preiser-Kapeller, 'Calculating the Middle Ages?', p. 103; MacCarron and Kenna, 'Viking Sagas: Six Degrees of Icelandic Separation', p. 13; MacCarron and Kenna, 'Universal Properties of Mythological Networks', pp. 1–6. MacCarron and Kenna, 'Network Analysis of the Íslendinga sögur', pp. 1–9.
144 This discussion is based on Jón Viðar Sigurðsson, *Viking Friendship*.

- Networking Power: The authority that individuals and organizations belonging to networks have over persons and collectives, in contrast to actors standing outside the networks.
- Network Power: power of the network.
- Networked Power: 'the power of social actors over other social actors in the network'.
- Network-making Power: power to influence the networks decisions, 'and the power to switch different networks following the strategic alliances between the dominant actors of various networks'.[145]

In his book *Ideology and Power in Norway and Iceland, 1150–1250*, Costel Coroban adjusts this model to make it fit medieval Norway in the following way:

- Networking power: the power of the Court over the kingdom.
- Network power: the power of the King over the barons in the Court.
- Networked power: the power of the barons over the kingdom.
- Network-making power: the power of the King over the kingdom.[146]

The problem with Castells' model and Coroban's adjustment is that they do not take into consideration the substantial overlapping of networks; all the most powerful men in a royal network belonged to several other networks as well. In the multipolar and multiparty conflicts that characterized the power game, overlapping friendship and kinship ties affected the developments and results.

It was these overlapping relationships that made it so difficult to wage war in Norway. The frequent intermarriages between the social elites for centuries meant that the overlaps of kinship were extensive. In addition to these kinship ties, there existed a strong friendship between members of the social elite, making it almost impossible to wage war in Norway. Furthermore, the *leiðangr* organization made it even more problematic to fight. The solution to this 'problem' was the *flokkr*.

The Rise of the *flokkr*

As already mentioned, Hakon the Broad-Shouldered, the ten-year-old son of Sigurd Mouth, was named king and chosen as the leader of his father's *flokkr* in 1157.[147] On 4 February 1161, King Inge Hunchback was killed in battle against Hakon the Broad-Shouldered and his men. After the battle, King Hakon the Broad-Shouldered controlled the whole kingdom

---

145 Castells, *A Network Theory of Power*, p. 773.
146 Coroban, *Ideology and Power in Norway and Iceland*, p. 103.
147 *Heimskringla III*, pp. 347, 407 (Olav Gudbrandsson), 411 (Oystein Oysteinsson).

and appointed his men to all the *sýslur* and towns (*kaupstaðir*) in the country.[148] He was now the sole ruler.

This meant that King Inge's former supporters not only lost their royal titles but were also cut off from royal revenues. As a consequence, Erling Skakke arranged a meeting. He sent messages to all the lords (*hǫfðingjar*) he knew had been confidential friends (*trúnaðarvinir*) of King Inge Hunchback, his *hirðsveit*, his *handgengnir menn*, and Gregorius Dagssons' *húskarlar*, who were the leading warriors in the realm at this time. Gregorius had been King Inge's closest adviser and had died some months prior in another battle against Hakon the Broad-Shouldered. The men mentioned by *Heimskringla* who participated in the meeting, besides Erling Skakke, were Jon Hallkelsson, Nikolas Skjaldvarsson,[149] and Arne, the king's brother-in-law. Jon Hallkelsson was, as we should remember, a son of Hallkell Huk, the man who had brought Harald Gille to Norway and later married his daughter. Nikolas Skjaldvarsson was King Magnus Barefoot's sister's son, and his *lendr maðr* and treasurer (*gjaldkeri*). Skjaldvar, Nikolas' father, had been *lendr maðr* for three kings: Magnus Barefoot, Oystein Magnusson, and Sigurd the Crusader. Nikolas had previously fought for King Hakon the Broad-Shouldered, but the reasons why he changed sides are unknown. Arne king's brother-in-law was married to Ingrid Ragvaldsdatter, the former queen of King Harald Gille.[150]

We do not know where the meeting was held, but it was probably in one of the towns in eastern Norway: Tønsberg, Hamar, Oslo, Sarpsborg, or Konghelle. When the participants met, they made an agreement (*bundu fastmælum*) to keep the *flokkr* united. That is, they gave each other promises to stay together. *Heimskringla* does not mention for how long a time this was supposed to last. It is, however, likely that the plan was to keep the *flokkr* together as long as King Hakon the Broad-Shouldered was alive.

Then the issues arose of whom they should take as their king. Erling Skakke spoke, asking whether it was the wish of the lords (*hǫfðingjar*) and other *lendir menn* that King Harald Gille's daughter's son, Simon Skalpr should become a king, and that his father Jon Hallkelsson should become the leader of the *flokkr*. Jon declined the offer. Then Nikolas Skjaldvarsson, King Magnus Barefoot's sister's son, was asked, but he also refused, saying that it was his counsel that they should take as their king a person who was descended from the royal line, but that they should also choose an intelligent man as the leader of the *flokkr*. Arne king's brother-in-law was then asked whether he was willing to have any of his sons, the half-brothers of King Inge Hunchback, accepted as king. He, however, pointed to Magnus

---

148 *Heimskringla III*, p. 369.
149 Arstad, 'Nikolas Skjaldvorsson'.
150 Arstad, 'Nikolas Skjaldvorsson'; Norseng, 'Arne på Ståreim'.

Erlingsson, King Sigurd the Crusader's daughter Kristin's son, and said that she had the best descent, entitling Magnus to the kingdom in Norway. Arne king's brother-in-law stressed that Magnus' father, Erling Skakke, was an intelligent man, determined and well tried in battles and a good ruler, and if the lords supported him, he would become a good leader. Many men agreed. Erling then stood and gave a speech saying that this was a dangerous and difficult task and that it was important that the group stood together, and that the person in charge needed strong safeguards from the men involved, and that they would not in the future oppose him or show him hostility. Everyone agreed to this and set up a *samband* (close and mutual agreement with clear obligations),[151] with full *trúnaði* (trust, loyalty). Erling then spoke again, accepted his role as the leader for the *flokkr*, and requested that they bind their relationships with oaths (*svardögum*).[152] Then the five-year-old Magnus Erlingsson was made king over the whole country at an assembly in the city, though we do not know which one. After that, everyone who was present and had been in the service of King Inge paid allegiance to Magnus (*gengu til handa honum*), and each of them kept the same titles (*nafnbætr*) as they had previously had with King Inge.[153]

There are some important problems with the source for this episode, especially regarding the dialogues. What is, however, important to us is that this is the first time a *flokkr* is known to have been founded, and oaths are here used to strengthen the ties between its members, a practice well known from, for example, Germany.[154] The decision to put Magnus Erlingsson on the throne was notable. As previously mentioned, this was the first time in Norwegian history that the son of a king's daughter was chosen to be king and he was a child too. Obviously, there had been some issues regarding the paternity of some of the previous kings,[155] but they had all convinced the people of Norway that they were kings' sons. There can be little doubt that the people of Norway, especially the social elite, knew that inheritance through the female line was not uncommon in Europe. To mention a few of the best-known examples: in England King Stephen (1135–1154), King Henry II (1154–1189); in Denmark Svend Estridsen (1047–1076); in Sweden Sverker the Elder (1130–1156), and St Erik (1156–1160). It is of interest to note that Erling Skakke's wife had

---

151 *Norges gamle love* V, 'samband'.
152 <http://malid.is/leit/svardagar> [accessed 4 April 20194).
153 *Heimskringla III*, pp. 374–75. Cf. *Eirspennill*, pp. 224–25; *Codex Frisianus*, pp. 360–61.
154 Oexle, 'Conjuratio und Gilde im frühen Mittelalter', pp. 151–214; Althoff, *Verwandte, Freunde und Getreue*, pp. 119–33.
155 Krag, 'Myten om Hårfagreættens "odel"', pp. 381–94.

a son with Sigurd Mouth, but his name never came up in the discussion in 1161. To eliminate that threat Erling Skakke had him killed shortly after.[156]

These events mark a watershed in the civil wars in Norway. Not only because of the breach with the old royal succession, but also because the use of a *flokkr* now became key to Norwegian politics. The *flokkr* that stood behind this coup also abandoned the idea of joint kingship, that kings should *rule together* and *divide* the royal revenues between them, and introduced the European model: Norway should have a single ruling king.

The *flokkr*, originally a unit in the kings' armies, was a warrior band under the leadership of a king. We don't have any information about the size of the *flokkar* in the civil wars, but they most likely consisted of only two to five hundred individuals. The kings and the lords who formed these *flokkar* were aware of the potential problems that could arise from overlapping friendship and kinship ties among their members. To avoid this, they tried to enlist men from the lower echelons of society who had no such ties to the social elite. However, as Hilde Nysether has pointed out, there were still comprehensive overlaps, especially among the leaders of these warrior bands. These overlapping social networks frequently served as a conflict-reducing mechanism during the period. They had a great impact on reducing the loss of life, especially through the granting of mercy, as will be discussed below. The activation of these networks allowed for negotiation and mediation, and the granting of mercy was often an important part of resolving conflicts. Overall, while the *flokkar* and their overlapping social networks did not prevent conflict from occurring, they did play an important role in reducing its impact and helping to resolve disputes.[157]

The importance of the role the *flokkr* played in the power game can best be seen in the fact that only three kings had *flokkar* before c. 1160, but all of the subsequent kings did.[158] The first time a *flokkr* was used in the power game *inside* Norway was around 1095 when lord Steigar-Thorir was worried about whether he would be able to establish a friendship with the newly appointed King Magnus Barefoot. Steigar-Thorir had previously fostered King Hakon Haraldsson and had supported him in his fight against Magnus Barefoot. He had followers and resources but he was old and infirm. He therefore founded a *flokkr* with Svend Haraldsson, a great

---

156 *Heimskringla III*, p. 410.
157 Nysether, 'Overlappende nettverk og det kontekstuelle fiendebildet under de norske "borgerkrigene"', pp. 133–50.
158 *Heimskringla I*, pp. 202, 244, 266, 296, 305, 357; *Heimskringla II*, pp. 51, 68, 97, 125, 155, 208, 347, 351, 353, 356, 363, 371, 372, 373, 387, 411; *Heimskringla III*, pp. 44, 54, 80, 187, 213–14, 260, 282, 304, 347, 353, 356, 364, 373–74, 383, 384, 385, 386, 387, 390, 391, 392, 393, 399, 408, 409, 411, 412, 416–17. For *Sverris saga*, *Bǫglunga saga* and *Hákonar saga* see for example: *Sverris saga*, pp. 13, 14, 18, 19, 20, 29, 31; *Hákonar saga Hákonarsonar I*; pp. 4, 5, 7, 32, 46, 173, 180; *Heimskringla III*, pp. 282 (Magnus the Blind), 304 (Sigurd Slembe), 347 (Oystein).

warrior and Viking of noble birth; he made Svend its leader and gave him the *hǫfðingjanafn*. Many noble men supported this *flokkr*. However, this uprising was crushed by King Magnus Barefoot.[159]

Another important reason for the use of *flokkr* was that the *leiðangr*, the 'official' army of the kingdom, could not be mobilized. The *leiðangr* was, as mentioned, a naval organization under the leadership of the king, used to defend the kingdom against outside aggression and to attack other kingdoms.[160] The householders were friends with all the kings in the country and could therefore not be summoned to fight for one king against the other. In the period c. 1130–1164 a *leiðangr* is only mentioned once in relation to the internal struggle. This happened in 1162 when King Hakon the Broad-Shouldered and Erling Skakke summoned the *leiðangr* from Trondheim and the western part of Norway respectively[161] — it was mustered twice to fight external enemies.[162]

After Magnus Erlingsson became king, *Heimskringla* and *Fagrskinna* narrate that Erling, with many of the *lendir menn* travelled to Denmark to meet King Valdemar. He was a cousin of Erling's wife Kristin. They came to an agreement that King Valdemar was to provide King Magnus Erlingsson with all the support from his kingdom that he needed in order to gain possession of Norway. In return, Valdemar was to have the 'rule in Norway that his previous relatives Harald Gormsson and Svend Tjugeskjegg had had [in the tenth century], the whole of the Viken as far north as Rygjarbit. This plan was confirmed by oaths and private agreements'.[163]

According to Saxo Grammaticus in Denmark, Erling, after King Inge's death and before Magnus Erlingsson was put on the throne, went to Jutland with his son. Saxo stresses that Magnus Erlingsson was closely related to Valdemar on his mother's side and that Erling gained generous amounts of provisions and great financial support from Valdemar. Erling then travelled back to Norway and put Magnus Erlingsson on the throne.[164]

The chronology of Erling's journey to Denmark is thus unclear. According to *Heimskringla* and *Fagrskinna*, Erling travelled after Magnus Erlingsson was named king, but *Gesta Danorum* suggests he travelled before. If we rely on Saxo's account, it is likely that the suggestion of putting Magnus Erlingsson on the throne in Norway had been made in Denmark, and that Valdemar had been involved in making that decision.

---

159 *Heimskringla III*, pp. 213–19.
160 Bjorkvik, 'Leidang', cols 432–59; Ersland and Holm, *Krigsmakt og kongemakt*, pp. 42–63.
161 *Heimskringla III*, pp. 378–80.
162 *Heimskringla III*, pp. 393–94, 404.
163 *Heimskringla III*, p. 375, 'en Valdimar skyldi hafa þat ríki í Noregi sem haft hǫfðu hinir fyrri frændr hans, Harald Gormsson ok Sveinn tjúguskegg: Víkina alla norðr til Rýgjarbits. Var þessi ráðagerð bundin eiðum ok einkamálum'. *Ágrip*, p. 348; Helle, *Norge blir en stat*, pp. 70–71.
164 *GD*, 14.29.12, 14.29.13.

Svend Estridsen, Valdemar's great-grandfather, who had established a new royal line in Denmark, was not a king's son but a son of King Knud the Great's daughter. Putting a king's daughter's son on the throne in Norway was a coup, and Erling needed support not only from Norwegian lords, but also from the most influential player in the North, King Valdemar, to carry out such a plan. Therefore, we can plausibly rely on Saxo regarding the chronology. The reason why the Old Norse saga authors place Erling's journey to Denmark after Magnus Erlingsson became king would then be that they were trying to stress Erling Skakke's part in this process.

King Hakon the Broad-Shouldered died in battle on 7 July 1162. The sagas do not inform us about what happened afterwards. It is likely that the *flokkr* that Erling was in charge of stayed together and planned their next move: to ensure full control over the throne and to get Magnus Erlingsson crowned.

Until 1104, Iceland and the rest of Scandinavia belonged to the archdiocese of Hamburg/Bremen, and from 1104 to 1152–1153 to that of Lund. In 1152–1153 the archbishopric of Nidaros (Trondheim), which included Norway and the Norse settlements on the islands in the West, was founded. The Church used this opportunity to secure three important concessions. The Church was to have complete authority over the clergy and their appointments, control over its property and finance, and be permitted to make its own decisions regarding its personnel and other matters.[165] The foundation of the archbishopric changed the power game in Norway. The archbishop became one of the most influential people in the realm. The kings of Norway, however, did not keep their promises. So, in order to ensure the coronation took place, Erling Skakke and Archbishop Oystein (1161–1188), King Inge's former treasurer, made a pact; the archbishop was to keep all the privileges that were promised when the archbishopric was founded in 1152–1153, and in return, the archbishop was to support Magnus Erlingsson.[166]

Magnus Erlingsson was crowned in 1163–1164; this was the first coronation in Scandinavia.[167] In the same year as the coronation or the

---

165 Danielsen and others, *Norway. A History from the Vikings*, p. 68.
166 The events in these years have been heavily debated among Norwegian historians, see for example: Helle, *Norge blir en stat*; Helle, *Under kirke og kongemakt*; Gunnes, *Erkebiskop Øystein*; Bagge, *Udsigt og innhogg: 150 års forskning om eldre norsk historie*; Bagge, *From Viking Stronghold*; Bagge, *Cross and Scepter*.
167 *Fagrskinna* narrates that when Erling was crowned King Valdemar was the 'mikil óvinr' Erling's because he has not kept his oath (*lagaeið*) and agreement (*sáttmála*) (*Ágrip*, p. 351.) Jón Loptsson, the most powerful Icelandic chieftain, was in Bergen when Magnus was crowned. That is not a coincidence. For the *flokkr* of Erling Skakke, it was crucial to gain as much support for the coronation as possible. William of Newburgh, in his *Historia rerum Anglicarum* (*The History of English Affairs*), mentions this event and King Sverre's usurpation in book three (*Chronicles of the Reigns of Stephen*, p. 228).

year afterwards, a new Law of Succession was introduced; it established the principle of male primogeniture — the country was to have one king who should be succeeded by his oldest legitimate son. According to Bagge, the law of succession shows the Church's impact, 'as well as the general ideology'. However, 'the immediate reason for passing the law was the need for the faction which had now gained the upper hand in protecting its new king, Magnus Erlingsson, against rival pretenders by stamping all his opponents as rebels and heretics'.[168] The Law of Succession was an attempt to 'secure' the throne for Magnus Erlingsson.[169]

In 1163, the *Gulathing law* was revised, and around the same time, 1163–1164 the *Canones Nidrosienses*, rules for the archbishopric, were established. It contains fifteen canons, which deal with various matters, including the clergy and war, lay investiture, advowson, elections of bishops and archbishops, as well as clerical marriages and celibacy.[170] That the coronation oath, the Law of Succession, the revision of the *Gulathing law* and *Canones Nidrosienses* were all undertaken within the same year is not a coincidence, instead it demonstrates a deliberate plan to consolidate the power of Magnus Erlingsson and found a new royal dynasty in Norway. It is likely that the plans for the events had been made when Erling Skakke visited King Valdemar in Denmark. The making of all the above-mentioned 'documents' took time, and the archbishop Oystein must have played an important role.

The *flokkr*'s Organization

The hierarchy of the *flokkr* was clearly defined, with the king or the person fighting for the throne and his advisers at the top. The lords, who were also advisers, were heavily involved in this process of establishing a *flokkr*. The person chosen by the *flokkr* as its leader, usually a king's son, became the king and was accepted as such at local assembly(ies). The task of the assemblies now became to sanction the *flokkr*'s decisions, rather than electing the king. The *flokkr* thus became the main 'producer' of kings. The first time this happened was when King Oystein's *flokkr* constituted a new *flokkr* and gave Hakon the Broad-Shouldered his royal name in 1159.[171]

---

168 Bagge, *From Viking Stronghold*, pp. 167–68.
169 Bagge, *From Viking Stronghold*, p. 41. 'To protect him against his rivals, by defining their claims as illegal and stamping them as rebels and heretics. Magnus was only seven years old and related to the dynasty through his mother, but he had the advantage from point of view of the Church that he was born in marriage'. Bagge, *Cross and Scepter*, p. 54. Cf. Tobiassen, *Tronfølgelov og privilegiebrev*, pp. 181–273.
170 Bagge, *From Viking Stronghold*, pp. 202, 294.
171 *Heimskringla III*, pp. 213, 214–15, 347, 407. See, for example, *Hákonar saga Hákonarsonar I*, pp. 172–73. 179, 283 (*einkamál*); Helle, *Norge blir en stat*, p. 55.

The only time we hear about the creators of a *flokkr* swearing oaths to ensure mutual loyalty among its leaders was when the *flokkr* around Magnus Erlingsson was created. It is, however, likely that this also happened when other *flokkar* were founded. Due to overlaps in family and friendship ties, such situations could easily lead to conflicts, and it was necessary for the leaders to obtain these assurances. Otherwise, they could risk standing alone in demanding situations.

The *flokkar* had goals that motivated their behaviour. The main goal was to gain control over the kingdom or, at the very least, not to lose control over the territory and royal revenues they already held. As previously mentioned, these conflicts were both multipolar and multilevelled, as is further discussed in Chapter 4 in this volume. It is important to bear in mind that, like the groups Fotini Christia studied in her book *Alliance Formation in Civil Wars*, the *flokkar* were not 'homogeneous' or immune to 'internal fractionalization'.[172] However, there were some differences between the *flokkar* and the Afghan groups. The number of *flokkar* in Norway was usually limited to two, and even though internal fractionalization occurred, their leaders seldom changed sides, unlike in Afghanistan.

The main elements in a *flokkr* were *húskarlar* and the *lið*. *Húskarlar* were warriors belonging to the households of kings and lords. The best-known group of *húskarlar* in the sagas pertaining to our period is the group of approximately ninety who fought for Gregorius Dagsson. Nothing is known about their social background or that of other *húskarlar*, but it is likely that most of them came from the lower strata of society, and some of them may have even come from Iceland.[173] The number of *húskarlar* entertained by lords other than Gregorius Dagsson is unknown, but it is probable that it would have been around twenty men per lord. According to the *Hirðskrá*, *húskarlar* were the oldest common name for *handgengnir menn*, but their position within the *hirð* was somewhat unclear. They could be used both as a fighting force and to carry out tasks requested by the king.[174] The *húskarlar* only made up a part of the fighting force in the

---

[172] Christia, *Alliance Formation in Civil Wars*, p. 4. Cf. Parkinson and Zaks, 'Militant and Rebel Organization(s)', p. 275.

[173] *Heimskringla III*, pp. 338, 339, 375. *Sverris saga* narrates that when Sverre Sigurdsson became king, seventy men became his men (*gengu honum til handa*), and some became *hirðmenn*, some *gestir*, and some *húskarlar* (*Sverris saga*, p. 16). Refsdal, *Dagsætta: en høvdingeslekt på 1100-tallet i Grenland*, pp. 75–77.

[174] In *Hirðskrá* it is stated that in the 'old times', it was the custom that all those men who paid homage to the king or received the sword from him (*varo handgegnir eða suærðtakarar*) were called *húskarlar* (*Hirdloven*, p. 108). *Skáldskaparmál* narrates that kings and *jarlar* have in their escort men called *hirðmenn* and *húskarlar*, but *lendir menn* also have *handgengna menn* in their service who in Denmark and Sweden are known as *hirðmenn*, but in Norway *húskarlar*. *Hirðmenn* were generally referred to as kings' *húskarlar* in ancient times (*Edda Snorra Sturlusonar*, p. 172). Lars Hamre ('Hird', cols 568–69) saw the term *húskarl* as an

flokkar; the majority belonged to the unspecific group of the *lið*, and they were usually recruited from men from the lower strata of society, including many who did not belong to any households.[175] According to the *Gulathing law*, there were a number of smaller *flokkr*-groups with not fewer than five persons. It is likely that on many occasions, they joined the *lið*.[176] The *flokkar* were frequently subdivided into companies (*sveitir*) under the leadership of a captain (*sveitarhǫfðingi*). These *sveitir* were often located on different royal farms and could be easily mustered in times of crisis. It is highly likely that the captains were also involved to some degree in local administration, although this is unclear. However, it is most likely that they came from the most respectable families in the country.[177]

The relationship between the leader of the *flokkr* and its members was reciprocal.[178] The retainers were expected to fight for their lords, and in return, they were provided with provisions, clothing, and arms. They also had the opportunity to raid farms belonging to the opposing king and his friends. Additionally, one way for a leader to show appreciation for his followers was through marriage. Kings could arrange marriages for their men to girls from respectable families or to wealthy widows. A notable example of this occurred after the battle between Sverre and Magnus Erlingsson at Fimreite in Sogn in 1184. Following his victory, King Sverre arranged marriages for many of his men with the widows of his fallen adversaries.[179] This was a smart tactic for the king, as it not only secured wealth for his men, but it also showed a willingness for reconciliation. None of the widows had to leave their farms, and they and their families retained their position in society. If the king had wanted to, he could have

---

indication of the relationship between the *húskarl* and his master. Helle, *Norge blir en stat*, p. 201; Love, *A Lexicon of Medieval Nordic Law*.

175 In the runic and skaldic corpus, *lið* had different meanings: the main one was a 'group of people', with other translations such as '"troop", "retinue", "help, assistance" and even "fleet"'. Jesch, *Ships and Men*, p. 187; Lindow, *Comitatus, Individual and Honor*, pp. 70–81; Lund, 'The Armies of Swein Forkbeard and Cnut: "leding or lið?"', pp. 105–18; Raffield, 'Bands of Brothers', pp. 324–29; Naderer, 'Love and Fear'; Raffield and others, *Ingroup Identification*, pp. 1–16; Lindow (Lindow, *Comitatus, Individual and Honor*, p. 74), claims that 'a lið was an expedition of a warrior band functioning abroad under a single leader'; Bagge, *From Viking Stronghold*, pp. 54–55.

176 *Den eldre Gulatingslova*, §§ 142, 152, 154, 167, 168, 183, 189, 202.

177 See, for example, *Heimskringla III*, pp. 281, 353, 355, 367, 368; *Hákonar saga Hákonarsonar I*, p. 12.

178 Relations between roles are 'the social linkages that define the nature, centralization, and hierarchy (if any) of the organization. In other words, relations form the backbone of organizational structure. They are often best defined in terms of their content: i.e., what specifically is flowing from one role to another. The content may be material (e.g., money or resources), behavioural (e.g., information exchange or giving orders), or social (e.g., family ties or distrust)'. Parkinson and Zaks, 'Militant and Rebel Organization(s)', p. 274.

179 *Eirspennill*, pp. 350, 613. Cf. *Codex Frisianus*, p. 523.

confiscated all their property, but instead, he chose a more diplomatic approach.

Additionally, the establishment of group identity through naming and symbols was a significant development in the evolution of the *flokkar*. Almost all the *flokkar* after 1177 had names such as *Birkibeinar, Baglar,* and *Heklungar,* and probably also a symbol (*hǫfðingjamerki*).[180] This created a sense of belonging and shared purpose among the members and strengthened their loyalty to their leader and fellow members. The use of symbols also made it easier for members to identify each other on the battlefield and during other group activities. The naming of the *flokkar* crated group identity and also made it easier for them to be recognized by others in society, which helped to establish their legitimacy and influence. Overall, the use of names and symbols played an important role in the development of the *flokkar* as a political force in medieval Norway.[181]

The reciprocal ties were crucial in the sense that it helped to establish trust and loyalty among the members of the *flokkar*. Forcing men to fight without these ties could lead to tragedy, as seen in the battle at Fyrileiv in 1134. In this battle, Kristrod, Harald Gille's half-brother, was killed by a householder from the same army:

> Then many that were standing nearby spoke, asking why he had done this so evil deed. He replied: 'Now he knows that, for they slaughtered my animals in the summer and took everything that was in the house, and forced me to go with them into their army. I had been planning this for him earlier if I had an opportunity. After that King Harald's troops began to take to flight, and he fled himself and all his troops.[182]

This illustrates the danger of fighting without a strong sense of shared purpose and loyalty to one another. The establishment of strong reciprocal ties helped to mitigate such risks and ensure that the members of the *flokkar* could fight together effectively and efficiently.

Although a large proportion of the *flokkar* consisted of individuals from the lower strata of society, their friendships and kinship ties overlapped significantly. This, as pointed out by Hilde Nysether and Louise Taylor, had an impact on the fighting during the Norwegian civil wars, as both kings and the men fighting for them exhibited mercy (*grið*) towards

---

180 *Sverris saga*, p. 226.
181 Cf. Jones, 'Changing Geographies of Governance and Group Identities in the Middle Ages', pp. 901–26; Sztompka, *Trust: A Sociological Theory*, p. 46; Buskens, *Social Networks and Trust*, pp. 5–8.
182 *Heimskringla III*, pp. 281–82, 'Þá mæltu margir er hjá stóðu hví hann gerði þetta it illa verk. Hann svaraðI, "Nú veit hann þat er þeir hjuggu bú mitt í sumar ok tóku allt þat er heima var en hǫfðu mik nauðgan í her með sér. Slíkt hugði ek honum fyrr ef ek fengi fǫng á." eptir þat kom flótti í lið Haralds konungs ok flýði hann sjálfr ok allt lið hans. Þá var fallið mart af liði Haralds konungs'. Translation in *Snorri Sturluson. Heimskringla 3*, p. 172.

their enemies. The most famous example of this is found in *Sverris saga*, where, during a battle, King Sverre granted *grið* to the same man three times, who each time returned to the group fighting against Sverre. The man was subsequently captured once more, and this time he was put to death.[183]

As a result of this situation, it was often unclear who the enemy was, and this ambiguity had an impact on the battles. It can be argued that the warriors were fighting for 'possibilities' rather than against a clearly defined enemy. The most common terms for 'enemy' in Old Norse are *óvinr* (not a friend) and *fjándi* (enemy). However, in the sagas, these words are rarely used to describe the relationships between the *flokkar*. The distinction between 'us' and 'them' was therefore often vague. Furthermore, the men in the *flokkar* not only knew each other across the lines of conflict, but they also recognized that the Other was in a similar situation to themselves, 'creating an empathic undercurrent in what was otherwise a tense and volatile situation defined by actual or potential violence'.[184] It is also worth noting that we do not have any accounts of heroes who fought bravely against the enemy or martyrs who died for the cause at the hands of the enemy in the Norwegian civil wars. As a result, only relatively few men were killed in battles during this period.

According to *Heimskringla's* account of Magnus Erlingsson's reign, Norway was prosperous during the first part of his rule, and the householders were wealthy and unaccustomed to a lack of freedom (*ófrelsi*) or the discontent (*ófriði*) caused by the *flokkar*. Instances of plundering (*rán*) were also widely known.[185] However, it is important to note that this statement should not be given too much weight, as the civil wars in Norway did not significantly impact the lives of most householders in the country. They were rarely subject to plundering, and as discussed in Chapter 5, the battles were fought primarily in and around the three main cities in the realm: Oslo, Bergen, and Trondheim.[186] As a result, most parts of the country were not affected by the civil wars at all.

Theodoricus Monachus wrote *De antiquitate regum Norwagiensium* (On the Old Norwegian Kings) around 1180. This work covers the history of Norway from of Harald Finehair *c.* 852 to the death of Sigurd the Crusader in 1130. According to Theodoricus Monachus, as mentioned in Chapter 1, after Sigurd's death, the kingdom fell into a state of decay

---

183 Nysether, 'Overlappende nettverk og det kontekstuelle fiendebildet under de norske "borgerkrigene"'; Taylor, *The Restraint of Violence*; *Sverris saga*, p. 261.
184 Jón Viðar Sigurðsson and Henrik Vigh, 'Who Is the Enemy?', pp. 51, 52–56; Nysether, 'Overlappende nettverk og det kontekstuelle fiendebildet under de norske "borgerkrigene"'.
185 *Heimskringla III*, p. 385.
186 e.g. *Heimskringla III*, pp. 283, 309, 384; Rosén, Frederik, and Helle Vogt, 'The War, and What Is Mine', pp. 99–114.

characterized by various wrongs, including killings, perjuries, parricides, desecrations of holy places, contempt for God, plundering of the clergy and the people, abductions of women, and other abominations. However, it is advisable not to accord too much significance to this statement, as the situation after Sigurd the Crusader's death was not much different from that in the years prior to it. Nevertheless, it is noteworthy that Theodoricus Monachus listed the abduction of women (*mulierum captiuationes*) among the wrongs that had taken place.[187]

There are no episodes in the sagas that mention the abduction of women in relation to the civil wars. However, that does not mean that the abduction of women was not a problem in Norway. The *Gulathing law*, which is the oldest law code in Norway and applies to West-Norway, was revised twice. The first revision was according to the tradition made by King Olav Haraldsson (1015–1028, after his death in 1030), known as the Olav-text, and the second revision was made around 1163, known as the Magnus-text, after King Magnus Erlingsson (1161–1184).[188] Paragraph 51, which is found in both revisions, states that if a man abducts (*tecr*) another man's betrothed woman and marries her, and both have consented to this, then the man who had affianced her should summon the thief to an assembly, and it was the duty of the *thing*-men to outlaw them both. However, if the woman claims that she did not give her consent, she has nothing to answer for.[189] Paragraph 32, which is only found in the later revision of the *Gulathing law*, states that those men who take other men's wives, betrothed women, or daughters by violence (*taca með rane*), without the consent of those who have authority over them or without their own consent, are all such men are outlawed (*ubotamenn*) and have forfeited their peace and wealth.[190] The abduction of women was obviously a problem in Norway. However, the above-mentioned paragraphs in the *Gulathing law* were addressing a general problem that existed in the country and cannot be linked to the civil wars.

It is also noteworthy that Theodoricus only mentions the abduction of women, and not rape. There are two recorded instances of rape in the sagas that date back to the period between 1130 and 1240.[191] However, the laws clearly indicate that rape was a serious crime.[192] It is striking

---

187 *Theodoricus*, pp. 126–27.
188 Helle, *Gulatinget og Gulatingslova*, pp. 17–20.
189 *Den eldre Gulatingslova*, § 51.
190 *Den eldre Gulatingslova*, § 32.
191 *Hákonar saga Hákonarsonar I*, pp. 18–19, 115; *Hákonar saga Hákonarsonar II*, p. 39. More episodes are known from sagas narrating the Icelandic Free State society (*c.* 930–1262/64), see for example Miller, 'Beating Up on Women and Old Men and Other Enormities'; Ljungqvist, 'Rape in the Icelandic Sagas'; Bell, 'Ok lá þar at óvilja hennar: A Reconsideration of Sexual Violence in the Old Norse World'.
192 Lyngvær, Kirsti. 'Kvinner og vold. En undersøkelse av norske middelalderlover', pp. 83–99.

that rape is seldom discussed in most sources on war. It is worth noting that the two instances of rape mentioned in the sagas involve high-born women, one of whom was married to a man who had been a close friend (*höfuðvinr*) of King Hakon Hakonsson throughout his life.[193] This suggests that the prevalence of rape during this period may have been higher than the sagas indicate. Nonetheless, we should not discount the importance of friendship and kinship ties in preventing rape. In many cases, women married to the 'enemy' were relatives, or married to a friend. Wrongdoing towards them could have consequences at a later time.

Conclusion

The 'conflict literature' stresses that there are two 'necessary conditions' for the start of a 'civil war: 1) the existence of social tensions and grievances, and 2) the feasibility of collective action to transform tensions into fighting'.[194] In early twelfth-century Norway, social tensions between political leaders existed, but this was not new, as it had been a part of the political system for a long time. What was different was that these tensions were transformed into actual fighting, which was made possible by the failure of the social networks of the kings and local lords with overlapping relationships to control the situation. Another important factor that prevented the tension between claimants to the throne from escalating was the fact that householders were friends to all the kings, which made it difficult for anyone king to summon the *leiðangr*, to help them in power struggles. The solution to this problem was the *flokkr*, a small unit of usually no more than a few hundred men, whose family and friendship ties with other *flokkar* prevented large-scale casualties in battles between them.

The struggle between Magnus the Blind and Harald Gille is best explained by Magnus' unwillingness to accept Harald as a co-regent — an explanation which echoes the results from the scholarly discussion that has lasted for more than a century. After the killing of Magnus the Blind and Sigurd Slembe, the royal network established peace in the country. It was not until after the death of Sigurd Mouth and Inge's foster fathers that the tension grew between Inge Hunchback on one side, and Sigurd Mouth and Oystein on the other. After the killing of Inge, Hakon the Broad-Shouldered, son of Sigurd Mouth, became the sole ruler of the country and under 'normal' circumstances he and the lords who fought against him would have started to work out a solution that would have 'normalized' the situation. This, however, did not happen, because of the coup by the most loyal supporters of King Inge Hunchback, who put

---

193 *Hákonar saga Hákonarsonar II*, p. 39.
194 Rohner, 'Reputation, Group Structure and Social Tensions', p. 189.

Magnus Erlingsson, the son of Erling Skakke and Kristin, daughter of Sigurd the Crusader, on the throne. This was the turning point in the history of the Norwegian civil wars. Erling Skakke and the people behind the coup abandoned the ideology of joint rulership — its main tenet had been that kings should *rule together* and *divide* the royal revenues between them — and introduced the common European model and ideology: a kingdom should have one single king. This rebellion was not successful; however, it created a struggle between the old and the new royal line for decades to come.

The background for these skirmishes were the extensive overlaps of kinship and friendship which helped to keep the struggles relatively contained and prevent them from escalating into more violent and destructive conflicts. This social structure created a system of alliances and loyalties that limited the extent of violence and helped to preserve the social order, even in times of political instability and conflict.

Works Cited

Primary Sources

Ágrip af Nóregskonunga sǫgum. Fagrskinna. Nóregs konunga tal, ed. by Bjarni Einarsson, Íslenzk fornrit, XXIX (Reykjavík: Hið íslenzka fornritafélag, 1985)

Biskupa sögur II, ed. by Ásdís Egilsdóttir, Íslenzk fornrit, XVI (Reykjavík: Hið íslenzka fornritafélag, 2002)

Chronica magistri Rogeri de Houedene Volume 3, ed. by William Stubbs, Cambridge Library Collection – Rolls: Volume 3 (London: Longman and Co, 1870)

Chronicles of the Reigns of Stephen, Henry II, and Richard I: Containing the First Four Books of the Historia rerum anglicarum (Reprod.) of William of Newburgh, ed. by Richard Howlett (London: Longman, 1884)

Codex Frisianus: en Samling af norske Kongesagaer, ed. by Carl Richard Unger (Christiania [Oslo]: Malling, 1871)

Danakonunga sögur, Skjoldunga saga, Knýtlinga saga, Ágrip af sögu danakonunga, ed. by Bjarni Guðnason, Íslenzk fornrit, XXXV (Reykjavík: Hið íslenzka fornritafélag, 1982)

Den eldre Gulatingslova, ed. by Tor Ulset, Bjørn Eithun, and Magnus Rindal, Norrøne tekster, 6 (Oslo: Riksarkivet, 1994)

Edda Snorra Sturlusonar, ed. by Heimir Pálsson (Reykjavík: Mal Og Menning, 1996)

Eddukvæði I–II, ed. by Jónas Kristjánsson and Vésteinn Ólason, Íslenzk fornrit (Reykjavík: Hið íslenzka fornritafélag, 2014)

Eirspennill, AM 47 fol., ed. by Finnur Jónsson (Kristiania: Den norske historiske kildeskriftskommission, 1916)

Gammelnorsk homiliebok, ed. by Erik Gunnes and Astrid Salvesen (Oslo: Universitetsforlaget, 1971)

GD = Saxo Grammaticus. Gesta Danorum: The History of the Danes: 1–2, ed. by Karsten Friis-Jensen, trans. by Peter Fisher (Oxford: Oxford University Press, 2015)

Grágás. Efter det Arnamagnæanske haandskrift, nr. 334 fol., Staðarhólsbók, ed. by Vilhjálmur Finsen (Copenhagen: Gyldendal, 1879)

Grágás. Stykker, som findes i det Arnamagnæanske haandskrift, nr. 351 fol. Skálholtsbók og en række andre haandskrifter, ed. by Vilhjálmur Finsen (Copenhagen: Gyldendal, 1883)

Hákonar saga Hákonarsonar I. Bǫglunga saga, ed. by Þorleifur Hauksson, Sverrir Jakobsson and Tor Ulset, Íslenzk fornrit, XXXI (Reykjavík: Hið íslenzka fornritafélag, 2013)

Heimskringla I, ed. by Bjarni Aðalbjarnarson, Íslenzk fornrit, XXVI (Reykjavík: Hið íslenzka fornritafélag, 1941)

Heimskringla II, ed. by Bjarni Aðalbjarnarson, Íslenzk fornrit, XXVII (Reykjavík: Hið íslenzka fornritafélag, 1945)

Heimskringla III, ed. by Bjarni Aðalbjarnarson, Íslenzk fornrit, XXVIII (Reykjavík: Hið íslenzka fornritafélag, 1951)

Heimskringla 3. Magnús Óláfsson to Magnús Erlingsson, ed. by Alison Finley and Anthony Faulkes (London: Viking Society for Northern Research, 2015)

Hirdloven til Norges konge og hans håndgangne menn. Etter AM 322 fol., ed. by Steinar Imsen (Oslo: Riksarkivet, 2000)

Islandske Annaler indtil 1578, ed. by Gustav Storm, Det Norske historiske Kildeskriftfonds skrifter, 21 (Christiania [Oslo]: Grøndahl & Søns Bogtrykkeri, 1888)

Jómsvíkinga saga, ed. by Þorleifur Hauksson and Marteinn Helgi Sigurðsson, Íslenzk fornrit, XXXIII (Reykjavík: Hið íslenzka fornritafélag, 2018)

Morkinskinna I–II, ed. by Ármann Jakobsson and Þórður Ingi Guðjónsson. Íslenzk fornrit, XXIII (Reykjavík: Hið íslenzka fornritafélag, 2011)

Norges gamle Love I–V, ed. by Rudolf Keyser and others (Christiania [Oslo]: Chr. Gröndahl, 1846–1895)

Orkneyinga saga. Legenda de sancto Magno. Magnúss saga skemmri. Magnúss saga lengri. Helga þáttr ok Úlfs, ed. by Finnbogi Guðmundsson, Íslenzk fornrit, XXXIV (Reykjavík: Hið íslenzka fornritafélag, 1965)

Scriptores minores historiæ Danicæ medii ævi: 2. hæfte, ed. by Martin Cl. Gertz (Copenhagen: G. E. C. Gad, 1918–1920)

Sturlunga saga I–II, ed. by Jón Jóhannesson, Magnús Finnbogason, and Kristján Eldjárn (Reykjavík: Sturlunguútgáfan, 1946)

Sverris saga, ed. by Þorleifur Hauksson, Íslenzk fornrit, XXX (Reykjavík: Hið íslenzka fornritafélag, 2007)

Theodoricus. De antiquitate regum Norwagiensium. On the old Norwegian kings, ed. by Egil Kraggerud (Oslo: Novus, 2018)

Secondary Studies

Althoff, Gerd, *Verwandte, Freunde und Getreue: Zum politischen Stellenwert der Gruppenbindungen im frühen Mittelalter* (Darmstadt: Wissenschaftliche Buchgesellschaft, 1990)

Amory, Frederic, 'The Historical Worth of *Rígsþula*', *Alvíssmál*, 10 (2001), 3–20

Andersson, Theodore M., 'Kings' Sagas (Konungasögur)', in *Old Norse-Icelandic Literature: A Critical Guide*, ed. by Carol J. Clover and John Lindow, Islandica (Ithaca: Cornell University Press, 1985), pp. 197–238

Andersson, Theodore M., *The Sagas of Norwegian Kings (1130–1265): An Introduction. Islandica LIX* (Ithaca: Cornell University Library, 2016)

Ármann Jakobsson, *Í leit að konungi. Konungsmynd íslenskra konungasagna* (Reykjavík: Háskólaútgáfan, 1997)

Arstad, Knut Peter Lyche, Nikolas Skjaldvorsson – Norsk biografisk leksikon (snl.no), 12. June 2020

Arstad, Knut, '"han var svag af Charakteer og uden ringeste Herskergaver, hvilket også fremgaar af hele hans Historie", En undersøkelse av Harald Gilles ettermæle', *Historisk Tidsskift* (N), 78 (1999), 435–60

Auður Magnúsdóttir, *Frillor och fruar. Politik och samlevnad på Island 1120–1400* (Gothenburg: Historiska Institutionen, 2001)

Bagge, Sverre, 'Borgerkrig og statsutvikling i Norge i middelalderen', *Historisk tidsskrift* (N), 65 (1986): 145–97

———, 'Borgerkrig og statsutvikling – svar til Hans Jacob Orning', *Historisk tidsskrift* (N), 93 (2015), 91–110

———, *Cross and Scepter: The Rise of the Scandinavian Kingdoms from the Vikings to the Reformation* (Princeton: Princeton University Press, 2014)

———, *From Viking Stronghold to Christian Kingdom. State Formation in Norway, c. 900–1350* (Copenhagen: Museum Tusculanum Press, 2010)

———, 'Mellom kildekritikk og historisk antropologi. Olav den hellige, aristokratiet og rikssamlingen', *Historisk tidsskrift* (N), 81 (2002), 173–212

———, *Mennesket i middelalderens Norge. Tanker, tro og holdninger 1000–1300* (Oslo: Aschehoug, 1998)

———, 'Samkongedømme og enekongedømme', *Historisk tidsskrift* (N) 54 (1975), 239–74

———, *Society and Politics in Snorri Sturluson's Heimskringla* (Berkeley: University of California Press, 1991)

———, 'Udsigt og innhogg: 150 års forskning om eldre norsk historie', *Historisk tidsskrift* (N), 75 (1996), 37–77

Bell, Jacob, 'Ok lá þar at óvilja hennar: A Reconsideration of Sexual Violence in the Old Norse World', *Journal of Family History*, 48 (2021), 3–29

Bjarni Guðnason, *Fyrsta sagan*, Studia Islandica. Íslensk fræði. Vol. 37 (Reykjavík: Bókaútgáfa Menningarsjóðs, 1978)

Bjørgo, Narve, Øystein Rian, and Alf Kaartvedt, *800–1536. Makt og avmakt. Selvstendighet og union: fra middelalderen til 1905*, Norsk utenrikspolitikks historie, 1 (Oslo: Universitetsforlaget, 1995)

———, 'Samkongedøme kontra einekongedøme', *Historisk tidsskrift* (N), 49 (1970), 1–33

Bjørkvik, Halvard, 'Krongodset i mellomalderen', *Historisk Tidsskrift* (N), 40 (1960–1961), 201–31

———, 'Leidang', in *Kulturhistorisk Leksikon for Nordisk Middelalder*, vol. x (Copenhagen: Rosenkilde og Bagger, 1965), cols 432–42

———, *Det norske krongodset i mellomalderen* (Trondheim: Tapir, 1968)

Bjørkvik, Halvard, and Andreas Holmsen, *Kven åtte jorda i den gamle leiglendingstida? Fordelinga av jordeigedomen i Noreg i 1661* (Trondheim: Tapir, 1972)

Blom, Grethe Authén, *Samkongedømme – enekongedømme – Håkon Magnussons hertugdømme*, Skrifter/Det Kongelige norske videnskabers selskab (Trondheim: Universitetsforlaget, 1972)

Bouchard, Constance Brittain, *'Those of my blood': Constructing Noble Families in Medieval Francia*, The Middle Ages series (Philadelphia: University of Pennsylvania Press, 2001)

Buskens, Vincent Willem, *Social Networks and Trust*, Theory and Decision Library, Game Theory, Mathematical Programming and Operations Research, Series C. Vol. 30 (Boston: Kluwer Academic, 2003)

Canning, Joseph, *A History of Medieval Political Thought* (London: Routledge, 2002)

Castells, Manuel 'A Network Theory of Power', *International Journal of Communication*, 5 (2011), 773–87

Christia, Fotini, *Alliance Formation in Civil Wars* (Cambridge: Cambridge University Press, 2012)

Cipolla, Carlo M. *Before the Industrial Revolution: European Society and Economy, 1000–1700*, 3rd edn (London: Routledge, 1993)

Coroban, Costel, *Ideology and Power in Norway and Iceland, 1150–1250* (Newcastle: Cambridge Scholars Publishing, 2013)

Crouch, David, *The Birth of Nobility: Constructing Aristocracy in England and France 900–1300* (New York: Routledge, 2005)

Danielsen, Rolf, Ståle Dyrvik, Tore Grønlie, Knut Helle, and Edgar Hovland, *Norway. A History from the Vikings to Our Own Times* (Oslo: Scandinavian University Press, 1995)

Drell, Joanna H., *Kinship and Conquest: Family Strategies in the Principality of Salerno during the Norman Period, 1077–1194* (Ithaca: Cornell University Press, 2002)

Duffy, Seán, Ailbhe MacShamhráin, and James Moynes (eds), *Medieval Ireland: An Encyclopedia* (New York: Routledge, 2005)

Duindam, Jeroen, 'Dynasties', *Medieval Worlds*, 2 (2015), 59–78

Ersland, Geir Atle, and Terje H. Holm, *Krigsmakt og kongemakt 900–1814* (Bergen: Eide, 2000)

Gade, Kari Ellen, '1235 Órækja meiddr ok heill gǫrr', *Gripla*, 9 (1996), 115–32

Ghosh, Shami, *Kings' Sagas and Norwegian History. Problems and Perspectives*, The Northern World. North Europe and the Baltic c. 400–1700 AD. Peoples, Economies and Cultures (Leiden: Brill, 2011)

Gluckman, Max, 'The Peace in the Feud', *Past and Present*, 8 (1955), 1–14

Green, Dennis Howard, *Language and History in the Early Germanic World* (Cambridge: Cambridge University Press, 1998)

Gunnes, Erik, *Erkebiskop Øystein, Statsmann og kirkebygger* (Oslo: Aschehoug, 1996)

——, *Kongens ære. Kongemakt og kirke i En tale mot biskopene* (Oslo: Gyldendal, 1971)

Haer, Roos, *Armed Group Structure and Violence in Civil Wars: The Organizational Dynamics of Civilian Killing* (London: Routledge, 2015)

Hamre, Lars, 'Hird', in *Kulturhistorisk Leksikon for Nordisk Middelalder*, vol. VI (Copenhagen: Rosenkilde og Bagger, 1961), cols 568–77

——, 'Retterbot', in *Kulturhistorisk Leksikon for Nordisk Middelalder*, vol. XIV (Copenhagen: Rosenkilde og Bagger, 1969), cols 108–10

Hansen, Lars Ivar, ''Ætten' i de eldste landskapslovene – realitet, konstruksjon og strategi', in *Norm og praksis i middelaldersamfunnet*, ed. by Else Mundal and Ingvild Øye (Bergen: Senter for europeiske kulturstudier, 1999), pp. 23–55

——, 'Slektskap', in *Holmgang. Om førmoderne samfunn. Festskrift til Kåre Lunden*, ed. by Anne Eidsfelt, Knut Kjeldstadli, Hanne Monclair, Per G. Norseng, Hans Jakob Orning, and Gunnar I. Pettersen (Oslo: Historisk institutt, Universitetet i Oslo, 2000), pp. 104–32

Helle, Knut, 'Brigida Haraldsdatter', in *Store norske leksikon* (Brigida Haraldsdatter – Store norske leksikon (snl.no)) 23. May 2021

——(ed.), *The Cambridge History of Scandinavia I. Prehistory to 1520* (Cambridge: Cambridge University Press)

——, *Gulatinget og Gulatingslova* (Leikanger: Skald, 2001)

——, 'Hvor står den historiske sagakritikken i dag?', *Collegium Medievale*, 24 (2011), 50–86

——, *Norge blir en stat 1130–1319*, Handbok i Norges historie, 3 (Bergen: Universitetsforlaget, 1974)

——, 'Den primitivistiske vendingen i norsk historisk middelalderforskning', *Historisk Tidsskrift* (N), 88 (2009): 571–609

——, *Under kirke og kongemakt: 1130–1350* Aschehougs Norgeshistorie, III (Oslo: Aschehoug, 1995)

Hødnebø, Finn and (eds), *Kulturhistorisk leksikon for nordisk middelalder I–XXII* (Oslo: Gyldendal, 1956–1978) (2. oppl. 1980–1982)

Holmsen, Andreas, *Norges historie. Fra de eldste tider til 1660* (Oslo: Gyldendal, 1939)

Hyams, Paul R., *Rancor and Reconciliation in Medieval England* (Ithaca: Cornell University Press, 2003)

Jensen, Janus Møller, 'Korstog mod de hedenske svenskere. Nye perspektiver på Kalmarledingen 1123/1124', *Collegium Medievale*, 31 (2018), 151–76

Jesch, Judith, *Ships and Men in the Late Viking Age: The Vocabulary of Runic Inscriptions and Skaldic Verse* (Woodbridge: Boydell Press, 2001)

——, *The Viking Diaspora*, The Medieval World (London: Routledge, 2015)

Jón Viðar Sigurðsson, 'The Appearance and Personal Abilities of goðar, jarlar, and konungar. Iceland, Orkney and Norway', in *West over Sea. Studies in Scandinavian Sea-Borne Expansion and Settlement Before 1300*, ed. by Beverly Ballin Smith, Simon Taylor, and Gareth Williams (Leiden: Brill, 2007), pp. 95–109

——, *Chieftains and Power in the Icelandic Commonwealth*, trans. by Jean Lundskær-Nielsen, The Viking Collection, 12 (Odense: Odense University Press, 1999)

——, *Frá goðorðum til ríkja: Þróun goðavalds á 12. og 13. öld*, Sagnfræðirannsóknir, B. 10 (Reykjavík: Bókaútgáfa Menningarsjóðs, 1989)

——, 'Forholdet mellom frender, hushold og venner på Island i fristatstiden', *Historisk tidsskrift*, 74 (1995), 311–30

——, 'Kings, Earls and Chieftains. Rulers in Norway, Orkney and Iceland c. 900–1300', in *Ideology and Power in the Viking and Middle Ages. Scandinavia, Iceland, Ireland, Orkney and the Faeroes*, ed. by Gro Steinsland, Jón Viðar Sigurðsson, Jan Erik Rekdal, and Ian Beuermann (Leiden: Brill, 2011), pp. 69–108

——, *Kristninga i Norden 750–1200*, Utsyn and innsikt (Oslo: Det Norske samlaget, 2003)

——, *Viking Friendship. The Social Bond in Iceland and Norway, c. 900–1300* (Ithaca: Cornell University Press, 2017)

Jón Viðar Sigurðsson and Anne Irene Riisøy, *Norsk historie 800–1536: frå krigerske bønder til lydige undersåttar*. Vol. 1, 2nd edn (Oslo: Det norske samlaget, 2022)

—— and Henrik Vigh, 'Who Is the Enemy? Multipolar Micropolitics', in *Medieval and Modern Civil Wars. A Comparative Perspective*, ed. by Jón Viðar Sigurðsson and Hans Jacob Orning. History of Warfare, 135 (Leiden: Brill, 2021), pp. 34–61

Jones, Rhys, 'Changing Geographies of Governance and Group Identities in the Middle Ages: The Role of Societal Interaction and Conflict', *Political Geography*, 19 (2000): 901–26

Krag, Claus, 'Magnus 3. Olavsson Berrføtt', in *Store norske leksikon* (Magnus 3. Olavsson Berrføtt – Norsk biografisk leksikon (snl.no)), 23. May 2021

——, 'Myten om Hårfagreættens "odel"', *Historisk tidsskrift* (N), 81 (2002), 381–94

——, *Norges historie fram til 1319* (Oslo: Universitetsforlaget, 2000)

Lambert, T. B., 'Introduction. Some Approaches to Peace and Protection in the Middle Ages', in *Peace and Protection in the Middle Ages*, ed. by David W. Rollason and T. B. Lambert, Durham Medieval and Renaissance Monographs and Essays (Durham: Durham University, 2009), pp. 1–16

Lawing, Sean B., 'Perspectives on Disfigurement in Medieval Iceland: A Cultural Study based on Old Norse Laws and Icelandic Sagas for the PhD' (Unpublished Doctoral Thesis, University of Iceland, 2016)

Lindow, John, *Comitatus, Individual and Honor. Studies in North Germanic Institutional Vocabulary*, University of California Publications in Linguistics, 83 (Berkeley: University of California Press, 1976)

Ljungqvist, Fredrik Charpentier, 'Rape in the Icelandic Sagas: An Insight in the Perceptions about Sexual Assaults on Women in the Old Norse World', *Journal of Family History*, 40 (2015), 431–47

Love, Jeffrey, and , *A Lexicon of Medieval Nordic Law* (Cambridge: Open Book Publishers, 2020)

Lund, Niels, 'The Armies of Swein Forkbeard and Cnut: "leding or lið"?', *Anglo-Saxon England*, 15 (1986), 105–18

Lunden, Kåre, *Norge under Sverreætten, 1177–1319. Høymiddelalder* (Oslo: Cappelen, 1976)

Luttwak, Edward N., 'Give War a Chance', *Foreign Affairs*, 78 (1999), 36–44

Lyngvær, Kirsti, 'Kvinner og vold. En undersøkelse av norske middelalderlover' ([Master's Thesis] Hovedfagsoppgave, Universitetet i Oslo, 1996)

MacCarron, Pádraig and Ralph Kenna, 'Network Analysis of the Íslendinga sögur – the Sagas of Icelanders', *The European Physical Journal B*, 86 (2013), 1–9

———, 'Universal Properties of Mythological Networks', *EPL (Europhysics Letters)*, 99 (2012), 1–6

———, 'Viking Sagas: Six Degrees of Icelandic Separation Social Networks from the Viking Era', *Significance*, 10 (2013), 12–17

Mann, Michael, *The Sources of Social Power: Vol. 1: A History of Power from the Beginning to A.D. 1760* (Cambridge: Cambridge University Press, 1986)

McManus, Damian, 'Good-Looking and Irresistible: The Hero from Early Irish Saga to Classical Poetry', *Ériu*, 59 (2009), 57–109

Miller, William Ian, 'Beating Up on Women and Old Men and Other Enormities: A Social Historical Inquiry into Literary Sources', *Mercer Law Review*, 39 (1988), 753–66

———, *Bloodtaking and Peacemaking. Feud, Law, and Society in Saga Iceland* (Chicago: University of Chicago Press, 1990)

Mitchell, Linda E., *Family Life in the Middle Ages* (Westport: Greenwood, 2007)

Moseng, Ole Georg, Erik Opsahl, Erling Sandmo, and Gunnar Pettersen, *Norsk historie I* (Oslo: Universitetsforlaget, 1999)

Mundal, Else, 'Kvinnesynet og forståinga av biologisk arv i den norrøne kulturen', in *Atlantisk dåd og drøm: 17 essays om Island/Norge*, ed. by Asbjørn Aarnes (Oslo: Aschehoug, 1998), pp. 153–70

Naderer, Max, 'Love and Fear: Debating Violence in the Political Culture of the "Civil War" Period in Norway and Denmark, c. 1130–1240' (Unpublished Doctoral Thesis, University of Oslo, 2020)

Norseng, Per G., 'Arne på Ståreim', in *Store norske leksikon* (Arne på Ståreim – Store norske leksikon (snl.no))

———, 'Erling Skakke', in *Store norske leksikon* (Erling Skakke – Store norske leksikon (snl.no))

———, 'Margrete Fredkulla', in *Store norske leksikon* (Margrete Fredkulla – Store norske leksikon (snl.no))

Nygård, Berit Marie, ''Ok óksu allir upp heima þar': fostringsinstitusjonens form, innhald og funksjon på Island i fristatstida' (Master's Thesis, Universitetet i Bergen, 1997)

Nysether, Hilde Andrea, 'Overlappende nettverk og det kontekstuelle fiendebildet under de norske "borgerkrigene"', *Collegium Medievale*, 32 (2019), 133–50

O'Donnell, Thomas Charles, 'The Affect of Fosterage in Medieval Ireland' (Unpublished Doctoral Thesis, University College London, 2017)

Oexle, Otto Gerhard, 'Conjuratio und Gilde im frühen Mittelalter. Ein Beitrag zum Problem der sozialgeschichtlichen Kontinuität zwischen Antike und Mittelalter', in *Gilden und Zünfte. Kaufmänn und gewerbliche Genossenschaften im frühen und hohen Mittelalter*, ed. by Berent Schwineköper (Sigmaringen: Thorbecke, 1985), pp. 151–214

Orning, Hans Jacob, 'Borgerkrig og statsutvikling i Norge i middelalderen – en revurdering', *Historisk tidsskrift* (N), 93 (2014), 193–216

——, 'Hvorfor vant kongene?', *Historisk tidsskrift* (N), 93 (2015): 285–92

Parkes, Peter, 'Fosterage, Kinship, and Legend: When Milk Was Thicker than Blood?', *Comparative Studies in Society and History*, 46 (2004), 587–615

Parkinson, Sarah E., and Sherry Zaks, 'Militant and Rebel Organization(s)', *Comparative Politics*, 50 (2018), 271–93

Patzold, Steffen, 'Konsens und Konkurrenz. Überlegungen zu einem aktuellen Forschungskonzept der Mediävistik', *Frühmittelalterliche Studien*, 41 (2007), 75–103

Pollington, Stephen, 'The Mead-Hall Community', *Journal of Medieval History*, 37 (2011), 19–33

Preiser-Kapeller, Johannes, 'Calculating the Middle Ages? The Project "Complexities and Networks in the Medieval Mediterranean and the Near East" (COMMED)', *Medieval Worlds*, 2 (2015), 100–27

Raffield, Ben, 'Bands of Brothers: A Re-appraisal of the Viking Great Army and its Implications for the Scandinavian Colonization of England', *Early Medieval Europe*, 24 (2016), 308–37

Raffield, Ben, Claire Greenlow, Neil Price, and Mark Collard, 'Ingroup Identification, Identity Fusion and the Formation of Viking War Bands', *World Archaeology*, 48 (2015), 1–16

Refsdal, Frank, *Dagsætta: en høvdingeslekt på 1100-tallet i Grenland*, Grenland allmennvitenskapelige bibliotek (Porsgrunn: Norgesforlaget, 2004)

Rohner, Dominic, 'Reputation, Group Structure and Social Tensions', *Journal of Development Economics*, 96 (2011), 188–99

Rosén, Frederik, and Helle Vogt, 'The War, and What Is Mine: Private Ownership in the Civil Wars in Norway and Denmark in the High Middle Ages', in *Medieval and Modern Civil Wars. A Comparative Perspective*, ed. by Jón Viðar Sigurðsson and Hans Jacob Orning, History of Warfare, 135 (Leiden: Brill Academic Publishers, 2021), pp. 94–123

Rüdiger, Jan. *All the King's Women: Polygyny and Politics in Europe, 900–1250. The Northern World* (Leiden: Brill, 2020)

——, *Der König und seine Frauen. Polygynie und politische Kultur in Europa (9.-13. Jahrhundert)*, Europa im Mittelalter, Vol. 20 (Berlin: de Gruyter, 2015)

Russell, Josiah Cox, 'Population in Europe 500–1500', in *The Fontana Economic History of Europe, Vol. 1*, ed. by Carlo M. Cipolla (London: Collins/Fontana, 1972), pp. 25–70

Sawyer, Birgit, 'The "Civil Wars" Revisited', *Historisk tidsskrift* (N), 82 (2003), 43–73

Schneidmüller, Bernd, 'Konsensuale Herrschaft. Ein Essay über Formen und Konzepte politischer Ordnung im Mittelalter', in *Reich, Regionen und Europa in Mittelalter und Neuzeit. Festschrift für Peter Moraw*, ed. by Paul-Joachim Heinig, Sigird Jahns, Hans-Joachim Schmidt, Rainer Christoph Schwinges, and Sabine Wefers (Berlin: Duncker & Humblot, 2000), pp. 53–87

Shepard, Jonathan, 'Networks', *Past and Present*, 238 (2018): 116–57

Skinner, Patricia, *Living with Disfigurement in Early Medieval Europe* (New York: Palgrave: 2017)

Skyum-Nielsen, Niels, *Kvinde og slave*, Scandinavian University Books, Vol. 3 (Copenhagen: Munksgaard, 1971)

Stafford, Pauline, *Queens, Concubines and Dowagers: The King's Wife in the Early Middle Ages*. Women, Power and Politics (London: Leicester University Press, 1998)

Staniland, Paul, 'Militias, Ideology, and the State', *Journal of Conflict Resolution*, 59 (2015), 770–93

——, *Networks of Rebellion: Explaining Insurgent Cohesion and Collapse*, Cornell Studies in Security Affairs (Ithaca: Cornell University Press, 2014)

Sundqvist, Olof, *An Arena for Higher Powers: Ceremonial Buildings and Religious Strategies for Rulership in Late Iron Age Scandinavia*, Studies in the History of Religions, 150 (Leiden: Brill, 2016)

——, 'Asarnas idrotter och religion', in *Zlatan frälsaren och andra texter om religion och idrott: en festskrift till David Westerlund*, ed. by Susanne Olsson, Olof Sundqvist, and David Thurfjell (Farsta: Molin & Sorgenfrei Förlag, 2014), pp. 122–38

Sveaas Andersen, Per., *Samlingen av Norge og kristningen av landet 800–1130*, Handbok i Norges historie, 2 (Bergen: Universitetsforlaget, 1977)

Sztompka, Piotr, *Trust: A Sociological Theory* Cambridge Cultural Social Studies (Cambridge: Cambridge University Press, 2003 [1999])

Taylor, Louisa, *The Restraint of Violence: Elite Conduct in England, Norway and Denmark in the High Middle Ages*, forthcoming

Tobiassen, Torfinn, 'Tronfølgelov og privilegiebrev. En studie i kongedømmets ideologi under Magnus Erlingsson', *Historisk tidsskrift* (N), 43 (1964), 181–273

KIM ESMARK

3. Messy Conflict

Socio-political Competition and War in Denmark c. 1128–1137

In the kingdom of Denmark, the twelfth-century 'civil war period' began around the same time as in Norway. It is usually said to have started off suddenly with an infamous political assassination. On 7 January 1131 Magnus, son and prospective heir of the long-reigning King Niels, lured his cousin Duke Knud Lavard, son of Niels' brother and royal predecessor Erik I the Good, to a meeting in the forest of Haraldsted in Central Zealand. When Knud turned up, he was ambushed by Magnus and a sworn band of associates, struck down, and killed.

The murder was the culmination of years of mounting tension between competing branches of the royal family. During the 1120s, Knud Lavard had built himself an impressive power base in the border region between Denmark and the Empire; Magnus and his friends long suspected him of aspiring to kingship. In the end they resolved to remove the threat by killing Knud off. Yet, as it turned out, the Haraldsted killing pushed the tensions into overdrive as powerful friends of the dead duke rallied behind his half-brother Erik the Unforgettable to take revenge. They had Erik elected king in the eastern Danish provinces of Zealand and Scania, but large sections of the lay and ecclesiastical elite remained loyal to King Niels and his son Magnus, especially in the western province of Jutland. Soon armies were fighting each other on both land and sea. The conflict — alternately labelled 'rebellion' (*seditio*), 'disturbances' (*pertubationes*) or 'internal wars' (*intestina bella*) by contemporary and near-contemporary Latin writers[1] — was brought to a sort of conclusion in the summer of

---

1 *Chronicon Roskildense*, p. 27; Helmold von Bosau, *Chronica Slavorum/Slawenchronik*, p. 192. Old Norse writers did not apply general classificatory terms to describe the struggles, but simply reported about warfare, fighting, harrying, battle (*hernaðr, orrusta*).

Kim Esmark (kesmark@ruc.dk) is associate professor in the Department of Communication and Arts, University of Roskilde.

1134 when Niels and Magnus died at the hands of Erik the Unforgettable's armies and allies and Erik himself ascended to sole rule.

In Danish historiography the 1131–1134 war is well-trodden territory. It is the first major political conflict of its kind where it is possible to follow it in reasonable detail thanks to a *relatively* extensive, albeit also difficult, highly selective, and partly interdependent, narrative source material. The *Roskilde Chronicle*, written no later than 1140 by an anonymous local cleric of Roskilde cathedral,[2] the Saxon priest Helmold of Bosau's *Chronicle of the Slavs* (early 1170s),[3] Svend Aggesen's *Short History of the Danish Kings* (c. 1185),[4] and Saxo Grammaticus' massive *History of the Danes* (completed c. 1210),[5] as well as the Old Norse *Knýtlinga saga* (compiled c. 1250),[6] all provide information — sometimes corroborating, sometimes complementary, sometimes incompatible — about the events and their context. Further evidence may be gathered from a few royal and episcopal charters issued around the time,[7] from near-contemporary German annals, and from scattered notices in the necrologies of the Cathedral church of Lund, later Danish annalistic records, and the Norwegian Kings' sagas. The hagiography, finally, of Knud Lavard, who was promoted as a martyr saint from the mid-1130s and officially canonized in 1169–1170, contains valuable information about the pre-history of the war.[8]

In most modern scholarly discussions, the war following the Haraldsted murder is construed as a kind of *Vorspiel* to or the first phase of a longer period of disruptive internal strife, which marked Denmark's transformation from a loosely organized Viking society to medieval Christian

---

2 *Chronicon Roskildense*; introduction and critical discussion in Gelting, 'Chronicon Roskildense', and Gelting, 'Forfatteren og hans tid'.

3 Helmold; introduction and critical discussion in Liljefalk and Pajung, 'Helmolds slaverkrønike'.

4 Sven Aggesen, *Brevis historia*; introduction and critical discussion in Christiansen, 'Sueno Aggonis'.

5 *GD*; introduction and critical discussion in Friis-Jensen, 'Saxo Grammaticus', and Gelting, 'Saxo in the Archives'.

6 *Knýtlinga saga* (all translations from *Knytlinga Saga. The History of the Kings of Denmark*, unless otherwise noted); introduction and critical discussion in Finnur Jónsson, *Knýtlinga saga*; Albeck, *Knytlinga*; Bjarni Guðnason, 'Introduction'. The saga was composed by an Icelandic author on the basis of various Latin chronicles (including Saxo), lost twelfth-century saga material, skaldic verses, oral traditions, and information obtained during the author's stay at the Danish royal court around 1240–1241.

7 Counting every royal and episcopal charter issued on Danish soil from the first known charter by King Knud II the Holy in 1085 to the end of the period discussed in this chapter as well as every reference to lost letters in narrative sources, it is impossible to muster more than some 15–20 documents. Private charters only start flowing in Denmark from around 1200.

8 Robert of Ely; *Historia S. Kanvti*; introduction and critical discussion in Friis-Jensen, 'Robertus Elgensis'; Chesnutt and Friis-Jensen, 'Sanctus Kanutus Dux', and Bergsagel, 'Kanute, cuius est Dacia?'.

monarchy.[9] In the words of one Danish historian, the 'horrifying process of events' after Magnus' killing of Knud Lavard ushered 'a political and social explosion of such fierceness, that it took a whole generation to provide the preconditions for a new stability'.[10] Erik the Unforgettable's takeover in 1134 never settled tensions and before long, armed hostilities broke out again. For some twenty-odd years, rival members of the royal lineage fought each other on-off. The decades of 'civil war' (or 'throne war', 'dynastic feud', 'kings' war', 'the long dynastic war' — historians' terms vary) supposedly exposed the Danish kingdom to political chaos as well as to external threats from the Empire against its status as an independent realm and Church province. Only when Valdemar I, son of Knud Lavard, was finally recognized as sole king in 1157, did the king and Church manage to realize what one influential synthesis has called a 'happy cooperation', which overcame 'the weaknesses in the national policy of the realm' and secured 'the progress of state formation', while 'the nation's leading forces united in firm rejection of German claims to overlordship'.[11]

In this chapter the war triggered by the Haraldsted murder will be treated in its own right, loosened from the narrative matrix of the civil war period and incipient state formation, and analysed from the perspectives set out in Chapter 1. The question to be pursued is plain and mundane: *What sort of conflict was this?* The chapter first seeks to outline the basic structures and axes of tension in the early twelfth-century field of power, focusing on the years leading up to Haraldsted. From here, the chapter moves on to the actual course of the war and the immediate aftermath in a chronologically ordered micro-political analysis of means, measures, and strategies employed by the actors. Borrowing a concept from international relations studies of modern civil war theatres, it will be argued that the conflict was inherently *messy*, e.g. polydimensional, driven and influenced by multiple agencies, fought for various purposes, difficult to control, and characterized by frequent side-switching, regional segmentation, cross-border interventions, and alliance formation. The chapter also argues that although it is convenient for many purposes to speak commonsensically of the war as having started with the killing of Knud Lavard in 1131 and ended with the death of Niels and Magnus in 1134, such temporal demarcations also misconstrue the dynamics of socio-political contests in this period.

---

9 This historiographical pattern very much mirrors the Norwegian one depicted in Chapter 2.
10 Breengaard, *Muren om Israels hus*, pp. 203–04. Skyum-Nielsen, *Kvinde og slave*, p. 71, likewise speaks of the period as 'the most perturbed quarter of a century since the days of Sven Estridsen'.
11 Christensen, *Kongemagt og aristokrati*, pp. 5, 49. For other key works within the nation-oriented, state evolutionist tradition, see Weibull, 'Nekrologierne fra Lund'; Koch, *Kongemagt og kirke*; Paludan, 'Flos Danie'; Fenger, *Kirker rejses alle vegne*.

Figure 3.1. Main regions and localities mentioned in the text. Map by author.

Aristocratic Networks: The Dark Matter of the Power Field

In order to grasp the dynamics underlying the Haraldsted event and what followed, it is necessary to first analyse, if only tentatively, the structure of power relations in the 1120s. What such an analysis reveals is that, rather than suddenly disrupting thirty years of peaceful reign under King Niels (a standard historiographical narrative), the assassination of Knud Lavard and the subsequent war came as a violent escalation or intensification of already well-established endemic tensions among the political elite, brought about in a context of genealogical accidents and disproportionate accumulations of power and resources.

If one takes contemporary representations seriously, medieval Danish power politics was very much a family matter. In the apt words of Thyra Nors:

In close reading the so-called political history of twelfth century Denmark appears as one big family brawl. All the time it is brothers or cousins who fight with each other for power. What historians traditionally have seen as political actions remain, if one sticks strictly to the text, nothing but manifestations of inheritance and succession claims.[12]

Although the sources (Latin more than Old Norse) inevitably tend to focus on *royal* brothers and cousins, competition for various forms of power or resources — land, wealth, reputation, ecclesiastical offices, useful relationships, military capacity, etc. — always involved those wider networks of magnates, who constituted 'the societal precondition for any kind of political activity'.[13] The top echelons — rich landowners, local lords, and commanders of armed retinues — were closely connected to members of the royal family through bonds of marriage, fosterage, and friendship, and for most practical purposes were on a par with the king. They not only lent their support to rulers and rival brothers and cousins of the royal kindred, but also exerted pressure on them in proactive pursuit of their own goals and interests — just as they experienced pressure themselves from the many individuals and families of slightly lower status, who formed their own power bases. When kings went into war or organized looting expeditions abroad, their armies consisted of contingents of warriors supplied by these magnates. 'Kin and mutual friendship between the king and his retainers of great men with private armies was continuously the core of the military system'.[14] This also applied to inter-dynastic war, the outcome of which, in the words of Niels Lund, 'was clearly decided by the support each side was able to muster from the magnates of the various provinces. They made and unmade kings, and the battles were fought by their forces'.[15] To understand the dynamics of the power field, one therefore needs to read through the royal bias of histories and records

---

12 'Den såkaldte politiske historie i det 12. århundredes Danmark tager sig tekstnært læst ud som ét stort familieslagsmål. Det er hele tiden brødre eller fætre, der kæmper indbyrdes om magten. Det som historikerne traditionelt har betragtet som politiske handlinger, er, hvis man holder sig strengt til teksten, intet andet end manifestationer af arve- og tronfølgekrav'. Nors, 'Slægtsstrategier', p. 59. See in the same vein Sawyer, 'The "Civil Wars" revisited', and Chapter 9 in this volume.
13 Breengaard, *Muren om Israels hus*, p. 207.
14 Hybel, *The Nature of Kingship*, p. 302. As Hybel rightly notes, the sources covering the years discussed in this chapter actually 'disclose an unprecendented gallery of great men with their own private military forces', but as Hybel seems to imply himself, this is probably due to a *mutation documentaire*; the 'more or less autonomous warlords' most likely had been there before the growth of written evidence from *c.* 1100 onwards (*The Nature of Kingship*, p. 277).
15 Lund, *Lið, leding og landeværn*, p. 296. In a comparative context it might be worth stressing that these magnates were not royal 'vassals' in any sense.

and consider the constant underlying push-and-pull of multiple competing elite groups on many levels.[16]

As for the 1120s, Danish historians usually single out three supposedly dominant kin-networks. The Trund family was based in Jutland. It was headed by the mighty Christiern Svensen, who according to the chronicler Svend Aggesen occupied a pre-eminent position in King Niels' entourage. Christiern's brother Asser, bishop of Lund since 1089, became Denmark's first archbishop in 1103–1104 when an independent Nordic ecclesiastical province was established and Lund elevated to the status of a metropolitan Church. In southern Zealand around Næstved, we find the enormously wealthy Peder Bodilsen and his brothers. Their mother Bodil may have been a daughter of one of King Erik the Good's concubines.[17] Around 1122–1123 Peder Bodilsen and his chaplain Nothold initiated a violent campaign for priestly celibacy in Zealand. Their harsh persecutions of priests were only suspended when in 1124 King Niels appointed a new bishop of Roskilde, who managed to mediate.[18] Also based in Zealand was the so-called 'Hvide family' (or 'Skjalm clan'), named by historians after Skjalm Hvide, a war leader who, according to family tradition, was able in the late 1090s to mobilize the entire island's naval forces for a revenge campaign of his own. Around 1100 King Erik the Good made Skjalm regional commander of Zealand and entrusted him with the upbringing of his son Knud Lavard. In the 1120s the family was led by Skjalm's sons, Knud Lavard's foster brothers.[19]

Scattered evidence of these three groups' resources, relationships, and socio-political activities both before and after Haraldsted clearly testify to their pre-eminent standing. Yet, although they may have 'dominated with a weight hardly ever matched by the nobility of any later period',[20] they were far from alone. Other figures and kin-networks evidently existed, but, besides a few names in scattered charters and diplomas, we do not know much about them.[21] As for identifiable individuals and families from the elite, we primarily possess information about those whose descendants two or three generations later got their story recorded for posterity by

---

16 Variations of this perspective have constituted a kind of 'under-current' in Danish historiography, see Paludan-Müller, 'To bemærkninger', Danstrup, 'Træk af den politiske kamp', Skyum-Nielsen, *Kvinde og slave*, Gelting, 'Forfatteren og hans tid', and most comprehensively Hermanson, *Släkt, vänner och makt*.
17 Liljefalk and Pajung, 'Bodil-slægten', p. 52; Hermanson, *Släkt, vänner och makt*, p. 155. The genealogical link remains speculative.
18 Nyberg, 'Kong Niels', pp. 377–79.
19 For a hypothesis that Skjalm's ancestry might be traced back to an old royal family from before the unification of the Danish realm, see Jaubert, 'Un ou plusieurs royaumes danois?'.
20 Gelting, 'Forfatteren og hans tid', p. 71.
21 *DD*, I:2, no. 32 and 34 (c. 1117); I:2, no. 64 (1135); I:2, no. 65 (1135). See also the discussion in Friisberg, *Hvem tilhører Danmark?*, pp. 91–92.

chroniclers or monastic scribes: Svend Aggesen was Christiern Svensen's grandson; Saxo wrote his history as a result of Skjalm Hvide's grandson Archbishop Absalon's commission; and the Bodilsen kindred, the Hvide family, and members of the Trugund clan had their *memoria* celebrated at privately founded *Hausklöster*.[22] Our view of actors and relations of force in the power field around 1130 is thus necessarily (dis-)coloured by the state of the field at a later time.[23] As for the 1120s, from the historian's perspective the vast majority of magnates may be said to have constituted a kind of 'dark matter' of the power field: like the dark matter hypothesized by astrophysics to account for the otherwise inexplicable gravitational effects of the observable objects in space, they are difficult to observe directly, but it is impossible to account for the visible movements within the field without recognizing their existence and practical impact.[24]

The Succession Issue

As we have already seen in Chapter 2, one recurrent instance where the exertion of magnates' political power became particularly evident was the process of royal succession. Succession always represented a highly critical moment in medieval politics. Who should succeed to the throne, who will enjoy the future benefits of *Königsnähe*, how will the shift in power influence the balance between groups and the relative value of established bonds and privileges? In this regard Scandinavia was certainly no different from the wider European scene. According to Thomas Bisson, '[p]ractically every princely house in Europe had its succession crisis in the century after 1060'. Many of them were attended by violent strife, and everywhere the accession of lord-princes depended on the good will of aristocratic supporters and on their ability to reward them. As aristocratic loyalties were guided first of all by 'familial and patrimonial interests', the inability of throne candidates to satisfy allies 'might give way to rebellion'.[25]

---

22 Hill, *Könige, Fürsten und Klöster*.
23 Names and memories about individual magnates sometimes also survived in stories preserved in later compilations, see for instance the case of King Knud II's conflict with Blood-Egil, earl of Bornholm, in *Knýtlinga saga*, pp. 153–67.
24 One possible way to overcome some of the limitations of the written sources and drag twelfth-century magnates out of the shadows may be explorations of the seemingly ever-richer archeological evidence; see, for examples, Poulsen and Sindbæk (eds), *Settlement and Lordship*; Hartvig and Poulsen, 'Contextualizing an Early Medieval Village'.
25 Bisson, *The Crisis*, pp. 186–91, quotations at p. 190 and p. 191. Bisson's compendium of dynastic succession crises covers the kingdoms and principalities of England, Flanders, Germany Tuscany, Poland, Léon-Galicia, Normandy, Maine, Anjou, Navarra, Carcassonne and Barcelona in the years between 1060 and 1140.

The Danish sources generally agree that the killing of Knud Lavard was motivated by fear amongst Magnus and his network that his powerful cousin might seek the kingship, when at some point King Niels died. Even though Magnus was the only living son of the ruling king, his succession to the throne was never a given. Just as in Norway, kingship in early twelfth-century Denmark had procedures for deciding who was to rule, but no formalized succession law. In principle, 'any member of the royal family could present himself as a candidate for the throne and it was a matter of no great concern if he descended from a king's son or daughter, or whether he had been born in wedlock or not. What mattered was his personal capabilities and the support of influential persons'.[26] As we'll see in Chapter 9, this kind of open succession order was not just a feature of Scandinavia, and it necessarily implied what has aptly been described as 'an extraordinary appeal to political activity',[27] not only among potential candidates from the royal stock, but equally importantly within the competing factions and networks around them.

Kings were formally elected and acclaimed by 'the people', that is magnates, householders, and armed retainers, at regional assemblies.[28] As a brief review of royal elections since the death of Niels' father King Svend II Estridsen (r. 1047–1076[29]) shows, even when successions were approved by consensus or at least without open strife, they took place in the shadow of intra-dynastic or regional opposition and so they functioned as occasions for measuring, testing, and adjusting hierarchies in the wider field of power.

Svend Estridsen left numerous sons, born both in and out of wedlock. Five of them succeeded him on the throne in turn.[30] In 1076 the choice was between Harald Hen and his younger brother Knud, who enjoyed particular support among the Scanians.[31] After a process allegedly involving threats, manipulations, and half-hearted suggestions of sharing power, Harald was able to muster more support at the deciding assembly in Jutland than Knud, who was temporarily exiled. Two years later a coalition

---

[26] Riis, 'The Significance of 25 June, 1170', p. 91.
[27] Breengaard, *Muren om Israels hus*, p. 203.
[28] Friisberg, *Hvem tilhører Danmark?*, p. 26. On the assembly places, see Chapter 5.
[29] For the dating of King Svend's death, see Sonne, 'Svend Estridsens politiske liv', p. 38.
[30] The earliest hagiographic text on Knud Lavard, written in the mid 1130s, claims that Svend Estridsen himself prescribed a seniority principle according to which his sons should succeed him in order of age (Robert of Ely, *De vita et miracvlis*, p. 235). Saxo also seems to refer to some kind of seniority system (Lind, 'Knes Kanutus', pp. 103–06). Sonne, 'Svend Estridsens politiske liv', pp. 33–36, considers this tradition untrustworthy. Rather than prescribing a succession order, King Svend's precautionary strategies to avoid succession strife included having a young son acclaimed co-ruler (but the boy died) and supporting other career paths for the many grown-up sons, either within the Church or as warlords in England. More on Svend Estridsen's progeny in Chapter 5.
[31] GD, 11.10.1–6; *Knýtlinga saga*, pp. 139–43; Ailnoth, *Gesta Swenomagni regis*, p. 90.

of Harald's brothers asked the Norwegian king for help to force Harald to share the kingdom with them. In Rome the pope warned against discord and advised Harald to curb dissatisfaction by offering his brothers lands and honours.[32] A contemporary skaldic verse preserved in the *Knýtlinga saga* explicitly relates how Svend Estridsen's sons were 'sorely unsettled' and that actual fighting took place.[33]

After Harald's death in 1080, Knud then gained the kingship with the consent of his brothers, possibly at the assembly in Viborg.[34] However, his controversial, centralizing reign, focused on Scania, became increasingly unpopular and ended in the summer of 1086, when rebels from Jutland killed him along with his brother Bent in a church in Odense. Another brother, Oluf, who had supposedly conspired with disadvantaged *primores* against Knud, was put on the throne by the Jutlanders.[35] Yet another brother, Erik the Good, spent time in exile in Russia and Sweden, until in 1095, when Oluf died, he returned home to receive kingship, 'elected by the whole army and acclaimed by the people'.[36] He was possibly welcomed by Asser of the Trugund family, since 1089 bishop of Lund and also a nephew of Erik's wife, Queen Bodil. Efforts by Odense ecclesiastics to promote the slain Knud as saintly martyr received willing support by Erik.[37]

When in 1103 Erik the Good passed away on Cyprus during a pilgrimage or crusade, he was succeeded by his brother Niels, who, in Saxo's somewhat belittling narrative, ascended to the throne in 1104 as a sort of fourth choice: Niels' elder brother Svend had sought election at the provincial assembly of Viborg in Jutland, but died from illness on the way to the meeting. A second candidate, Erik the Good's son Harald Kesja, who had acted as regent during his father's journey abroad, was rejected by the magnates, allegedly on account of his harsh and unjust government.[38] Ubbe, another older brother of Niels, was then acclaimed king at the assembly at Isøre, but afterwards renounced the honour, leaving the throne for Niels.[39] Besides a few scant references to regional divisions, the sources

---

32 *DD*, I:2, no. 18 (1078).
33 *Knýtlinga saga*, pp. 144–45, see also pp. 139–43.
34 *GD*, 11.11.1; *Knýtlinga saga*, p. 145.
35 *GD*, 11.13.4; 12.1.1.
36 Ailnoth, *Gesta Swenomagni regis*, p. 130: 'totius exercitus electione et populi acclamation'.
37 Esmark, 'Spinning the Revolt'; Esmark, 'Hellige ben i indviet ild'; Esmark, 'Miracle and Mandate'.
38 *GD*, 12.8.2. Another tradition, transmitted in the *Knýtlinga Saga*, pp. 239–40, has Harald Kesja 'generally liked' as deputy ruler, albeit mainly because of his father's popularity.
39 *GD*, 12.8.1–3.

reveal no details about the specific groups and factions which decided the series of royal elections.[40]

From his accession in 1104 until the crisis unleashed by the Haraldsted killing, King Niels seems to have ruled without open contention.[41] As time went by, however, it was only natural that influential people began speculating and strategizing about who would succeed. The ageing monarch's unusually long reign left an unusual amount of time for prospects and their networks to cultivate ambition and build alliances. Moreover, Svend Estridsen's many sons and daughters, born as a result of relationships with numerous young women from illustrious families,[42] had produced an unusual abundance of potential royal candidates — a genealogical coincidence which in itself tended to create tension as it expanded the space of possible strategies within the power field. Thus, in the mid-1120s at least five of Magnus' cousins could potentially lay claim to kingship: Knud Lavard, son of King Erik the Good; Knud's half-brothers Erik the Unforgettable and Harald Kesja, also sons of Erik the Good; Karl, son of St Knud; and Henrik Skadelar, son of Niels' brother Svend, who died on the way to being elected king in 1104. We shall return to this group of cousins shortly.

New Assets, Rising Stakes

The succession issue was further complicated by certain overall socio-structural transformations. The early twelfth-century power field saw the formation of new assets or accumulation points, which modified competitive options and strategies while raising the stakes and challenging existing balances.

One key development concerned ecclesiastical offices. A permanent diocesan structure in Denmark was not established until c. 1060 during the reign of King Svend Estridsen. At that time many, if not most, bishops and higher clerics were imported from abroad, but gradually they came to be

---

40 Nils Hybel's claim (*The Nature of Kingship*, pp. 352–53), that the realm ruled by King Svend Estridsen and his successors was merely 'variable areas controlled by a political party [...], under royal leadership', and that all up until 1157 'in reality the country was split up into various territories ruled by a complicated pattern of different power blocks', may seem overstated, but deservedly challenges much traditional historiography's no less overstated ideas of continuity and coherence within the early Danish regnal polity.

41 Hermanson, 'Danish Lords and Slavonic Rulers', p. 3, claims that 'King Niels was constantly threatened by royal usurpers, as there were no established succession-rules', but mentions no specific threats. After his death, however, some writers directly or indirectly disputed the legitimacy of Niels' accession, see Robert of Ely, *De vita et miracvlis*, p. 235, and Helmold von Bosau, *Chronica Slavorum/Slawenchronik*, p. 188.

42 *GD*, 11.7.1.

recruited from indigenous aristocratic families. At the same time grants of land and privileges made cathedral churches centres of not only religious prestige, but also territorially based wealth. For the first time, then, high ecclesiastical offices, distributed by the king, became really attractive gains for groups within the elite.

The eight dioceses in Denmark were suffragans of Hamburg-Bremen until 1103–1104, when King Erik the Good persuaded the papacy to establish a separate ecclesiastical province with authority over the churches of Denmark, Norway, and Sweden. The episcopal see of Lund was raised to metropolitan status and Bishop Asser of the Trugund family became its first archbishop. All up until the 1160s, however, the archbishops of Hamburg-Bremen continued to threaten the independence of the Nordic Church province, and even had it abolished between 1133 and 1137 (more on this later).[43] Even so, the establishment of an archbishopric in Lund introduced a new, hitherto unparalleled, position in the field of power next to the great earls and the king himself.[44]

Another important development was the early growth of urban communities. While this used to be regarded as a post-1150 phenomenon, more recent research suggests that the first half of the twelfth century already constituted 'an essential period for the formation of towns' in Denmark.[45] As will be discussed in more detail in Chapter 5, the number of towns was much higher in Denmark than in Norway, and they were also more numerous than the written sources depict. The growth and transformation of trade (from luxury products to wider assortments of goods) relied on personal networks of merchants and town potentates. These potentates were primarily kings and princes, but also local/regional magnates, who profited from the commercial activities in return for providing protection and peace.[46] The most important towns saw a gradual formation of semi-formalized communities of merchants and builders, which were capable in the struggles after 1131 of acting, negotiating, and even organizing militarily.[47]

---

43 Breengaard, *Muren om Israels hus*, pp. 211–23, 237–39, 276–86; Gelting, 'Da Eskil ville være ærkebiskop', pp. 184–97, 214–23.
44 Compare the establishment of an independent Norwegian archbishopric in the 1150s described in the foregoing chapter.
45 Kristensen and Poulsen, *Danmarks byer i middelalderen*, p. 67. This period saw the first appearance of towns as motif on coins, and recent studies point to a general increase in the use of coinage at the end of King Niels' reign, most markedly in the provinces of Jutland and Zealand (Poulsen, *Mønt og magt*, pp. 193, 203).
46 Kristensen and Poulsen, *Danmarks byer i middelalderen*, p. 94. At the time of Peder Bodilsen, for instance, Næstved was already a regular town with church, assembly square and mill (p. 69).
47 Kristensen and Poulsen, *Danmarks byer i middelalderen*, p. 145.

Like high ecclesiastical offices, control of or association with towns became a new distinguishing resource to be pursued in the game of power. In fact, as accumulation points the two tended to overlap as the most important urban communities evolved in cathedral towns. Thus, before 1150 Lund was the largest town in the realm, followed by the episcopal centres of Roskilde, Viborg, Ribe, and Schleswig.[48]

King Niels and Queen Margrethe: Networks and Socio-Political Strategies

In Danish historiography, King Niels has sometimes been regarded a 'weak' king. Yet, if twelfth-century kingship essentially rested on social power, that is, the ability to maintain the loyalties of family members and other magnates and to even out imbalances between competing factions,[49] then Niels must be considered a 'strong' ruler, at least until the late 1120s, when things eventually got out of hand. The case of Ubbe may exemplify the strategies by which Niels forged bonds with key people. Ubbe, possibly a distant member of the royal kin,[50] married Ingrid, Niels' daughter by a concubine,[51] and was assigned the earldom of 'the small islands', e.g. modern Lolland-Falster. Today this region is considered a socio-economically deprived 'peripheral area', but in the twelfth century it occupied a geo-strategically key position at the nexus of trade routes and military frontlines between Denmark, Wendish territories, and the Baltic Sea. As son-in-law and regional commander, Ubbe would show himself to be an ever-faithful ally of Niels during the war against Erik the Unforgettable. As shown in much more detail by Lars Hermanson, it was this kind of personal alliance rather than any system of formal delegation of offices that constituted royal power at this time.[52]

During the course of his long reign, Niels furthermore had the opportunity to install a number of bishops, which ensured for him the long-term support within the Church hierarchy and within the aristocratic families who were entrusted with the ecclesiastical offices. Thus, around the years 1120–1125, Niels appointed men from his own circle as bishops of Odense, Viborg, Ribe, and Roskilde.[53] He particularly favoured the

---

48 Kristensen and Poulsen, *Danmarks byer i middelalderen*, p. 73. Urban development was also stimulated by monastic foundations and by the building by magnates of private churches which later became parish churches (pp. 63, 89; Poulsen, 'Mønt og magt', p. 184).
49 Gelting, 'Forfatteren og hans tid', pp. 77–78.
50 Hermanson, *Släkt, vänner och makt*, p. 141.
51 *GD*, 13.1.4.
52 Hermanson, *Släkt, vänner och makt*, pp. 51–91, 141–47.
53 Nyberg, 'Kong Niels', pp. 367–69. Before that Niels may even have appointed Bishop Ketil of Vendsyssel and Ulkil of Aarhus, but that remains speculative.

church of Odense, home of the saintly cult of King Knud,[54] possibly to counter the weight of the archbishopric of Lund, where Asser owed his position to Niels' predecessor King Erik the Good.[55] The bishopric of Roskilde, granted to one Peder, chaplain of Niels' son Magnus, provided the king with a much needed foothold in the province of Zealand, where his position otherwise seem to have been weak.

Around the time of his accession in 1104, King Niels married Margrethe Fredkulla ('Peace-maiden'), daughter of King Inge Stenkilsson of Sweden, and a young widow after the death of King Magnus Barefoot of Norway in 1103. Queen Margrethe, whose formidable position in the power field is analysed in greater depth in Chapter 6, showed herself to be a most able politician and effectually became Niels' co-regent. A key asset of Margrethe's was her substantial inheritance. Around 1125 the last male member of the Swedish royal Stenkil family died, leaving the throne vacant and Margrethe in control of the family's landed estates in Sweden.[56] Margrethe's sisters Kristina and Katarina and her niece Ingrid were also among the heirs. These women all married princes and potentates in Denmark and neighbouring realms. According to Saxo, Margrethe was the architect behind this marriage strategy, which aimed to consolidate the kinship ties between Magnus and his cousins and to divide the Stenkil inheritance in order to keep the peace.[57] Kristina married Prince Mstislav of Novgorod, an important political centre and trading junction to the east of Scandinavia. Kristina died in 1122, but before that her daughters Malmfrid and Ingeborg had married, respectively, Sigurd the Crusader (co-king and from 1123 sole ruler of Norway) and Duke Knud Lavard. Katarina was wedded to Bjorn Ironside, son of Harald Kesja, while Margrethe's niece Ingrid became the wife of Henrik Skadelar.

Niels and Margrethe had two sons, Magnus and Inge, both born around 1105 or shortly thereafter. Their names betray a multistranded dynastic investment. Inge was the first-born, baptized when Margrethe's father King Inge Stenkilsson still ruled Sweden, the name therefore possibly pointing to aspirations towards Swedish kingship. Magnus — a Norwegian kings' name — was also known by the name Svend,[58] a traditional Danish royal name and specifically the name of King Svend Estridsen, grandfather

---

54 *DD*, I:2, no. 32; I:2, no. 34; I:2, no. 35; Ailnoth, pp. 81–82.
55 Nyberg, 'Kong Niels', pp. 363–64.
56 Margrethe's father King Inge died c. 1110, his nephews and co-ruling successors Philip and Inge c. 1118 and 1125. The possessions were located in Dalshus-Bohuslän, Western Götaland and Mälardalen (Hermanson, *Släkt, vänner och makt*, p. 112, n. 192; Skyum-Nielsen, *Kvinde og slave*, p. 65).
57 *GD*, 13.1.4, and Chapter 6 in this volume.
58 According to Ailnoth and *Necrologium Lundense*, see Olrik, *Knud Lavards Liv*, p. 59, and Steenstrup, 'Dobbelte navne'.

of all the royal cousins. Inge, however, died early,[59] and from then on Magnus' succession to Danish royal power seems to have been Niels' and Margrethe's main political goal.[60] During the 1120s they worked to construct a powerbase for their son, which would make his claim to the throne possible. In the *Knýtlinga saga* he was remembered as 'the biggest man in the whole of Denmark', always surrounded by 'a large following'.[61] Yet he was also younger than his cousins and therefore possibly some steps behind in the race.

Cousins and Competitors

It is difficult to assess the strategies and relative political strength of the royal cousins in the years leading up to Haraldsted. Not only are they very unequally represented in the sources, but the complex ways they were connected through ties of blood and marriage and the fact that their networks extended beyond the borders of the realm left plenty of room for manoeuvre (Fig. 3.2).[62]

Born 1084, Karl, son of King St Knud, was much older than Magnus. After his father's violent death in 1086, Karl's mother Adela, daughter of Count Robert I of Flanders, escaped with her infant son to her home country, where Karl grew up to attain the honour of count with ties to leading European princely dynasties.[63] In Flemish charters he proudly designated himself 'Karl, son of St Knud, King of the Danes'. Whether that ever indicated some sort of aspiration to Danish kingship or not, Karl hardly enjoyed much support among the Danish elite. Many, especially in Jutland, still claimed the rebellion against his father was justified and looked with scepticism at Knud's sanctification.[64] As it was, Karl ended up being killed before the altar himself during the famous internal disputes in Bruges in 1127. According to the annals of Lund, the assassination happened 'on the advice of Magnus, son of King Niels' (*per consilium Magni, filii Nicolai regis*).[65] This is hard to believe, and the major account of

---

59 GD, 13.1.3. Witnessed by Queen Margrethe, Magnus, and various magnates, King Niels made a pious donation to the church in Odense for the benefit of Inge's soul (*DD*, I:2, no. 34).
60 Nyberg, 'Kong Niels', p. 386.
61 *Knýtlinga saga*, pp. 248–49.
62 Hermanson, 'Danish Lords and Slavonic Rulers', p. 9: 'In this respect "socio-political borders" associated with individuals and groups were of greater importance than national frontiers'.
63 Hermanson, *Släkt, vänner och makt*, p. 140.
64 Esmark, 'Spinning the Revolt', p. 24.
65 *DMA*, p. 56. Annalistic recording began in Lund around 1130. The adapted and extended version of the *Annales lundenses* known today was compiled *c.* 1265 on the basis of various

MESSY CONFLICT 111

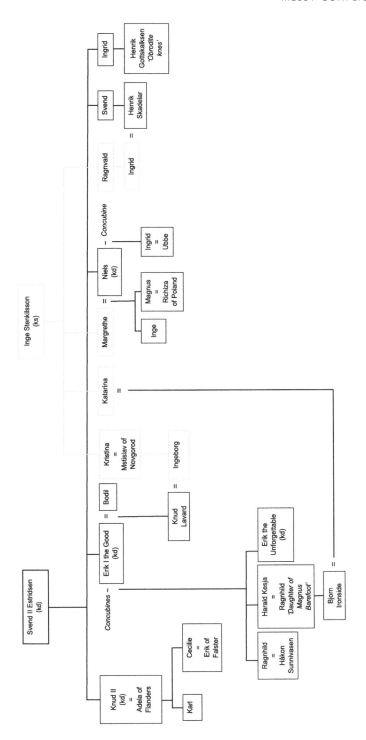

Figure 3.2. Key political actors discussed in the text. Figure by author.

Karl's death from Flanders makes no mention of it.[66] Still, the claim may well reflect rumours, suspicions, and conspiracy theories prevalent within the Danish elite around the time.

Far more threatening to the succession plans of Niels' and Margrethe's network was Knud Lavard, son of Erik the Good and Queen Bodil. Born c. 1096, he was about 10 years older than Magnus. From his father Knud inherited friendship ties with important Danish magnates. As a small boy, he was placed in the custody of Skjalm Hvide, earl of Zealand, and as the events after Knud's murder would show, Skjalm's sons, Knud's foster brothers, seem to have expected much from their family's bond to a main branch of the royal family.[67] Other pre-eminent nobles associated with Knud Lavard included Erik of Falster, a Zealand-based potentate, who was married to Cecilia, sister of Karl of Flanders, and who at some point won the title of prefect of the Swedish Götar;[68] and Hakon Sunnivasen, son of a Jutland magnate and a mother of Norwegian high aristocratic descent, who was rewarded for having avenged the killing of one of Erik the Good's brothers with the hand of Erik's daughter Ragnhild (making Hakon and Knud Lavard brothers-in-law).[69]

After his early years with the Skjalm family, Knud Lavard spent some years at the court of Lothar of Supplinburg, duke of Saxony — a friendship tie that came to be of great importance, when Lothar was later elected German king in 1125 and crowned emperor in 1133.[70] Around 1115, Knud acquired the earldom or duchy of Schleswig. According to Helmold, this was by King Niels' royal appointment, whereas Saxo claimed that he had simply bought the position from his uncle.[71] The cathedral town turned out to be a golden egg. Despite its modest size, Schleswig was already Denmark's most important trading centre, populated by Frisians, but also by people from Saxony, Iceland, Bornholm, and other places.[72] Located on the northern bank of the Schlei river, it functioned as the main transit harbour for Scandinavian ships transporting goods between Rus, the Baltic, the North Sea, and Western Europe, and the town also connected

---

older versions as well as other sources (*DMA*, pp. xi–xiii; Kristensen, *Danmarks ældste annalistik*, pp. 109, 118).

66 Galbert of Bruges, *De multro, traditione et occisione gloriosi Karoli*.
67 On the socio-political institution of fosterage in Scandinavia, see Chapter 2.
68 Hermanson, *Släkt, vänner och makt*, pp. 138–40.
69 *GD*, 12.3.6; *Knýtlinga saga*, pp. 230–31; Hermanson, *Släkt, vänner och makt*, p. 168.
70 According to Helmold von Bosau, *Chronica Slavorum/Slawenchronik*, p. 188, Knud was sent to Lothar's court out of fear that King Niels might plot against his life, because he, Knud, had been designated as Niels' successor by Erik the Good in 1102. The story seems unfounded.
71 Helmold von Bosau, *Chronica Slavorum/Slawenchronik*, p. 188; *GD*, 13.3.2. For the dating of Knud's acquisition of the title, see the thorough discussion in Lind, 'Knes Kanutus', pp. 111–14. *Knýtlinga saga*, pp. 232–33, claims Knud was granted the earldom already as a boy by his father Erik the Good.
72 Blomkvist, *The Discovery of the Baltic*, p. 130.

to land-based routes.[73] Knud became *senior* and *defensor* of the town's communal organization, the *hezlagh*.[74] He built two watchtowers and a *castellum*, which served as a toll station and prison, and from visits in Saxony he learnt how to bar the harbour entrance and tax visiting merchants as well as collecting legal fines and tribute on land. As lord of the town Knud furthermore won a reputation for brutally fighting local robbers and Wendish pirates who were attracted by Schleswig's commercial activities.[75] The considerable financial income raised from the engagement in trade made it possible for Knud to entertain a large retinue of armed men, for whom he was the *hlaford* or *lavard*, the 'provider of bread'.[76]

In 1117 Knud married Ingeborg, daughter of Prince Mstislav of Novgorod and Queen Margrethe's sister Kristina. The marriage linked Knud's branch of the royal family to that of Niels, but more importantly it also strengthened the profitable trade routes to Novgorod, where the wedding was celebrated.[77] Along with Ingeborg came a substantial share in her Swedish Stenkil inheritance, offering Knud a certain foothold in Sweden as well.[78] As mentioned above, Saxo credits Queen Margrethe for having orchestrated the marriage, but memories preserved in the *Knýtlinga saga* suggest it might have come out of Knud's own initiative, motivated by trade-political concerns, mediated by a travelling merchant, and relying on connections established during his father King Erik the Good's stay in Rus in the late 1080s.[79] If so, Margrethe most likely approved of the marriage as well.

If Knud Lavard was thus already in the mid-1120s ranked among the most important princes in the realm, he became an acute source of fear in 1127–1128 when he attained the title of *knes* — king or prince — of the Obodrites, a Wendish confederacy in modern Mecklenburg and Holstein. Henrik Gottskalksen, son of King Niels' and Erik the Good's sister Ingrid and thus a cousin of Knud's, who had ruled the Obodrites since the 1090s, died and so did his two sons. The *knes* of Obodritia was a vassal of King Lothar, at whose court Knud had spent his youth. Knud approached the German ruler who 'for a lot of money' (*multa pecunia*) agreed to confer

---

[73] Kristensen and Poulsen, *Danmarks byer i middelalderen*, pp. 61, 92; Lind, 'Knes Kanutus', p. 122; *DD*, I:2, no. 45.

[74] Kristensen and Poulsen, *Danmarks byer i middelalderen*, pp. 99, 102.

[75] *Knýtlinga saga*, pp. 242–44; Robert of Ely, *De vita et miracvlis*, pp. 236–37; *Historia S. Kanvti*, pp. 191–92; *DRHH*, III, p. 711, n. 2.

[76] Skyum-Nielsen, *Kvinde og slave*, p. 69.

[77] Lind, 'De russiske ægteskaber', pp. 234–36.

[78] According to *GD*, 13.1.4, the inheritance was divided between Margrethe herself or Magnus (1/3), Ingeborg (1/3), and Ingrid Ragvaldsdatter (1/3), who married Magnus' cousin Henrik Skadelar.

[79] *Knýtlinga saga*, pp. 212–13, 244–48; Lind, 'Knes Kanutus', p. 123; Hermanson, *Släkt, vänner och makt*, pp. 119–20.

upon him all power of the Obodrite realm and receive him *in hominem*, e.g. as his vassal.[80]

Having achieved the knesdom of the Obodrites, Knud Lavard proceeded to recruit new troops in the area and to attack and subject the neighbouring Wagrians, bolstering his extended powerbase by building castles and by cultivating friendly relations with the local Church.[81] Further cementing his frontier-zone network he also established bonds of friendship with Duke Vartislav I of Pomerania, a vassal of Lothar's like Knud himself.

From around 1127–1128, Knud Lavard thereby stood out as 'a Baltic-Sea prince of a very high dignity'.[82] Having gradually established himself as a semi-independent regional power broker in the border zone between Denmark, the Wendish territories, and the Baltic Sea, he possessed considerable economic and military resources, and a protective multi-edged alliance network comprising Danish magnates, Slavic potentates, the princely house of Novgorod, and the German king. At King Niels' royal court and among magnates associated with Magnus, this disproportionate amassing of wealth and influence evidently caused envy and worry. In the laconic words of the *Knýtlinga saga*, they thought Knud 'had too many friends' (*hans vinir holzti margir*).[83]

Three more figures weighed heavily in the game of power. Born c. 1080, Harald Kesja — the son of a concubine of Erik the Good — was almost Niels' peer in age. As mentioned above, he was appointed deputy ruler of the kingdom by his father around 1102,[84] but subsequently denied royal election by the magnates. Harald's powerbase lay in the province of Zealand. In the swampy area just north of Roskilde he had erected a wooden *castrum*, Haraldsborg, from where he and his large retinue of men, according to Saxo, plundered and tormented both town and countryside.[85] Yet, Harald was also remembered for having increased the power of the church of Roskilde and for having been a close friend of King Niels, at whose court he stayed for long periods.[86] Harald's wife was Ragnhild, daughter of King Magnus Barefoot of Norway (d. 1103). He had numerous sons, many of whom were already full-grown men in the 1120s, among them Bjorn Ironside, who was also linked to King Niels' network through his marriage, mentioned above, with Katarina, sister of Queen Margrethe.

---

80 Helmold, *Chronica Slavorum/Slawenchronik*, p. 188. For a critical discussion of Saxo's alternative version of Knud's acquisition of Obodritia (*GD*, 13.3.2–8), which downplays the role of the German king, see Lind, 'Knes Kanutus', pp. 115–17.
81 Helmold, *Chronica Slavorum/Slawenchronik*, p. 190.
82 Hermanson, 'Danish Lords and Slavonic Rulers', p. 6.
83 *Knýtlinga saga*, p. 248.
84 *Knýtlinga saga*, pp. 232, 239; *GD*, 12.6.5; *Historia S. Kanvti*, p. 189.
85 *GD*, 13.4.1.
86 *Knýtlinga saga*, p. 241.

Like Harald Kesja, Erik the Unforgettable was a half-brother of Knud Lavard; his mother had been a concubine and he had supposedly been raised in a foster family of less impressive status.[87] During Erik the Good's pilgrimage, Erik accompanied his father 'along with other men of rank'.[88] In the 1120s he fell out with Harald Kesja in yet another intra-familial inheritance dispute. After plundering and arson in Zealand, the two half-brothers were reconciled, in Saxo's narrative thanks to the mediation of Knud Lavard.[89] The *Knýtlinga saga* claims that, contrary to Harald Kesja, Erik the Unforgettable was 'not so well-liked' (*ekki jafnkærr*) by King Niels.[90] Other sources suggest he was close to Knud Lavard, whom he might have followed on military expeditions and who entrusted him with some kind of regional command or estate management on 'the minor islands' (Lolland-Falster), possibly making him a rival there of the above-mentioned Ubbe, King Niels' son-in-law.[91]

Henrik Skadelar, finally, a son of King Niels' brother Svend, whose untimely death through sickness prevented him from gaining kingship in 1104, was a similar age to Knud Lavard.[92] Thanks to Henrik's marriage with Queen Margrethe's niece Ingrid, he possessed considerable lands in Sweden, and was closely connected to Niels', Margrethe's and Magnus' network. Historians have speculated whether Henrik perhaps hoped to win the title of earl or even king of Sweden, if Magnus managed to become Danish king after Niels.[93] With regard to such ambitions, Henrik may have felt threatened by Knud Lavard, who besides his southern border empire also had a foot in Sweden on account of his marriage with Ingeborg, Queen Margrethe's niece. Evidence from the time of his descendants suggests Henrik's main resources lay in Jutland.[94]

How did Magnus compare, first of all, with his imposing cousin Knud Lavard? From his mother, Magnus would inherit the main part of the Stenkil estates in Sweden. It has been suggested that a failed Danish-Norwegian expedition (known as the 'Kalmar-leding') against heathens in the lordless border region of Småland in 1123 was perhaps intended to establish a position for Magnus in Sweden.[95] The Swedish kingdom at this time was a loose confederation of regions: Western Götaland, Eastern Götaland, and Svealand. Royal power was weak, lacking the support of

---

87 *GD*, 12.6.5.
88 *Knýtlinga saga*, p. 233.
89 *GD*, 13.4.2.
90 *Knýtlinga saga*, p. 241.
91 Robert of Ely, *De vita et miracvlis*, p. 237; *GD*, 13.7.4; Hermanson, *Släkt, vänner och makt*, p. 144.
92 Hermanson, *Släkt, vänner och makt*, p. 114.
93 Hermanson, *Släkt, vänner och makt*, p. 113.
94 Hermanson, *Släkt, vänner och makt*, p. 170.
95 Harrison, *Sveriges historia*, pp. 190–91; Skyum-Nielsen, *Kvinde og slave*, p. 65.

an ecclesiastical organization, and the socio-political elites were divided in their loyalties between the Danish and Swedish kings. Economically Western Götaland in particular was more closely connected to the Danish province of Scania than to the eastern parts of Sweden.[96]

As mentioned before, the Swedish throne was left vacant in 1125, and in 1128–1129 Magnus had himself acclaimed king of the Götar. His claim to Swedish rule was no doubt legitimized by his maternal descent.[97] The election of Magnus probably felt natural in Western Götaland, an area already familiar with Danish overlordship. The formal right to elect the Swedish king, however, lay with the *thing*-men of the north-eastern province of Svealand. They refused the Danish prince, opting in his place for a local magnate of unknown lineage, who also won recognition in Eastern Götaland, but he was killed when he entered the western part of the kingdom. The regional segmentation of Sweden stands out clearly here. In the absence of a regular king in Eastern Götaland and Svealand, the local lawmen and chieftains decided to rule themselves. Magnus' move for the Swedish throne was probably meant to equal Knud's title of Obodrite *knes*, but his authority probably did not extend beyond Western Götaland, and the lordship of a thinly populated, economically weakly-integrated Swedish province was never comparable to his cousin's Baltic Sea empire.[98] To balance Knud Lavard it was necessary to direct attention towards the south.

Perhaps as a direct response to Knud Lavard's acquisition of the Obodrite lordship, Magnus thus in 1128 married Richiza, twelve year old daughter of Duke Boleslaw III of Poland — an alliance that may have been based on connections established many years before between King Niels and the Polish duke.[99] Duke Boleslaw had long been an enemy of the princes of Novgorod, Knud Lavard's in-laws,[100] and to the west he had for decades worked to subject Pomerania, ruled by Knud's *amicus* Duke Vartislav, with the aim of gaining control of the trade around the mouth of the Oder river.[101] Magnus' marriage to Richiza therefore created a forceful alliance directed against Knud's border empire west of Pomerania. Two 'parallel Danish-Slavic alliances' or 'competing systems of alliances' confronted each other.[102] Immediately after the betrothal — the wedding process still not completed — the Danish and Polish allies launched an

---

96 Line, *Kingship and State Formation*, pp. 63–64.
97 GD, 13.5.1.
98 Line, *Kingship and State Formation*, pp. 80–82; Skyum-Nielsen, *Kvinde og slave*, p. 65.
99 GD, 13.5.2. For the dating of the marriage to 1128 according to Polish sources, see Lind, 'Knes Kanutus', pp. 117–18; Nyberg, 'Kong Niels', p. 376, suggests 1127, while Line, *Kingship and State Formation*, p. 80, has 1129.
100 Lind, 'De russiske ægteskaber', pp. 244–45.
101 Hermanson, 'Danish Lords and Slavonic Rulers', p. 6.
102 Lind, 'Knes Kanutus', p. 117; Hermanson, 'Danish Lords and Slavonic Rulers', p. 6.

attack against Duke Vartislav and lured him into imprisonment. If we are to believe Saxo, the Pomeranian lord was only released thanks to the mediation of Knud Lavard.[103]

Escalating Tensions, Open Crisis

From here on tensions only increased.[104] The sources present different versions of the events leading up to the killing at Haraldsted and the exact chronology is impossible to clarify. The main process, however, is clear: the contest between Magnus and Knud Lavard for honour and support intensified. According to the *Knýtlinga saga*, it was basically a competition for popularity, for securing the friendship of the leading men of the realm. If Knud succeeded in becoming 'so well-liked that all the best men in Denmark became friends with him as much as with King Nikolas [Niels] and his son Magnus', the ruler and his heir presumptive would no longer be able to trust their own network.[105]

The competition unfolded in various arenas. Turning to traditional strategies for demonstrating leadership and accumulating reputation, booty, and followers, both Magnus and Knud Lavard tried to surpass each other as successful warlords during plundering expeditions in Swedish territory.[106] At the same time, rivalries also played out in symbolic forms at assemblies and ceremonies, that is the public sphere of the power field. Here Knud Lavard is said to have presented himself with an air and attitude of great self-esteem. In the circles around Magnus, this was interpreted as if Knud reckoned himself the equal and natural successor of King Niels. Saxo, for instance, relates that at the occasion of Magnus' and Richiza's wedding in 1128 — celebrated in Ribe, where the harbour provided the town with precious goods from abroad and therefore formed a fitting location for the feast — Knud Lavard was among the guests and provoked envy and anger by pretentiously showing off in extravagant Saxon clothing. According to the somewhat anecdotal narrative, Henrik Skadelar, now clearly siding with Magnus, directly threatened Knud, who responded by mocking Henrik's boorish appearance (*rusticitas*).[107]

Helmold likewise tells of a confrontation between King Niels and Knud Lavard at a public assembly (*colloquium*) in Schleswig. Here, on his

---

103 Lind, 'Knes Kanutus', pp. 118–19.
104 Hermanson, *Släkt, vänner och makt*, pp. 94–99.
105 'svá vinsæll … at allir inir beztu menn í Danmǫrk váru hans vinir eigi minni en Níkuláss konungs eða Magnúss, sonar hans'. *Knýtlinga saga*, p. 250, see also pp. 241–42, 248–49.
106 GD, 13.5.5.
107 GD, 13.5.4. Jezierski, 'Convivium', p. 151, suggests Knud's Saxon outfit was a conscious public statement about his status and network in Northern Germany.

home ground, Knud, 'king of the Obodrites' (*rex Obotritorum*) allegedly posed as if he was a monarch of equal rank with the Danish ruler, sitting on a throne with a crown on his head, surrounded by his entourage, and breaking the etiquette by not standing up to greet his uncle, but opting to exchange kisses with him in the space between their seats as if they were perfect equals in dignity. This was a 'spectacle' (*spectaculum*) which humiliated Niels and aroused 'unbelievable anger' (*incredibile dictu est, quanto ira*) at his own court.[108]

Again according to Saxo, King Niels is said to have summoned Knud Lavard before another assembly, which, according to one of Saxo's sources, Knud's saintly legend, took place in Ribe (possibly in 1129). In front of the attending magnates, Niels accused Knud of having usurped the title of king and of disregarding the norms of succession. Yet, Knud supposedly received his uncle uncloaked and held the dismounting king's stirrup in a submissive gesture which recalled the German *Stratordienst* (a rhetorical attempt by Saxo, perhaps, to counter Helmold's image of an all-too-proud Knud) and vehemently denied all accusations.[109] Helmold furthermore relates how King Niels called on 'all the princes of the realm' (*universos principes regni*) — possibly at this same assembly in Ribe — to reconcile the conflicting youth and turn dissent into peace, which they did, at least for some time.[110] Helmold's reference to some sort of mediation process involving wide circles of the Danish elite attests to the seriousness of the crisis and once again hints at the 'dark matter' of the power field.

As some historians have argued, it is by no means certain that Knud Lavard was actually aiming for the throne. His position as lord of Schleswig and *knes* of the Obodrites had already made him a strong, independent regional prince. Rather than the Danish kingship, this might very well have been his political project.[111] Even so, King Niels and his allies might have feared the competition of Knud's emerging polity, which 'would have appeared as an instant great power on the Baltic, as well as an embryonic "European" state of the West Slavic nation'.[112] However, setting aside Knud's own intentions, his network of friends, especially in Zealand, probably hoped to launch him as their candidate for the throne. Despite formal peace agreements, Magnus and his circles certainly continued to worry about the schemes of the duke and the many nobles who congregated around him, and started a conspiracy. United by oath, Magnus, his

---

108 Helmold von Bosau, *Chronica Slavorum/Slawenchronik*, p. 190. Analysis in Jezierski, 'Convivium', pp. 150–52.
109 GD, 13.5.8–14; *Historia S. Kanvti*, pp. 193–94; *DRHH*, I, p. 308, n. 48. On Stratordienst, see Althoff, *Die Macht der Rituale*, p. 141, and *Family, Friends and Followers*, p. 137.
110 Helmold von Bosau, *Chronica Slavorum/Slawenchronik*, p. 192.
111 Lind, 'Knes Kanutus', p. 103.
112 Blomkvist, *The Discovery of the Baltic*, p. 138.

cousin Henrik Skadelar, King Niels' son-in-law Ubbe, and Hakon, Ubbe's son, laid plans to eliminate Knud. Hakon Sunnivasen was amongst the conspirators too; as noted before, he had links to both camps, but now chose to go with Magnus.[113] To what extent King Niels was involved or knew about the conspiracy remains unclear.

A decisive switch seemingly occurred when around 1129–1130 Queen Margrethe suddenly died. As mentioned earlier, she was credited by Saxo as having worked to maintain the bonds of peace between the various branches of the royal family: all the way back from the moment when Knud Lavard, as a boy, had become his junior cousin Magnus' baptismal sponsor, up to the present crisis, she had acted the unifying figure.[114] The moment she disappeared, animosities were let loose.[115] In direct contrast to Saxo, however, Helmold claims Queen Margrethe was actively inciting her son Magnus to kill his cousin.[116] Maybe both stories carry a ring of truth, reflecting two phases: the first years of trying to bridge competing interests and secure peace, and then, when Knud Lavard grew just too powerful (the turning point being his accession to the Obodrite knesdom), the queen changed her mind?[117]

The crisis provoked by Queen Margrethe's death was mirrored and possibly accentuated by the concomitant upheavals at the royal court of Norway described in the previous chapter. The progressively more mentally unbalanced King Sigurd the Crusader repudiated his wife, Queen Malmfrid, niece of Queen Margrethe and sister of Knud Lavard's wife Ingeborg, and when he died in March 1130, a succession crisis began, as we saw in Chapter 2, between his son Magnus the Blind and his nephew Harald Gille.

As for the actual assassination at Haraldsted, the vividly dramatized accounts differ in their details, but the main points are clear.[118] Gathered

---

113 *GD*, 13.5.6–7; 13.6.1. The sworn pact might have been intended to strengthen Magnus' network rather than actually aiming at Knud Lavard's life from the start, cf. *DRHH*, I, pp. 310–11, n. 52. In that case the pact may be likened to the German *coniuratio* or Norwegian *flokkr* discussed in Chapters 2 and 8.
114 For Knud as Magnus' baptismal sponsor, see Robert of Ely, p. 237.
115 Hermanson, *Släkt, vänner och makt*, p. 96; Olrik, *Knud Lavards liv*, pp. 61–62; *GD*, 13.5.7. More on Queen Margrethe's mediating efforts in Chapter 6.
116 Helmold von Bosau, *Chronica Slavorum/Slawenchronik*, pp. 190–92.
117 According to an entry in the Næstved annals (*DMA*, p. 83), Margrethe had already died in 1117, which would undermine the narratives of both Saxo and Helmold as well as — consequently — the interpretative framework adopted here on the basis of Hermanson, *Släkt, vänner och makt* (see Nors, 'Review'). Recent research, however, convincingly dismisses the Næstved entry and strongly suggests Margrethe lived until the end of the 1120s (Haastrup and Lind, 'Dronning Margrete Fredkulla').
118 Robert of Ely, *De vita et miracvli*, p. 239; *Historia S. Kanvti*, pp. 197–200; Helmold von Bosau, *Chronica Slavorum/Slawenchronik*, p. 192; *GD*, 13.6.1–9; *Knýtlinga saga*, pp. 252–55. Useful discussion in Friisberg, *Hvem tilhører Danmark?*, pp. 135–36.

at a Christmas feast in Roskilde or Ringsted, attended by many nobles and possibly King Niels himself, Magnus assured Knud of his friendship and the two exchanged gifts. After the party Knud lodged at the manor of his friend Erik of Falster near Haraldsted. From here he was lured into the woods and killed by Magnus, Henrik Skadelar and their band of accompanying warriors. One of Knud's hagiographers has Magnus roaring in Knud's face the second before his men split the duke's head: 'Knud, whose is Denmark?' (*Kanute, cuius est Dacia?*).[119] Another tradition, preserved in the *Knýtlinga saga*, relates that Knud's own followers were dead drunk (*dauðdrukknir*) and unable to fight back.[120] Magnus afterwards went to Roskilde, while friends of Knud found his body and brought it to Erik of Falster's manor nearby.

Mobilizing for Conflict: Networks and Officializing Strategies

The killing of Knud Lavard had eliminated the single most powerful rival to Magnus' succession to the kingship. But the assassination at Haraldsted not only hit Knud himself. It also struck a blow to the various groups and individuals who shared bonds with him, who had invested loyalty in the patronage and possible future political prospects of the Schleswig lord. We should not think of this network as constituting a unified party or alliance. Besides their diverse ties to Knud, his kinsmen and in-laws, his foster family in Zealand, his friends and associates among the Danish magnates, his German vassal lord, the Obodrites, and the townsmen of Schleswig did not necessarily share interests, and may have looked at the assassination and the potential re-configuration of the power field from very different angles. Magnus and his party perhaps expected the network to disintegrate once the unifying figure was taken out. That scheme crashed, however, when shortly after the murder a coalition of Knud Lavard's friends and relatives in Zealand under the leadership of Erik the Unforgettable united in a call for revenge.

According to *Knýtlinga saga*, Erik the Unforgettable was abroad somewhere when reports of Haraldsted started circulating, but the moment he became aware of the events, he took swift action. 'When the news reached him he gathered all the willing support he could get. He then travelled to Denmark, where upon his landing he summoned an army'.[121] Erik's call

---

119 *Historia S. Kanvti*, p. 199.
120 *Knýtlinga saga*, p. 255.
121 'En er hann frétti þessi tíðendi, þá safnar hann liði at sér ǫllu því, er hann fekk ok honum vildi fylgja. Hann fór síðan til Danmerkr, ok er hann kom í land, þá krafði hann sér liðs'. *Knýtlinga saga*, pp. 256–57 (translation modified).

apparently met with a widespread response. In the telling words of the saga, he was able to reap the benefit of his brother Knud and their father Erik the Good's *vinsælda*, literally their 'having many friends'. Many of those who had been friends (*vinir*) of Knud and Erik the Good reckoned that on the back of Haraldsted, Erik the Unforgettable 'had a big score to settle' (*mikils eiga at hefna*) with the king and his son. Having thus gathered a sufficiently strong force by activating old networks, Erik set out to attack King Niels' men at various places in Denmark, and significantly damaged Niels' power.[122] The image of the revolt (*seditio*) as a justified act of vengeance is shared by the chronicler Svend Aggesen, who relates how Erik, 'incited by God's finger, was aroused to the fights of war against his uncle King Niels, for the revenge of his brother'.[123] Helmold likewise reports how Erik the Unforgettable hurried across the realm and 'gathered a multitude of Danes who looked with disgust at the nefarious murder of Knud'.[124]

Presumably though, there was more to the process of mobilizing allies and forming a coalition strong enough to challenge Magnus and his father than this. The most detailed account of the immediate aftermath of the murder, that of Saxo's, points to a more complicated process, centring in the initial phase not on military exploits, but on symbolic power, specifically the winning over the hearts and minds of the wider population of *thing*-men and their leaders.[125] Like any other political event or action, the murder at Haraldsted was also the object of interpretative struggles, or what Bourdieu calls *officializing strategies*.[126] In the words of Stephen D. White, every war in this kind of society presupposes an idea of vengeance and threat, and as there is no vengeance without some kind of wrongdoing which demands retribution, every war presupposes a story that qualifies and justifies the war as an act of revenge. The confection and officialization of a story of the war which conforms to one of the kinds of war that could be recognized by aristocratic political practices therefore constitutes an integral element of the conflict.[127] Whoever wanted to avenge Knud Lavard's

---

122 *Knýtlinga saga*, pp. 256–57. On the meaning of the term *vinsæll*, see Jón Viðar Sigurðsson, *Viking Friendship*, pp. 22, 57, 123, 131.
123 Sven Aggesen, *Brevis historia*, p. 132: 'in fratris ultionem Henricus cum prefato patruo suo regnante Nicolao, domini instigatus digito, ad pugne certamina suscitatur'.
124 Helmold von Bosau, *Chronica Slavorum/Slawenchronik*, p. 192; 'congregavit multitudinem Danorum execrantium inpiam mortem Kanuti'.
125 Symbolic power defined as 'the power to constitute the given by stating it, to act upon the world by acting upon the representations of the world'. Bourdieu and Wacquant, *An Invitation to Reflexive Sociology*, p. 148.
126 Bourdieu, *The Logic of Practice*, p. 109. The term was developed in the context of Bourdieu's ethnographic fieldwork in Kabylia. It is applied in a medieval context by, for instance, White, 'Inheritances and Legal Arguments', p. 97; Esmark, 'Just Rituals'; Esmark, 'Double Records'.
127 White, 'Un imaginaire faidal', pp. 175–76. More on the inherently perspectival character of war in Chapter 9.

death or counter its effects on the balance of power had to convince wider circles that Magnus' killing was indeed a shameful and criminal act which necessitated retribution.

Certainly, the assassination at Haraldsted — just like the killing of King Magnus the Blind discussed in the previous chapter — was a radical political act. Despite endemic tensions, it was highly unusual for core members of the Danish royal kindred to suffer a violent death. As far as the records go, since the days of Svend Estridsen it had only happened twice: in 1086, as mentioned earlier, rebels killed King Knud, the later saint. No friends of the unpopular king, however, ventured to take revenge, and Knud's brother Oluf was quickly installed as new ruler. Around 1100, Bjorn, a brother of Knud Lavard's father King Erik the Good, was killed at a public assembly; in that case, Hakon Sunnivasen took revenge on behalf of King Erik and was rewarded for that with the hand of the king's sister Ragnhild.[128] Furthermore, Magnus had not killed a stranger, but a close kinsman, who even happened to be his own *pater spiritualis*. Thus, whether *Knýtlinga saga*'s assertion that Haraldsted was perceived by many as 'the foulest of crimes' (*nidingsverk*), a transgression of norms which cast shame upon the perpetrators and made honest men reconsider their loyalty to King Niels and his son, is factually correct or not, it must at least have been possible to represent it as such.[129]

Knud Lavard's Burial Place

According to Saxo, the initial steps in the process were taken not by Erik the Unforgettable, but by Knud Lavard's foster brothers, the sons of Skjalm, 'who had been very close to Cnut [Knud] through their upbringing together',[130] and whose main residences at Fjenneslev and Bjernede were located just a few kilometres from the murder scene. Saxo obviously had every motive for exaggerating the role played by the ancestors of his own patron Archbishop Absalon,[131] but the Skjalm sons might well in fact have been among the first to learn about the fate of Knud Lavard.[132] They reportedly sought out King Niels in Roskilde, to ask his permission to bury their dead foster brother in the cathedral town. As emphasized by Knud's

---

128 *GD*, 12.3.6.
129 *Knýtlinga saga*, p. 255.
130 *GD*, 13.7.1. 'quibus multa ad eum ex educationis communione familiaritas erat'.
131 Absalon was Saxo's single most important source and 'camera eye' for the parts of the chronicle covering contemporary history (from the 1140s onwards) — to the degree that *Gesta Danorum* has been labelled the 'memoirs of Absalon' (Mortensen, 'A Thirteenth-Century Reader', p. 348). See, however, also Gelting, 'Saxo Grammaticus', for the chronicler's substantial use of archival sources.
132 *DRHH*, I, p. 315, n. 64.

vita, Roskilde was the episcopal see of Zealand, the foremost town of the island, home of Denmark's patron saint Lucius and burial seat of both bishops and kings, including, notably, Svend Estridsen, grandfather of each and every potential successor to King Niels.[133] In addition, the town also happened to be Knud Lavard's own birthplace.[134] In other words, Roskilde was a place loaded with familial and religio-political significance relevant to the present conflict. Allowing the murdered duke to be buried there would be akin to *officially* recognizing his *de facto* position almost on a par with the king, and, by implication, to recognizing the dignity of his family, friends, and followers.

King Niels declined the request, according to Saxo, by hypocritically pointing out the risk of provoking urban unrest. At the sight of Knud's corpse, the townsmen of Roskilde would probably rage against Magnus when he turned up, whereupon the pious ceremony would turn into violence and confusion.[135] But perhaps Niels never had to excuse himself. According to Knud Lavard's *vita*, the magnates (*meliores* — no names given), who wanted Knud buried at Roskilde, felt compelled to abandon their plans for sheer fear of 'the tyrant' (*tyrannus*) King Niels.[136] Distrust and uncertainty no doubt loomed large on both sides. At any rate, Knud Lavard's body was instead taken to the humble abbey church of Ringsted, close to Haraldsted, and interred before the high altar there.

Mobilizing Public Opinion at District Assemblies in Zealand

Friends and associates of Knud now turned to the local district assemblies to publicly accuse Magnus of the murder of their *amicus*, and to 'rouse the people's rage against the ruffian's highly iniquitous action'.[137] Besides the Skjalm clan again, Saxo mentions Hakon Sunnivasen, who had switched over to take a clear anti-Magnus stance (after having initially been part of Magnus' *conuiratio*), and the powerful Peder Bodilsen of Næstved. While both the Skjalm sons and Hakon Sunnivasen were closely related to Knud Lavard and his father, it is less clear from the extant sources why Peder Bodilsen joined their ranks at this stage. Like Hakon and the Skjalm sons, Peder is, however, referred to by Saxo as Knud's friend (*amicus*). Perhaps

---

133 *Historia S. Kanvti*, p. 201. As well as Svend Estridsen, Harald Bluetooth and Svend Forkbeard were buried at Roskilde. All bishops of Roskilde — except Sven Nordman, who died at Rhodos on pilgrimage — were interred here. *Danske helgeners levned*, p. 141, notes 1–2.
134 Robert of Ely, *De vita et miracvli*, p. 234.
135 Saxo, 13.7.1; Esmark, 'Just Rituals', pp. 245–48.
136 *Historia S. Kanvti*, p. 201.
137 GD, 13.7.4. 'aduersum iniquissimum percussoris actum uulgi iram erigere cupiendo'.

his regional affiliation also played a role? Whatever the reasons may have been for Peder's choice of sides, it strengthened the cause of Knud Lavard's avengers considerably. Saxo writes that Hakon, Peder, and the Skjalm sons visited 'every popular assembly' (*popularium ubique conciliis*). The impression conveyed is clearly that of a campaigning tour across the island of Zealand aimed at addressing and involving as many people as possible.

As will be discussed in more detail in Chapter 4, in twelfth-century Denmark, as elsewhere in Scandinavia, the assembly (*thing* in Old Danish, *placitum*, *ius* or *concilium* in Latin) functioned as a key arena for sociopolitical and judicial transactions. At the highest level, each of the three major regions or law provinces of the kingdom had its own provincial assembly. In the eastern province of Scania, the assembly met in Lund, while in the central region of Zealand it convened in Ringsted, and in the western province of Jutland (including Funen) it gathered in Viborg. These were the places where kings were elected, laws confirmed, and major conflicts negotiated and settled.

Each province, then, was divided into districts (*herreder*), each of which were centred around their own local assembly (*herreds-thing*). The province of Zealand, for instance, comprised some thirty-odd districts. In principle, all free men from a district would attend its local assembly, which worked as a multifunctional arena for the negotiation and determination of any issue of communal concern. It was also a venue for military mobilization, which may be particularly relevant in this case.[138] Later sources describe how the spatial arrangements at the assembly reflected social status and power relations. The most prominent men of the community (magnates and wealthy peasants) would be seated in the middle, where speeches, testimonies, and oath takings took place, while lesser men would make up the surrounding crowd standing behind them.[139]

Such were the arenas where, according to Saxo, the vengeful magnates showed up to complain about Magnus' misdeed. As a special gimmick, explicitly aimed at provoking emotional responses among the crowds, they allegedly displayed Knud's bloodied clothing to trigger anger and revenge.[140] Saxo probably borrowed this particular motif (also known from Icelandic sagas) from Appian or Suetonius, and the gimmick reappears later in the chronicle on similar occasions.[141] All the same, even if Saxo is most likely making things up at this point, the fictitious scene is no less

---

[138] Cf. Saxo's report that Skjalm Hvide around 1100 used the local assemblies to mobilize the entire fleet of Zealand to follow him on a private campaign of revenge (*GD*, 12.4.1).
[139] *DD*, II:5, no. 229 (1302).
[140] *GD*, 13.7.4.
[141] Miller, *Bloodtaking and Peacemaking*, p. 47. Kjær, 'Political Conflict', pp. 81–82, referring to Appian and Suetonius. On the specific functions of the motif in the narrative economy of the chronicle and on Saxo's views and authorial uses of ritual and symbolic action, see Esmark, 'Just Rituals'.

likely reflecting in a more general manner the means and techniques that political actors might turn to at assemblies in order to influence audiences and generate support.

Saxo adds that rumours of Knud Lavard's saintliness, corroborated by various miracles, also helped to convince people, but this seems to be a retrospective projection from after the rise of Knud's cult.[142] Rather more important was the fact that when Hakon Sunnivasen, Peder Bodilsen, and the sons of Skjalm turned up at local assemblies in Zealand, they were already well-known, awe-inspiring figures. In their capacity as rich landowners with widespread possessions in various Western and Southern Zealand districts, they would have attended these assemblies many times before, arriving with escorts of armed retainers and dominating proceedings along with their local social peers.[143] In the 1120s, Peder Bodilsen in particular had used local district assemblies in Zealand to mobilize his violent campaign for priestly celibacy.[144] At least within their own heartlands the magnates were capable of activating patrimonial structures that connected them with multiple lesser men and householders and reached deep into the local social body. In other words, the crowds Knud Lavard's friends were addressing at the assemblies were presumably often inclined (socially predisposed) to respond favourably to their call.[145]

Conviction at the Provincial Assembly

According to Saxo, the main battle for the official representation of Knud Lavard's death supposedly took place at the provincial assembly of Zealand, which, as mentioned above, convened in Ringsted, only some five km from the spot where the duke had been slain and the place he was buried. Here Erik the Unforgettable along with his half-brother Harald Kesja entered the scene and presented a concerted plea, 'full of pathos'

---

142 Exactly when claims about Knud's status as holy martyr were first articulated is not clear, but stories of miracles hardly played any role at the time of the initial mobilization for revenge in 1131. After the war (1135–1137), Knud's first hagiographer, Robert of Ely, writing on the commission of Knud's avenger, Erik the Unforgettable, reported that Knud was healing all sorts of diseases (*De vita et miracvli*, p. 241). The Roskilde Chronicle, written no later than 1140, says nothing about Knud's sainthood.

143 For the structure of landholding in Zealand and the specific landed possessions of the Bodilsen and Skjalm families, see Ulsig, *Danske adelsgodser*; Liljefalk and Pajung, 'Bodilslægten'; Nørlund, 'Klostret'. Hakon's main power base possibly lay in the island of Funen (*GD*, 14.2.15).

144 *Chronicon Roskildense*, pp. 25–26; Breengaard, *Muren om Israels hus*, p. 202.

145 The sources of course hardly offer any concrete views whatsoever into these local, micropolitical processes. They are in essence deduced from the general socio-anthropological model of twelfth-century society which informs the analysis. This is of course no different from analyses based on, say, a legal-minded, state-evolutionist perspective, or other models.

and 'tearful oratory', to the assembly crowd.[146] Their motives for throwing themselves into the contest varied, Saxo claims. While Erik was driven by wild anger and thoughts of revenge, Harald was more occupied by ideas of exploiting the crisis to achieve kingship for himself.[147] Saxo's partisan comment about the mixed motives of the two may best be read as reflecting the plurality of criss-crossing drivers that were a fundamental feature in such conflicts and which also applied to political actors of lesser status. It also exemplifies the ways medieval authors — and, we may assume, political protagonists — would distinguish between legitimate and illegitimate drivers, in this case censoring Harald's motivation as being too self-interested. Whether Erik's feelings of wrath were 'honest' or not is impossible to know and beside the point: Knud's death had weakened Erik's prospects dramatically, and in the political culture of the time a public display of anger was a well-founded means of communicating and strategizing in such a situation.[148]

At any rate, as much as the assassination at Haraldsted had relieved Magnus of his most potent rival, it now exposed his royal father and him to the dangers of a perfectly legitimate revenge feud. The proceedings at the Ringsted assembly are known from Saxo's account only. It is not clear precisely how claims and accusations were framed or exactly which legal or normative framework would be applicable at the time.[149] Magnus apparently had made no attempts to conceal his deed and probably aimed to have it recognized as the result of open fight or manslaughter. If so, the dead man's kinsmen were obliged to seek compensation or retribution. In fact, as the killer and victim were first cousins, the whole affair might be represented as a private family matter, in which case Niels as head of the kindred could be seen as responsible for settling the conflict — as indeed he had mediated between his son and nephew at the assembly in Ribe a year or so before.[150]

As it turned out, Magnus never showed up at the assembly. The atmosphere was heated and the mood of the crowds uncertain, whereupon Archbishop Asser advised him to stay in Roskilde. Even King Niels hesitated but went to Ringsted with the primate, who seemed to assume a mediating role — later on, when his kinsmen in Jutland joined the rebellion, Asser would side with Erik.

The assembly site in Ringsted was located at some hills just outside town. Niels still found it unsafe to show up in person before the impassioned gathering, so he stayed in town and sent men out to observe and

---

146 *GD*, 13.7.4 and 13.7.6.
147 *GD*, 13.7.4.
148 White, 'The Politics of Anger'; Barton, '"Zealous Anger"'.
149 The first written Danish laws were compiled from the 1170s onwards.
150 *DRHH*, I, pp. 315–16, n. 65, and pp. 317–18, n. 69.

report from the proceedings, where the machinations of Erik and Harald met with success. The multitude at the assembly was outraged about the killing of Knud Lavard and soon pronounced their condemnation of the absent defendant, Magnus, who was convicted and condemned to exile.

King Niels himself was not initially targeted. In spite of Saxo's allegations, it is unclear whether he was actually suspected of being an accomplice to his son's crime at the time.[151] The assembly, however, left him no choice but to consent to the conviction of Magnus and to swear henceforth to avoid the company of his outcast son. The king's counsellors recommended that he accept these conditions, believing that the public hatred towards Magnus would soon ease off and make it possible for him to return. The pacified assembly then adjourned. Niels went off to Jutland, presumably to assure himself of the loyalty of his supporters in that region. Magnus left the realm, heading off to Götaland, where, for what it was worth, he still held the title of Swedish king.[152]

Up to this point the tensions seem to have been settled by negotiation and agreement. Yet, soon afterwards, Niels was encouraged by his advisers to override the oath in Ringsted and summon his son to come back. The decision to kill Knud Lavard had been made with the counsel of these advisers (says Saxo), implying a considerable investment on their part in Magnus' future kingship. They could not allow the prince to fade away in exile without compromising their own position. King Niels, as well, must have seen the alienation of his own son and heir as potentially impairing his own position. Also, Niels at this point must have felt confident that he could trust the majority of the magnates, especially in Jutland, as well as the bishops. Yet, Magnus' premature return 'again roused the storm which had been calmed by his departure'.[153] By inviting the exile home, King Niels effectively suspended the verdict of the Ringsted assembly and laid himself open to accusations of both perjury and complicity. The dissociation of the king from the leaders of the assembly communities in Zealand accelerated and played into the hands of the group of avengers. Erik and Harald issued a joint condemnation of both father and son and took to open rebellion.

We only know about the assembly process and the condemnation of Magnus from Saxo's account, which is easily read as a sort of retrospective *Verrechtlichung*, aimed at providing a revolt against a ruling king with the legitimizing guise of legal procedure. But although the particulars of his

---

151 Except for Robert of Ely, Knud's first hagiographer, the sources closest in time to the events of 1131 do not suggest that Niels was considered to be an accomplice to his son's misdeed.
152 *GD*, 13.7.8.
153 *GD*, 13.8.1.

narration should be taken *cum grano salis*,[154] its basic outline of the struggle for Knud's burial place and the proceedings at the assembly demands consideration as an apt example of officializing strategies. Sources chronologically closer to the events like the Roskilde Chronicle or Helmold of Bosau clearly indicate that the majority of the lay and ecclesiastical elite remained loyal to King Niels.[155] The task of Knud's avengers was by no means an easy one, then. Saxo may try to convey the impression of a 'people' (*populus*) unanimously lamenting the death of the all-popular duke and demanding action, but to mobilize enough support to actually challenge a sitting king and his son would have taken a lot of political work. Obviously, this work did not only take place at public assemblies. We can only imagine the numerous parallel private meetings, circulation of messengers, etc. whereby the circles around Knud Lavard laboured to persuade potential allies to join their cause. But such efforts would certainly be furthered by having the essentially private, interest-driven enterprise transmuted into a disinterested, publicly praiseworthy, and therefore legitimate enterprise. Such officializing effects could be created by honouring collective customs and discourses of political contest at the public assembly. There, the particularist claims raised against Magnus and his party could be consecrated by wider communities and thus become 'collectively shouldered and approved'.[156]

In the present case Erik the Unforgettable's course was considered just by many, as it corresponded to collective norms of revenge: Magnus was in the wrong and King Niels had made himself an accomplice by sheltering his outlawed son. Others, like the Roskilde chronicler, who rejected the very legitimacy of revenge, could never acknowledge the claims of the avenging faction.[157]

A Kingdom Split

We now move on to the phase of overt warfare.[158] Building on the preceding months' political mobilization, primarily in Zealand, Knud Lavard's

---

154 For instance, Niels' recall of Magnus might have been perfectly legal, as the king at least from 1085 was entitled to payment for restitution of legal status and rights, cf. *DRHH*, I, p. 319, n. 70.
155 Cf. Koch, *Kongemagt og kirke*, p. 160.
156 Bourdieu, *The Logic of Practice*, p. 238. In Bourdieu's view, officializing strategies apply particularly to societies without a *de facto* monopoly of legitimate violence, where 'specifically political action can only be exerted through the officialization effect' (p. 109).
157 Breengaard, *Muren om Israels hus*, pp. 203–04.
158 An exact chronology of events is difficult to establish, in the following I shall rely mainly on the reconstructions of primarily Skyum-Nielsen, *Kvinde og slave*, pp. 71–77, and Breengaard, *Muren om Israels hus*, pp. 210–23.

associates had Erik the Unforgettable acclaimed as king. According to a near-contemporary entry in the annals of Colbaz, it took place in April in the province of Scania.[159] Saxo records that Erik was elected simultaneously by the Zealanders and the Scanians. Erik, however, was unable to receive kingship at Isøre. The harbour of Isøre, located at the entrance to Isefjord in Northern Zealand, was where the *ledings*-fleet used to assemble and where, according to the chronicler Svend Aggesen, 'it was old custom for the whole multitude of Danes to convene for royal inaugurations so that the high name of king was obtained with the consent of everybody'.[160] Saxo himself relates how kings had been acclaimed at the special assembly of Isøre since ancient times, and specifically reports on the royal inaugurations there in 1076 and 1104.[161] The exceptional royal legitimacy associated with the assembly of Isøre and its tradition of universal ('trans-provincial') consent, escaped Erik, then, and he had to settle for a more limited — hence more political — acclamation at the provincial assemblies of Zealand and Scania.[162]

It is possible that Niels reacted to his nephew's claim to kingship by formally making Magnus king as well, thus bolstering his son's position as heir to the crown. In the *Annales ryenses*, compiled in the late thirteenth century on the basis of various earlier monastic records, an entry notes that 'while still alive [...] King Niels made his son Magnus king of the Danes as well as the Goths'.[163] Also, in early 1134 Magnus was received at the imperial court as *rex Danorum* (more on this below). At any rate, bringing into play segmentary dynamics which are explored in more detail in the next chapter, the kingdom was now effectively split into two parts, a western part (Jutland), still in the hands of King Niels, Magnus, and the magnates supporting them, and an eastern part (Zealand, Scania) dominated by the vengeful faction under Erik the Unforgettable's leadership. All the same, the picture of a neatly ordered divide is deceiving, as we shall see: territorial control remained precarious at best, and rather than fight

---

159 *DMA*, p. 9.
160 'Nec est pretereundum, quod hec prisca ueterum inualuerit consuetudo, ut ad regum inaugurationes in Iisore Danorum uniuersa turba conflueret, ut eo in loco assentientibus omnium suffragiis regium nomen rerumque summam obtinerent'. Sven Aggesen, *Brevis historia*, p. 125. See also Chapter 5 in this volume.
161 *GD*, 3.3.1 (ancient); 11.10.2–4 (Harald Hén); 12.8.2 (Niels).
162 When in 1146 Erik's son Svend was in competition for the crown with Knud, son of Magnus, he was elected in Zealand and again Saxo implies that it was a break with earlier custom and ancient usage not to secure agreement from the whole realm — 'true power lay in the will of the entire body of society' (*ius uero penes populari arbitrii communitatem consistere*). *GD*, 14.3.1.
163 *Annales ryenses*, compiled *c*. 1250: 'Viuente adhuc predicto Nicolao rege filius eius Magnus factus est rex Danorum atque Gottorum'. *DMA*, p. 164.

to conquer land, the warring parties fought to destroy opposing networks and win allies.

Erik the Unforgettable's claim to kingship was condemned as outright usurpation by the Roskilde chronicler, but was defended by Saxo: one could not attack the king without royal leadership — that is, without someone around whom the resistance against King Niels and his son could congregate.[164] Anyway, as sons of the former King Erik the Good, both Knud's half-brothers Erik and Harald Kesja qualified, but the *populus* (or, rather, the leading magnates) opted for Erik, even if he was Harald's junior. The choice was made easy, claims Saxo, by Harald's notorious greed and sexual immorality.[165] The Roskilde chronicler instead points to the effects of Erik's superior oratory.[166] As mentioned before, Harald also seems to have been quite close to his uncle King Niels — a *kærr vin*, in the words of *Knýtlinga saga* — at least in the early part of his reign, when he served for a long time in the king's retinue (*hirðar*).[167] Maybe the avenging magnates did not have faith in his commitment to actually depose King Niels so as to make way for Knud Lavard's friends? Harald could easily have supported the claim for revenge without endorsing a full-scale revolt. Furthermore, Harald was not only very wealthy, but also the father of no fewer than twelve sons. Perhaps the prospect of having to deal with the sharing of power and resources among such a huge flock of future pretenders to the throne simply did not appeal to the leading men? At any rate, when Harald realized that he had been bypassed by his younger brother, he eventually jumped ship.[168] Conversely, his most important son, the powerful Bjorn Ironside, remained with Erik.[169] If the formal election of a king was meant to cement the unity of the rebellious faction, it thus caused cracks as well.

Besides the acclamation of Zealanders and Scanians, Erik also managed to establish some support in Jutland. The Roskilde chronicler — weary and despairing about the political upheaval in general — reports that '[a]fter having assembled all perfidious and infamous men, Erik went off to Jutland, where from a part of the people he usurped, by way of false

---

164 *Chronicon Roskildense*, p. 27; *GD*, 13.8.2. Indeed, as argued by John Comaroff, protest and resistance against a ruler only evolve into a civil war if there emerges an opponent or aspirant who brings into play the segmentary principle touched upon in Chapter 1 (Comaroff, 'Reflections', p. 300; see also Orning and Vigh, 'Constant Crisis').
165 Saxo's critique of Harald's alleged life with concubines was probably meant to compromise the status of his progeny and thereby delegitimize potential claims to the throne by descendants of Harald's line in Saxo's own time.
166 *Chronicon Roskildense*, p. 27.
167 *Knýtlinga saga*, p. 241.
168 Skyum-Nielsen, *Kvinde og slave*, p. 71, thinks this happened right after Erik's election, while Saxo, as we shall see, places Harald's turn in 1132, after Erik's faction had suffered a string of military backlashes (cf. also Koch, *Kongemagt og kirke*, p. 161).
169 Sven Aggesen, *Brevis historia*, p. 132; Bjorn Ironside was husband of Katharina, sister of Queen Margrethe Fredkulla.

promises, the name of king'.[170] Erik's feeble foothold in Jutland meant that he could take the war to his opponents' territories rather than the other way around. Thus, for the first couple of years military activities would concentrate on Jutland. However, rather than actually gaining ground there, Erik suffered defeat after defeat.

The Passage of War: Spring 1131 to Spring 1132

As we have seen, Knud Lavard's network extended well beyond the borders of the Danish realm. From the very start, warfare therefore came to involve actors that historians have often termed 'foreign' or 'exterior' (as opposed to 'domestic' or 'inland'), although they belonged to the same system of alliances with the Danish magnates and royal princes.

Among those outside the realm who might have responded to the call to avenge Knud's death — or who sought to exploit the occasion for other political purposes — were Lothar of Supplinburg, king of the Germans. Erik the Unforgettable obviously saw a potential ally of considerable potency here and allegedly wrote to the German ruler, begging him by entreaties as well as by promises of payment to join in a military alliance (*societas belli*), to avenge the death of his friend (*amicus*), and to punish Magnus' killing of a kinsman.[171] According to German sources, Lothar was indeed affected by the reports of Haraldsted. 'When he got the horrible message', writes Helmold, 'Emperor Lothar and his wife Richenza were very saddened that a man connected to the Empire with such close bonds of friendship had fallen'.[172] Lothar therefore soon led a huge army against the Danish realm 'to avenge the death of this best of men (*optimus vir*), Knud'. The near-contemporary annals of Erfurt likewise report that Lothar took action after having been contacted by Erik:

> King Lothar went to Denmark with his assembled army because of the internal wars that went on there. The Danish king's son had killed his father's brother's son, because he feared that if once he was thrust aside himself, this man would take over rule, for the father of the killed man had previously been king. For that reason Lothar, after having been urged by the killed man's brother, took to arms against such

---

170 *Chronicon Roskildense*, p. 27: 'Igitur Hericus collectis omnibus perfidis et sceleratis in luciam uenit ibique \per) partem populi falsis promissionibus regium nomen sibi usurpauit'.
171 *GD*, 13.8.5.
172 Helmold von Bosau, *Chronica Slavorum/Slawenchronik*, p. 192: 'Audito enim sinistro hoc nuntio Lotharius imperator cum coniuge sua Rikenza non modice contristati sunt, eo quod corruerit vir imperio amicicia coniunctissimus'. Helmold titles Lothar emperor, but the imperial title was not conferred on the German king until 1133.

huge impiety/disloyalty and led his army towards the Danish realm to avenge the shedding of innocent blood.[173]

This was probably in late summer of 1131. King Lothar, however, never entered into any sort of binding pact with Erik. Nor did he aim to coordinate military efforts.[174] The bonds that connected him to Knud permitted him to act in his own right, and he most likely did not want to share the benefit of this position with Erik or others.[175] In late summer, then, a German army, supposedly numbering 6000 fighting men, moved towards the ramparts of the Danevirke, which marked the southern border of the Danish realm, while Niels and Magnus gathered a huge defensive force. In the end, the impending clash of arms came to nothing, as Lothar settled for compensation. Satisfied by the promise of a payment of no less than 4000 marks, guaranteed by the provision of hostages, he returned with his troops to Germany 'in glorious triumph' (*cum triumpho glorioso*).[176] According to both Helmold and Saxo, Magnus had to perform a submissive act of homage to receive impunity, without implying military service or transformation of Denmark into a German fief.[177]

German observers dwelt upon the Danes' awe at the sight of the splendid shining arms of the invading army (and their resulting fear of battle), while Saxo asserted that the Germans were too few to actually storm the ramparts, and therefore feared getting stuck in a prolonged siege, but it

---

173 *Annales Erphesfurdenses*, p. 538. 'Rex Lotharius congregato exercitu in Daniam proficiscitur, propter intestina bella quae gerebantur in ea. Filius quippe regis Daniae patrui sui filium occiderat, quia hunc quandoque se depulso regnaturum esse timuerat. Nam pater occisi antea rex fuerat. Hinc ergo rex Lotharius ab occisi fratre interpellatus, adversus tam immanem impietatem arma corripuit, ad ulciscendum sanguinem innocentem contra partes Daniae exercitum movit'.
174 Saxo's assertions to the contrary (*GD*, 13.8.6) appear unfounded.
175 Breengaard, *Muren om Israels hus*, p. 210. The bonds of vassalage between Knud Lavard and Lothar are completely suppressed by Saxo, who insists that Lothar did not engage himself in the feud to avenge the crime, but rather to exploit the dynastic disruption in Denmark for his own benefit.
176 *Annales Erphesfurdenses*, p. 538. For the amount of the compensation, see *Annales Patherbrunnenses*, p. 157. To finance the massive compensation payment as well as the war in general, King Niels devalued the silver coin (Skyum-Nielsen, *Kvinde og slave*, p. 72).
177 Skyum-Nielsen, *Kvinde og slave*, p. 72, n. 10. Gelting, 'Da Eskil ville være ærkebiskop', p. 185, thinks Lothar refrained from demanding an oath of homage from King Niels to avoid humiliating Erik the Unforgettable, who had just taken the name of king. In the *Annales Patherbrunnenses*, p. 157, Lothar's expedition against the Danes is represented as a successful coercive act, which forced the Danes to plead for mercy (*deditio*), and it is likened (... *simili modo* ...) to Lothar's attack and subjugation in the same year of the revolting Slavs (*rebellelantes Sclavos*). Did the annalist thus see Magnus' assassination of Knud Lavard, Lothar's vassal, as a simple revolt against the king of the Obodrites? Both expeditions are certainly construed as a kind of re-ordering 'police action'. Cf. *Annales Magdeburgenses*, p. 184: the Saxon king leads expedition against the Danes, is given hostages and thus 'powerfully defeats them' (*eosque ... potenter devicit*).

is likely that in fact both sides preferred an agreement to the costs and risks of battle.[178] King Lothar not only cashed in a considerable amount of money, but showed himself ready as lord to honour social obligations to avenge his vassal by 'forcing the Danes to surrender'[179] — without even having to actually fight. Niels and Magnus, on their side, managed to ward off the threat of an alliance between Lothar and Erik and were now able to concentrate their forces on combating the latter. Erik, on the other hand, allegedly became 'totally sick at heart' (*summam animi ęgritudinem*), when he realized that he would receive no assistance from the German king.[180]

In that same summer of 1131 Erik, still master of the eastern provinces, went to Jutland himself and moved towards Schleswig, Knud Lavard's main bastion.[181] On his way, however, he encountered King Niels's forces at Jelling and was defeated in battle.[182] Saxo anecdotally blames the naiveté of Erik, whom he says was fooled by Niels' ally Bishop Thord of Ribe.[183]

From Jelling, Erik and his men somehow managed to escape southwards to reach Schleswig, where he succeeded in mobilizing his dead half-brother's old network: remembering Knud's good lordship, says Helmold, the townsmen received Erik well and promised to fight to the death for him. Soon afterwards, Schleswig was besieged from both land and sea by Niels and Magnus' large army. The townsmen turned to Count Adolf II of Holstein, offering him 100 marks if he would help them defend Schleswig. The count's father, Adolf I, had presumably been an ally of Knud's during the expeditions in the 1120s against the Wagrians.[184] Magnus, however, undertook negotiations with the count as well, offering him an equivalent amount of money for *not* interfering. Having consulted with the leading men (*maiores*) of his realm, the count finally opted to support the townsmen of Schleswig because of the trade bonds which united the town and the county of Holstein (it's the economy, stupid!). Yet, the Holsteiner troops quickly suffered a huge defeat at the hands of Magnus' army and were forced to retreat back over the river Eider.[185] Erik had no choice but to give up Schleswig.[186]

---

178 On the function in this regard of Magnus' *homagium*, see Esmark, 'Just Rituals', p. 249.
179 'eos ad dedicionem coegit', *Die Reichskronik des Annalista Saxo*, p. 594.
180 *GD*, 13.8.6.
181 Breengaard, *Muren om Israels hus*, p. 210.
182 *DMA*, p. 56.
183 *GD*, 13.8.4.
184 But also, occasionally, an enemy: Around 1130 Count Adolf I apparently attacked Knud's stronghold in Alberg/Segeberg (Olrik, *Knud Lavards Liv*, p. 151).
185 Helmold von Bosau, *Chronica Slavorum/Slawenchronik*, p. 194; *GD*, 13.8.6.
186 Helmold places the siege of Schleswig in the winter of 1133–1134, but this does not fit with the — albeit brief — information in the more contemporary *Chronicon Roskildense*, p. 27, nor does it make sense in the general context: as we shall see below Erik in late 1133 was hardly capable of launching an offensive in southern Jutland (cf. *DRHH*, I, p. 320, n. 73; Olrik, *Knud Lavards liv*, p. 254; Skyum-Nielsen, *Kvinde og slave*, p. 72, n. 14).

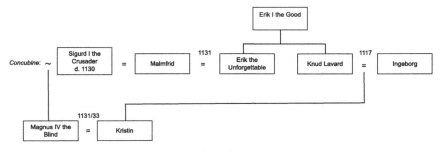

Figure 3.3. The double marriage alliance of 1131/33. Figure by author.

Abandoning hopes of creating an alliance with Knud Lavard's German network, Erik instead turned to the royal court of Norway for support. Upon Knud Lavard's death, Erik had become guardian of Kristin, Knud's elder daughter, who was still a minor. The wardship proved valuable when envoys arrived from King Magnus the Blind of Norway, asking for the young girl's hand. The political content of the proposal is spelled out by Saxo in *Klartext*: 'Erik, in hope of gathering more strength, treated this mission agreeable and was very cheerful at their reception, since he was eager to enlist the aid of a neighbouring people by benefitting from a marriage alliance'.[187] Due to Kristin's young age the marriage was not completed until 1133, but the parties in fact settled for a double union, as Erik agreed to marry Malmfrid, former wife and queen of King Sigurd the Crusader of Norway and sister of Knud Lavard's widow Ingeborg. In other words, by marrying Malmfrid Erik might also have aimed to recreate the links to Novgorod, where Ingeborg resided with Valdemar, her infant son with Knud Lavard. As for the Norwegian king's motives for linking up with the Danish rebel leader, he might have hoped to bolster his position in face of his half-uncle and co-ruler Harald Gille, who, as described in Chapter 2, seems to have enjoyed greater popularity among the Norwegian nobles than Magnus himself. Perhaps he also saw an opportunity to destabilize the Danish kingship as such by supporting a rival king. For the time being, however, Erik's new alliances did not materialize in terms of money or manpower (Fig. 3.3).

During the winter of 1131–1132 hostilities were put on hold as normal.[188] As spring approached, King Niels started gathering new troops among the Jutlanders while Erik recruited men in the eastern provinces. Yet the picture of a clear frontline is deceptive. On both sides of the territorial divide, important magnates, both lay and ecclesiastical, either switched

---

187 GD, 13.8.7.
188 GD, 13.9.1.

sides or at least strove to keep both doors open. Most significantly, in Northern Jutland Christiern Svensen, head (or 'clan leader'[189]) of the all-powerful Trund family, brother of Archbishop Asser, and for a long time a prominent member of King Niels' entourage, openly sided with Erik and his associates.[190] Bishop Peder of Roskilde, on the other hand, firmly located in the heart of Erik's Zealand domain, but a former chaplain of Magnus' and ordained bishop by King Niels in 1124, was secretly sympathetic towards the old king. Erik's brother and original co-avenger Harald Kesja, all the while, drifted towards Niels' side. Saxo's description of the muddled situation is worth quoting in full:

> Through his hatred of Magnus, Christiern had defected from Niels and pledged to assist Erik with might and main. However, Peder, the bishop of Roskilde, was a follower of Erik in his person, but of Niels in his heart, adhering to the former through dread, but to the latter because of his affection for him. Harald's allegiance, on the other hand, wavered this way and that, swaying between dislike and a sense of guilt; with reflections of shame and embarrassment he avoided Niels' camp, but, likewise, refused to be one of his brother's housecarls, since he envied and hated the way Erik had been preferred to himself. Consequently he and two of his sons, both of proven qualities, accompanied Erik's side, but more for appearance's sake than from goodwill towards him; because Harald saw himself outstripped by his brother in a bid for the realm, the aversion he felt for him was no slighter than his ill-feeling towards his brother's slayer.[191]

In the discourse deployed by Saxo, ambiguous stances and side-switching are consistently represented with reference to emotions: hate, envy, fear, affection, shame, guilt, embarrassment, personal aversion, ill-feeling. In another register we might alternatively seek to rationalize the movements of the main political actors in terms of strategizing networks and the balance

---

189 Hybel, *The Nature of Kingship*, p. 279.
190 GD, 13.9.2; Sven Aggesen, *Lex castrensis*. Was Erik's aforementioned acclamation as king by some people in Jutland, reported by the Roskilde chronicler, somehow connected to Christiern's turn? Why Christiern denounced his friendship with King Niels is not explained. Did he perhaps fear that Magnus' network would become too dominant if Erik the Unforgettable was crushed?
191 GD, 13.9.1.: 'Is Magni odio a Nicolao deficiens enixe se Erico affuturum spoponderat. Petrus uero, Roskyldensium pontifex, Ericum corpore, Nicolaum animo comitabatur, metu alterum, alterum charitate complexus. Sed Haraldi fauor inter ruborem et odium uarie fluctuatus est. Ut enim Nicolai castra uerecunda pudoris meditatione uitabat, ita fratris prêlationem perosus militiam eius inuidia detrectabat. Itaque partes eius cum duobus spectatê indolis filiis specie magis quam beniuolentia prosequebatur. Neque enim ei parcius aduersum germanum, a quo se in regni petitione superatum uidebat, quam in fratris interfectorem odium erat.' (transl. modified).

of power.[192] Harald Kesja presumably had stood with his brother Erik the Unforgettable to take revenge for the killing of Knud Lavard, but as the friends of the dead duke had opted for Erik as king and leader of their faction, Harald might have seen better prospects for himself in Niels' camp. Bonds of blood did not prevent his sons from taking the opposite stance. Bishop Peder owed his episcopal office and therefore also his allegiance to King Niels. Yet, as underlined by Carsten Breengaard, throughout the war the Danish bishops generally positioned themselves pragmatically in accordance with the prevailing power relations within their bishoprics. As long as Erik ruled eastern Denmark, the bishop of Roskilde would seek to avoid any confrontation. Likewise, Bishop Adelbjorn of Schleswig, Knud Lavard's main powerbase, was known to sympathize with Erik and the avengers, but was forced to support the opposing side, when Niels gained control of Schleswig.[193]

The Passage of War: 1132 to 1133

The annals and chronicles report a handful of military incidents in 1132, the outcome of which combined to maintain the regional east-west division of the kingdom so far. In southern Jutland, Erik's attempt to get hold of Schleswig had failed, but the decision by Christiern Svensen and the powerful Trund network to join his cause offered new opportunities in the northern part of the region. According to Saxo, the mighty potentate 'assembled a team of his connections and resolved to do battle with the king'.[194] As noted by Niels Lund, Christiern's move reminds us about the nature and scale of the conflict: leading magnates of the realm possessed sufficient means of their own, both in terms of economic and socio-political capital, to raise an army, which could actually pose a serious threat to a ruling king.[195] As it turned out, however, King Niels' other followers in Jutland remained loyal and managed to conquer Erik's new allies in what Saxo calls a 'terrific slaughter' (*ingentem stragem*) at Rønbjerg in Northern Jutland. Christern himself was captured and imprisoned in the castle at the mouth of the river Schlei outside Schleswig.[196]

As in Norway, ships played a key role in the conflict with regard to both communication and mobility (more on this in Chapter 4). Accordingly, Niels had divided his troops so as to be able to fight both on land

---

192 Cf. the logic studied by Frederik Barth and discussed in a Scandinavian civil war context by Bagge, 'The Structure of the Political Factions'.
193 Breengaard, *Muren om Israels hus*, pp. 219–20.
194 GD, 13.9.2: 'necessariorum manu contracta acie regem aggredi statuebat'.
195 Lund, *Lið, leding og landeværn*, p. 218.
196 GD, 13.9.4; Sven Aggesen, *Brevis historia*, p. 132; DMA, p. 56.

MESSY CONFLICT   137

and sea.[197] While the king himself concentrated on combating Christiern Svensen's army on the Jutland mainland, his son Magnus attempted to take the war to Erik's territory by leading a fleet towards Zealand. The manoeuvre failed, however: the ships were caught by surprise by enemy vessels and Magnus suffered a crushing defeat in a sea battle near the island of Sejrø and only just managed to escape alive himself.[198]

Still unaware of his allies' defeat at Rønbjerg and eager to exploit the Sejrø victory, Erik then led his entire fleet deep into the Limfjord — according to Saxo in the hope of finally conquering Jutland. His men went ashore, but soon learnt the disappointing news about Christiern Svensen's fate and were forced to retreat quickly to avoid King Niels' approaching troops.[199] The armies nevertheless ended up in battle at Onsild bridge some 20 km north of the cathedral town of Viborg, and once again Niels' forces prevailed. Erik was close to being captured himself, but was rescued — according to a family tradition preserved by Svend Aggesen — thanks to the courageous intervention of Christiern Svensen's brother Agge (the chronicler's father) and Harald Kesja's son Bjorn Ironside.[200]

According to Saxo, it was around this time that Harald Kesja finally opted to abandon his brother and commit himself to King Niels.[201] Saxo represents Harald's defection as treason and claims that he was lured by secret assurances and promises of lofty positions.[202] But as we have seen, Harald had most likely started to contemplate his turn when he was deselected as king of the eastern provinces.

As described earlier, Harald's main stronghold was Haraldsborg, a wooden castle north of Roskilde. Regardless whether his reputation as a local robber baron holds true, Haraldsborg posed an obvious threat to Erik's domination of Zealand.[203] As Harald sought to aid King Niels' cause by strengthening the fortifications, Erik therefore reacted by laying siege to the castle with a large detachment of Zealanders, but his men were unable to break the defence until they were assisted by Saxon craftsmen residing in Roskilde.[204] These men knew how to construct a ballista, a weapon

---

197 GD, 13.9.2.
198 DMA, p. 56; Chronicon Roskildense, p. 27; GD, 13.9.2–3.
199 GD, 13.9.4.
200 Sven Aggesen, Brevis historia, p. 132.
201 GD, 13.9.7.
202 GD, 13.9.5.
203 GD, 13.4.1. According to the memory transmitted in the Knýtlinga saga, pp. 256–57, Harald never considered joining Erik's course, but rather stayed loyal to King Niels, who appointed him ríki (lord) of Zealand, throughout.
204 GD, 13.9.5–7. DMA, pp. 57, 101. The dating of events is generally somewhat confused in the Danish annals, thus some place the destruction of Harald's castle in 1133. For 1132, see Olsen, Borge i Danmark, p. 33. Breengaard, Muren om Israels hus, p. 210, believes the Saxons were merchants.

hitherto unknown in Denmark, but frequently used during sieges in Saxony and elsewhere.[205] With the aid of this 'castle destruction machine' (*machina de destructionem castri*[206]), Harald's bastion was soon conquered and demolished.[207]

In 1132 the conflict also saw its first high status ecclesiastical casualty. Thus, during autumn Erik landed a sea-borne force near the cathedral town of Viborg, where his men came upon Bishop Eskil in the village church of Asmild and killed him on 20 October, while he was reading the canonical hours.[208] This was the first ever killing of a bishop in the kingdom since its Christianization. Eskil had long belonged to King Niels' circle who had ordained him in 1122.[209] As mentioned earlier, bishops were not only spiritual shepherds but also warleaders, so what might look like a blasphemy may have been regarded — outside clerical circles — as just part of ongoing acts of war. The sequence of events is difficult to establish with any certainty, but it seems most likely that the killing of Bishop Eskil took place during a sort of hit-and-run attack late in the year, after the campaigns in Jutland mentioned before and the destruction of Haraldsborg.

At any rate, the end of 1132 saw the status quo maintained: Erik's failed offensives in Jutland meant that King Niels, Magnus, and their supporters were now in full control of the whole western region, including the important town of Schleswig.[210] On the other hand, Niels' and Magnus' attempts to take the war to Zealand had been successfully averted by Erik, who had destroyed his defected brother's stronghold near Roskilde and whose position as king of eastern Denmark remained unaltered.

How the balance of power was evaluated by the conflict's key actors — magnates and warriors behind the rival candidates to the throne — is never systematically accounted for in the sources and escapes detailed reconstruction. Yet, somehow the impression is that Erik's campaigning

---

205 On castles and fortifications in twelfth-century Denmark, see Chapter 5 in this volume.
206 *DMA*, p. 101.
207 The military details of the Haraldsborg siege are only known from Saxo, who probably based his account on local tradition (*DRHH*, I, pp. 322–23, n. 84).
208 *Necrologium lundense*, p. 100; *Vita et Miracula*, p. 263; *Chronicon Roskildense*, p. 29. Which year the bishop was killed had been subject to debate. While the necrology has 1133, the Roskilde chronicler states that it happened two years before (*duobus annis ante*) the slaughter at Fotevig, that is, in 1132. Skyum-Nielsen, *Kvinde og slave*, p. 76, has 1133, Nyberg, 'Kong Niels', p. 368, has '1132 or 1133' following *Series episcoporum*, p. 120, while Breengaard, *Muren om Israels hus*, p. 226 and *DRHH*, I, p. 322, n. 82 have 1132. The general context and Erik's situation in the autumn of 1133 (see below) makes 1132 the most plausible date.
209 Nyberg, 'Kong Niels', speaks of Eskil of Viborg and Peder of Roskilde, both installed by Niels, as 'people from his own circle', pp. 368–69.
210 Skyum-Nielsen, *Kvinde og slave*, p. 72.

in Jutland had drained his resources, and that in 1133 his star began to fade.[211]

Despite the demolition of Haraldsborg, doubts about the prospects of the royal challenger seem to have grown among his followers. Niels and his Jutlanders, to the contrary, grew in confidence and finally succeeded in bringing the war to Erik's power bases. 'Yearning', in the words of Saxo, 'to take vengeance for the long-standing insult of his subjects' desertion' (*diutinam deficientis a se regni ulcisci cupiens iniuriam*) — that is, to punish disloyalty to him as king — Niels and his army arrived with one hundred ships somewhere near Roskilde. In a violent battle at Værebro, some 15 km north of the town, they completely defeated Erik's forces. The Roskilde chronicler explicitly attributes Niels' triumph to the fact that 'the majority of the people' (*maior pars populi*) in Zealand, headed by Bishop Peder of Roskilde, favoured Niels.[212] If the chronicler is right, the shift in the balance of power between the old king and his challenger, which was now clear for all to see, was not so much caused by the military showdown at Værebro. Rather, the decisive factor seems to have been the loss of faith among Erik's networks in his luck, and as a result many of his Zealand followers started seeping away from him. The actual battle then merely confirmed these underlying movements.

The aftermath of Værebro saw an apparently unusual act of brutality. Harald Kesja, who seemingly pursued his own personal feud within the war, demanded of King Niels, his lord, that Erik's capture of his castle earlier in the year should be met with severe retribution. Niels' men consequently ravaged (*deuastauit*) the town of Roskilde and delivered the Saxon ballista-builders to the mercy of Harald, who as a particularly degrading mark of infamy had the tips of their noses cut off.[213]

In late summer, the rebellion thus appeared to have been crushed in every practical sense. Along with his wife Malmfrid and little son Svend, whose mother was a concubine, Erik fled to the easternmost province of Scania in a desperate last attempt to mobilize support. The Scanians, however, who supposedly had been the first to acclaim Erik king in April 1131, turned down his appeals and expelled him from the region.[214] After the failed expeditions to Jutland and the loss of Zealand, the avenger of Knud Lavard no longer looked like a winner. To add insult to injury, Erik,

---

211 Breengaard, *Muren om Israels hus*, p. 210.
212 *Chronicon Roskildense*, p. 27; GD, 13.11.1.
213 *Chronicon Roskildense*, p. 27; GD 13.11.2; according to some annalistic entries, Roskilde was 'depopulated' (*depopulata est*), DMA, p. 75. DRHH, I, pp. 324–25, n. 88.
214 GD, 13.11.1.; *Chronicon Roskildense*, p. 27.

who now seemed to be ever on the run, earned himself the dishonourable nickname of 'Harefoot'.[215]

From Scania, Erik, Malmfrid, and their company journeyed northwards to Norway.[216] Kristin, Knud Lavard's daughter, who had been betrothed to King Magnus in 1131, had come of age and presumably she had already been sent to the Norwegian court to complete the marriage alliance.[217] Erik therefore must have expected a friendly welcome.

King Niels had sought to strengthen his network through marriage as well. Following Queen Margrethe Fredkulla's death in 1129 or 1130, he entered marriage with Ulvhild, young daughter of a Norwegian earl and widow of Margrethe's late father King Inge of Sweden (Fig. 3.4). The marriage might have been an attempt to hold on to the Stenkil inheritance and perhaps even consolidate Magnus' precarious (and in terms of actual presence almost fictive) position as king of the Götar.[218] Around 1132 or 1133, however, the Götar took advantage of the internal feuding in Denmark and denounced Magnus' kingship, opting instead to appoint the local non-royal magnate Sverker. To complete the failure of Niels' arrangement, Ulvhild chose to leave him in favour of this very Sverker. While this strengthened the latter's position considerably, Magnus' feeble claim to the same throne melted into thin air.[219]

As it turned out, Erik the Unforgettable's Norwegian alliance likewise proved abortive. According to the Roskilde chronicler, King Magnus initially vowed to help, but changed his mind, when Erik arrived, deprived him of his goods, drove his retinue away, and had him isolated in chains. From his imprisonment, however, Erik managed to send messages to friends back home, reminding them of the numerous gifts and benefits he previously had supplied them with — an invocation of the norms of reciprocity and of past relations rather than future prospects. Soon Erik's friends came by ship to Norway and freed him from custody.[220] On his way back Erik possibly met with Harald Gille, King Magnus' half-uncle, co-ruler, and rival, and the two men were later reported to have become sworn brothers.[221]

---

215 Skyum-Nielsen, *Kvinde og slave*, p. 72; cf. Helmold von Bosau, *Chronica Slavorum/ Slawenchronik*, pp. 192–94.
216 *Chronicon Roskildense*, p. 27.
217 *GD*, 13.11.1.
218 For the idea that Niels possibly married Ulvhild very shortly after Margrethe's death, *before* the murder at Haraldsted, see Chapter 6.
219 According to an anecdote of Saxo's (*GD*, 13.10.1.), Ulvhild was courted and abducted by Sverker. As Magnus is not mentioned in any Swedish medieval king list, it is doubtful whether he ever wielded any actual power among the Götar.
220 *Chronicon Roskildense*, pp. 27–28. More on Erik's Norwegian alliance and captivity in Chapter 6.
221 *DRHH*, I, p. 325, n. 89 and Chapter 2 in this volume.

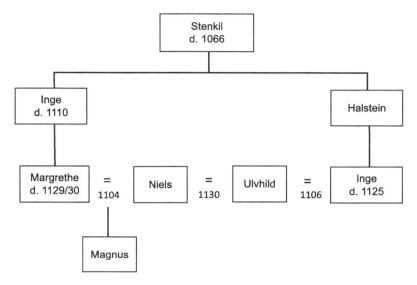

Figure 3.4. King Niels' marriage with Ulvhild, c. 1130. Figure by author.

Why King Magnus betrayed Erik is not clear. In Saxo's lively account, the Norwegian king was bribed by King Niels, but perhaps he simply shied away from investing in a man who at this time appeared to be about to lose everything.[222] Saxo adds to the story: King Magnus' wife Kristin, Knud Lavard's daughter, warned Erik about her husband's treason and was later repudiated by Magnus and sent back to Denmark for this.[223] But anyway Erik had escaped; the friends who rescued Erik came from 'his most faithful Lolland' (*fidissimam sibi Lalandiam*), the far south of the realm where he apparently still enjoyed some support.[224] Having arrived there and wishing to re-establish himself as a figure still to be reckoned with, Erik captured Ubbe, King Niels' son-in-law and earl (*prefectus*) of the minor islands, and had him hanged like a thief. This way Erik took revenge on one of the sworn associates behind the murder of Knud Lavard and simultaneously 'gave clear notice of his return' (*clarum reditus sui indicium dabat*).[225] If Saxo's story carries any truth, it testifies again to the mobility and opportunities for shipborne hit-and-run tactics offered by the water-dominated

---

222 Bagge, *From Viking Stronghold*, p. 48.
223 *GD*, 13.11.12.
224 Erik later granted land in Lolland to one of his important followers in return for military service (*DD*, I:2, no. 99).
225 *GD*, 13.11.4–7.

geography of Denmark, and the related difficulties of effectively controlling large territories.

From Norway or Lolland, Erik continued to Scania, where he learnt that King Niels planned to celebrate Christmas in Lund, presumably to demonstrate his recovery of all the provinces, and therefore had gathered large provisions in the town. Erik, however, reached Lund first and seized the goods. Niels decided to stay in Zealand, where he began collecting foodstuffs from people there instead.[226]

The Passage of War: 1134

From having been almost concluded, the conflict had come alive again. In early 1134 Erik was firmly re-established in Scania and had settled in Lund where he ordered the cathedral town to be fortified with walls and ditches. The leading Scanians regretted their former attitude and unanimously consented to welcome him back, 'saying that they would live and die with him' (*dicentes se uelle uiuere et mori cum eo*).[227] Presumably Erik won over the Hallanders as well.[228] Archbishop Asser of Lund also sided with him, even if that alliance set the prelate against the majority of the Danish higher clergy. The Roskilde chronicler famously blamed Asser for lacking firmness and turning in whatever direction the wind happened to blow.[229] But Asser probably aligned his course with that of his kinsmen: his brother Christiern was still imprisoned by Niels in southern Jutland, while his other brother Agge seems to have been in Scania with Erik.[230] Old loyalties to Erik's father Erik the Good, during whose reign Asser was made Denmark's first metropolitan, may have played a role as well. *Knýtlinga saga* — always attentive to the socio-political factor of friendship bonds — relates that Asser 'gave Eirik a warm and respectful welcome, offering him all the support at his disposal, for the archbishop had been a close friend (*mesti vinr*) of Eirik's father, King Eirik the Good'.[231] The saga also has Asser joining Erik's army with 'many of his kinsmen and other members of his retinue'.[232] The archbishop's support of Erik in Scania was hardly a reversal (as many historians have suggested), but rather expressed his basic stance during most of the conflict. When, for instance, around New Year 1132–1133 the archbishop decided to have his great donation

---

226 *GD*, 13.11.7.
227 *Chronicon Roskildense*, p. 28.
228 *Knýtlinga saga*, pp. 258–59.
229 *Chronicon Roskildense*, p. 28.
230 Sven Aggesen, *Brevis historia*, p. 135.
231 *Knýtlinga saga*, p. 259: 'tók vel ok sæmiliga við Eiríki ok fekk honum allan þann styrk, er hann hafði fǫng á, því at erkibiskup hafði verit inn mesti vinr Eiríks konungs ins góða, fǫður hans'.
232 *Knýtlinga saga*, p. 260: 'Mikill frændabálkr hans ok svá annat lið'.

to the church of Lund (made at the inauguration of the crypt in 1123) attested in writing, the charter was dated 7 January in commemoration of the day of Knud Lavard's death.[233]

How Erik managed so quickly to recreate a power base in the province from where he had been expelled less than half a year before remains a puzzle. Neither the Roskilde chronicler, who sees the Scanians turning simply 'as if led by penance' (*quasi penitencia ducti*),[234] nor any other source provide sufficient information about the local micro-politics to really explain the sudden changes. The dynamics, however, probably resemble those analysed in Chapter 4 on the basis of more informative Norwegian texts. Somehow Erik must have been able to persuade his former followers that he was not done for yet. Again, one also needs to consider the logistical obstacles to sustained control of large territories (lack of infrastructure and permanently garrisoned fortifications, limited number of troops, etc.). Niels, Magnus, and Harald Kesja may have routed Erik's army in Zealand, but he had managed to escape, and as soon as he could mobilize new troops, he could show up unexpectedly anywhere (as he did at Asmild and Lolland), try his luck with a surprise attack or simply usurp power within an unguarded area (as at Lund).[235]

Saxo reports that Niels tried to obstruct Erik's build-up of troops by ordering his forces to patrol the shores of Zealand. The province was still the bastion of many of Knud Lavard's old associates, who had granted Erik kingship three years earlier. The defeat at Værebro and Erik's flight from the island probably had made many reconsider their stance, but hearing about Erik's renewed control of Scania some might have suspected a second chance coming up. Taking advantage again of his naval superiority, Niels therefore 'issued his soldiers with orders to watch the coastal stretches of Zealand in order to prevent anyone crossing over [Øresund] to Erik'.[236] Yet, as one would imagine, the blockade was not effective. Saxo tells a story of one particular knight (*miles*), who had previously served the avenging king and who, with the help of his own retainers (*satellites*), secretly managed to make his way across the water to Scania, 'where he

---

233 *DD*, I:2, no. 56. Cf. Breengaard, *Muren om Israels hus*, p. 220: 'Asser did not shift politics from new year 1134, but stood openly on Erik's side throughout that part of the feud, where Erik had dominion of Scania'.
234 *Chronicon Roskildense*, p. 28.
235 Cf. Breengaard, *Muren om Israels hus*, p. 211: 'By placing smaller, heavily armed groups in an area without military potential or organization it was possible to dominate the place for a long time. Therefore, it hardly has required much military effort on the part of Erik to settle in Lund and dominate all Scania, while slowly building up his military potential for the purpose of a more offensive course'.
236 *GD*, 13.11.11. 'Nicolaus maritima Sialandiê loca, nequis ad Ericum transiret, a militibus obseruari iussisset'.

brought welcome aid to Erik' (*gratam Erico opem attulit*).[237] The story is anecdotal, of course, but it may reflect a more general pattern. Some of the Saxons, for instance, who had suffered from Harald Kesja's harsh treatment in Roskilde, are mentioned in German sources as having gone to Scania to fight on Erik's side.[238] As is well known, nothing succeeds like success,[239] and this is how the *Knýtlinga saga* author imagined the process: 'the more Eirik's strength increased, the more unpopular Nikolas and Magnus became, and a good many people shifted their allegiance and service to Eirik'.[240]

The information in the Danish annals about the plundering of Roskilde by Wendish pirates in early 1134 confirms the picture of King Niels' limited territorial control.[241] A Rus' chronicle relates how around this same time — spring 1134 — Niels or some of his allies took travelling merchants from Novgorod as hostages, presumably to put pressure on Erik the Unforgettable's father-in-law Prince Mstislav.[242]

On top of the pressure from Erik's reinvigorated regime in Scania, Niels and Magnus also had to deal with King Lothar, who had been crowned emperor in Rome in June 1133. The German ruler was supposedly angered by the mutilation of Saxons during the looting of Roskilde and even contemplated invading Denmark again for that reason.[243] Niels and Magnus therefore decided to seek reconciliation and to secure Lothar's consent to Magnus' succession.

Thus, at the imperial Easter celebration in Halberstadt 15 April 1134, Magnus — represented in German records as either king of the Danes or 'one of the leaders of the Danes' (*quidam de primoribus Danorum*)[244] — appeared before Lothar to make amends for the Roskilde mutilations and 'gave himself over to the Emperor's power' (*in potestatem imperatoris tradit*).[245] To obtain mercy, one annalist reports, the son of King Niels of the Danes paid an enormous amount of gold and silver for the many Germans living in Denmark that he had killed, mutilated, tortured, or

---

237 *GD*, 13.11.11. Translation modified.
238 *Annales Patherbrunnenses*, p. 160.
239 The dictum famously connected to the Scandinavian civil wars in Bagge, *Society and Politics*, p. 96.
240 *Knýtlinga saga*, p. 259: 'því meirr sem óx afli Eiríks því meiri var óvinsæld þeira Níkuláss ok Magnúss, ok snørusk þá margir menn til hlýðni ok þjónostu við Eirík'.
241 *DMA*, p. 57. At exactly what time of the year the sacking took place is uncertain. Olrik, *Knud Lavards liv*, p. 260, thought it was 'in the beginning of 1134', probably because the annalists usually placed the event *before* the battle of Fotevig in June 1134 (see below).
242 Lind, 'De russiske ægteskaber', p. 236.
243 *Annales Patherbrunnenses*, p. 160: 'Rex Danorum pluribus advenis Teutonicis terram suam incolentibus truncationes membrorum facit. Hac de causa imperator expeditionem super eum movere intendit'.
244 *Die Reichskronik des Annalista Saxo*, p. 597; *Annales Magdeburgenses*, p. 184.
245 *Annales Patherbrunnenses*, p. 160.

chased away while Lothar had been occupied by a military expedition to Rome (in mid-1133). The Danish delegation also offered hostages.[246] In return Lothar resolved to invest Magnus with both a knighthood and the kingship and crowned him king of the Danes.[247] Magnus' position as the legitimate co-ruler of Denmark was hereby firmly recognized by the lord of the man whom Magnus had killed three years earlier. In return for this grace, Magnus agreed to receive the kingdom of Denmark in fief from the emperor and swore an oath to the effect that Danish kingship could be transmitted to his successors by imperial permission only.[248] As discussed in more detail in Chapter 8, Magnus carried the emperor's sword in a public ceremonial demonstration of his subordination. For Lothar, the internal conflict among the Danish elite had proven to be yet another opportunity to change the balance of power between the empire and the Danish kingdom in his own favour.

The talks in Halberstadt between the emperor and Magnus' Danish mission perhaps touched upon another issue. Ever since the establishment in 1103–1104 of a separate Danish Church province (including Norway and Sweden), the metropolitan Church of Hamburg-Bremen had worked to re-subjugate their former Nordic suffragans. The complicated Romano-German power struggle triggered by the papal schism in the early 1130s finally paved the way. Thus, in May 1133 Pope Innocent II issued bulls declaring that the Nordic Church province had been abolished. The decision was a result of an alliance between King Lothar, always a steadfast supporter of Hamburg-Bremen, and Innocent II, who had to provide something in return for Lothar's support against his rival for the holy see, Anacletus. Letters were sent to Archbishop Adelbero of Hamburg-Bremen, Archbishop Asser of Lund, the bishops of Sweden, and King Niels.[249] Yet, the bulls were formulated ambiguously (impressing obedience to Hamburg-Bremen on the Danish clergy, but without explicitly annulling the rank of Asser or Lund) and it is uncertain whether the letters actually reached Scandinavia at all.[250] If they did, Magnus would have had to accept the papal decision when supplicating Lothar in Halberstadt.[251] At the same time, however, the fact that the papal letter was sent to King Niels (rather than to Erik) suggests that in late spring 1133 the emperor recognized the

---

246 *Annales Erphesfurdenses*, p. 539. Hostages: *Annales Patherbrunnenses*, p. 160.
247 *Annales Erphesfurdenses*, p. 539. Knighthood: *Annales Magdeburgenses*, p. 184.
248 *Annales Patherbrunnenses*, p. 160: 'Imperator pascha Halverstad peragit. Ibi rex Danorum veniens sese in potestatem imperatoris tradit, obsides dat, iuramentum facit, se successoresque suos nonnisi permissu imperatoris succesorumque suorum regnum adepturum'. According to Skyum-Nielsen, *Kvinde og slave*, p. 76, this did not imply paying of tribute, or courtly or military service, it was simply the way political alliances were made.
249 *DD*, I:2, nos 57–61.
250 Breengaard, *Muren om Israels hus*, p. 221; Skyum-Nielsen, *Kvinde og slave*, pp. 74–75.
251 Gelting, 'Da Eskil ville være ærkebiskop', pp. 188–89.

old man as the legitimate ruler of the Danes. King Niels might therefore have supported the degradation of the see of Lund in order to assure himself of imperial support with respect to his own position and to Magnus' succession, and in order to counter Erik's archiepiscopal ally.[252]

Gamechanger at Fotevig

Having made peace with the emperor on largely submissive terms, Magnus, now his father's co-ruler, hurried back to Denmark to resume fighting with Erik and the Scanians. According to the Roskilde chronicler, King Niels called up the naval army (*leding*) from all the lands that were subject to him — e.g. Jutland, Funen, and Zealand — and instructed all noble men (*meliores*) to follow him to Scania in the first days of June, where they would aim to celebrate Pentecost.[253] Helmold likewise applied a discourse of 'Scanians' versus 'all the Danes', emphasizing the regional segmentation.[254] Magnus, Harald Kesja, and Henrik Skadelar were the most prominent of those gathered. Also on board the assembled 'innumerous fleet' (*innumera classe*)[255] were six bishops as well as a huge gathering of lower clergy from all over the realm. The *expeditio* thus constituted an impressive show of force when on 4 June it landed near the bay of Fotevig in southern Scania. Perhaps this was in fact the main purpose: to demonstrate to the locals that they were about to face a vastly superior power and thus had better abandon their allegiance to the royal challenger? Or perhaps Niels and Magnus expected Erik's troops to be quickly overrun and therefore wanted all their key lay and ecclesiastical followers to be present to consolidate things at a subsequent general assembly?[256]

But the concentration of numerous important people at one place also rendered Niels' and Magnus' side vulnerable. As it proved, the invading army was caught out by a surprise attack almost immediately after its arrival. Erik's troops must have been informed about the fleet's landing site near Fotevig Bay. Marine archaeological finds suggest they blocked the entrance to the bay, forcing the incoming ships to disembark in a

---

252 Nyberg, 'Kong Niels', pp. 383–85.
253 *Chronicon Roskildense*, pp. 28–29. Saxo has Niels gather 'the whole Danish fleet except the Scanian' (*prêter Scaniam omni Danica classe*, GD, 13.11.8) and claims that Scanians later boasted about their crushing of the entire Danish forces (GD, 14.3.2).
254 Helmold von Bosau, *Chronica Slavorum/Slawenchronik*, p. 194.
255 Helmold von Bosau, *Chronica Slavorum/Slawenchronik*, p. 194.
256 Niels Lund, 'Bisperne ved Fodevig'. Friisberg, *Hvem tilhører Danmark?*, pp. 109–10, and Hybel, *The Nature of Kingship*, p. 277, are probably right, that the bishops were there as war leaders rather than as pastors.

somewhat disorderly fashion.[257] Erik then broke out from his camp in Lund,[258] fell upon Niels' and Magnus' men at the village of Hammer close to the bay area while they were still stationed at the beach, and completely destroyed them before they were able to organize for battle or slip away in their vessels. Things apparently developed into a slaughter rather than a regular clash of arms. As well as countless ordinary warriors,[259] Magnus himself was killed along with his cousin — and co-assassin from Haraldsted — Henrik Skadelar and several other prominent lay nobles. The clergy in particular suffered unusually heavy casualties as 'no other war was more prolific in its squandering of bishop's blood'.[260] No fewer than five bishops and sixty priests were put to death on the shores. Bishops Peder of Roskilde, Thord of Ribe, Ketil of Vestervig, and Henrik of Sigtuna (an exiled Swedish prelate) all died at Fotevig, while Adelbjorn of Schleswig would expire less than two years later from his wounds. A subdeacon from the cathedral chapter of Lund was one of the few casualties reported on the Scanian side.[261] King Niels himself, who in the words of the Roskilde chronicler 'watched some [of his men] getting caught, others mutilated, some killed, others drowned in the water', barely managed to escape in a ship accompanied by Harald Kesja.[262] From having been close to quashing the rebellion, the ruling monarch in one sudden stroke on the holy day of Pentecost found himself 'defeated and robbed of both son and heir'.[263]

The element of surprise seems to have been an important factor behind Erik's triumph — as it seems to have been in most such skirmishes (more on this in the next chapter). The loyalty and — according to some sources — renowned soldiery of the Scanians may have played a role as well.[264] The landing troops, on the other hand, is said by one usually well-informed German annalist to have been caught by fear and hesitation as they disembarked.[265] If there is any truth in this, it may be that some of the Zealanders who found themselves summoned to war against the

---

257 Lund, 'Bisperne ved Fodevig', p. 15. Cf. also the remark in *Chronicon Roskildense*, 29, that Niels' and Magnus' troops were incautious and disordered upon their arrival.
258 *Annales Erphesfurdenses*, p. 539.
259 Mass graves have been found at Hammernäs near Fotevig, Skyum-Nielsen, *Kvinde og slave*, p. 76.
260 *GD*, 13.11.11.: 'Neque bellum aliud crebriorem pontificum cruorem absumpsit'.
261 *Chronicon Roskildense*, p. 29; *Necrologium lundense*, pp. 75–76: 'Apud uillam Hamar occisi sunt in prelio Magnus filius regis Nicolai, et episcopi, Petrus Roskeldensis, Thore Ripensis, Catelo vvendilensis, Henricus Sictunensis et Brant subdiaconus, frater noster, cum plerisque melioribus danie'. 60 priests: *Die Reichskronik des Annalista Saxo*.
262 *Chronicon Roskildense*, p. 29: 'uidens alios capi, alios membris detruncari, alios interfeci, alios aquis submergi'.
263 Sven Aggesen, *Brevis historia*, p. 134: 'victus, nato pariter et herede orbatus'.
264 Sven Aggesen ascribes a special *probitas* (a term often used synonymously with *virtus*) to the Scanian people.
265 *Annales Erphesfurdenses*, p. 539.

man whom they three years earlier elected king might not have felt entirely devoted to the cause. If Saxo is right to assert that some of them had in fact already defected and joined Erik's army, Niels' and Magnus' Zealanders might even have had to face friends and kinsmen on the other side.[266]

What is more, Erik had managed to reinforce his army of Scanians (and defected Zealanders) with contingents of Germans, not only some of those who had suffered persecution in Roskilde, but also 300 mounted Teutonic knights.[267] Supposedly, this elite combat force in particular caused disruption among the invaders and effectively decided the outcome of the clash. Organized fighting by heavily armed horsemen in the 'chivalric' style was still a novelty in Scandinavia at the time, and there is some reason to believe that it did create a shock effect.[268] According to German annals, the knights were led by 'a son of Erik's sister' (*Erichi sororis filius*).[269] The sister may have been Ragnhild, married to Hakon Sunnivasen, one of the magnates who co-initiated the revenge feud in early 1131 (cf. above). Erik the Lamb, who a few years later would succeed Erik the Unforgettable as Danish king, was their son.[270] Who provided the 300 knights and how they were recruited and paid is impossible to say.[271]

---

266 According to memories transmitted in the *Knýtlinga saga*, troops, including 'many great chieftains', had come with Erik from Zealand (*Knýtlinga saga*, p. 260). Dilemmas arising from having to fight friends and kinsmen — a built-in feature of this kind of war — are analysed in more detail in Chapters 2 and 4.
267 *Annales Erphesfurdenses*, p. 539; *Die Reichskronik des Annalista Saxo*; GD, 13.11.8.
268 As noted by Lund, 'Bisperne ved Fodevig', p. 12, the Danes evidently knew about large-scale mounted warfare and most likely had encountered it in clashes with Wendish armies, but it does not seem to have been *practised* in Denmark before the battle at Fotevig, where it 'overturned all common rules of warfare' (Fenger, *Kirker rejses alle vegne*, p. 76). On knighthood and mounted warfare in twelfth-century Denmark, Heebøll-Holm, 'Priscorum quippe curialum'; Heebøll-Holm, 'Saxo og 1100-tallets danske krigskunst'; Friisberg, *Hvem tilhører Danmark?*, pp. 110–14.
269 *Annales Erphesfurdenses*, p. 539.
270 The German annalist calls him David, but double names were perfectly normal in Denmark up until the latter part of the twelfth century, cf. Steenstrup, 'Dobbelte Navne'. For an alternative view that the annalist was simply reworking the biblical myth of David vs Goliath (playing on the meaning of the Latin name Magnus), see Bolvig, 'Hvis blot kong Niels kendte sine egne kræfter', p. 24.
271 Gelting, 'Da Eskil ville være ærkebiskop', p. 189, contemplates whether the knights might have been sent by Emperor Lothar, who thus played double games in Halberstadt. Bolvig, 'Hvis blot kong Niels kendte sine egne kræfter', has questioned — somewhat unpersuasively — whether the German mercenaries actually were mounted knights or rather just ordinary footsoldiers. Bolvig convincingly identifies the issue of horses and human control of horse power as a literary *Leitmotif* throughout book 13 of Saxo's *Gesta Danorum* (the part of the chronicle that deals with the reign of King Niels), but that does not in itself exclude the possibility that Saxo had it right about the mounted horsemen (in fact, the chronicler may have got the idea for the *Leitmotif* from the role mounted warfare played at Fotevig …). Also, Bolvig is unable to explain why German annalists used the term *milites* which in the twelfth century would normally mean 'knights'.

Redistribution, Cleansing, and Renewed Tensions

From the beaches of Fotevig, Niels and Harald Kesja escaped back to Zealand, where the old king sought to encourage his followers, and then continued to Jutland. Here Niels gave Harald a share in half the kingdom and honoured him with the title of king; according to Saxo, this was to make sure there was an heir to the realm who could continue fighting Erik.[272] Surrounded by a retinue of faithful men, Niels then travelled to Schleswig, where the townsmen presumably had sworn fidelity to him. Harald smelt deceit and decided to stay away, and he was right: while the urban clergy received Niels' company amicably, the members of the town gild (*hezlag*) and others, who considered themselves to have been friends of the murdered Knud Lavard, killed the king and his men inside the town on 25 June.[273]

When Erik the Unforgettable learnt about Niels' death, he immediately went to Schleswig, where he freed his imprisoned ally Christiern Svensen and bestowed rich gifts on the townsmen in reward for their deed. While still in town, Erik appointed friends and allies to the many bishoprics that were vacant after the Fotevig bloodshed. The important see of Roskilde was granted to Eskil of the Trund clan, nephew of Archbishop Asser and provost at the cathedral chapter of Lund, while in Jutland Ribe went to Nothold, protégé of Peder Bodilsen, and Vestervig to Self, most likely also a follower of Erik's. Bishop Ulkil of Aarhus, one of the few prelates who apparently survived Fotevig, was removed from office on the same occasion and replaced by Erik's man Illugo. When the following year Schleswig's bishop Adelbjorn expired from wounds inflicted at the battle, Erik nominated his own chaplain Rike to succeed him.[274] Rikulf, a wealthy magnate who had served Erik in war, became bishop of Odense.[275] The see of Viborg, finally, vacated by Erik's killing of Bishop Eskil during his raid in 1132, was taken over by Svend, canon of the Viborg chapter and brother of Archbishop Asser and Christiern Svensen. Whether Svend was ordained already by King Niels during the war or by Erik after the victory at Fotevig is not clear,[276] but the end result was that in the late summer of 1134, Erik

---

272 *Chronicon Roskildense*, p. 29; GD, 13.11.13.
273 *Chronicon Roskildense*, pp. 29–30; GD, 13.11.13–14; Helmold von Bosau, *Chronica Slavorum/Slawenchronik*, p. 196; *Necrologium lundense*, p. 79; DMA, p. 57; *Knýtlinga saga*, pp. 262–63, claims Saxon troops who were by chance residing in Schleswig participated in the regicide.
274 *Chronicon Roskildense*, p. 30; Skyum-Nielsen, *Kvinde og slave*, p. 78; Breengaard, *Muren om Israels hus*, p. 226.
275 DD, I:2, no. 99.
276 The exact date of Bishop Svend's inauguration is unknown. The Roskilde chronicler does not include Svend among the list of Erik's bishops, cf. *Series episcoporum*, p. 120, and Nyberg, 'Kong Niels', p. 368. As argued by Breengaard, *Muren om Israels hus*, p. 226, however,

the Unforgettable's network had occupied each and every episcopal see in the realm. Erik also distributed secular honours. Peder Bodilsen's brother Jorgen, for instance, was made earl of the Minor Islands.[277]

Erik's elder brother Harald Kesja, however, was still roaming around and gathering support and encouragement from factions in Jutland, who refused to lay down their arms and give up their hopes of revanche. In late 1134, while Erik was in Scania, they had Harald acclaimed king at an assembly in Urnehoved, not far from Schleswig. Erik evidently realized the dangers of his brother's popularity and set off to Jutland on a quick winter raid. In a sort of hit-and-run action he effectively kidnapped his brother and then had him executed in a most degrading way.[278]

Having thus done away with all the major rivals as well as having distributed gifts and the spoils of war to members of the networks which had helped him on his way to power, Erik celebrated Christmas in Lund. Here, on the fourth anniversary of Knud Lavard's death, he gave thanks to God and the saints for his victory at Fotevig and for having gained kingship, and instituted a mass for his own salvation by making a huge donation of estates, primarily located in Scania, to the church of his associate, Archbishop Asser.[279] The charter issued at the occasion reads as a highly political document. Pronouncing, in the words of Lars Kjær, 'the official verdict on the conflict promulgated by Erik and his supporters', the text aims to justify Erik's own rebellion against a ruling king while at the same time criminalizing any future attempt to rise against the throne, now occupied by him.[280]

Efforts to recast the unmistakably political death of Knud Lavard as a holy martyrdom also received Erik's eager support. Signalling a new 'politicizing of monasticism' — hitherto monks had been of limited interest to those in power[281] — Erik reorganized and endowed the priory of Ringsted, Knud's burial place, in commemoration of his brother. The gift ceremony in front of the altar at Knud's very tomb was attended by leading magnates from the king's network like Peder Bodilsen, members of

---

the Trund family's stance in the war and Erik's weakened position in Jutland in 1133 suggest that Svend's ordination happened *after* Niels' defeat. If ordained by Niels, Svend's episcopacy perhaps attempt to restore bonds to Trund family? Or perhaps the family was divided? Olrik's suggestion, *Knud Lavards liv*, p. 257, that Svend was installed by Erik the Unforgettable immediately after his assault on Viborg makes no sense.

277 Friisberg, *Hvem tilhører Danmark?*, p. 50.
278 GD, 14.1.4.
279 *Chronicon Roskildense*, p. 30; DD, I:2, no. 63. Among the attendants to the donation ceremony were Queen Malmfrid, Erik's son Svend, Archbishop Asser and a visiting bishop from Norway.
280 Kjær, 'Political Conflict', pp. 72–77 (quotation at p. 72); Breengaard, *Muren om Israels hus*, pp. 227–28.
281 Nyberg, *Monasticism*, pp. 95, 103.

the Hvide and Trund families, 'and many others' (*aliisque cumpluribus*).²⁸² The donation charter does not speak expressly of Knud as a martyr saint, but around the same time Erik also commissioned the composition of a regular saint's life, written by the Ringsted-based English monk Robert of Ely.²⁸³ Although Robert's *vita* has only survived in fragments, its negative portrait of Niels and Magnus stands out prominently. As a piece of 'hard ideological work'²⁸⁴ it aimed to officialize the story of the war promoted by Erik the Unforgettable and his network.

Erik and his followers, however, still carried fears that opposing factions might come back to challenge their newly won hegemony. At the occasion of Harald Kesja's capture and execution, eight of his sons were caught as well and taken to Scania. These sons might have sought revenge for the killing of their father at some point. In August 1135, after consultation with his Scanian friends, Erik resolved to have the children killed off.²⁸⁵ Harald's two oldest sons, Bjorn Ironside and Erik Deacon, had stayed loyal to Erik ever since the war started in 1131, as mentioned earlier. Supposedly they had tried to persuade their father to seek exile in Norway, and in 1136 Erik had them drowned at the castle of Schleswig, apparently determined to purge the family tree of every possible future rival and/or — as claimed by Saxo — pressured into taking these drastic measures by his powerful Trund-ally, Christiern Svensen.²⁸⁶ Memories of the post-Fotevig process of purging enemies recirculated in *Knýtlinga saga* stress how Erik showed himself to be ruthless towards 'all those with whom he thought he had a score to settle', in particular those who had been the closest friends (*mestir vinir*) of King Niels and Magnus.²⁸⁷

Erik's 'energetic clean-up work'²⁸⁸ and assertion of rule did not mean an end to warfare. Shortly after Fotevig, Erik became involved in the internal struggles in Norway as he joined forces with his oath-brother Harald Gille against Magnus the Blind — only to later re-unite with Magnus against Harald Gille's sons. As related in the previous chapter, Erik's forces raided Oslo during the campaigns. Such continued military activity and the opportunities for plunder no doubt helped the king to sustain his

---

282 *DD*, I:2, no. 65; Hermanson, *Släkt, vänner och makt*, p. 161.
283 Bergsagel, 'Kanute, cuius est Dacia?'; Bysted, 'The Creation of a Cult Site'; Skyum-Nielsen, *Kvinde og slave*, p. 82.
284 Kjær, 'Political Conflict', p. 77.
285 The murder of the eight children might have taken place at the island of Sorø, home base of Erik's allies among the Skjalm family, see Andersen, 'En ø som hedder Suer'.
286 *Chronicon Roskildense*, p. 30; *GD*, 14.1.1–2 and 4; Skyum-Nielsen, *Kvinde og slave*, p. 79. One of Harald Kesja's sons, Oluf, escaped Erik's purge, and later (1139–1142) won recognition as king in Scania during a revolt against Erik's nephew and successor, King Erik the Lamb (*GD*, 14.2.5).
287 *Knýtlinga saga*, p. 263: 'alla þá menn, er hann þóttisk stórsakir við eiga' (see also pp. 265–66).
288 Gelting, 'Da Eskil ville være ærkebiskop', p. 195.

popularity and to keep disengaged warriors from causing trouble.[289] Erik might even have aimed for the Norwegian throne.[290] In 1136 he also led expeditions to Rügen to the south of Denmark and supposedly forced the local heathen Wendish people to convert to Christianity.[291] Further south, Emperor Lothar had crowned Niels' son Magnus only a few months before Fotevig and made the Danish king his vassal. A royal mission to the imperial court at Magdeburg around Pentecost 1135 most likely served to clarify relations, renew the vassalic bond, and have Erik's Danish kingship acknowledged by the German overlord.[292]

Yet, for all the efforts by Erik and his associates to assert the new balance of power, tensions remained. Erik's reputation, as most famously expressed by the Roskilde chronicler, became that of a cruel Caesarean ruler, who, swollen by pride (*superbia*) and jealous of competitors, exceeded the limits of power.[293] Despite attempts by other writers like Saxo to burnish his image, memories of Erik's unbalanced rule lived on. Svend Aggesen, whose Trund kindred had stood behind Erik, accused him of having been aroused by winning kingship and of having forgotten about the original motive of revenge, while *Knýtlinga saga* states that Erik the Unforgettable 'once he felt secure in his kingdom, was harsh and severe with the people of Denmark', and that his tyranny grew so bad 'the noblemen thought it intolerable'.[294]

The king's conduct seemingly nourished opposition and even resulted in cracks in his own alliances. Thus, if Saxo is to be trusted, in 1136 or early 1137, Eskil — nephew of Archbishop Asser, bishop of Roskilde, and allegedly the most influential man in Zealand — rose against King Erik.[295] Eskil's revolt (*seditio*) received support from the mighty Peder Bodilsen. Perhaps Eskil's contribution to the Bodilsen family's foundation of a *Hauskloster* in Næstved in 1135 had helped develop their friendship?[296] The two magnates gathered sufficient backing among the Zealanders to temporarily force the king out of the province. Old friends among the Skjalm clan, however, refused to join Bishop Eskil's and Peder Bodilsen's

---

289 GD, 14.1.5 and 14.1.8. More on this problem in Chapter 6.
290 *Knýtlinga saga*, pp. 266–68; Friisberg, *Hvem tilhører Danmark?*, p. 152.
291 GD, 14.1.6–7; *Knýtlinga saga*, pp. 265–66; Skyum-Nielsen, *Kvinde og slave*, p. 79.
292 Skyum-Nielsen, *Kvinde og slave*, p. 79; Gelting, 'Da Eskil ville være ærkebiskop', p. 189; DRHH, III, pp. 712–13, n. 8.
293 *Chronicon Roskildense*, p. 31.
294 GD, 14.1.9; Sven Aggesen, *Brevis historia*, p. 134; *Knýtlinga saga*, p. 265: 'var harðr ok stirðr við fólk allt í Danmǫrk, þegar hann þóttisk festask í ríkinu'; 'ríkismenn þóttusk varla þola mega'.
295 GD, 14.1.11. The revolt is only known from Saxo's account, which has made some historians dismiss it as fiction (cf. Breengaard). I follow Skyum-Nielsen, *Kvinde og slave*, p. 81, Gelting, 'Da Eskil ville være ærkebiskop', especially pp. 192–93, and DRHH, III, p. 717, notes 20 and 21.
296 DD, I:2, no. 64; Skyum-Nielsen, *Kvinde og slave*, p. 80.

coalition — a reminder that alliance formation remained a fluid and dynamic process, which was always related to specific issues and settings, balances and constellations. In the end, the revolt collapsed as King Erik returned from Jutland with a huge naval force. The subsequent negotiations were mediated by the elders of the Trund family — Eskil's father Christiern Svensen and his uncle Archbishop Asser — and the rebellious bishop got off the hook by paying a huge fine. Peder might have had to leave Zealand for a short while, but his basic position seems to have remained unaltered by the conflict.[297] Thus, he was able, more or less singlehandedly, to decide the outcome of the major dispute that erupted in 1137–1138 over the succession to the archbishopric in Lund following the death in May 1137 of Archbishop Asser.[298] At that time, King Erik the Unforgettable was dead as well, having been killed in September 1137 in full public view at an assembly in southern Jutland. His ecclesiastical friends in Scania bemoaned his death: in the martyrology of Lund cathedral the murder at the assembly was described as a martyrdom.[299] Whether the kingslayer was a member of Erik's own retinue, as claimed by Saxo, or a local magnate, who avenged wrongdoings committed by the ruler against his father, as related in *Knýtlinga saga*, the king was overtaken by the same constant crisis, the same tensions and factional rivalries that structured the power field in this society throughout the period.[300] Once again, it was up to prominent magnates (*Knýtlinga saga*'s *ríkismenn*) and their networks of friends and followers to negotiate the royal succession and the distribution of power.

Messy Conflict

What sort of conflict was this, then? The struggle between the parties headed by Niels/Magnus and Erik the Unforgettable betrayed no ideological antagonisms. This was never a conflict between opposing visions of politics, religion, or society, but a fight for power between groups and individuals within the elite that for all practical purposes shared the same basic

---

297 Saxo's insistence that Peder Bodilsen had died before King Erik's return is positively wrong as Peder witnessed charters issued in 1140 and 1142, see *DD*, I:2, nos 78 and 84.
298 *Chronicon Roskildense*, p. 32; Gelting, 'Da Eskil ville være ærkebiskop'.
299 Breengaard, *Muren om Israels hus*, pp. 39–44. Breengaard does not, however, see the celebration of King Erik as an expression of political partisanship, but as part on an ongoing specifically *ecclesiastical* campaign for criminalization of rebellion against the throne.
300 *Chronicon Roskildense*, p. 31; Sven Aggesen, *Brevis historia*, pp. 136–37; *GD*, 14.1.13; *Knýtlinga saga*, p. 269. Erik the Unforgettable's son Svend took revenge for his father's murder some ten years later.

socio-political norms and outlooks.[301] The reported (or invented) speech of one householder, in the *Knýtlinga saga*, at the elective assembly in 1076, probably strikes the basic chord: to receive acclamation as ruler a king must prove himself in battle and military command; he must be prudent, energetic, eloquent, and stylish; he must possess both restraint and the will to strike down injustice; and as he gathers much wealth, he must also be generous and give away freely. Who from the royal family, then, was judged to be best endowed with these qualities, was a matter for discussion and decision among 'all the best people' of the realm, 'the kind who ought to have some say in what's to be done'.[302] Any self-interested claim to power, appeal to public opinion, or fight for support and legitimacy had to be represented and officialized within the flexible confines of this commonly shared *doxa*.[303] In other words, nothing really divided the parties of the war besides the simple issue, condensed in dramatic form in the alleged outburst by Magnus at Haraldsted: *Whose is Denmark?* A question which applied as much to the configuration of aristocratic networks as to the royal contestants themselves.

Kingship constituted the most important accumulation point in the power field. Competition for the throne and for its benefits among friends and followers of royal family members was thus built into the structures and workings of the power game — its constant crisis.[304] Its dynamics can be traced backwards through the reigns of King Niels and his predecessors, albeit in less detail as the sources are scarcer. Most of the time, things remained in a state of *coopétition*, and opposition was handled peacefully or at least without large-scale violence. Yet, tensions were always looming and sometimes escalated into armed hostilities. When this did happen in early 1131, it was seemingly down to the coincidence of a series of contextual factors: genealogical chance had put an unusual number of able

---

301 Cf. Gelting, 'Forfatteren og hans tid', pp. 57, 77; Friisberg, *Hvem tilhører Danmark?*, pp. 23–24. This evidently runs counter to classic interpretations by the likes of Weibull, Arup, and Koch, as well as to the recent reinvocation of political ideas as motivating force among the Danish aristocracy in Kjær, 'Political Conflict': arguing explicitly against the networks-and-interest perspective of the present book, Kjær describes the revolt against King Niels in 1131 as a 'popular cause' undertaken by politically and religiously concerned magnates.

302 *Knýtlinga saga*, p. 141: 'alla ina beztu menn, þá er nǫkkurs eru ráðandi'. This part of *Knýtlinga saga* supposedly derives from a late twelfth-century saga about St Knud, the king. Its discourse on kingship is, however, strikingly similar to the one found in the early twelfth-century skaldic poems transmitted throughout the saga.

303 Obviously, religious norms and clerical discourse increasingly played into this doxa. See, for instance, the analyses of biblical rhetoric in Erik the Unforgettable's abovementioned charters to Lund and Ringsted in Kjær, 'Political Conflict', pp. 72–77, and Breengaard, *Muren om Israels hus*, pp. 227–30.

304 One might perhaps think of kingship as a kind of central bank of economic and symbolic credit, and the socio-political competition as a contest for controlling the board of the bank (the royal court) and its decisions and arrangements.

candidates for the throne forward at the same time; the unusual accumulation of power by Knud Lavard and his network threatened to overturn the balance of power and caused extraordinary fear among rival factions; the system of marriage alliances aimed at reducing tensions within the royal family collapsed with the death of Queen Margrethe and the concomitant intensification of the Norwegian succession crisis; all of this happened in a socio-economic conjuncture of rising stakes and modification of the rules of the power game by the introduction of new accumulation points (towns, bishoprics).

Even after Haraldsted, the crisis might have been averted by negotiation and some kind of power sharing deal, but in the end micro-political power and interests which are impossible to map satisfactorily caused things to accelerate into open conflict and large-scale war. Personal enmities, miscalculations, and overreactions — always more important in this kind of society, because less mediated by institutional structures — no doubt played their part as well.

The resulting war came to involve a multitude of variously interlinked parties and networks. Some were mobilized by the main contestants under the competing banners of 'justifiable war for revenge' and 'illegitimate rebellion against a ruling king' — whether one perceived the reaction to Knud Lavard's murder to be one or the other very much depended on personal adherence, invested loyalties, and the situated evaluation of options and interests.[305] Others were drawn into the conflict for other reasons, sometimes seizing the moment to pursue their own aims, sometimes simply pressurized into choosing sides. Although labelled 'internal' by both medieval and modern historians, the war was never limited to being an altogether inner Danish affair. In fact, frontiers between realms were of less importance than 'socio-political borders', the structure and outreach of networks and personal alliances.[306] 'Foreign' actors — the German emperor, the count of Holstein, the kings of Norway, the Swedish magnates, the Russian merchants, etc. — were only really 'foreign' in an anachronistic sense of nation state optics. As analysed in more detail in Chapter 4, borders between realms and polities were fluid, separated by wide border areas and regions beyond the direct domination of kings. One fought to help or control people, not to subject land.[307] In this respect, war did not differ from the structure of more peaceful competition for power.

Militarily the war was very much about hit-and-run manoeuvres and surprise attacks. Territorial control was difficult to uphold. Even the decisive clash at Fotevig seems to have been the result of a surprise attack more

---

305 On the competing representations of wars involving the Crown, see the more detailed analysis of examples from England in Chapter 9.
306 Hermanson, 'Danish Lords and Slavonic Rulers', p. 9.
307 Harrison, *Sveriges historia*, pp. 217–18.

than a regular pitched battle. Castles and sieges played minor roles, while ships and mobility seemingly were more important. For the first time since the conversion, bishops were assassinated or suffered death in combat — a testament to their growing relevance to the power game. Also for the first time, town communities engaged actively in military exploits. Otherwise, we are left more or less in darkness with regard to the scope and scale of the actual fighting. The sources reveal very little about how warriors were recruited. In most cases big men would mobilize their network of kinsmen and associates — like when Christiern Svensen 'assembled a team of his connections' (note 193 above) — who presumably, then, turned up with their bands of housecarls. As the conflict wore on, however, the need no doubt rose for extra troops. Helmold relates how, during the dynastic wars of the 1150s, King Svend III (r. 1146–1157), son of Erik the Unforgettable, provided a local Holsteinian warlord with money to equip daring men with a helmet, a shield, or a horse. This company then harassed the lands of the local count, who had opted to support Sven's opponent, Knud, son of Knud Lavard's assassin, Magnus.[308] Perhaps such raisings of armies *ad hoc*, on the spot, under the command of local big men, applied to the 1130s as well? Warriors could also be recruited from abroad. The German knights at Fotevig are one example; another case is provided by Snorre Sturlason, who relates how in 1139 rival claimants to the Norwegian throne were allowed to recruit warriors in the Danish province of Jutland.[309] There are no traces in the accounts of tightly organized, oath-bound warbands with names and symbols like the Norwegian *flokkar* discussed in the foregoing chapter.[310] How many troops battles and skirmishes involved, how combat unfolded in practice, or how many casualties a 'terrific slaughter' like Rønbjerg in 1132 implied, is difficult to say. The narratives, all written from the self-sufficient class perspective of aristocratic privilege, also remain silent about plunder and other possible sufferings of non-combatants. For these aspects, we have to look to the better-illuminated conditions in Norway analysed in the next chapter.

It is hard to resolve an intra family feud and apparently, the hatred between the main rivals for the throne was uncompromising. From the moment armed warfare commenced, there were no negotiations between Niels/Magnus and Erik the Unforgettable. Among the supporters of each camp, however, switching sides or cautious sitting-on-the-fence appears to have been relatively common. Whole provinces (as represented at regional

---

308 Helmold von Bosau, *Chronica Slavorum/Slawenchronik*, pp. 232–34.
309 Skyum-Nielsen, *Kvinde og slave*, p. 86. Skyum-Nielsen hypothesizes (*Kvinde og slave*, p. 103) that the general demographic growth in Denmark in the period 'created a ragtag proletariat, that could be bought for war service and moved down during the civil wars'.
310 Even the Icelandic *Knýtlinga saga*, whose sources and literary examples included the Norwegian kings' sagas, does not speak of *flokkar* in its accounts of Danish dynastic wars.

assemblies, that is) and even leading men of the Church might change sides in the course of the conflict. In the actual struggles, social or diplomatic strategies thus seem to have been no less important than military ones: the warring parties incessantly worked to activate, strengthen, and extend their networks, near and far, while at the same time trying to undermine ties between their opponents, ward off potential intervention from third parties, and lure potential defectors into their own camp. Strategies of persuasion and promise, gift and payment, conducted in private or at public assemblies and feasts, were all integral to the conflict. In the end, although sources tend to focus on the main protagonists of the royal family, it is difficult to rationalize the manoeuvres and changes of luck during the war other than as movements within the 'dark matter' of the power field, that is the many, mostly nameless, aristocratic groups whose loyalties and leanings decided the balance of force among the contenders for the throne.

Just as the war unleashed in 1131 merely intensified the already existing structural dynamics of socio-political competition, these dynamics also continued after the formal end of the war in 1134. Magnus' massive defeat and death at Fotevig and the Schleswig townsmen's killing of King Niels left Erik the Unforgettable in power. However, the brutal purge of Niels' and Magnus' supporters and the overly one-sided exaltation and accommodation of Erik's network at the expense of other groups seemingly challenged the norms of balance and equity and certainly left numerous nobles deprived of their former wealth and rank. Embittered by feelings of betrayal and loss, these people could only hope for revenge and redistribution.[311] Even some of those who had ended up on the winning side in 1134, but found themselves insufficiently rewarded, might have looked towards the possibility of a new deal. In that sense, the effects and results of the war already carried the seeds of continued tension.

---

311 Cf. Gelting, 'Forfatteren og hans tid', p. 77: 'The exaltation of one group of magnates at the cost of another group created an imbalance in the power distribution, that fed new hate and new struggles'.

Works Cited

Primary Sources

Ailhnoth, *Gesta Swenomagni regis et filiorum eius passio gloriasissimi Canuti regis et martyris*, ed. by Martin Cl. Gertz, *Vitae Sanctorum Danorum* (Copenhagen: G. E. C. Gad, 1908–1912), pp. 77–136

Annales Erphesfurdenses Lothariani, ed. by Oswald Holder-Egger (Hannover, 1899)

Annales Magdeburgenses, ed. by G. H. Pertz, MGH, XVI (Stuttgart, 1859)

Annales Patherbrunnenses, ed. by Paul Scheffer-Boichorst (Innsbruck, 1870)

Chronicon Roskildense, ed. by Martin Cl. Gertz, in *Scriptores minores historiæ danicæ medii ævi*, I (Copenhagen: G. E. C. Gad, 1917–1918), pp. 1–33

Danske helgeners levned, trans. by Hans Olrik (Copenhagen: Karl Schønberg, 1893–1894)

DD = *Diplomatarium Danicum*, ed. by Herluf Nielsen and others (Copenhagen: Ejnar Munksgaards forlag, 1938–)

Die Reichskronik des Annalista Saxo, ed. by Klaus Nas (Hannover: Hahn, 2006)

DMA = *Danmarks middelalderlige annaler*, ed. by Erik Kroman (Copenhagen: Selskabet for Udgivelse af Kilder til Danmarks Historie, 1980)

DRHH = Saxo Grammaticus, *Danorum Regum Heroumque Historia*. Books X–XVI, trans. and commentary by Eric Christiansen, 3 vols (Oxford: B.A.R., 1980)

Galbert of Bruges, *De multro, traditione et occisione gloriosi Karoli, comitis Flandriarum*, ed. by Jeff Rider (Turnhout: Brepols, 1994)

GD = Saxo Grammaticus. *Gesta Danorum. The History of the Danes*, ed. by Karsten Friis-Jensen, trans. by Peter Fischer (Oxford: Oxford University Press, 2015)

Helmold von Bosau, *Chronica Slavorum/Slawenchronik*, ed. and trans. by Heinz Stoob (Darmstadt: Wissenschaftliche Buchgesellschaft, 1973)

Historia S. Kanvti dvcis et martyris, ed. by Martin Cl. Gertz, *Vitae Sanctorum Danorum* (Copenhagen: G. E. C. Gad, 1908–1912), pp. 189–204

Knýtlinga saga, ed. by by Bjarni Guðnason, *Danakonunga sögur*, Íslenzk fornrit, 35 (Reykjavík: Íslenzka fornritafélag, 1982), pp. 91–321

Knytlinga Saga. The History of the Kings of Denmark, trans. by Hermann Pálsson and Paul Edwards (Odense: Odense University Press, 1986)

Necrologium Lundense. Lunds Domkyrkas Nekrologium, ed. by Lauritz Weibull (Lund: Berlingska Boktryckeriet, 1923)

Robert of Ely, *De vita et miracvlis S. Canvti Dvcis libri III*, ed. by Martin Cl. Gertz, *Vitae Sanctorum Danorum* (Copenhagen: G. E. C. Gad, 1908–1912), pp. 234–41

Series episcoporum ecclesiae catholicae occidentalis, Series VI, II: Archiepiscopatus Lundensis, ed. by Helmut Kluger (Stuttgart: Hiersemann, 1992)

Sven Aggesen, *Brevis historia regum Dacie*, ed. by Martin Cl. Gertz, *Scriptores minores historiæ Danicæ medii ævi* (Copenhagen: G. E. C. Gad, 1917–1918), vol. I, pp. 94–141

──, *Lex castrensis sive cvrie*, ed. by Martin Cl. Gertz, *Scriptores minores historiæ Danicæ medii ævi* (Copenhagen: G. E. C. Gad, 1917–1918), vol. I, pp. 64–93
Vita et miracvla sancti Ketilli, ed. by Martin Cl. Gertz, Vitae Sanctorum Danorum (Copenhagen: G. E. C. Gad, 1908–1912), pp. 260–75

Secondary Studies

Albeck, Gustav, *Knytlinga. Sagaerne om Danmarks konger* (Copenhagen: Nyt Nordisk Forlag, 1946)
Althoff, Gerd, *Family, Friends and Followers: Political and Social Bonds in Early Medieval Europe* (Cambridge: Cambridge University Press, 2004)
──, *Die Macht der Rituale. Symbolik und Herrschaft im Mittelalter* (Darmstadt: WBG, 2003)
Andersen, Harald, 'En ø som hedder Suer', *Skalk*, 6 (2002), 13–16
Arup, Erik, *Danmarks Historie 1: Land og folk til 1282* (Copenhagen: Hagerup, 1925)
Bagge, Sverre, *From Viking Stronghold to Christian Kingdom. State Formation in Norway, c. 900–1350* (Copenhagen: Museum Tusculanum, 2010)
──, *Society and Politics in Snorri Sturlason's Heimskringla* (Berkeley: University of California Press, 1996)
──, 'The Structure of the Political Factions in the Internal Struggles of the Scandinavian Countries During the High Middle Ages', *Scandinavian Journal of History*, 24 (1999), 299–320
Barton, Richard E., '"Zealous Anger" and the Renegotiation of Aristocratic Relationships in Eleventh- and Twelfth-Century France', in *Anger's Past: The Social Uses of an Emotion in the Middle Ages*, ed. by Barbara Rosenwein (Ithaca: Cornell University Press, 1998), pp. 153–70
Bergsagel, John, 'Kanute, cuius est Dacia? Knud Lavard, *dux danorum*: Murdered or Martyred?', in *Of Chronicles and Kings. National Saints and the Emergence of Nation States in the High Middle Ages*, ed. by John Bergsagel, David Hiley, and Thomas Riis (Copenhagen: Royal Library, 2015), pp. 73–90
Bisson, Thomas, *The Crisis of the Twelfth Century. Power, Lordship, and the Origins of European Government* (Princeton and Oxford: Princeton University Press, 2009)
Bjarni, Guðnason, 'Introduction', in *Danakonunga sögur*, ed. by Bjarni Guðnason, Íslenzk fornrit, 35 (Reykjavík: Hið íslenzka fornritafélag, 1982), pp. lxxi–clxxxvii
Blomkvist, Nils, *The Discovery of the Baltic. The Reception of a Catholic World-System in the European North (AD 1075–1225)* (Leiden: Brill, 2004)
Bolvig, Axel, 'Hvis blot kong Niels kendte sine egne kræfter', *Skalk*, 3 (1973), 18–27
Bourdieu, Pierre, *The Logic of Practice* (Oxford: Polity Press, 1990)

——— and Loïc J. D. Wacquant, *An Invitation to Reflexive Sociology* (Cambridge: Polity Press, 1992)

Breengaard, Carsten, *Muren om Israels hus: regnum og sacerdotium i Danmark 1050–1170* (Copenhagen: G. E. C. Gad, 1982)

Bysted, Ane L., 'The Creation of a Cult Site for Knud Lavard in Ringsted: Foundation or Reformation?', in *Ora Pro Nobis. Space, Place and the Practice of Saints' Cults in Medieval and Early-Modern Scandinavia and Beyond*, ed. by Nils Holger-Petersen, Mia Münster-Swendsen, Thomas Heebøll-Holm, and Martin Wangsgaard Jürgensen (Odense: Syddansk Universitetsforlag, 2019), pp. 13–23

Chessnutt, Michael and Karsten Friis-Jensen, 'Sanctus Kanutus Dux', *Medieval Nordic Literature in Latin*, <https://wiki.uib.no/medieval/index.php/Sanctus_Kanutus_Dux> [accessed 26.01.2024]

Christensen, Aksel E., *Kongemagt og aristokrati* (Copenhagen: Ejnar Munksgaards Forlag, 1946) [rev. edn, 1968]

Christiansen, Eric, 'Sueno Aggonis', *Medieval Nordic Literature in Latin*. <https://wiki.uib.no/medieval/index.php/Sueno_Aggonis> [accessed 26.01.2024]

Comaroff, John, 'Reflections of the Political Theology of Conflict: From Medieval Scandinavia to the Global Future', in *Nordic Medieval Civil Wars in a Comparative Perspective*, ed. by Hans Jacob Orning and Jón Viðar Sigurðsson (Leiden: Brill, 2021), pp. 279–308

Danstrup, John, 'Træk af den politiske kamp 1131–82', in *Festskrift til Erik Arup den 22. November 1946*, ed. by Astrid Friis and Albert Olsen (Copenhagen: Gyldendal, 1946), pp. 67–87

Esmark, Kim, 'Double Records: Officializing Dispute Settlement in Twelfth Century Denmark', in *Records and Processes of Dispute Settlement in Early Medieval Societies – Iberia and Beyond*, ed. by Isabel Alfonso, José Andrade, and André Evangelista Marques (Leiden: Brill, 2023), pp. 387–410

———, 'Hellige ben i indviet ild – den rituelle sanktifikation af kong Knud IV, 1095', in *Gaver, ritualer, konflikter – et rettsantropologisk perspektiv på nordisk middelalderhistorie*, ed. by Hans Jacob Orning, Lars Hermanson, and Kim Esmark (Oslo: Unipub, 2010), pp. 161–210

———, 'Just Rituals: Masquerade, Manipulation, and Officializing Strategies in Saxo's Gesta Danorum', in *Rituals, Performatives, and Political Order in Northern Europe, c. 650–1350*, ed. by Wojtek Jezierski, Lars Hermanson, Hans Jacob Orning, and Thomas Småberg (Turnhout: Brepols, 2015), pp. 237–68

———, 'Miracle and Mandate: A Case Study of Sanctification at the Intersection of Ritual and Law', *The Mediaeval Journal* (TMJ), 11.2 (2021), 64–94

———, 'Spinning the Revolt. The Assassination and Sanctification of an 11th-Century Danish King', in *Rebellion and Resistance*, ed. by Henrik Jensen (Pisa: Pisa University Press, 2009), pp. 15–32

Fenger, Ole, *Kirker rejses alle vegne: 1050–1250*, 2nd edn (Copenhagen: Politiken-Gyldendal, 2002)

Finnur, Jónsson, *Knytlingasaga, dens Kilder og historiske Værd* (Copenhagen: Høst og Søn, 1900)
Friis-Jensen, Karsten, 'Robertus Elgensis', *Medieval Nordic Literature in Latin* <https://wiki.uib.no/medieval/index.php/Robertus_Elgensisd> [accessed 26.01.2024]
——, 'Saxo Grammaticus', *Medieval Nordic Literature in Latin* <https://wiki.uib.no/medieval/index.php/Saxo_Grammaticus> [accessed 26.01.2024]
Friisberg, Claus, *Hvem tilhører Danmark? Kampen om kongemagten 1074 til ca. 1202* (Gråsten: Vestjysk Kulturforlag, 2018)
Gelting, Michael H., 'Chronicon Roskildense', *Medieval Nordic Literature in Latin* <https://wiki.uib.no/medieval/index.php/Chronicon_Roskildense> [accessed 26.01.2024]
——, 'Da Eskil ville være ærkebiskop af Roskilde. Roskildekrøniken, Liber daticus Lundensis og det danske ærkesædes ophævelse 1133–1138', in *Ett annat 1100-tal*, ed. by Peter Carelli, Lars Hermanson, and Hanne Sanders (Gothenburg: Makadam Förlag, 2004), pp. 181–229
——, 'Forfatteren og hans tid', in *Roskildekrøniken*, trans. by Michael H. Gelting, 2nd edn (Højbjerg: Wormianum, 2002), pp. 39–94
——, 'Saxo Grammaticus in the Archives', in *The Creation of Medieval Northern Europe: Christianisation, Social Transformations, and Historiography: Essays in Honour of Sverre Bagge*, ed. by Leidulf Melve and Sigbjørn Sønnesyn (Oslo: Dreyers Forlag, 2012), pp. 322–45
—— 'Uløste problemer. Adam af Bremen, Saxo Grammaticus og Knytlinga saga', *Scandia*, 77.2 (2011), 126–42
Haastrup, Ulla, and John H. Lind, 'Dronning Margrete Fredkulla: Politisk magthaver og mæcen for byzantisk kunst i danske kirker i 1100-talets begyndelse', in *Medeltidens genus: kvinnors och mäns roller inom kultur, rätt och samhälle: Norden och Europa ca. 300–1500*, ed. by Lars Hermanson and Auður Magnúsdóttir (Gothenburg: Acta Universitatis Gothoburgensis, 2016), pp. 29–71
Harrison, Dick, *Sveriges historia 600–1350* (Stockholm: Norstedt, 2009)
Hartvig, Anders, and Bjørn Poulsen, 'Contextualizing an Early Medieval Village: An Aristocratic Family in Southern Jutland, its Landed Wealth, and its Connection to a Central Danish Thing Place', *Danish Journal of Archeology*, 11 (2022), 1–23
Heebøll-Holm, Thomas, 'Priscorum quippe curialum', *Historisk Tidsskrift* (D), 109 (2009), 21–69
——, 'Saxo og 1100-tallets danske krigskunst – Riddere, armbrøster og tyskere', in *Saxo og hans samtid*, ed. by Thomas Heebøll-Holm and Per Andersen (Aarhus: Aarhus Universitetsforlag, 2012), pp. 113–32

Hermanson, Lars, 'Danish Lords and Slavonic Rulers. The Elite's Political Culture in the Twelfth-Century Baltic', in *The European Frontier: Clashes and Compromises in the Middle Ages*, ed. by Jörn Staecker (Lund: Almqvist & Wiksell International, 2004), pp. 107–13

——, *Släkt, vänner ock makt: en studie av elitens politiska kultur i 1100-talets Danmark* (University of Gothenburg: Historiska institutionen, 2000)

Hill, Thomas, *Könige, Fürsten und Klöster: Studien zu den dänischen Klostergründungen des 12. Jahrhunderts* (Frankfurt am Main: Peter Lang, 1992)

Hybel, Nils, *The Nature of Kingship c. 800–1300. The Danish Incident* (Leiden: Brill, 2018)

Jaubert, Anne Nissen, 'Un ou plusieurs royaumes danois?', in *Les élites et leurs espaces*, ed. by Philippe Depreux, François Bougard, and Régine Le Jan (Turnhout: Brepols, 2007), pp. 135–54

Jezierski, Wojtek, 'Convivium in terra horroris: Helmold of Bosau's Rituals of Hostipitality', in *Rituals, Performatives, and Political Order in Northern Europe, c. 650–1350*, ed. by Wojtek Jezierski, Lars Hermanson, Hans Jacob Orning, and Thomas Såberg (Turnhout: Brepols, 2015), pp. 139–74

Jón Viðar, Sigurðsson, *Viking Friendship. The Social Bond in Iceland and Norway, c. 900–1300* (Ithaca: Cornell University Press, 2017)

Kjær, Lars, 'Political Conflict and Political Ideas in Twelfth-Century Denmark', *Viking and Medieval Scandinavia*, 13 (2017), 61–100

Koch, Hal, *Kongemagt og kirke. 1060–1241* (Copenhagen: Politikens forlag, 1963)

Kristensen, Anne K. G., *Danmarks ældste annalistik: Studier over lundensisk Annalskrivning i 12. og 13. århundrede* (Copenhagen: Historiske Institut ved Københavns Universitet, 1969)

Kristensen, Hans Krongaard, and Bjørn Poulsen, *Danmarks byer i middelalderen* (Aarhus: Aarhus University Press, 2016)

Liljefalk, Lone, and Stefan Pajung, 'Bodil-slægten – en sydsjællandsk gåde', *Personalhistorisk tidsskrift*, 1 (2013): 46–60

——, 'Helmolds Slaverkrønike som kilde til Danmarks, Vendens og Nordtysklands historie', *Historisk Tidsskrift* (D), 113.1 (2013), 1–38

Lind, John H., 'Knes Kanutus. Knud Lavard's Political Project', in *Of Chronicles and Kings: National Saints and the Emergence of Nation States in the High Middle Ages*, ed. by John Bergsagel, David Hiley, and Thomas Riis (Copenhagen: Royal Library, 2015), pp. 103–28

——, 'De russiske ægteskaber: Dynasti- og alliancepolitik i 1130'ernes danske borgerkrig', *Historisk Tidsskrift* (D), 92 (1992), 225–63

Line, Philip, *Kingship and State Formation in Sweden, 1130–1290* (Leiden: Brill, 2014)

Lund, Niels, 'Bisperne ved Fodevig', *Skalk*, 2 (1998), 12–15

——, *Lið, leding og landeværn. Hær og samfund i Danmark i ældre middelalder* (Roskilde: Vikingeskibshallen, 1996)

Miller, William Ian, *Bloodtaking and Peacemaking. Feud, Law, and Society in Saga Iceland* (Chicago: University of Chicago Press, 1990)
Mortensen, Lars Boje, 'A Thirteenth-Century Reader of Saxo's Gesta Danorum', in *The Creation of Medieval Northern Europe. Christianisation, Social Transformations, and Historiography: Essays in Honour of Sverre Bagge*, ed. by Leidulf Melve and Sigbjørn Sønnesyn (Oslo: Dreyers forlag, 2012), pp. 346–55
Nors, Thyra, 'Review: Lars Hermanson, Släkt, vänner och makt', *Historisk Tidsskrift* (D), 101.2 (2001), 571–80
——, 'Slægtsstrategier hos den danske kongeslægt i det 12. århundrede: svar til Helge Paludan', *Historie* (2000), 55–68
Nyberg, Tore, 'Kong Niels – skitse til en biografi', *Historisk Tidsskrift* (D), 107.2 (2007), 353–88
——, *Monasticism in North-Western Europe, 800–1200* (Aldershot: Ashgate, 2000)
Nørlund, Poul, 'Klostret og dets gods', in *Sorø: Klostret, skolen, akademiet gennem tiderne*, ed. by Mouritz Mackeprang and William Norwin, vol. 1 (Copenhagen: J. Frimodts forlag, 1924–1931), pp. 53–131
Olrik, Hans, *Knud Lavards Liv og Gærning* (Copenhagen, 1888)
Olsen, Rikke Agnete, *Borge i Danmark* (Herning: Sandberg & Schultz AB, 1986)
Orning, Hans Jacob and Henrik Vigh, 'Constant Crisis', in *Nordic Medieval Civil Wars in a Comparative Perspective*, ed. by Hans Jacob Orning and Jón Viðar Sigurðsson (Leiden: Brill, 2021), pp. 1–33
Paludan-Müller, Casper, 'To bemærkninger i Anledning af Prof. F. Hammerichs nyeste Skrift: En Skolastiker og en Bibeltheolog fra Norden', *Ny Kirkehistoriske Samlinger*, 3 (1864–1866), 430–33
Paludan, Helge, 'Flos Danie. Personer og standpunkter i dansk politik under kong Niels', *Historie*, 7 (1967), 497–525
Poulsen, Bjørn, and Søren Michael Sindbæk (eds), *Settlement and Lordship in Viking and Early Medieval Scandinavia* (Turnhout: Brepols, 2011)
Poulsen, Thomas Guntzelnick, 'Mønt og magt. Danmarks monetarisering 1074–1241' (Unpublished Doctoral Thesis, University of Aarhus, 2020)
Riis, Thomas, 'The Significance of 25 June, 1170', in *Of Chronicles and Kings. National Saints and the Emergence of Nation States in the High Middle Ages*, ed. by John Bergsagel, David Hiley, and Thomas Riis (Copenhagen: Royal Library, 2015), pp. 91–102
Sawyer, Birgit, 'The "Civil Wars" Revisited', *Historisk Tidsskrift* (N), 82.1 (2003), 43–73
Skyum-Nielsen, Niels, *Kvinde og slave. Danmarkshistorie uden retouche* (Copenhagen: Munksgaard, 1971)
Sonne, Lasse C. A., 'Svend Estridsens politiske liv', in *Svend Estridsen*, ed. by Lasse C. A. Sonne and Sarah Croix (Odense: Syddansk Universitetsforlag, 2016), pp. 15–38

Steenstrup, Johannes, 'Dobbelte Navne – Erik Lam – David', *Historisk Tidsskrift* (D), 6.4 (1892–1894), 729–41

Ulsig, Erik, *Danske adelsgodser i middelalderen* (Copenhagen: Gyldendalske boghandel, 1968)

Weibull, Lauritz, 'Nekrologierne från Lund, Roskildekröniken och Saxo. Grunddrag i Danmarks historia under det 12. århundradet', *Scandia*, 1 (1928), 86–112

White, Stephen D., 'Un imaginaire faidal. La représentation de la guerre dans quelques chansons de geste', in *La vengeance, 400–1200*, ed. by Dominique Barthélemy, François Bougard, and Régine le Jan (Rome: École française de Rome, 2006), pp. 175–98

——, 'Inheritances and Legal Arguments in Western France, 1050–1150', *Traditio*, 43 (1987), 55–103

——, 'The Politics of Anger', in *Anger's Past: The Social Uses of an Emotion in the Middle Ages*, ed. by Barbara Rosenwein (Ithaca: Cornell University Press, 1998), pp. 127–52

HANS JACOB ORNING

4. Constant Crisis in Norway, 1202–1208*

Introduction: 1202

1202 marks a watershed in Scandinavian history, as two kings and one earl died after having governed their respective realms for decades: in Denmark Knud Valdemarsson died after twenty years' rule, in Sweden Birger Brosa after twenty-eight years as earl and leading man of the realm, and in Norway Sverre Sigurdsson after twenty-three years as king. However, these deaths had very different results in the three Scandinavian realms. In Denmark, power was smoothly transferred from the deceased Knud to his brother Valdemar, whereas in Norway and Sweden the ruler's death led to intense power struggles, often termed 'civil wars'. Yet it is only in Norway that we can follow this in detail, as the Swedish and Danish sources are very sparse for this period.[1] Here a period of political struggles and division followed Sverre's death, lasting — depending on the criteria used — until 1208, 1217, 1227, or 1240.[2]

This chapter will focus on the period from 1202 to 1208 in Norway which has been considered as a climax of the Norwegian civil wars, but

---

* The theme of this chapter has been further explored in the book *Constant Crisis: Deconstructing the Civil Wars in Norway, c. 1180–1220* (Ithaca, NY: Cornell University Library, 2024). The book elaborates on the chapter by expanding the time frame and themes under scrutiny.
1 In Sweden, three major battles were fought in 1205, 1208, and 1210, which suggests that the death of Birger had severe political consequences, see Line, *Kingship and State Formation in Sweden*, pp. 94–109; Brandt, 'Slaget ved Gestilren'; Lundberg, 'Lena och Gestilren'.
2 The civil wars were traditionally considered to have ended when Hakon Hakonsson became king in 1217, see Bull, 'Borgerkrigene i Norge og Håkon Håkonssons kongstanke'. A more recent generation pushed the civil wars up to the quashing of the Ribbung rebellion in 1227, see Holmsen, *Norges historie*, pp. 252–57, whereas others see the civil wars as lasting until 1240, see Bagge, 'Borgerkrig og statsutvikling'.

Hans Jacob Orning (h.j.orning@iakh.uio.no) is professor of medieval history in the Department of Archaeology, Conservation, and History, University of Oslo.

New Perspectives on the 'Civil Wars' in Medieval Scandinavia, ed. by Hans Jacob Orning, Kim Esmark, and Jón Viðar Sigurðsson, Comparative Perspectives on Medieval History, 1 (Turnhout: Brepols, 2024), pp. 165–212

BREPOLS ⁕ PUBLISHERS   10.1484/M.CPMH-EB.5.137261

has curiously remained somewhat in the shadow in Norwegian historiography, probably because it is bookended by the two towering figures King Sverre Sigurdsson (r. 1179–1202) and King Hakon Hakonsson (r. 1217–1263), who are the main protagonists in their respective lengthy sagas. Two developments have been considered to have occurred in this period. First, factions allegedly became more permanent in composition and more territorially based in Norway, with the Birkibeinar in Trøndelag, the Baglar in Viken, and the western part of the country as an in-between area. Concomitant with the establishment of more coherent and territorially defined groups, conflicts allegedly became more violent than previously, resembling wars. Therefore, the climax of the civil wars reflected a twofold development: from loose groups to fixed parties, and from personal, small-scale feuds to large-scale wars.[3]

I will depart from this view in two ways. First, this interval will be analysed not as a phase of war implying a political breakdown, but as a period of intensified conflict in society. Here I will work from the assumption that conflict in varying intensities is always present in society, and that it is usually informally regulated by a principle of balance. The concept 'constant crisis' will be used to frame conflict this way (see Chapter 1). Second, I will study conflict at various levels of society. The dynastic issue is the prime focus in the sources, but this is only one of several dimensions of the conflicts which occurred in this period. Here I will study conflicts at multiple levels ranging from local to transregnal: this chapter will use the concept 'segmentary opposition' to modify the images of fixed parties in this period (see Chapter 1).

I will use the unusually detailed and polyphonic *Bǫglunga sǫgur* to analyse the complex interweaving of conflict into the political culture of the period 1202–1208. The focus of the source is on the political struggle between the Birkibeinar and the Baglar in Norway, but its details reveal much about other dimensions of the conflict, such as tensions within each group and across group boundaries — all of which will be explored in the following. Finally, the saga also hints at a transnational dimension of the struggles, which I do not have space to pursue in this chapter. One caveat should be given here: referring to *Bǫglunga sǫgur* in the plural stems from the fact that the saga is found in two different versions, one short (S) and one long (L). The main manuscripts for the short version of *Bǫglunga sǫgur* are *Eirspennill* and *Flateyjarbók*. The long version is based on Peder Clausson Friis's translation published in 1633, and some smaller fragments written in Old Norse. The short version covers the period 1202–1210, while the longer version includes incidents up to 1217. The provenience and bias of the two versions has been much debated. Helle holds the

---

3 Bagge, 'Borgerkrig og statsutvikling' and Bagge, *From Viking Stronghold*, pp. 63–65. See also Chapter 2, this volume.

shorter version to be the older, while Magerøy argues the opposite.[4] The longer version has been considered to have a Birkibeinar bias; for the shorter, opinions differ on whether it is neutral or pro-Baglar.[5] This issue will not be pursued in this chapter, because the question of bias tends to accompany a view that different versions are products of 'parties', which is exactly what this study will raise doubts about. As far as I can see, the two texts do not offer very different versions of the events they recount. In the following discussion, I will therefore use both versions of the saga, assuming that both offer valuable and fairly reliable information on the past.[6] The issue of date is not critical for this study, since both versions deal with a recent past about which they, considering the amount of detail in both accounts, had ample information, and since the theme here is the political culture rather than the historicity of specific events. The exact dating of the writing of the saga is impossible. Helle holds it to have been written while Skule Bardsson had a strong position, i.e. before 1223; Magerøy is more cautious, but thinks that the saga cannot have been written long after the events had taken place, considering the detailed narrative.[7]

Us vs. Them: Who Are we Fighting?

On a 'national' or regnal level, the segmentary opposition lay between the Birkibeinar and the Baglar. These groups had existed for a long time when *Bǫglunga sǫgur* starts in 1202. The Birkibeinar had been established by King Sverre in 1177, probably as a continuation of a group led by Oystein Møyla in 1176–1177. The Baglar group was formally founded in 1196, but precursors can be found in earlier groups in opposition to the Birkibeinar, such as the Heklungar (1177–1184), the Eyjarskeggjar

---

4 According to Knut Helle, the short version is older, Helle, *Omkring Bǫglunga sǫgur*. Hallvard Magerøy has opposed this view because he thinks that the long version is more historically correct than the short one, Magerøy, *Soga om birkebeinar og baglar I*, pp. 47–58, 178–209.
5 Helle believes that the short version can be counted as neutral (Helle, *Omkring Bǫglunga sǫgur*, pp. 80, 84), whereas Magerøy sees it as pro-Baglar (Magerøy, *Soga om birkebeinar og baglar I*, pp. 178, 188–93). It is assumed that the long version arose in a Birkibeinar context. Concerning age, I tend to agree with Helle in that the longer version is more recent, see Orning, *Unpredictability and Presence*, pp. 41–42.
6 *Bǫglunga sǫgur* has recently been edited by Þorleifr Hauksson, Sverrir Jakobsson and Tor Ulset in the Íslenzk fornrit series. See *Hákonar saga Hákonarsonar 1*; *Bǫglunga saga*. However, I will not use this edition, because it has divided the short and long versions into two separate parts. This makes it impractical for the purpose of this chapter, where comparison between the two parts is central. For that reason, I will work from the edition by Magerøy, *Soga om birkebeinar og baglar: Bǫglunga sǫgur: 2* (hereafter *Bǫglunga sǫgur*) which presents the two versions in parallel. References are to pages.
7 Helle, *Omkring Bǫglunga sǫgur*, pp. 91–92; Magerøy, *Soga om birkebeinar og baglar I*, pp. 206–07.

Figure 4.1. Scandinavia in the Civil War period. Map by author.

(1193–1194), the Kuflungar (1185–1188), and other minor groups.[8] In this section I shall study the relationship *between* groups, and therefore operate from a premise that these groups were relatively stable, whereas in the next two sections I shall discuss the permeability of the groups. My aim is to show how intentions to achieve superiority repeatedly failed, not primarily due to the lack of determination among the participants or to coincidental factors, even if such factors certainly could play a role, but because topographical, military, and sociopolitical structures made long-term dominance by one faction hard to achieve. The structural factors worked in favour of a balance of power, not dominance by one party over another. Moreover, I will argue that the fact that dominance was not achieved by one group does not mean that the situation was out of control and that society was torn apart by conflict and war. The situation was one of 'constant crisis' where conflicts were ever-present, and where they normally cemented social relations rather than upsetting them (Fig. 4.1).

The Power Struggle Year by Year

When viewing the struggle between the Birkibeinar and the Baglar in 1202–1208 from a bird's eye view, it is clear that Viken was the stronghold

---

8 Helle, *Norge blir en stat*, pp. 90–93. The continuity is traceable partly in that the royal candidates descended from Magnus Erlingsson, partly in the identity and ancestry of the leading men in the groups.

of the Baglar, Trøndelag the Birkibeinar, while the western part of Norway was more fluid in its affiliation. This pattern was formalized in the settlement at Kvitingsøy in 1208, discussed in more detail in Chapter 7, in which the Birkibeinar gained two thirds of the country (Trøndelag and the western part of the country), the Baglar one third (Viken).[9] However, using a fixed territorial division does not give a satisfactory picture of the political power play in this period, because it reifies one form of territorial (and possibly institutionalized) power. The fact that a pattern in the struggle is discernible *a posteriori* does not mean that this pattern was an acknowledged principle among the actors. On the contrary, they always tried to gain dominance by outmanoeuvring one another, implying that the balance of power at any time had the potential to transform into something else. Moreover, the division was not stable, but continuously a target of challenge and conflict. The best way of demonstrating the dynamic whereby one group never achieved lasting dominance over the other is by analysing the movements and tactics of the parties. In the following, I shall trace the movements of the Birkibeinar and Baglar in the period 1202–1208 year by year, paying particular attention to the forces working against total victory and against territorial power. This will simultaneously give the reader a synopsis of the main events in the period 1202–1208.

King Sverre's last feat before dying in March 1202 was to conquer Viken by besieging Tønsberg.[10] However, the Baglar did not perish even if many of their leaders had to surrender to Sverre. Parts of the group still remained in Oppland, the inland part of the country. From here they made attacks on the western coast. The death of King Sverre could have dealt a major blow to the Birkibeinar, but the successful instalment of his son Hakon Sverresson as king resulted in the opposite: the Baglar were dispirited and killed their king, Inge Magnusson, accepting Hakon as their king. As a result, in 1203 Hakon travelled safely all over the country. From his winter base in Nidaros, he sailed to Viken, and from there to Bergen, where he spent the subsequent winter.

However, the Birkibeinar success was ephemeral. At New Year 1204 King Hakon died in mysterious circumstances. After that, the Birkibeinar quickly retreated to Nidaros, where they elected a new king, Guttorm, son of Sverre's son Sigurd Lavard, leaving a small group behind in Bergen. Some months later Guttorm died suddenly and Inge Bardsson was elected king. Under such calamitous conditions it turned out that the surrender of the Baglar was only limited, and probably only included parts of the group, since many warriors had left for Denmark and Sweden after Hakon had been made king in 1202. In Denmark, a band of Baglar was evidently awaiting a favourable occasion, which came when Hakon died. Erling

---

9 *Bǫglunga sǫgur*, pp. 116–18. See Chapter 7 for 1208 as the first territorial division of Norway.
10 *Sverris saga*, pp. 267–78.

Stonewall, who claimed to be son of Magnus Erlingsson, had refused to be elected king of the Baglar when Hakon was alive, but now he was made king. The band headed for Viken, which they won easily, and continued to the western part of the country, where they ousted the Birkibeinar from Bergen. As 1204 came to an end, the Birkibeinar stayed in Nidaros, the Baglar in Viken, while Oppland was populated by both groups, and the western part was an intermediate zone — probably closest to the Baglar.

Early in 1205 the Baglar made a surprise attack on Stavanger, but they returned when the major Birkibeinar fleet came southwards and continued all the way to Viken. The Baglar were forced to withdraw to Denmark — one faction going to Halland and another to Jutland. Thus, in spring 1205, the Birkibeinar looked like victors as they controlled all of Norway. However, their success was shortlived, as the Baglar travelled incognito in smaller groups to Norway. Some of them made guerrilla attacks at various places, while the majority conquered Nidaros, which lay open for the taking with no Birkibeinar leaders present. The Birkibeinar in Viken now sailed to Nidaros as fast as possible, while a faction remained in Bergen on the way northwards. Notified of these movements, the Baglar headed back to Viken and Oppland.

1206 started out with an open scenario. The Baglar were once again firmly installed in Viken, where they had built numerous large ships during the winter. In the previous spring, they had been chased by a superior Birkibeinar fleet, and this was not something they wanted to see repeated. In April they raised the sails of their new-built fleet, opting for Nidaros. The result was the Norwegian 'blood feast' on 22 April 1206, where the Birkibeinar celebrating a royal wedding were taken by surprise and almost ninety men were killed. Unluckily for the Baglar, King Inge managed to escape, and as soon as he had gathered troops nearby, the Baglar left town and sailed southwards. On their way, they encountered the fleet of Hakon Galen, who was on his way from Bergen. Hakon Galen avoided battle and swiftly returned to Bergen, while the bulk of the fleet headed for Nidaros.

Bergen now developed into a centre of attention for both the Birkibeinar and the Baglar. When the Baglar approached Bergen from the north, the Birkibeinar had taken refuge in a fortified castle they had recently erected. The numerically superior Baglar stayed in town, and in the end the Birkibeinar withdrew from Bergen in what resembles a rout. The Baglar fleet sailed northwards, and they caught the remainder of Hakon Galen's fleet by surprise in Moldefjord, resulting in the largest slaughter of the period where 200 Birkibeinar were killed. When 1206 came to an end, the Baglar had the upper hand against the Birkibeinar. The Baglar were firmly installed in Viken, and Erling Stonewall considered spending the winter in Bergen, a sure sign that they controlled the western part of the country. Hakon Galen evidently realized the impending danger, and started a programme of shipbuilding, emulating the successful Baglar strategy from the previous year.

However, early in 1207 Erling Stonewall died. In a disputed dynastic succession, the common people trumped the retainers and had the experienced Filippus Simonsson elected as the new king. The Birkibeinar acted on the news of the demise of Erling by attacking Viken, and forcing the Baglar to leave as they had done two years earlier — this time not to Denmark but to Bergen. Here the Baglar managed to win the castle from the Birkibeinar and burnt it down. Hearing the news that Hakon Galen was on his way, they went back to Viken, where they had some indecisive encounters with Inge. Now Hakon Galen sailed to Viken to assist his brother Inge, whereas the Baglar sailed the opposite direction, avoided Hakon Galen, and came to Bergen where they had no trouble conquering the castle that Hakon had rebuilt for a third time.

Since all the Birkibeinar were gathered in Viken, Nidaros was defenceless. The Baglar sailed there without encountering any resistance, and Filippus was acclaimed king at the Eyrathing. After that they sailed southwards, crossing paths with the northbound Birkibeinar fleet and continuing all the way to Viken. Now it must have seemed fairly evident that it was impossible for one group to conquer and expel the other. True, the Birkibeinar had had the upper hand most of the time — and even supremacy in 1203. However, their efforts at hitting the Baglar on their home territory had proven fruitless, and the attempts to pursue them in 1206–1207 were unsuccessful, even in a vulnerable situation of dynastic succession among the Baglar.

The Structural Factors

In the power struggle between the Birkibeinar and the Baglar in the period from 1202 to 1208, both groups aimed for dominance by routing and reducing their opponent as much as possible. Sometimes a group succeeded in expelling the other from its core area for some time. This happened when the Birkibeinar conquered Viken in 1202, 1203, 1205, and 1207, and when the Baglar took Nidaros in 1206. However, the long-term success of such victories was quite limited, and the reasons for this were twofold.

First, ousting a group from an area could lead the expelled group to turn to guerrilla warfare. When Sverre had subdued the Baglar after a lengthy siege in 1201–1202, the latter sought refuge on an inland island in Oppland, and from there they attacked Birkibeinar strongholds in a guerrilla-like manner. The same happened after the Baglar were beaten in Viken in 1205. Then they divided up into smaller bands who inflicted damage on a lot of places by targeting unexpectedly and brutally. This guerrilla strategy was probably not intended to win popular support in an area, but it was effective in undermining the basis of Birkibeinar support, as it was next to impossible to put up an efficient defence against such instant attacks, which thus demonstrated the inability of the Birkibeinar to protect the population.

A second negative result of subduing a group too harshly was that they could seek refuge abroad. In 1202 Hakon Sverresson was elected king so swiftly and successfully that the Baglar lost most of their support, and a group of Birkibeinar assisted by local peasants ambushed and killed the Baglar king and his retinue. The saga states that the Baglar 'fled away, some to Sveaveldi, some to Denmark, others to their relatives, some urged quarter from King Hakon. The whole group was then dissolved, and there was good peace'.[11] However, the subsequent events demonstrated that this was a euphemism, as shortly thereafter Erling Stonewall appeared in Skanør in Scania and claimed to be a son of Magnus Erlingsson:

> When the Baglar heard this [that a son of King Magnus was there], those who previously had been with the Baglar tried to find him. When they met, they offered to raise an armed group and take him as their leader. They said that they would not be short of men when it is noticed that we have a son of King Magnus as leader.[12]

There evidently existed a pool of potential opponents outside Norway awaiting the right occasion to strike. They stayed calm so long as Hakon Sverresson was king, probably because he had widespread support. Accordingly, in that instance Erling refused to be their king. In the long version, he argued that 'all people are now in friendship with King Hakon and therefore I have little desire to start such an enterprise without a larger force than I can now expect', whereas in the short version he argued that 'he did not want to raise a *flokkr* against King Hakon or make war in the country as long as he [Hakon] was king of Norway'.[13] However, as soon

---

11 *Bǫglunga sǫgur*, p. 10. Only the long version has this reference in full: 'flydde, en part til Suerrig, en part til Danmarck, oc en part til deres Frender, oc nogne søgte forligelse hos King Hagen, oc bleff da alt det Folck oc den hob adspred oc forstøret'. The short version gives a briefer account which, however, does not contradict the longer one: 'Eftir þat eyddisk flokkrinn allr. Stukku þeir ór landi er mest váru sakbitnir, sumir suðr til Danmerkr en sumir lengra braut'.
12 *Bǫglunga sǫgur*, p. 14. Once again L is denser: 'Der de adsprede Bagler, som vaare komne mange der til Marcket, det hørde, da sellede de sig til hannem, oc vilde tagit hannem til deris Høffding, oc sagde sig ville faa Folck nock, naar de hafde en Høffding som vaar Kong Magni Søn'. S only has 'Buðusk honum þegar margir menn til fylgðar'.
13 *Bǫglunga sǫgur*, p. 14, L: 'Kong Hagen hafuer yndist oc venskab aff alt Folcket i Norrig, oc som mig er sagt, er Baglernis Høfdinger den største part gaaet hannem til haande; thi begynder jeg ingenlunde denne handel med saa liden mact oc styrcke'. S: 'hann sagðisk eigi vilja reisa flokk móti Hákoni konungi eða gera óróa í landi meðan hann væri konunr yfir Nóregi'. This was much the same as the way in which King Sverre had (allegedly) refused to become leader of the Birkibeinar in 1177 (*Sverris saga*, pp. 14–16).

as Hakon Sverresson died the following winter, the situation changed. According to the saga, the Baglar were re-established because now the former Baglar who had formerly been granted quarter by Hakon Sverresson 'did not expect to gain any peace from the Birkibeinar'[14] — probably hinting at the unrelenting attitude they expected of Hakon Galen.[15] Yet it must have been more important that the reason why Erling had refused the offer in 1203 — namely the popularity of Hakon Sverresson — had vanished. As the Birkibeinar were weakened by divided leadership, the prospect of Baglar success was altogether more likely, not least since the Danish king supported them. The opportunity to go abroad, in particular to Denmark, was an important 'safety valve' for conquered parties in Norway and served to maintain a balance of power between contending parties.[16]

We should therefore make a sharp distinction between what applies respectively at the intentional and the structural level of the struggles between Birkibeinar and Baglar in this period. People do not need to be peaceful to maintain a stable society, because this is a matter of how violence *works* in society. On the level of intentions, both parties opted for victory. In our period, the Birkibeinar were most often on the offensive, as in 1203, 1205, and 1207 when they managed to expel the Baglar from Viken (this strategy had also been pursued by King Sverre in his last three years as king). Yet, if the Baglar had the opportunity, such as in 1206, they pursued the goal of domination with no less determination than the Birkibeinar (above all, this had been the case in the years 1198–1199, in an earlier phase of the war, when the Birkibeinar were confined to Trøndelag).[17]

However, seen in a structural perspective, the dominant pattern that emerges from the struggle is one of balance between the two opposing forces. The Birkibeinar usually had the upper hand, but it was a big leap from being *relatively* stronger to becoming *supreme*. In *Bǫglunga sǫgur*, attempts to secure supremacy repeatedly failed, and resulted in the opposing group resorting to guerrilla warfare or seeking foreign support. The underlying cause as to why supremacy failed was that in order to stay in power in an area, a group had to be present there. They could not rely on the local population or on a smaller armed group to hold an area if confronted by the enemy. Hence, in order to be sufficiently strong, they

---

14 *Bǫglunga sǫgur*, p. 19. Both versions have this meaning, but S depicts a more unrelenting attitude of the Birkibeinar: 'þótti þeim þá sér ekki friðvænligt með Birkibeinum'; in L: 'strax søgte alle Baglerne til hannem som hafde værit hos hannem om Vinteren tilforn'.
15 A similar unrelenting attitude marked Erling Skakke, and Snorre claims that it contributed to keep opposition groups together (*Heimskringla* 3, pp. 241–42).
16 See Chapter 2. Brathetland emphasizes the foreign support, in particular from Sweden, around 1200 more than previous research has done. See Brathetland, 'Nettverksmakt', pp. 286–94, 323–27. See also Orning, *Constant Crisis*.
17 *Sverris saga*, pp. 234–35.

had to be present with adequate numbers and leaders. A group could divide its forces into sub-groups, and in some cases the groups managed to operate with numerous armies or fleets that were efficiently able to face the opposing group, but such division of forces was a risky strategy that made the group vulnerable.[18]

This implies that each group had to prioritize what region(s) they wanted to hold, and that the opposing group could take advantage of this and seek out the region(s) not prioritized. Moreover, it took two parties to make a confrontation. It has often been stated that in naval warfare the principle of military dominance applied, so that the group with the most and best ships ruled most of the coastline and could tap it for economic and military resources.[19] However, fleets could avoid confrontation if they were insecure about their strength vis-à-vis their opponents'. This dynamic became evident when the Baglar, in spite of being weakened and divided after Erling Stonewall's death early in 1207, had few problems avoiding clashes with the Birkibeinar. In this game of cat-and-mouse, the mouse was usually free to run away, and an alternative to continuing the chase was to make a compromise with the mouse. Late in 1207, the clerical leaders brought the two parties to the negotiating table, not to disturb the balance of power, but to cement it.

One could argue that the settlement between the Birkibeinar and Baglar and the resulting territorial division in 1208 ended the 'constant crisis' by formalizing the relationship into a territorial division. However, this would be confounding formal arrangements with practical policies. The tug-of-war between the Birkibeinar and Baglar continued after 1208, epitomized in the Baglar insistence on giving Filippus the title of king.[20] The struggle resurfaced in full when Hakon Hakonsson was elected king in 1217, and thereafter gave rise to a new opposition group in the Viken region: the Ribbungar.[21] Finally, the struggle between King Hakon and his second-in-command, the earl Skule Bardsson, should be interpreted as another 'constant crisis' that would persist until Skule's rebellion in 1239 which was put down the following year.[22]

'Constant crisis' is an apt description of the political struggles between the Birkibeinar and Baglar in this period. Conflicts were intense, but they were seldom conclusive. The reason was that several factors worked against one group achieving lasting dominance over the other. One is

---

18 See more in the section on the 'We-Group'.
19 This is a major point in Bagge, 'Borgerkrig og statstutvikling' (but less in *From Viking Stronghold*, p. 134).
20 *Bǫglunga sǫgur*, pp. 118–19.
21 See Arstad, 'Rex Bellicosus' on the military and political threat and strength of the Ribbungar.
22 Orning, 'Feud in the State'.

topographical. Norway was too large a realm to be effectively governed by one group, given that governing also meant being present, if not permanently, at least sufficiently that local populations felt that they were being protected efficiently against rival groups. Another factor is military. I have not analysed military resources systematically in this section, but the strategies available — plunder, battle, and fortifications — generally worked against establishing dominance on a permanent, territorial basis. Battles could be easily avoided, both on land and sea, and this period saw no major battles, only ambushes. Fortifications were seldom able to withstand sieges, and even less to control regions. Plunder was risky and an ineffective means of gaining support. Splitting up armies seldom proved to be efficient, and the same goes for using situational superiority to pursue an opponent too harshly.[23]

I have argued elsewhere that joint rulership over Norway in the period 1035–1157 should not be regarded as a sign of disorder or chaos, but rather on the contrary as characteristic of a particular dynamic that worked in favour of the groups keeping one another in check.[24] The same goes for the constant crisis characteristic of this period, as the inconclusive power struggle between Birkibeinar and Baglar in effect constituted a power balance that was quite stable, in spite of the intensity of struggles and the intentions of the parties involved. The sociopolitical factors working against supremacy will be analysed in the next two sections.

The We-Group: Who Are We Fighting for?

So far, the struggle between the Birkibeinar and Baglar has been scrutinized as a constant crisis. While my conclusions so far diverge from the usual account of this period as an unstable one, they are in line with the traditional view of regarding armed groups as the main constituents of political action. In the following, I will question the solidity of group cohesion by studying segmentary opposition at intra-group level.

The practice of creating a group, a *flokkr*, as discussed in Chapter 2, is described in our sources in most detail in connection with Erling Skakke, who established a group to oppose the power of Hakon the Broad-Shouldered in 1161.[25] This suggests that Erling's strategy of establishing a group of men with a specific purpose of overturning the group in power was a new one. Group labels were first only applied to groups opposing

---

23 See Orning, *Constant Crisis* on these military issues.
24 Orning, 'Conflict and Social (dis)order'.
25 The term *flokkr* is used a few times before 1161, but never with the same detail as with Erling. Legally, a *flokkr* consisted of at least five persons, see *Den eldre Gulatingslova* §§ 154, 168.

Erling Skakke, but from *Sverris saga* onwards all groups had names.[26] Labelling groups is peculiar to Norway in comparison to Denmark and Sweden. The use of the term *flokkr* and the labelling of such groups attest to the importance of creating political action groups, and the quarrel over names also hints that group names served as identity markers.[27]

Yet the armed groups were not massive, enclosed entities, in two respects: they were not the only identity markers, and they were not easily circumscribed. What constituted the basic glue of the group was primarily having a common leader and enemy. Still, people were not only bound to leaders but also to other men, and their enmities did not necessarily run along the same lines as group affiliations. In this section, I shall investigate tensions within each group at the top level of leadership. The subsequent section will scrutinize overlapping connections between the groups, partly by looking at the connections between 'hardliners' and 'softliners', partly in terms of personal relationships which transcended group boundaries. I will treat the power struggles among the Birkibeinar and the Baglar separately, not because they operated according to different principles, but because it gives a tighter analysis of each camp. Birkibeinar tensions were most intense from 1202 to 1204, whilst among the Baglar tensions were most apparent from 1204 to 1207. Yet the constant crisis as a process of grouping, sub-grouping and re-grouping within both groups lasted for the whole period from 1202 to 1208 (after which it continued too, first during the co-rule of two kings and then after 1217 more candidly under the rule of a sole monarch).[28]

---

26 Opponents of Erling Skakke were labelled Markusmenn, Hettusveinar, and Birkibeinar, see Helle, *Norge blir en stat*, pp. 69–72.

27 Labels brought along expectations about how to behave and contributed to forming people's identities. The term 'Birkibeinar' (Birchlegs) signifies 'using birch as shoes'. This humble origin Sverre used actively in his efforts to mobilize his men, and to remind them of their social climbing and of the courage expected from them. 'Baglar' means bishop's hats, and referred to this group's close connection to the Church, a bond that they exploited actively in their fight against Sverre as a heretic. The 'Eyjarskeggjar', the Island Beards, were called so because they were established in the Orkneys, but the saga adds that 'they wanted to be called Gullbeinar' (*Sverris saga*, p. 181), meaning 'gold bones'. Magnus Erlingsson's group was labelled 'Heklungar', signifying 'inheritors of a cloak', originating in that they found a cloak after an old beggar woman filled with silver (*Sverris saga*, pp. 65–66). One might suppose that Magnus was not very content with this association, but given that the saga was written from their enemies' perspective, we shall never know if they themselves protested against this name and labelled themselves differently.

28 See Orning, 'Feud in the State', on the informal power struggle between Hakon Hakonsson and Skule Bardsson up to 1240.

Constant Crisis among the Birkibeinar

As also emphasized in Chapters 2 and 3, a king's death was always a decisive and pivotal moment in medieval history, because power to a large degree was personalized. This was certainly the case when Sverre died after a quarter of a century as king. As a king, Sverre constantly had to convince the Birkibeinar about which course of action to pursue,[29] but his leadership of the group was never disputed in his saga. His death demonstrates how vulnerable the situation was for the Birkibeinar — not only in terms of the threat from the Baglar, but also from inner divisions. Sverre himself had prepared for the scenario by writing letters making his son Hakon his successor.[30] The immediate problem after he passed away was that Hakon was resident in Nidaros — approximately two weeks' journey from Sverre's place of death in Tønsberg. As soon as Sverre had died, his sister's sons Hakon Galen and Peter Stoype sailed as quickly as possible from Tønsberg to Nidaros carrying Sverre's letters to Hakon.[31] Upon arrival in Nidaros, they were immediately asked by the Birkibeinar there about the king's disease, and they responded that the king was feeling much better.[32] Then they got to talk with Hakon alone and told him about his father's death and gave him the letters. After that, Hakon gathered the retinue, told them the news and was acclaimed leader of the retinue, and subsequently the Eyrathing was summoned and Hakon was made king.[33] A king's death opened up a scenario where conflict could erupt at any level, and as this episode illustrates, the innermost circle only encompassed the king's closest relatives. Even the retinue could turn against the king at vulnerable moments. On this occasion, the Birkibeinar managed to quash uncertainties quickly by making Hakon king before anyone had time to protest.

Yet tensions within the Birkibeinar camp were not defused once and for all. Now a new conflict flared up within the Birkibeinar group, caused by the widowed queen Margrethe. On Sverre's death, she had immediately travelled from Nidaros to Oslo, intending to go to Götaland, where she had her relatives — she was daughter of the deceased Swedish King Erik the Saint. An even more critical matter was that she brought along her and Sverre's daughter Kristin. Therefore Peter Stoype sailed to Oslo and

---

29 Bagge, *From Gang Leader*, pp. 20–51.
30 *Sverris saga*, pp. 278–79.
31 *Bǫglunga sǫgur* here refers to *Sverris saga*, where the letter is set up by Sverre on his deathbed. It concerned the governance of the realm and declared that Sverre had no other sons alive than Hakon (*Sverris saga*, pp. 278–79).
32 *Bǫglunga sǫgur*, p. 4.
33 *Bǫglunga sǫgur*, p. 4.

managed to separate Kristin from her mother, using trickery.[34] Margrete was furious but could do nothing; according to the saga, she screamed her accusations at Peter while sailing away to her relatives.[35]

A reasonable hypothesis is that the manoeuvre of forcefully separating Margrete from her daughter would alienate her from the Birkibeinar, as she had powerful relatives in Sweden.[36] However, having Margrete at court was evidently prioritized, as King Hakon wrote a letter urging her and her daughter to come back, stating that, 'they should receive the largest honour by him'.[37] Margrete accepted the invitation and came back to the Birkibeinar together with her niece Kristin Nikolasdatter before Christmas 1203. King Hakon went far in trying to please her. He had prepared a separate table for her, but 'the queen seldom ate together with the king'.[38] On Christmas Eve, tension escalated into open confrontation when she did not turn up for the feast. Ultimately she did appear, The king got his will in the end, but shortly afterwards the king died; all indications pointed towards poisoning, with Margrete as the instigator. She had to clear herself through an ordeal by hot iron, but the ordeal failed and Margrete had to leave the retinue, this time for good.[39]

Since Margrete had been the source of conflict in the Birkibeinar camp, one could imagine that her departure would have cooled tensions among the Birkibeinar. However, conflicts continued to erupt after she was gone. Partly the repercussions stemmed from her interference, since after Peter Stoype had kidnapped Kristin Sverresdatter from Margrete, the long version of the saga tells that Margrete 'harboured great hatred towards Peter Stoype and all those who had come to take the maiden, but she made herself good friends with Hakon Galen and put her trust in him

---

34 *Bǫglunga sǫgur*, pp. 7–8. L spells out the dangers inherent in Margrete taking Kristin out of the country: 'Birkebenerne siuntis det icke være raadeligt, at Kongens Daatter skulde drage aff Landet' (*Bǫglunga sǫgur*, p. 7). S only refers to the forced take-over of Kristin: 'tók hana at nauðigri dróttningu' (*Bǫglunga sǫgur*, p. 8).

35 *Bǫglunga sǫgur*, pp. 7–8.

36 However, in 1202 Sverker the younger was in power in Sweden. Margrete belonged to the competing royal line — the Erik lineage. See Line, *Kingship and State Formation in Sweden*, pp. 104–07.

37 *Bǫglunga sǫgur*, p. 11. This is only referred in L: 'de skulde blifue holden i største act oc ære hos hannem'.

38 *Bǫglunga sǫgur*, p. 15. The formulation is from L: 'det skede sielden at hun gick til Bords med Kongen'. It also adds that 'hand lod holde hende et besynderligt Kiøcken oc Bord', underlining the break of norms. S is shorter, focusing on the bad relationship between the two of them: 'Lagðisk heldr þungt á með þeim Hákoni konungi' (*Bǫglunga sǫgur*, p. 16). On norms for feasting, see articles in Jezierski and others, *Rituals, Performatives and Political Order*.

39 *Bǫglunga sǫgur*, p. 10.

in all cases that she considered important'.[40] After Margrete left, Hakon Galen continued to have a close relationship with her relative Kristin Nikolasdatter. This indicates that Margrete created a split in the core of the Birkibeinar faction or exploited an already-existing rift.

However, Margrete might have been a symptom rather than a cause of the Birkibeinar tensions. Peter Stoype and Hakon Galen had operated in tandem to secure the smooth transfer of power from Sverre to his son Hakon, as well as on previous occasions,[41] but the prospect of conflict between the two is not in itself very surprising. For one thing, brothers fought one another without hesitation for the throne, as with the sons of Harald Gille in the 1150s (see Chapter 2) or the grandsons of Svend Estridsen in Denmark in the 1130s (see Chapter 3). For another, it probably helped fuel the conflict that the brothers came from different branches of Sverre's already very disputed family. Hakon Galen was the son of Sverre's sister Cecilia, the daughter of King Sigurd Haraldsson, and Folkvid lawman in Vermland. Cecilia had divorced Folkvid after Sverre became king; she went to Norway and married the magnate Bard Guttormsson from Rein in Trøndelag. This branch of the family was very powerful, in particular in Trøndelag. Peter Stoype was the son of one of Sverre's sisters from the Faroes.[42] Coming from Sverre's maternal line on the one hand gave him stronger connections to Sverre, but on the other hand he had less power and limited networks in Norway, as his grandfather was Unas the comb-maker from the Faroes, and his grandmother Gunnhild's relationship to King Sigurd was openly disputed even in Sverre's presence.[43] Thus, whereas Hakon Galen prospered as a result of family ties to the uppermost elite in Trøndelag, Peter Stoype could only draw on his connection to the deceased king. However, at some time he strengthened his networks by marrying Ingeborg, daughter of the former opponent King Magnus Erlingsson, even if it is uncertain how a bond with the opposing royal family would help here.[44]

The tension between Hakon and Peter intensified after the sudden death of Hakon Sverresson in 1204 after ruling for only one and a half

---

40 *Bǫglunga sǫgur*, p. 15. 'Dronningen hafde stor had oc vrede til Peter Steiper, oc alle de andre som hafde værit med hannem Øster til Oslo oc hente hendis Dotter fra hende, Men hun maatte saare vel lide Hagen Galin, oc hafde aldhendis trøst til hannem'. S has nothing on this.
41 Hakon and Peter also operated in tandem against the Baglar in 1199 (*Sverris saga*, p. 237). Peter was leading the guests in 1201 (*Sverris saga*, p. 268).
42 *Sverris saga*, p. 5.
43 Peter is mentioned first in 1193 as a Birkibeinar leader, possibly already in 1184 if he can be the Svina-Peter mentioned who had the same by-name as his father (*Sverris saga*, p. 148). See Helle, 'Gunnhild 1': 'en av hans yngre søstre ble gift med en Svina-Stefan og med ham fikk sønnen Peter Støyper, kanskje identisk med den Svina-Peter som i *Sverris saga* opptrer som en fullvoksen mann 1184'.
44 *Bǫglunga sǫgur*, p. 28.

years. To be sure, the saga does not record outright strife, as it records neutrally the result decided by the bishop, the retinue and the 'best men' in Bergen. The shorter version refers more magnates, six in total, with Hakon and Peter as the leading ones.[45] In the longer version, a more detailed arrangement is described: Hakon Galen was to govern the realm and the retinue on behalf of the new king — the infant Guttorm, son of Sverre's son Sigurd lavard, whereas Peter Stoype and Einar Kongsmag were to foster the king and watch over him.[46]

Moreover, they sent a letter to Nidaros stating that Inge Bardsson was to govern Trøndelag.[47] Inge was brother of Hakon Galen with the same mother (Sverre's sister), but Inge's father was the magnate Bard Guttormsson from Trøndelag. The tensions involved are revealed in the concluding remark in the longer saga about the election: 'In this way they managed to keep the group united'.[48] It is no doubt that Hakon Galen was now the strong man, and that this was not something everyone was comfortable with. No one could match Hakon's combination of lineage and experience in having led the retinue for several years. Peter Stoype had similar experience, but a weaker pedigree (due to the reduced legitimacy and power of Sverre's maternal line), whereas Guttorm and Inge were in better dynastic positions but had much less experience than Hakon.

The election of Guttorm as king served to balance these various considerations. On the one hand, it allowed Hakon Galen a prominent position, which was necessary in order to satisfy him, as well as to be able to counter the military threat from the Baglar. On the other hand, the appointments of Peter Stoype and Einar Kongsmag as guardians to the king, and of Inge as governor in Trøndelag, served to counter the threat from Hakon Galen to become too powerful.

This carefully crafted arrangement ended abruptly with King Guttorm's death later in 1204. Once again, suspicion of poisoning came to the fore, now with Kristin Nikolasdatter, Hakon Galen's close accomplice, as the prime suspect. However, the suspicions never resulted in any trial, as with Margrete, suggesting that this might have been just rumours — in

---

45 *Bǫglunga sǫgur*, pp. 18–19: 'þat sama vár tóku Birkibeinar sér konung þar í Björgyn, son Sigurðar lávarðs, þann er Guthormr hét. Hann var þá barn at aldri. En fyrir flokkinum váru þessir höfðingjar: Hákonn galinn, systursonr Sverris konungs, Pétr steypir, annarr systursonr hans, hann átti Ingibjörgu, dóttur Magnúss konungs. Þessir váru ok höfðingjar með flokkinum; Sigurðr konungsfrændi, Eyvindr prestsmágr, Einarr konungsmágr, Hróarr konungsfrændi ok marta annarra ríkismanna' (*Bǫglunga sǫgur*, p. 7).
46 *Bǫglunga sǫgur*, p. 18: 'skulde Hagen Galin regere Riget oc det Kongelige Hof paa hans vegne, oc Peter Steiper oc Einer Kongens maag skulde opfostre oc take vare paa Kongen'.
47 *Bǫglunga sǫgur*, p. 19.
48 *Bǫglunga sǫgur*, pp. 18–19: 'i saa maade holt de Krigsfolcket til sammen' (only in L).

particular since the saga author seems to be somewhat biased against Hakon Galen.[49]

When debating who should be elected king after Guttorm, most people seem to have wanted Hakon Galen as king.[50] However, the swiftness and efficiency that had characterized the elections of Hakon Sverresson and Guttorm Sigurdsson backfired, probably because of diverging opinions among the leading men. The saga attributes the dissent to Archbishop Eirik Ivarsson, partly over a non-specified conflict, partly as a result of Hakon's close connection with Kristin Nikolasdatter.[51] The absence of a consensus amongst the inner circle of magnates and prelates resulted in the summoning of the popular assembly, the traditional king-making assembly at Eyrathing. The late and reluctant involvement of the assembly shows how much royal elections now had become a matter to be decided by the elite. The summoning of the popular assembly opened up the field for unpredictable and therefore potentially dangerous measures for the ones involved, since now discussions were to take place in a public forum, not in private.[52] According to the longer version, the candidates were: Hakon Galen, Inge Bardsson, Sigurd kongsfrende, Roar kongsfrende, and Peter Stoype.[53] Out of these, all but Roar had the same position as King Sverre's sister's sons,[54] but they were mentioned in two rounds: first the offspring of Sverre's paternal line (Hakon, Inge, Sigurd), then those from his maternal one (Peter, Roar). Peter Stoype had a potential advantage in being married to Ingeborg, daughter of the former opponent King Magnus Erlingsson — at least the relationship was by now worth considering, in the context of the forthcoming election.[55]

The magnates still had the option to find a consensus candidate, but they did not succeed.[56] The result was that the decision was left for the peasants at the assembly. The field was by now limited to three contenders:

---

49 Bǫglunga sǫgur, p. 25. See Lunden, Norge under Sverreætten, pp. 153–54, 167, on Hakon Galen as the candidate for war.

50 In S, both retainers and peasants wanted Hakon as king: 'Vildu flestir liðsmenn ok bændr Hákon til konungs kjósa' (Bǫglunga sǫgur, p. 28). In L, however, only the magnates favored Hakon: 'den første part gafue deris stemme oc samtycke paa Hagen Jarl Galin' (Bǫglunga sǫgur, p. 27).

51 Bǫglunga sǫgur, pp. 27–28. It might have to do with the reconciliation that Hakon Sverresson had made with the Church in 1202. For the reconciliation, see Norges Gamle Love Indtil 1387: 1, pp. 444–45. Coming from a magnate family in Trøndelag, Eirik probably also had personal reasons for supporting Inge, who came from the same region.

52 See Althoff, Spielregeln, on the pre-planning of such meetings.

53 Bǫglunga sǫgur, p. 28.

54 We don't know about Roar's pedigree, but he might have been son of one of Sverre's (half-)sisters at the Faroes, putting him on par with Peter. See Brathetland, 'Roar Kongsfrende'.

55 Bǫglunga sǫgur, p. 28.

56 Bǫglunga sǫgur, pp. 28–29.

Hakon, Inge, and Sigurd. This narrowing down reveals that the decisive element for eligibility was to be offspring from Sverre's paternal line. Sigurd was considered fair-minded but not strong. The argument in favour of Hakon was that he was an able leader who was capable of fighting the foreign army threatening Norway, and the magnates wanted him as king.[57] However, the peasants preferred Inge whose father came from Trøndelag, and in the longer version it is added that they did not want a man with Gothic lineage (Hakon Galen was son of the Swede Folkvid) as king.[58] The peasants won, and Inge was elected king.

How unpredictable was this result? Maybe not so much as it may seem, since the assembly was held in Trøndelag, where Inge Bardsson had his power base, as his father Bard was a leading magnate. It is a plausible hypothesis that the tactic of involving the popular assembly was instigated by Inge's supporters in order to remove the decision from the retinue, where a majority favoured Hakon. The fear that Hakon Galen would become too strong soon turned out to be very real, as when the followers in the royal retinue were to renew their oath of allegiance to the king [Inge], the long version states that there was 'murmur among Hakon earl's friends and followers',[59] who claimed he was better suited to lead the army than Inge. They evidently had the power to back their claim, because the result was that Hakon was appointed earl and leader of the army, and was to have half of the income of Norway. Hence, in reality the two were put on a par. Whereas Inge had the highest formal position, Hakon had the military power, and economically they were on equal terms.

After 1204, the Birkibeinar entered a more stable period in that King Inge served as king until his death in 1217. However, in practice nothing changed very much, because up to Hakon Galen's death in 1214 the leadership of the Birkibeinar was, for all practical purposes, divided. Moreover, after the settlement with the Baglar in 1208 they shared power with the Baglar leader Filippus Simonsson. Hakon strengthened his position by marrying Kristin Nikolasdatter in 1205, thus solidifying the link to Sweden.[60] One reason for the marriage taking place then, after several years of a close relationship, might be that Archbishop Eirik, who had been an opponent of the connection between Hakon and 'the Swedish lady', had resigned earlier in 1205, and his successor Tore Gudmundsson proved to be a more pragmatic man.[61] Moreover, Hakon's rival Peter Stoype moved

---

57 This is strongest formulated in L: 'Lænshøfdingerne vilde icke andet, end at hafue Hagen til Konge' (Bǫglunga sǫgur, p. 28). S has a more modest version: 'var þat ráð liðsmanna at Hákoni bræðr sínum gæfi Ingi konungr jarlsnafn' (Bǫglunga sǫgur, p. 30).
58 Bǫglunga sǫgur, p. 28.
59 Bǫglunga sǫgur, p. 29: 'ny knur for Hagen Jarls skyld'.
60 Bǫglunga sǫgur, p. 36. The Swedish connection was reinforced by the presence of Erik Knutsson at the wedding (Bǫglunga sǫgur, pp. 35–36), future king of Sweden.
61 Bǫglunga sǫgur, p. 78.

to Stavanger that year as *sýslumaðr* to succeed Einar Kongsmag, who had been ambushed and executed by the Baglar.[62] This position was no promotion for Peter, as it removed him from the power struggle, where he (and Einar) had played central roles as foster fathers for King Inge.

Yet between 1204 and 1208 no outright tensions appear in the relationship between Inge and Hakon. The reason is probably that the saga focused on the struggle against the Baglar in this period, and that the threat from the Baglar encouraged internal cohesion. We see a clear pattern in the Birkibeinar camp in these years, where Hakon Galen acted as supreme military commander and spearhead against the Baglar, while Inge stayed behind as a backup, mostly on home ground in Trøndelag. The division of forces could render the Birkibeinar vulnerable. After the Baglar had been chased to Denmark in 1205, they returned to Norway in the winter and managed to pass Hakon unnoticed and ambush Inge in Trøndelag.[63] In 1207, too, the Baglar had ample scope for operating in-between the Birkibeinar armies positioned in Oslo and Bergen. Yet even if the Birkibeinar were not altogether successful in fighting the Baglar, being able to split into two fairly strong and coherent armies was a strength, not a weakness.[64]

Joint or divided leadership created a lot of tensions that made for dramatic encounters. However, this condition of 'constant crisis' within the Birkibeinar group constituted an efficient form of governance, partly because it kept power-hungry leaders at bay, and partly as it allowed for forces to be spread out. In the following more detailed discussion about the Baglar, we shall see that it also was conducive for arriving at sound political solutions.

Constant Crisis among the Baglar

Constant crisis in terms of inner-group tensions and conflicts was not peculiar to the Birkibeinar alone. It was equally prevalent among the Baglar, although it took on a somewhat different form as a result of the group being more on the defensive and involving foreign actors more actively than the Birkibeinar did. *Sverris saga* depicted the Baglar group on the verge of collapse as the result of Sverre's lengthy siege of the Baglar at Berget in 1202. The besieged Baglar leader Reidar Sendemann sent desperate messages to the faction in Oppland requesting that they come

---

62 *Bǫglunga sǫgur*, pp. 36–38.
63 *Bǫglunga sǫgur*, pp. 56–57.
64 In the autumn of 1205, the Birkibeinar chased the Baglar out of Viken, and Inge thereafter sailed to Trøndelag, while Hakon Galen ventured all the way to Halland to track down the Baglar, staying in Bergen for the wintertime (*Bǫglunga sǫgur*, pp. 39–46). Two years later, the Birkibeinar once more sailed to Viken. Now Inge remained in Viken to keep the Baglar out, while Hakon Galen travelled to Bergen (*Bǫglunga sǫgur*, pp. 90–94).

to their rescue, but to no avail as the group on Oppland considered the chances of defeating Sverre to be small.[65] Here the internal split among the Baglar proved to be beneficial for the group as a whole, since instead of aiding their companions, which would probably have led to defeat, the division opened up new fronts in other places. *Sverris saga* depicts the Baglar manoeuvres as a failure, but the less biased *Bǫglunga sǫgur* shows that they were quite successful, as the saga starts out by claiming that the Baglar were in power in 1202 on the western coast all the way from Bergen to Trondheim.[66]

However, the swift and successful election of Hakon Sverresson as Birkibeinar king put the Baglar under increased pressure.[67] Seeing that they were bound to lose, Baglar retainers and local peasants joined forces and killed King Inge Bardsson on Helgøya.[68] Here again it is likely that division within the Baglar camp fulfilled a productive purpose, in that it prevented them from fighting a struggle that they were bound to lose.

Hakon Sverresson's sudden death in 1204 created new opportunities. Now a rift surfaced between the two leaders Erling Stonewall and Bishop Nikolas Arnesson which was to persist with varying levels of intensity until Erling's death in 1207. Erling's main asset was that he was the son of a king, namely Magnus Erlingsson, even though this was disputed among the Birkibeinar.[69] This made him a candidate for royal power, a candidature which was warmly embraced by the Baglar from the very start. Already when Erling first appeared in Denmark in the summer of 1203 and claimed to be a king's son, the Baglar offered him the throne. At that time, he refused the offer, arguing that Hakon Sverresson was king of Norway (short version) or that he was too strong in Norway (long version).[70] It is noteworthy that the shorter version argues from a perspective of legitimacy (Hakon was acclaimed king), whereas the longer version brings along a purely pragmatic argument for not accepting the throne (the Birkibeinar are too strong). Regardless, Hakon Sverresson's death changed the situation, and a group of Baglar sailed to Erling in Copenhagen: 'Then

---

65 As the leader of the Oppland faction Sigurd Jarlsson said: 'Let us not run right into hell even if Reidar wants to show us the way'. (*Sverris saga*, p. 274).
66 *Bǫglunga sǫgur*, p. 3.
67 L states that 'their group became smaller each day, as all the people submitted to King Hakon' ('bleff deris hob dagligen jo mindre oc mindre, thi alt Landsfolcket gaff sig under K. Hagen', *Bǫglunga sǫgur*, p. 7). S has nothing on this.
68 The joining of forces is clearest in L: 'Bønderne paa Opland forsamlede sig met nogne aff Kongens suorne Mend' (*Bǫglunga sǫgur*, p. 9). However, also S has both groups contributing to the homicide: 'þar var hann svikinn af sínum mönnum sjálfs [...] Ingi var drepinn af bóndum'. Yet it puts more emphasis on a Gunnar, who betrayed him.
69 *Hákonar saga Hákonarsonar* made a huge point in 'proving' the falsity of Erling's ancestry (*Hákonar saga Hákonarsonar I*, pp. 308–09). However, this doubt was probably not very different from the one associated with King Sverre.
70 *Bǫglunga sǫgur*, p. 14, short and long version respectively.

a *flokkr* was established. When this news was spread, many of the men came who had previously followed the Baglar'.[71] They then sent for their friends in Viken who came to Aalborg.

Nikolas Arnesson was Erling's main rival. He was not a king's son, but as the son of the queen widower Ingrid Ragvaldsdatter and the magnate Arne from Ståreim, he was part of the uppermost Norwegian elite with close bonds to the royal family; for instance, King Inge Haraldsson (the Hunchback, d. 1161) was his half-brother. He was also related to the Danish King Valdemar II (the Victorious).[72] However, Valdemar was equally closely related to Erling.[73] Nikolas was appointed bishop in Oslo in 1190, a position he later combined with the royal office of *sýslumaðr*.[74] He had supported the Baglar since they were formed in 1196. As a bishop, Nikolas was of course excluded as a royal candidate, so he supported his relative Filippus Simonsson, son of his sister Margrete. Hence, Nikolas was a major player as a result of his lineage, offices and networks, including transnational ones, and a man firmly situated on the anti-Birkibeinar side.[75]

The opposition between Erling and Nikolas/Filippus certainly was an acute political issue of power and support that could easily weaken the Baglar. However, it can also be seen as a more constructive 'constant crisis' in that they balanced one another and involved complementary legitimizing resources. Their potential reciprocal strength can be seen already at the royal election. As/if a king's son, Erling profited from his royal blood. However, his descent was disputed, and as a bishop Nikolas possessed the spiritual means for deciding the issue through an ordeal. This gave Nikolas a power he did not hesitate to grab, and the saga explores the conflicts and negotiations at great length. It would be obvious to interpret the internal conflicts in which the contenders did their best to outmanoeuvre one another as a sign of Baglar weakness. This particularly goes for Nikolas, whose intrigues were laid bare in the saga in a rather unflattering fashion.[76]

---

71 *Bǫglunga sǫgur*, p. 19. S: 'þá hófsk flokkrinn. En er þat spurðisk þá dreif mart manna til þeira, þat er áðr hafði fylgt Bǫglum'; L: 'Der denne Tidende spurdis til Danmarck, da vaar Erling Stenveg i Kiøbenhafn, oc strax søgte alle Baglerne til hannem som hafde værit hos hannem om Vinteren tilforn, oc fick hand snart en Flock forsamlet'.
72 Valdemar's grandmother Kristin was sister of Nikolas' grandfather Ragvald, who were children of Inge Stenkilsson. Thus, they were second cousins.
73 Valdemar's mother Ingeborg was a sister of Erling's great grandmother Malmfrid.
74 *Sverris saga*, pp. 170–71.
75 See Brathetland, '*Nettverksmakt*', pp. 294–97, 305–10 on clerical networks.
76 Both versions of Bǫglunga sǫgur go into much detail on this issue. There are no big differences, although L is as usual more detailed than S (*Bǫglunga sǫgur*, pp. 20–24). Erling was eager to undergo an ordeal, but Nikolas postponed the case several times, because he wanted it to take place in the presence of the Danish king Valdemar, whom he expected would back him up. However, Valdemar initially declared that he would support Erling, but as a result of Nikolas' insistence that Erling was an impostor who would only arouse dissent in Norway, Valdemar agreed to come to Norway to support Filippus, provided that they

However, if we leave aside the details of the power struggle and focus instead on the *result* of these entanglements, the interpretation changes. The intrigues were not futile, as they brought along a solution where the two main rivals came to an agreement to share power, whereby Erling's controversial royal pedigree was confirmed; and they even managed to gain the support of the Danish king for their case. The compromise solution signalled Baglar cohesion, not fragmentation.

The tension among the Baglar leaders was not over with the election, but on the contrary formed part of the 'constant crisis' that characterized the Baglar leadership in this period. In the autumn they sailed to Bergen, and here Erling, according to the saga, made a quite comical figure, and his opinion was disregarded in favour of Nikolas' at a meeting among the ship leaders.[77] Thus, Erling's overwhelming support at the royal election did not guarantee him the dominant voice thereafter. Yet, these discussions were not necessarily a symptom that the Baglar were weakened. For one thing, Nikolas was a much more experienced war leader than Erling, and there are good reasons to assume that Nikolas' alternative was the better one. Nikolas' superior advice emerges more clearly the following spring, when the Birkibeinar sailed to Viken with a large fleet and many Baglar were intent on resistance. Here he argued that 'there was no other option than to withdraw to Denmark and not fight the superior Birkibeinar force'.[78] This was probably a correct judgement, as it was not until they had built ships in the winter 1205–1206 that we hear that the Baglar were able to compete with the Birkibeinar at sea.

A second advantage of having several leaders was demonstrated in that the Baglar were able to split the group into three operative units, led by Erling, Nikolas, and Filippus respectively. One faction travelled up north to Nidaros where Erling was acclaimed king, another went to the western part of Norway conducting surprise attacks, while a third faction travelled more slowly from Denmark.[79] Not all of these operations were equally

---

themselves consented. Arriving in Norway, however, Valdemar discovered that the Baglar leaders and the local peasants objected to Filippus, as they wanted a king's son as their king. Whereas Nikolas had intended Valdemar to intervene as arbiter in the royal election, the King's support for Erling now forced him to change tactics. This involved seeking out Erling in private, telling him that Valdemar would not support him unless he succeeded in proving his royal lineage, making this approval conditional on Nikolas' cooperation, which again was made conditional on Filippus being appointed earl. Valdemar himself was suspicious of Nikolas now: he was keen on seeing that Erling succeeded in the ordeal and had the church guarded by armed followers, but Nikolas was still in control, as he was the one checking whether Erling's hand was unaffected by the hot iron.

77 *Bǫglunga sǫgur*, pp. 30–34.
78 *Bǫglunga sǫgur*, p. 39. Here S and L are fairly similar. S: 'Sagði Nikolás byskup at ekki var annat ráð en fara undan suðr til Danmerkr ok berjask eigi við ofrefli'; L: 'Bisp Niclaus raadde dennem at drage til Danmarck, oc stride icke mod Ofuermacten'.
79 *Bǫglunga sǫgur*, pp. 39–43.

successful, and none of the groups had the power to confront the Birkibeinar openly. However, operating in small bands carried the advantage that they could travel incognito and launch devastating surprise attacks on the Birkibeinar in many places simultaneously. A precondition for this guerrilla warfare was split leadership combined with the professional element.

A unique insight into the decision-making process among the Baglar is given in the saga description of their expedition from Viken to Nidaros in April 1206. First the tactic of sailing northwards was discussed, and four ship commanders refused to go, in spite of Erling's request.[80] Nearby Bergen the ship leaders had a meeting, where the majority, including the king, wanted to attack Hakon Galen in town without warning, but Reidar Sendemann objected and was heard.[81] Approaching Nidaros, Arnbjorn Jonsson and Reidar wanted to wait for two ships which were delayed, but then Erling received plaudits for attacking while they were still unnoticed. In the following meeting, Lodin Stallare suggested a strategy for the attack that passed uncontested.[82]

The constant haggling about decisions among the Baglar during this campaign might look like a sign of weak leadership, in particular since there seems to have been no predictability over who had the final say. For instance, King Erling sometimes got his will, other times not, and the same goes for the other leaders. However, this conclusion should be qualified. First, as mentioned in the previous case, this 'split leadership' allowed the Baglar to divide their forces into smaller parts that worked effectively by themselves. As such, it can be interpreted as a lesson in how spreading responsibility fostered accountability. Second, as long as it did not split the group, discussing matters without one person having the automatic final say was probably a good way of finding the optimal decisions.[83] This emerges clearly in this campaign, as the Baglar tactic of ambushing the Birkibeinar in Nidaros in April 1206 resulted in almost ninety Birkibeinar killed, which ranks second highest in terms of numbers of deaths in battle in the period 1204–1208.[84] We can of course not be sure

---

80 *Bǫglunga sǫgur*, p. 48.
81 *Bǫglunga sǫgur*, p. 51. The issue came up once more when they heard that Hakon Galen wanted a fight, the king urging for a confrontation, but once again Reidar was successful (*Bǫglunga sǫgur*, p. 51).
82 *Bǫglunga sǫgur*, p. 54. However, once again agreement was not unanimous, because as soon as the attack started, two Baglar leaders disagreed and almost started a fight among themselves (*Bǫglunga sǫgur*, p. 57).
83 The argument that open, rational discussions provide the best milieu for finding optimal solutions is made strongly by Jürgen Habermas. See Habermas, *The Theory of Communicative Action 1*, pp. 295–305.
84 In the numerically most important battle, 200 Birkibeinar were killed after a surprise attack in Moldefjord (*Bǫglunga sǫgur*, pp. 75–77).

of what would have happened had decisions been different, but there are reasons to believe that the options turned down — to attack Hakon Galen in Bergen, and to postpone the attack on Nidaros — would have been less effective than the course taken, since that would have diminished the element of surprise in the attack. In order to kill enemies, it was decisive to catch them by surprise, since an inferior force would always try to escape, and the norms for showing mercy to opponents were strong if they asked for it (see more on mercy later). The fact that the Baglar did not manage to trap King Inge was not due to failed tactics, but to chance.[85]

In support of the beneficial effects of the 'open' climate for Baglar leaders, the long-term trend after 1204 was that the Baglar never made any serious tactical blunders, and managed to mobilize resources so that they could compete on equal terms with the Birkibeinar even if their core area was smaller. The death of Erling Stonewall in the winter of 1207 put a halt to the Baglar expansion. What would have happened had he lived longer we shall never know, but it might be that the advantageous effects of the collective leadership of the Baglar could have been fully realized. At least, the last we hear before Erling died is that, upon receiving news about the Birkibeinar building ships, Erling, Reidar, and Filippus started to build ships 'that were much bigger than anyone that had been built in Norway previously'.[86]

The death of Erling unleashed both external and internal threats. His death was kept secret for a week, and meanwhile a ship sailed quickly to Filippus in Bergen to tell 'the earl the news, but to the public it was said that the Danish king wanted to meet with the earl'.[87] Just as after the death of King Sverre, only the core group was trustworthy in such a situation. However, contrary to the events after Sverre's death, the Baglar did not come to a rapid agreement about the succession. On the one hand, Earl Filippus was next in line to Erling, and he was a grown, experienced man. On the other hand, Erling had left two underage sons, who were directly descended in the male line from Magnus Erlingsson. Filippus received support from his relative Nikolas Arnesson, who rallied to Tønsberg and held a secret meeting with the most powerful peasants, allegedly obtaining

---

85 The saga depicts in vivid detail how close they came: Inge had to flee under chaotic conditions, he was close to being revealed by townspeople, and he barely managed to swim across the Nidelv to get into safety on the other side (he might even have obtained a permanent injury during the flight). Yet he escaped, and the loss of ninety men did not change the balance of power between the parties in any significant way (*Bǫglunga sǫgur*, pp. 56–63).

86 *Bǫglunga sǫgur*, p. 80. Here the two versions are in accordance. S: 'þau váru miklu meiri en fyrr hefði slík ger verit í Nóregi'; L: 'de vaare større end nogen skib hafde værit før bygt i Norrig'.

87 *Bǫglunga sǫgur*, p. 81. S: 'En alþýðunni var sagt at Danakonungr vildi hitta hann'; L: 'lode sig høre for Almuen, at Dane Kongen vilde tale med Grefuen'.

everyone's consent to the election, while Reidar Sendemann and the retinue supported Erling's sons.[88] Here it is interesting to note that as soon as the leaders realized that internal divisions could end up destroying the group, they quickly rallied behind one candidate — Filippus. To be sure, discussions within the Baglar camp continued after Filippus became king,[89] but there was a difference between conflicts putting the existence of the group in jeopardy, and ongoing tensions between leaders about what strategies and tactics to adopt.

Disagreements, divisions, and negotiation could at times be catastrophic to a group. However, under normal conditions such tensions were not symptoms of deviation from normal practice within the armed groups, but an inherent property of their smooth functioning. They serve as a reminder that 'constant crisis' among leaders was often more beneficial for military and political success than strong leadership, partly because it frequently brought better grounded decisions, and partly because, by spreading out responsibilities, it allowed for broader participation and commitment. One could argue that this view only reformulates the established standpoint that consensual governance was a better political arrangement than kingship without limits, which is often juxtaposed with tyranny. However, a main point here is that division of leadership worked better even in a context of conflicts among leaders — and thus of non-consensus/dissent, and that it even could surpass governance by able sole rulers.

Us and Them: What Are We Fighting for?

So far, I have concentrated on conflicts between or within the Birkibeinar and Baglar groups, arguing that such tensions were almost endemic and can be interpreted as a 'constant crisis' that normally served to keep a rough balance between and within the groups, attesting to a profound stability beneath the intense power struggles. However, these groups should not be viewed as closed entities. In the previous section, I showed that there were persistent tensions at their very core. In the following, we shall see that the boundaries between the groups were no more solid than their internal cohesion, because the groups were in themselves constructs of a double order. Firstly, groups were established as attempts to

---

88 *Bǫglunga sǫgur*, pp. 82–86.
89 In their first encounter with the Birkibeinar after the royal election, Filippus was overruled by Arnbjorn Jonsson who wanted to fight against the Birkibeinar — an unwise decision as it turned out (*Bǫglunga sǫgur*, p. 92). Filippus evidently did not become the too-strong leader that the Birkibeinar earl Hakon Galen threatened to turn into. The episode shows that the existence of multiple advice did not automatically mean that the best advice was taken.

create unity among people with diverging interests by emphasizing their common bond to a leader as well as their common cause against an enemy. Secondly, the groups can be viewed as products of the kings' sagas, which were written as arguments in favour of a royal way of regarding politics, implying a privileging of conflicts which took place between royally led groups operating within national borders. Hence, the Birkibeinar and Baglar were the result of kings dividing between friends and enemies, insiders and outsiders, based on royal criteria for inclusion and exclusion. To what degree did they succeed in this endeavour?

Robert Bartlett has argued that it is anachronistic to separate the state's 'public' conflicts (*bellum*) from the individuals' 'private' conflicts (*guerra*), and to 'relate the existence of enmity to the weakness of the state'.[90] Such dichotomies are modern constructs deduced from the Weberian definition of the state as having the monopoly on legitimate violence, whereas Bartlett insists that state violence in the Middle Ages is not public violence reappearing, but 'private violence writ large'.[91] However, even if 'state conflict' was no different from 'private conflict' apart from in scale, there was an inherent potential for conflict between them, because 'private' interests could run counter to those of the king/'state'. In medieval society, it was beyond a king's realistic and even theoretical ambition to act as the protector of everyone in his realm — ideological claims for a *monopoly* of royal power did not appear until after the Middle Ages, with Jean Bodin and Thomas Hobbes. Yet kings aimed to make the bonds linking other men to them more binding than bonds based on kinship, friendship, and patronage to others than themselves.[92] Such efforts to privilege royal bonds ran counter to the social logic of networks guiding people's lives, where it was the bonds and networks that each person established and maintained that were decisive in determining his or her welfare and fortunes.[93] This means that royal attempts to impose their bonds as superior to other bonds necessarily had to meet with resistance, passive or active.

Bǫglunga sǫgur does not have very many examples where royal obligations clashed with private ones. This could be interpreted as a sign that the royal bond was increasingly successful in attaining primacy, and this is indeed how it has normally been interpreted.[94] Yet, since the kings' sagas

---

90 Bartlett, 'Mortal Enmities', p. 210. See also Alice Taylor, *The Shape of the State*, pp. 1–4 on the anachronistic division between public and private agents.
91 Bartlett, 'Mortal Enmities', p. 210.
92 This is also known from Europe, for instance in the social institution 'liege homage'. See Bloch, *Feudal Society*, 1, pp. 214–18.
93 For studies applying this perspective, see Esmark and others, *Nordic Elites in Transformation II: Social Networks*; Jón Viðar Sigurðsson, *Viking Friendship*; Hermanson, *Friendship, Love, and Brotherhood*.
94 The state formation process in Norway as described in Bagge, *From Viking Stronghold*; Helle, *Norge blir en stat*; Lunden, *Norge under Sverreætten*.

saw events from a royal point of view, there is nothing surprising in that struggles were described as being fought between contending parties led by kings and motivated by their mortal enmities. The kings' sagas had a ready-made answer to the question 'what are we fighting for?': 'for the king'.[95]

What *is* surprising, given this bias, is that the sagas do occasionally render episodes where private bonds ran counter to royal ones, since that in effect undermines the image that both the kings and the sagas fed on. We can glimpse the complexities of the motivational issue through the fact that the kings knew that they had to persuade others to follow them.[96] And the reason why people followed them was not some kind of unconditional loyalty, but that they gained concrete advantages and favours from doing so. People made their own judgements, implying that they also had other motives for fighting than serving kings. The sagas were not particularly interested in pursuing such motives, but sometimes they came to the fore.

In the following, I shall divide such alternative motivations into three categories, which can roughly be attributed to specific groups. First, I shall discuss the role played by 'private' bonds, i.e. personal bonds based on kinship, friendship, and clientelism that summoned men brought along when participating in armed groups, and which could make them exploit struggles for their own personal benefit.[97] Second, the motive of material enrichment will be investigated. The quest for booty has accompanied warfare from day one, but it has often been concealed because the glory of fighting thrives better on prowess than on greed.[98] As Strickland formulates it, 'the burning of fields or attacks on peasantry gained the warrior more material profit than martial glory'.[99] Material gain was probably most important for armed retainers who had bound their destiny to that of their leader, and for whom perpetuating a condition of war was vital for their material survival. Third, I will explore this material motive on a more subtle level, namely as part of the hegemony of a martial class that based their social hegemony on military dominance — the *milites*

---

[95] Kings' sagas shared the royal goals explicitly in forewords where they set out to glorify the past deeds of great men (see prologues to *Heimskringla* and *Sverris saga*). More indirectly, the royal perspective in kings' sagas is revealed in statements that they only recounted incidents where kings were involved (*Heimskringla* 3, pp. 241–42; *Sverris saga*, pp. 111, 255; *Hákonar saga Hákonarsonar* I, p. 254).

[96] In *Sverris saga* King Sverre constantly had to argue actively to convince his men to fight for him (Bagge, *From Gang Leader*, pp. 21–50). This goes also for *Heimskringla* (Bagge, *Society and Politics*, pp. 64–100).

[97] For such a perspective on modern warfare, see Cramer, *Civil War is not a Stupid Thing*.

[98] See Verbruggen, *The Art of Warfare*, pp. 49–51; more generally in Christie and Yazigi, *Noble Ideals and Bloody Realities*.

[99] Strickland, *War and Chivalry*, p. 290.

or *nobiles* in Latin terminology.¹⁰⁰ The king in many respects belonged to this culture, but it clashed with royal aims on two points. First, the noble culture was inherently a(nta)gonistic and individualistic / self-assertive — in contrast to the image of the king as the peacemaker. Second, it was international and without fixed borders, and thus did not divide groups on a national/regnal basis. These three alternative motivations for fighting are most certainly underrepresented in the kings' sagas as compared to the royal perspective, and we should therefore not focus on their representativity or statistical significance but on their *exemplary* character.¹⁰¹

The Primacy of Personal Bonds

The kings' sagas were about kings, and saga writers explicitly stated that this ruled out incidents where kings were absent or that had no impact on royal affairs.¹⁰² However, sagas were also historical accounts about the past with a particular interest in conflict, and therefore private or individual matters were of concern if they impinged on royal politics. This is not to say that private bonds necessarily meant a clash with the bond to the king, but rather that personal issues could interfere with the priorities of the king. In April 1206, the Baglar ambushed the Birkibeinar in Nidaros and chased them relentlessly, and in the heat of the fight a Baglar discovered that he had killed an opponent who was his brother. The long version rendered his response on realizing the mistake this way: 'Then he threw away his sword and behaved badly'.¹⁰³ The reaction of the slayer leaves no doubt that it was a mistake, and shows that family ties were far more important than royal ones.¹⁰⁴

So why did brothers choose to join opposing groups, when they risked putting family members in peril? One reason may be that the risk involved in this strategy was not very high, and that they were outweighed by the advantages that this strategy offered. Normally, in a situation of choice between king and kin anyone would go for the familial ties, and that would be perfectly legitimate and understandable. *Sverris saga* relates an episode where Magnus Erlingsson told one of his supporters who had a Birkibeinar father that he would kill the father unless the son made him switch sides.¹⁰⁵ When Sverre heard about this, he wrote a letter back threatening to kill

---

100 See Duby, 'The Origins of Knighthood'.
101 Orning, *Unpredictability and Presence*, pp. 39–40, 326–29.
102 *Heimskringla* 3, pp. 241–42; *Sverris saga*, pp. 111, 255; *Hákonar saga Hákonarsonar* I, p. 254.
103 *Bǫglunga sǫgur*, p. 63. L: 'thi kastede and Suærdet fra sig, oc gremmede sig ynckeligen'.
104 At this ambush we also notice the very variable help given to the Birkibeinar by the locals (a concubine of Inge threatening to reveal his hideout) and even professionals (a man refusing to help Inge fleeing).
105 *Sverris saga*, pp. 69–70.

other people as retaliation if Magnus implemented his threats. It all came to naught, demonstrating that kings who tried to prioritize the royal bond on behalf of private bonds were clearly acting unwisely and against common opinion.

Another reason why close family members joined different groups is that it was a way to hedge their bets, as it would ensure that part of the family would be on the winning side regardless of who won. The advantage of having relatives in the opposing camp is discernible in conflict situations, where these bonds could be activated to mitigate antagonism.[106] When the Birkibeinar leader Dagfinn Bonde was besieged in Bergen in 1207, he contacted Gyrd, his brother-in-law among the Baglar, who then acted as a mediator negotiating favourable terms for Dagfinn.[107]

One type of situation where the importance of personal bonds could clash with royal interests was in granting pardon to conquered enemies in the aftermath of battle, as then kings who had incited their men to fight relentlessly during battle would turn completely around and go for general amnesty. Both of these absolutes were alien to most people fighting for the king, because they would also have their own personal motives for engagement. In *Bǫglunga sǫgur*, the peace treaty between the Birkibeinar and Baglar in 1208 became more acceptable when those opposing peace decided to go abroad to plunder.[108] In two general quarters in 1202 and 1227, the schism between royal and private interests emerges even clearer. When Sverre proposed to grant general quarter to the Baglar after a lengthy siege in 1202, the Birkibeinar objected: 'now we shall accept to receive our father's or brother's killer and give him quarter and seat beside us'.[109] Sverre then gave a speech underlining his own tribulations, including an appeal to give mercy in order to receive God's mercy: 'You have a soul you as well as me, and that you must not forget. No man will call you cowards for that sake'.[110] The saga makes no reference to resistance to the king's order but given that it ran counter to the men's urge for vengeance, it is reasonable to infer that not all were willing to comply. In *Hákonar saga Hákonarsonar*, a similar general quarter was granted to the Ribbungar after protracted fighting in 1227, and here the saga openly stated that there were some men among the Ribbungar 'whom the quarter could not protect'.[111] For them the royal decree had no value, and they had to flee the country.

---

106 *Heimskringla* 3, pp. 194–95; *Hákonar saga Hákonarsonar* II, p. 73.
107 *Bǫglunga sǫgur*, p. 107.
108 *Bǫglunga sǫgur*, pp. 117–19.
109 'nú skyli taka fǫðurbana eðr bróðurbana sína ok gefa grið og skipa síðan í hálfrými hjá oss'. (*Sverris saga*, p. 277).
110 'Eigu þér ekki síðr sálur en ek ok eigið þess at minnask. Engi maðr mun kalla yðr at heldr bleyðimenn fyrir þessa sök'. (*Sverris saga*, p. 277).
111 'er sér væntu engra griða.' (*Hákonar saga Hákonarsonar* I, p. 329).

An advantage of giving mercy was that the pardoned person amassed a debt to the grantor. This bond of gratitude could turn him into a supporter.[112] Switching sides was common on the battlefield. Seeing their own group being beaten, both individuals (such as Jon Hallkjellsson and an unnamed man who got mercy thrice during battle, the latter was killed the fourth time)[113] and groups (such as the Birkibeinar after having been beaten by the Kuflungar)[114] changed sides without much ado. A conquered or outnumbered party would not, and was not expected to, fight until the bitter end. It goes without saying that if one's group had been decisively conquered or the alternative was to be killed, switching sides was acceptable. However, how valuable was the support of conquered opponents who had been forced to change sides? For one thing, they could plead that an oath was extracted under coercion and therefore void.[115] More importantly, such men would often return to their armed groups. An illustrative example of this in Bǫglunga sǫgur comes from the siege in Bergen in 1206, where the Birkibeinar stayed in the castle with 600 men, and the Baglar had 2000 men in town. First the saga records that many men from the Birkibeinar switched sides to the Baglar, presumably because the latter had the upper hand in town and in the region. However, their new loyalty did not prove long-lasting, because when the Birkibeinar made a surprise attack chasing the Baglar through town, former Birkibeinar who were now fighting for the Baglar ran into churches, only to run out again a moment later as Birkibeinar.[116] The shallowness of switching sides is illustrated in that when the former Birkibeinar hornblower (*lúðrsveinn*) was forced to join the Baglar, he openly sabotaged his Baglar companions by not blowing the horn. It was not until he rejoined the Birkibeinar that he blew the horn loudly again (the motif of horn-blowing was probably a saga cliché,[117] but that does not make it less significant). The confused state created by the shifting sides is illustrated when the Birkibeinar started beating up a bunch of Baglar in a narrow pass, and it turned out that there were many

---

112 This is the gist of the argument in Bagge's analysis of *Heimskringla*: as today's enemy might be tomorrow's ally, one might just as well give quarter. See Bagge, *Society and Politics*, in particular pp. 64–110.
113 *Sverris saga*, pp. 121, 261.
114 *Sverris saga*, pp. 161–62.
115 This principle was laid down in canon law in Pope Gregor IX's *Liber Extra* from 1234 (1.40.4). See Richard Helmholz, 'Pope Innocent III and the Annulment of Magna Carta'. The most famous instance of this in the kings' sagas is Harald Gille's oath breaking in 1130 (*Heimskringla* 3, p. 170).
116 *Bǫglunga sǫgur*, pp. 71–72.
117 Horn blowers had an important function to signal battle, see for instance *Sverris saga*, p. 81, and *Sverris saga*, p. 121 on problems of fighting without a horn blower. For another poor horn blower who improved upon royal goading, see *Hákonar saga Hákonarsonar II*, p. 95.

Birkibeinar among the targets. In such a situation, the best strategy was probably to avoid engagement and to stay alert.

The frequency of switching sides could prompt a conclusion that group or royal affiliation was unimportant. In my opinion this is a premature conclusion. First, stating that side switching was common is not the same as stating it was without costs. The sagas give ample evidence that switching sides was a delicate issue that impinged on the evaluation of a man's moral character, and therefore had to be carefully framed not to be 'misunderstood' as stemming from cowardice or cynicism.[118] Second, there was a paradox in switching sides. On the one hand, any leader would hope that enemies joined their own ranks if they beat them, instead of having to kill them because they would remain disloyal. On the other hand, they would denounce the same mechanism if it worked in favour of the opponent. The crux of the issue was that as long as the defeated parties were pardoned, party affiliation remained superficial, at least it did not exclude other allegiances, and it did not carry with it an expectation to fight to death.

The Quest for Booty

The quest for booty is not often referred to in the sagas. One reason for this is probably that plunder of peasants was relatively less common in medieval Norway than in most of Europe. Strickland stresses that ravaging of peasants in medieval Europe was not considered unchivalric, as 'the actions and gestures that comprised "chivalrous" behaviour were never intended to be applied to the lesser orders'.[119] This attitude towards peasants contrasts with that of the sagas. King Sverre, according to his saga, was an ardent opponent of plundering peasants, and he allegedly solved this problem once and for all in the first phase of his career when he set up a test that separated the men who wanted to follow him because they believed in his cause from those who were only concerned with plunder.[120] Sverre's pruning attests to different attitudes to and relations with peasants from that normal elsewhere in Europe, but his precaution did of course not eliminate plunder as an integral part of warfare. For one thing, the aim

---

118 An example from *Sverris saga* is Torstein Kugad, who switched sides twice. On the one hand, such persistent side switching attests to the weak allegiance and ample opportunities for maneuvering. On the other hand, Torstein had to frame his side switches carefully in order not to be 'misunderstood' for being a coward or unreliable man (*Sverris saga*, pp. 166–67, 205–07). See also King Harald Hardruler's side switching in Morkinskinna, where he took great care to qualify and legitimize it so that it did not impair his moral character (*Morkinskinna*, pp. 151–54).
119 Strickland, *War and Chivalry*, p. 289.
120 *Sverris saga*, p. 19.

of acquiring material goods was normally fully compatible with fighting for the king, and in particular for armed followers it was a main cause for attaching themselves to the king in the first place. For another, the hunt for booty could sometimes clash with the interests of the king, and conflicts would flare up over the distribution of booty after battle, and on what should be considered the most important goal of fighting — booty or victory.[121]

In the long version of *Bǫglunga sǫgur*, the fight for booty is clearly exposed in the Baglar's siege of the castle in Bergen in spring 1207. As the Birkibeinar were residing in the castle with only a few men and little provisions, the Baglar considered their prospects of success in a siege to be good, whereas the Birkibeinar were correspondingly pessimistic.[122] Then the Birkibeinar sent the newly elected Archbishop Tore to try to mediate a settlement. Tore argued that the Baglar should 'let the Birkibeinar have free pass with life and goods',[123] and that their reward lay in erasing the castle. 'The Baglar answered variously to this',[124] the saga states — a minimal mode of expressing that a decision was controversial. While some were positive, 'some said that much of the townsmen's goods was in the castle, and they expected to have that as booty',[125] and that they would be able to conquer it easily. The final decision was left to King Filippus, who was expected to arrive soon afterwards. Filippus accepted the archbishop's terms for surrender, but when the Birkibeinar walked out of the castle, 'the Baglar murmured against King Filippus for taking away from them all the booty that they could have shared, because they would certainly have won the castle if he had not come'.[126] As a response to the discontent, Filippus made the men swear an oath that they had not taken out more than what they owned.[127]

---

121 *Sverris saga* refers one outright quarrel on the distribution of booty where Sverre was furious with his followers and wanted to decide himself (*Sverris saga*, p. 205). Once the Birkibeinar lost track of an opponent because he threw out money while fleeing (*Sverris saga*, p. 89). Yet typically the saga mentions the motive in episodes where the Birkibeinar disregarded it, as when leaving their property behind when attacked by Magnus Erlingsson's men (*Sverris saga*, p. 53).
122 *Bǫglunga sǫgur*, pp. 94–97.
123 *Bǫglunga sǫgur*, p. 96. L: 'lade Birkebenerne affdrage frj oc fellig, med Liiff oc Gods'.
124 *Bǫglunga sǫgur*, p. 96. L: 'Baglerne suarede ulige der til'.
125 *Bǫglunga sǫgur*, p. 96. L: 'der vaar megit aff Bymendenis Gods inde paa Slottet, huilcket de ventede sig til byte'.
126 *Bǫglunga sǫgur*, p. 98. L: 'Baglerne knurrede imod K. Philippus, oc sagde, at hand skilde dem ved deris Roff oc Byte, thi de hafde vel vundet Slottet, om hand hafde icke der kommet'.
127 *Bǫglunga sǫgur*, p. 98. The terms were stipulated by Archbishop Tore, and his peacemaking capacities were honoured. However, the fact that they built on a blatant lie (Tore argued that the Birkibeinar had provisions for two years, which he knew was not so) was not considered badly.

In this instance, it is not specified who argued against giving mercy, but other episodes can shed light on the identity of those more concerned with booty than with mercy. On their way to Bergen in 1207, the Baglar got news that the Birkibeinar were nearby, including two *sýslumenn*. They then attacked them and killed most of them. 'Nikolas of Lista gave mercy to both Olavs [the *sýslumenn*], but when the armed followers heard about this, they killed them.'[128] Two years earlier, the Baglar ambushed the *sýslumaðr* Einar Kongsmag in Stavanger, who fled into the church. Einar swore an oath that he would never fight Erling Stonewall. 'The leaders wanted to keep the pardon, but the armed followers were in charge', and Einar was executed.[129] Why did the followers insist that Einar was killed? The prospect of booty was probably not affected by the execution, since the Baglar took 'a lot of *leidang* which Einar had collected [...] and much goods owned by the Birkibeinar and townsmen'.[130] It is likely that they would have taken this booty regardless of Einar's fate.

What this episode hints at is that the armed followers were not only concerned with booty, but more generally with perpetuating the struggle with the Birkibeinar, probably because that was a precondition for extracting resources from others — directly as plunder of opponents or more indirectly as 'protection money'.[131] The interest in keeping up fighting is fully revealed in the aftermath of the settlement between the Birkibeinar and Baglar at Kvitingsøy in 1208, most fully detailed in the long version:

> Now there was murmuring among the Birkibeinar and Baglar, because there were many excellent men who had lost all their properties and money in the conflict. They then decided that the next spring they were to plunder in the Sudreys [Hebrides] to win goods. People from both groups declared that they would join in this venture.[132]

---

128 *Bǫglunga sǫgur*, pp. 94–95. Only in S: 'Nikolás af Lista gaf grið hvárumtveggja Óláfi. En er liðsmenn urðu þess varir þá veittu þeir þeim atgöngu ok drápu þar'.
129 *Bǫglunga sǫgur*, p. 38. 'Vildu höfðingjar halda grið við hann, en liðsmenn réðu'.
130 *Bǫglunga sǫgur*, p. 38. The formulation is from S: 'þar tóku þeir leiðangr mikinn er Einarr hafði saman dregit um allt Rogaland ok mikit fé annet er Birkibeinar áttu ok bæjarmenn'. L does not specify the leidang, probably because this was extinct in the seventeenth century: 'Baglerne finge stort roff oc bytte i Stavanger'.
131 Cf. the concept of 'protection racket' developed by Tilly, 'War Making and State Making as Organized Crime'.
132 *Bǫglunga sǫgur*, pp. 117–18. The formulations are from L: 'Der bleff et stor bulder blant Birkebenerne oc Baglerne, fordi der vaar mange ypperlige Mænd som hafde mist alt deris Gods oc Pendinge I den Feide, da bleff det Raad paafundet, at om Someren der efter skulde de drage Vester til Suder Øer I Røfuerii at forhuerfe sig Gods oc Pendinge igien, oc de lafuede skibe til paa begge sider'. S has more briefly: 'þat sumar fóru þeir í víking í Suðreyjar' (*Bǫglunga sǫgur*, p. 119). However, it specified that three Birkibeinar and five Baglar prepared the expedition. A related mechanism can be seen after the settlement between the Baglar and Birkibeinar in 1218, when men from the Baglar who had not

It is difficult to find a clearer expression of the diverging motives for fighting than this episode. The king might promulgate in solemn words that the struggle was for the throne, but for many of his armed retainers fighting was an end in itself. When the condition of armed struggle was threatened by conclusive peace agreements, previous divisions into friends and enemies dissolved, giving way to a new division between peacemakers and warmakers. Such a realignment could ultimately erode the existing sociopolitical structure by revealing the shallowness of group enmities.[133] One way of minimizing the role of this potentially disruptive force in the saga was to restrict it to the lower segments of the army — to the rank-and-file warriors as opposed to the 'noble' leaders who fought for something larger than material gains, namely the throne. Yet, from the description above it is by no means certain that the men who joined forces only came from the lower classes. On the contrary, this must be reckoned as a rhetorical strategy of the saga author, and an indication of his own class bias.

An Elite Community

In 1202, King Hakon Sverresson issued a letter of reconciliation with the Church, where he painted the present situation in gloomy colours:

> Now neither learned nor unlearned fear God or good men. Rather, every man now lives as he pleases in a lawless order, because the laws are neglected, but robbery prevails, bad customs increase and good ones are squeezed.[134]

Norwegian historians have often taken this statement as a reliable description of the contemporary realities, and lauded the parties for finally coming to terms so that the 'lawless order' could be terminated — 'to the best of the populace', as King Hakon ended the letter.[135] As discussed in Chapter 7, the men of the Church also played an active part in settling the conflict in 1208. Late in 1207 Bishop Nikolas appeared in a new role as mediator,[136] and it turned out that in the summer of 1207, Nikolas had visited Archbishop Tore Gudmundsson, who had become archbishop in

---

obtained new honours / offices were frustrated, but there they joined a new rebel group (*Hákonar saga Hákonarsonar I*, p. 228).

133 Cf. Schmidt, *The Theory of the Partisan*.
134 'Rædazt nu huarke lerdir ne olerdir gud ne goda men. Helldr lifuir nu huer sem lystir vndir lagha lausre skipan. þui at logh lægiazt. en ran rikia. vsidir vaxa. en sidir tynaz.' (*Norges Gamle Love* I, pp. 444–45).
135 See Helle, *Under kirke og kongemakt*, 70; Johnsen, *Fra ættesamfunn til statssamfunn*, pp. 91–92; Paasche, *Kong Sverre*, pp. 109–10.
136 *Bǫglunga sǫgur*, p. 112.

1206 after the controversial Eirik. 'Then there were exchanges of letters between [Birkibeinar and Baglar].'[137]

This interpretation of peacemaking as emanating from a concern for the common good was vehemently criticized by historians of a Marxist bent, most notably Kåre Lunden, who argued that the settlements in 1202 and 1208 did not signify the end of the civil war, but the establishment of a new form of dominance. In Lunden's view, King Sverre's role in Norwegian history was as 'a 25 years' permanent political and military shock', who taught the magnates that 'it created strife and destruction, not peace, if one single fraction [...] too relentlessly strove to monopolize all the resources of the kingdom for themselves'.[138] For Lunden, the civil wars brought the leading classes together, as it served as a lesson that it was better to extract resources from the working population by uniting under a king who could collect contributions legitimately, than to fight internally over them.

Lunden's class perspective on the struggles is a welcome correction to the naïve interpretation of these incidents as launching a new era of peace, but there are reasons to be suspicious of the view that the upper classes now finally 'understood' how much they had in common. One of Lunden's examples of an incipient class formation is *Bǫglunga sǫgur*'s description of lifting the siege in Bergen in 1207. Here the saga writer gives a detailed account in the long version of how the Birkibeinar came out of the castle door with their goods, with Baglar standing on each side: 'He [Filippus] took the maiden Kristin, daughter of King Sverre, by her hand and led her out of the gate'.[139] For the saga writer and his audience, the whole episode was a foreshadowing of the union of the warring parties one year later, after which Filippus and Kristin would share a marital bed.

However, this does not mean that this type of class identity was a new one. Such a community should rather be considered as an intrinsic part of elite culture throughout the period, and an aspect that could surface in various ways.[140] Sometimes this community was grounded in personal bonds, such as with Dagfinn Bonde and Gyrd, who belonged to different groups but could still communicate and make common cause in a strained

---

137 'Hófusk þá upp bréfsendingar millum manna' (*Bǫglunga sǫgur*, p. 113). On the importance of clerics in this phase of the conflict, see Brathetland, '*Nettverksmakt*', pp. 294–97. For a more secular view on Nikolas, see Orning, *Unpredictability and Presence*, pp. 214–19.
138 'et 25-årig, permanent politisk og militært sjokk', som lærte stormennene at 'det skapte strid og ødeleggelse, ikke fred, om én enkelt fraksjon [...] altfor overmodig forsøkte å monopolisere alle kongedømmets ressurser for seg'. Bønder og bymenn lærte at 'det kunne være det minste av to onder å akseptere regulære oppofrelser til en statsmakt som var sterk nok til å sikre noenlunde orden og fred'. Lunden, *Norge under Sverreætten*, pp. 137–38.
139 L: 'hand tog Jomfru Christin Suerris dotter ved haanden, oc ledde hende ud aff porten' (*Bǫglunga sǫgur*, p. 97).
140 Some of the first sources to Nordic history, skaldic poems, are primarily vehicles for cherishing and remembering noble deeds. See Frank, *Old Norse Court Poetry*.

situation where group interests diverged.[141] At the settlement of Kvitingsøy in 1208, the former enemies Peter Stoype and Reidar Sendemann must have found it easier to reconcile considering that they were brothers-in-law, married to daughters of Magnus Erlingsson.[142] Other times, as when 'Nikolas of Lista gave mercy to both Olavs' we do not know about their relations other than that they belonged to the elite, as these two Olavs were *sýslumenn*. The inclination to grant mercy to opponents cannot be reduced to a consequence of personal bonds, as it was a more general drive among the elites. The Baglar who wanted to pardon Einar Kongsmag in 1205 were elite members like him, but not related to him. One reason that they were more reconciliatory than the ordinary fighters who wanted to execute him, might be that they hoped that Einar would switch sides and thus become a resource for the Baglar in the future, which was not an unrealistic scenario (see later on switching sides). Another may be that by offering mercy in the church and making Einar swear an oath of non-commitment, norms of noble — one could maybe even say chivalrous — conduct had been respected by both parts. This is exactly what Einar addressed in his famous last words on being executed: 'Dirty and treacherous is the Baglar mercy becoming now'.[143]

These elite norms were certainly not inviolable, but they played a part in how the elite framed their identity and dominance.[144] The noble community across group divisions emerged clearly in the episode where the Birkibeinar surrendered the castle in Bergen in 1207 as related above. It also surfaced three years earlier, when Erling Stonewall had led the Baglar fleet to Bergen, and tried to prevent fighting by arguing that 'they [the Birkibeinar] are our men', but here he received only ridicule in response. Why do we see these opposite reactions to the pointing out of an elite community across groups? Probably because its significance was highly contextual and ambiguous. In 1207 a unified elite worked in the same direction as the kings: towards reconciliation, in contrast to the unrelenting attitude of the armed followers who demanded booty and strife. In 1204, however, it undermined the efforts to maintain mortal enmities between the Baglar and Birkibeinar.

Marxist historians have tended to lump together all members of the elite in a 'dominant class', and to see internal strife within this upper class as superficial compared with inter-class conflicts, and as functional

---

141 *Bǫglunga sǫgur*, p. 107.
142 *Bǫglunga sǫgur*, p. 28.
143 *Bǫglunga sǫgur*, p. 38. Only in L: 'Kranck oc suigfuld er Baglernis fred oc lejde'. This has been reckoned as one of the few 'saga-worthy' utterances in the saga (Magerøy, 'Føreord', p. 272).
144 Strickland, *War and Chivalry*, pp. 330–40.

to the system as a whole.[145] In my opinion, this view conflates royal and noble interests too much. In their enigmatic combination of aggressive self-assertion and shared values, the elites promoted a condition of 'constant crisis' that was alien to the king's aim to determine the conditions for peace and war. In the previous section, we saw that a noble community could be consistent with royal peacemaking (in 1207), but not always (as in 1204). The same goes for noble self-assertion, which could be nicely attuned to royal warmaking when the king wanted to have people fight for him, but contrarily could pose more of a problem in times of peace, such as after the settlement at Kvitingsøy in 1208. Whereas kings had previously striven to uphold enmities, now was the time for burying the battle axe.[146] For the magnates, it meant that their community across group boundaries now had full potential to unfold. However, the new condition of peace left less room for letting tensions play out, both within and across former group divisions.

Yet peace did not put a lock on elite rivalry; it just promoted a variant and less overtly violent form of constant crisis. The first major tension to surface concerned the position of the Baglar leader Filippus in the new arrangement. He had to renounce the royal title, and the saga made him resign without protests. However, his intended spouse Kristin Sverresdatter was more uncompromising,[147] and some former Baglar insisted on calling Filippus king after 1208. Filippus probably did not protest very wholeheartedly against this labelling.[148] Here a compromise was carved out that reflects how royal and noble concerns were balanced: Filippus was still called king among the Baglar, allegedly in secret, but no more secretly than as to be known to the saga author.[149]

Another threat to the royal peace after 1208 was the power struggle between King Inge and Hakon Galen, which in reality had been going on since 1204. After 1208 it crystallized on two occasions. First, Hakon

---

145 Andreas Holmsen called internal conflicts within the upper class 'surface waves' ('overflatekrusninger'). Holmsen, *Norges historie*, p. 274. Kåre Lunden drew attention to that elites needed to show moderation, and that the king was useful in order to curb tensions within the elite (Lunden, *Norge under Sverreætten*, pp. 137–38). For criticism of this perspective in that it tends to posit a self-fulfilling system where both harmony and conflict shows the system at work: Hay, *Albion's Fatal Tree*; Lacey, *The Royal Pardon*.
146 *Bǫglunga sǫgur*, pp. 116–18. The country was separated into three parts: two for the Birkibeinar and one for the Baglar — of which the Birkibeinar part was divided between Inge and Hakon Galen. That in reality meant a three-part separation of Norway, with one king and two earls (see Chapter 7 in this volume).
147 The description in the saga might have been stylized so as to represent Kristin as a strong-willed independent woman in the vein of the Icelandic family sagas. On the other hand, Kristin's objections do make sense considering the other strong female agents in this period.
148 A more formal aspect of this tension was Filippus' unwillingness to give up the royal seal (*Bǫglunga sǫgur*, p. 118).
149 *Bǫglunga sǫgur*, pp. 118, 124.

Galen tried to gain the royal title for himself.[150] Inge resisted this attempt firmly, but Hakon achieved an agreement that the one who lived longest of them should inherit the other, and that when both were deceased, the one son born in wedlock should inherit the throne.[151] The latter paragraph in reality meant acknowledging Hakon's superiority, since he in contrast to Inge had legitimate children. Hakon Galen's second attempt to undermine Inge's power allegedly consisted of encouraging the peasants in Trøndelag, Inge's core area, to rebel against him. The saga states that 'Hakon earl and archbishop Tore were strongly suspected for having goaded the peasants into rising against the king'.[152] The rebellion became so powerful that Inge had to retreat, and it was only after Hakon's death in 1214 that Inge was able to suppress the peasants.[153] The saga also refers to Hakon Galen as the instigator of an assassination attempt against the king.[154] These tensions have either been regarded as echoes from the previous period of strife threatening to overthrow the fragile peace arrangement of 1208, or as a consequence of Hakon Galen's intrigues.[155] As for the latter interpretation, it is doubtful that the saga is trustworthy in these accounts, as it contains a decidedly anti-Hakon tone.[156] A similar tension between brothers played out among the Baglar, when Filippus's brother Andres came from Denmark and ended in a skirmish which Filippus managed to suppress effectively.[157] More important, I think that such tensions are better interpreted as more or less permanent internal rivalries among the elites which concerned matters of honour and the sharing of power rather than dynastic affairs, and which were not necessarily so detrimental or disruptive for the sociopolitical order. Such an ambiguity has been neatly framed by Pierre Bourdieu:

> It tends to be forgotten that a fight presupposes agreement between the antagonists about what it is that is worth fighting about; those points of agreement are held at the level of what 'goes without saying', they are left in the state of *doxa*, in other words everything that makes the field itself, the game, the stakes, all the presuppositions that one tacitly and

---

150 *Bǫglunga sǫgur*, pp. 122–23.
151 *Bǫglunga sǫgur*, p. 124.
152 *Bǫglunga sǫgur*, p. 125. L: 'Denne opreisning imod Kongen bleff Hagen Jarl oc Erckebisp Tore megit misstencke fore, at de skulde hafue opvect hannem aff Bønderne'.
153 *Bǫglunga sǫgur*, pp. 126–27.
154 *Bǫglunga sǫgur*, pp. 125–26.
155 Arstad, 'Håkon Galen'; Lunden, *Norge under Sverreætten*, pp. 148–54.
156 After Hakon's death in 1214, his widow Kristin immediately travelled back to Sweden, indicating that the network around Hakon had disintegrated after his death. This meant that when *Bǫglunga sǫgur* was written, there were no one to defend Hakon's reputation.
157 *Bǫglunga sǫgur*, p. 127.

even unwittingly accepts by the mere fact of playing, of entering the game.[158]

The internal rivalries that persisted after the formal peace treaty in 1208 can be regarded as a 'constant crisis' within the elite that reflected their double-bind relationship to one another as a community and competitors. Moreover, even if the elites partook in the royal endeavour, their position needs to be separated more firmly from the king's than Marxist historians have done. The pre- and post-1208 situation illustrates the tensions lucidly: before 1208 the threat was that magnates rallied for communal interests in situations of conflict, after 1208 inversely that they opted for conflict during conditions of peace. In reality, the relationships between kings and elites was always characterized by ambiguity.

The Illusion of Mortal Enmity

A king's effort to implement his understanding of mortal enmity as the criterion for action ran into many difficulties, as men had numerous, complex, and sometimes contradictory motives for behaving in the way they did. Kings could not seriously challenge the primacy of personal bonds if they should happen to run counter to the royal affiliation. They also had to take into account that their followers, in particular armed retainers with modest private social standing and resources, were inclined to use the struggle to gain material wealth. Finally, the magnates shared values and norms that often were irreconcilable with a strict division between Birkibeinar and Baglar. Usually, it was possible for kings to handle these varying concerns and manoeuvre between them. After all, reality is always more complex than ideal states. However, on certain occasions the split in motives was revealed, often to the detriment of the royal cause. This was an age where no one was willing to die for their king or fatherland. The embryo of this thought is detectable in royal speeches,[159] but in battle it goes without saying that no man would set consideration for the realm above his individual concerns. As Bagge formulates it concerning King Sverre, '[h]e appeals to individual wishes for gain, not to loyalty or patriotism'.[160]

Yet the fact that the bond to the king was not ubiquitous (which no one would expect it to be) does not mean that it was not important. The crux is that it was not fixed as a focal point above politics, but firmly enmeshed in politics, and this was also what gave it its strength. During

---

158 Bourdieu, 'Some Properties of Fields', pp. 73–74.
159 On Sverre's speeches, see Bagge, *From Gang Leader*, pp. 25–33; more generally in Knirk, *Oratory in the King's Sagas*.
160 Bagge, *From Gang Leader*, p. 26.

negotiations between Sverre and Magnus in Nidaros in 1180, men from the two groups 'sat down and drank together at Brattøra, because even if they served in two armies, many of them were related or in-laws or had been friends previously'.[161] Previously we saw that enmity could be mitigated, or at times eroded, by a series of personal factors. Here we see that enmity was also constrained in space and time. Warriors could perfectly well on given occasions disregard their enmities and sit together sharing drinks and values. Only after the kings had failed to reach an agreement did they stop drinking and become enemies again. Enmity was contextual, not absolute, and hence the crucial issue was how to define a situation. Warriors were expected to be fierce in battle, and this constituted their ultimate *raison d'etre*, but as we saw above, they could act differently in other situations. Actually, the same goes for kings, as in line with King Sverre's slogan according to William of Newburgh: 'ferus ut leo, mitis ut agnus' — fierce as a lion, mild as a lamb.[162]

Still, this was not simply an issue of war versus peace, as criss-crossing lines of friendship and enmity made the situation considerably more complex. At a skirmish at Tittelsnes in 1207, Peter Stoype's ship rowed straight at Reidar Sendemann's. 'Why are you devils rowing in our way tonight?' a man on Reidar's ship uttered, throwing a stone onto Peter's ship, whereupon they then decided to back out.[163] They did not know — as the saga author did — that shortly thereafter a settlement would be made, and Peter and Reidar would join forces to go to Jorsal together.[164] However, what the opposing forces at Tittelsnes did know was that they fought men with whom they had a lot in common.[165] For instance, the two leaders Peter and Reidar were brothers-in-law, as both were married to daughters of Magnus Erlingsson (Reidar to Margrete, Peter to Ingeborg). Moreover, part of the warrior ethos consisted in knowing when *not* to fight, and in a chaotic situation as on this dark night at Tittelsnes, every measure was probably taken to minimize risk, at least until the situation became more perspicuous. As this was not an age when anyone was expected to risk their life for their king, the king's men needed to be certain about their prospects of success. 'Mortal enmity' could be a powerful keyword for fighting in a situation where the odds for victory were good, but not so much from an inferior position. Hence, mortal enmity was a

---

161 'Settusk allir saman út á Brötteyri, drukku þar ok töluðusk við, þó at þeir væri í tvennum flokkum. þá váru þeir margir frændr eða mágar eða höfðu fyrr verit vinir' (*Sverris saga*, p. 94).
162 William of Newburgh, *History*, book 3, chapter 6. The slogan was very similar to Sverre's request to the Birkibeinar to be 'as lambs in peacetime, but cruel as lions when it is war' (*Sverris saga*, p. 160).
163 *Bǫglunga sǫgur*, p. 111. Only in S: 'Hví róa djöflar yðrir fyrir oss í nótt?'.
164 *Bǫglunga sǫgur*, pp. 118, 120.
165 This is in line with the division Stephen Morillo draws between intracultural and intercultural wars, in Morillo, 'A General Typology of Transcultural Wars'.

reality in this society, but a varying and fluctuating one, just as the question 'Why are we fighting?' cannot be given one single, universal answer. In short, this was a society of constant crisis, where everything was in flux, but a flux that constrained as much as it fuelled conflict.

Conclusion

The period 1202–1208 has usually been regarded as a climax of the Norwegian civil wars, and therefore as a period of widespread violence and disorder. This chapter has departed from that view, not by disproving that the period was a violent one, but by arguing that conflicts — violent or not — by and large played a constructive role in society. Adopting the concept of 'constant crisis', I have demonstrated, as in other chapters, that conflict and tension was an integral aspect of society, which was foremost structured according to a principle of balance. This principle operated at a structural level, not an intentional one, and is therefore compatible with the fact that people could be violent and opt for supremacy. The central issue is that dominance for numerous structural reasons was difficult to achieve, so that balance of power was the normal condition. Moreover, it means that politics was neither without rules nor governed by a set of fixed *Spielregeln*. Since the struggling parties aimed at dominance, they did not follow any 'rules' guaranteeing balance. Rather, their efforts were blocked by obstacles that they themselves (and most historians) tended to view as conflict-triggering, but which we from a structural perspective can impute their proper function as conflict-restraining.

Constant crisis is most visible in the struggle for national supremacy between the Birkibeinar and Baglar. However, constant crisis was a recurring dynamic at different levels of society, because there were no primordial social or political units, but a flow of informal groups which formed and disbanded, or rather, were activated and de-activated according to context. Networks constituted the foundation of group formation, but as sociopolitical bonds they were neither ossified nor institutionalized and people were part of multiple networks, exactly what network was activated in a conflict was impossible to predict. Conflicts could occur at various levels, engaging networks at local, armed group, national / regnal or supra-national levels.[166] Moreover, informal group formation could be based on kinship, friendship, warrior identity or an elite community. In this chapter, I have focused on networks and oppositions on the national / regnal and armed group level.

---

166 This has been labelled segmentary opposition in this chapter.

In the first part, I discussed the struggle between the Birkibeinar and Baglar for national hegemony. Here my main point was that topographical and military factors worked in favour of a balance of power, which of course is another way of saying 'a perpetual power-struggle for power'. Regardless of how messy these conflicts were, I argued that the biggest threat to stability under this condition was not fighting in itself, which was fairly regulated and modest (not only because mercy was usual but also because the groups were on the alert), but the prospect that one party tried to dominate the other. The last scenario would typically result in an escalation of warfare, in terms of guerrilla-style warfare or the involvement of agents from outside Norway. Hence, on a structural level constant crisis was often more stable than the dominance of one group. Moreover, even an apparent victory, as that of the Birkibeinar in 1208 and even more in 1217, did not alter the fundamental condition of constant crisis in the leading strata.

In the second part, I argued that this constant crisis was not limited to the national arena, but cut straight to the core of the armed groups themselves. *Bǫglunga sǫgur* goes into detail about military tactics and strategies, no doubt because these occasions were often characterized by quarrels and potential factionalizing. Once again it is easy to see the persistent tugs-of-war within each group for influence and power as symptoms of disorder, but these processes in my view attest to a political culture where power struggles could have a stabilizing and even fertilizing effect. For one thing, the persistent struggle for hegemony within the groups secured participation and influence from a large segment of the group, not only from the dominant faction. For another, in the Baglar case it is even possible to argue that the fluctuating power structures facilitated an environment which enabled the best argument to be accepted.

In the final part, I drew attention to the fact that the Birkibeinar and Baglar were not monolithic units, so that the dimension of tension must be expanded to include bonds and interests crossing group boundaries. Motives for joining the armed groups were complex and varying, and, whereas this should not make us conclude that leaders were powerless, it shows the limitations of their power, and more basically the importance of negotiation and compromise for finding viable solutions. It went without saying that kings had to take into account that people had private causes for fighting (or not fighting), that retainers were focused on booty, and that elites had a community of interest that stretched beyond group boundaries. It must have been common knowledge that people fighting in armed groups did so for different reasons, and normally this would be no problem. However, at certain point such ruptures would manifest themselves, necessitating compromises to be made.

What remains to complete the analysis of constant crisis is to investigate networks on local levels, including those connecting local communities to the armed groups, and supra-national networks, of which those stretching into Sweden are of particular importance in this period. These issues are too big to be treated here, but I will conclude with some brief observations on these issues.

First, there is the relationship between the armed groups and the local communities on whose support they were dependent in the last instance. We cannot draw firm borders between members of the armed groups and local populations, as armed men also were part of local communities, albeit in varying degrees depending on their role and commitment. The various and differing commitment of group members to the group can be illuminated in *Bǫglunga sǫgur*'s description of where the Baglar ventured following the assassination of the Baglar King Inge in 1204: 'some to Denmark, others to their relatives, some urged quarter from King Hakon'.[167] It is likely that the men travelling abroad were the core members who either had few private resources or magnates who had staked everything on Baglar success and had few firm connections to the Birkibeinar. For them there was no exit option if their group lost. However, for those who sought pardon or returned home, the defeat was not necessarily crushing. The former were probably powerful men whose allegiance was important or mercenaries choosing to find a new master, the latter probably men of lesser importance who could engage or disengage in the struggle more freely. What they had in common is that they were less committed to the cause and had made sure that they had an 'exit option'. There must have been a thin line between commitment and safeguarding in this period.[168] Commitment was necessary in order to gain part in an eventual victory, but given that no group were predestined to win, the need to have an exit option was equally urgent. We have seen that some families solved this by having one man in each camp, so that they would be on the victor's side no matter the result. Others probably tried to 'stay on the fence' as long as they could, staying attentive to what direction the winds were blowing.[169] In fact, this uncertainty was built into the political system, as the practice of switching sides allowed for extreme flexibility. However, the result of this was that nothing really changed very much, even if one part gained what looked like an overwhelming victory. Constant crisis was the normal

---

[167] The full reference in L: 'en part til Suerrig, en part til Danmarck, oc en part til deres Frender, oc nogne søgte forligelse hos Kong Hagen' (*Bǫglunga sǫgur*, p. 10). S has a shorter version, see footnote 10.

[168] Two former war leaders — Gudolv of Blakstad and Ragvald Hallkjellsson — experienced the dangers of transgressing this line, as they were killed by angry local peasants after they settled down (*Hákonar saga Hákonarsonar I*, pp. 209–10, 321).

[169] See Vigh, 'Crisis and Chronicity' on this aspect; Orning and Vigh, 'Constant Crisis' on comparison of modern and medieval evidence; Kilcullen, *The Accidental Guerilla* on the sliding transition between full-scale members of military group and supporters with local affiliations.

condition. There was endemic rivalry, but how much did that affect the local communities? Local peasants could be summoned to the army, and being in the vicinity of armed groups was probably not a pleasant experience. However, it should be borne in mind that the struggles that we have followed took place in a geographically far-flung region where the impact of war was not necessarily very substantial, and that summoned peasants were normally not expected to partake actively in armed combats.[170] One could even argue that one purpose of *Bǫglunga sǫgur* was not to decide who was right, Birkibeinar or Baglar, but to argue that armed groups and warfare was decisive, set against a set of local communities mostly intent on avoiding the whole issue of war and factions.

Second, there is the supra-national dimension, the links which connected with places or people outside of Norway. These have usually been treated as 'external impulses', with the implication that the 'internal' and national matter is the primordial.[171] By relegating agents from outside Norway to the role of 'external', we also imply that they can appear and disappear, and thus can be absent, in contrast to what goes on 'internally'. Thus, we already marginalize the Scandinavian field by our terminology. However, demonstrating the importance of broadening the field to include Scandinavia is another matter, which is difficult for many reasons: partly because Sweden and Denmark are devoid of narrative sources for the period around 1200, and partly because *Bǫglunga sǫgur* focuses on dynastic issues within Norway. The claims of the Danish kings to be overlords of Norway are well known, and even if they were not explicitly mentioned in *Bǫglunga sǫgur*, the role of King Valdemar for the Baglar was so vital that to rule him out as a factor in power relations in Norway would be naïve. Less known is the Swedish presence in Norway. It did not stop when the widowed queen Margrete fled to Götaland in 1204. Her niece Kristin Nikolasdatter, granddaughter of King St Erik, perpetuated the link to Sweden in tandem with Hakon Galen, whose father was Swedish, and who had close connections to King Erik of Sweden (r. 1208–1216). Hakon was Norway's most powerful man after 1204, and it was his death prior to King Inge's that prevented him from becoming king of Norway. Had that happened, a union with Sweden could have been pushed forward more than a century. But that is another story.

---

170 Twice *Bǫglunga sǫgur* mentions *leidangsmenn* being killed, probably because this was considered unusual (*Bǫglunga sǫgur*, pp. 90, 93).

171 Jens Arup Seip formulated this dichotomy in the image of the seed and the soil, Seip, 'Problemer og metode', p. 37). Even if later historians have objected to this image, they have largely followed the model of separating internal and external factors.

Works Cited

Primary Sources

Bǫglunga sǫgur = *Soga om birkebeinar og baglar: Bǫglunga sǫgur: 2*, ed. by Hallvard Magerøy (Oslo: Solum/Kjeldeskriftfondet, 1988)
Den eldre Gulatingslova (see full reference on p. 87 in JVS bibliography)
Hákonar saga Hákonarsonar 1; Bǫglunga saga, ed. by Sverrir Jakobsson and Tor Ulset, Jubileumsutgave (Reykjavík: Hið Íslenska Fornritafélag, 2013)
Heimskringla III, ed. by Bjarni Aðalbjarnarson, Íslenzk fornrit, 28 (Reykjavík: Hið Íslenska Fornritafélag, 1951)
Heimskringla 3, ed. and trans. by Alison Finlay and Anthony Faulkes (London: London: Viking Society for Northern Research, 2015)
Magerøy, Hallvard, *Soga om birkebeinar og baglar: Bǫglunga sǫgur: 1*. Vol. 1 (Oslo: Solum, 1988)
——, *Soga om birkebeinar og baglar: Bǫglunga sǫgur: 2*. Vol. 2 (Oslo: Solum, 1988)
Morkinskinna: The Earliest Icelandic Chronicle of the Norwegian Kings (1030–1157), ed. and trans. by Theodore M. Andersson and Kari Ellen Gade, Islandica, Vol. 51 (Ithaca, NY: Cornell University Press, 2000)
Norges Gamle Love Indtil 1387: 1, ed. by P. A. Munch and Rudolph Keyser, Vol. 1 (Christiania [Oslo]: Chr. Grøndahl, 1846)
Sverris Saga, ed. by Þorleifur Hauksson, Íslenzk fornrit, 30 (Reykjavík: Hið Íslenska Fornritafélag, 2007)
William of Newburgh, *History, Books 1–5*, The Internet Medieval Sourcebook, <https://sourcebooks.fordham.edu/basis/williamofnewburgh-intro.asp> [accessed 6 May 2023]

Secondary Studies

Althoff, Gerd, *Spielregeln Der Politik Im Mittelalter: Kommunikation in Frieden Und Fehde* (Darmstadt: Wissenschaftliche Buchgesellschaft, 1997)
Arstad, Knut and Peter Lyche, 'Håkon Galen', in *Norsk biografisk leksikon*, <https://nbl.snl.no/H%C3%A5kon_Galen> [accessed 8 May 2021]
——, 'Rex Bellicosus: Strategi, taktikk og feltherregenskaper i Norge på 1200-tallet: En analyse av krigføring i middelalderen samt militært og politisk lederskap sett gjennom karrierene til Sigurd Erlingsson, Knut Håkonsson, Skule Bårdsson og Håkon Håkonsson' (Unpublished Doctoral Thesis, University of Oslo, 2019)
Bagge, Sverre, 'Borgerkrig og statsutvikling i Norge i middelalderen', *Historisk tidsskrift* (N), 65.2 (1986), 145–97

―――, *From Gang Leader to the Lord's Anointed: Kingship in Sverris Saga and Hákonar Saga Hákonarsonar*, The Viking Collection, Vol. 8 (Odense: Odense University Press, 1996)

―――, *From Viking Stronghold to Christian Kingdom: State Formation in Norway, c. 900–1350* (Copenhagen: Museum Tusculanum Press, 2010)

―――, *Society and Politics in Snorri Sturluson's Heimskringla* (Berkeley: University of California Press, 1991)

Bartlett, Robert, 'Mortal Enmities', in *Feud, Violence and Practice: Essays in Medieval Studies in Honor of Stephen D. White*, ed. by Belle Stoddard Tuten and Tracey Lynn Billado (Farnham: Ashgate, 2010), pp. 197–212

Bloch, Marc, *Feudal Society*, vol. 1 (London: Routledge, 1975)

Bourdieu, Pierre, 'Some Properties of Fields', in *Sociology in Question*, ed. by Pierre Bourdieu, trans. by Richard Nice (London: Sage Publications, 1993), pp. 72–77

Brandt, Troels, 'Slaget ved Gestilren: En dansk synsvinkel i lys av "glemte" udenlandske kilder', 2006, <http://gedevasen.dk/gestilren.html> [accessed 8 May 2021]

Brathetland, Bente, 'Nettverksmakt: Sosiale band og nettverk i dei norske innbyrdesstridane 1130–1208' (Unpublished Doctoral Thesis, University of Bergen, 2019)

―――, 'Roar Kongsfrende', in *Norsk biografisk leksikon*, <https://nbl.snl.no/Roar_Kongsfrende> [accessed 2 December 2020]

Bull, Edvard, 'Borgerkrigene i Norge og Håkon Håkonssons kongstanke', in *Samfunnsmaktene brytes*, ed. by Andreas Holmsen and Jarle Simensen, Norske historikere i utvalg (Oslo: Universitetsforlaget, 1969), pp. 24–37

Christie, Niall, and Maya Yazigi, *Noble Ideals and Bloody Realities: Warfare in the Middle Ages* (Leiden: Brill, 2006)

Cramer, Christopher, *Civil War is Not a Stupid Thing: Accounting for Violence in Developing Countries* (London: Sage Publications, 2006)

Duby, Georges, 'The Origins of Knighthood', in *The Chivalrous Society*, trans. by Cynthia Postan (Berkeley: University of California Press, 1977), pp. 158–71

Esmark, Kim, Lars Hermanson, and Hans Jacob Orning, *Nordic Elites in Transformation II: Social Networks* (London: Routledge, 2020)

Frank, Roberta, *Old Norse Court Poetry: The Dróttkvætt Stanza* (Ithaca: Cornell University Library, 1978)

Habermas, Jürgen, *The Theory of Communicative Action 1: Reason and the Rationalization of Society* (Boston: Beacom Press, 1984)

Hay, Douglas, *Albion's Fatal Tree: Crime and Society in Eighteenth-Century England* (New York: Pantheon Books, 1975)

Helle, Knut, 'Gunnhild 1', in *Norsk biografisk leksikon*, <https://nbl.snl.no/Gunnhild_-_1> [accessed 8 May 2021]

―――, *Norge blir en stat: 1130–1319*. 2nd edn (Bergen: Universitetsforlaget, 1974)

———, *Omkring Böglungasögur*, Årbok (Universitetet i Bergen: Trykt Utg.) (Bergen, 1958)
———, *Under kirke og kongemakt: 1130–1350* (Oslo: Aschehoug, 2005)
Helmholz, Richard, 'Pope Innocent III and the Annulment of Magna Carta', *Journal of Ecclesiastical History*, 69.1 (2018), 1–14
Hermanson, Lars, *Friendship, Love, and Brotherhood in Medieval Northern Europe, c. 1000–1200*, The Northern World, 85 (Leiden: Brill, 2019)
Holmsen, Andreas, *Norges historie: fra de eldste tider til 1660*, 4th edn (Oslo: Gyldendal, 1977)
Jezierski, Wojtek, Lars Hermanson, Hans Jacob Orning, and Thomas Småberg, *Rituals, Performatives, and Political Order in Northern Europe, c. 650–1350*, Ritus et Artes, 7 (Turnhout: Brepols, 2015)
Johnsen, Arne Odd, *Fra ættesamfunn til statssamfunn* (Oslo: Aschehoug, 1948)
Jón Viðar, Sigurðsson, *Viking Friendship: The Social Bond in Iceland and Norway, c. 900–1300* (Ithaca and New York: Cornell University Press, 2017)
Kilcullen, David, *The Accidental Guerrilla: Fighting Small Wars in the Midst of a Big One* (Oxford: Hurst & Company, 2009)
Knirk, James E., *Oratory in the Kings' Sagas* (Oslo: Universitetsforlaget, 1981)
Lacey, Helen, *The Royal Pardon: Access to Mercy in Fourteenth-Century England* (York: York Medieval Press, 2009)
Line, Philip, *Kingship and State Formation in Sweden, 1130–1290*, The Northern World, 27 (Leiden: Brill, 2007)
Lundberg, Stig, 'Lena och Gestilren', <https://web.archive.org/web/20090214223003/http://stiglundberg.org/lena-och-gestilren/b/> [accessed 9 November 2021]
Lunden, Kåre, *Norge under Sverreætten, 1177–1319: Høymiddelalder*, Norges historie (Oslo: Cappelen, 1976)
Magerøy, Hallvard, 'Føreord til *Soga om baglarar og birkebeinar*', in *Norges kongesagaer 3*, trans. by Dag Gundersen and Finn Hødnebø (Oslo: Gyldendal, 1979), pp. 269–70
Morillo, Stephen, 'A General Typology of Transcultural Wars', in *Transcultural Wars from the Middle Ages to the 21st Century*, ed. by Hans Henning Kortüm (Berlin: Akademie, 2006), pp. 29–42
Orning, Hans Jacob, 'Conflict and Social (Dis)Order in Norway, c. 1030–1160', in *Disputing Strategies in Medieval Scandinavia*, ed. by Lars Hermanson, Kim Esmark, Hans Jacob Orning, and Helle Vogt (Leiden: Brill, 2013), pp. 45–82
———, *Constant Crisis: Deconstructing the Civil Wars in Norway, c. 1180–1220* (Ithaca, N.Y.: Cornell University Library, 2024)
———, 'Feud in the State: The Conflict between Haakon Haakonson and Skule Baardsson', in *Emotion, Violence, Vengeance and Law in the Middle Ages, Essays in Honor of William Ian Miller*, ed. by Kate Gilbert and Stephen D. White (Leiden: Brill, 2018), pp. 202–24

──, *Unpredictability and Presence: Norwegian Kingship in the High Middle Ages*, The Northern World, 38 (Leiden: Brill, 2008)

Orning, Hans Jacob and Henrik Vigh, 'Constant Crisis', in *Nordic Medieval Civil Wars in a Comparative Perspective*, ed. by Jón Viðar Sigurðsson and Hans Jacob Orning (Leiden: Brill, 2021), pp. 1–33

Paasche, Fredrik, *Kong Sverre*, Aschehougs Fontenebøker (Oslo: Aschehoug, 1966)

Schmitt, Carl, *The Theory of the Partisan: Intermediate Commentary on the Concept of the Political* (New York: Telos Press Publishing, 2007)

Seip, Jens Arup 'Problemer og metode i norsk middelalderforskning', in *Problemer og metode i historieforskningen*, ed. by Jens Arup Seip (Fakkel-Bok. Oslo: Gyldendal, 1983), pp. 15–78

Strickland, Matthew, *War and Chivalry: The Conduct and Perception of War in England and Normandy, 1066–1217*, Cambridge Studies in Medieval Life and Thought (New York: Cambridge University Press, 1996)

Taylor, Alice, *The Shape of the State in Medieval Scotland 1124–1290* (Oxford: Oxford University Press, 2016)

Tilly, Charles, 'War Making and State Making as Organized Crime', in *Bringing the State Back In*, ed. by Peter Evans, Dietrich Rueschemeyer, and Theda Skocpol (Cambridge: Cambridge University Press, 1985), pp. 169–91

Verbruggen, Jan Frans, *The Art of Warfare in Western Europe During the Middle Ages: From the Eighth Century to 1340*, 2nd edn, rev. and enl. (Woodbridge: Boydell Press, 1997)

Vigh, Henrik, 'Crisis and Chronicity: Anthropological Perspectives on Continuous Conflict and Decline', *Ethnos*, 73.1 (2008), 5–24

Part II

Thematic Analyses

JENNY BENHAM, LARS HERMANSON, AND
BJØRN POULSEN

Introduction to Part Two

The first part consisted of extended case studies which highlighted that politics in the twelfth and thirteenth centuries in Scandinavia should be studied as a series of networks, and that conflicts were a more or less permanent feature of the societies in this period. This implies that it easily becomes misleading to distinguish too strictly between different realms, as well as between periods of (civil) war and peace. Departing from these perspectives, the chapters in this part turn to various thematic aspects of the political processes in this period. The analytical framework is consistently inter-Nordic as the authors apply and indeed connect evidence gathered from both Norway, Denmark, and Sweden — and with a view to European parallels as well.

In Chapter 5 Bjørn Poulsen unpacks the material and spatial foundation of conflict across Scandinavia through a registration of central places (towns, assembly sites, royal manors, fortifications), lines of communication, and battlefield topographies, as they are recorded in narrative sources and documented by archaeological evidence. He discusses how the Nordic landscapes differed not only from those of central Europe but also from each other. With regard to military logistics and the potential for rapid deployment, guerrilla tactics, and exile routes, power and the control of space were intimately connected to the sea. In the northern world ships were all-important. More so in Norway (the long coastline) and Denmark (the many islands) than in Sweden (endless forest land), but in every case ships remained a precondition for maintaining regional networks. In Denmark kings and magnates built strongholds of stone inspired by European models. In Norway this was less common, and the role of castles and siege warfare in Scandinavia never compared to what we know from wider Europe. Towns were also more numerous in Denmark than in Norway and, especially, Sweden. Royal palaces (*kongsgårde, curiae*) in towns provided key places for localized kingship, but the spatial distances limited political centralization. What Poulsen demonstrates is that, differences aside, spaces, places and centres across Scandinavia were created and functioned within the context of competing networks and 'constant crisis'. The waterborne communication routes implied that the whole region was closely intertwined across regnal boundaries.

As we saw in all the case studies in part one, marriage constituted an indispensable component of network formation. Dynastic strategizing and accumulation of status and resources very much centred on the exchange of women between elite groups. In Chapter 6 Lars Hermanson approaches this theme from a gender perspective and investigates how and by what means twelfth century high-status women in Scandinavia were able to act upon, exercise control of, and indeed transform power relations. Tracing the socio-political trajectory as well as the subsequent memorialization of Margrethe, princess of the Swedish Stenkil dynasty and queen of first Norway, then Denmark, and of her nieces and their progeny, Hermanson shows how the shape of genealogies and networks change considerably if we take highborn women as our analytical point of departure. Rather than being simply passive transmitters of royal blood and ancestry, women of the elite had decisive functions, both in real life and after their death, in the construction, transformation and preservation of social networks and symbolic capital. The case of Margrethe in particular demonstrates exactly how closely Swedish, Norwegian, and Danish elites were intertwined. As Hermanson concludes, the medieval succession struggles which we have grown used to think of as 'civil wars' within a national or proto-national context were in effect always inter-Nordic intra-elite conflicts.

How rivalling kings and their followers attempted to make peace and put an end (albeit often temporarily) to armed hostilities is the subject of Chapter 7. Here Jenny Benham delves into the agreement of Kvitingsøy in 1208, which — as briefly mentioned in Chapter 4 — was concluded between three royal claimants to the Norwegian crown and supposedly aimed to settle the long-lasting factional strife between Birkibeinar and Baglar. The recording of the agreement is analysed within a broad comparative context of Scandinavian and European peace treaties from 800 to 1250. Specific attention is devoted to the issue of power sharing and partition of realms. According to which principles did parties to peace settlements divide territories and resources? On the basis of this investigation Benham sees the 1208 agreement as conforming in many ways to European ideas and practices. That includes the knowledge, displayed by the author of the record, of canon and Roman law, and also the means and measures applied by the consenting parties to prevent new conflict from breaking out: the choice of location for peace talks, and the symbolic acts and gestures surrounding the reconciliation ceremonies, which aimed first of all at the fostering of personal relations — between rival rulers and between members of their supporting networks.

BJØRN POULSEN

5. Spatial Practices in the Twelfth and Early Thirteenth Century Scandinavian Power Game

In the Scandinavian 'constant crisis' (or the 'coopétition') of the twelfth and thirteenth centuries which is the topic of this book, spaces, places, and centres were created, existed, and became part of and agents in the developments. The physical landscape of the North evidently set the limits with its mountains and plains, but human practice and strategy gave meaning to spaces and places.[1] The enormous spatial distances in the Scandinavian realms in themselves limited the possibilities of central government, gave impulse to royal violence in distant places and, on the other hand, created possibilities for local forces.[2] Exactly this interaction between space and practice forms the core of this chapter. It will aim to sketch the geographical and travel patterns of Nordic participants in the twelfth- and thirteenth-century power game.

This will be undertaken in two ways. First and foremost, space will be described from the narrative texts which mirror the world view of contemporary observers. Secondly, such views are to some degree going to be confronted with what is not in the narrative texts, that is with physical *realia* as we know them from geography and the archaeological and other historical source material. The focus will be on the most condensed, compact, places of the period, namely towns.

As a consequence of the situation of the sources, the realms of Norway and Denmark are the main areas covered, while Sweden receives less consideration. Two narrative texts are central: Snorre Sturluson's *Heimskringla*

---

1 See Harrison, *Medieval Space*; Le Jan, *Coopétition*.
2 Orning, *Unpredictability and Presence*; Lamberg, Hakkanen, and Haikari, *Physical and Cultural Space in Pre-Industrial Europe*.

> **Bjørn Poulsen** (hisbp@cas.au.dk) is professor of medieval and early modern history in the School of Culture and Society, University of Aarhus.

New Perspectives on the 'Civil Wars' in Medieval Scandinavia, ed. by Hans Jacob Orning, Kim Esmark, and Jón Viðar Sigurðsson, Comparative Perspectives on Medieval History, 1 (Turnhout: Brepols, 2024), pp. 217–264
BREPOLS ❧ PUBLISHERS   10.1484/M.CPMH-EB.5.137262

and the Danish *Gesta Danorum* by Saxo Grammaticus.[3] They are supplemented with other texts such as *Fagrskinna, Morkinskinna, Sverris saga, Bǫglunga sǫgur, Knýtlinga saga, Chronicon Roskildense*, and Adam of Bremen. Here we shall be looking for, using Lefebvre's words, *spatial practice*, especially mediated through *representations of space*, that is through the understanding of the selected authors, their perception of the world one may say.[4] It shall, however, constantly be considered whether the literary gaze, which most often is that of victorious kings, is really rooted in reality. Other sources, such as archaeological finds, will, as said, be drawn on too. In this way, it is hoped that we can attain an understanding of the spatiality which the political processes of the time created and crystalized around.

It is only possible to a limited degree to contrast the large narrative sources with other written material such as charters. The charters are generally few, although if they had existed in larger numbers they would, no doubt, have unmasked the selective worldview of the chroniclers. A single example can be given. An extant charter from 1140 documents the privileges given by the Danish king Erik the Lamb to the monastery of S. Peter in the town of Næstved. The charter tells us that it has been negotiated and confirmed in the South Zealand manor of Eggeslevmagle, owned by the Danish magnate Peder Bodilsen.[5] This manor, significantly, is not mentioned in our most important narrative source, Saxo Grammaticus' *Gesta Danorum*, presumably because Saxo focusses rather exclusively on another magnate family of Zealand, the 'Hvide family' and their manors. On a general level, the source from 1140 reminds us of one of the important gaps in our material, namely that towns are much more present in the written sources as places of political action than rural manors.[6]

---

3 In the following, I quote from the English translations by Finlay and Faulkes *Snorri Sturluson, Heimskringla*, vol. 1–3, cited as *Heimskringla* 1–3), and *Saxo Grammaticus. Gesta Danorum. The History of the Danes*, vol. 2, edited by Friis-Jensen and translated by Peter Fisher (Oxford, 2015), cited as *GD*. For a comparison of the two narrative texts, see Sverre Bagge, 'Fortelling, makt og politikk hos Saxo og Snorre'. On the concrete, annalistic and well-documented last part of Saxo's text, see Gelting, 'Saxo Grammaticus in the Archives'.

4 Lefebvre, *The Production of Space*. Cf. Fabian, 'The Spatial Turn within Social and Cultural Studies'; Aalto, 'The Connection between Geographical Space and Collective Memory'.

5 *Diplomatarium Danicum*, ed. by Herluf Nielsen and others (Copenhagen: Ejnar Munksgaards forlag, 1938–), cited as *DD*, I:2, no. 78. Cf. *DD*, I:2, no. 84 — Elias, the provost of Eggeslev(magle) in the company of Peder Bodilsen. Liljefalk and Pajung, 'Bodil-slægten – en sydsjællandsk gåde', pp. 46–60.

6 A point that Dick Harrison makes from Merovingian sources. Harrison, *Medieval Space*, p. 5.

Regions, Paths, Routes

The following concentrates on the Scandinavian scene, and hereby largely ignores distant places such as Jerusalem, Rome, and Constantinople. These places formed part of the macrospace of the Scandinavian game of power, but they may as a consequence of their sacrality or holiness be termed 'qualitatively different spaces'.[7] They were situated far away but, nevertheless, were familiar. Snorre Sturlason knew well that a sea stretched from Gibraltar to the Holy Land, 'Jórsalaland'. Rome, naturally, because of its papal see, formed a centre in the spatial practice and thinking of the time. High-ranking clergymen along with ordinary pilgrims constantly moved between Rome and Scandinavia.[8] The goal here, however, is to see what the more local types of conflict, rivalry, and negotiation were about, partly as perceived by contemporaries, partly as the result of inevitable and visible materiality. The focus is on what may termed the region or microspace, the empirically known world (Fig. 5.1).[9]

One of the simple, but clear, understandings of recent research in spatiality is that places come into existence in a confluence of paths and routes. Places, maybe temporary ones, are constituted through connections and networks, which on the other hand in their totality constitute regions.[10] The paths could be wild, as when the rebellious Sverre after Easter 1177 with his armed group, the Birkibeinar, took 'strange paths' 'through a wood that is thirteen miles long'. He came to 'Eksherred'. As they departed from there they had to cross just as long a wood before they came to a place named 'Malung'. From here, there was fifteen miles more covered with woods to reach 'Jarnberaland'. In all the woods there was no food except meat from birds and elk".[11] This was a long detour to reach a goal. In Sweden, 'Svíþjóð', there was, Snorre writes, 'forested land, and there is so much uninhabited forest that it takes many days to cross it'.[12] During the widespread guerrilla warfare in Norway, the paths often followed risky terrain which led to unknown places. In Denmark spies

---

[7] Cf. Harrison, *Medieval Space*, p. 12; Steen, *Ferd og Fest*, pp. 100–03; Sverrir Jakobsson, 'Hauksbók and the Construction of an Icelandic World View'; Bjarni Einarsson, 'Reisebeskrivelser'; Kålund, 'En islandsk Vejviser for Pilgrimme fra 12. århundrede'; Jensen, 'Vejen til Jerusalem'.

[8] For instance, around 1130 Sigurd Slembe took off to Rome, Jerusalem, and the River Jordan (*Morkinskinna*, p. 368). Erling Skakke was also in Jerusalem at the River Jordan (*Morkinskinna*, p. 390). One of the humbler travellers was, according to *Sverris saga*, Sverre's mother, Gunnhild, who in the mid-twelfth century is said to have travelled to Rome. *Sverris saga*, p. 7. Cf. Finnur Jónsson and Jørgensen, 'Nordiske Pilegrimsnavne'.

[9] Harrison, *Medieval Space*, p. 2.

[10] Ingold, *The Perception of the Environment*; Ingold, *Lines*.

[11] *Sverris saga*, p. 14. Contrary to Danish saints' *vitae*, Norwegian sources have accounts of people getting lost in woods.

[12] *Heimskringla* 1, p. 35.

Figure 5.1. Scandinavia in the Civil War period. Map by author.

could also take quite unexpected routes, as did one Magnus Saksesen, who in 1134, as related in Chapter 3, according to Saxo, let himself be lowered down the steep cliffs of Stevns Klint and then sailed across the Sound to Scania in a small rowing boat to bring to his lord, Erik the Unforgettable, important information.[13]

On the other hand, well-used inland routes existed too, which were based on hard-earned experience and 'routinization'.[14] Narrow mountain passes were vital for intra-regional trade, but some of the routes were large regional roads (Old Norse: *allmannavegr*, Old Danish *athæl wægh*), with

---

13 GD, 13.11.1.
14 Sindbæk, *Ruter og rutinisering*.

bridges crossing rivers.[15] Often the large roads were combined with ferries and shipping. For instance, between Viken and Trøndelag the main traffic was inland, while transport from Viken to Bergen normally went along the coast.[16]

The Ship as a Precondition for Controlling Space

It is certainly possible to define coherent and integrated regions such as Jutland, Scania, Viken, the western part of Norway, the Trøndelag-Mälar area, and Götaland-Uppland, but communication between regions was essential. Ships and ship technology constituted the precondition for the Danish and Norwegian realms that emerged in the Iron and Viking Age. It was certainly not evident that the realms should stay united, but the ship gave mobility and speed, which was necessary to reign over several regions.[17]

Both Denmark and Norway are characterized by their long coasts. Correctly, Adam of Bremen around 1075 writes that 'the land of the Danes is nearly completely cut into islands'.[18] This geography could easily result in several fragmented lordships or realms, such as Western Norway and Viken, or as happened in Denmark after 1146 where the country was divided at the Little Belt. Against this geographical background, the large ships of the time were, so to speak, the materialization of power, connecting space with power. Tellingly, *Sverris saga* informs us that in the 1180s King Magnus Erlingsson was 'alone in holding all ships and therefore he received taxes and duties from all land south of Trondheim'.[19]

The written sources abound with references to sailing, and from them and archaeology we can discern ship types and developments in ship technology.[20] Already around the year 1000 ships could functionally be divided into war ships and merchant ships; the sizes of both types of ships grew constantly. Commercial ships travelled mostly under sail, while rowing was essential for war ships. Quite traditional ships of the same type as Viking Age ships still existed in the twelfth century. Snorre recorded that the Norwegian king Oystein Magnusson (1103–1123) built a large ship

---

15 Pilø, Finstad, and Barrett, 'Crossing the Ice'; Steen, *Ferd og fest*; Matthiessen, *Hærveje*; Ropeid, 'Veg'; Fenger, 'Veje'; Brink, 'Forntida vägar'; Poulsen-Hansen, 'Middelalderens veje'.
16 Elgvin, 'Reiser'.
17 Heebøll-Holm, 'Medieval Denmark as a Maritime Empire'.
18 *Adam von Bremen. Hamburgische Kirchengeschichte*, p. 226, 'provintia Danorum tota fere in insulas dispertita est'.
19 *Sverris saga*, p. 73.
20 Christensen, 'Skibstyper'; Zilmer, 'The Representation of Waterborne Traffic in Old Norse Narratives'; Bill, 'Scandinavian Warships and Naval Power'; Englert, *Large Cargo Ships in Danish Waters 1000–1250*; Larre, 'The Transformation of Naval Warfare in Scandinavia'.

in Trondheim: 'it was built in shape and after the fashion in accordance with how Ormr inn langi had been, which Olav Tryggvason had had made. It also had a dragon-head on the front and a curved tail at the back and both were gilded'.[21] The Danish bishop Absalon sailed a magnificent ship; around 1160, he came to Isøre at the mouth of Isefjord with a 'dragon ship' which the 'Norwegian king had given to [King] Valdemar [I] as a sign of their friendship'.[22] When these kinds of long ships appeared together in a fleet, there was every reason to be on guard. In Trondheim in the 1170s, it was nervously said: 'Father-in-law, some fishermen that have come in are saying that longships were sailing in along the fiord, and people suppose that it must be Birkibeinar'.[23]

Power was, to a large degree, connected to the sea. A strange example of that is the use of Isøre in the Isefjord, a liminal place, without any settlement and with little centrality in relation to inland settlement, but with direct access to the strait of Kattegat and a fine anchorage.[24] Here fleets from all the Danish regions could gather. According to Saxo, this is the place where in 1103 the Danish naval fleet gathered and elected a new king, King Niels.[25] And already in 1076, after the death of King Svend Estridsen, the acclamation of a new king had taken place at Isøre, where 'the vast expanse of Ocean is admitted into a narrow mouth, where the raging seas are pushed and squeezed through a tight entrance between the headlands'.[26] Around 1160 Bishop Absalon had his fleet at Isøre, and in 1169, according to the same author, this was where Absalon met the Norwegian lord Erling Skakke, when he came from the north.[27]

Fleets could form the basis of peaceful meetings, but certainly also be involved in fighting. One of the tax collectors of the Baglar party, who operated in the northern part of Norway (Nordland), was very unlucky that he, with his twenty-oar ship, 'Gullbringen', was waylaid by six ships

---

21 *Heimskringla* 3, p. 123.
22 GD, 14.25.5.
23 *Heimskringla* 3, p. 258.
24 It is, however, clear that Isøre had importance as an outer port for Roskilde. *Knýtlinga saga* describes the place in connection with tenth century events; see Sørensen, *Vikingernes havn*. The use of Isøre as a 'port' seems to have ended in the twelfth century. The placename 'Borreholm' together with finds of tile indicates an early castle here. On liminality as a factor in the location of assembly places, see Semple and Sanmark, 'Assembly in North West Europe', p. 528. A corresponding liminal place where a number of Nordic royal meetings took place is Konghelle in southern Norway at the Göta älv (before the town was founded in early twelfth century). Helle, *Norsk Byhistorie*, p. 58. Carlsson (ed.), *Bohuslän som gränslandskap*, p. 47. Cf. also the meeting place of the Nordic kings, which is mentioned in tenth century saga texts, at the islands of Brännöarna (Brenneyjar, Alvaskären), near present-day Göteborg.
25 GD, 12.8.2.
26 GD, 11.10.3.
27 GD, 14.42.2.

of his enemies, the Birkibeinar. He and all of his men were killed. This was only a small incident, but larger sea battles were not rare along the Norwegian coasts.

In 1139 a Danish-Norwegian fleet was defeated at Holmengrå (Hordaland) by the Norwegian king Inge Hunchback.[28] The Norwegian pretender Hakon the Broad-Shouldered was killed on his way towards Bergen in a sea battle at Sekken in 1162.[29] A smaller battle at sea took place in 1178 at Hattehammeren, west of Trondheim, where men of this town attacked four ships of the Birkibeinar.[30] One of the most decisive battles in Norwegian history occurred in 1184 in the Sogndalsfjorden at Fimreite. King Sverre Sigurdsson was attacked here by his opponent King Magnus Erlingsson. Magnus came from Bergen with a score of ships but Sverre was victorious with fewer vessels, and during the fight King Magnus was killed.[31] In 1194, again there was a large battle at sea at Florvåg (Hordaland) where a fleet from the Orkneys, on its way towards Bergen, was defeated by King Sverre.[32] Danish sea war in the period was mainly directed against enemies on the southern shore of the Baltic. But internal fighting did occur. One of the larger Danish sea battles took place in 1132, when Magnus Nielsen with his fleet sailed from the town of Aarhus against Erik the Unforgettable. Erik the Unforgettable lay at anchor at Sejrø, where he, according to Saxo, attacked the fleet of Magnus, surrounded it and destroyed it, even though Magnus escaped.[33]

The Ship as a Precondition for Regions

The possession of fleets and the control of shipping routes formed the precondition for royal rule: the long coast of Norway and the many Danish islands could only be governed with ships. Norwegian medieval history is heavily connected with ships going up and down the coasts, and Danish history likewise is full of examples of the interregional use of the internal Danish waters. This is the case with the Great Belt (Storebælt) where, as recounted by Saxo, Duke Knud Lavard in 1120s had the experience of his ships being chased by pirates, 'when the ship lay halfway between the two coasts'.[34] And it is also true for the Little Belt (Lille Bælt), where Knud's son Valdemar in the mid-1150s crossed the frozen waters with

---

28 Helle, *Norge blir en stat*, p. 44.
29 Helle, *Norge blir en stat*, p. 57.
30 Helle, *Norge blir en stat*, p. 81.
31 Helle, *Norge blir en stat*, p. 85.
32 Helle, *Norge blir en stat*, p. 91.
33 *Chronicon Roskildense*, p. 27; GD, 13.9.2; Skyum-Nielsen, *Kvinde og slave*, p. 72.
34 GD, 13.3.1.

great difficulty in a small boat.[35] Additionally, sailing was part of Danish commercial and militarily violent interaction with the peoples of the southern Baltic.

In the context of this book the most important region is, however, that which revolved around the Kattegat Strait. The region comprised the southern parts of Norway with the landscape of Viken (Vik) around the Oslo fjord and the (now Swedish) Bohuslän. At the mouth of Göta älv the Danish realm began, and further inland lay the Swedish area of Götaland. Between southern Norway, Denmark and to some degree Götaland there was frequent and direct communication; to an extent, it is possible to speak of a Kattegat region, united by routes that did not respect the borders of kingdoms and in fact became integrated exactly because of internal crisis in the kingdoms.[36] If anywhere, it was here that geographical centre of the multipolar Nordic power field was situated, it was here that most Nordic power networks overlapped.[37]

An archaeological find that illustrates the exchange which took place here is the more than 36 m long ship found in 1997 in Roskilde, which dates to c. 1025. Although this colossal ship ended up in Denmark, most probably as war booty, it had been built in the Norwegian Viken area.[38] Non-peaceful communication across the Kattegat is touched on in connection with Snorre's description of Harald Hardruler (r. 1045–1066) in Oslo: 'Staying there [in Oslo] was very convenient for guarding the land from the Danes, and also for incursions into Denmark'.[39] The sea could be crossed by hostile fleets, as in 1165 when the Danes sailed to Norway and plundered, and the Norwegian magnate Erling Skakke there upon gathered a fleet, most likely with the participation of rebellious Danes, followed the Danes and defeated them at the mouth of the East Jutland river Djurså.[40] The Danish king could arrive with his fleet in Norway, as for instance in 1204, when he according to *Bǫglunga sǫgur* came to Tønsberg with 300 ships.[41] Often it was difficult to say whether the presence of the Danish king was part of a foreign war or an internal struggle. As Orning argues: 'Danish kings sometimes played such an important part in conflicts in Norway that it would be misleading to classify them as external to the rivalry going on within the confines of the Norwegian realm'.[42]

---

35 *Knýtlinga saga*, pp. 282–84.
36 Steen, *Ferd og fest*, pp. 95–97.
37 Jón Viðar Sigurðsson, 'Jyllandshavet ca. 870–1035'; Petersen, 'Skagerrak and Kattegat in the Viking Age', pp. 307–17. For religious connections see *Vitae Sanctorum Danorum*, pp. 3–20 (Sanctus Theodgarvs confessor).
38 Bonde and Stylegar, 'Roskilde 6 – et langskib fra Norge'.
39 *Heimskringla* 3, p. 83.
40 Poulsen, 'Søslagene på Kolindsund'.
41 *Soga om baglarar og birkebeinar*, p. 287.
42 Orning, 'Conflict and Social (Dis)order', p. 55.

Many cases, however, document the direct routes between Norway and Denmark and to a lesser degree Götaland, as exile routes or links to new alliances, often confirmed through marriage. If things got too problematic at home, one could, as the Danish pretender Erik the Unforgettable did after he was defeated at Værebro in 1133, flee to Norway (see Chapter 3). Saxo tells us that Erik sailed to Norway 'in a single vessel'.[43] Further, Saxo reports that King Knud (Magnussen) in 1150 escaped from Viborg to Aalborg and from there went on to his stepfather King Sverker in Lödöse at the Götaelv.[44] In reverse, as discussed in Chapter 2, King Harald Gille in 1134 fled from Norway to Denmark after he had lost the battle at Fyrilev, and left his Norwegian realm to Magnus Sigurdsson. Harald was given the Danish province of Halland as a fief by the Danish king.

In Denmark, Aalborg in Northern Jutland was an important place in this regional network. Adam of Bremen notes that 'if one boards a ship in Aalborg or Vendsyssel one can sail to the town of Wig [Oslo or Tønsberg?] in one day'.[45] Aalborg became a sort of accepted safe haven. If a wife had to run away from her husband, like the wife of the Dane Henrik the Lame, she could go to Aalborg to try to flee to Norway.[46] If Norwegians wanted to get away from bitter conflicts at home, they sailed to Aalborg,[47] just as Olav Ugjæva (the Unlucky) did. Snorre tells that he went to Aalborg (Álaborg), 'the next winter after that. And the following spring Óláfr caught an illness that led to his death, and he is buried there at the Church of Our Lady (Maríukirkja), and the Danes call him a saint'.[48] In 1135 it was Sigurd Slembe who reached Denmark from Norway. Snorre reports that 'he stayed in Álaborg during the winter'. After his subsequent, terrible death his corpse was transferred to Aalborg, to 'the Church of Our Lady (Maríukirkja) there in the town. The provost Ketill, who was in charge of Maríukirkja, told Eiríkr that Sigurðr was buried there'.[49] In 1170 the Norwegian chief Erling Skakke with his ship ventured even further down the east coast of Jutland, namely to the town of Randers to seek the Danish king in his hall. The result of the meeting was an agreement with the king, and generally it was the rule that the Baglar party, to which Erling belonged, were supported by Danish kings. Therefore, members of the group often went to Denmark. In 1204 some of them retreated to

---

43 *GD*, 13.11.4.
44 *GD*, 14.5.2.
45 *Adam von Bremen. Hamburgische Kirchengeschichte*, p. 267. Cf. Englert, 'Rejsehastighed over Kattegat og Skagerrak'.
46 *GD*, 13.4.3.
47 Cf. Harald Gille, who went to Denmark in 1134.
48 *Heimskringla* 3, p. 256; Steen, *Ferd og fest*, p. 96. The author of *Fagrskinna* notes Aarhus as the place where he died (*Fagrskinna*, p. 358).
49 *Morkinskinna*, pp. 371, 387; *Heimskringla* 3, pp. 190, 197. Ketill is Danish Kjeld, see *Vitae Sanctorum Danorum*, pp. 252–83 (Sanctus Ketillvs confessor).

Copenhagen and from here they sent messages to Viken in Norway stating that they should all gather in Aalborg to prepare a military expedition against Oslo. Next year, the Baglar were in Aalborg and from there they sailed to Viken.[50]

Swedish Götaland was located in another periphery of the Kattegat region. Here the royal Eriks and Sverker families ruled; they participated in the larger Scandinavian power game, and therefore welcomed high-born refugees from Norway and Denmark. The Danish pretender Oluf Haraldsen, for instance, was in Götaland in the early 1140s.[51] The Danish King Knud V also, it was said, took refuge in Lödöse in Götaland in 1150, and a couple of members of the Danish royal family, who had rebelled in vain against their king in 1176, had to flee by ship from Randers to Götaland.[52] The Norwegians likewise also went to the Swedish king. After a battle between King Inge and Magnus the Blind, the latter fled to Götaland and so did other rebels at the same time.[53]

The third key area of the Kattegat region, the Sound, was situated further to the south. The central point in the Sound region was the international herring markets which had evolved on the southern coast of Scania, which was then part of Denmark. Here thousands of people met at the Haløre market or Skanør from the mid-twelfth century, many of whom were Norwegians; it was only gradually that Germans became the majority of visitors.[54] In 1196 Bishop Nikolas Arneson of Oslo and Archbishop Eirik of Nidaros (Trondheim) travelled to this place to meet a group of rebellious Baglar from Viken.[55] Six years later, in 1203, as discussed in Chapter 4, Erling Stonewall was in Skanør to discuss with a large group of Norwegians whether they should start a war with the ruling Norwegian king. This did not happen immediately, and Erling Stonewall went to the emerging centre of Copenhagen on the Zealand bank of the Sound.[56]

Nordic policy in the twelfth to thirteenth centuries retained much of its dynamic precisely because of the political geography made possible by the Kattegat and Sound regions. People who sought power and possessed ships could easily switch sides in the area. They could deescalate conflicts, but also find a place to build up troops and initiate new campaigns. The open space between Norway and Denmark by its very existence created possibilities for movement that furthered change in the power game.

---

50 *Soga om baglarar og birkebeinar*, p. 286.
51 GD, 14.2.9.
52 GD, 14.54.16.
53 Helle, *Norge blir en stat*, p. 55.
54 Eriksson, *Skånemarkedet*; Jahnke, *Das Silber des Meeres*.
55 *Sverris saga*, p. 129.
56 *Soga om baglarar og birkebeinar*, pp. 281–82, 286. On Copenhagen see Hanna Dahlström, Poulsen, and Olsen, 'From a port for Traders to a Town of Merchants'.

Law Communities as Creators of Regional Meeting Places

If we move to the level of individual kingdoms, it is possible to observe more limited networks and assembly practices, which created public spaces. The space of law and power in Denmark and Norway was partly constituted by the kingdoms but also, and more important, by the 'pre-state' law provinces. In Norway we can, quite early, identify the areas of Gulathing, Borgarthing, Trøndelag (Frostathing) and Eidsivathing; in Denmark four provinces had written laws in the twelfth to thirteenth centuries: Scania, Zealand, Funen, and Jutland. Archaeologically it is possible already in the Viking Age to observe differences between the areas, which mirror diverging identities and possible law systems.[57]

The places where the men of the regional areas gathered, and which constituted their sense of community, were the assembly places, where delegates from the various districts in each region met to make legal judgements and pass laws. Æilnoth of Canterbury's description of Jutland's centre, Viborg, is presumably accurate: 'here often large groups from Jutland assemble, partly to negotiate common matters, partly to discuss whether the laws are just and valid and to give them firmness. Whatever is agreed upon by the unified voice of the crowd cannot without punishment be set aside anywhere in Jutland'.[58] The twelfth- and thirteenth-century laws are naturally themselves witnesses to the assemblies, but there is little doubt that the history of these assemblies goes back into the Iron Age, before the Viking period.[59] If we turn to our primary sources for this connection, the works of Snorre and Saxo, it is clear that they regarded such assemblies as extremely important public spaces. They appear as central for the legitimatization for all persons who sought power, and ultimately for the acquisition of royal power.

A central place for acclaiming kings in Norway was, according to Snorre, the Eyrathing at the mouth of the Nidelv Trondheimsfjord, which was the central place for the whole area of Trøndelag. Snorre records that in 1028 King Knud the Great was made king at the Eyrathing, and that Magnus the Good in 1035 was likewise acclaimed at the same assembly.[60] According to Snorre, Hakon Magnusson was still able to gather

---

57 Sindbæk, 'Kulturelle forskelle, sociale netværk og regionalitet i vikingetidens arkæologi'.
58 *Vitae Sanctorum Danorum*, p. 111.
59 Christensen, *Vikingetidens Danmark*; Helle, *Gulatinget og Gulatingslova*; Nørgård Jørgensen, Jørgensen, and Gebauer Thomsen, 'Assembly Sites for Cult, Markets, Jurisdiction and Social Relations'; Iversen, 'Concilium and Pagus'; Iversen, 'The Thing in Trøndelag'; Semple and Sanmark, 'Assembly in North West Europe'; Sanmark, *Viking Law and Order*; Iversen, 'Between Tribe and Kingdom'; Hartvig and Poulsen, 'Contextualizing an Early Medieval Village'.
60 *Heimskringla* 3, p. 6; Taranger, 'Om Kongevalg i Norge'.

the Eyrathing in 1093: 'and at this assembly Hákon asked for the title of king for himself, and this was granted him, insofar as the farmers took him as king over half the country, which is what his father Magnús had had'.[61] Oystein Haraldsson, Snorre further states, in 1136 got the farmers (*prændir*) to acclaim him king at this assembly.[62] Presumably, it was also here that Hakon Sigurdsson in 1159 was made king.[63] In 1162 we hear that Erling Skakke had the Eyrathing gathered and succeeded in getting them to acclaim his son Magnus Erlingsson king, and in 1163 Sigurd Sigurdsson Markusfostre was successful in being accepted as king there.[64] Later, too, in 1202 Hakon Sverresson, the son of King Sverre, was acclaimed as king at the Øyrating, and in 1205 Erling Stonewall became king here.[65] However, other assemblies could be used. In 1136 Inge was first acclaimed as king at Borgarthing, the assembly for the area of Viken, and was only subsequently confirmed as king at the Øyrating.[66] And in 1130 Harald Gille was 'accepted as king over half the country' at the Haugating outside Tønsberg, while the other part of the country fell to Magnus the Blind after a meeting in Oslo.[67] King Sverre was first acclaimed as king at the assembly in Bohuslen in 1177, and only later at the Øyrating.

For the Danish kings, the regional assembly of Viborg had a central role.[68] This was certainly the opinion of Snorre, who, in connection with his description of King Magnus the Good's acclamation here in 1042, noted: 'That is where the Danes have chosen themselves kings in both ancient and modern times'.[69] As in 1046, when the Norwegian King Harald Hardruler tried to become king of Denmark, Snorre tells us that the king wanted to bring his army to 'to Vébjargaþing and having himself accepted as king over the realm of the Danes'.[70] In Saxo's text, we read that King Erik the Good chose to announce his pilgrimage to Jerusalem at the assembly at Viborg, and after his death in 1103 the Viborg assembly seems to have become a regular place for choosing a new king. In 1146 Knud (and maybe Svend) and in 1154 Knud and Valdemar were made kings in Viborg.[71] Viborg was, however, not always the chosen locality. Already in 1076 after the death of King Svend Estridsen, Isøre, as noted above, was presumably

---

61 *Heimskringla* 3, p. 127.
62 *Heimskringla* 3, p. 197.
63 *Heimskringla* 3, p. 234.
64 *Heimskringla* 3, pp. 240, 245.
65 *Soga om baglarar og birkebeinar*, p. 272.
66 *Heimskringla* 3, p. 186.
67 *Heimskringla* 3, p. 170. See Chapter 2.
68 For the following see Erich Hoffmann, *Köningserhebung und Thronfolgeordnung*, pp. 23–190.
69 *Heimskringla* 3, p. 21.
70 *Heimskringla* 3, p. 63.
71 Kristensen, 'Knud Magnussens krønike', p. 443; GD, 14.16.4; Skyum Nielsen, *Kvinde og slave*, p. 137.

the place where the acclamation took place, and in 1104, a new king was acclaimed by the army at Isøre.[72]

In general, according to Saxo, there were no fixed places for the acclamation of Danish kings. In 1131, Harald Kesja sought to be accepted as king at the regional assembly in Ringsted on Zealand, and as described in Chapter 3, he was later acclaimed king at the southern Jutland assembly at Urne.[73] The period with several kings at the same time is mirrored in Saxo's description of Harald Kesja's son Oluf Haraldsen who 1140 was acclaimed at the Scania assembly in Arnedal (outside the town of Lund), and in his notice that Svend and Knud were acclaimed at the regional assemblies of Scania, Zealand, and Jutland.[74] Saxo tells us that in 1182 Knud VI was traditionally acclaimed at the regional assembly of Viborg but also that he afterwards encountered some protests when he sought further acclamation at the Urne assembly in southern Jutland.[75]

Both in Norway and in Denmark claimants to the throne, according to the sources, sought the acclamation of the 'people' at opportune places, even if it is clear that some places were more prestigious than others. Only the Danish Isøre, however, was in principle for the whole realm, and it is clear that the existence of several regional assemblies could further the system of several kings. In addition to this possibility of conflict, it can be added that Norwegian candidates to the Danish throne during the eleventh century sought acclamation at Danish assemblies. As mentioned above, Snorre tells us that this was the case with Magnus the Good and Harald Hardruler. Such a procedure, according to both Saxo and Snorre, was also vital in King Valdemar I's attempt to become ruler of Norway in 1165–1166. Saxo writes that Valdemar, 'when he reached the town of Borg (present-day Sarpsborg),[76] assumed the royal title, which the citizens of Viken had resolved to confer on him, and there held an assembly of the populace'. Snorre, as well as Saxo, depicts Valdemar's arrival in Tønsberg, but with rather different details. Saxo tells how 'the citizens of Tønsberg [...] received him in their district and paid their respects with a most distinguished procession'. Snorre, on the other hand, recounts the story that after the arrival of the king in Tønsberg, 'King Valdemar called an assembly there on Haugar, but no one attended from the surrounding districts. Then King Valdemar made a speech'.[77]

---

72 GD, 12.8.2.
73 GD, 14.1.4. It has wrongly been argued that it was only after 1192–1197 that the Urne assembly achieved its position of a regional assembly. Andersen, Rex imperator, pp. 53, 70–73.
74 GD, 14.2.5 and 14.3.3.
75 GD, 16.1.1.
76 In Østfold, to the east of Oslo Fjord; it was the general assembly site of the inhabitants of Viken.
77 GD, 14.29.18, 14.38.2; Heimskringla 3, p. 252.

The regional assemblies had many ordinary and daily functions, but they were also central in negotiations between the ruler and the population. Saxo tells us in passing, though it can hardly be coincidental, that Knud Magnussen, in the in the three-king situation in 1157, went to the regional court of Zealand in Ringsted, 'which, as it happened, was taking place that day, thronged with milling crowds of people'.[78] After the killing of King Knud in Roskilde in the same year, Saxo said of King Valdemar that he 'proceeded to Viborg' where 'he [king Valdemar] spoke before the assembly about Svend's guile'.[79] Ruler-people negotiations at the assembly are also seen when Erling Skakke had taken Bergen and immediately called the assembly: 'Straightway in the morning Erlingr had all his troops called out onto Eyrar by trumpet for an assembly, and at the assembly Erlingr brought charges against the Þrœndir, accusing them of treason against the king and himself, and naming them as responsible'.[80] In situations of conflict and fighting, the assemblies were apparently essential for securing support.[81] The interplay between the people and the ruler at the assembly are probably given in most detail in Saxo's history of the rebellion against Absalon in Scania in 1180–1182. Here the Scanian regional assembly at Arnedal, outside Lund, is the place where the king and bishop tried to talk to the leaders of the rebellious people.[82] Unlucky royal officials were 'shamefully handled ... by a ferocious assembly' at the Scania assembly during the rebellion and had to flee from the crowd.[83]

Beneath these regional assemblies, there was a large number of local assemblies which were often used in lordly negotiations with the rural and urban populations. Around 1157 Gregorius in Konghelle gathered 'a large assembly with landowners and townspeople and requested troops'.[84] A typical town meeting, presumably what we from the laws know as a *moth*, appears in 1157, where we have the story in Saxo of how Svend acted in the town of Roskilde: 'At daybreak Svend gathered the townsfolk (*ciuibus*) together and complained that his rivals had made a treacherous attempt on him during the night; he showed them his bloody cloak'.[85] Saxo also tells us about the assemblies of the small territorial units, the *herreder*, *herredsting*. This happened in connection with the complaints raised after the murder of Knud Lavard in 1131 (see Chapter 3). The situation was set out as follows: 'Sunniva's son, Hakon, along with Peder, whose mother was Bodil, and the sons of Skjalm pursued the hideous

---

78 *GD*, 14.18.1.
79 *GD*, 14.19.3.
80 *Heimskringla* 3, p. 251.
81 *GD*, 14.19.3.
82 *GD*, 14.13.1; Skovgaard Petersen, 'Saxo som samtidshistoriker'.
83 *GD*, 15.4.1.
84 *Heimskringla* 3, p. 215.
85 *GD*, 14.18.11.

crime by framing serious accusations in every popular assembly'.[86] Among the many flattering words attributed to Bishop Absalon by Saxo are that he was a most elegant and flawless speaker at the local assemblies, the *herredstingar*.[87]

In the fight for recognition and legitimization in the realm and the regions, the assemblies were central places. They were filled with symbolic value. The assemblies stood as markers of identity; in fact they constituted the regions as such. Acclamation at the assemblies was therefore essential in order to become a king, and speeches at the assemblies were frequently a form of power negotiation.

Meeting at the Battlefield

If words and negotiations were of no use, if overlapping networks collided, one could gamble and seek power in a violent way by going into battle on land, creating landscapes of conflict.[88] Battles were deliberately sought; leaders generally tried to defeat the enemy in open battle with larger forces.[89] Terror against the rural population, on the other hand, was not a common tactic in internal struggles, although defenceless women and children were killed in large numbers during fighting in Norwegian towns.[90]

The warring parties could go to the manors and large farms in the countryside which do not appear much in the sources. But in these situations they do occur. A very large battle took place in 1134 outside the royal manor of Fyrileiv in Viken between the armies of the two Norwegian kings Magnus the Blind and Harald Gille.[91] A raid was carried in 1167, when Erling Skakke was resting in the presbytery (*præstegård*) of Rydjøkul (Sørum, Romerike) and he was surprised by Norwegian warriors supported by Danes. In Denmark that sort of surprise could also take place. In 1135 Erik Kesja, who had been acclaimed king, was attacked by King Erik the Unforgettable on his manor, presumably in the Kolding region, and was beheaded together with his eleven sons (see Chapter 3).[92] A few years later, in 1139 the bishop of Roskilde was caught and killed by the son of Harald Kesja, Oluf, on his manor Ramløse in northern Zealand.[93] Later,

---

86 GD, 13.7.4 (while Harald went to the regional assembly in Viborg).
87 GD, 14.21.3.
88 There is a rich European literature on medieval battlefields. Keegan, *The Face of the Battle*; Curry, *Agincourt*; Williams, 'Landscape and Warfare in Anglo-Saxon England'; Creighton and Wright, *The Anarchy*.
89 Arstad, 'The Use of Castles as Military Strongholds'; Arstad, 'Rex Bellicosus', p. 522.
90 Arstad, 'Rex Bellicosus', p. 524; Brødholt and Holck, 'Skeletal Trauma'.
91 Scott, 'Kongs- og lendmannsgårder i Viken', p. 36.
92 GD, 14.1.4; Orluf, 'Hvor dræbtes Harald Kesja?'; Skyum Nielsen, *Kvinde og slave*, p. 79.
93 GD, 14.2.10. The bishop's manor in the village of Ramløse was later known as Hovgård.

the same Oluf Haraldsen was killed in 1141 by King Erik the Lamb, while he was resting at the royal manor of Årstad in Halland.[94]

Large-scale battles could also occur on the periphery of the main sphere of power, as happened when King Knud in 1151 fought against King Svend in the west Schleswig marshes, near the later town of Husum. Sometimes small trading places and harbours appear as battlefields in the sources. This is the case with the West Zealand harbour of Boeslunde in south-west Zealand where, in 1158, Bishop Absalon and his retinue met Slavic forces.[95] A battle nearly also took place in 1156 at the important harbour on the Seløyene, an island group off the south coast of Norway (Agder), between King Inge Hunchback and King Oystein; but it was stopped when Oystein paid tribute to the other party.[96]

In general, however, battles often occurred when armies were on their way towards a town, seeking lordship over it. The importance of towns is made clear by the location of battlefields. External enemies such as Slavic looters naturally went directly to the towns in order to get rich. As did Prince Ratibor I, Duke of Pomerania, when he, in a politically motivated raid, plundered Roskilde in Denmark and Konghelle in Norway in 1135.[97] But it appears to be characteristic that domestic battles were fought outside towns. Admittedly, control of the towns was the goal, but the battles took place in the vicinity rather than inside the towns. As a pretender Hakon the Broad-Shouldered advanced on King Inge Haraldsson in Oslo, and said: 'King Ingi then went out onto the ice with his army and set up his battle line in front of the town'.[98] The fight ended with Inge being killed by his nephew. In another situation, as Harald Gille returned to Konghelle, he was met by 'the landed men [*lendir menn*] and the citizens', who 'drew up a line of battle above the town'.[99] 1161 was the year of two battles near towns, namely first on the ice at Ekeberg outside Oslo and secondly at Tønsberg. In 1177, two armies, each consisting of a couple of thousand men, met at Re in Vestfold. One of the armies, the Birkibeinar, were seeking to take Tønsberg but were crushed by the forces of King Magnus Erlingsson. On the other hand, in 1179, the king of the Birkibeinar, King Sverre, won

---

94 *GD*, 14.2.12. The dating to 1141, Skyum Nielsen, *Kvinde og slave*, p. 84. It is, however, possible that it took place in 1143. On the royal manor of Årstad, Halland, see Nilsson, 'Hallandslistan i kung Valdemars jordebok'.
95 *GD*, 14.21.4. On Boeslunde as early medieval trading place see Jørgensen, 'Stormandssæder og skattefund i 3.-12. århundrede'; Ulriksen, Schultz, and Mortensen, 'Dominating the Landscape', p. 7.
96 *Morkinskinna*, p. 402. The fleet of the Baglar in 1207 at the Seløyene. *Soga om baglarar og birkebeinar*, pp. 316–17.
97 Cf. Hermanson, 'Kungahälla och Europa', pp. 33–34. In *Annales Lundenses* the attack on Roskilde is dated to 1135: *DMA*, p. 57.
98 *Heimskringla* 3, p. 228.
99 *Heimskringla* 3, p. 173.

the famous battle at Kalvskinnet at Trondheim. It was at this battle that Erling Skakke died, and from then on, the Trondheim region was ruled by Sverre.[100]

In 1181, King Magnus Erlingsson tried to take back Trondheim with a large force; the fighting took place at a narrow place, Illevollene, outside the town. Thanks to his superior tactics, Sverre was the absolute winner. In 1206, the Baglar attacked Trondheim; Erling Stonewall took the town by surprise while King Inge Bardson's sister was celebrating her marriage there. The Baglar took a lot of war booty. Fortunes, however, were later reversed in the same year when the Birkibeinar attacked the Baglar in Bergen, while they were besieging the castle of the town. In 1207, the Birkibeinar made similar assaults on Tønsberg and Oslo.

Likewise, in Denmark, battlefields were deliberately chosen in order to capture towns, though the actual fighting took place outside the town. Snorre tells that, in 1043–1044, while Svend Estridsen was staying in the town of Aarhus he sought battle with King Magnus the Good, and, 'then he brought his troops out of the town and prepared for battle'.[101] A skaldic verse has more precise information that the battle took place 'south of Áróss'.[102]

The main town of twelfth century Denmark was Lund in Scania, and as discussed in Chapter 3, the most decisive Danish battle of that century was fought in 1134 at the bay of Fotevig. It clearly represented an attempt to take Lund. Initially, King Niels was forced to leave Lund by Erik the Unforgettable. As Niels returned and disembarked on the coast of Scania, his forces were massacred. Niels had to flee, and Erik retained lordship over the town of Lund and the whole region of Scania.[103] Some years later, in 1142 Oluf Haraldsen, who had become king in 1140, lost a battle against King Erik the Lamb in Scania at Glumstorp, also near Lund.[104]

The royal town of Roskilde often constituted the prize in battles on Zealand. The bridge of Værebro, 14 km north of Roskilde, is the only suitable crossing over the 30 km long Værebro river if one comes from the north along the eastern bank of the Roskilde Fjord. Here Erik the Unforgettable and his army were defeated in 1133 and he had to flee.[105] The winner, King Niels, who had come from the north with a fleet of 100 ships, went on and 'ravaged Roskilde'.[106] A little more to the north, in 1139, marching against Roskilde, at the river Bydinge between the

---

100 Blom, 'Trondheim bys historie', p. 159.
101 *Heimskringla* 3, p. 28.
102 *Heimskringla* 3, p. 38.
103 GD, 13.11.8–10; Crumlin-Pedersen, *Pugna Forensis*.
104 GD, 14.2.8.
105 GD, 13.11.1.
106 *Chronicon Roskildense*, p. 27 ('Roskildam deuastatuit'). The fleet of King Niels was presumably stopped by a sea defence at Skuldelev. Crumlin-Pedersen, *Søvejen til Roskilde*.

Arresø and Roskilde Fjord, Oluf Haraldsen was defeated.[107] During the wars between Svend, Knud, and Valdemar after 1146, Knud tried several times to march on Roskilde. In 1146 or 1147, he suffered a defeat by his rival Svend, 'in the very bloody battle' outside the royal manor and town of Slangerup; presumably he too came from the north, as the place is situated at a bottleneck between Helsingør and Roskilde.[108] Again in 1150, Knud, who had invaded from the Sound coast (near Copenhagen), lost a battle at (Høje) Tåstrup, 11 km to the east of Roskilde, and was driven away again.[109]

In Jutland the regional assembly and royal centre of Viborg constituted the much-desired goal for claimants to the throne. In 1152 (or 1151) King Knud marched on the road (*Hærvej*) towards Viborg and was defeated by King Svend's soldiers at Gedbæk, outside Viborg.[110] In 1157, Svend came from the east, from a position in the town of Randers, trying to take Viborg. But the river Gudenå forced him south, and again he found himself south of Viborg on the same road, the *Hærvej*, at Grathe Moor, where Valdemar's forces met him on 23 October. King Svend fled and was killed. A chapel was erected at the place of the battle.[111]

To Conquer a Town

If a hostile army reached a town, it did not necessarily have to fight much to take it. Town walls and fortifications were not common in the first part of the twelfth century, and one may also question whether they were effective. Towns in Scandinavia were apparently at the mercy of attacking enemies, both external and internal.

In 1123, King Sigurd the Crusader plundered both the Danish (Scanian) town of *Tumaþorp* (Tommerup) and Swedish Kalmar without problems.[112] The above-mentioned raid in 1135 on Konghelle by the Slavic Prince Ratibor I was brutal. Snorre records that brought 'five hundred and fifty Wendish warships, and on every warship there were forty-four men and two horses'. Although 'the merchants armed themselves and defended themselves well and valiantly for a long time', this did not help. Snorre's account of the Slavic attack continues thus: 'They took all the wealth that

---

107 GD, 14.2.9.
108 GD, 14.3.4; Skyum Nielsen, *Kvinde og slave*, p. 137; Andrén, *Den urbana scenen*, p. 178.
109 GD, 14.3.13; Skyum Nielsen, *Kvinde og slave*, p. 138.
110 GD, 14.4.5.
111 Fabricius, 'Den jyske krig i Efteraaret 1157'; Skyum Nielsen, *Kvinde og slave*, p. 144.
112 *Heimskringla* 3, p. 161; Jönsson and Wallebom, *Tommarp och Simrishamn*. The attacks were strategically placed as both places were important outlets for iron from the northern Scanian woodlands. Ödman, 'Skånskt järn från malm till marknad'.

was there in the fortification. They went in to Krosskirkja and plundered it of all its finery'.[113]

In the internal Danish struggles of the first part of the twelfth century, it is evident that towns often were conquered without fighting. King Niels could in 1133 plunder Roskilde without resistance, and fairly typically King Knud in 1150 captured Roskilde, 'as it lay unprepared'.[114] In Norway fighting did not just occur in the vicinity of towns. There are many more examples of street fighting, such as when Erling Skakke took Trondheim in 1162: 'Erlingr and his men ran into the town, and they were told that Óttarr birtingr's son Álfr hroði, a landed man [*lendr maðr*] was still sitting and drinking with his men. Erlingr made an attack on them. Álfr was killed and nearly all his men. Few other men fell, for most had gone to church'.[115] This scene exactly matches the beginning of the battle of Kalvskinnet in 1177; the prelude was a feint where the Birkibeinar warriors were chased through Trondheim by the Baglar.[116] In 1206 the Baglar succeeded in going unseen into Trondheim and successfully chasing all Birkibeinar, including King Inge, through the lanes and streets and into the fields.[117]

Only a few towns were fortified as a result of the constant violence. Through the archaeology and written sources, we can, however, follow the building of walls around the large Danish episcopal towns. Lund was fortified in 1134, as was Roskilde around the same time or even a couple of years earlier.[118] It is said that King Svend in 1147, after an embarrassing failure of a crusade against the Slavs, occupied Zealand and 'encircled Roskilde, which was destitute of walls, with a rampart and ditch'.[119] Even if Knud later, as just mentioned, returned to Roskilde and took the town, at his first attempt the town successfully prevented him and his army from entering and 'closed its gates to him'.[120] Viborg was fortified in the period between a battle near the town in 1150 and another just south of it in 1151.[121] Saxo says about Svend: 'he resolved to withstand siege in Viborg, a town which he had recently improved with defence works'. After this, King Svend was so convinced that the town could not be taken that 'he resolved to withstand siege in Viborg, a town which he

---

113 *Heimskringla* 3, pp. 176–77.
114 *Chronicon Roskildense*, p. 27; GD, 14.3.12.
115 *Heimskringla* 3, p. 251.
116 Blom, 'Kong Olavs by, ca. 1000–1537', p. 158.
117 *Soga om baglarar og birkebeinar*, pp. 304–06.
118 Kristensen and Poulsen, *Danmarks byer i middelalderen*, pp. 76–78; Birkebæk and Høj (eds), *Roskilde Bys Historie – tiden indtil 1536*, pp. 67–171. Cf. *Chronicon Roskildense*, p. 28: 'Eo tempore Lund muro et uallo iussu Herici est circumdata'.
119 GD, 14.3.9: 'uallo fossaque complectitur'.
120 GD, 14.3.11.
121 Hjermind and Kristensen, 'Svend Grathes vold'.

had recently improved with defence works'.[122] Only a little later, he used the same tactic to defend himself in the episcopal town of Odense on Funen, 'the inhabitants of which he won for his sake through promises of protection'.[123] The Danish town defences of the twelfth century played an important role but only for a very short time, and their existence mirrored the most intense period of fighting between the claimants to the throne.

In Norway, the large town of Trondheim for a long period was completely without fortifications. Archbishop Oystein (d. 1188) was the first to attempt to build timber defences to close off access to the town.[124] Sarpsborg or Borg presumably from its foundation by King Olav Haraldsson in 1016 had an earthwork wall as protection in west, but this was not the rule.[125] Some kind of early fortification is, however, mentioned at Konghelle, where Sigurd the Crusader (r. 1103–1130) 'had buildings erected in the royal palace grounds within the fortifications. He imposed on all the areas that were in the vicinity of the market town, and also on the citizens, that every twelve months each man nine winters old or older was to carry to the fortification five stone war-missiles or another five stakes, and these must be sharpened at one end and five ells high'.[126] In the 1130s, Snorre mentions that Magnus the Blind in Bergen sought to protect himself against his rival Harald Gille: 'He had a ballista set up out on Hólmr, and he had iron chains and some timber booms made and placed across the bay over below the royal palace. He had caltrops forged and thrown across onto Jóansvellir, and no more than three days over Yule were kept sacred so that no work was done'.[127]

Towns as Royal Seats

Both in Norway and in Denmark, a system of royal farms, halls, and manors existed in rural areas, used by the ambulatory king. From here power was exercised, and, through both simple violence and local negotiation, revenue was kept for the kings.[128] Many of the manors were, no doubt, frequently visited by the rulers. It is hardly accidental that both a Danish and a Norwegian king died on royal manors in the periphery: Olav Kyrre in 1093 at the manor of Haukbœr in Bohuslän (Håkeby, in Tanum)

---

122 *GD*, 14.5.5–6.
123 *GD*, 14.17.8.
124 Blom, 'Kong Olavs by, ca. 1000–1537', p. 158.
125 Fischer, *Norske kongeborger*, vol. 1, pp. 25–27.
126 *Heimskringla* 3, p. 169. Cf. Andersson, *Kungahälla*.
127 *Heimskringla* 3, p. 175.
128 Orning, 'Den materielle basis for den norske kongemaktens utvikling i høymiddelalderen'; Poulsen, 'Den danske konges indtægter i middelalderen'; Orning, 'Festive Governance'; Skre, *Rulership in 1st to 14th century Scandinavia*.

while travelling on the 'Kungsvägan' from Konghelle to Oslo, and Svend Estridsen on the road 'Hærvejen' through Jutland on the small manor of Søderup in Sønder-Jutland (near the later town of Aabennraa).[129]

But instead of this kind of local rural presence, already in the eleventh and twelfth centuries, there is a marked tendency for kings to stay in royal palaces (*kongsgårde*) located in towns.[130] Therefore, the importance of rural manors dwindled; tellingly, it was during the first years of his reign that King Sverre (1177–1202) was a guest at rural centres. His saga tells us: that in the Gudbrandsdal 'half a month of provision (*veitsle*) was given him and his whole army on the royal manor of Steig'. It was done in this way because the king as a rebel had to avoid the towns. As soon as he had control and full power, he stayed in towns just like other rulers of this period.[131]

It was only in the second part of the twelfth century that a more permanent place for the burial of Danish kings came into existence with the choice of Ringsted, and it was also then that the Norwegian kings selected Bergen as the fixed location for royal burials. The question is whether earlier general patterns exist in the way those in power used towns. At least, it can be said that royal power and town life soon became deeply intertwined. In a contemporary skaldic verse, recounting events in the year 1044, the Danish King Svend Estridsen was tellingly termed 'Lund's overlord'.[132] Danish and Norwegian towns had the status of towns precisely because they had royal protection.[133]

The Danish kings could choose to stay in different towns, but, in the view of the Zealander Saxo, the town of Roskilde was their most important centre. Saxo tells us that Danish kings from Svend Estridsen onwards stayed here.[134] In the period after the killing of Knud Lavard in 1131, Roskilde still, according to Saxo, constituted a safe place for the murderer, King Niels' son Magnus. Here royal individuals apparently could relax, when the nearby regional assembly apparently was too dangerous. In 1131 King Niels thought that in respect to the life of his son Magnus 'it would be dangerous for him to enter the assembly [in Ringsted]'. It is said that he 'did not dare expose his own or his son's retinue to the violence of the mob'.[135] The town of king and bishop, Roskilde, was set against a town,

---

129 *Heimskringla* 3, p. 126; GD, 11.9.1. In the 1170s King Valdemar the Great held meetings, where he 'was surrounded by all the Danish aristocracy' at his manor in Viby, outside Aarhus. GD, 14.54.25.
130 Iversen, 'Eiendom, makt og statsdannelse'; Orning, *Unpredictability and Presence*.
131 Steen, *Ferd og fest*, p. 137.
132 *Heimskringla* 3, p. 32.
133 Some Danish towns had bishops or lay magnates as town lords. Kristensen and Poulsen, *Danmarks byer i middelalderen*, pp. 152–53.
134 GD, 11.7.12.
135 GD, 13.6.8–13.7.3. See Chapter 3.

Ringsted, controlled by broader groups in society. Roskilde, according to Saxo, was also the more or less stable residence of King Svend.[136] King Valdemar the Great could, as when he in 1160 demanded oaths of allegiance, gather all magnates of the country in Roskilde, and Saxo tells us that the king regularly stayed here and 'heard mass in the church of the Supreme and Highest Trinity'.[137] Other important royal towns with royal residences before 1157 included, according to Saxo, the episcopal towns of Lund, Schleswig, Ribe, Aarhus, Viborg, and Odense, as well as Slagelse (in the diocese of Roskilde).[138] The places mentioned by Saxo can be correlated with the royal itineraries reconstructed from royal charters. Such a reconstruction has, for instance, been undertaken for the reign of King Valdemar I (1157–1182). The picture is, to some degree, similar to Saxo's, as charters were issued in the towns of Roskilde, Ringsted, and Lund, but new places are added, like the manor and town of Slangerup, the castle and town of Søborg, and rural centres like the manors of Søllested and of Hjulby, both on Funen, and the Jutland monastery of Tvis.[139]

If one examines Saxo's text, it is evident that Viborg in Jutland became central during the internal struggles of the 1150s, when both Knud and Svend resided there, as well as Valdemar I (the Great).[140] New royal residences, such as Ringsted and Vordingborg, were adopted during Valdemar the Great's actual reign. Before he became sole ruler in 1157, Valdemar had already, according to Saxo, stayed in Ringsted, and later on he was there almost permanently.[141] It was there, at the festival of St John, on 25 June 1170, that Valdemar arranged the canonization of his father Knud Lavard and had the whole Danish aristocracy, including the archbishop of Lund and two messengers sent by the Norwegian king — Bishop Helge of Oslo and Bishop Stefan of Uppsala — show deference to the king. At Ringsted one would find the king 'celebrating the festival amid a great concourse of the aristocracy'.[142] Vordingborg with its first wooden castle, built in the mid-eleventh century, gained a special position as a naval base during the campaigns against the Slavs, but it was also the place where the king could assemble the aristocrats of the realm for a common meeting.[143] Saxo tells

---

136 GD, 14.14.5–14.15.1.
137 GD, 14.33.3, 14.54.8, 14.54.11, 14.56.1.
138 GD, 13.4.2 (Schleswig), 13.5.4 (Ribe), 13.9.2 and 14.54.22 (Aarhus), 14.36.1 (Slagelse).
139 Riis, 'Det middelalderlige danske rejsekongedømme indtil 1332'; Riddersporre, 'Alltid på våg'. On Hjulby as royal manor, see Henriksen, 'Er Hjulby Nyborgs forgænger?'; Henriksen, 'Før Nyborg'.
140 GD, 14.16.4, 14.54.17.
141 GD, 14.14.4, 14.22.4.
142 GD, 14.49.12.
143 GD, 14.34.5. Wille-Jørgensen, *Kongens borg*, pp. 53–79.

us that it was actually at the castle of Vordingborg that, in 1182, the king died.[144]

The royal palaces (*kongsgårde*) in towns represented the incarnation of localized kingship. There the king sat enthroned, gave his gifts, and governed. In a number of Danish towns, Saxo explicitly mentions the royal manors or palaces, which were often attached to a main church. This was, for instance, the case in Roskilde, where it is said that Svend Estridsen moved from the cathedral to his palace.[145] In Odense, Saxo mentions the royal palace in the 1150s as the place where King Svend rested when crossing Funen.[146] In Snorre's text, a royal Danish hall in Randers is mentioned. It was there that the Norwegian magnate Erling Skakke suddenly appeared before the royal throne. 'Just then dishes were being carried in, and the doors were open'.[147] Baths (saunas) in connection with the palaces are mentioned at Odense and Roskilde.[148] The summer feast in Roskilde in 1157 involved both the palace and the bath of Sven's retainer Thorbern; it is mentioned in Saxo's description of it. It is said that the three kings, Svend, Knud, and Valdemar, 'spent the night in sport and revelry' and it is described how the hall was set up with long tables.[149] In Schleswig, the royal palace (*aula regia*) has been fairly securely located by archaeologists in the centre of the town, near the cathedral. During the reign of King Erik the Unforgettable, there was mention of 'the fortress of Schleswig'. This may have been the castle Jurisborg on the Möweninsel in the waters just outside the town, which is known to have been an important royal residence around 1200.[150] As well as the royal palaces in towns, bishop's manors also existed, such as the aristocratic stone house, a *palatium*, which in the late twelfth century the archbishops of Lund had built in Åhus on the south coast of Scania.[151]

The Norwegian kings in particular divided their time between three or four towns. Their palaces in these towns are often mentioned by Snorre, and generally, as in Denmark, they were connected to a major church. One of them was in Trondheim, where King Harald Hardruler in the mid-eleventh century built a palace and a church, an early Our Lady's Church (Mariakirken). The open space in the palace was, according to

---

144 *GD*, 15.6.6–8.
145 *GD*, 11.7.11–12. On the location of the royal palace in Roskilde, see Moltke (ed.), *Roskilde domkirke. Københavns amt. Danmarks kirker*, pp. 12–13.
146 *GD*, 14.16.4–5, 14.17.10. Cf. Christensen, Bjerregaard, and Runge, 'Odense before and after the Canonization of Cnut'.
147 *Heimskringla* 3, p. 253.
148 *GD*, 14.17.10.
149 *GD*, 14.18.2–3.
150 *GD*, 14.1.1. Cf. Olsen, *Danske middelalderborge*, p. 31; Rösch, Müller, and Dörfler, 'Castrum quod Slesvig villam speculator'.
151 Ödman, *Borgar i Skåne*, pp. 167–69.

Snorre, a place for negotiations: 'King Haraldr was in his palace and was standing out on a balcony'. It is also made clear that this was the place for judgement of a thief.[152] The area of Viken was administered from rural royal manors, as well as palaces in Tønsberg, Oslo, Borg, and Konghelle. Snorre says that Sigurd the Crusader built a palace in Konghelle, 'within the fortifications'.[153] The most detailed description is of the royal hall in Bergen, which in the twelfth century became the centre of the western part of Norway.[154] Magnus Erlingsson's coronation took place there in 1162: 'Erlingr skakki had preparations made in the royal palace for a great banquet, and the great hall was hung with precious cloths and tapestries and adorned in the most expensive way. Then the court and all the people in the king's service were given entertainment. There was a huge number of guests and many leaders there. Magnús then received consecration as king from Archbishop Oystein, and there were present at the consecration five other bishops and the legate and a huge number of clerics. Erlingr Skakke and twelve landed men [*lendir menn*] with him swore legally binding oaths together with the king. And on the day that the consecration took place, the king and Erlingr had as their guests the archbishop and the legate and all the bishops, and this banquet was the most glorious. Father and son gave out there many great gifts'.[155]

Bǫglunga sǫgur makes it clear that in 1206 a tower had been built at the Bergen palace with a bell to serve as an alarm.[156] Additionally in Norway, just as in Denmark, the royal palaces in the episcopal towns co-existed with similar solid buildings built by the bishops. From the twelfth century, the archbishop's manor in Trondheim was surrounded by a stone wall.[157]

The royal palaces were places for communal eating and drinking, for wielding of power and for negotiation, and for showing power and friendship.[158] In the texts, there are clear seasonal patterns evident. In Saxo's *Gesta Danorum*, we see King Valdemar in Roskilde observing the celebration of Easter with all important aristocrats of his country, 'holding a feast, at which everybody was at the highest good humour'.[159] In general, kings tended to spend longer in one place in the winter. This was, of course, a consequence of the cold Nordic climate, but it was also caused by a tendency to cease warfare in winter, since among other issues, sailing was not possible when ice covered the sea. Saxo's words on the situation in 1131 after the killing of Knud Lavard are illuminating: 'The winter

---

152 *Heimskringla* 3, p. 73.
153 *Heimskringla* 3, p. 169.
154 Iversen, 'Eiendom, makt og statsdannelse'.
155 *Heimskringla* 3, p. 249.
156 *Soga om baglarar og birkebeinar*, pp. 304–05.
157 Nordeide, ,Erkebispegården i Trondheim'.
158 Cf. Kjær, 'Gaver og gæstebud'; Kjær, 'Feasting with Traitors'.
159 *GD*, 14.56.1.

months, then, were spent peacefully, but hostilities began to brew again as the season for them returned'.[160] For winter and especially for Yule food and supplies, *veizlr*, had to be collected. In 1134 old King Niels had planned to celebrate Christmas in Lund, but unluckily his rival Erik (the Unforgettable) 'seized the whole outlay which had been gathered to make provision for the monarch'. Niels then had to transfer the feast to Roskilde, where he 'collected foodstuffs by public assistance'.[161] In 1135, the contemporary *Chronicle of Roskilde* recorded that King Erik 'travelled to Scania and spent Christmas there'. Now that he was the sole ruler of the country, he could have a peaceful Christmas in Lund.[162]

A famous Danish Christmas feast took place in 1130, when Prince Magnus planned to assassinate his rival Duke Knud Lavard. *Knýtlinga saga* states that King Niels, the father of Magnus collected *veizlr* for his Yule stay in the town of Ringsted in the winter of 1130.[163] It is also clear in the nearly contemporary *vita* of St Knud Lavard, and later in Saxo (who builds on the *vita*), that both imagined a large feast; on that occasion, however, they place it in Roskilde.[164] Part of the feast was, according to Saxo, a public meeting, as it was the place for a gathering of the most important men of the realm: 'After gathering together a throng of noblemen in Zealand and inviting Knud to a banquet at Roskilde for the holy celebration of Christ's nativity'.[165] Saxo further tells that the 1130 feast for the Danish lords lasted four days.[166] Later royal Danish Christmas feast are, among others, mentioned in 1187 and 1201.[167]

The Norwegian kings routinely stayed in town during the winter, especially at Christmas. Snorre's text is full of evidence of this and of the collection of provisions, *veizlr*. After 1066 King Olav Kyrre donated land near Konghelle, Oslo, Tønsberg, Borg (Sarpsborg), Bergen, and Trondheim to the aristocrat Skule who wished for 'properties that are situated close to the market towns in which you, king, are accustomed to stay and receive Yule feasts'.[168] We hear of Harald Hardruler that 'King Haraldr stayed the winter in Niðaróss' and that 'King Haraldr stayed during the winter in Oslo

---

160 *GD*, 13.9.1.
161 *GD*, 13.11.7. Kjær, 'Gaver og gæstebud', p. 196.
162 *Chronicon Roskildense*, p. 30 ('ibique Natale Domini peregit').
163 *Knýtlinga saga*, p. 252.
164 The place, Haraldsted, where Knud was killed is only 6 km north of Ringsted. Haraldsted was according to Robert of Ely's vita (*Vitae Sanctorum Danorum*, p. 234) and Saxo delegated to the high-ranking Erik, *præfectus* of Falster, and presumably functioned as a royal residence near the regional assembly (Hermanson, *Släkt, vännor och makt*, pp. 138–40. King Svend III was at Haraldsted in 1148, *DD*, I:2, no. 101. The manor figures in 1231 as a royal possession, *bona regalia*, in King Valdemars Survey.
165 *GD*, 13.6. 3.
166 *GD*, 13.6.5.
167 Kjær, 'Gaver og gæstebud', pp. 193–94.
168 *Heimskringla* 3, p. 119.

and sent men of his into Upplǫnd to collect the taxes and land dues and the fines payable to the king'.[169] It is said of King Oystein that in 1115 he 'remained for a large part of the winter in Borg (Sarpsborg)'.[170] Magnus the Blind and Harald Gille were recorded as having in 1134 'both stayed the fourth winter north in Kaupangr (Nidaros / Trondheim), and each invited the other to a banquet'.[171] Later on one meets Magnus the Blind 'going north to Bergen and settling down there for the winter'.[172] Snorre tells us that King Hakon Sigurdsson (1157–1162) 'was in Kaupangr over Yule, and his men had a fight one evening during Yule in the royal hall, early in the Yule season, and seven men were killed and many were wounded'.[173] In a similar fashion, it was noted that Hakon the Broad-Shouldered (1159–1162) 'stayed in Þrándheimr during the winter', while Erling Skakke and his son Magnus in other years spent the winter in Tønsberg.[174] King Magnus Erlingsson gave a banquet in Tønsberg 'over Yule'.[175] Hakon Sverreson's Yule feast in Bergen 1203–1204 is well known; this was when 'King Hakon served Yule *veitsle* with many good things' but unfortunately died.[176] The winter season, to a high degree, was the time for staying and feasting in towns, while during the summer one could fight.

Towns as Places of Rule and Sacrality

Towns can be defined by having central military and political importance, but also by their possession of sacral-cultic functions.[177] All such kinds of centrality were very important to kings and pretenders. Kings eagerly sought legitimacy from the sacral life of the towns, but it was also vital to rule towns in order to obtain regional acclamation and followers as happened during the assemblies.

Initially there was no link between towns and assemblies for the simple reason that the assemblies, at least generally, were older than towns. But gradually as towns became centres for king and church organizations, such connections were established. The motive of the power holders was clearly that it gave them access to and to some degree the possibility of governing the activities of the assembly, that is, to develop a degree of royal jurisdiction.

---

169 *Heimskringla* 3, pp. 84, 96.
170 *Heimskringla* 3, p. 156.
171 *Heimskringla* 3, p. 170.
172 *Heimskringla* 3, p. 172.
173 *Heimskringla* 3, p. 224.
174 *Heimskringla* 3, pp. 236, 240, 241.
175 *Heimskringla* 3, p. 260.
176 *Soga om baglarar og birkebeinar*, pp. 282–84.
177 Irsigler, 'Annäherungen an den Stadtbegriff', p. 28.

In Norway the Frostathing remained in the countryside, while the Borgarthing from the earliest time was situated in the town which Olav Haraldsson had founded and built a wall around, namely Borg (Sarpsborg). The assembly of royal acclamation, Eyrathing, was also closely connected to the emerging town of Trondheim. In Denmark, town and regional assemblies were already united in the Jutland town of Viborg during the reign of Knud the Great.[178] One can only speculate about the situation in Odense on Funen, where the existence of the regional assembly is only documented late, but a combination of the regional assembly and town seems clear in the case of Ringsted from the eleventh century onwards.[179]

Towns in some cases enabled royal and would-be royal negotiations with whole regions at the assemblies. It was, however, far from the only factor which made the towns so central for the legitimization of rulers. Churches were also very important. All towns became centred around churches, but for several of the towns their function as Christian centres was absolutely fundamental to their existence. Towns with cathedrals, centres of dioceses, were created in Denmark and Norway during the twelfth century. In Denmark, the connection between town and episcopal residence was very pronounced, as it was also in Norway where the bishops moved to the towns. The two archiepiscopal seats, Lund (1103/1104–) and Trondheim (1152/1153–), must be ranked first as public spaces in the kingdoms, in line with the regional assemblies.[180]

If we look at Denmark, Saxo's sources and his general interests determine a strong focus on the dioceses of Lund and Roskilde; but on the other hand all Danish dioceses are mentioned in his text. The eleventh century building of the cathedrals of the Trinity in Roskilde and of St Lawrence are given relatively detailed descriptions.[181] Other churches are often mentioned. Based on the Roskilde Chronicle, Saxo not only tells us of the building project around 1086 of the Cathedral of the Trinity in Roskilde by Bishop Svend, but also of his monasteries in Ringsted and Slagelse.[182] St Alban's Church of Odense and the cathedral of the town, where after 1095 the tomb of St Knud was located, has a certain but not very decisive role in Saxo's text.[183] He does not mention rural monasteries; this may be because they were not consciously drawn into the political life of the kingdom. Even the monastery of Sorø, which became a Cistercian

---

178 Hjermind, Iversen, and Kristensen, *Viborg Søndersø 1000–1300*.
179 Kristensen and Poulsen, *Danmarks byer i middelalderen*, pp. 61–63. On late tenth century Odense, see Runge and Henriksen 'The Origins of Odense'.
180 Brendalsmo and Jón Viðar Sigurðsson, 'The Social Elites and Incomes from Churches c. 1050–1250'.
181 GD, 11.12.5–7.
182 GD, 12.1.5.
183 GD, 11.14.7, 11.15.3. See *S. Knuds kirke. Odense domkirke*.

monastery through the actions of his patron Absalon, is not mentioned in his *Gesta Danorum*.

The building of churches and monasteries in towns by Norwegian kings is very often mentioned by Snorre. The most important of these towns, Trondheim (Nidaros), where the body of St Olav rested, is far from alone in the text.[184] Sigurd the Crusader's building activity in Konghelle offers Snorre the possibility to report on a royal church here: 'Inside the fortification there King Sigurðr had Krosskirkja built. It was a timber church and very carefully constructed in materials and workmanship. When Sigurðr had been king four and twenty winters, Krosskirkja was consecrated. Then the king deposited there the Holy Cross and many other holy relics. It was known as Kastalakirkja (Fortification Church).'[185] The many churches were served by priests, and this made it possible to arrange religious processions in the towns. It created the possibility of establishing a spatial and physical relationship between rulers, their subjects, and the churches — and to create new ties.

Saxo tells, how King Svend, when King Valdemar in the 1150s visited him in Odense, 'received him with a religious procession, bringing sacred objects to their meeting'. The negotiations between the two rivals, according to Saxo, still took place 'in the chancel of the church of St Alban'; this was the church where St Knud had been killed and which was situated very near the royal palace of the town.[186] In Trondheim, a tradition evolved that the shrine of St Olav should be present at the acclamation of kings. *Bǫglunga sǫgur* describes the situation in 1204 when Inge Bardsson was acclaimed king: 'The shrine of St Olav was carried out, and followed to the assembly by archbishop Eirik and the canons'. The archbishop and the canons led the procession and secured the sacrality of the royal acclamation.[187] Olav was also an ally in warfare. In 1177 when King Sverre marched against Trondheim, the town opposed him with an army that carried 'the mark of Olav before them in the fight'. The king's banner had been taken out of Christchurch to support the warriors.[188]

The choice of burial place and memorial church for deceased kings was very important for their staging, legitimization, and the creation of memory. Therefore, Snorre and Saxo routinely gives us information on this topic. It was only in rare cases that royal burials were not in towns. The two exceptions are kings slain in battle, namely King Oystein, who

---

184 *Heimskringla* 3, pp. 71, 125, 154.
185 *Heimskringla* 3, p. 169. Cf. Andersson, *Kungahälla*. Johnsen, 'Fra den eldste tid til 1252', p. 114.
186 *GD*, 14.17.10.
187 *Soga om baglarar og birkebeinar*, p. 291. See Andås, 'Prosesjoner i byrommet i høymiddelalderens Norge'.
188 Blom, 'Kong Olavs by, ca. 1000–1537', p. 154.

was buried at Foss in Bohuslen, and King Svend Grathe, who was placed in a humble grave at the moor of Grathe Moor, outside Viborg.[189] Svend Estridsen, according to Saxo, died at a rural royal manor but was buried in Roskilde, where the local bishop established 'a tomb in the cathedral of the Trinity'.[190] In this connection, Roskilde is mentioned as 'that sanctified locality, which Danish kings have revered according to ancient custom, habitually provided a residence for them in their lifetime and a resting place when they met their fate'.[191] In spite of these words, Roskilde was not continually used as a burial place for kings in the period under examination here.[192] The next Danish king, Harald Hen, in 1080 was buried in the newly built basilica in Dalby, Scania.[193] King St Knud was laid to rest in Odense where he was killed in 1086, and also for the subsequent kings no fixed traditions were established.[194]

A fixed and sacral resting place for Danish kings was first established after the killing of Knud Lavard in 1131 and his subsequent burial in Ringsted. Interestingly, as described in Chapter 3, the heirs of the deceased Knud Lavard tried, according to Saxo, to persuade King Niels to allow them to bury his corpse in Roskilde. Their idea must have been that this was the real place for a man of royal blood to rest.[195] Instead, the relatives had to be satisfied with Ringsted, which with the burial in 1182 of Knud Lavard's son Valdemar the Great was for a time the place of royal entombment.[196] From the accession of Valdemar, the church of the monastery in Ringsted became a centre of the royal cult and miracles in the Danish realm. This was marked by the canonization of Knud Lavard on 25 June 1170, when all the important members of the Danish aristocracy were gathered there. It was only natural that the king was buried there too. As Saxo says, the town of Ringsted was ancient, and contained the grave of the king's father.[197]

In Norway the most important royal tomb was, no doubt, the grave of St Olav, the oldest royal Nordic saint.[198] As noted c. 1075 by Adam of

---

189 *Heimskringla* 3, p. 213.
190 *GD*, 11.9.4; *Chronicon Roskildense*, p. 23. Andersen, 'Sven 2. Estridsen og Gunhild'.
191 *GD*, 11.9.1.
192 Knud Magnussen (d. 1157) is buried in Roskilde. Engberg, 'Knud 3. Magnussen'.
193 Nyborg, 'Sven 2. Estridsen og Gunhild'.
194 1103 Erik the Good buried on Cyprus, 1134 Niels in Schleswig, 1137 Erik the Unforgettable in Ribe, 1146 Erik the Lamb in Odense, 1157 Svend Grathe at Grathe Moor. See *Danske kongegrave*, pp. 191–93.
195 *GD*, 13.7.1. According to Robert of Ely's vita, Knud Lavard was born in Roskilde (*Vitae Sanctorum Danorum*, p. 234, and see Chapter 3 in this volume).
196 1182: Valdemar the Great; 1202: Knud 6; 1241: Valdemar the Victorious; 1250: Erik Plough-Penning. Karin Kryger, 'S. Bendt i Ringsted, helgengrav og kongebegravelse', Kryger (ed.), *Danske kongegrave*, pp. 253–71.
197 *GD*, 15, 6.10 (1493).
198 Ekroll, 'St Olavs skrin i Nidaros'; Mortensen, 'Writing and Speaking of St Olaf'.

Bremen, 'there are the relics of the martyr St Olav. By his grave the Lord exposes prominent miracles and because of this people come from afar'.[199] The golden shrine of the saint was already mentioned in skaldic verses in the 1030s, and Snorre tells us of King Olav Kyrre: 'King Óláfr had a stone minster built in Niðaróss and sited it in the place that King Óláfr's body had at first been buried, and the altar was placed over where the king's grave had been. It was consecrated as Christchurch. After that King Óláfr's shrine was also conveyed there and placed over the altar there'.[200] Olav's grave and shrine are central to Snorre's text, mirroring the fact that Olav's cult in the second half of the twelfth century had become an accepted symbol for the kingdom of Norway. The Norwegian kings guarded this treasure and developed an almost corporeal relation to it, as is made clear from the fact that the eleventh century kings allowed the nails, hair, and beard of the saint to be cut.[201] Trondheim, and especially the cathedral of the town, the Christchurch, almost naturally became the burial place for a long line of Norwegian kings. Magnus the Good (d. 1047) was, however, buried in the St Clemens Church, and Harald Hardruler (d. 1066) was laid to rest in Our Lady's Church (Mariakirken) of the town.[202] A tendency to choose Oslo first becomes apparent upon the selection of the St Hallvard's cathedral there as the burial place of Sigurd the Crusader (d. 1130), Magnus the Blind (d. 1139), and Inge Hunchback (d. 1161).[203] A quite new Norwegian tradition was instituted at the death of King Sverre with his burial in the Christchurch of Bergen. It signified that this town was the new political centre of Norway.[204]

A Network of Towns

Urban places with regional assemblies, cathedrals, and royal burials constituted central goals in the power game of the time, but there was a whole network of other towns. Around 1075 the German clerk Adam of Bremen mentions a number of Danish towns, namely Aalborg, Aarhus, Helsingborg, Ribe, Roskilde, Schleswig, Viborg together with the Norwegian Trondheim and 'Vig' (Oslo or Tønsberg).[205] And the Anglo-Norman writer Orderic Vitalis in 1135 knew of six towns in Norway: Bergen,

---

199 *Adam von Bremen. Hamburgische Kirchengeschichte*, pp. 121, 159.
200 *Heimskringla* 3, p. 125.
201 *Heimskringla* 3, pp. 60, 107.
202 *Heimskringla* 3, pp. 63, 120.
203 *Morkinskinna*, p. 387: 'King Magnus's body brought to Óslo and buried in Saint Hallvard's Church, next to his father'. Müller, 'Østnorske basilika-anlegg: en sammenligning'.
204 The king of the Baglar Erling Stonewall (died 1207) was, however, buried in Tønsberg. *Soga om baglarar og birkebeinar*, p. 314.
205 *Adam von Bremen. Hamburgische Kirchengeschichte*.

Konghelle, Trondheim, Borg (Sarpsborg), Oslo, and Tønsberg.[206] Later, the thirteenth-century texts of both Snorre and Saxo give accounts of a number of towns in their homelands, but it is clear that Snorre had the greatest interest in documenting them, and that he mentions most of those that existed. Saxo, on the other hand, makes a radical selection, and in general was not at all interested in the many new Danish towns that appeared in the period 1150–1200. Presumably this mirrors the fact that the oldest towns were still dominant players in the power game which was the topic of Saxo's chronicle. Saxo mentions several towns in Norway, and Snorre also refers to some Danish towns. These 'foreign' towns are naturally an expression of the geographical knowledge of the authors, and their spatial perception; but their occurrence in the texts is first and foremost a product of real traffic. The selection of towns in the neighbouring countries was certainly connected with important lines of shipping in the Kattegat region.

If one takes a look at the archaeological and written sources, it is clear that, in the twelfth century, there were considerably more towns than those revealed by Snorre and Saxo, and also that there was quite a lot of difference between Norway and Denmark in terms of the number of towns. In Norway, there were the eleventh century towns of Tønsberg, Trondheim, Hamar, Konghelle, Skien, Borg (Sarpsborg), Oslo, Bergen (Bjørgvin), and probably also Borgundkaupangen.[207] During the twelfth century, Vágar (Nordland) and Stavanger were founded.[208] But no more than eleven towns can be counted. In Denmark there were more towns in the eleventh century or had grown up just after the year 1100, namely the Jutland towns of Schleswig, Flensburg, Horsens, Randers, Varde, Viborg, Aalborg, and Aarhus, the Zealand Copenhagen, Næstved, Roskilde, Slagelse, and Ringsted, as well as the Scanian Borgeby (on the coast of the Sound), Helsingborg, Lomma, Lund, and Tommarp (Danish: Tommerup). There was a total of eighteen towns, and in the following fifty years at least twelve more were founded. From the period c. 1150–1200, the following new founded Danish towns were: Hjørring, Grenå, Haderslev, Kolding, Ringkøbing, Tønder, Vejle, Kalundborg, Slangerup, Store Heddinge, Søborg, and Vä.[209] Thus in Denmark at the end of the twelfth century there were nearly three times as many towns as in Norway. Amongst the Nordic towns which were part of the Kattegat network, Lödöse should be mentioned. This place,

---

206 Helle, *Norsk Byhistorie. Urbanisering gjennom 1300 år*, p. 41.
207 Andersson, Hansen, and Øye, De første 200 årene – nytt blikk på 27 skandinaviske middelalderbyer; Helle, *Bergen bys historie*; Schia, *Oslo innerst i viken: liv og virke i middelalderbyen*; Brendalsmo and Molaug, 'To norske byer i middelalderen'.
208 Brendalsmo and Paasche, 'Stavanger – før det ble en by'.
209 Kristensen and Poulsen, *Danmarks byer i middelalderen*, pp. 117–19.

situated at the Göta älv near Konghelle, became a town during the twelfth century as well.[210]

The town network was much denser in Denmark than in Norway, therefore. One of the consequences of this was that Norwegian people became much more regionally tied to single towns, while the Danes were part of networks with several centres. Only in Denmark could neighbouring towns vie for power, such as for example the Zealand towns for Roskilde and Ringsted. In both Norway and Denmark, towns were, however, important for power holders because they gave access to resources and taxes. We have just touched upon the fact that the role of towns was not quite the same in the Nordic countries as it was in central and southern Europe. During wars and fighting, relatively little was done to establish control over towns, and battles did not take place within the walls of towns but outside them. But generally, towns came to constitute *points d'appui* for local, regional, and international wealth and men. Their space was ideal for building up power bases.

Into the Compact Castle

Towns became pivotal points in the medieval Nordic conflicts, and conflicts were thus localized to places with a degree of permanency. It became crucial to control central localities like Lund, Roskilde, Trondheim, and Bergen, and a new form of 'compact' power can be said to have come into existence, corresponding to similar tendencies of the period.

The most physical effect of the tendency towards 'compactness' was a new type of castle. Iron Age and Viking Age fortifications had been characterized by their large area.[211] In Denmark they were only surrounded by earth walls, while in Norway it was possible to use natural rock formations. One of these ancient fortifications is actually mentioned as being in use in Saxo's text. Around 1157, he tells that 'the Falster community, with their small population, were protecting themselves behind the communal defence works against an enormous Wendish fleet'.[212] There is every reason to identify this fortification with the large 'folk castle' (*folkeborg*) of 'Falsters Virke', which goes back to the Iron Age.[213] Most probably Mildeborg, a 'walled fortification' in West Schleswig, should be included in this group

---

210 Harlitz, 'Urbana Systemoch riksbildning i Skandinavien', p. 150. Lödöse is seen as dominated by Norwegian power in the period 1150–1190.
211 Gammelborg on Bornholm is a fine example. In Norway the so-called 'bygdeborger' were used up to the eighteenth century. Nordeide, 'Norske festningsverk i middelalderen', p. 128.
212 GD, 14.22.1.
213 Thorsen, 'En to-tre folkeborge – en på Lolland, og to på Falster'. The place is presently (2020) being excavated <https://videnskab.dk/kultur-samfund/kaempe-vikingeanlaeg-paa-falster-opdaget-fra-luften-var-overset-i-100-aar> (visited 04.06.2020).

of large area fortifications, manned by the population of a whole region. It was from Mildeborg that King Knud, aided by the regional Frisian population, fought against King Svend.[214]

From the eleventh and twelfth century, much smaller and more compact castles were built, initially mostly as wooden constructions. Some of them were Norwegian. An early stronghold seems to have stood near the royal Maria church in Oslo and may have been of the so-called 'motte and bailey type'.[215] Another early example is the 'large castle' *'kastala mikinn'* in Borg (Sarpsborg), which was presumably built in the first half of the eleventh century by King Olav Haraldsson.[216] An ecclesiastical wooden castle was built by Archbishop Oystein at Trondheim. In Denmark, in contrast to Norway, lay aristocrats, and not only the king and bishop, could build castles.[217] An early royal Danish castle is the relatively undocumented eleventh to twelfth century castle in Helsingborg.[218] From the twelfth century, there were many 'motte and bailey' castles in Denmark.[219] Haraldsborg, which King Erik the Good's son Harald Kesja had built just outside Roskilde, was this type of fortification, with a wooden tower.[220] That the castle had administrative duties in relation to the town is most likely, even if it was not mentioned by Saxo. This was also the case with a wooden castle near Ribe, which in 1148–1149 was built by King Svend Grathe's counsellor, Riber Ulf, 'Ulf Ripensis'.[221] In the same area Bishop Helias (1142–1162), according to the Chronicle of the bishops of Ribe, fortified the episcopal manors, presumably in a similar way.[222] Such private wooden fortifications were undoubtedly promoted by the period's state of constant crisis.

Soon more solid stone constructions gained popularity, following European models. In Denmark around 1130 a stone tower, the so-called 'Bastrup tower', was built in northern Zealand, a donjon held by a person who was close to King Niels, and who is mentioned around 1130: 'Ebbe de

---

214 *GD*, 14.7.2, 14.7.8.
215 Eriksson, *Maktens boningar*, pp. 118–20. Brendalsmo and Molaug, 'To norske byer i middelalderen'.
216 Fischer, *Norges kongeborger*, pp. 13–15, 25–27, 32–36; Stibeus, 'Sigurd Jorsalafars kastell och Ragnhildsholmen'.
217 For general a view on Danish medieval castles see la Cour, *Danske borganlæg til midten af det trettende århundrede*, vol. 1–2; Olsen, *Danske middelalderborge*.
218 Thomasson, 'Av samma penning Helsingborg 3 mark'. On the possibility that the Helsingborg castle was from the Viking-Age, see Weidhagen-Hallerdt, 'A Possible Ring Fort from the Late Viking Age Period in Helsingborg'.
219 Ödman, *Borgar i Skåne*, p. 16.
220 *GD*, 13.4.1, 13.9.5; Lindahl, 'Haraldsborg-skatten'; Olsen, *Danske middelalderborge*, pp. 38–39.
221 Søvsø, 'Riber Ulfs borg'.
222 *Ribe Bispekrønike*, p. 28.

Bastorp', most probably of the Hvide family.[223] A large castle with towers and walls of stone was erected by Archbishop Eskil during the years 1137–1155 in Søborg in North Zealand.[224] On the island of Bornholm the large royal castle of Gammelborg was extended with a large stone wall during the 1140s, but it was soon given up and the more modern Lilleborg, a curtain wall castle in a lake, succeeded it.[225] From the mid-twelfth century, such European-style stone castles dominated in Denmark. Some of them were built in towns. This for instance was the case with the castles which were built after Valdemar the Great gained power.[226] Vordingborg, built in the mid-twelfth century as a simple wooden construction and in stone in the 1190s, has already been mentioned, but there is reason to highlight three other constructions, which were mentioned by Saxo.[227] One of these is Kalundborg, where the aristocrat Esbern Snare is said to have given the town 'protection of a new fortification' and cleared the harbour of pirates.[228] On Funen, Knud Prislavson, a son of King Valdemar's sister, Saxo notes, established a fortress or a town (*urbs*), presumably in Svendborg.[229] And finally, the castle, which Saxo's hero bishop Absalon had built in Copenhagen in 1167, can be mentioned.[230] The process of castle building led to the situation of the thirteenth century, when Denmark was densely covered by and ruled from such constructions.

In Norway, the early building of castles, and especially of stone castles, is much less common than in Denmark.[231] An early Norwegian construction, which was possibly of stone, was built by King Sigurd the Crusader in Konghelle in the first decades of the twelfth century. This border castle, the so-called 'kastala', possibly a motte and bailey structure, was, however, not standing for long.[232] King Sverre erected two stone castles that were both named Sverresborg — Sverre's castle. In the winter of 1182–1183,

---

223 Randsborg, 'Bastrup – Europe. A Massive Danish Donjon from 1100'; Olsen, *Danske middelalderborge*, pp. 34–36. The lord of the castle may be identified as Ebbe Skjalmsen Hvide (Hermanson, *Släkt, vänner och makt*, p. 74). Another castle built by a member of the Hvide family (Peder Thorstensen (d. 1175), is Pedersborg in Lake Sorø (Olsen, *Danske middelalderborge*, pp. 36–37). On the stone tower of Gammelborg at the river Schlei see Wille-Jørgensen, *Kongens borg*, p. 197.
224 Pavón, 'Søborg – ærkebiskop Eskils borg i Nordsjælland'.
225 Olsen, *Danske middelalderborge*, pp. 48–49.
226 Olsen, *Danske middelalderborge*, pp. 61–78.
227 Other examples are the royal castle Sprogø and archbishop's castle Skeingeborg in Scania. Engberg and Frandsen, *Valdemar den Stores borg på Sprogø*; Ödman, *Borgar i Skåne*, pp. 130–33.
228 GD, 14.36.5; Olesen, 'Vestborgen Castle in Kalundborg'.
229 GD, 14.44.1.
230 GD, 14.34.6, 14.35.1, 14.49.1.
231 Nordeide, 'Norske festningsverk i middelalderen'; Eriksson, *Maktens boningar*.
232 Stibeus, 'Sigurd Jorsalafars kastell och Ragnhildsholmen'; Eriksson, *Maktens boningar*, pp. 120–23.

Sverre was occupied with the defence of his town Trondheim; he built a solid castle on a mountain, east of his royal palace.[233] Shortly afterwards, in the mid-1180s the king built the castle in Bergen, which was also situated close to royal palace there.[234] 'Berget' (the Mountain) in Tønsberg was the location of a certain type of fortification, two 'kastala' (with a church) from the mid-twelfth century, but these was not stone constructions.[235] The castle in Trondheim was destroyed in 1197, while the castle in Bergen met its fate in 1207. After that stone castles in Norway are not encountered in the sources before the 1220s.

As a consequence of the very existence of the stone castles and their passive strength, contemporary texts describe a new kind of spatial behaviour, the siege. An early example is the royal siege of the archbishop's castle of Søborg in 1161, which after holding out for a long time ended with an agreement with the inhabitants of the castle 'that they and their possessions would remain unscathed', and therefore 'they handed over the evacuated fortress to the king'".[236] Another case is the story of how the men on Absalon's castle 'Sigosta' (Søfde) in the Sövdesjön near Lund prepared themselves for a siege: they 'rounded up horses, others collecting any wagons that happened to be available, blocked the ford which stretched in front of the island, shallows which Absalon later had protected with brickwork; other began to gather rocks suitable for hurling'.[237]

The sling stones testify to the development of new techniques to defend and conquer castles, which consequently forced the castle builders to build higher and more solid walls. Catapults are mentioned several times in the sources. Already mentioned is the *ballista*, which Magnus the Blind in the 1130 placed outside Bergen.[238] Saxo carefully describes how the castle of Harald Kesja, Haraldsborg, at Roskilde, in 1133 was destroyed by Erik the Unforgettable using a 'ballistic device', which Erik learned to use 'from the Saxons who lived in Roskilde' (more on this in Chapter 3). Here we have direct import of military technology.[239] The most detailed descriptions of the capturing of castles is, however, as discussed in Chapter 4, the Norwegian saga's description of battles around the castles in Bergen and Trondheim in the late twelfth and early thirteenth centuries. Here

---

233 Eriksson, *Maktens boningar*, pp. 123–25.
234 Fischer, *Norske kongeborger*, pp. 98–100; Eriksson, *Maktens boningar*, pp. 125–26.
235 Eriksson, *Maktens boningar*, pp. 68–70. Brendalsmo and Molaug, 'To norske byer i middelalderen – Oslo og Tønsberg før ca. 1300'.
236 GD, 14.26.12. Cf. Chapter 8 dealing with the right to 'unhindered withdrawal'.
237 GD, 15.4.8; Stille, *Saxos skånska stridsskildringar*; Ödman, *Borgar i Skåne*, pp. 122–24.
238 *Heimskringla* 3, p. 175.
239 GD, 13.9.6. Cf. Heebøll-Holm, 'Saxo og 1100-tallets danske krigskunst: riddere, armbrøster og tyskere'.

we are given vivid pictures of the use of fire and assault, and, in Bergen, of attempts to tear down a castle so it could be taken out of the power struggle.

The Logic of Space and Place

There is a military logic behind the change in fortifications, from uncomplicated constructions covering large areas to small ones which were high and compact. In the first part of the period examined here, fighting in both Norway and Denmark was primarily on foot with bows, spears, axes, and swords. An analysis of skeletal material from Norway, which is believed to represent victims of the twelfth-century internal power struggles of the realm, describes the range of injuries: 'The sword seems to be responsible for the majority of injuries, but there are signs of blows from a variety of weapons ... The trauma patterns reveals many frontal and parietal injuries, indicating that regular hand-to-hand fighting probably had taken place in most cases'.[240]

In Denmark, heavy cavalry based on the continental model was increasingly used during the twelfth century.[241] The constant conflict of the period as well as the newly introduced chivalric ideology were no doubt drivers behind the new military techniques. This development was certainly more marked in Denmark than in Norway where the general naval military service remained crucial for much longer. However, in both countries a clear professionalization of the army took place, which to a large degree came to consist of men who were either tax-free or received pay.[242] The warriors were better trained, better armed, and smaller forces could therefore do more. The castle in Bergen could, according to the sagas, around 1200 be defended by only 100–200 men, and other castles demanded even fewer men.[243]

It is quite clear that castles were of relatively little importance in twelfth-century Norway compared to Denmark. This became even more evident from the first part of the thirteenth century. While Danish royal castles from around 1200 became necessary for the administration of local territory and the development of large-scale taxation, in Norway the castles did not prove themselves to be an effective means of getting control of their surroundings.[244] Warfare with ships for a long time remained the

---

240 Brødholt and Holck, 'Skeletal Trauma'.
241 Heebøll-Holm, 'Priscorum quippe curialum, qui et nunc militari censentur nomine'; Malmros, *Bønder og leding i valdemarstidens Danmark*.
242 Ersland and Holm, *Krigsmakt og kongemakt 900–1814*, p. 38.
243 *Soga om baglarar og birkebeinar*, pp. 292–94.
244 Orning, *Unpredictability and Presence*, pp. 302–04.

most suitable in the wide and long country of Norway. Mobility and not stability remained the keyword in the Norwegian territory.[245] In Norway, however, as in Denmark the towns became more important for all rulers with regard to the extraction of revenues and as fixed sacral points. In Norway as well as Denmark, a development towards compactness thus could be seen in the power games around densely populated towns as well as in the growing castellation process, but both processes were most pronounced in Denmark.

Another aspect of this process is a tendency toward a different power game that no longer freely took place in a common Nordic space of the Kattegat region. Territorial boundaries tied to national states (and national archbishoprics) became more pronounced and furthered the density of geographies of power. As stressed by Hans Jacob Orning, during the twelfth century there was an unclear division between power centre and periphery.[246] This division became clearer, and the territories could better be internally exploited as rulers organized and fixed human activities' spatial territories. The strengthening of borders led also to a new form of war. Where twelfth- and early thirteenth-century Norwegian military warfare, as stressed by Knut Arstad, stretched from the Arctic Circle to Denmark, warfare from then on — both Norwegian and Danish — became increasingly a border phenomenon.[247]

Simply put, in this new society face-to-face meetings became less common, while institutions were somewhat more important. Partly, the constant journeys of kings to rural manors was reduced and towns became their favourite residences; some of them developed into the political centres of the realms with solid castles. Partly, there is little doubt that writing came to be more important, and the predominant role of orality thus was reduced. From Saxo and the Norwegian sagas as well as the surviving documents, it seems clear that charters and letters gained ground in the year around 1200. Saxo, for instance, gives us an account of King Valdemar who was hunting on the island of Samsø. From there, he wrote a letter to Zealand to his adviser bishop Absalon and asked him to come to him to discuss the government of the realm.[248] Saxo also has an example of a false, forged letter.[249] In the same way *Bǫglunga sǫgur* is filled with information about letters, which were transported by ship or by carriers up and down the Norwegian coasts. Thanks to such written information, the need for the personal royal presence was less pressing, and social distance,

---

245 Orning, 'Borgenes blindsoner'.
246 Orning, *Unpredictability and Presence*, p. 310.
247 Arstad, 'The Use of Castles as Military Strongholds in the Norwegian Civil Wars'.
248 GD, 15.4.11. King Valdemar resided on the castle Gammel Brattingsborg: *Borgene på Samsø. En arkæologisk jagt på historien bag øens fem middelalderborge*, pp. 63–85.
249 GD, 14.26.11.

on the other hand, could be stressed. Increasing literacy can be said to have expressed a development of new spatial rules.[250] Royal — and aristocratic — power was somewhat more present in particular spaces as an active agent as the friction of distance diminished, but power on the other hand gradually became more distant, more abstract. Spatial practice and its use of centres and mobility changed in Scandinavia during the twelfth and early thirteenth century in constant interaction with the political history of the time.

250 Cf. Nedkvitne, *The Social Consequences of Literacy in Medieval Scandinavia*.

Works Cited

Primary Sources

Adam von Bremen. *Hamburgische Kirchengeschichte*, ed. by Bernhard Schmeidler, 3rd edn (Hannover and Leipzig: Hannsche Buchhandlung, 1917)

Chronicon Roskildense, ed. by Martin Cl. Gertz, *Scriptores minores historiæ danicæ medii ævi*, I (Copenhagen: G. E. C. Gad, 1917–1918), pp. 1–33

DD = *Diplomatarium Danicum*, ed. by Herluf Nielsen and others (Copenhagen: Ejnar Munksgaards forlag, 1938–)

DMA = *Danmarks middelalderlige annaler*, ed. by Erik Kroman (Copenhagen: Selskabet for Udgivelse af Kilder til Danmarks Historie, 1980)

Fagrskinna = *Ágrip af Nóregskonunga sǫgum. Fagrskinna. Nóregs konunga tal*, ed. by Bjarni Einarsson, Íslenzk fornrit, 29 (Reykjavík: Hið Íslenska Fornritafélag, 1985)

GD = Saxo Grammaticus. *Gesta Danorum. The History of the Danes*, ed. by Karsten Friis-Jensen, trans. by Peter Fischer (Oxford: Oxford University Press, 2015)

Heimskringla I–III, ed. by Bjarni Aðalbjarnarson, Íslenzk fornrit, 26–28 (Reykjavík: Hið Íslenska Fornritafélag, 1941–1951)

Heimskringla 1–3, ed. by Alison Finlay and Anthony Faulkes (London: Viking Society for Northern Research, 2011–2015)

Knýtlinga saga = *Danakonunga sǫgur, Skjoldunga saga, Knýtlinga saga, Ágrip af sǫgu danakonunga*, ed. by Bjarni Guðnason, Íslenzk fornrit, 35 (Reykjavík: Hið Íslenska Fornritafélag, 1982)

Knytlinga Saga. The History of the Kings of Denmark, trans. by Hermann Pálsson and Paul Edwards (Odense: Odense University Press, 1986)

Morkinskinna I–II, ed. by Ármann Jakobsson and Þórður Ingi Guðjónsson. Íslenzk fornrit, 23 (Reykjavík: Hið Íslenska Fornritafélag, 2011)

'Ribe Bispekrønike', in *Kirkehistoriske Samlinger*, ed. by Ellen Jørgensen, ser. 6., vol. 1, 1933–1935: 23–33

Soga om baglarar og birkebeinar, in *Norges kongesagaer* 3, trans. by Dag Gundersen and Finn Hødnebø (Oslo: Gyldendal, 1979)

Sverres saga in *Norges kongesagaer* 3, trans. by Dag Gundersen and Finn Hødnebø (Oslo: Gyldendal, 1984)

Vitae Sanctorum Danorum, ed. by Martin Gertz (Copenhagen: Gad, 1908–1912)

Secondary Studies

Aalto, Sirpa, 'The Connection between Geographical Space and Collective Memory in Jómsvíkinga saga', in *Contacts and Networks in the Baltic Sea Region. Austmarr as a Northern mare nostrum, ca. 500–1500 AD*, ed. by Maths Bertell and Kendra Wilson (Amsterdam: Amsterdam University Press, 2019), pp. 67-87

Andås, Margrete Syrstad, 'Prosesjoner i byrommet i høymiddelalderens Norge', in *(GEN)KLANGE, Essays om kunst og kristendom: tilegnet Nils Holger Petersen på 70-årsdagen*, ed. by Lars Nørgaard, and Kristoffer Garne (Copenhagen: Publikationer fra Det Teologiske Fakultet, 2016), pp. 47–55

Andersen, Michael, 'Sven 2. Estridsen og Gunhild', in *Danske Kongegrave*, vol. 1, ed. by Karin Kryger (Copenhagen: Museum Tusculanum Press, 2014), pp. 167–73

Andersen, Per, *Rex imperator in regno suo: dansk kongemakt og rigslovgivning i 1200-tallets Europa* (Odense: Syddansk Universitetsforlag, 2005)

Andersson, Hans, *Kungahälla* (Stockholm: Riksantikvarieämbetet och Statens Historiska Museer, 1981)

——, Gitte Hansen, and Ingvild Øye, *De første 200 årene – nytt blikk på 27 skandinaviske middelalderbyer* (Bergen: Universitetet i Bergen Arkeologiske Skrifter, 2008)

Andrén, Anders, *Den urbana scenen. Städer och samhälle i det medeltida Danmark* (Malmö: CWK Glerup, 1985)

Arstad, Knut, 'Rex Bellicosus. Strategi, taktikk og feltherre-egenskaber i Norge på 1200-tallet. En analyse af krigsføring i middelalderen samt militært og politisk lederskap sett gjennom karriene til Sigurd Erlingsson, Knut Håkonsson, Skule Bårdsson og Håkon Håkonsson' (Unpublished Doctoral Thesis, University of Oslo, 2019)

——, 'The Use of Castles as Military Strongholds in the Norwegian Civil Wars of the 12th and 13th Centuries', in *Castles at War (Castles of the North 1)*, ed. by Rainer Atbach, Lars Meldgaard Jensen, and Leif Plith Lauritsen (Bonn: Magt, Borg og Landskab, 2015), pp. 26–37

Bagge, Sverre, 'Fortelling, makt og politik hos Saxo og Snorre', in *Saxo og Snorre*, ed. by Jon Gunnar Jørgensen, Karsten Friis-Jensen, and Else Mundahl (Copenhagen: Museum Tusculanum Forlag, 2010), pp. 167–85

Bill, Jan, 'Scandinavian Warships and Naval Power in the Thirteenth and Fourteenth Centuries', in *War at Sea in the Middle Ages and the Renaissance*, ed. by John B. Hattendorf and Richard W. Unger (Woodbridge: Boydell and Brewer, 2003), pp. 35–51

Birkebæk, Frank A., Ernst Verwohlt, and Mette Høj (eds), *Roskilde bys historie – tiden indtil 1536* (Roskilde: Roskilde Museum, 1992)

Bjarni, Einarsson, 'Reisebeskrivelser', in *Kulturhistorisk Leksikon for Nordisk Middelalder*, vol. XIX (Copenhagen: Rosenkilde og Bagger, 1975), cols 28–30

Blom, Grethe Authén. *Trondheim bys historie*, 1 (Trondheim: F. Bruns Bokhandels Forlag, 1956)

Bonde, Niels, and Frans-Arne Stylegar, 'Roskilde 6 – et langskib fra Norge', *Kuml. Årbog for Jysk Arkæologisk Selskab* (2011), 247–62

Brendalsmo, Jan, and Jón Viðar Sigurðsson, 'The Social Elites and Incomes from Churches c. 1050–1250', in *Nordic Elites in Transformation, vol. 1. Material Resources*, ed. by Bjørn Poulsen, Helle Vogt, and Jón Viðar Sigurðsson (New York and London: Routledge, 2019), pp. 248–74

———, and Knut Paasche, 'Stavanger – før det ble en by', *Historisk tidsskrift* (N), 96 (2017), 103–23

———, and Petter Molaug, 'To norske byer i middelalderen – Oslo og Tønsberg før ca. 1300', *Collegium Medievale* (2014), 134–99

Brink, Stefan, 'Forntida vägar', *Vägar och vägmiljöer: Bebyggelsehistorisk tidskrift*, 39 (2000), 23–64

Brødholt, Elin T., and Per Holck, 'Skeletal Trauma in the Burials from the Royal Church of St Mary in Medieval Oslo', *International Journal of Osteoarcheology*, 22 (2012), 201–18

Carlsson, Helene (ed.), *Bohuslän som gränslandskap. Före och efter Roskildefreden*. Bohusläns Museum Rapport. 2012: 47 (Uddevalla: Bohusläns Museum, 2013)

Christensen, Aksel E., *Vikingetidens Danmark* (Copenhagen: Gyldendal, 1969)

Christensen, Arne Emil, 'Skibstyper', in *Kulturhistorisk Leksikon for Nordisk Middelalder*, vol. xv (Oslo: Gyldendal, 1970), cols 491–93

Christensen, Jakob Tue, Mikael Manøe Bjerregaard, and Mads Runge, 'Odense before and after the Canonization of Cnut', in *Life and Cult of Canute the Holy – The First Royal Saint of Denmark*. Report from an Interdisciplinary Research Seminar in Odense November 6th to 7th 2017, ed. by Steffen Hope, Mikael M. Bjerregaard, Anne H. Krag, and Mads Runge (Odense: Odense University Press, 2019), pp. 10–25

Creighton, Oliver, and Duncan Wright, *The Anarchy: War and Status in 12th-century Landscapes of Conflict* (Liverpool: Liverpool University Press, 2017)

Crumlin-Pedersen, Ole, *Pugna Forensis. Arkeologiska kring Foteviken, Skåne 1981–1983* (Malmö: Länsstyrelsen i Malmöhus Län i samarbejde med Vikingeskibshallen i Roskilde, 1984).

———, *Søvejen til Roskilde* (Roskilde: Vikingeskibshallen, 1978)

Curry, Anne, *Agincourt. A New History* (Stroud: Tempus, 2005)

Dahlström, Hanna, Bjørn Poulsen, and Jesper Olsen, 'From a Port for Traders to a Town of Merchants: Exploring the Topography, Activities and Dynamics of Early Medieval Copenhagen', *Danish Journal of Archaeology*, 1.7 (2018), 69–116

Ekroll, Øystein, 'St Olavs skrin i Nidaros', in *Ecclesia Nidrosiensis 1153–1537*, ed. by Steinar Imsen (Trondheim: Tapir akademiske forlag, 2003), pp. 325–49

Elgvin, Johannes, 'Reiser', in *Kulturhistorisk Leksikon for Nordisk Middelalder*, vol. xiv (Oslo: Gyldendal, 1969), cols 15–19

Engberg, Nils, and Jørgen Frandsen, *Valdemar den Stores borg på Sprogø* (Højbjerg: Wormianum, 2011)

———, 'Knud 3. Magnussen', in *Danske Kongegrave*, vol. 1, ed. by Karin Kryger (Copenhagen: Museum Tusculanum Press, 2014), pp. 249–51

Englert, Anton, *Large Cargo Ships in Danish Waters 1000–1250. Evidence of Specialized Merchant Seafaring prior to the Hanseatic Period* (Roskilde: Viking Ship Museum, 2015)

——, 'Rejsehastighed over Kattegat og Skagerrak i vikingetiden', *Ressourcer og kulturkontakter: Arkæologi rundt om Skagerrak og Kattegat*, ed. by Liv Appel and Kjartan Langsted (Gilleleje: Gillejele Museum, 2011), pp. 101–15

Eriksson, Anna-Lena, *Maktens boningar. Norska riksborgar under medeltiden* (Stockholm: Almqvist & Wiksell International, 1995)

Eriksson, Henning S., *Skånemarkedet* (Højbjerg: Wormianum, 1980).

Ersland, Gejr Atle, and Terje Holm, *Krigsmakt og kongemakt 900–1814*, Norsk Forsvarshistorie, vol. 1 (Oslo: Fagbokforlaget, 2000)

Etting, Vivian (ed.), *Borgene på Samsø. En arkæologisk jagt på historien bag øens fem middelalderborge* (Odense: Syddansk Universitetsforlag, 2018)

Fabian, Louise, 'The Spatial Turn within Social and Cultural Studies. Spatial Theory as an Interdisciplinary Praxis', in *What is Theory? Answers from the Social and Cultural Sciences*, ed. by Hervé Corvellec (Stockholm: Liber and CBS Press, 2013), pp. 283–98

Fabricius, Knud, 'Den jyske krig i Efteraaret 1157', *Historisk Tidsskrift* (D), 7.3 (1900–1902), 369–87

Fenger, Ole, 'Veje', in *Kulturhistorisk Leksikon for Nordisk Middelalder*, vol. XIX (Copenhagen: Rosenkilde og Bagger, 1975), cols 622–24

Finnur, Jónsson and Ellen Jørgensen, 'Nordiske pilegrimsnavne i Broderskabsbogen fra Reichenau', *Aarbøger for nordisk Oldkyndighed og Historie*, 3rd ser., vol. 13 (1923): 1–36

Fischer, Gerhard, *Nidaros erkebispestol og bispesete: 1153–1953. B. 2 2: Norges kirker Domkirken i Trondheim Kirkebygget i middelalderen* (Oslo: Land og kirke, 1955)

——, *Norske kongeborger*, vol. 1, Norske minnesmerker (Oslo: Gyldendal, 1951)

Gelting, Michael, 'Saxo Grammaticus in the Archives', in *The Creation of Medieval Northern Europe. Essays in honour of Sverre Bagge*, ed. by Leidulf Melve and Sigbjørn Sønnesyn (Oslo: Dreyers Forlag, 2012), pp. 322–45

Harlitz, Erika, 'Urbana system och riksbildning i Skandinavien. En studie av Lödöses uppgång och fall ca. 1050–1646' (Unpublished Doctoral Thesis, University of Gothenburg, 2010)

Harrison, Dick, *Medieval Space. The Extent of Microspatial Knowledge in Western Europe during the Middle Ages* (Lund: Lund University Press, 1996)

Hartvig, Anders, and Bjørn Poulsen, 'Contextualizing an Early Medieval Village: An Aristocratic Family in Southern Jutland, its Landed Wealth, and its Connection to a Central Danish Thing Place', *Danish Journal of Archaeology*, 11 (2023), 1–23

Heebøll-Holm, Thomas, 'Medieval Denmark as a Maritime Empire', in *Empires of the Sea. Maritime Power Networks in World History*, ed. by Rolf Strootman, Floris van den Eijnde, and Roy van Wijk (Leiden/Boston: Brill, 2019), pp. 194–218

——, 'Priscorum quippe curialum, qui et nunc militari censentur nomine: riddere I Danmark i 1100-tallet', *Historisk Tidsskrift* (D), 109.1 (2009), 21–69

———, 'Saxo og 1100-tallets danske krigskunst: riddere, armbrøster og tyskere', in *Saxo og hans Samtid*, ed. by Per Andersen and Thomas Hebøll-Holm (Aarhus: Aarhus Universitetsforlag, 2012), pp. 113–32

Helle, Knut, *Bergen bys historie. Bind 1* (Bergen: Alma Mater, 1982)

———, *Gulatinget og Gulatingslova* (Leikanger: Skald, 2001)

———, *Norge blir en stat 1130–1319*, 3rd edn (Oslo: Universitetsforlaget, 1993)

———, *Norsk byhistorie. Urbanisering gjennom 1300 år*, Part 1 (Oslo: Pax, 2006)

Henriksen, Mogens, 'Er Hjulby Nyborgs forgænger?', *Fynske Minder* (2002), 155–86

———, 'Før Nyborg', *Skalk* (2003), 11–17

Hermanson, Lars, 'Kungahälla och Europa. Stadens symboliska betydelse inom 1100-talets politiska maktspel', in *Bohuslän som gränslandskap. Före och efter Roskildefreden*, ed. by Helene Carlsson Bohusläns museum Rapport 2012:47 (Uddevalla: Bohusläns Museum, 2013), pp. 33–43

———, *Släkt, vänner ock makt: en studie av elitens politiska kultur i 1100-talets Danmark* (University of Gothenburg: Historiska institutionen, 2000)

Hjermind, Jesper, and Hans Krongaard Kristensen, 'Svend Grathes vold', *MIV*, 14 (1986), 84–89

———, Mette Iversen, and Hans Krongaard Kristensen, *Viborg Søndersø 1000–1300. Byarkæologiske undersøgelser 1981 og 1984–1985* (Højbjerg: Wormianum, 1998)

Hoffmann, Erich, *Köningserhebung und Thronfolgeordnung in Dänemark bis zum Ausgang des Mittelalters* (Berlin: de Gruyter, 1976)

Ingold, Tim, *Lines: A Brief History* (London: Routledge, 2007)

———, *The Perception of the Environment* (London: Routledge, 2000)

Irsigler, Franz, 'Annäherungen an den Stadtbegriff', in *Europäische Städte im Mittelalter*, ed. by Ferdinand Opll and Christoph Sonnlechner (Innsbruck/Wien/Bozen: Studien Verlag, 2010), pp. 15–30

Iversen, Frode, 'Between Tribe and Kingdom – People. Land, and Law in Scandza AD 500–1350', in *Rulership in 1st to 14th Century Scandinavia. Royal Graves and Sites at Avaldsnes and beyond*, ed. by Dagfinn Skre (Berlin: de Gruyter, 2020), pp. 245–304

———, 'Concilium and Pagus – Revisiting the Germanic Thing-System of Northern Europe', *Journal of the North Atlantic*, 5 (2013), 5–17

———, 'Eiendom, makt og statsdannelse. Kongsgårder og gods i Hordaland i yngre jernalder og middelalder' (Doctoral thesis, University of Bergen, 2004)

———, 'The Thing in Trøndelag in Late Iron Age and Medieval Times', *Gunneria*, 81 (2017), 71–108

Jahnke, Carsten, *Das Silber des Meeres. Fang und Vertrieb von Ostseehering zwischen Norwegen und Italien (12.-16. Jahrhundert)* (Weimar: Böhlau, 2000)

Jensen, Janus Møller, 'Vejen til Jerusalem. Danmark og pilgrimsvejen til det Hellige Land i det 12. århundrede: En islandsk vejviser', in *Ett annat 1100-tal. Individ, kollektiv och kulturella mönster i medeltidens Danmark*, ed. by Peter Carelli, Lars Hermanson, and Hanne Sanders (Gothenburg: Makadam Förlag, 2004), pp. 284–337

Johnsen, Arne Odd, *Fra den eldste tid til 1252* (Oslo: Land og kirke, 1955)

Jón Viðar Sigurðsson, 'Jyllandshavet ca. 870–1035: de danske kongenes mare nostrum', in *Et fælles hav – Skagerrak og Kattegat i vikingetiden. Seminar på Nationalmuseet, København 19.- 20. september 2012*, ed. by Anne Pedersen and Søren M. Sindbæk (Copenhagen: Nationalmuseet, 2015), pp. 24–36

Jönsson, Lars, and Ulrika Wallebom, *Tommarp och Simrishamn – Österlens medeltida städer* (Simrishamn: Österlens museum, 2006)

Jørgensen, Anne Nørgård, Lars Jørgensen, and Lone Gebauer Thomsen. 'Assembly Sites for Cult, Markets, Jurisdiction and Social Relations. Historic-Ethnological analogy between North Scandinavian Church Towns, Old Norse Assembly Sites and Pit House Sites of the Late Iron Age and Viking Period', *Arkæologi i Slesvig | Archäologie in Schleswig*, Haderslev (2010), 95–112

Jørgensen, Lars, 'Stormandssæder og skattefund i 3.-12. Århundrede', *Fortid og Nutid* (1995), 83–110

Kålund, Kristian, 'En islandsk Vejviser for Pilgrimme fra 12. Århundrede', *Aarbøger for nordisk Oldkyndighed og Historie*, 3rd ser., vol. 3 (1913), 51–105

Keegan, John, *The Face of the Battle. A Study of Agincourt, Waterloo and the Somme* (London: Penguin Books, 1984 [1976])

Kjær, Lars, 'Feasting with Traitors: Royal Banquets as Rituals and Texts in Medieval Scandinavia', in *The Power of Practice. Rituals, Performatives, and Political Order in Northern Europe, c. 650–1350*, ed. by Wojtek Jezierski, Lars Hermanson, Hans Jacob Orning, and Thomas Småberg (Turnhout: Brepols, 2015), pp. 269–94

——, 'Gaver og gæstebud. Avaritia og liberalitas i Gesta Danorum', in *Saxo og hans Samtid*, ed. by Per Andersen and Thomas Hebøll-Holm (Aarhus: Aarhus Universitetsforlag, 2012), pp. 183–213

Kristensen, Anne Katrine Gade, 'Knud Magnussens krønike', *Historisk Tidsskrift* (D), 3.12 (1968–1969), 432–52

Kristensen, Hans Krongaard, and Bjørn Poulsen, *Danmarks byer i middelalderen* (Aarhus: Aarhus University Press, 2016)

Kryger, Karin (ed.), *Danske Kongegrave*, vol. 1 (Copenhagen: Museum Tusculanum Press, 2014)

——, 'S. Bendt i Ringsted, helgengrav og kongebegravelse', in *Danske Kongegrave*, vol. 1, ed. by Karin Kryger (Copenhagen: Museum Tusculanum Press, 2014), pp. 253–71

la Cour, Vilhelm, *Danske borganlæg til midten af det trettende århundrede*, vols 1–2 (Copenhagen: Nationalmuseet, 1973)

Lamberg, Marko, Marko Hakkanen, and Janne Haikari (eds), *Physical and Cultural Space in Pre-Industrial Europe. Methodological Approaches to Spatiality* (Lund: Nordic Academic Press, 2011)

Larre, Beñat Elortza, 'The Transformation of Naval Warfare in Scandinavia during the Twelfth Century', *Journal of Medieval Military History*, XVIII (2020), 81–98

le Jan, Régine, *Coopétition. Rivaliser, coopérer dans les sociétés du haut Moyen Âge (500–1100)* (Turnhout: Brepols, 2018)

Lefebvre, Henri, *The Production of Space* (La Production de l'espace) (Oxford: Blackwell, 1991 [1974])

Liljefalk, Lone, and Stefan Pajung, 'Bodil-slægten – en sydsjællandsk gåde', *Personalhistorisk Tidsskrift* (2013), 46–60

Lindahl, Fritze, 'Haraldsborg-skatten', in *Strejflys over Danmarks bygningskultur – festskrift til Harald Langberg*, ed. by Robert Egevang (Copenhagen: Nationalmuseet, 1979), pp. 213–33

Malmros, Rikke, *Bønder og leding i valdemarstidens Danmark* (Aarhus: Aarhus Universitetsforlag, 2019)

Matthiessen, Hugo, *Hærvejen. En tusindårig vej fra Viborg til Danevirke* (Copenhagen: Gyldendal, 1930).

Moltke, Erik (ed.), *Roskilde Domkirke. Københavns Amt. Danmarks Kirker*, vol. 3 (Copenhagen: Gad, 1944–1951)

Mortensen, Lars Boje, 'Writing and Speaking of St Olaf: National and Social Integration', in *Saints and their Lives on the Periphery: Veneration of Saints in Scandinavia and Eastern Europe (c. 1000–1200)*, ed. by Haki Antonsson and Ildar H. Garipzanov (Turnhout: Brepols, 2010), pp. 207–18

Müller, Inger Helene Vibe, 'Østnorske basilika-anlegg: en sammenligning' (Unpublished Doctoral Thesis, University of Oslo, 1971)

Nationalmuseet (ed.), *S. Knuds kirke. Odense Domkirke* (Copenhagen: Syddansk Universitetsforlag, 1990)

Nedkvitne, Arne, *The Social Consequences of Literacy in Medieval Scandinavia* (Turnhout: Brepols, 2004)

Nilsson, Ing-Marie, 'Hallandslistan i kung Valdemars jordebok: nya perspektiv på Hallands tidigmedeltida skattesystem', *Lund Studies in Historical Archaeology* (2016), 191–96

Nordeide, Sæbjørg Walaker, 'Erkebispegården i Trondheim. Beste tomta i by'n Trondheim' (Unpublished Doctoral Thesis, University of Oslo, 2003)

———, 'Norske festningsverk i middelalderen', in *From Nature to Script. Reykholt, Environment, Centre, and Manuscript Making*, ed. by Helgi Þorláksson and Þóra Björg Sigurðardóttir (Reykholt: Snorrastofa, 2012), pp. 117–40

Nyborg, Ebbe, 'Sven 2. Estridsen og Gunhild', *Danske Kongegrave*, vol. 1, ed. by Karin Kryger (Copenhagen: Museum Tusculanum Press, 2014), pp. 175–82

Ödman, Anders, *Borgar i Skåne* (Lund: Historiska media, 2002)

———, 'Skånskt järn från malm till marknad', in *Medeltida danskt järn. Framställning av och handel med järn i Skåneland och Småland under medeltiden*, ed. by Sven-Olof Olsson (Halmstad: Högskolan i Halmstad, 1995), pp. 146–55.

Olesen, Martin Borring, 'Vestborgen Castle in Kalundborg – Coastal Defence, Royal Stronghold or Naval Base for the Crusade', in *Building a Castle – Preparing for War or Keeping the Peace? (Castella Maris Baltici XIII)*, ed. by Nils Engberg, Vivian Etting, Lars Meldgaard Sass Jensen, Claus Sørensen, and Dorthe Wille-Jørgensen (Bonn: Magt, Borg og Landskab, 2018), pp. 18–28

Olsen, Rikke Agnete, *Danske middelalderborge* (Aarhus: Aarhus universitetsforlag, 2011)

Orluf, Frederik, 'Hvor dræbtes Harald Kesja?', *Danske Studier* (1953), 54–64

Orning, Hans Jacob, 'Borgenes blindsoner', *Klassekampen*. 4 June 2018, 12–13

———, 'Conflict and Social (Dis)order in Norway, c. 1030–1160', in *Disputing Strategies in Medieval Scandinavia*, ed. by Kim Esmark, Lars Hermanson, Hans Jacob Orning, and Helle Vogt (Leiden: Brill, 2013), pp. 45–82

———, 'Festive Governance: Feasts as Rituals of Power and Integration in Medieval Norway', in *Rituals, Performatives, and Political Order in Northern Europe, c. 650–1350*, ed. by Wojtek Jezierski, Lars Hermanson, Hans Jacob Orning, and Thomas Småberg (Turnhout: Brepols, 2015), pp. 175–208

———, 'Den materielle basis for den norske kongemaktens utvikling i høymiddelalderen', *Historisk Tidsskrift* (N), 3.84 (2005), 455–69

———, *Unpredictability and Presence – Norwegian Kingship in the High Middle Ages* (Leiden: Brill, 2008)

Pavón, Martin, 'Søborg – ærkebiskop Eskils borg i Nordsjælland', *Aarbøger for Nordisk Oldkyndighed og Historie, 2011–2012* (2013), 263–91

Petersen, Anne, 'Skagerrak and Kattegat in the Viking Age – Borders and Connecting Links', in *Northers Worlds – Landscapes, Interactions and Dynamics. Research at the National Museum of Denmark* (Proceedings of the Northern Worlds Conference Copenhagen 28–30 November 2012), ed. by Hans Christian Gulløv (Copenhagen: University Press of Southern Denmark, 2014), pp. 307–17

Pilø, Lars, Espen Finstad, and James H. Barrett, 'Crossing the Ice: An Iron Age to Medieval Mountain Pass at Lendbreen, Norway', *Antiquity*, 94.374 (2020), 437–54

Poulsen-Hansen, Kamma M., 'Middelalderens veje – set fra et arkæologisk synspunkt', *Vejhistorie. Tidsskrift for Dansk Vejhistorisk Selskab*, 19 (2011), 3–11

Poulsen, Bjørn, 'Den danske konges indtægter i middelalderen', in *Statsudvikling i Skandinavia i middelalderen*, ed. by Sverre Bagge, Michael H. Gelting, Frode Hervik, Thomas Lindkvist, and Bjørn Poulsen (Oslo: Dreyer, 2012), pp. 55–75

Poulsen, Thomas Guntzelnick, 'Søslagene på Kolindsund', *Museum Østjylland. Årbog* (2015), 119–31

Randsborg, Klavs, 'Bastrup – Europe. A massive Danish Donjon from 1100', *Acta Archaeologica*, 74 (2003), 65–122

Riddersporre, Mats, 'Alltid på våg. Valdemar den stores uppehållsorter enligt Saxo och diplom', *Fortid og Nutid* (1988), 17–26

Riis, Thomas, 'Det middelalderlige danske rejsekongedømme indtil 1332', in *Middelalder, metode og medier, festskrift til Niels Skyum-Nielsen*, ed. by Karsten Fledius, Niels Lund, and Herluf Nielsen (Viborg: Jysk selskab for historie, 1981), pp. 115–36

Ropeid, Andreas, 'Veg', in *Kulturhistorisk Leksikon for Nordisk Middelalder*, vol. XIX (Copenhagen: Rosenkilde og Bagger, 1975), cols 617–21

Rösch, Felix, Ulrich Müller, and Walter Dörfler, 'Castrum quod Slesvig villam speculator. Untersuchungen zur Möweninsel in der Schlei vor Schleswig', *Zeitschrift für Archäologie des Mittelalters*, 42 (2014), 117–58

Runge, Mads, and Mogens Bo Henriksen, 'The Origins of Odense – New Aspects of Early Urbanisation in Southern Scandinavia', *Danish Journal of Archaeology*, 7 (2018), 2–68

Sanmark, Alexandra, *Viking Law and Order. Places and Rituals of Assembly in the Medieval North* (Edinburgh: Edinburgh University Press, 2017)

Schia, Erik, *Oslo innerst i viken: liv og virke i middelalderbyen* (Oslo: Aschehoug, 1991)

Scott, Ida, 'Kongs- og lendmannsgårder i Viken ca. 800–1240 – i et rikssamlingsperspektiv' (Master's Dissertation, University of Oslo, 2016)

Semple, Sarah, and Alexandra Sanmark, 'Assembly in North West Europe: Collective Concerns for Early Societies?', *European Journal of Archaeology*, 16.3 (2013), 518–42

Sindbæk, Søren M., 'Kulturelle forskelle, sociale netværk og regionalitet i vikingetidens arkæologi', *Hikuin*, 35 (2008), 63–84

——, *Ruter og rutinisering: Vikingetidens fjernhandel i Nordeuropa* (Copenhagen: Multivers Academic, 2005).

Skovgaard Petersen, Inge, 'Saxo som samtidshistoriker. Det skånske oprør', *Scandia* (2008), 31–45

Skre, Dagfinn, *Rulership in 1st to 14th Century Scandinavia. Royal Graves and Sites at Avaldsnes and beyond* (Berlin: de Gruyter, 2020)

Skyum-Nielsen, Niels, *Kvinde og slave* (Copenhagen: Munksgaard, 1971)

Steen, Sverre, *Ferd og fest. Reiseliv i norsk sagatid og middelalder* (Oslo: Frydenlunds bryggeri, 1929)

Stibeus, Magnus, 'Sigurd Jorsalafars kastell och Ragnhildsholmen', in *Kungahälla. Problem och forskning kring stadens äldsta historia*, ed. by Hans Andersson, Kristina Carlsson, and Maria Vretemark (Uddevalla: Bohusläns museum, 1989), pp. 149–74

Stille, Arthur, *Saxos skånska stridsskildringar* (Uppsala: K. Vitterhets Historie och Antikvitets Akademi, 1922)

Sverrir Jakobsson, 'Hauksbók and the Construction of an Icelandic World View', *Saga Book*, 31 (2007), 12–38.

Sørensen, Kurt, *Vikingernes havn: sagnet om Isøre – havnen og landskabet* (Nykøbing: Engel, 2009)

Søvsø, Morten, 'Riber Ulfs borg', *Arkæologi i Slesvig/Archäologie in Schleswig*, 2 (2014), 191–203

Taranger, Absalon, 'Om kongevalg i Norge i sagatiden', *Historisk Tidsskrift* (Norwegian), 5th ser. (1934–1936): 110–66, 273–308

Thomasson, Joakim, 'Av samma penning Helsingborg 3 mark – landskapet, urbaniseringen och Helsingborg', *META Historiskarkeologisk tidskrift* (2021) 165–88

Thorsen, Sven, 'En to-tre folkeborge – en på Lolland, og to på Falster', *Lolland-Falsters historiske Samfund. Årbog*, 89 (2001), 5–16

Ulriksen, Jens, Maja K. Schultz, and Morten F. Mortensen, 'Dominating the Landscape – The Emblematic Setting of Borgring and the Viking Age Ring Fortresses of Denmark', *Danish Journal of Archaeology*, 9 (2020), 1–22

Weidhagen-Hallerdt, Margareta, 'A Possible Ring Fort from the Late Viking Age Period in Helsingborg', *Current Swedish Archaeology*, 17 (2009), 187–204

Wille-Jørgensen, Dorthe, *Kongens borg. 123 års arkæologi på Vordingborg* (Gylling: Danmarks Borgcent, 2014)

Williams, Thomas J. T., 'Landscape and Warfare in Anglo-Saxon England and the Viking Campaign of 1006', *Early Medieval Europe*, 23.3 (2015), 329–59

Zilmer, Kristel, 'The Representation of Waterborne Traffic in Old Norse Narratives: The Case of the Baltic Sea', *Viking and Medieval Scandinavia* (2006), 239–74

LARS HERMANSON

6. The Memory of Margrethe

Noblewomen as Power Agents in Multi-Party Conflicts c. 1120–1170

Constitutionally oriented historians often based their studies on a distinction between state and society — between public and private. In recent decades, however, the pendulum has swung towards actor-related historical analyses where scholars focus on people by investigating their action strategies and mental world. Gender studies has gained a prominent position in this broader power analysis influenced by theories represented by, for example, Michel Foucault and Pierre Bourdieu.[1] It is no longer self-evident that the concept 'historical actor' is synonymous with a man. The interdependence between men and women is often accentuated by historians dealing with how various resources were used for political action in medieval society. Still, noblewomen are often interpreted as pawns in the marriage market, contributing to the upward or downward mobility of families.

This view has been nuanced by gender-oriented scholarship, which states that women could be seen as 'transmitters of power'.[2] Yet this interpretation is somewhat problematic since it is based on a traditional view of public power as an invariable constant linked to politics and the material distribution of resources. Men are seen as more or less independent of 'the private sphere', which means that one often disregards the fact that power

---

1 See e.g. Foucault, *History of Sexuality*; Bourdieu, *Masculine Domination*. For critical views on Foucault's perspectives see e.g. King, 'The Prisoner of Gender'. For a critical discussion on Bourdieu's *Masculine Domination*, see e.g. Krais, 'On Pierre Bourdieu's *Masculine Domination*'.
2 Sjöberg, 'Kvinnans sociala underordning – en problematisk historia', pp. 169, 172–73; Andersson, *Kloster och aristokrati*.

Lars Hermanson (lars.hermanson@history.gu.se) is professor of history in the Department of Historical Studies, University of Gothenburg.

in medieval society rested on couples.[3] It always takes two to tango. The partner's scope for manoeuvre was to a large extent dependent on social and symbolic forms of capital linked to multiple roles within families. Hence women's capacity for practising agency risks being eclipsed if they are merely seen as transmitters of power. Here the dynamics of power will be analysed from a Bourdieusian perspective by focusing on the interplay between social and symbolic forms of capital.[4] Thus, we have to discuss how women and men interacted on the political scene.

This chapter investigates how and through what means noblewomen acted in and transformed Scandinavian power relations during the intra-elite conflicts of c. 1120–1170. In order to focus on and highlight female agency, an agent is thus defined as a person, who for various reasons, is capable of exercising some control over the social relations of which he or she is a part, which in turn entails an ability to change them.[5] For the purposes of this chapter, this entails a focus on how different kinds of resources were accumulated and strategically used by noblewomen in a society marked by constant crises. Special attention will be paid to how the memorialization of noblewomen was used as a basic constituent in the production and reproduction of symbolic and social capital. The main thesis is that women in life and after death had decisive functions in the construction, transformation, and preservation of networks. Here the Swedish princesses Margrethe Ingesdatter and her niece Ingrid Ragvaldsdatter, who were introduced in Chapter 3, will form points of departures.

Queen Margrethe: An Unpredictable Success Story?

Margrethe played a prominent role in the Scandinavian political arena already as young teenager when her father, the Swedish king Inge Stenkilsson, married her to the Norwegian king Magnus Barefoot in 1101. The alliance was formed in order to settle a conflict about disputed border areas,

---

3 Many studies of medieval queenship emphasize the role of the household as the foundation for monarchy. This implies a focus on intersectional relationships of king and queen with distant kin, noble families, household members, clergy, etc. In her research survey on medieval queenship Theresa Earenfight states that 'Studying queens prompted a shift of the power axis to a horizontal plane where networks, affiliations, and alliances at court and in the household were tangible sources of power, influence, and agency'. Earenfight, 'Medieval Queenship', p. 2.
4 Bourdieu, *Outline of a Theory of Practice*; Bourdieu, *The Logic of Practice*.
5 Sewell, 'A Theory of Structure', p. 158. Referring to the views of Sewell, 'agency' stands for 'the actor's capacity to reinterpret and mobilize an array of resources in terms of cultural schemas other than those that initially constituted the array' (p. 157). On the dynamics of power and the interplay between agency and structure, see Bourdieu, *Outline of a Theory of Practice*, pp. 78–86; 159–97; Bourdieu, *The Logic of Practice*, pp. 52–65; 80–97; 112–21. On female agency in the Middle Ages, see Erler and Kowaleski, 'Introduction', pp. 1–6.

with the Danish king Erik the Good acting as mediator. Old Norse sources relate that Margrethe received the disputed areas as a dowry (*heimanfylgje*) and she was thereafter called 'the Peacemaiden' (Fredkulla).[6] Her husband was killed in Ireland and shortly afterwards she was remarried to Erik the Good's brother and successor, the Danish king Niels Svendsen.[7] It could be argued that the pact between King Niels and Inge Stenkilsson ought to be seen as a pure political settlement wherein the economic aspects were not salient. Niels was then a recently elected king in urgent need of a powerful ally.[8] No dowry is mentioned in the sources, but we can assume that the young queen had limited control over her material resources since she was subordinated to her husband's guardianship.[9] Her natal family were in 1105 still in full possession of the Swedish royal *patrimonium*. Thus, at this stage there was nothing that distinguished Margrethe from other Scandinavian queens. She was primarily a transmitter of power in her capacity as a symbol of the political alliance between two royal families. However, during the following years the tables were turned between Niels and Margrethe, due to a remarkable chain of events linked to transfers of inheritance and the socio-political mechanisms of bilateral kinship.

Niels managed to stay on the throne for nearly thirty years, which must be considered as an unusually long reign for a medieval monarch who ruled a society marked by constant crises. Yet, as pointed out in Chapter 3, he owed a great debt of gratitude to his wife Margrethe for being in power for so long. When she died at the end of the 1120s, Niels only managed to stay for power for a few more years before he was ousted and slaughtered by his opponents. If we read sources such as *The Legend of Knud Lavard*, Helmold of Bosau, and Saxo Grammaticus, it is actually more appropriate to speak about 'the reign of the couple Margrethe and Niels' than 'King Niels' reign', which is the most common phrase used by Danish historians.[10] For instance, *The Legend of Knud Lavard* states that Niels 'lacked the foresight and capacity for rulership' which was needed

---

6 Theodoricus, p. 27; *Ágrip*, p. 67; *Morkinskinna*, p. 307; *Fagrskinna*, p. 250. In Europe where marriages were arranged between warring families as parts of settlements the brides were sometimes termed as *obses pacis* meaning 'pledge of peace' or 'hostage of peace'. Bartlett, *Blood Royal*, p. 14.
7 The short marriage to Magnus Barefoot did not result in any offspring.
8 Niels had outmanoeuvred his elder half-brother Harald Kesja who had ruled Denmark during Erik the Good's pilgrimage to Jerusalem. Erik died in Cyprus in 1103. For more on Niels' accession to kingship, see Chapter 3.
9 It is possible that she brought the dowry from her first marriage with her into the next which implies that the disputed border areas came under the control of Niels. Another possibility is that the dowry went back to Margrethe's father after the death of Magnus Barefoot. On the use of dowries and morning-gifts in medieval Europe, see e.g. Hughes, 'From Brideprice to Dowry in Mediterranean Europe', pp. 262–96; Ward, *Women in Medieval Europe, 1200–1500*, pp. 40–44.
10 Hermanson, *Släkt, vänner och makt*, p. 110.

to be able to rule the realm and therefore foreigners considered that the Danish leadership was dependent on 'female virtue (*virtute feminea*)'.[11]

According to Saxo, the peace in the Danish realm was solely due to Queen Margrethe's proactive measures. He writes that she wanted to create a stronger family feeling among the young royal kinsmen

> through the aid of family ties, [she] joined in marriage the daughter of her brother Regnald to Henrik, and her sister's daughter, Ingeborg to Cnut. She divided the inheritance from her father (*paterna vero bona*) into exactly equal parts and distributed these fairly, one to herself, the others to her nieces, the wives I just mentioned. From this act there rose a quarrel between the Danes and Swedes, which was quickened by several further sources of enmity, and it has lasted right to this day, clinging to its old hatred.[12]

When she lay on her deathbed, the hatred between 'the excited young men', i.e. her son Magnus Nielsen and his cousins Henrik Svendsen and Knud Lavard, had reached a critical stage that severely threatened the peace.[13] Saxo says that the Queen then called Knud Lavard to her and urged him to 'foster the peace of the country, and concord among his kinsmen'. She is described as 'the most kindly nourisher of family affection' and Margrethe further tells Knud that, while in health, she had eagerly tried to warn and stop those who 'would try to destroy [...] the mutual affection of the royal family'.[14] Knud swore to uphold the peace and Saxo states that Margrethe 'reassured by such loyalty, declared that she would die with her mind in rest'.[15] Saxo not only stresses the queen's role as a protector of the peace, but also gives prominence to her achievements as a devoted benefactor of the Church. In her role as representing a sacral office Margrethe used her wealth by enriching 'the churches of God with great estates' and

> but also put all her energies into increasing their splendour and to altering the priests' needy way of life by investing them with choice

---

11 *Historia S. Kanvti*, p. 190.
12 GD, 13.1.4. 'Cui mater ampliorem propinquorum fauorem affinitatum beneficio creare cupiens Henrico Regnaldi fratris / Kanuto Ingiburgam sororis filiam coniugio copulauit. Paterna uero bona in equales admodum portiones partitione redegit, unam sibi, ceteras nuptis, quas prefatus sum, diuisionis parilitate contribuens. Hinc Danorum Sueonumque dissensio orta ac deinde compluribus inimicitiarum incrementis coalita ad hoc usque tempus ueteris odii tenacissima perseuerat'.
13 Henrik's father Svend and Knud Lavard's father Erik the Good were brothers of Magnus's father Niels (see Chapter 3).
14 GD, 13.5.6. 'Adiecit quoque existere, qui regie familie charitatem odio disiicere niterentur, se uero plenis salubritatis monitis pestiferos talium instinctus pressisse'.
15 GD, 13.5.6. 'Illa promissionis beneficio delectata tante fidei securam equo se animo obituram asseruit'.

adornments. In order to deck the faith in grander fashion, she took it upon herself to produce richly bordered chasubles and other pastoral vestments, which were then provided for the use of ecclesiastics.[16]

A couple of observations can be made based on Saxo's depiction of Queen Margrethe. To begin with: she cannot simply be interpreted as a 'transmitter' of power.[17] There is no doubt that she fulfils the criteria for being an agent. With no intervention from her husband, Margrethe is portrayed as the sole social engineer of the marriage alliances between the Swedish and the Danish royal families. The Queen is in full control of her inheritance and seems to be able to do what she wants with her paternal estates (around 1125 her father King Inge's nephews and successors Philip and Inge the Younger were both dead, see below). Normally this freedom of action was reserved for widows. Furthermore, not only did she use her exceptional wealth for political peace-making purposes. Margrethe was also capable of transforming her resources into a symbolic and cultural capital by acting as a generous benefactor of the Church, which obviously must have lent her an outstanding charisma.[18] Hence she was situated firmly within the imagined community of the Danish realm.

However, it cannot be ignored that Saxo traces the origins of the conflicts of his age to the politics of Queen Margrethe. She is portrayed as a peacemaker with good intentions while living, but when dead her political legacy turned out to be a kind of Pandora's box, which suddenly opened as soon as she had drawn her last breath. Moreover, it is interesting to note that the disputes emanating from Margrethe's failed peace policy are depicted in an ethnic, bipolar framework when the author states that the enmities which later took place were between Danes and Swedes.

---

16 GD, 13.1.5. 'non solum diuinarum edium opes latifundiis auxit, sed et totis uiribus ad augendum earum' splendorem incubuit, sacerdotalisque cultus inopiam exquisito ornamentorum genere permutauit. Enimuero quo rem diuinam ornatiorem efficeret, pallas laticlauias ceteraque sacerdotii insignia condere atque sacrorum usibus erogare cure habuit'.

17 Parallels could be drawn between the view of women as transmitters and Bruno Latour's actor-network-theory which emphasizes the distinction between intermediaries and mediators. Similarly to transmitters, intermediaries only transport or replicate the force of another unit without transformation. On the contrary, mediators do things by triggering new unpredictable consequences through concatenations. Latour, *Reassembling the Social*, pp. 58–60. Moreover, Latour underscores 'the under-determination of action', which means that he accentuates the uncertainties about 'who and what is acting'. Latour, *Reassembling the Social*, pp. 44–45. Thus, from Latour's perspective Margrethe could be interpreted as a mediator in an unpredictable success story that caused transformation through a series of new interconnections.

18 For a discussion on the medieval European queen as peacemaker, intercessor, and benefactor, see Huneycutt, 'Medieval Queenship'. Sean Gilsdorf, in a study of the Carolingian and Ottonian elite, has shown that queens often acted as intermediaries in their capacity as affines with bonds of affection and obligations to different networks. Gilsdorf, *The Favor of Friends*, pp. 114–24.

So what lay behind the unique political position of Queen Margrethe, and how should we interpret Saxo's explanation about the origins of the hostilities between Danes and Swedes? Margrethe is a formidable example of how medieval lordship was intertwined with kinship. Therefore, the first step has to be to take a closer look at kinship and inheritance and how these resources were accumulated and transformed into various forms of capital.

If we compare the Norwegian king's socio-political strategies around the year 1100 with his Danish counterpart, we can trace some common traits. As stated in Chapter 2, royal dynastic lineage was not a determinant for Norwegian kingship due to the frequent use of concubinage.[19] Margrethe's first husband, Magnus Barefoot, mainly built his power on vertical alliances of friendship with local magnate families. Some of these pacts were confirmed through ties of concubinage or fosterage resulting in a motley family tree (again, see Chapter 2). Polygynous reproduction resulted in a numerous progeny that gave the king opportunities to spread the risks of the emergence of overly strong power centres by delegating honourable assignments to local lords all over the realm. Through this short-term strategy, Magnus Barefoot successfully built his own powerbase, but his relationships with concubines did not enlarge his material resources. He should be seen foremost as a classical 'Viking-king', who gained material wealth through an aggressive policy of expansion built on conquests and plundering.

King Magnus's childless marriage with Margrethe meant that he was able to control her dowry, but when he died these border areas may have been transferred into her new marriage with the Danish King Niels. Like the Swedish King Inge, Magnus had also formed an alliance with the Danish royal family by marrying his daughter Ragnhild to Niels's brother Harald Kesja. Ragnhild's mother Thora was, however, a concubine, which implies that in this case the elements of symbolic and material capital were modest. Seen from a Danish point of view, Niels's marriage to Margrethe gave him a stronger position in relation to his competitor Harald, since it was far more lucrative considering the symbolic and material resources which were included in the bargain.[20] This was probably a contributory factor that can explain why Niels managed to consolidate and legitimize his disputed accession to the throne.

---

19 See also, Rüdiger, *All the King's Women*, pp. 74–119, 206–24. For parallels to the use of concubinage in medieval Iceland, see Auður Magnúsdóttir, *Frillor och fruar*.
20 According to Tore Nyberg, Niels' marriage to Margrethe took place shortly after Magnus Barefoot's death in 1103. Nyberg, 'Kong Niels. Skitse til en biografi', p. 362. However, other scholars claim that the marriage took place in 1105. The year of Niels's accession is uncertain, see e.g., Nyberg, 'Knud, Danmarks konge – 900 år efter helgenkåringen', pp. 5–14.

In a similar way to the Norwegian family tree, the Danish royal family, which was descended from Svend Estridsen (d. 1076), must also be considered to be fairly complex, due to the practices of bilateral kinship and polygyny.[21] Svend Estridsen's royal heritage came from the maternal side.[22] His marriage to the Swedish princess, Gunhild, resulted in increased material and symbolic resources. But the marriage was dissolved, since the couple, according to the Church, were too closely related.[23] Like Magnus Barefoot, Svend Estridsen had numerous progeny. As discussed in Chapter 3, all five royal successors from 1076 to Niels's death in 1134 were bastard sons of Svend. Additionally, he had at least nine other 'illegitimate' sons and an unknown number of daughters.[24]

Though Svend managed to create a firm personal powerbase founded on vertical bonds (based on concubinage and fosterage) with regional magnates, an unavoidable outcome of this strategy was the fragmentation of the family estate. Hence, the offspring of Svend competed for a limited share of resources. Some of his successors increased their royal prestige by marrying foreign noble princesses. For instance, Knud (r. 1080–1086) married Adela of Flanders, who in Ailnoth's *vita* is referred to as *imperatorii generis nobilissium*.[25] Though this was a highly prestigious and potent alliance between the Danish king and Adela's father, Robert of Flanders (which provoked fear in England), it probably did not enhance Knud's material resources to any great extent.[26]

In contrast, Knud's younger brother Niels succeeded in combining social, economic, and symbolic forms of capital by marrying Margrethe. Her natal family's strategies differed somewhat from Svend Estridsen and

---

21 For definitions of the term 'polygyny', see Rüdiger, *All the King's Women*, pp. 9–15.
22 His mother Estrid was a daughter of Svend Forkbeard and sister to Knud the Great. She was married to the earl Ulf, who was murdered at Knud's instigation. Estrid made a large donation to Roskilde cathedral after her husband's death and thereby, like Queen Margrethe, she earned a reputation as a devoted benefactor of the Church. Lind, 'Nordic and Eastern Elites', p. 113.
23 Adam, 3.15.126. Gunhild did not remarry. Instead she became a devoted benefactor of the Church. Adam calls her 'the most saintly (*sanctissima*) queen Gunnhild'. Adam of Bremen, p. 126. On Svend Estridsen's divorce, see Lund, 'Sven Estridsen's Incest and Divorce'.
24 Some of these daughters were married to foreign princes, such as Sigrid who was married to the Slavic prince Gudskalk. Adam, 3.18.130; 3.50.157. However, it is here important to notice that the depiction of Svend's sons as 'illegitimate' is heavily dependent on Saxo. Older sources such as Adam of Bremen associate Svend with at least three lawful marriages in addition to his marriage with Gunnhild. Bolin, 'Kring mäster Adams text. Interpretation och kommentar', pp. 230–44. Thyra Nors states that Saxo is the only source which emphasizes the illegitimacy of all of Svend's children. Nors, 'Ægteskab og politik i Saxos Gesta Danorum', p. 13. See also Rüdiger, *All the King's Women*, pp. 55–64.
25 *Historia S. Kanvti*, p. 93.
26 Though she was remarried to Roger of Apulia, Adela continued to honour her Danish conjugal family by sending precious gifts to Knud's grave in Odense. *Historia S. Kanvti*, p. 133.

Magnus Barefoot. Perhaps it only had to do with unexpected occurrences linked to 'genealogical accidents', but her parents Inge's and Helena's marriage policy was based on a trans-regnal network, including Scandinavian royal families, the Russian Monomakids, and even the Byzantine imperial family.[27] Compared to the Norwegian and Danish polygynous families, it is possible that Margrethe's kin was marked by a specific noble and sacral charisma.[28] Yet it was first and foremost genealogical accidents that prepared the way for Margrethe's unique position, which meant that she became an eligible match for Niels. Inge's and Helena's only known son, Ragvald, died at a fairly young age, but he was not too young to have a daughter named Ingrid, who was married to the Danish prince Henrik Svendsen. Thus, her dowry was controlled by him. King Inge died c. 1110. After his and Ragvald's death, the inheritance was in the hands of his daughter Margrethe and her two sisters Kristina and Katarina. Kristina was married to the *kniaz* Mstislav of Kiev (Mstislav-Harald), who probably had highly limited (if any) control over her tangible assets.[29] She died, according to *The First Novgorod Chronicle*, in 1122.[30] The youngest sister Katarina was later married to a Danish prince, Harald Kesja's son Bjorn Ironside (see below).[31] Unfortunately the sources give no information of how she handled her properties. Perhaps Katarina was subordinated to her more powerful elder sister Queen Margrethe (see Fig. 6.1).

The political situation in Sweden after the death of King Inge c. 1110 is wrapped in mystery. Perhaps his son Ragvald gained the throne a short while before his death.[32] We know that the Crown later went to Inge's nephew Philip. He died in 1118 and another nephew, Inge the Younger, was king until c. 1125. They had no male heirs, implying that the Swedish

---

27 Their granddaughter, Evpraksiia, was married to the Byzantine emperor's son, Alexios Komnenos. Lind, 'Nordic and Eastern Elites', p. 117. On the concept 'genealogical accident', see Preiser-Kapeller, 'Calculating the Middle Ages?', p. 114.
28 Hermanson, 'Det tidiga Vreta. En helig plats i ett europeiskt maktsystem', pp. 235–36. On various forms of charismatic legitimacy based on e.g. holy status, see Jezierski, 'Introduction: Nordic Elites in Transformation, c. 1050–1250', pp. 1–35.
29 *Morkinskinna*, pp. 328–29. Marriages to foreign princes foremost increased the symbolic capital. Transactions of land through dowries were for natural reasons not a salient feature. Thus, these marriages could be a strategy to keep the *patrimonium* intact.
30 *The Chronicle of Novgorod*, 1122. A.M. 6630, p. 10.
31 Son of Harald Kesja and grandson of Magnus Barefoot. Bjorn was, according to the anonymous Roskilde chronicle and the chronicle by Svend Aggesen, executed in 1135 by King Erik the Unforgettable. *Chronicon Roskildense*, p. 31; Sven Aggesen, *Brevis historia*, p. 134 (more on this in Chapter 3). We do not have any information on Katarina and what happened to her dowry. Perhaps she outlived Margrethe by a couple of years and maybe her inheritance was confiscated by her husband's murderer, Erik the Unforgettable.
32 The Swedish archaeologist, Markus Lindberg, asserts that Ragvald died before his father. Lindberg, 'Det ligger en kung begraven. Vreta klosterkyrka som gravplats', p. 128.

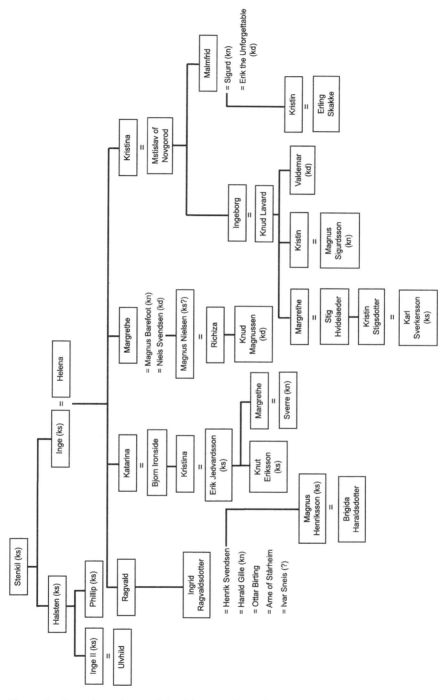

Figure 6.1. Genealogical tree of Stenkil. Figure by author.

throne was vacant until 1128, when Margrethe's son Magnus was elected king of Götaland, as related in Chapter 3.[33]

So, what does this complicated chain of marriage alliances and genealogical accidents tell us? Firstly, Inge may have succeeded in keeping the royal *patrimonium* largely intact, but perhaps his and Helena's strategy was not that good, since it led to the extinction of the male line of the family. His daughters were a great asset, but daughters without brothers unavoidably led to a situation where new players, i.e. in-laws (*mágr, magh*), entered into the Swedish political game. By contrast Inge's more promiscuous colleagues, Magnus Barefoot and Svend Estridsen, had an endless supply of male heirs. These 'bastards', on the other hand, had to share the royal cake with each other. In this competitive situation, the princes who had managed to become in-laws to the Stenkil family were the ones who had the most favourable positions.[34] In the case of Denmark, it is evident that while Margrethe was alive, she managed to maintain the peace between the royal kinsmen who were allied with her family, but not between the brothers Harald Kesja and Erik the Unforgettable, who in the 1120s lacked strong ties to the Stenkil family, and who may have been feuding with each other.[35]

Secondly, it now becomes clearer why *The Legend of Knud Lavard* states that during Niels's reign the leadership of the Danish realm relied on female virtue.[36] Due to genealogical accidents, Margrethe had in the middle of the 1120s turned into an accumulation point of social, symbolic, cultural, and material forms of capital. The greater part of the Stenkil-*patrimonium* was then hers. In a 'legal' sense or according to 'customary practices', Niels ought to have controlled her dowry. Yet according to Saxo, Margrethe exercised full control over her social and material resources when she arranged peace-keeping marriages and portioned out shares of the patrimony to her nieces.[37] Thus she cannot be interpreted simply as

---

33 *GD*, 13.5.1.
34 Margrethe's father Inge was son of King Stenkil. The descendants of Stenkil used to be called 'the Stenkil-family', or 'the Stenkil *ätt* (kin)', or simply 'the Stenkils'.
35 *GD*, 13.4.2. According to Saxo, their brother Knud Lavard rebuked them and decided that the patrimony should be divided equally among Harald and Erik. It seems a bit strange that Knud had the power to decide this. However, any alteration in the distribution of family land had to be sanctioned with the consent of the whole family. *DRHH*, p. 302, n. 35. Perhaps Knud was given authority to decide in his role as mediator. It is also important to keep in mind Saxo's ambition to promote the royal branch descending from Knud Lavard.
36 *Vitae Sanctorum Danorum: S. Canutus dux*, p. 190.
37 It is important to make a distinction between 'rules of inheritance' and how they were used in practice, i.e. how they were adapted to various situations. Hansen, 'The Concept of Kinship'; Sawyer, 'Fromheten, familjen och förmögenheten', pp. 42–48; Gelting, 'Odelsrett–lovbydelse–bördsrätt–retrait lignager'. We must also note that most historians' interpretations of these 'rules' or 'customs' are based on sources compiled in the thirteenth century.

a transmitter of power. It makes more sense to see her as a transformer and catalyst of various forms of power resources. The queen was a core member because of her favourable position based on material wealth and a considerable number of social connections which she was able, not only to control, but also to change.[38] Her husband Niels's position was for most of his reign dependent on Margrethe. Though he was formally the ruler of the realm, he was nevertheless in a vulnerable position. His greatest assets against his equal royal challengers sprang from his role as the husband of a rich and well-connected queen.

The Legend of Knud Lavard and Saxo are both tendentious sources in the sense that they strive to promote Margrethe's charisma on the expense of Niels'.[39] However, the Queen's power and public role are also confirmed by contemporary sources. Margrethe was the first woman in Scandinavia to have her name stamped on coins and she was also the first royal woman to appear in Nordic charters. Her name was the first mentioned in the line of prominent witnesses who confirmed King Niels's donation to the churches of Odense.[40] Additionally the German chronicler Helmold of Bosau relates that Margrethe actively participated in one of the critical political meetings between King Niels and Duke Knud Lavard during the growing succession crisis in 1128–1129.[41]

Margrethe's public functions were also prominent in her role as a symbol of piety. Saxo's depiction of the Queen as a devoted benefactor of the churches is confirmed by foreign contemporary scribes who had heard about her reputation for piety.[42] Bernard Gineste has, for instance, shown that the French canon, Thibaud d'Étampes of the Benedictine monastery Saint-Étienne, tried to enter into Margrethe's service *c.* 1112–1116.[43] The

---

38 On the network concept 'core member' and mechanisms for centrality to individual nodes, see Preiser-Kapeller, 'Calculating the Middle Ages?', pp. 102–03.

39 More contemporary sources such as Ailnoth's legend of St Knud (*c.* 1111–1112) do not depict King Niels as a weak ruler. In the *Roskilde Chronicle* (*c.* 1140) he is described as '*mansuetus et simplex, minime rector*' (*Chronicon Roskildense*, p. 25), a portrait that has been much debated among Danish historians.

40 *DD*, I:2, no. 34; Hermanson, *Släkt, vänner och makt*, pp. 100–01.

41 Helmold, p. 99. Perhaps she was supposed to act as a mediator or intercessor between the two cousins. However, Helmold, as mentioned in Chapter 3, in contrast to Saxo, does not give the Danish queen a peace-making function. Her role is rather the opposite in that she advises her son Magnus to murder Knud. However, it is possible that Helmold has confused Margrethe with Niels's second wife/mistress Ulvhild given that Margrethe could well have been dead at that point. Hermanson, *Släkt, vänner och makt*, p. 94 n. 135. On the depictions of the frictions at the meeting, see, Jezierski, '*Convivium in terra honoris*', p. 151, and Chapter 3 in this volume.

42 On women's management of the public image and symbolic capital of the family, see Bourdieu, *Masculine* Domination, pp. 99–100.

43 Gineste, 'Thibaud d'Étampes', pp. 43–44; 54–55. See also Haastrup and Lind, 'Dronning Margrete Fredkulla', pp. 33–34.

Danish queen seems to have acted as a benefactor of the Norman abbey, and Thibaud turned to her in order to escape from the complicated rules of celibacy.

Ulla Haastrup and John Lind have emphasized Queen Margrethe's role as a founder of churches in Denmark. They argue, for instance, that the mural paintings in Vä Church in Scania depict images of the royal donors, Margrethe and Niels. It is the only fresco-painting in northern Europe to show a female founder carrying a model of a church.[44] Additionally Haastrup and Lind identify the noblewoman dressed in a Byzantine outfit depicted on a mural painting in Målöw Church as Queen Margrethe.[45] Hence, there are several indications that she not only used her resources for peace-keeping purposes but also for honouring God, which could be seen as just another side of the coin. Consequently, Margrethe transformed her wealth into social, cultural, and symbolic forms of capital.[46] The latter contributed the most to her charisma as representing the holy mission associated with high medieval queenship.[47] It was thus above all Margrethe's wealth and the way she used it that distinguished her from her contemporary female counterparts in Scandinavia.

From a socio-political point of view, as Jón Viðar Sigurðsson states in Chapter 2, Magnus Barefoot based his rule on vertical bonds. This was also characteristic of Svend Estridsen and his royal offspring. It is suggestive that Saxo only adds King Niels's marriage policy as a short supplement to Margrethe's deeds where he states that 'Furthermore, a mistress is reported to have borne Niels a daughter, Ingrid, who was later married off to a man named Ubbe.'[48] As shown in the first chapters of this book, the networks of Magnus Barefoot and the male scions of Svend Estridsen were founded on domestic ancestors, while the Swedish royal network was 'transregnal'. Yet one may say that Queen Margrethe's proactive marriage policy made an important contribution by also making the Norwegian and Danish networks transregnal. As mentioned above, Saxo's depiction of

---

44 Haastrup and Lind, 'Dronning Margrete Fredkulla', p. 44. The alleged depiction of Niels is showing a man carrying a reliquary.
45 Haastrup and Lind, 'Dronning Margrete Fredkulla', p. 67. Margrethe's Byzantine appearance could be explained due to the Stenkil-family's connections with the Eastern Empire. Foreign dress most likely served to project an imperial image to the public. Parallels could be drawn with Knud Lavard, who, according to Saxo, attended a Danish wedding ceremony dressed 'in the Saxon fashion and more elegant than anyone else', 'in ueste Saxonica ceteris cultior progrederetur'. *GD*, 13.5.4.
46 On women's role as being responsible for the conversion of economic capital into symbolic capital/'signs of distinction', see Bourdieu, *Masculine Domination*, pp. 98–102.
47 Stafford, *Queens, Concubines, and Dowagers*; Klaniczay, *Holy Rulers, and Blessed Princesses*. For an overview of research on medieval queenship, see Earenfight, 'Medieval Queenship', pp. 1–9. On the symbolism of medieval marriage, see Engh, *The Symbolism of Marriage*.
48 *GD*, 13.1.4. 'Preter hec Ingritha Vbboni cuidam postmodum denupta Nicolao ex pellice nata proditur'.

Margrethe for posterity is ambivalent. She is, on the one hand, portrayed as a peace-keeper, but on the other hand, the author says that her family policy led to a permanent antagonism between Danes and Swedes.

It is nonetheless obvious that Margrethe left both a social and a symbolic memory for future generations, which had great impact on their strategies and the frictions that followed.[49] Following the network-theorist Johannes Preiser-Kapeller, we may draw the conclusion that the 'social system of the elite had a "memory" with regard to conflicts, which influenced the severity of further conflicts'.[50]

Ingrid Ragvaldsdatter — A Noblewoman in the Middle of the Scandinavian Power Field

The memory of Margrethe was principally maintained by her nieces Ingrid, Malmfrid, Ingeborg, and Kristina. These female descendants of the Swedish Stenkil family constituted basic nodes within a macro-network comprising nearly all Nordic royal contenders during the twelfth century. Affiliation with this genealogical pool was thus a prerequisite for political success. The extinction of the Stenkil family's male line in the 1120s meant that Margrethe's nieces after her death were transformed into accumulation points and transmitters of wealth and royal prestige. During the following decades, clusters were formed and reformed around these central actors in the Scandinavian field of power.[51] It led to fractionalization and increased competition for resources that had repercussions well into the thirteenth century.

These conditions could partly explain the duration and multipolarity of the Scandinavian intra-elite conflicts. As previously mentioned, Saxo notes that Margrethe's death led to a prolonged discord between Danes and Swedes. However, to an equal degree these disputes also involved the Norwegians. From Saxo's point of view, one might say that Queen Margrethe's nieces were 'gold boxes' which soon turned out to be 'Pandora's boxes'. Still there are reasons to be sceptical about the author's depiction of these women as merely troublemakers. In many political situations they were also troubleshooters. On account of their multiple social connections, they occasionally acted as mediators or intercessors and thereby Margrethe's

---

49 One may here paraphrase Ernst Kantorowicz's famous transpersonal trope in *The King's Two Bodies*, 'The King is dead. Long live the King' with a female analogue, i.e. 'The Queen is dead. Long live the Queen'. Kantorowicz, *The King's Two Bodies*, p. 412.
50 Preiser-Kapeller, 'Calculating the Middle Ages?', p. 112.
51 On concepts used in network theory such as 'cluster', 'nodes', etc., see Preiser-Kapeller, 'Calculating the Middle Ages?', pp. 100–27.

female relatives sometimes had a stabilizing effect on strained political relations.

Among Margrethe's nieces, it is only possible to survey the life and doings of Ingrid Ragvaldsdatter, since the information about the other nieces is very scanty. She is probably the best example of Nordic serial-monogamy given that she was married four times and on top of this she also had an extramarital liaison. These relationships resulted in nine known sons who all participated in the Scandinavian intra-elite conflicts. Ingrid Ragvaldsdatter was politically active as the Danish and Norwegian Queen and dowager from the 1120s to the 1160s. Her life story may seem somewhat extreme, but considering her vulnerable position given that she lacked male protectors on her natal family's side, Ingrid needed husbands who could safeguard her properties and secure her offspring's rights. She is a good example of what it meant to be a queen consort in a society of constant crises. If they did not die in childbirth, noblewomen often outlived their men by several years. Three of Ingrid's partners faced violent deaths linked to power struggles over succession. Additionally, many of her sons were killed in battle or executed before she died in the end of the 1160s. Thus, remarrying was most likely the best survival tactic and the most effective way to secure her properties and to facilitate guardianship of her children's rights.

Ingrid grew up at the Swedish royal court, but was married already as a child to the Danish prince Henrik Skadelar Svendsen. He was killed in battle against the pretender to the Danish throne, Erik the Unforgettable in 1134 (see Chapter 3). Shortly afterwards Ingrid became Queen consort of Norway when she was remarried to the Norwegian king Harald Gille. After the killing of Harald two years later, she managed to maintain her position as queen of Norway by consolidating her power through vertical marriage alliances with regional magnates. Of these marriages, the first was with the *lendr maðr* Ottar Birting who was murdered in 1146–1147. The second (and last of all her marriages) was with the powerful magnate Arne of Ståreim. This chain of relationships developed into an extended family, which to a great extent contributed to the multipolarity that characterized the discord within the Scandinavian elite. Families of this kind meant that interpersonal bonds overlapped, which inevitably lead to conflicts of loyalties (Fig. 6.2).

An example of intersecting loyalties is, for instance, the complications that preceded Ingrid's marriage to Harald Gille in the autumn of 1134. Marriage alliances were often rapidly arranged in situations caused by genealogical accidents. The potential candidate to the throne, Erik the Unforgettable, was in desperate need of powerful allies after the assassination of his brother Knud Lavard in 1131 (Chapter 3). He therefore made a treaty with Harald Gille's enemy and co-ruler, the Norwegian king Magnus Sigurdsson. The pact was initiated through a betrothal between

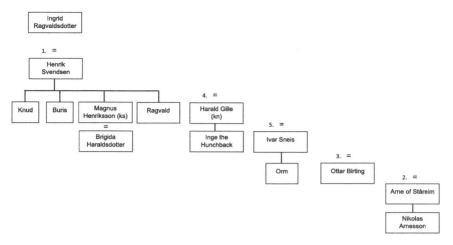

Figure 6.2. Ingrid Ragvaldsdatter's family. Figure by author.

Magnus and Kristin Knudsdatter, who was the daughter of Knud Lavard and Ingeborg.[52] The arrangement was confirmed when Erik shortly afterwards married Ingrid's cousin Malmfrid, queen dowager of Sigurd the Crusader.[53]

During the strife in Denmark, Erik and his wife Malmfrid were in 1133 forced to take refuge in Norway where they sought support from their ally Magnus Sigurdsson. This put the combatants' wives in a tricky situation. For instance, Kristin was caught in a dilemma where she had to choose between being loyal to her conjugal family or to her natal relatives. Saxo says that she disclosed that her husband Magnus was planning to betray and murder Erik and Malmfrid during their stay in Norway. According to Saxo, Magnus's plan was to change sides by allying with King Niels.[54] Obviously, Kristin felt obliged to warn her uncle and aunt that their lives were in danger. This led the Norwegian king to repudiate his wife, who later was sent back to Denmark.[55] According to Snorre Sturluson, things went badly for Magnus after this incident. The author states that 'He came to be greatly disliked by her (Kristin's) relatives'.[56] Hence, Magnus Sigurdsson was deprived of all support from the female representatives of the powerful Stenkil family.

---

52 Due to Kristin's young age, the marriage was not confirmed until 1133. In Scandinavia marriage was normally allowed from twelve years of age.
53 The Norwegian king Sigurd the Crusader (r. 1103–1130) was half-brother of Harald Gille.
54 GD, 13.11.1.
55 GD, 13.11.4.
56 Heimskringla III, p. 170.

Harald Gille's marriage to Ingrid Ragvaldsdatter in 1134 was a countermove against his opponent which was made feasible after the death of her husband. Erik the Unforgettable's victory at the battle of Fotevig in Denmark implied that Harald Gille henceforth was backed up by the new Danish king and finally he managed to seize the crown from Magnus Sigurdsson. He was brutally punished by Harald who instructed his servants to have him blinded, mutilated, and castrated (Chapter 2). Magnus was thereafter called Magnus the Blind. During this chain of events, Ingrid Ragvaldsdatter can easily be seen as a pawn in the political game; she was married off to a man who was allied with Erik the Unforgettable, i.e. the one who had slaughtered her previous husband, Henrik Svendsen. From this perspective she can mainly be seen as a war-trophy which Harald Gille brought to Norway.

However, according to the Danish sources, Ingrid does not seem to have been very much attached to Henrik. For Ingrid's activities as Danish princess, we have to rely on Saxo's fairly tendentious account which is coloured by his negative attitude towards Henrik Svendsen and his allies. Her marriage with Henrik was arranged in order to establish an alliance with the Swedish royal family. After the extinction of the male line of the Stenkil family, Henrik failed to secure powerful Swedish allies. His greatest asset in the competition against his Danish rivals was his guardianship of Ingrid's dowry. Perhaps that is why Saxo tells a story about how Ingrid became 'tired of her husband' and therefore, dressed in man's clothes, tried to flee from him together with a young lover. The attempted escape failed and the author writes that Henrik suspected his opponent, the powerful duke Knud Lavard, to be the instigator of his humiliation, though Knud was totally innocent.[57]

Perhaps Saxo's story was only intended to dishonour Henrik and throw suspicion on the noble blood of his offspring. However, one cannot deny the fact that if Ingrid's alleged escape had succeeded, Henrik's position would have been severely weakened. As her husband, he only controlled Ingrid's dowry, and he did not have any rights of possession. Hence, Knud Lavard had much to gain if the plan had worked. Spoiling marriages through dishonouring acts performed towards the enemy was during the Middle Ages a dangerous (due to the honour-based violence it risked to unleash) but cost-effective strategy, because it did not require a large amount of resources. Another example of this symbolic form of violence is Saxo's somewhat obscure statement that the Swedish king Sverker the Elder (r. 1130–1156) had sent 'love-messages' to King Niels's new wife

---

57 *GD*, 13.4.3.

Ulvhild 'and then secretly abducted her, and had her as his mate (*connubium*)'.[58]

After Queen Margrethe's death, her son Magnus Nielsen had a strong position as the direct heir and owner of a large part of his mother's inheritance. As husbands, Henrik's and Knud's positions were dependent on their wife's material resources which they did not have full rights to. But in contrast to Henrik, Knud Lavard had powerful foreign allies, and that was probably why Henrik chose to align with Magnus (see Chapter 3).

During the time of Ingrid's marriages with Henrik Svendsen and Harald Gille, she is mostly to be seen as a transmitter of power. However, after the killing of Harald Gille, she immediately took the initiative to act as an authoritative Norwegian queen, by having her young son, Inge the Hunchback, proclaimed king at an assembly.[59] She was backed up by a strong group of magnates who previously had been loyal to Harald. This conglomeration, constituted by a high-born queen aligned with a couple of powerful *lendir menn* acting as the protectors and spokesmen of a five-year-old king, proved to be successful. It was made even stronger when her stepson, the three-year-old Sigurd Mouth, was proclaimed co-regent.[60] This alignment was solid for several reasons. Ingrid used a strategy similar to her male royal predecessors, i.e. she based her positions on vertical relationships with regional magnates.

Thereby she was only to a limited extent put under male tutelage. It meant that Ingrid's word carried weight in the group of counsellors that surrounded the child-kings. It was, so to speak, a win-win-situation for Ingrid and her loyal magnates. The queen's noble charisma lent legitimacy to the faction, in that she stood as a guarantor of family continuity which resembled a kind of royal 'lineage' by representing the memory of Harald.[61] Furthermore, the commemorative tradition of her deceased husband was strengthened by reputations of martyrdom. The synergetic effects among the magnates were that they gained *Königsnähe* (or rather '*Königinsnähe*'), political influence and material resources by acting as

---

58 *GD*, 13.10.1. 'Hic Suerco Vlwildam Noricam, quam Nicolaus in matrimonium emortua Margareta receperat, amatoriis primo legationibus sollicitatam, mox uiro furtim abstractam ad suum usque connubium perduxit'.
Through this rendering Saxo manage to kill two birds with one stone. He dishonours King Niels and his family at the same time as he portrays Sverker as a bride-stealer and a lecher. Saxo further tells that Karl Sverkersson was a son of Sverker and Ulvhild, and by that he hints that Karl was a bastard. In the same passage, Saxo also calls Sverker 'a Swede of modest origins' (*mediocri inter Sueones*). On symbolic violence and tactics used in European 'feudal warfare', see e.g. Algazi, 'Pruning Peasants'; Barthélemy, 'Feudal War in Tenth-Century France'.
59 *Heimskringla III*, p. 186.
60 *Heimskringla III*, p. 186.
61 Harald's claim to the throne was disputed. He had a somewhat obscure Irish background and was therefore in need of all the status and legitimacy he could get.

counsellors, protectors, and administrators of the royal domain. The relationships between the queen and her magnates were cemented through fictive ties of kinship when the most prominent leaders in the group were entrusted to carry out the duty to act as foster-fathers of the young kings (see Chapters 2 and 3).[62] Thereby, intimate personal bonds of loyalty were created. Ingrid was soon also married to one of them, the *lendr maðr* Ottar Birting; and when he was murdered, she married another member of the cluster, Arne of Ståreim.[63]

During the minority rule, Ingrid could act as peacemaker by keeping up the balance between different factions. The factions were dependent on its core member, Ingrid herself, who then was able to control her own material resources. This meant that, at least for a while, hereditary enmity could be kept in reins. Hence, the queen was able to practice agency, in the sense that she exercised control over the social relations of which she was a part and she also had the ability to change them. Like her male royal colleagues, Ingrid created her own aristocracy and thereby managed to prepare the ground for her son Inge. Sources such as *Heimskringla* give the impression that Ingrid kept her prominent position in the group of counsellors who surrounded her son Inge throughout his reign.

Ingrid's extended family were scattered all over the three Nordic realms.[64] She had several conjugal families, which meant that her activity, centred on safeguarding her son's rights, had a great impact on the Scandinavian game of thrones.[65] Around the year 1160 one might say that Ingrid stood at the height of her power. Her son Inge was king of Norway, while her son Magnus Henriksson had gained the throne in Sweden, where he ruled together with his brother, Earl Ragvald. In Denmark her two other sons Knud and Buris had been entrusted with prominent positions by King Valdemar I.[66] Due to their royal ancestry and loyal support, the King had honoured them with fiefs linked to titles of honour.[67] Their

---

62 Grohse, 'Strength through Weakness', pp. 255–57.
63 *Heimskringla III*, p. 199.
64 In contrast to kings who foremost were grounded in one realm, queens were parts of international families and cross-cultural exchanges of symbolic, social, and symbolic forms of capital.
65 For discussions on motherhood as an expression of power, influence, and agency, see e.g. McNamara, 'Women and Power through the Family Revisited'; Fleiner and Woodacre, *Virtuous or Villainess?*
66 Knud and Buris principally based their power on their paternal inheritance. In a charter issued in 1163, Buris donates land inherited from his father, Henrik Svendsen, for the foundation of the Cistercian abbey Tvis in Jutland. *DD*, 1:2, no. 152. Hence the brothers active in Denmark may primarily have based their positions on their paternal inheritance, while the brothers Magnus and Ragvald claimed their maternal inheritance in Sweden. Another possibility is that Buris and perhaps Knud were sons of concubines. Buris is a Slavic name.
67 Hermanson, *Släkt, vänner och makt*, p. 228.

political prowess later developed into a severe threat against Valdemar's own position.

Nevertheless, in a state of constant crises dominant positions could change in a twinkling. Ingrid is an example of the 'vulnerability of elite arrangements' which, according to Preiser-Kapeller, is 'especially salient in cases of genealogical accidents'.[68] In 1161 Inge Hunchback was killed by his opponents.[69] A couple of months later Magnus Henriksson and his brother Ragvald were slain in encounters with the pretender to the Swedish throne Karl Sverkerson. Ingrid had to flee to Denmark together with the *lendr maðr* Erling Skakke.[70] He was married to Ingrid's first cousin once removed, Kristin, who was daughter of Sigurd the Crusader through his marriage with Malmfrid.[71] In Denmark Ingrid, backed up by her son Buris, actively used her family connections with Valdemar in order to get Danish support for proclaiming Erling's and Kristin's young son, Magnus Erlingsson, as the rightful heir of the Norwegian crown. Valdemar agreed to her request and Erling later managed to get his son recognized as king of Norway. Magnus Erlingsson was the first crowned sovereign in Scandinavia, and also the first Norwegian king who accessed the throne by pleading royal descent on the maternal side (see Chapter 2).[72] Erling Skakke's prowess as kingmaker was thus grounded on the intercession of Ingrid Ragvaldsdatter.

After the above-mentioned episode, there is no more information to be found about Ingrid's life. Her son Knud died in 1162 and her other son Buris may have intended to start an uprising against Valdemar in 1166–1167. He had strong support from his relatives in Norway and probably from his mother in Denmark. Nonetheless, his intention failed. Buris was imprisoned and possibly blinded, and he was removed from the political scene.[73] Ingrid died at the end of the 1160s, but her memory was upheld by

---

68 Preiser-Kapeller, 'Calculating the Middle Ages?', p. 114.
69 Ingrid's son with Ivar Sneis, Orm, must then have fled to his half-brothers Magnus and Ragvald in Sweden. *Heimskringla III*, p. 198.
70 GD, 14.29.12; *Heimskringla III*, p. 234. Among the group that went to Denmark, there were also Magnus Erlingsson, Ingrid's two sons, her husband Arne of Ståreim, and a group of magnates.
71 Kristin Sigurdsdatter later had an important diplomatic function as mediator in a war between Erling Skakke and Valdemar. Snorre says that she sailed to Denmark in order to meet King Valdemar. He received his kinswoman well. Kristin sent a delegation to Norway with the mission to get Erling to travel to the Danish king for a reconciliation. *Heimskringla III*, p. 253. Erling later went to Denmark where he reached a settlement with Valdemar on the grounds that he became the Danish king's earl. *Heimskringla III*, p. 254.
72 This was not a new phenomenon in Denmark. Kings such as Svend Estridsen's and Erik the Lamb's claims for the throne were legitimated through maternal lines. In Sweden kings such as Magnus Nielsen and Magnus Henriksson did the same. Also, Erik Jedvardsson and Karl Sverkersson legitimated their claims through marrying into the Stenkil-family.
73 Hermanson, *Släkt, vänner och makt*, pp. 236–37.

groups which had a large impact on Nordic politics during the following centuries. Her son, Bishop Nikolas Arnesson, was a core member of the so-called Baglar-faction, which elected her grandson Filippus Simonsson as king of Norway in 1207 (see Chapter 4).

In Sweden Ingrid's cluster lost its power when her sons Magnus and Ragvald were killed. Yet the power struggle in the Swedish kingdom came to be dominated by other factions linked to Ingrid's cousins Kristina and Ingeborg. Also, her stepdaughter, Brigida Haraldsdatter (daughter of Harald Gille and a concubine), played an important role in both Swedish and Norwegian politics (see Chapters 2 and 4). Like her stepmother, Brigida could be termed serially-monogamous, since she first was married to the Swedish earl Karl Sunesson, secondly to Magnus Henriksson, and finally to the powerful Swedish earl Birger Brosa, who had a balancing position between clusters, not solely in Sweden, but also in the two other Nordic realms.[74]

Uses of the Stenkil Legacy in Sweden, c. 1130–1170

In order to get a deeper understanding of how the memory of Margrethe was used by other factions, we have to shift focus from women as agents to the role of men as husbands. In what ways were they in a state of dependence in relation to their wives? In the following the issue will be discussed in light of the intra-elite conflicts in Sweden after the extinction of the Stenkil family's male line.

In previous research, the Swedish wars of succession have been interpreted as a bipolar conflict between two different dynasties (*ätter*): the Sverker family and the Erik family. This prolonged discord, which lasted more than 100 years, has also been placed within a dualistic territorial framework. It has been asserted that the Sverkers came from the province of Östergötland, while the powerbase of the Eriks was located in Västergötland. Thus, in comparison with Norway and Denmark, this dynastic and territorial dualism stands out as different, considering that the Norwegian and the Danish royal combatants were more or less descended from the same stock. In addition, it is not possible to distinguish clear-cut regional territories linked to specific branches of the Norwegian or Danish royal families.

It is here important to bear in mind that the prevalent readings of the civil strife in Sweden are based on a male perspective, wherein the Swedish opposing parties are viewed as more or less formed in line with an agnatic system. Consequently, since the Sverker family's progenitor originated

---

74 *Heimskringla III*, p. 204.

from Östergötland, the 'lineage' belonged to that province, whereas the head of the Erik family came from Västergötland and consequently the dynasty is supposed to have been rooted in that province. Ancestral lands have been placed on a par with paternal estates as the main determinant for the combatant's resources and courses of action. The role of maternal inheritance has been of secondary importance in previous research. If we replace this male-oriented and provincial approach with a gender perspective, another depiction emerges, wherein the conditions of power do not diverge to any great extent from the political circumstances in the neighbouring countries.

All pretenders to the Swedish throne claimed affiliation with the Stenkil family through female links. Erik Jedvardsson, the founder of the so-called Erik-dynasty, formed a cluster through marrying Kristina, daughter of Katarina and the Danish prince Bjorn Ironside (see Fig. 6.1).[75] She was most probably a woman endowed with considerable resources. Her mother had, like Queen Margrethe, inherited large estates in Sweden and, as we will see later, Kristina was fully capable of defending them on her own. Erik Jedvardsson's marriage to Kristina meant that he was guardian of her dowry. Thus, it was principally through his role as an in-law of the Stenkil family that he could claim accession to the Swedish throne.[76]

The Sverker family enhanced their royal legitimacy through the same genealogical pool. However, their association with the Stenkils was somewhat weaker. The Swedish king Sverker the Elder used a strategy based on couple relationships with royal dowagers who previously had been queens in Denmark. He seized the opportunity to heighten his royal status by marrying (or perhaps abducting, see above) King Niels' Queen Ulvhild. After her death in the end of the 1140s, he married King Niels's son

---

75 *Knytlingesaga*, p. 117. As mentioned above, Katarina's husband Bjorn Ironside was executed in 1135. We do not know when Katarina died. If she survived her husband, she must in her role as widow have had full control of her inheritance. The Swedish literary historian Bengt R. Jonsson identifies Erik Jedvardsson's wife with Kristin Knudsdatter, i.e. Valdemar I's older sister who was repudiated by the Norwegian king Magnus Sigurdsson. According to his thesis, Erik's son Knud was named after his grandfather, Knud Lavard. Jonsson, 'Erik den helige. Gammalt helgon i ny belysning', pp. 282–93. This identification has not convinced other scholars since it could not be verified in the sources. See e.g. Lovén, 'Sigridlev och godsrikedomen i Stenkilsätten', pp. 161–62.

76 Erik may also have had royal blood on his father's side (or mother's), though we do not know who his father Jedvard was. Some scholars claim that he was of English descent. Others argues for links to the old royal dynasty from Svealand. It is here worth considering Saxo's mention of a king elected by the Svear as a countermove to the election of Magnus Nielsen as king of Götaland *c.* 1128. Saxo never mentions his name. *GD*, 13.5.1. Swedish scholars have identified him with a Ragvald Roundhead; this identification is, however, based on late medieval sources. One may hypothesize that Saxo's anonymous king could have been the father of Erik. Ragvald Roundhead has often been misinterpreted as Ingrid Ragvaldsdatter's father.

Magnus Nielsen's previous wife, the Polish princess Richiza. His liaison with Ulvhild lent him symbolic prestige, but it is difficult to say to what extent the alliance increased his material resources. According to *Fagrskinna*, Ulvhild's first marriage was with the Swedish king Inge the Younger.[77] The couple did not have any known children, which implies that Ulvhild in her role as queen dowager could have possessed considerable material assets in Sweden. Richiza's royal prestige was high, as she was the daughter of the Polish Prince Boleslaw III Wrymouth (Piast dynasty) and had previously been married to Magnus Nielsen and thereafter to Volodar of Minsk.[78]

Richiza's symbolic significance also encompassed Sweden, as she had been queen of Götaland in her marriage with Magnus Nielsen. Yet it is doubtful if she in any sense contributed to the enhancement of Sverker's economic resources. Richiza had no property at her disposal which derived from her natal family, but it is not unlikely that she inherited estates in Götaland in her capacity as a widow of Magnus Nielsen.[79] Nonetheless Karl Sverkersson, the son of Sverker and Ulvhild, tried to form a cluster by aligning with the Stenkil family.[80] He married the Danish princess Margrethe Stigsdatter who was a granddaughter of Kristina and daughter of Ingeborg (Fig. 6.3).[81] This association provided an entry, not solely to the material assets of the Stenkils, but also an opportunity to take

---

[77] *Fagrskinna*, p. 236. Ulvhild Hakonsdatter's father was Hakon Finnsson, a member of the powerful Norwegian Tjotta-family.

[78] For unknown reasons Richiza was probably divorced from Volodar of Minsk. Their daughter, Sophia Volodarevna (a scion of the Polotsk dynasty), was later married to Valdemar. Lind, 'De russiske ægteskaber: Dynasti- og alliancepolitik i 1130'ernes danske borgerkrig', pp. 251–53. Other scholars argue that Rikissa was married to Vladimir of Novgorod. On this debate, see Gallén, 'Vem var Valdemar den Stores drottning Sofia?', pp. 273–87; Lind, 'De russiske ægteskaber: Dynasti- og alliancepolitik i 1130'ernes danske borgerkrig', pp. 244–45.

[79] Their son Knud Magnussen visited his mother and stepfather Sverker in Sweden in order to obtain support in the Danish wars of succession. However, his mission failed. *GD*, 14.5.2; Rønning, 'The Politics of Exile in Northern Europe'. Saxo further tells us that Knud made another, more successful attempt. Together with Valdemar (later king) they went to Sweden to 'look after their properties' there. Their real mission was, however, to establish an alliance with King Sverker. Knud was to marry Sverker's daughter Helena and Saxo writes that the Swedish king was so amused by the alliance that he offered them the opportunity to be his heirs at the expense of his own sons. *GD*, 14.14.3. Saxo's information about Sverker's generous offer seems highly doubtful, but at least we learn that both Valdemar and Knud had properties in Sweden. Knud's estates derived from his father and grandmother and Valdemar's from his mother Ingeborg. Through Knud's marriage to Sverker's daughter he increased his material resources by controlling her dowry.

[80] Burislev was the offspring of Sverker's marriage with Richiza (and half-brother to the Danish king Knud Magnussen). Kol and Burislev were rival royal candidates in Sweden after Knut Eriksson's killing of Karl Sverkersson. They posed a severe threat to Knut well into the 1170s.

[81] Margrethe's father was the magnate Stig, a member of the Hvide-clan. This link explains why the offspring of this aristocratic family in the beginning of the thirteenth century took an active part in the Swedish civil wars.

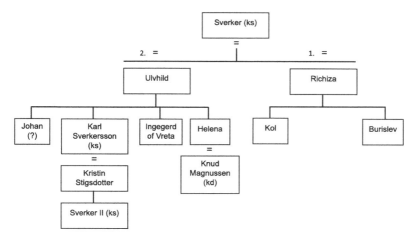

Figure 6.3. Genealogical tree of Sverker the Elder. Figure by author.

advantage of the family's symbolic prestige and to get powerful back-up from Denmark. Still, it is important to bear in mind that Erik Jedvardsson and Karl Sverkersson were married into the Stenkil family. Thus, they were dependent on their women in the sense that they could control their ancestral lands but they were not able to dispose of the rights of possession to the properties (Fig. 6.3).

When it comes to rights of inheritance to the Stenkil estates, the sons of Ingrid Ragvaldsdatter, Magnus and Ragvald, had far more favourable positions compared to both Erik Jedvardsson and Karl Sverkersson. As cognates they were lineal descendants of the Stenkil family. When Magnus Henriksson entered the Swedish political scene in the mid-1150s, his rights to the throne and the royal ancestral lands were strong. In addition, he was backed up by his mother, Queen Ingrid of Norway. Swedish historians have tended to portray him in line with a national framework as a gruesome 'Danish' king-slayer who was behind the assassination of King Sverker in 1156 and four years later attacked Erik Jedvardsson outside a church in Uppsala and had him beheaded.[82] However, Magnus could not be seen as an intruder, given that ever since the reign of Queen Margrethe the offspring of Stenkil were acting inside a Scandinavian field of power which embraced all the three Nordic kingdoms. His marriage to Harald Gille's daughter Brigida not only strengthened his support from Norway,

---

82 This depiction is probably coloured by *The Legend of Saint Erik*, compiled in the second part of the thirteenth century. Like Magnus Henriksson, the 'Swedish' kings Karl Sverkersson and Knut Eriksson were king-slayers but their posthumous reputation was never stained for these reasons. They have instead been portrayed as righteous avengers.

but probably also gave him advantages in Sweden thanks to Brigida's status as the widow of the Swedish earl Karl Suneson. Serially-monogamous women possessed considerable amounts of social forms of capital which often made them a good match. Still, Magnus Henriksson's kingship in Sweden was short-lived. In 1161 he and his brother Ragvald were slain in battles against Karl Sverkerson. As a result, the cluster centred around Ingrid Ragvaldsdatter was also removed from the Swedish political scene.

Moreover, there was another faction that gained advantages from Ingrid's constellation. Members of the noble Bjälbo family had held prominent positions in the Swedish realm ever since the end of the eleventh century. They had royal blood on the maternal side through the Danish king St Knud's daughter Ingegerd, who was married to a Swedish magnate named Folke. This couple were the progenitors of the Bjälbo clan, whose members in later sources are called 'Folkungar'. Though prominent indeed, these magnates did not appear as claimants of the Swedish throne, perhaps because they lacked close affinity to the Stenkil family. However, after the fall of Magnus Henriksson his widow Brigida was remarried to Birger Brosa, grandson of Folke. In that way Birger managed to get a share of the Stenkil legacy. Though married to the wife whose husband Karl Sverkersson had killed, Birger Brosa established an alliance with the Swedish king by marrying his daughter to Karl Sverkerson's son, Sverker the Younger.

In 1167 Karl Sverkersson was killed by Knut Eriksson, son of Erik Jedvardsson. During the long reign of Knut Eriksson (1167–1195/1196), Birger Brosa consolidated his power by holding the office of earl of the Swedes. He was also brother-in-law to the Erik family.[83] The couple Birger Brosa and Brigida came out to be a stabilizing factor in the Swedish field of power, probably thanks to their multiple connections with various royal groupings in the Scandinavian realms. This favourable position also meant that the powerful dyad became a balancing factor in the Nordic political arena. Birger Brosa and Brigida's court was frequently visited by Norwegian and Danish pretenders who were seeking support or protection because of ties of kinship and friendship. When Knut Eriksson died at the end of the twelfth century, Birger Brosa remained in power by appearing as the new king Sverker the Younger's (r. 1196–1208) earl. This clearly indicates that Birger's political prowess rested on his ability to create overlapping bonds between the three dominating clusters which all claimed affiliation with the Stenkil family. Thanks to his connections with nearly all influential royal and aristocratic families the Swedish earl emerged into a Scandinavian lord whose all-seeing eye kept a strict watch to make sure that the balance of power in the Nordic realms did not turn to his disfavour.

---

83 His son Magnus was married to Knut Eriksson's daughter Sigrid.

All things considered, the interpretation of the Swedish wars of succession as a bipolar conflict between two rivalling territorially based 'dynasties' has to be reassessed. Viewed from a gender perspective, the struggles should instead be seen as a game of thrones marked by multipolarity.[84] Political constellations were constantly rearranged in response to the transformation of social relationships. The prevalent male-centred perspective on the conflicts risks creating an impression that the opposing parties were formed in line with an agnatic system. That was certainly not the case, since all the contenders claimed a similar descent on the maternal side. In short, one may draw the conclusion that the disputes revolved around only one unit, the Stenkil family and its ramifications. Four powerful clusters were formed on the basis of female representatives. The political strategies were to a great extent shaped in line with a cognatic system. Hence the Swedish wars of succession demonstrate the openness of kinship and lineages discussed in Chapter 2. As an extension of this, it means that we have to abandon the national framework when interpreting Nordic intra-elite wars. These disputes were more or less always Scandinavian-wide conflicts, because the families were so closely intertwined. In line with the argument set out in Chapter 2 of this volume that medieval royal power was embedded within the social system, we may conclude that the Swedish realm was marked by multipolarity, and hence could be considered as an elastic formation in constant state of negotiation and realignment.

As a further consequence, we also have to reassess the depiction of the Swedish kingdom as marked by a territorial dualism. The Stenkil-patrimony was scattered all over the realm.[85] The Sverker family may have had their paternal inheritance concentrated in the province of Östergötland and the heartland of the Erik family's landed property may have been located in Västergötland. However, the still predominant perception of Sweden as a 'kin-society' is misleading. Bonds of kinship were subject to constant negotiation and manoeuvering. Property, too, had a relational nature, implying that the structure, location, and ownership of land-holdings were perpetually transformed.[86] As in Denmark and Norway, the Swedish kinship system was basically bilateral in structure.[87] Hence, if we take into account female family-members' hereditary estates and dowries, the territorial dualism becomes less distinct. Practical kinship

---

84 After the murder of Sverker the Elder in 1156, Magnus Henriksson was probably active in Sweden as a challenger to Erik Jedvardsson. Simultaneously Karl Sverkersson's reign was marked by a threat from Knut Eriksson. Finally, Knut Eriksson was threatened by the pretenders Kol and Burislev.
85 Lovén, 'Sigridlev och godsrikedomen i Stenkilsätten', pp. 158–59.
86 Orning and others, 'Networks', p. 307.
87 Hansen, 'The Concept of Kinship according to the West Nordic Medieval Laws', p. 180.

was the factor that shaped the constellations of power in twelfth century Sweden.

The principles of bilateral kinship gave scope for multiple legitimating strategies. Overlapping bonds could be a way to success, but they could also have triggering effects and conduce prolongations of conflicts. However, during the twelfth and thirteenth centuries the emphasis on patrilineal descent and primogeniture was a Europe-wide development.[88] Male entails were seen as a guarantee for peaceful successions and a way to prevent the fragmentation of family estates. Thereby, with support from the Church, it was calculated that intra-elite wars and violence could be avoided. Though twelfth century Scandinavia was marked by a cognatic kinship system, the feuding family members always had a desire to officialize their kin by preserving lineage and creating dynastic continuities linked to temporal family constellations.

The development towards agnatic systems reduced noblewomen's possibilities for practising agency. In a 'pure' agnatic system, women could simply be seen as transmitters of power, or, as Jennifer Ward writes 'pawns in the marriage market, contributing to the upward or downward mobility of families'.[89] In this system, noblewomen's ability to act was restricted to the marital family. However, as shown above, women such as Queen Margrethe and her niece Ingrid Ragvaldsdatter played important roles in providing for family stability, both from the conjugal and the natal point of view. In twelfth century Scandinavia, the interdependency between noblemen and women was a salient feature for the creation of family continuity. The foundation of monasteries and acts of religious devotion are good examples of how women and men interacted in order to construct and officialize memorable family traditions.

From Cluster to Cloister: Monasteries as Accumulation Points in a Society of Constant Crises

Around the year 1100 the marital couple King Inge Stenkilsson and Queen Helena made a large donation for the foundation of a monastic community in Vreta, located in the province Östergötland in south-east Sweden. Helena, i.e. the mother of Queen Margrethe and her siblings, stands out as the first mother in the *memoria* tradition that surrounded the Stenkil family. In fact, it would be more appropriate to talk about 'the Helena family' if one judges by the twelfth century sources. Her origins are debated, but there is no doubt that she was of high royal birth.

---

88 Ward, 'Noblewomen, Family, and Identity in Later Medieval Europe', pp. 250–55.
89 Ward, 'Noblewomen, Family, and Identity in Later Medieval Europe', p. 254.

In Abbot William of Æbelholt's written defence of the Danish princess Ingeborg, who was repudiated by the French king Philip Augustus in 1194, the abbot calls attention to the princess's noble descent from Queen Helena.[90] She is also referred to in William's genealogy, compiled in honour of the Danish royal family.[91] Helena was undoubtedly an important symbol of sacral queenship and royal blood in all the three Nordic realms. It entailed that the clusters which were aspiring for kingship by profiting from the Stenkil legacy had to acquire their share of the symbolic capital represented by Helena.

During the 1160s Vreta abbey was converted into a nunnery. In Scandinavia, as in other parts of Europe, monasteries played a central role for aristocratic families that strove to improve their prestige by affiliating with other noble families or more distant relatives. Monasteries were intimately linked, not only to their patron saint, but also to their male or female founders. Associations with an abbey were reached through gifts, patronage, and refoundations. Prestigious gifts, such as large donations of land, confirmed hierarchies and enhanced noble and pious status. The most respected gift of all was to donate a child to a monastery.

The Swedish historian, Catharina Andersson, has shown that among the noble Swedish families, donations of daughters to nunneries were far more common than donations of sons.[92] When an aristocratic daughter entered a nunnery, she was endowed with a dowry to which the monastic community, in its capacity as her guardian, had full rights of possession.[93] Thus, it was a highly expensive gift, but it not only paid off in counter-gifts, such as prayers, masses for the dead, and salvation of the donor's souls; it also served as an entrance into the legacy of the abbey's founding family. Gifts of land had a similar function, but donations of children or the admission of grown-up family members established a direct social link to the abbey and to its founders. Thereby, both a spiritual and social bond was created. Hence, those who donated pious gifts to Vreta also became intimately associated with the sacral and royal family of Inge Stenkilsson and Helena.[94] During the fierce Nordic intra-elite wars, monasteries were used as accumulation nodes of symbolic, cultural, economic, and social forms of capital. Consequently, religious institutions offered an opportunity for the creation of continuity, tradition, and royal legitimacy.

---

90 Will. ep. II 22, pp. 501–03.
91 *Wilhelmi abbatis genealogia*, p. 182.
92 Andersson, 'Gifts and Society in Fourteenth Century Sweden', pp. 226–31.
93 Andersson, *Kloster och aristokrati*, p. 261; Andersson, 'Gifts and Society in Fourteenth Century Sweden', pp. 226–31.
94 On royal sacral networks in Europe around the year 1100, see Hermanson, 'Det tidiga Vreta. En helig plats i ett europeiskt maktsystem', pp. 219–40.

The Polish medievalist Grzegorz Pac has argued that noblewomen played a crucial role for the creation of devotional communities stretching across Europe.[95] Women acted as founders of religious houses, and their donations were often superior to the ones made by their husbands or male relatives. Constance B. Bouchard has noted that in eleventh- and twelfth-century France, aristocratic women often initiated their husbands into the religious houses of their natal families.[96] The Swedish historian Anders Emanuelsson has pointed towards similar patterns in Scandinavia, where women's donations to local churches often exceeded the ones made by men.[97] In this context high-born women cannot simply be seen as transmitters of power alone since their noble status often exceeded that of their husbands. The foundation of religious houses and large donations were fairly often initiated and accomplished by women. With reference to Karl Hauck's concept of *Geblütsheiligkeit*, i.e. the link between sanctity and familial affinity, and the idea of *beata stirps*, Grzegorz Pac asserts that women should be seen as the main strategists behind the ennobling processes within the top echelons of medieval society.[98] The wide circle of benefactors with relationships to a religious house could, according to Pac, be termed an 'imagined community', a concept that he borrows from Benedict Anderson's discussion on the formation of collective identities.[99]

As shown in the first part of this chapter, Queen Margrethe definitely qualifies as belonging to this category of female familial strategists. She was a member of a Europe-wide devotional community. She was the first woman to appear in a Scandinavian charter, and it is significant that Margrethe issued the diploma in her capacity as a generous benefactor of the Church in Odense. Likewise, the oldest preserved charter from Sweden, the so-called Viby-document issued *c.* 1164–1167, deals with transactions of land made by a woman. It announces a dispute-settlement between a noble-born dowager named Doter and her only son Gere.[100] Doter is denominated as *deo dicata*, i.e. a woman consecrated to God, implying that she in widowhood had the intention of entering into a nunnery. The dispute was about whether her donation of the farm Viby to the monks of Alvastra monastery should be returned to her son after her death, or if the

---

95 Pac, 'Communities of Devotion across the Boundaries'.
96 Bouchard, *Sword, Miter, and Cloister*, p. 147. According to Bouchard, French magnates often tried to improve their noble status by marrying women of more powerful families. A common strategy was thus to give patronage to the same religious houses that the wife's family had patronized.
97 Emanuelsson, 'Kyrkojorden och dess ursprung'.
98 Pac, 'Communities of Devotion across the Boundaries', p. 128.
99 Pac, 'Communities of Devotion across the Boundaries', p. 124. See also Elisabeth van Houts' discussion on constructions of collective memory through collaboration between men and women. Houts, *Memory and Gender in Medieval Europe, 900–1200*, pp. 89–95, 147–50.
100 *SDHK*: 200.

brothers had eternal rights of possession to the income of the estate. The controversy was settled by Archbishop Stephan in favour of the monks. This charter shows that a noble widow could act in line with her own agenda with powerful support from ecclesiastical dignitaries.

As stated above, Scandinavian princely families were more or less always in a state of constant crisis. But religious houses offered an opportunity to create family traditions, and to officially align with noble ancestors. During the Scandinavian wars of succession, victories on the battlefield were often followed by generous donations to religious institutions. For instance, after Erik the Unforgettable and his allies' victory at the battle of Fotevig in 1134, the monastic communities in Ringsted and Næstved were founded in the following year. Likewise, after the battle of Grathe Moor in 1157, Valdemar founded the Cistercian abbey Vitskøl as an expression of gratitude to God for granting him the glorious victory. Simultaneously the king made large donations to other religious houses, such as Esrum Abbey.[101]

Swedish examples of the same phenomenon are the religious acts performed by the kings Magnus Henriksson and Karl Sverkersson. Ingrid Ragvaldsdatter's son Magnus Henriksson successfully defended his rights of inheritance by killing the 'usurper' Erik Jedvardsson in 1160. After the victory he donated large domains mainly in the province of Östergötland to Vreta monastery.[102] The monastic community had been in decline since the reign of King Inge and Queen Helena. The royal couple Sverker the Elder and his wife Ulvhild mainly acted as benefactors for abbeys such as Alvastra and Lurö. Magnus's donations could therefore be interpreted as symbolic legitimating acts, wherein he displayed his affiliation with the Stenkil family. The 'rightful heir' of the Stenkils had succeeded to the throne, and the gifts could be seen as both a socio-political strategic act and a performance of sacral confirmation.

However, the donations were made in a critical situation. Magnus' position on the throne was by no means secure. The avengers of Sverker the Elder and Erik Jedvardsson both posed a serious threat to him. Though his claim to royal legitimacy had powerful support from Norway and Denmark, he had to secure his rule on Swedish soil. The royal donation

---

101 Hermanson, *Släkt, vänner och makt*, p. 167.
102 Rasmus Lundvigsson, *Brevis historica narratio*, D 18. The information is to be found in two registers of donations (one in Swedish, the other in Latin) reproduced in the sixteenth century, but the original was most probably compiled in 1170. Ahnlund, 'Vreta klosters äldsta donatorer'; Lovén, 'Vreta år 1162. Donatorslängden och årboken'. The donations could have begun already in the 1150s, but since Magnus is called king in the list, the transaction must have been made after the death of King Sverker the Elder in 1156. The fact that Magnus donates estates in honour of his brother earl Ragvald's soul suggests that this gift was given in 1161. Ragvald was, according to Snorre Sturluson, alive in the beginning of that year. Lovén, 'Vreta år 1162. Donatorslängden och årboker.', p. 209.

to Vreta was a way to establish territorial control in the heartlands of the Stenkil family, by declaring them as holy ground which belonged to the Church and were protected by the king. All the same, Magnus's imagined community soon collapsed, when he was killed by Karl Sverkersson.

His assassin and royal successor used a similar, but perhaps even more sophisticated strategy. In 1162, i.e. the year after his victory over Magnus, Karl Sverkersson proclaimed himself as *fundator* of Vreta, which was then converted into a Benedictine nunnery.[103] According to the Swedish art historian Christian Lovén, monasteries could accumulate founders over periods of time and he asserts that the term *fundator* could mean 'important donor' as well as 'founder'.[104]

Karl Sverkersson's 'refoundation' of Vreta is seen as a male initiative. Nevertheless, four prominent women played a crucial part in the donation. To begin with, Karl's most prestigious gift to Vreta was his daughter, who entered into the nunnery with a considerable dowry deposited for her lifelong stay within the walls. She did not, however, need to feel abandoned by her family, since Karl's sister, Ingegerd, also moved in together with her and simultaneously was appointed prioress of the converted cloister. Christian Lovén states that Ingegerd indeed ought to have been designated *fundatrix* in the sources since her pious gift widely exceeded her brother's.[105] A queen also joined the nunnery. Ingegerd's sister Helena, widow of the murdered Danish king Knud Magnussen, became a nun in Vreta and so did a woman named Ragnhild, who was a widow of Karl Sverkerssons' brother Johan and mother of King Kol who tried to succeed his uncle on the throne in the 1170s.[106]

Magnus Henriksson attempted to revive the monastic community in Vreta through large donations in order to build a heavenly fortress that could strengthen his position in relation to rival claimants to the Crown. He laid the material foundation for its wealth, but he never had the time to endow Vreta with social resources, perhaps because Magnus did not have access to suitable relatives who could act within the walls. Karl's and most possibly also Ingegerd's strategy of converting Vreta into a nunnery was undoubtedly a clever move. Through this act the religious house was transformed from being primarily an 'imagined community' for royal clusters to a majestic institution controlled by the offspring of Sverker the Elder.

Ingegerd was active as prioress of Vreta right up to her death in 1204, implying that this powerful institution was also controlled by the

---

103 *ASM*, p. 356.
104 Lovén, 'Vreta år 1162. Donatorslängden och årboken', p. 199. Refoundations of abbeys was, according to Lovén, quite common in the British Isles and in continental Europe.
105 Lovén, 'Vreta år 1162. Donatorslängden och årboken', p. 210.
106 Ahnlund, 'Till frågan om den äldsta Erikskulten i Sverige', p. 317.

Sverkers during the long reign of Knut Eriksson.[107] Ingegerd sat safe and untouchable behind the holy walls and from there could look after the political and material interests of her family. As prioress of an influential monastic institution, she could not solely be seen as a transmitter of power. Ingegerd possessed all that was needed to practice real agency. Karl Sverkersson's takeover of Vreta was by all means a large socio-political and material investment. The conversion of Vreta into a nunnery meant that the religious house was virtually invaded by noblewomen related to the Sverker family. Nevertheless, Karl basically used the same strategy as his adversary Magnus Henriksson. By profiting from the Stenkil-legacy linked to Vreta, the Sverkers could enhance and confirm their affiliation with the founder-couple King Inge and Queen Helena.

The Alvastra monastery located in the province of Östergötland was, according to a Danish source, founded by Sverker the Elder's wife Ulvhild in 1143.[108] Yet another source mention that the Cistercian abbey was founded by both Sverker and Ulvhild.[109] Alvastra has often been described as a *Hauskloster* of the Sverkers as it served as a royal mausoleum for Sverker the Elder and his scions.[110] The abbey was certainly an important symbol for the family, but it lacked strong connections to the Stenkils. Through the conversion of Vreta, Karl Sverkersson found a remedy for this weakness.

Takeover of monasteries was not only a method practised by the Sverker family. At Sverker and Ulvhild's instigation a Cistercian abbey was in the 1140s established on the island Lurö in Lake Vänern. Due to bad environmental conditions, the brothers later had to move to Varnhem in the province of Västergötland, where the Erik family had a strong position. The Danish Chronicle of Vitskøl abbey (*Narratiuncula*) tells that a high-born woman named Sigrid donated lands to the monks, but after her death they were seriously harassed by Erik Jedvardsson's wife and Sigrid's relative (*consanguinea*) Kristina.[111] The monks fled to Denmark, where

---

107 Ahnlund, 'Vreta klosters äldsta donatorer', p. 302.
108 *Exordium magnum*, p. 258.
109 *Narratiuncula*.
110 Brian P. McGuire asserts that the term *Hauskloster* concedes too much to the founders since the Cistercians tried to keep their distance from lay society. McGuire, 'Cistercian Origins in Denmark and Sweden', p. 96.
111 *Narratiuncula*, pp. 138–39. Christian Lovén argues that Sigrid was daughter of the Swedish king Inge and his queen Helena. Lovén, 'Sigridlev och godsrikedomen i Stenkilsätten'. Valdemar II's cadastre, compiled in the beginning of the thirteenth century, mentions a conglomeration of estates in Sweden called *Sigridslev* that still was a part of the Danish king's inheritance. *Kong Valdemars jordbog*, fol. 29 v. According to Lovén *Sigridslev* derived from Sigrid and he asserts that Sigrid was Valdemar's great-aunt. Lovén, 'Sigridlev och godsrikedomen i Stenkilsätten', pp. 159–60. Brian P. McGuire explains Kristin's harassment by drawing parallels to Valdemar I's relative Margrethe, who opposed the monks of Veng abbey in Denmark because she, according to *The Øm Abbey Chronicle*, wanted to make

they, thanks to Valdemar I's benevolence, in 1158 got the opportunity to establish Vitskøl monastery. Some of the brothers were, however, later called back to Varnhem when Kristina suddenly changed her mind, and soon monks from Alvastra joined the brotherhood. Obviously, she had by then realized that her family was in great need of a religious house. Varnhem abbey was during the following years transformed into a *Hauskloster* of the Eriks, probably as a countermove to the monastic foundations made by the Sverkers.[112] During the thirteenth century another cluster represented by the earl Birger Magnusson of the Bjälbo clan transformed Varnhem once again. Birger was, due to his first marriage with a sister to the king Erik Eriksson, buried in Varnhem. Thus, not only foundations of monasteries, but also refoundations and takeovers, played a significant part in the Swedish wars of succession.

The socio-political role of monasteries could also be viewed in light of prevailing tensions between the noblewomen's conjugal and natal families. A high-born lady in a society of constant crises had a vulnerable position. Several of the women discussed in this chapter lost their husbands in battle, implying that they had to find new protectors as soon as possible. They also risked being abused and dishonoured through bride-stealing (*brudrov*), that was intended to desecrate the reputation of the enemy's family and throw suspicion on its progeny. Saxo, for example, tells a story about how Sverker the Elder's son Johan abducted the Danish prince Karl Eriksen's wife and widowed sister when their guardian was away. Johan brought them to Sweden where he raped them. However, his father Sverker urged him to send them back. This 'shameful deed' dishonoured not only Karl Eriksen, who was grandson of St Knud, but also the reigning Danish king, Svend Grathe, who, according to Saxo, for this reason started a war against the Swedes.[113]

---

her own monastic foundation of women. McGuire argues that the early Cistercians were wary of getting involved with women. Hence Scandinavian noblewomen may have regretted their initial support and because of the Cistercians' dissociation from women they changed their attitude towards the monks. McGuire, 'Cistercian Origins in Denmark and Sweden'. The above-mentioned Sigrid, the benefactor of Varnhem, according to the Vitskøl narrative, changed her mind and drove away the monks on the instigation of a 'powerful man' (perhaps Erik Jedvardsson or Sverker). However, when she was stricken with leprosy, Sigrid once again changed her mind and invited them back. McGuire, 'Cistercian Origins in Denmark and Sweden'.

112 Perhaps Kristina changed her attitude towards the Cistercian monks after the killing of her husband in 1160. Varnhem could then be interpreted as an important element in the building up of a *memoria*-tradition in honour of Erik Jedvardsson. However, Erik's remains were enshrined in Uppsala, located in Eastern Sweden, and the Chronicle mentions explicitly that Kristina *and* King Erik became more friendly towards the monks. The source is only preserved in a copy from the seventeenth century.

113 GD, 14.10.1. Saxo further tells that also the Swedes were furious because of Johan's deed and therefore had him slaughtered at an assembly. The Norwegian monk Theodoricus

There are several examples of noble women who returned to their natal family after their husbands' deaths. This indicates that political alliances were based on couples and, due to their conditional character, women always had to maintain contact with their natal families. The Danish duke Knud Lavard's wife Ingeborg returned to Rus while pregnant, after her husband's assassination in 1131. Magnus Nielsen's wife Richiza returned to Poland after 1134, and Knud Magnussen's wife Helena returned to Sweden after his death in 1157. While Richiza chose to remarry, Helena went for the other option available for dowagers, i.e. entering into a monastery. Abbeys could be a safe haven for noblewomen in times of crises. In a papal letter from Celestine III, it is mentioned that the Swedish king Knut Eriksson in his youth with the consent of his kinsmen was betrothed to a woman who was of 'the highest noble birth in the realm'. However, when Knut's father Erik was killed by Magnus Henriksson, Knut had to go into exile. Then, according to the letter, through the consent of the couple's kinsmen Knut's betrothed was as a 'protective measure' placed in a monastery. Later when Knut Eriksson had defeated his enemies, he requested the Pope to absolve her from the vow of chastity so they could unite in 'matrimonial love'.[114]

A return to the natal family was not without risks. When the Norwegian king Sverre died in 1202, his wife Margrethe, who was a daughter of Erik Jedvardsson, packed her belongings to return to Sweden (see Chapter 4). *Soga om baglarar og birkebeinar* tells that the recent widow brought her daughter Kristin with her and another high-born lady, Kristin Nikolasdatter, who came from the Swedish province of Värmland. All the same, the noblemen at the Norwegian royal court would not let her daughter leave the country. A magnate named Peter Stoype abducted Kristin behind her mother's back.[115] The reason for the abduction was probably that the king's daughter was too valuable to be brought out of the country. The Norwegians could not allow that such an important potential bride would

---

enumerates abductions of women as one out of several abominations that tormented Norway in the conflicts that erupted after the death of the king Sigurd the Crusader. *Theodoricus*, p. 53.

114 SDHK: 269/1193. The Swedish scholar Nils Ahnlund hypotheses that Knut Eriksson's wife could have been a certain Cecilia, sister of Karl Sverkersson. Ahnlund, 'Vreta klosters äldsta donatorer', pp. 307–08. See also Kjellberg, 'Erik den heliges ättlingar och kronpretendenter bland dem', p. 357; Schück, 'Från Viby till Bjälbo', pp. 200, 215; Line, *Kingship and State Formation in Sweden 1130–1290*, p. 495. We will never get a straight answer to that, but from wider Scandinavian perspective it sounds quite plausible that there was an attempt to create an alliance between the Sverker-family and the Erik-family in order to meet the threat from Magnus Henriksson. The genealogical consequences of Ahnlund's hypothesis is, however, rather overwhelming. For instance, Knut Eriksson would have been responsible for the killing of his wife's brother and the couple's offspring would have been on the maternal side direct descendants of Sverker the Elder.

115 *Soga om baglarar og birkebeinar*, pp. 278–79.

come under the control of the Swedes to be used as an instrument in their marriage policy.[116] Hence, royal women, such as Margrethe Eriksdatter and the previously mentioned Kristin Knudsdatter, had to perform balancing acts between their conjugal and natal families. Overlapping bonds were sometimes lucrative, but they could also be dangerous. In a society of constant crises, women and men always had to be proactive by making calculations in case of genealogical accidents. Monasteries were an alternative to remarriage, but could, as the case of Knut Eriksson shows, also function as temporary safe havens in critical situations.

Noblewomen and the Dynamics of Power in Twelfth Century Scandinavia

In the introduction to this chapter, it was noted that medieval noblewomen often have been interpreted as transmitters of power. However, it is important to bear in mind that this concept has been borrowed from studies based on late medieval and early modern sources. The conditions in twelfth century Nordic societies differed from those of later periods. In late medieval society the agnatic kinship system meant that the possibilities for women to practice agency were reduced. Some medievalists have used Pierre Bourdieu's twin notions of 'official' and 'practical' kinship. Practical kinship is thus defined as 'private', situational, and strategic, while official kinship is 'the formal representation of genealogical relationships made by outside observers'.[117] During the late Middle Ages, it is possible to trace a process wherein official kinship became more important, at the expense of practical kinship.

Moreover, we must pay attention to the fact that the concept 'transmitters of power' is based on an analysis of power that draws a rather sharp distinction between a 'public' and a 'private' sphere. When dealing with the twelfth century, it is not possible to operate with this demarcation.[118]

---

116 Hermanson, 'Kvinnorna runt Birger jarl', p. 95. Sverre's successor Hakon later invited Margrethe back to the royal court. She agreed but during her stay in Norway she was surrounded by suspicion and was accused of poisoning the king. Margrethe's lady-in-waiting, the noblewoman from Värmland had also returned to the Norwegian court but was accused of performing witchcraft against the child-king Guttorm. *Soga om baglarar og birkebeinar*, pp. 280–81, 282–84, 288–90.

117 Esmark and others, 'Kith and Kin', p. 15. For a thorough discussion of these concepts, see Esmark and others, 'Kith and Kin'; Esmark, 'Officielt, praktisk, strategisk'; Bourdieu, *Outline of a Theory of Practice*. On kin-based action groups (i.e. practical kinship), see Tanner, *Families, Friends, and Allies*, p. 9.

118 On the validity of the public-private distinction in the history of medieval women, see e.g. Erler and Kowaleski, *Women and Power in the Middle Ages*, pp. 4–5; Fradenburg, 'Introduction'; Freccero, 'Marguerite de Navarre', p. 132.

Some of the examples discussed in this chapter may be seen as anomalies, as for instance Ingrid Ragvaldsdatter. Still, one cannot deny that nearly all political manoeuvres performed during the Nordic wars of succession involved family relations.

The Scandinavian field of power has here been interpreted as a scene where members of the elite, men *and* women, competed for what they considered their rights. Noblewomen were not active on the battlefields, but, in their capacity as wives, concubines, mothers, widows, mediators, diplomats, and devoted benefactors of the Church, they played active parts in the conflicts. Above all, they had crucial communicative functions. The noblewomen's extended families meant that they could build allegiances and nurture alliances. By these means they exercised an influence as powerful as any official authority.[119]

It is important here to consider the medieval dynamics of power. in this pre-capitalist society, power rested on a total social system including political, social, economic, and sacral elements.[120] This suggests that the validity of the public–private distinction loses its meaning, and the interpretation of women as merely transmitters of power has to be nuanced. Many studies of medieval noblewomen revolve around concepts, such as marginality, subordination, misogyny, etc.[121] However, this somewhat one-sided focus risks giving a distorted depiction, since these conceptions more or less presuppose a distinction between public and private. Hence it could be argued that these views are based on a simplified picture of the relationships of power between men and women.

This chapter has focused on power and agency, i.e. the diverse and refined ways in which power was transferred and social status maintained within families and across generations. In line with Pierre Bourdieu's emphasis on practice and social dynamics, this part of the book has served to illustrate how various resources were accumulated and strategically used by noblewomen and men.[122] In this context, social and symbolic forms of capital played significant roles. In twelfth-century Scandinavia

---

119 Parallels could here be drawn to the political roles of noblewomen in twelfth century England, see e.g. Johns, *Noblewomen, Aristocracy and Power*; SLtt, 'The Boundaries of Women's Power'. On women's official functions of presentation and representation, reception and hospitality, see Bourdieu, *Masculine Domination*, pp. 99–100.
120 On the concept total social system/phenomenon, see: Hermanson, *Friendship, Love, and Brotherhood in Medieval Northern Europe*, p. 16; Mauss, *The Gift*, pp. 17–45; Polanyi, *Primitive, Archaic, and Modern Economies*, pp. 207–335.
121 For a discussion on the marginalization of powerful women, see Fradenburg, 'Introduction', pp. 5–6.
122 Bourdieu, *Outline of a Theory of Practice*; Bourdieu, *The Logic of Practice*. In Bourdieu's studies of the Berbers of Kabylia women appear as objects of exchange in the matrimonial market 'defined in accordance with male interests to help to reproduce the symbolic capital of men', implying that women are transformed into gifts. Bourdieu, *Masculine Domination*, pp. 42–49, 98–102.

these resources were closely interlinked. Memory could, for instance, be interpreted as a symbolic form of capital that was used by members of the elite in order to enhance status, justify rights, or to legitimate claims to power.

Memory was thus used in practice for creating families, networks, and clusters. Noblewomen, such as Margrethe Ingesdatter and Ingrid Ragvaldsdatter, were prominent objects of memory, but they also played crucial roles themselves in constructions of social networks. They were, so to speak, both objects and agents. Consequently this implies that memory could also be used as a form of social capital. This is a key feature of Bourdieu's theoretical framework: various forms of capital may overlap or be converted from one form to another, just as one and the same particular resource may function as different kinds of capital in different contexts. This obviously applies to the Middle Ages, where one must be aware of the close interaction between the two forms of capital. Monasteries, for instance, could be interpreted as amalgamations of both symbolic and social resources. In a society of constant crises, religious houses were not only used to preserve family traditions and to establish continuities, but also to officialize new social relationships between living and deceased members of the elite. Monasteries were pious foundations established and supported by noblewomen and men, but simultaneously they could be used as tools in multipolar conflicts. These foundations were accumulation nodes for economic, social, and symbolic capital. Likewise, noblewomen functioned as accumulation points in their capacity as transmitters of honour, family names, and other forms of capital. However, they are to be seen as proactive accumulation points, possessing the capability to act on their own.

A Bourdieusian framework has here been used in order to show that high-born women in certain contexts had the capacity to practise agency.[123] They played important symbolic and active roles in the Scandinavian field of power and their participation could partly explain the multipolarity of intra-elite wars. Simultaneously, the roles of noblewomen could help to elucidate why it is misleading to use the nation-bound concept 'civil wars'. It was very much due to the women's extensive families that the conflicts took place on an all-encompassing Nordic arena.

---

123 On queenship, gender, power, influence and agency, see e.g. Earenfight, 'Without the Persona of the Prince'; Fößel, 'The Political Traditions of Female Rulership in Medieval Europe'.

Works Cited

Primary Sources

Adam of Bremen, *History of the Archbishops of Hamburg-Bremen*, trans. by Francis J. Tschan (New York: Columbia University Press, 1959)

Ágrip = *Ágrip af Nóregskonungasogum. A Twelfth-Century Synoptic History of the Kings of Norway*, ed. and trans. by Matthew James Driscoll (London: Viking Society for Northern Research, 2008)

ASM = *Annales Suecici medii aevi, Svensk medeltidsannalistik*, ed. by Göte Paulsson (Lund: Gleerup bokförlag, 1974)

Chronicle of Novgorod 1016–1471, trans. by Robert Michell and Neville Forbes (London: Royal Historical Society, 1914)

Chronicon Roskildense, ed. by Martin Cl. Gertz, *Scriptores minores historiæ danicæ medii ævi*, I (Copenhagen: G. E. C. Gad, 1917–1918), pp. 1–33

DD = *Diplomatarium Danicum*, ed. by Herluf Nielsen and others (Copenhagen: Reitzel, 1938–)

DRHH = Saxo Grammaticus, *Danorum Regum Heroumque Historia*. Books X–XVI, trans. and commentary by Eric Christiansen, 3 vols (Oxford: BAR International Series 84, 1980)

Exordium magnum: Exordium magnum cisterciense sive narratio de initio cisterciensis ordinis, ed. by Bruno Greisser (Rome: Editiones Cisterciensis, 1961)

Fagrskinna, a Catalogue of the Kings of Norway, trans. by Alison Finlay (Leiden: Brill, 2004)

GD = Saxo Grammaticus. *Gesta Danorum. The History of the Danes*, ed. by Karsten Friis-Jensen, trans. by Peter Fischer (Oxford: Oxford University Press, 2015)

Heimskringla III, Snorri Sturluson, trans. by Alison Finlay and Anthony Faulkes (London: Viking Society for Northern Research, 2014–2017)

Historia S. Kanvti dvcis et martyris, ed. by Martin Cl. Gertz, *Vitae Sanctorum Danorum* (Copenhagen: Gad, 1908–1912), pp. 189–204

Knytlingesaga. Knud den Store, Knud den Hellige, deres mænd, deres slægt, trans. by Jens Peter Ægidius (Copenhagen: Gad, 1977)

Kong Valdemars Jordebog, ed. by Svend Aakjær (Copenhagen: Samfund til udgivelse af gammel nordisk litteratur, 1980)

Morkinskinna: The Earliest Icelandic Chronicle of the Norwegian Kings (1030–1157), trans. with introduction and notes by Theodore M. Andersson and Kari Ellen Gade (Ithaca: Cornell University Press, 2000)

Rasmus Lundvigsson, *Brevis historica narratio*, D 18. in Nils Ahnlund, 'Vreta klosters äldsta donatorer', *Historisk tidskrift* (S), 65 (1945), 320

Soga om baglarar og birkebeinar, in *Norges kongesagaer 3*, trans. by Dag Gundersen and Finn Hødnebø (Oslo: Gyldendal 1979)

SDHK = *Svenskt diplomatariums huvudkartotek över medeltidsbreven*. Riksarkivet: <https://riksarkivet.se/sdhk>

Helmold = *Helmoldi Presbyteri Bozoviensis Cronica Slavorum*. Scriptores Rerum Germanicarum 2, ed. by Johann Martin Lappenberg and Bernhard Schmeidler (Hannover: Impensiis bibliopolii Hahniani, 1909)

Narratiuncula de Fundatione Monasterij Vitæscholæ in Cimbria, ed. by Martin Cl. Gertz, *Scriptores minores historiæ Danicæ medii ævi* (Copenhagen: Gad, 1917–1918), vol. II, pp. 138–42

Sven Aggesen, *Brevis historia regum Dacie*, ed. by Martin Cl. Gertz, *Scriptores minores historiæ Danicæ medii ævi* (Copenhagen: Gad, 1917–1918), vol. I, pp. 94–141

Theodoricus = *Theodoricus Monachus, Historia de Antiquitate Regum Norwagensium. An Account of the Ancient History of the Norwegian Kings*, trans. by David and Ian McDougall (London: Viking Society for Northern Research, 1998)

Vitae Sanctorum Danorum, ed. by Martin Cl. Gertz (Copenhagen: G. E. C. Gad, 1908–1912)

Will. ep. = *Epistolae abbatis Willelmi* (*Diplomatarium Danicum* 2:3), ed. by C. A. Christensen, Herluf Nielsen, and Lauritz Weibull (Copenhagen: Reitzel, 1977)

Wilhelmi abbatis genealogia regvm danorvm, ed. Martin Cl. Gertz, *Scriptores minores historiæ Danicæ medii ævi* (Copenhagen: Gad, 1917–1918), vol. I, pp. 176–85

Secondary Studies

Ahnlund, Nils, 'Till frågan om den äldsta Erikskulten i Sverige', *Historisk tidskrift* (S), 68 (1948), 297–320

——, 'Vreta klosters äldsta donatorer', *Historisk tidskrift* (S), 65 (1945), 301–51

Algazi, Gadi, 'Pruning Peasants. Private War and Maintaining the Lords Peace in Late Medieval Germany', in *Medieval Transformations. Texts, Power, and Gifts in Context*, ed. by Esther Cohen and Mayke B. de Jong (Leiden: Brill, 2000), pp. 245–74

Andersson, Catharina, 'Gifts and Society in Fourteenth Century Sweden', in *Disputing Strategies in Medieval Scandinavia*, ed. by Kim Esmark, Lars Hermanson, Hans Jacob Orning, and Helle Vogt (Leiden: Brill, 2013), pp. 219–46

——, *Kloster och aristokrati: Nunnor, munkar och gåvor i det svenska samhället till 1300-talets mitt* (Gothenburg: Historiska institutionen, Göteborgs universitet, 2006)

Auður Magnúsdóttir, *Frillor och fruar: Politik och samlevnad på Island, 1120–1400* (Gothenburg: Historiska institutionen, Göteborgs universitet, 2001)

Barthélemy, Dominique, 'Feudal War in Tenth-Century France', in *Vengeance in the Middle Ages. Emotion, Religion, and Feud*, ed. by Susanna Throop and Paul Hyams (Farnham: Ashgate, 2010), pp. 105–14

Bartlett, Robert, *Blood Royal. Dynastic Politics in Medieval Europe* (Cambridge: Cambridge University Press, 2020)

Bolin, Sture, 'Kring mäster Adams text. Interpretation och kommentar', *Scandia*, 5 (1932), 230–44

Bouchard, Constance B., *Sword, Miter, and Cloister. Nobility and the Church in Burgundy, 980–1198* (Ithaca: Cornell University Press, 1987)

Bourdieu, Pierre, *The Logic of Practice*, trans. by Richard Nice (Cambridge: Cambridge Polity Press, 1990)

——, *Masculine Domination*, trans. by Richard Nice (Cambridge: Cambridge Polity Press, 1998)

——, *Outline of a Theory of Practice*, trans. by Richard Nice (Cambridge: Cambridge University Press, 1977)

Earenfight, Theresa, 'Medieval Queenship', *History Compass*, 15.3 (2017), 1–9

——, 'Without the Persona of the Prince: Kings, Queens, and the Idea of Monarchy in Late Medieval Europe', *Gender and History*, 19 (2007), 1–21

Emanuelsson, Anders, 'Kyrkojorden och dess ursprung. Oslo biskopsdöme perioden ca. 1000–1400' (Unpublished Doctoral Thesis, University of Gothenburg, 2005)

Engh, Line Cecilie, *The Symbolism of Marriage in the Early Christianity and the Latin Middle Ages* (Amsterdam: Amsterdam University Press, 2019)

Erler, Mary, and Maryanne Kowaleski, 'Introduction A New Economy of Power Relations: Female Agency in the Middle Ages', in *Gendering the Master Narrative. Women and Power in the Middle Ages*, ed. by Mary Erler and Maryanne Kowaleski (Ithaca: Cornell University Press, 2003), pp. 1–16

—— (eds), *Women and Power in the Middle Ages* (Athens: University of Georgia Press, 1988)

Esmark, Kim, 'Officielt, praktisk, strategisk: Hviderne og slægtskabets former og funktioner i middelalderens danske elite', *Praktiske Grunde. Nordisk tidsskrift for kultur- og samfundsvidenskab*, 3–4 (2019), 99–130

——, and , 'Kith and Kin. Ties of Blood and Marriage', in *Nordic Elites in Transformation, c. 1050–1250*, vol. II: *Social Networks*, ed. by Kim Esmark, Lars Hermanson, Hans Jacob Orning (Abingdon and New York: Routledge, 2020), pp. 11–32

Fleiner, Carey, and Elena Woodacre (eds), *Virtuous or Villainess? The Image of the Royal Mother from the Early Medieval to the Early Modern Era* (Basingstoke: Palgrave Macmillan, 2016)

Fößel, Amalie, 'The Political Traditions of Female Rulership in Medieval Europe', in *The Oxford Handbook of Women and Gender in Medieval Europe*, ed. by Judith M. Bennett and Ruth M. Karras (Oxford: Oxford University, 2013), pp. 68–83

Foucault, Michel, *History of Sexuality* (London: Vintage, 1990)

Fradenburg, Louise Olga, 'Introduction: Rethinking Queenship', in *Women and Sovereignty*, ed. by Louise Olga Fradenburg (Edinburgh: Edinburgh University Press, 1991), pp. 1–13

Freccero, Carla, 'Marguerite de Navarre and the Politics of Maternal Sovereignty', in *Women and Sovereignty*, ed. by Louise Olga Fradenburg (Edinburgh: Edinburgh University Press, 1991), pp. 132–49

Gallén, Jarl, 'Vem var Valdemar den Stores drottning Sofia?', *Historisk tidskrift för Finland*, 61 (1976), 273–87

Gelting, Michael H., 'Odelsrett–lovbydelse–bördsrätt–retrait lignager: Kindred and Land in the Nordic Countries in the Twelfth and Thirteenth Centuries', in *Family, Marriage and Property Devolution in the Middle Ages*, ed. by Lars I. Hansen (Tromsø: Department of History, University of Tromsø, 2000), pp. 133–65

Gilsdorf, Sean, *The Favor of Friends: Intercession and Aristocratic Politics in Carolingian and Ottonian Europe* (Leiden: Brill, 2014)

Gineste, Bernard, 'Thibaud d'Étampes', *Cahiers d'Étampes-Histoire*, 10 (2009), 43–58

Grohse, Ian Peter, 'Strength through Weakness. Regent Elites under Kings Inge, Sigurd, and Magnus Haraldsson', in *Nordic Elites in Transformation, c. 1050–1250*, vol. II: *Social Networks*, ed. by Kim Esmark, Lars Hermanson, and Hans Jacob Orning (Abingdon: Routledge, 2020), pp. 252–70

Haastrup, Ulla, and Lind, John H., 'Dronning Margrete Fredkulla. Politisk magthaver og mæcen for byzantisk kunst i danske kirker i 1100-tallets begyndelse', in *Medeltidens genus. Kvinnors rätt och mäns roller inom kultur, rätt och samhälle. Norden och Europa ca. 300–1500*, ed. by Lars Hermanson and Auður Magnúsdóttir (Gothenburg: Kriterium, 2016), pp. 29–72

Hansen, Lars Ivar, 'The Concept of Kinship according to the West Nordic Medieval Laws', in *How Nordic are the Medieval Nordic Laws? Proceedings from the First Carlsberg Conference on Medieval Legal History*, ed. by Per Andersen, Ditlev Tamm, and Helle Vogt (Copenhagen: Djøf Publishing, 2011), pp. 177–206

Hermanson, Lars, *Friendship, Love, and Brotherhood in Medieval Northern Europe* (Leiden: Brill, 2019)

——, 'Kvinnorna runt Birger jarl', *Birger Magnusson. Den siste jarlen* (Skara: Västergötlands museums förlag, 2006), pp. 87–102

——, *Släkt, vänner och makt: En studie av elitens politiska kultur i 1100-talets Danmark* (Gothenburg: Historiska institutionen, Göteborgs universitet, 2000)

——, 'Det tidiga Vreta. En helig plats i ett europeiskt maktsystem', in *Fokus Vreta kloster. 17 nya rön om Sveriges äldsta kloster*, ed. by Göran Tagesson and others (Stockholm: Statens historiska museum, 2010), pp. 210–42

Houts, Elisabeth M. C. van, *Memory and Gender in Medieval Europe 900–1200* (Basingstoke: Macmillan, 1999)

Hughes, Diane Owen, 'From Brideprice to Dowry in Mediterranean Europe', *Journal of Family History*, 3 (1978), 262–96

Huneycutt, Lois, 'Medieval Queenship', *History Today*, 39.6 (1989), 16–22

Jezierski, Wojtek, '*Convivium in terra honoris*: Helmold of Bosau's Rituals of Hostipitality', in *Rituals, Performatives, and Political Order in Northern Europe, c. 650–1350*, ed. by Wojtek Jezierski, Lars Hermanson, Hans Jacob Orning, and Thomas Småberg (Turnhout: Brepols, 2015), pp. 139–74

——, 'Introduction: Nordic Elites in Transformation, *c.* 1050–1250, Legitimacy and Glory', in *Nordic Elites in Transformation, c. 1050–1250*, vol. III: *Legitimacy and Glory*, ed. by Wojtek Jezierski, Kim Esmark, Hans Jacob Orning, and Jón Viðar Sigurðsson (Abingdon: Routledge, 2021), pp. 1–35

Johns, Susan M., *Noblewomen, Aristocracy and Power in the Twelfth-Century Anglo-Norman Realm* (Manchester and New York: Manchester University Press, 2003)

Jonsson, Bengt R., 'Erik den helige. Gammalt helgon i ny belysning', in *Scandinavia and Christian Europe in the Middle Ages*, ed. by Rudolf Simek and Judith Meurer (Bonn: Hausdruck der Universität Bonn, 2003), pp. 282–93

Kantorowicz, Ernst H., *The King's Two Bodies. A Study in Mediaeval Political Theology* (Princeton: Princeton University Press, 1966 [1st edn 1957])

King, Angela, 'The Prisoner of Gender: Foucault and the Disciplining of the Female Body', *Journal of International Women's Studies*, 5 (2004), 29–39

Kjellberg, C. M., 'Erik den heliges ättlingar och kronpretendenter bland dem', *Historisk tidskrift* (S), 43 (1923), 351–75

Klaniczay, Gábor, *Holy Rulers, and Blessed Princesses: Dynastic Cults in Medieval Central Europe* (Cambridge: Cambridge University Press, 2002)

Krais, Beate, 'On Pierre Bourdieu's *Masculine Domination*', *Travail, genre et sociétés*, 1 (1999), 214–21

Latour, Bruno, *Reassembling the Social. An Introduction to Actor-Network-Theory* (New York: Oxford University Press, 2007)

Lind, John H., 'Nordic and Eastern Elites. Contacts Across the Baltic Sea. An Exiled Clan', in *Nordic Elites in Transformation, c. 1050–1250*, vol. II: *Social Networks*, ed. by Kim Esmark, Lars Hermanson, and Hans Jacob Orning (Abingdon: Routledge, 2020), pp. 104–24

——, 'De russiske ægteskaber: Dynasti- og alliancepolitik i 1130'ernes danske Borgerkrig', *Historisk tidsskrift* (D), 92 (1992), 225–63

Lindberg, Markus, 'Det ligger en kung begraven. Vreta klosterkyrka som Gravplats', in *Fokus Vreta kloster. 17 nya rön om Sveriges äldsta kloster*, ed. by Göran Tagesson and others (Stockholm: Statens historiska museum, 2010), pp. 111–36

Line, Philip, *Kingship and State Formation in Sweden 1130–1290* (Leiden: Brill, 2007)

Lovén, Christian, 'Sigridlev och godsrikedomen i Stenkilsätten', in *Medeltida storgårdar. 15 uppsatser om ett tvärvetenskapligt forskningsproblem*, ed. by Olof Karsvall and Kristofer Jupiter (Uppsala: Kungl. Gustav Adolfs Akademin för svensk folkkultur, 2014), pp. 145–64

—— , 'Vreta år 1162. Donatorslängden och årboken', in *Fokus Vreta kloster. 17 nya rön om Sveriges äldsta kloster*, ed. by Göran Tagesson and others (Stockholm: Statens historiska museum, 2010), pp. 199–218

Lund, Niels, 'Sven Estridsen's Incest and Divorce', *Viking and Medieval Scandinavia*, 13 (2017), 115–44

Mauss, Marcel, *The Gift: Forms and Functions for Exchange in Archaic Societies*, trans. by Ian Cunnison (London: Cohen & West Ltd, 1966 [1st edn 1923])

McGuire, Brian P., 'Cistercian Origins in Denmark and Sweden: The Twelfth Century Founders', in *Itinéraires du savoir de l'Italie à la Scandinavie: X^e–XVIe siècle: études offertes à Elisabeth Mornet*, ed. by Corinne Péneau (Paris: Publications de la Sorbonne, 2009), pp. 85–97

McNamara, Jo Ann, 'Women and Power through the Family Revisited', in *Gendering the Master Narrative. Women and Power in the Middle Ages*, ed. by Mary Erler and Maryanne Kowaleski (Ithaca: Cornell University Press, 2003), pp. 17–30

Nors, Thyra, 'Ægteskab og politik i Saxos Gesta Danorum', *Historisk tidsskrift* (D), 98 (1998), 1–33

Nyberg, Tore, 'Knud, Danmarks konge – 900 år efter helgenkåringen', *Fynske Årbøger* (2001), 5–14

—— , 'Kong Niels. Skitse til en biografi', *Historisk tidsskrift* (D), 107 (2007): 353–88

Orning, Hans Jacob, and others, 'Networks', in *'It's all about inheritance', On Gender, Sámi, Bourdieu, and other Important Categories in Lars Ivar Hansen's Research*, ed. by Sigrun Høgetveit Berg and others (Tromsø: Speculum Boreale nr. 17, 2017), pp. 307–12

Pac, Grzegorz, 'Communities of Devotion across the Boundaries. Women and Religious Bonds on the Baltic Rim and in Central Europe, Eleventh–Twelfth Centuries', in *Imagined Communities on the Baltic Rim, from Eleventh to Fifteenth Centuries*, ed. by Wojtek Jezierski and Lars Hermanson (Amsterdam: Amsterdam University Press, 2016), pp. 123–54

Polanyi, Karl, *Primitive, Archaic, and Modern Economies: Essay of Karl Polanyi*, ed. by George Dalton (New York: Beacon Press, 1968)

Preiser-Kapeller, Johannes, 'Calculating the Middle Ages? The Project *Complexities and Networks in the Medieval Mediterranean and the Near East* (COMMED)', *Medieval Worlds*, 3 (2015), 100–27

Rønning, Ole-Albert, 'The Politics of Exile in Northern Europe: The Case of Knud V of Denmark', in *Nordic Elites in Transformation, c. 1050–1250*, vol. II: *Social Networks*, ed. by Kim Esmark, Lars Hermanson, and Hans Jacob Orning (Abingdon: Routledge, 2020), pp. 271–84

Rüdiger, Jan, *All the King's Women. Polygyny and Politics in Europe, 900–1250* (Leiden: Brill, 2020)

Sawyer, Birgit, 'Fromheten, familjen och förmögenheten. Kristnandets följder för kvinnor i det medeltida Skandinavien', in *Hans och hennes. Genus och egendom i Sverige från vikingatid till nutid*, ed. by Maria Ågren (Uppsala: Historiska institutionen, 2003), pp. 37–59

Schück, Adolf, 'Från Viby till Bjälbo. Studier i Sveriges historia under 1100-talets senare hälft', *Fornvännen* (1951), 197–218

Sewell, William Hamilton, Jr., 'A Theory of Structure: Duality, Agency, and Transformation', in *Practicing History: New Directions in Historical Writing after the Linguistic Turn*, ed. by Gabrielle M. Spiegel (New York: Routledge, 2005), pp. 143–65

Sjöberg, Maria. 'Kvinnans sociala underordning – en problematisk historia. Om makt, arv och giftermål i det äldre samhället', *Scandia*, 63.2 (1997), 165–92

Slitt, Rebecca, 'The Boundaries of Women's Power: Gender and the Discourse of Political Friendship in Twelfth-Century England', *Gender and History*, 24 (2012), 1–17

Stafford, Pauline, *Queens, Concubines, and Dowagers. The King's Wife in the Early Middle Ages* (Athens: University of Georgia Press, 1983)

Tanner, Heather J., *Families, Friends, and Allies: Boulogne and Politics in Northern France and England, c. 879–1160* (Leiden: Brill, 2004)

Ward, Jennifer, 'Noblewomen, Family, and Identity in Later Medieval Europe', in *Nobles and Nobility in Medieval Europe*, ed. by Anne J. Duggan (Woodbridge: The Boydell Press, 2002), pp. 246–62

JENNY BENHAM

7. Peacemaking and Negotiations in High Medieval Scandinavia

The Norwegian civil wars period is a crowded marketplace for the historian. With its small corpus of narrative evidence, almost every facet of the period 1130–1240 has been combed for details to explain the causes and course of the conflict(s); the organization and character of the kings, the elite, and the Church; the more practical matters of strategy and tactics; and, in particular, the role and importance of the civil wars period for state formation.[1] Less attention has been paid to those, admittedly fewer, occasions when claimants to the individual kingdoms attempted to end conflict. One such occasion is the agreement at Kvitingsøy in 1208, concluded between the three claimants Inge Bardsson, his half-brother Hakon Galen ('the Crazy'), and Filippus Simonsson (see Chapter 4). Described by Sverre Bagge as a division between 'two factions', the Baglar and the Birkibeinar, a careful examination of this agreement and the circumstances surrounding its conclusion suggests a need to rethink this claim. This chapter aims to refocus the historiography of the agreement, and to put it into a wider comparative and methodological framework of how agreements between rulers were concluded in the early and high Middle Ages. In reconsidering the content of the agreement — that the kingdom would be divided in three, that Filippus would renounce his royal title and seal, that Filippus would swear obedience to King Inge, and that Filippus would marry Kristin, the daughter of King Sverre — it reveals that the issue of two factions is far from the only context within which

---

1 For a few examples of this extensive literature, see Bagge, *From Viking Stronghold to Christian Kingdom*; Bagge, *From Gang Leader to the Lord's Anointed*; Orning, 'Conflict and Social (Dis)order'; Orning, *Unpredictability and Presence*; Helle, *Norge blir en stat*; Lunden, *Økonomi og samfunn*.

Jenny Benham (BenhamJ@cardiff.ac.uk) is Reader in medieval history in School of History, Archaeology and Religion, University of Cardiff.

New Perspectives on the 'Civil Wars' in Medieval Scandinavia, ed. by Hans Jacob Orning, Kim Esmark, and Jón Viðar Sigurðsson, Comparative Perspectives on Medieval History, 1 (Turnhout: Brepols, 2024), pp. 309–340
BREPOLS PUBLISHERS   10.1484/M.CPMH-EB.5.137264

to view its purpose and aim. Instead, all three leaders played a larger role than scholars have often acknowledged, showing a complex military and social context. The chapter will further consider the significance of certain practices recorded in the agreement, such as the amnesty clause, and its significance for how we view war and peace as concepts and the transition from conflict to peace. The agreement at Kvitingsøy appears in *Bǫglunga sǫgur*, which was written shortly after the events it portrays by an unknown author or authors. It survives in two versions — a short version (A) and a fuller version (B) — with the first covering only the years 1202–1209, while the second covers the years from the death of King Sverre in 1202 until the death of King Inge in 1217.[2] Ultimately, this chapter aims to show that the agreement is important not only in what it can tell us about negotiations and occasions for peacemaking in medieval Scandinavia, but also in how a close reading of *Bǫglunga sǫgur* provides a new perspective on the author's purpose in writing and his retelling of events in early thirteenth-century Norway.[3]

Partitions

In 1208, only the portion that would come to Filippus, depicted as the candidate of the Baglar faction, is defined. The author states that he would have Oppland and the Vik but not further north than Rygjarbit and not further south than Svinesund.[4] In an earlier stage of the negotiations, while Bishop Nicholas — apparently the foremost negotiator — was trying to encourage Filippus to agree to the deal, the bishop is recorded as saying that the Vik was a better region than Trondheim (in the Trøndelag) because the latter was experiencing years of dearth and famine.[5] No further attempt is made to either define the different portions or to justify their existence. This is also a feature of previous partitions between claimants to the Norwegian throne. For instance, when the Icelander Snorre Sturlason recorded in *Heimskringla* the division between Magnus the Blind and Harald Gille after the death of Sigurd the Crusader in 1130, he says only that each received half of the kingdom and that Magnus, in addition, received 'the ships and table service and things of value and all the money that King Sigurðr had had'.[6] This is similar to the eleventh-century agreement

---

2 Magerøy, 'Bǫglunga sǫgur', p. 61; Magerøy, 'Føreord til Soga om baglarar og birkebeinar', pp. 269–70.
3 *Bǫglunga sǫgur*, 2 vols, ed. by Hallvard Magerøy (Oslo, 1988); *Soga om baglarar og birkebeinar*, in *Norges kongesoger*, vol. 3, ed. by Halvdan Koht and Gunnar Pedersen (Oslo, 1979).
4 *Bǫglunga sǫgur* II, pp. 116–17; *Soga om baglarar og birkebeinar*, pp. 330–31.
5 *Bǫglunga sǫgur* II, pp. 113–14; *Soga om baglarar og birkebeinar*, p. 329.
6 *Heimskringla* 3, p. 170.

between Magnus the Good and Harald Hardruler, when, according to Snorre, King Magnus offered Harald 'a settlement and friendship, and Haraldr was to have a half share of Norway along with King Magnús, while the wealth of both of them was to be shared half and half between the two of them'.[7] Exactly which part of the kingdom each king ruled over is never specified in either of these agreements. Perhaps Snorre did not know — he was after all writing in the mid-thirteenth century and perhaps reflected more contemporary events and practices, rather than the past long gone — or else there was simply an expectation that his audience would know.

Despite this lack of specificity, it is evident that there was a memory of Rygjarbit as the edge of one sphere of influence before 1208, but seemingly not originally a Norwegian one. In the early 1160s the Norwegian claimants to the throne were jostling for support and the Danish king, Valdemar I, eventually struck a deal with the Norwegian earl, Erling Skakke, according to which he would obtain the dominion of Norway which his earlier kinsmen, Harald Gormsson and Svend Forkbeard had had; that is, all of Viken up to Rygjarbit in return for his assistance in securing the kingship for Erling's son Magnus.[8] There could be many reasons why Snorre, writing in the thirteenth century, chose to depict Rygjarbit as the boundary mark of an area traditionally under Danish rule. However, given his close connection to King Hakon Hakonsson, the idea was probably to discredit any claimant to the Norwegian throne who had garnered Danish support — an issue that was still live when Snorre was writing. Nevertheless, other evidence indicates that Rygjarbit was indeed a traditional boundary marker. According to the author of the *Historia Norvegiae*, likely writing shortly before Snorre in the late twelfth or early thirteenth century, this area was one of four law provinces of Norway: 'The first law province in the east is called Viken and extends from the bounds of Denmark right to the place known as Rygjarbit'.[9] Hence, Rygjarbit was an immediate point of reference, and the particular shares of the partition corresponding to known law provinces makes sense considering the importance of assembly election for the Norwegian kingship.[10]

One could contrast all of this with the partition of the kingdom of Denmark in 1157 between the three rival kings Svend, Knud, and Valdemar. Saxo records how it was decided that all should use the royal title and then divided the kingdom into the three parts of Jutland, Scania,

---

7 *Heimskringla* 3, pp. 56–58.
8 'Saga of Magnus Erlingsson', in *Heimskringla*, p. 790.
9 'Prima patria Sinus Orientalis dicitur, a terminis Dacie oriens, et usque ad locum, qui Rygiarbit appellatur, extenditur', *Historia Norwegie*, pp. 54–55.
10 Ødegaard, 'State Formation, Administrative Areas, and Thing Sites'. For an excellent discussion of the rules to the Norwegian kingship, see Tollefsen, 'Scandinavian Kingship Transformed', pp. 37–54.

and the islands of Zealand and Funen. Jutland, according to Saxo, was 'as abundant in its number of inhabitants as in its wide expanses', and as Valdemar had the first choice, he opted for this part. Svend demanded Scania, according to Saxo, because he did not want to receive the middle ground between his co-rivals. The islands — 'a smaller share' — fell to Knud.[11] Obviously, Saxo is portraying the story from the perspective of the eventual winner, and hence the only share that is justified to the audience is that of Jutland, which was Valdemar's choice. The German contemporary, Helmold, whose *Chronicle of the Slavs* was written in the early 1170s and hence before Saxo, seems to imply a slightly different reason for this particular division, namely that Svend received or asked for Scania because it was deemed to be superior in arms and men.[12] Presumably the reason for this comment is that Helmold was favourably disposed to Svend, who had a German wife and had spent some time at the German court together with Frederick Barbarossa before the latter became king in 1152. Indeed, throughout the short narrative about Danish events of the 1150s, Helmold clearly portrays Svend as the rightful king of Denmark. Nevertheless, while the two writers disagreed about whose share of the kingdom was the best, they seem to be in agreement that Zealand was the lesser share.[13] Saxo notes that this share had been awarded by Frederick Barbarossa to Knud during his arbitration of the conflict over the Danish throne earlier in the process, and was to be held from Svend on the condition that Knud renounced his claim to the royal title.[14] Helmold does not state what Knud received at this earlier arbitration, merely that he was subjected to Svend ('eidem hominio subactis').[15] The implication is therefore that whoever possessed the Zealand share was less than the other two. Possibly this was the reason why the author of *Knýtlinga saga* recorded that Valdemar and Knud joined their shares together.[16]

Having several claimants to a kingdom is hardly unique to Denmark and Norway in the medieval period, nor the fact that this caused conflicts. Neither is it unique to Scandinavia that efforts to resolve such conflicts frequently focused on the division of land (property), rights, and resources between the parties. From the best-known such partition, that at Verdun in 843 dividing the large Carolingian empire between the three brothers Lothar, Louis the German, and Charles the Bald, we know that already

---

11 GD, 14.17.1; *Knýtlinga saga* also follows this division, see *Knýtlinga saga*, p. 112. Available in English as *Knytlingasaga: The History of the Kings of Denmark*, p. 154.
12 *Helmold von Bosau Slawenchronik*, pp. 302–03. Helmold makes no specific mention of the provinces of Halland and Blekinge, which presumably also fell to Svend as they, like Scania, were on the opposite side of the Sound in what is now Sweden.
13 GD, 14.17.15; *Helmold von Bosau Slawenchronik*, pp. 302–03.
14 GD, 14.8.2. See also *Knytlingasaga*, p. 150.
15 *Helmold von Bosau Slawenchronik*, pp. 254–55.
16 *Knytlingasaga*, p. 154.

holding possession of a particular territory was a basic principle guiding any divisions. No text of the Treaty of Verdun has survived into modern times, but the contemporary Nithard, who does not record the Treaty of Verdun, nevertheless states that any division was to be effected excluding Italy, Bavaria, and Aquitaine; that is, the parts where Lothar, Louis, and Charles respectively already held royal power.[17] That this principle held firm is, furthermore, evidenced by what the annalists of Fulda and St Bertin say about the terms of the treaty.[18] The exact allocations in the division of the Treaty of Verdun are usually reconstructed with the help of a series of subsequent partitions and treaties; in particular, that agreed at Meerssen in 870. The division at Meerssen is recorded in the *Annals of St Bertin* by Hincmar, archbishop of Rheims, who was an eyewitness, and in it he lists each share in terms of ecclesiastical provinces and then counties, before finally outlining some additional cities and settlements as well as an area, defined by rivers and roads, which was put to arbitration.[19] This tallies with the evidence explored by Ganshof, showing that, in 843, the commission of leading men had made inventories (*descriptiones*) of the realm, after which the division at Verdun was made on several principles including proximity to the lands already held by each king, equivalences between portions, and resources to distribute to followers.[20]

According to Ganshof, the reason why equal partition was so important was because the kings relied upon these offices, lands, and rights for subsistence and for the exercise of their imperial or royal power.[21] From a practical point of view, it seems likely that such considerations also underpinned partitions in Norway and Denmark, and the claimants received either that which they already possessed or those parts from which they drew their supporters or other resources. Moreover, it seems likely that conflicts primarily arose in those areas where these rights and claims overlapped. In the same way, Hincmar said that with the partition of Meerssen of 870, the areas where the parties could not agree were put to arbitration.[22] However, at first glance, the principles underpinning the divisions at Verdun and elsewhere do not seem to hold for the evidence we have for Denmark. We know that at the start of their conflict in 1146, Svend initially asked to be recognized as king by the Zealanders and Knud by the Jutlanders.[23] This makes sense, as it is evident from elsewhere in

---

17 Nithard, *Histoire des fils de Louis le Pieux*, pp. 116–43. For a summary of the context, content, and legacy of Verdun, see Benham, 'The Treaty of Verdun, 843'.
18 *Annales Bertiniani*, p. 29; *Annales Fuldenses*, p. 33.
19 'Treaty of Meerssen (870)', pp. 193–95; *The Annals of St-Bertin*, pp. 168–69.
20 Ganshof, 'The Genesis and Significance of the Treaty of Verdun (843)'.
21 Ganshof, 'The Genesis and Significance of the Treaty of Verdun (843)', p. 302.
22 *The Annals of St-Bertin*, pp. 168–69. On the role and function of arbitration panels, see Benham, *International Law in Europe, 700–1200*, pp. 35–36, 202–04.
23 GD, 14.3.1.

Saxo's text that the lands of Svend's father, Erik the Unforgettable, lay on the island of Zealand and he drew significant support and supplies from it.[24] It is hence odd that the division in 1157 awarded this part to Knud rather than to Svend. At the point of election, Saxo further portrays the Zealanders as declaring a wish to elect the same candidate as the Scanians, and to achieve this Svend reminded them of how the latter had supported his father to the kingship (cf. Chapter 3).[25] This makes it appear that the reason why Svend received Scania was because it was an area from which he drew significant support. But Saxo's motivation for depicting how the Zealanders and Scanians joined forces to elect Svend seems to be to discredit Eskil, archbishop of Lund and predecessor to Saxo's own patron Absalon, and his role, as well as that of his family, in leading the Scanians astray.[26] This is a theme running through the narrative, which mattered at the point that Saxo was beginning to compile the *Gesta*, as it explained the involvement of Eskil's family in the rebellion of Scania (1180–1182) in opposition to the Hvide family of Saxo's patron Absalon. In other words, Saxo's depiction of Scania and the Scanians is that of a struggle between these two families, and he, naturally, wanted to show that the eventual winners of this struggle, the Hvide family, supported the eventual winner of the conflict over the Danish kingdom. This winner was neither Svend nor Knud — the two front runners in the earlier part of the conflict — but Valdemar. Hence, Saxo uses the election of Svend by the Scanians and Zealanders to show that Eskil rebelled against Svend and withdrew his support, but says very little about any actual support for Svend in this area.[27] Saxo's narrative thus shows some of the problems of trying to ascertain the basis of any partition from a single source written some time after the events it portrays, when earlier decisions by the eventual 'winners' might make uncomfortable reading or at the very least disrupt the providential nature of historical writing.

If it is not entirely clear why Svend chose or was awarded Scania at the partition in 1157, the historian can fare a little better with the other two parts. As described in Chapter 3, Valdemar's father, Knud Lavard, had been governor of Schleswig on Jutland and this same office was later awarded to Valdemar by his rival Svend.[28] Saxo further notes that in 1154 Valdemar and Knud assumed their royal titles with the approval of the Jutlanders, and that, after the murder of Knud in 1157, this was also the area to which

---

24 *GD*, 14.8.3. This also explains why the author of the *Annales Ryenses* thought that Svend had been awarded this particular share. *Annales Ryenses*, p. 81.
25 *GD*, 14.3.2.
26 On this rebellion, see Hermanson, 'How to Legitimate Rebellion and Condemn Usurpation of the Crown', pp. 123–24.
27 *GD*, 14.3.3.
28 *GD*, 14.4.1. Again, the exact territory and jurisdiction on Jutland that this entailed is not clear.

Valdemar fled, indicating that he could garner support from it.[29] Hence there can be no question that the reason why Valdemar chose this share was because this was an area where he already held some possessions and from where he could draw most of his supporters and resources. Similarly, Knud's award of Zealand likely stemmed from the fact that this was the share awarded in the arbitration by Frederick Barbarossa, which, as he had indicated in a letter to Frederick's predecessor Conrad III, was part of his paternal inheritance.[30] However, it is also clear that Zealand (and the islands) was the share where the rights and claims of Svend and Knud overlapped, and it is evident that this played a part both in what Knud received at the partition and in their conflicts. Consider, for instance, what Saxo tells us about the arbitration undertaken by Frederick I between Svend and Knud in 1152. According to Saxo, the estates of Svend's father on Zealand were excepted from the agreement, and so were the lands that would be held by Knud, 'treating these as his private property'.[31] At the settlement in 1157, there is no mention of these estates. Nonetheless, it is evidently significant that despite having received Scania, Svend, upon killing Knud at the feast of Roskilde, drew together an army, not from Scania, but from Zealand and the islands.[32] Furthermore, a significant part of the conflict, military engagements as well as negotiations, took place in this same area.[33] From all of this then, it would appear that the principles — possession, supporters, resources — underpinning partition agreements elsewhere in Europe held true, in the main, for the partition of the kingdom of Denmark in 1157. Indeed, the arbitration award of Frederick I in 1152, which was based on what the claimants had themselves asked for and what they possessed at that time, provided the legal template for all subsequent attempts to reconcile the claimants.[34]

For Norway, it is not until we reach the reign of Hakon Hakonsson (1217–1263) that we have a sufficiently detailed narrative to give us an idea of the principles underpinning agreements detailing the division of the kingdom of Norway. Hakon's reign saw at least three such partitions. At the first, in 1217, there were three contracting parties: the incumbent king, Filippus, who had also been one of the parties to the 1208 agreement and who was supported by the Baglar faction; Earl Skule, who was the half-brother of the previous king, Inge Bardsson, had received all the king's

---

[29] GD, 14.16.4, 14.19.1–3; *Knytlingasaga*, p. 158. Even the compiler of the *Annales Ryenses*, who erroneously thought that Valdemar had been awarded Scania at the partition in 1157, says that he fled to Jutland after the murder of Knud. *Annales Ryenses*, p. 81.
[30] DD, I:2, no. 104.
[31] In other words, the patrimony was separate from any other lands acquired. GD, 14.8.3 (and also editor's footnote at p. 66).
[32] GD, 14.18.11, 14.19.4.
[33] For a few examples, see GD, 14.3.3–4, 14.3.10–12, 14.14.5, 14.16.4–9.
[34] For a discussion of this arbitration, see Benham, *International Law in Europe*, pp. 196–221.

property and had also appropriated that of Hakon Hakonsson's father and grandfather, and was seemingly a member of the Birkibeinar faction; and Hakon Hakonsson, a grandson of King Sverre, who was also supported by the Birkibeinar faction and put forward by them — supposedly to the earl's surprise — as the rival claimant to the throne.[35] Hence, the kingdom was partitioned in three, with Filippus retaining the part he already possessed, the Vik and Oppland, as per the 1208 agreement, showing that this particular principle was the basis of at least part of the division. Hakon received the title of king, and Skule and the new king each received a third of the kingdom, although which third is never divulged. However, the negotiations seem to have focused on what the author calls 'skattlanda', the outlying lands paying tribute and tax to the kingdom.[36] Similarly, when Filippus shortly afterwards died, the foremost concern of his supporters in negotiating a settlement with Hakon and Skule was that they would be allowed to keep the districts ('syslr') that they had held under Filippus. Some were afterwards disgruntled at having received others, as were the householders of those districts, who clearly resented the extraction methods of (and possibly the amounts held by) these men.[37] At the partition of 1223, concerns also centred around each claimant receiving a share equitable in terms of fixed units of land for payments of taxes ('skipreiðr'), and, in addition, there seems to have been an effort to consider the borders of ecclesiastical provinces, presumably because of how tithes were paid.[38] However, there was less emphasis on what each party already held, and the author of the saga suggests that King Hakon drew popular support from the whole kingdom ('allr múgr [...] bæði norðr í landi ok suðr'), while the great landholders ('stórmenni') were divided in their loyalties between Hakon, Skule, and various other claimants.[39] Nevertheless, the fact that the saga author records how after the agreement, King Hakon took the most trustworthy men from the north with him to the Vik and there rewarded them with offices, clearly indicates that this was the area perceived as the heartland of a Norwegian king with its capital at Tønsberg.[40] What is obvious from all of this is that, just like most European partitions, there was an economic basis to the agreements and divisions of the kingdom in Hakon's reign, and that each share had to be as financially viable as the next so that each claimant to the Norwegian throne could sustain and reward his followers.

---

35 *Soga om Håkon Håkonsson*, p. 45.
36 *Soga om Håkon Håkonsson*, pp. 46–47; *Hákonar saga Hákonarsonar*, pp. 319–20. On these 'skattlanda', see Wærdahl, *Incorporation and Integration*, pp. 70–71, 79–81.
37 *Soga om Håkon Håkonsson*, pp. 49–50; *Hákonar saga Hákonarsonar*, pp. 324, 326.
38 *Hákonar saga Hákonarsonar*, pp. 336–37. On skipreiður being a unit of land for paying tax, see Ødegaard, 'State Formation, Administrative Areas, and Thing Sites', pp. 47–48.
39 *Hákonar saga Hákonarsonar*, pp. 325, 336–37.
40 *Hákonar saga Hákonarsonar*, p. 337.

It seems unreasonable to suppose that earlier partitions of the Norwegian kingdom were not made on similar grounds. Sverre Bagge has certainly argued that power-sharing between two or more kings in the period 1030 to 1157 was based on a division of wealth and power rather than a physical dividing up of the kingdom.[41] However, while this seems true, we should also consider that something had to be the source of wealth and power. Snorre indicates that at the partition in the eleventh century Harald chose by lot, as if neither party had a prior claim or reason to choose a particular half:

> Finally he came to face his kinsman Haraldr with two canes in his hand, saying this: 'Which of the canes here do you wish to have?' Then Haraldr replies: 'The one that is nearer to me'. Then spoke King Magnús: 'With this cane I give you half the realm of Norway with all its dues and taxes and all the possessions that belong to it on this condition, that you shall be as lawfully king as I everywhere in Norway'.[42]

We should of course not believe this fictitious version of events, but what is evident is that, although Snorre describes both kings as being kings everywhere, he did not mean to indicate that the source of their wealth and power was not based on a physical division. In fact, he is quite clear that it was, and that each king drew dues and taxes from his share and held possessions in it. Similarly, in 1208, the principles of possession, supporters, and resources probably underpinned the agreement between Inge, Filippus, and Hakon. We know at the very least that the portions given to each roughly equated to what they already held, and, if it is possible to assume anything from this, that they drew support and resources from those same areas. The principles of possession, supporters, and resources hence lay at the heart of agreements that partitioned kingdoms.

The Settlement of 1208

Whilst the partition of the Norwegian kingdom in 1208 dealt with the thorny issue of what Inge, Filippus, and Hakon already held and how to ensure that each had enough resources for his subsistence and exercise of power, this division had implications for their supporters which were not always favourable. In particular, the agreement had an amnesty clause, stipulating that 'whatever injuries have been received on either side, whether to people or goods, no one shall demand compensation, vengeance or

---

41 Bagge, *From Viking Stronghold to Christian Kingdom*, pp. 40–41. On this issue see also Bjørgo, 'Samkongedøme og einekongedøme'; Bagge, 'Samkongedømme og enekongedømme'.
42 *Heimskringla* 3, p. 58.

appropriation for'.[43] By cancelling opportunities for redress, Inge, Filippus, and Hakon hence disposed of the rights of individuals without offering any compensation, and this shows a clear concept of princes having the authority (over all their followers) and jurisdiction (over all of their lands) to conclude treaties with each other and with other foreign entities: in other words, they were the 'state'.[44] This is quite a significant point, showing that Bagge's notion of two factions does not reflect reality, and that we should think carefully before designating Norway as a unitary kingdom in this period.[45] The author further reports that the supporters of the leaders were unhappy, because many had lost their money or property in the war.[46] The solution, the men agreed, would be to raid the Orkneys and the Scottish isles to recuperate some of the losses incurred from the partition. The year after, in the summer of 1209, some men from both sides duly took twelve ships and set sail for the joint raid. The plan may have been a good one, but it soon went awry. According to the author of the saga, the men disagreed, were beaten soundly, and returned to Norway in disarray, only to be severely chastised by the bishops for their raiding and violence.[47] This particular attempt at diverting violence elsewhere may have been unsuccessful, but as a concept, it was one which was tried and tested. It reflects, as an example, how successive civilizations have tried to deal with the problem of mercenaries during peace time. Hired soldiers were often left behind in the peace process, no longer entitled to compensation for losses incurred nor to wages from their employment.[48] Such displaced groups posed a serious threat to peace and security, as they often resorted to self-help in the form of plunder when not employed, and hence they became the targets for legislation as well as condemnation from the

---

43 *Bǫglunga sǫgur* II, p. 117. It is worth noting that the wording of this is remarkably similar to the amnesty clause in the treaty between the English king, Æthelred II, and the three Viking leaders, one of whom was Olav Tryggvason, king of Norway c. 995–1000. For this treaty, see *Die Gesetze der Angelsachsen* I, p. 224.
44 On amnesty clauses in the medieval period, see Benham, *International Law in Europe*, pp. 99–103. There is an extensive literature on sovereignty and the challenges of amnesty and human rights in later historical periods. For examples, see McEvoy and Mallinder, 'Amnesties in Transition', pp. 413–15; Haltern, *Was bedeutet Souveränität?*, pp. 75–97; Lyons, 'Ineffective Amnesty'; Scharf, 'From the eXile Files:', pp. 342–47; Steiger, 'Peace Treaties from Paris to Versailles', pp. 84–87.
45 On factions, see also Chapter 4.
46 The two versions of the saga respectively record this as that the men 'hafde mist alt deris gods oc pendinge i den feide'; 'er félausir varu ok hǫfðu þó nafnbœtr'. *Bǫglunga sǫgur* II, pp. 117–18.
47 *Bǫglunga sǫgur* II, pp. 118–20.
48 See, as an example, William of Newburgh's comments on this issue in the middle of the twelfth century, following the conflict during King Stephen's reign. *The History of English Affairs, Book II*, pp. 14–15. Several scholars have noted that the distinction between mercenaries and other groups of military men was often not entirely clear. For a discussion with reference to relevant literature, see DeVries, 'Medieval Mercenaries'.

Church.[49] Many medieval agreements consequently included payments and rewards in land, money, or offices, which then disincentivized men from plunder and ensured an economic basis to their existence even in peace time.[50] The author of the *Bǫglunga sǫgur* shows how during the conflict, fighting men were rewarded through plunder and movable property. For instance, after the capture of Nidaros, the Baglar faction divided the town into four before ransacking it, or at least stripping it of valuables, and the proceeds were then divided among the men in such a way 'that no one received less than three or four marks worth of goods'.[51] The agreement of 1208 evidently offered supporters the opportunity for more adequate, substantial, and permanent compensation for their losses from the conflict, but it was not to be, and the failure of the subsequent raid rubbed salt into their wounds. Redress then, whether for damages or injuries, for buying peace or having a ruler's mercy, for recovering costs of military campaigns, or for just facilitating trade in some way or another, stood at the heart of achieving peaceful relations in the medieval period; and its denial was a driver of conflict.[52]

Redress and amnesty are useful issues for thinking about and understanding the many competing demands of transitioning from conflict to peace. Some supporters were evidently disappointed by the amnesty clause, but there are signs that at the highest, inter-ruler level, the agreement of 1208 attempted to balance some of these demands. We can see this by exploring the stipulation that Filippus renounce his royal title and seal, and have whatever title King Inge would give him. In addition, the author records how Filippus was to swear fealty to Inge and to follow him both within and without the realm.[53] It is possible that renouncing the royal title rather than sharing it between different claimants was a new feature in negotiations for the Norwegian kingdom, as no previous agreement contained such a stipulation. Probably it also betrays the ecclesiastical outlook of an author influenced by European ideas of Christian kingship. Some such ideas had surfaced already in the 1160s, as discussed in Chapter 2, when Archbishop Oystein, who had been educated in Paris, tried to promote Christian kingship by striking a deal with Earl Erling Skakke over the coronation of his son Magnus as king, and it manifested itself in the *Law of Succession* of 1163. This document was an attempt at regulating

---

49 For examples, see *Die Urkunden Friedrichs I*, III, no. 575. 'Canons of the Third Lateran Council 1179', at <www.papalencyclicals.net/Councils/ecum11.htm> [accessed 10 October 2017], c. 27. On the context, see Géraud, 'Les routiers au douzième siècle'.
50 For some comparative European examples, see *Diplomatic Documents Preserved in the Public Record Office, 1101–1279*, pp. 12–13; *Le Liber Censuum de l'église romaine* I, p. 422.
51 *Soga om baglarar og birkebeinar*, p. 308.
52 For a fuller discussion of displacement and its relation to redress, war, and peace, see Benham, *International Law in Europe*, pp. 56–79, 98–99, 102–05.
53 *Bǫglunga sǫgur* II, pp. 116–17; *Soga om baglarar og birkebeinar*, pp. 330–31.

the royal succession by introducing concepts of legitimacy, primogeniture, suitability, and election. The idea was that from now on the kingship could only be held by one person at a time, and perhaps, most importantly, it was intended to make the traditional path — essentially kin-right and election at an assembly — to kingship illegal. For this purpose, it included a clause excommunicating any claimant, and his supporters, who sought the kingship in any other way than how the text specified.[54] The reduction of Filippus's status then appears as a long-term strategy by Norwegian churchmen to conform to the Christian ideal of kingship and to reduce conflict by limiting and eliminating competition over the crown.

That asking Filippus to renounce his royal title and seal was a significant request is evident, and it was one that required some form of redress to balance out the slight to his honour and loss of material and symbolic status. The recompense seems to have come in the form of another feature of the agreement; namely, the marriage between Filippus and Kristin, the daughter of the former king, Sverre. The saga author describes the negotiations for the marriage as being a pre-requisite for the agreement at Kvitingsøy. He describes how Bishop Nicholas of Oslo arranged a meeting with King Inge, Earl Hakon, and their men, and presented the case: 'King Filippus, our kinsman, has offered to forsake all enmity between you and to ally in brotherhood if you would allow him to marry Kristin, the daughter of King Sverre'.[55] When the other side replied that Inge would have to be sole king, the final meeting at Kvitingsøy was quickly arranged and the parties agreed that the kingdom would be divided in three, that Filippus's share would extend from Rygjarbit to Svinesund, that he would marry Kristin but would renounce his royal title and seal. That the bishop had never really expected the initial proposal to be accepted and that the recompense would be the marriage is clear from the depiction of how Bishop Nicholas initially met with his nephew, Filippus, to propose the agreement. At that meeting he describes Kristin as a 'daughter of [King] Sverre, who was born here in the realm', and notes that if they had sons together that would be valuable in the future.[56] As with so many other marriage alliances, the idea was to by-pass a claim, whether to a particular land or a title, at the heart of a conflict but giving both sides a stake in keeping the agreement through the claims of any future heir. As argued elsewhere, this was a tried and tested strategy, and one can surmise that, in this case,

---

54 *Norske middelalderdokumenter*, p. 34. On the traditional path to kingship, see Tollefsen, 'Scandinavian Kingship Transformed', pp. 40–43.
55 *Bǫglunga sǫgur* II, p. 114; *Soga om baglarar og birkebeinar*, p. 329.
56 *Bǫglunga sǫgur* II, pp. 113–14; *Soga om baglarar og birkebeinar*, p. 329.

it reflected the ideas of kingship as perceived by the author.[57] However, that the marriage also came with other material benefits is certain, and these would have gone a long way towards redressing those demands for peace that Filippus had to agree to. In the spring of 1209, the wedding between Filippus and Kristin was held in Oslo. Present was Margrethe, Kristin's mother and Sverre's widow, who arrived from Götaland even though she was severely ill and passed away a couple of weeks after the wedding.[58] Kristin clearly inherited her mother's property and movable goods in Sweden, as Filippus promptly sent his men to the provinces of Värmland and Västergötland to secure these. It would seem then, that Filippus, in return for agreeing to renounce his claim to the royal title, was amply recompensed; symbolically through the marriage and the potential of an heir with a royal claim, and materially through the dowry and the property and possessions acquired through Kristin's mother.[59]

Despite these efforts to balance some of the competing demands of the peace and the amnesty, the stipulation to renounce Filippus's royal title and seal came to be used as a justification for further conflict. This can be seen clearly in the saga author's description of the wrangle over King Filippus's seal — an important symbol of royal authority. The author shows that Filippus was very reluctant to surrender the seal, despite this being one of the main terms of the agreement. Filippus initially claimed that, while he wanted to renounce the enmity between the parties and accept the terms to which he had agreed, his seal had remained in Oslo with his chancellor 'where you can collect it'.[60] However, when King Inge sent one of his men, Dagfinn, to retrieve the royal seal from Filippus, the latter refused on the grounds that his counsellors and great men were not present and consequently asked Dagfinn to wait. A few days later, Filippus summoned an assembly where he announced the agreement he had concluded with Inge, that he had promised to relinquish his title and seal, and that Inge's men were there to collect it. Now, however, Filippus claimed that he would never have agreed to this were it not for the fact that the Birkibeinar had turned up at the conference with more men than had been agreed beforehand. The assembled followers then decided that the Birkibeinar had broken their word and that they would never allow anyone who took the seal away to rest; indeed, anyone among them who allowed it would have their hand chopped off. With this, Dagfinn realized he would

---

57 Benham, *Peacemaking in the Middle Ages*, p. 203. See also Watkins, *After Lavinia*, pp. 82–86, 108; Diggelmann, 'Marriage as Tactical Response'; Diggelmann, 'Marriage, Peace, and Enmity in the Twelfth Century', pp. 240–48.
58 *Bǫglunga sǫgur* II, pp. 119–20; *Soga om baglarar og birkebeinar*, p. 338.
59 More generally on the role of women, see Chapter 6.
60 *Bǫglunga sǫgur* II, pp. 116–17; *Soga om baglarar og birkebeinar*, pp. 330–31.

not receive the seal and asked Filippus to be allowed to return to Inge with the reply.[61]

Here, the author conflated the idea of Christian (sole) kingship with notions of law and justice as they were being developed in the twelfth and early thirteenth century. According to Roman law, usurping a seal or a royal title was '*crimine maiestas*' and hence part of the development of the crime of treason. There is no mention of the royal seal or its link to treason in the law of Gulathing, and it is possible that the idea came to Norway via England. We know, for instance, that John of Salisbury specifically notes the link, using Justinian's *Digest*, in the *Policraticus* — often described as a so-called mirror of princes — and the crime is later also found in the English legal treatise known as *Glanvill*, compiled towards the end of the twelfth century.[62] However, the false oaths of the Birkibeinar also made them an 'enemy of mankind' — a concept, which like '*crimine maiestas*', is linked to treason and unchristian behaviour in established peace theory.[63] The whole point of designating someone as having broken an oath and therefore as having acted in an unchristian manner was that this justified any action against them as self-defence. In the twelfth century, Isidore's insistence that to defend oneself — as a natural inclination — was a just act, mixed with Augustine's emphasis on 'just wars avenge injuries (*iusta bella ulciscuntur iniurias*)', became enshrined in Gratian's *Decretum*.[64] In short, the demand to return the seal was depicted as being not only an illegal but also an unchristian act, and the refusal by Filippus and his men and the subsequent resumption of conflict was couched in the Christian justification of self-defence.

The author of *Bǫglunga sǫgur* was deeply familiar with the Christian context of the just war theory through the works of Augustine and Gratian, and applied it to the content and circumstances of the agreement of 1208 to explain why conflict continued.[65] On a practical level, however, the failure of the leaders to provide redress for their followers goes a long way towards explaining why this agreement failed to transition the kingdom into a more lasting peace. In fact, if we compare it to other treaties between rulers or between claimants to a particular kingdom in the period 700–

---

61 *Bǫglunga sǫgur* II, p. 118; *Soga om baglarar og birkebeinar*, pp. 336–37.
62 *The Digest of Justinian*, 48: 4.1–4; John of Salisbury, *Policraticus*, VI: 25; *The Treatise on the Laws and Customs of the Realm of England Commonly Called Glanvill*, p. 171.
63 For a discussion of this with references to relevant literature, see Benham, *International Law in Europe*, pp. 57–58, 147–53. See also Magnou-Nortier, 'The Enemies of the Peace', pp. 60, 67–68.
64 Cox, 'The Ethics of War up to Thomas Aquinas', pp. 103–10; Russell, *The Just War in the Middle Ages*, pp. 18–20.
65 On the knowledge and reception of Gratian in Norway in this period, see Winroth, 'Decretum Gratiani and Eystein's *Canones Nidrosienses*'; Taylor, 'Bishops, War, and Canon Law', pp. 268–69; Bagge, *From Viking Stronghold to Christian Kingdom*, p. 202.

1250, one thing that is surprising is that the terms of the agreement at Kvitingsøy, as they have come down to us in the saga, are primarily aimed at or deal with the three main leaders: Inge, Hakon, and Filippus. For instance, the amnesty clause is not followed by any stipulations showing how disputes over redress between their supporters would be resolved going forward. Nor is there a sense that the peace and the amnesty were flexible enough to allow certain regions to be inside or outside of them at different times — a particularly surprising absence, given how sparsely populated the kingdom was. It is also surprising because of the need, at the periphery of each share, for individuals who could take up arms as well as lay them down, and resolve disputes and interactions relating to property, inheritance, and redress, without one of the contender's direct involvement. Though one could argue that the provincial laws provided such a framework, it is important to note that neither the laws of Gulathing nor those of Frostathing deal with cross-provincial or cross-factional matters, primarily because both texts anticipate a sole king. The terms of the agreement of 1208 then, conform in many ways with known European ideas and practices, but our knowledge of it has inevitably been shaped by the author of the saga and by the continued conflict.

As has become clear, agreements are often an expression of the right to determine what was legal and just in war and peace. As such, they are also in some ways frozen inside the times and circumstances in which they were concluded, and, one could argue, as a consequence, that their usefulness was quickly outstripped by subsequent events. However, transitioning from conflict to peace was about more than the terms of what was agreed. Consensus — the need to agree, confirm, guarantee, and enforce peace collectively and collaboratively — was one of the keys to resolving conflict in the medieval period. Face-to-face meetings were an important aspect of this, intended to foster cordial relations by plugging into the wider cultural and social context of the period, in which men showed their honour and status through feats of war and displays of camaraderie and largesse. Indeed, a main way to secure and maintain peace and to prevent future conflict was for rulers to foster personal relations with each other and their followers at these gatherings.[66] Hence, the final part of this chapter will focus on the location of the meeting and the gestures and symbolic acts surrounding the event, with the intention of examining the extent to which there was a real attempt at reconciliation and to foster future peace.

---

66 Benham, *Peacemaking in the Middle Ages*, p. 36.

The Location of Meetings

In 1208 the place of meeting (*fundr*) between Kings Filippus and Inge, and Earl Hakon Galen, seems to have taken place on the island of Kviting, the modern Kvitsøy, in the sea outside the town of Stavanger.[67] The island had perhaps been used as a meeting place already in the eleventh century, as Snorre records that King Olav Haraldsson and a certain Erling Skjalgsson were also reconciled there.[68] This accords well with what we know about meeting places elsewhere in medieval Europe. Sites on rivers — or as in 1208, at sea — seem to have been common meeting places, with favoured locations including islands, bridges, trees, and even boats anchored in the middle of rivers.[69] These locations reflected the fact that the participants claimed equal status, perceived or real, in their negotiations with each other. At first glance, this also seems to be the case in 1208, with the location of the meeting between Filippus, Inge, and Hakon Galen on the island of Kviting lying roughly halfway — as a ship sails — between the area of the Vik (with the towns Tønsberg and Oslo), held by Filippus, and the area of Trøndelag (with Nidaros), which was the heartland of Inge.[70] Furthermore, this halfway location makes sense from the perspective of who the mediators were: Bishop Nicholas of Oslo and Archbishop Tore of Nidaros. It is also significant that this location was in what we might think of as the conflict march, that is, the area which both kings were trying to control and where most of the military engagements occurred.[71] Earl Hakon held substantial possessions here, and hence his role was perhaps more central to the agreement and events than is often thought. Indeed, it might be important that the location of this meeting was not in the heart of this area, but rather on its southern edge, as if in a frontier region or 'march'. That the meeting took place in such a 'march' further tallies with what we know about negotiations and meetings between those claiming equal status in other contested areas, such as the Vexin between the duchy of Normandy and the kingdom of France.[72]

---

67 *Bǫglunga sǫgur* II, p. 116; *Soga om baglarar og birkebeinar*, p. 330.
68 *Heimskringla* 2, p. 48.
69 For some examples, see Benham, *Peacemaking in the Middle Ages*, pp. 21–37; Dalton, 'Sites and Occasions of Peacemaking', pp. 14–15; Voss, *Herrschertreffen im frühen und hohen Mittelalter*, pp. 38–87; Kolb, *Herrscherbegegnungen im Mittelalter*, pp. 58–71; Ganshof, *The Middle Ages: A History of International Relations*, p. 127.
70 A useful map can be found in Jón Viðar Sigurðsson and Riisøy, *Norsk Historie 800–1536*, p. 79.
71 The struggle over Bergen, which was situated in this 'conflict march', is a good example. For this, see *Soga om baglarar og birkebeinar*, pp. 292, 298–300, 318–20, 324.
72 On this see, Benham, *Peacemaking in the Middle Ages*, pp. 23–32. For an excellent study of this march, see Power, *The Norman Frontier*. On space more generally in Scandinavia, see Chapter 5.

However, while the meeting in 1208 may, on the basis of location, seem to be that of equals, the additional details about it tell a different story. For instance, the author of the saga divulges that at this meeting, King Filippus was anchored outside the island of Nød and King Inge and Earl Hakon were anchored at the island of Kviting. Men initially went between the two locations to negotiate before the kings met in person.[73] At this point, the author does not, in fact, say that the meeting took place at Kvitingsøy; rather, this is inferred from an earlier statement that the meeting would take place there. However, if this was also where Inge and Hakon were anchored, that is significant and indicates a different relationship than a meeting between equals. The model of such meetings and one of the best descriptions can be found in the *Five Books of Histories* by the eleventh-century Burgundian monk, Ralph Glaber, in which he details the peace conference of 1023 between the German Emperor Henry II (r. 1002–1024) and the king of the Franks, Robert II the Pious (r. 996–1031). Glaber records how the advisers of both kings regarded it as improper for either of the two kings 'to humiliate himself by crossing to the other as though to aid him'. The problem was so serious that for a while the kings considered going by boats and meeting mid-river.[74] Evidently, the act of crossing over to another participant was not desirable if a ruler wished to preserve his equality of status in the negotiations.[75]

With regard to the meeting in 1208, it is important to point out that the saga author, despite asserting that the two parties were anchored by different islands, never actually says that Filippus crossed onto the island of Kviting itself, and the statement that the meeting would take place there is rendered, in the shorter version at least, in the (dative) plural form of 'Hvitingseyjum' (lit. the white islands).[76] This seemingly indicates a small archipelago of the same name as the largest island within it, which might suggest that the actual meeting took place on an unnamed island that lay between the two islands where the parties were anchored. Nevertheless, since the manuscripts for both versions of the saga are not original, it is impossible to argue with any certainty what the exact status between the parties was, based on the language. Although it may seem unimportant whether or not the exact location of the meeting can be established, we know that to medieval and modern commentators alike, the site of the meeting directly influenced what would happen next in the peacemaking

---

73 *Bǫglunga sǫgur* II, p. 116; *Soga om baglarar og birkebeinar*, p. 330.
74 *The Five Books of Histories*, in *Rodulfus Glaber Opera*, pp. 108–09.
75 For a summary of similar conferences and the symbolism behind them, see Voss, *Herrschertreffen*, pp. 69, 75–77; Schneider, 'Mittelalterliche Verträge auf Brücken und Flüssen'; Benham, *Peacemaking in the Middle Ages*, pp. 21–37; Benham, 'Walter Map and Ralph Glaber'.
76 *Bǫglunga sǫgur* II, p. 116.

process, with that between equals being characterized by exchanges rather than one-sidedness.[77]

In 1208 there can be no doubt that, even if the location indicates equality, other details narrated about this meeting do not. For instance, the author of the saga states that at the meeting, the Birkibeinar had many more men than the Baglar faction, despite the fact that we know that equal negotiations are usually facilitated by an equal number of supporters, as described, most famously, by Nithard in the negotiations for the Treaty of Verdun.[78] The implied superiority of the Birkibeinar party conveyed through this detail is found also in the content of the agreement, with Filippus renouncing his royal title and swearing fealty to King Inge.[79] As discussed in Chapter 4, Inge and Hakon were in a better negotiating position. Moreover, Kåre Lunden has stressed their military superiority, presumably referring to the fact that the king and the earl spent the winter of 1207–1208 in Filippus's heartland at Tønsberg and the Vik, even though it should be noted that military success waxed and waned greatly leading up to the agreement.[80] Indeed, if the meeting had been one of Inge and Hakon trying to assert their advantageous position, a more suitable location would have been in the Vik, or even to have asked Filippus to come to the Trøndelag, because meetings between inferiors and superiors always took place inside one or the other's territory.[81] Likely, the location reflected the waxing and waning of their military successes, and in particular, the fact that neither side could 'win' the conflict.[82]

The relative status between participants in peacemaking was an important issue in Scandinavia as elsewhere in Europe. That it manifested itself not only in the locations of meetings is also evident. Take, as an example, what Snorre says about the partition of Norway between Harald Hardruler and Magnus the Good in the eleventh century: 'I [Magnus] give you half the realm of Norway with all its dues and taxes and all the possessions that belong to it on this condition, that you shall be as lawfully king as I everywhere in Norway'. This seemingly indicates that the two were equal. However, Snorre continues: 'But when we are all together, I shall have precedence in greetings and service and in seating. If there are three of us

---

77 Benham, *Peacemaking in the Middle Ages*, pp. 61–62.
78 *Bǫglunga sǫgur* II, p. 116; *Soga om baglarar og birkebeinar*, p. 330; Nithard, *Histoire des fils de Louis le Pieux*, Bk. IV, ch. 4. Translation in *Nithard's Histories* in *Carolingian Chronicles*, p. 171.
79 *Bǫglunga sǫgur* ii, pp. 116–17; *Soga om baglarar og birkebeinar*, p. 330.
80 Lunden, *Norge under Sverreætten*, pp. 158–59; *Bǫglunga sǫgur* II, pp. 110–12; *Soga om baglarar og birkebeinar*, pp. 326–27.
81 Benham, *Peacemaking in the Middle Ages*, pp. 44–62.
82 A similar context surrounds the partition of the English kingdom between Edmund Ironside and Knud in 1016, as well as that between King Stephen and Duke Henry (later Henry II) in 1153. For a discussion of the former, see Benham, 'Battle-Writing and Commemoration', pp. 28–30.

of this rank, I shall sit in the middle. I shall occupy the royal berth and dock. You shall also stand by and support our rule in the role in which we have set you, as the person in Norway that we had thought no one would have been as long as our skull had remained up above the ground'.[83] The portrayal here is that Magnus was higher in status than Harald. It is impossible not to sense that this reflected the situation as it was, or had been, in thirteenth-century Norway around the time that Snorre was compiling *Heimskringla*, rather than in the eleventh century, especially as he anticipates a third claimant. Particularly interesting is the idea that if there were three, Magnus, taking precedence in rank, would sit in the middle. We also find this in Saxo's description of the peace concluded between the three Danish rivals Svend, Knud, and Valdemar in 1157. In detailing the feast of Roskilde to celebrate the conclusion of peace and the division of the Danish kingdom, Saxo notes that Svend took a seat with Valdemar and Knud on either side, 'apparently a mark of respect for his seniority'.[84] Saxo's rather scornful tone here makes sense in the context of the time of composition — when Valdemar had consolidated his own position as sole king and ensured the survival of his dynasty in the succession. In contrast to these two descriptions of one king claiming precedence, in 1208, the author of *Bǫglunga sǫgur* states that King Inge sat down first and then the bishop and archbishop sat opposite him. King Filippus wanted to sit next to Inge but Hakon pushed him out of the way and sat between them.[85] If applying the model of seating arrangements offered by Snorre in *Heimskringla* and Saxo in the *Gesta Danorum* to events in 1208, the man highest in rank was neither Inge nor Filippus but rather the earl, Hakon Galen. We cannot, of course, know the motives of the author of *Bǫglunga sǫgur* and as such it is impossible to say what his intention with this description was, even though it is tempting to speculate that Hakon's position as the *de facto* military leader of the Birkibeinar meant that he was the real power broker.[86] In any case, the most interesting thing in all of this is that it seems that the location of the meeting and the tripartite division, indicating equality, are at odds with the context of the meeting and the request that Filippus renounce his title, which implies a relationship along the superior-inferior scale.

---

83 *Heimskringla* 3, p. 58.
84 GD, 14.18.3.
85 *Bǫglunga sǫgur*, p. 116; *Soga om baglarar og birkebeinar*, p. 330.
86 On the frequent disputes over seating arrangements, mostly at banquets, see Bullough, *Friends, Neighbours and Fellow-Drinkers*, pp. 13–15.

The Gestures and Ceremonies of Peacemaking

Perhaps the oddest thing about the context of the meeting at Kvitingsøy is that, as an event of reconciliation, it was not followed by many of the usual trappings we expect of these events, such as banquets, the giving of gifts, or other displays or ceremonies intended to show off the new, peaceful, relationship between the parties. In other words, there was in 1208 an almost complete lack of the displays of camaraderie through which great men usually fostered those personal relations with each other and their followers, that prevented conflict and ensured that any peace concluded was kept. As discussed elsewhere, Glaber's depiction of the lavish meeting in 1023 is the clearest example of this, but it can be seen even if we limit our view to conflicts and negotiations for peace between rival claimants to a kingdom.[87] John of Worcester, as an example, thought that the peace concluded between Edmund Ironside and Knud of Denmark in 1016 was guaranteed through an exchange of hostages, pledges, and oaths as well as garments and weapons.[88] Similarly, Henry of Huntingdon described the conclusion of peace between King Stephen and Duke Henry in 1153 at the end of the civil war in England as a lavish series of ceremonies. According to the chronicler, after the agreement had been 'strengthened by oaths', Duke Henry was received in Winchester and the *adventus* (the ceremonial entry), which was led by King Stephen, was glittering 'with bishops and famous men, and applauded by a countless multitude of the people'.[89] Henry was then adopted by the king as his son and made heir to the kingdom, before the parties relocated to London for a similarly splendid procession and ceremony. A while later, the two reconvened in Oxford, where, at the king's command, the English magnates paid homage and fealty to the duke as the heir, saving only the honour and faith which they owed to King Stephen during his lifetime.[90]

We can observe similarly opulent descriptions in the Scandinavian sources. Snorre, for instance, details how both Magnus the Good and Harald Hardruler, accompanied by sixty men each, held elaborate feasts and gave gifts, including gold, silver, weapons, and clothing, on two separate days following their agreement in the mid-1040s.[91] The partition of Denmark between Svend, Knud, and Valdemar in 1157 was confirmed by oaths, and Saxo further details how the claimants 'stretched their hands towards heaven and called on the Creator of the universe to heed their

---

87 For a summary of this, see Benham, 'Peace, Security and Deterrence', pp. 129–30.
88 *The Chronicle of John of Worcester*, II, pp. 492–93.
89 Henry, Archdeacon of Huntingdon, *Historia Anglorum*, IV, p. 37.
90 Henry, Archdeacon of Huntingdon, *Historia Anglorum*, IV, pp. 37–38.
91 *Heimskringla* 3, pp. 58–59. This description is very similar in format to that of the peace conference in 1023 by Glaber, for which see *The Five Books of Histories*, pp. 108–09.

covenant' while bishops threatened to excommunicate anyone who broke the pact.[92] Shortly afterwards a great feast was held in Roskilde, with a banquet, games, and music. However, although this feast was presumably intended to reflect the reconciliation and peace between the three rivals, it ultimately led to the murder of Knud.[93]

In comparison to these descriptions, the 1208 conclusion of peace seems low-key. According to the saga author, following the agreement, the parties 'swore the reconciliation oaths (*sættareiðana*). First, swore King Inge, Filippus and Hakon, and, thereafter, twelve landed men (*lendir menn*) and twelve district men (*sýslumenn*) on each side' — all indicating the equality among the contracting parties, the engagement of different sections of society in keeping the terms, and the creation of a complicated web of obligations that was not only individual but also communal.[94] The assembly was then closed 'and peace (*grið*) was agreed and mercy (*tryggðir*) given ... and the day after Filippus was betrothed to Kristin king's daughter'.[95] The failure of the saga author to elaborate on this or to detail any of the trappings of peacemaking is noteworthy. It certainly seems incorrect to argue that he had no interest in detailing such things, when several other events are described accompanied by significant displays and symbolic gestures. Take for instance, the portrayal of the election of King Guttorm in 1204 during which the four-year-old king girded Earl Hakon with a sword symbolizing the military function of his office and status in the realm.[96] Even more detailed is the capitulation of Bergen in 1207 to King Filippus, also discussed in Chapter 4. Here, in a depiction remarkably similar to the surrender of Jerusalem to the forces of Saladin in 1187, the author divulges that each man was allowed to leave with his goods and money, and that, as they did so, the Baglar men lined up along the road to watch. The most high-born women were grouped together and led out separately, and were given into the care of the archbishop, who had negotiated the capitulation.[97] At a second surrender of Bergen, it was similarly agreed that the Birkibeinar men would make a formal gesture of submission and come out 'without weapons and without outerwear'. Only a certain Dagfinn kept his helmet on, and the day after they had to swear fealty ('trúnaðareiða') to King Filippus.[98] As Althoff and others

---

92 *GD*, 14.17.15.
93 *GD*, 14.18.3; *Annales Ryenses*, p. 81; *Radulphi Nigri Chronica. The Chronicles of Ralph Niger*, p. 89. There is a large historiography on the feast in Roskilde. For two examples, see Kjær, 'Feasting with Traitors'; Malmros, 'Blodgildet i Roskilde historiografiskt belyst'.
94 Benham, 'Peace, Security and Deterrence', pp. 125–26.
95 *Bǫglunga sǫgur* II, p. 117; *Soga om baglarar og birkebeinar*, pp. 331–32.
96 *Soga om baglarar og birkebeinar* p. 284.
97 *Soga om baglarar og birkebeinar*, pp. 320–21. On the surrender of Jerusalem, see *Chronique d'Ernoul et de Bernard le Trésorier*, pp. 228–31.
98 *Bǫglunga sǫgur* II, 107–08; *Soga om baglarar og birkebeinar*, p. 325.

have shown, such ritual surrenders were common across the whole of the medieval West, and hence the details offered here reinforce the fact that the author was neither unaware of nor uninterested in what could be communicated visually.[99] In fact, it is likely that he understood — and possibly it suited his purpose of composition — the ambiguous message of these depictions in terms of being victor and vanquished, with the Birkibeinar appearing at once emasculated and shamed, but also as showing a humility to which the Baglar king, Filippus, had to respond with mercy so as not to strike at the heart of his own office as king.[100]

Given all this then, and also how little we know about the author and his purpose in writing, there are few possibilities for exploring the relative silence of the author on the displays of peacemaking. We can, of course, consider the date of composition. According to Magerøy, *Bǫglunga sǫgur* exists in two versions — a short version (A) and a fuller version (B) — and it was written in two parts: the first, covering the years 1202–1209, and a second covering the years after 1209 until the death of King Inge in 1217. The A-version covers only the first part while the B-version contains both.[101] The A-version was written down shortly after the last event it portrays, and as it contains none of the elaborations about seating arrangements in 1208 or the ritual surrenders in Bergen, one could speculate that the reason it is so concise is because it was written down as events happened.[102] This compares to other such narratives, including the late twelfth-century English chronicler Roger of Howden, whose *Gesta Regis Henrici Secundi* is often terse and was likely compiled as Roger went about his business in the service of King Henry II of England. However, in the *Chronica*, which was begun after 1192, Roger rewrote (but also continued) the work in the *Gesta*, adding details and commentary that cannot be found in the earlier work.[103]

Viewing *Bǫglunga sǫgur* in a similar light, the few visual signs of reconciliation could hence explain the brief depiction in the A-version but

---

99 Althoff, 'Das Privileg der deditio'; Althoff, 'Satisfaction'; Koziol, *Begging Pardon and Favor*, pp. 181–87; Mansfield, *The Humiliation of Sinners*, pp. 277–78.
100 On the issue of Christo-mimetic traits such as humility and love in peacemaking, see Benham, *Peacemaking in the Middle Ages*, pp. 96–97; Benham, 'Walter Map and Ralph Glaber', pp. 11–15. On the ambiguity of gestures of submission and rituals more generally, see Benham, *Peacemaking in the Middle Ages*, pp. 90–106; Althoff, 'The Variability of Rituals in the Middle Ages', pp. 71–88.
101 Magerøy, 'Bǫglunga Sǫgur', p. 61; Magerøy, 'Føreord til Soga om baglarar og birkebeinar', pp. 269–70.
102 Magerøy, 'Bǫglunga sǫgur', pp. 48–53 argues the opposite based on the superior chronology and narrative transmission, but the lack of references to the textual transmission means that this remains a contentious point. For a brief discussion of the date and provenance of Bǫglunga sǫgur, see Chapter 4.
103 One example of this the Treaty of Azay in 1189, for which see Benham, 'Writing Peace, Writing War'.

also the, fuller, B-version. As this latter version was written after 1217, when conflict broke out again, and the author continuously describes resistance to peace in the years between 1208 and 1217, one could argue that there simply was no need to depict elaborate displays of reconciliation between the parties in 1208 because peace proved elusive. Moreover, viewed in this way, the comments in the B-version about the jostling between Filippus and Hakon over the seating arrangements in 1208 — the only visual details divulged about the actual meeting — perhaps take on a deeper meaning, with the saga author continuously emphasizing their attempts to sow the seeds of discord in the years after the agreement. For instance, according to the author, Filippus refused to give up his royal seal, a key part of the agreement, which caused significant tension between the two sides, and attempts at further meetings for reconciliation resulted in the building of ships that became known as 'peace breakers or agreement wreckers'.[104] Similarly, the author states that Hakon not only attempted to make himself king but also often implied that Filippus had broken the agreement. In addition, the earl was implicated in a rebellion in Trøndelag shortly before his death.[105] While comments such as these likely reflected the continued competition for power between various potential claimants to the throne within the extended family of King Inge and Earl Hakon after 1217, especially through Inge's brother Skule and Hakon's son, Knut, they also reflect the date of composition of the two versions of the saga, as well as the author(s)'s perception of whether or not peace had in fact been achieved with the 1208 agreement. The latter is particularly important in thinking about what factors influenced how the author depicted the context in which that agreement was made and how peaceful relations were fostered. Compare, for instance, what Snorre says about peace following the eleventh-century agreement between Magnus the Good and Harald Hardruler: 'King Magnús and King Haraldr both ruled Norway the next winter after their settlement, and each of them had his own following. During the winter they travelled round Upplǫnd receiving banquets and were sometimes both together, and sometimes each on his own'. From this, it would appear that there was peace, for a time at least as Snorre also acknowledges that the harmony did not last long, but also that the two attempted to prevent conflict by fostering that personal relationship between them.[106] Hence, it likely made sense for Snorre, and to his audience, to set the agreement between Magnus and Harald within a context of peacemaking more generally and include all its trappings. Snorre may have gone one step further in describing the start of the civil wars period. In 1130, with no visual signs of reconciliation and

---

104 Bǫglunga sǫgur II, pp. 118–19, 124; Soga om baglarar og birkebeinar, pp. 336–37, 342–43.
105 Bǫglunga sǫgur II, pp. 122–25; Soga om baglarar og birkebeinar, pp. 340–43.
106 Heimskringla 3, p. 60.

no details given of the context of peacemaking, Snorre, nonetheless, stated that Harald Gille and Magnus (the Blind) 'ruled the land for some time in peace' following their agreement to divide the kingdom between them. Here, Snorre may have been more concerned about their actual intentions to keep any peace concluded, because he finishes by saying that this was done 'though their thoughts ran on very different lines'.[107] In the next chapter, he follows this up by saying that during the fourth winter after the agreement, 'each [king] invited the other to a banquet', though without divulging whether either banquet actually happened, 'and yet battle was always on the point of breaking out among their followers'.[108] Snorre is thus clear that hostile tension and intention was enough to not express this agreement, and hence the relationship between the kings, through displays of peace and reconciliation. By contrast, Bǫglunga sǫgur does not seem to depict any stages of peace over the whole of the realm. Only once does the author mention that there was peace, but specifies that this applied only to the part which Filippus held, and he seemingly uses it to show that Filippus was a good Christian king who dispensed justice wisely among the local people.[109] The statement stands in stark contrast to his depiction of the parts held by Inge and Hakon, which are described as conflict-ridden throughout the period, and also of the lack of peaceful relations between the candidates. Hence, while modern commentators frequently describe the period following the meeting on the island of Kviting until Inge's death in 1217 as one of peace, it is less certain that contemporaries, or at least the author of Bǫglunga sǫgur, viewed it that way.

Conclusion

By setting the reconciliation of 1208 into a context of Scandinavian and European agreements in the period 800 to 1250, and comparing what is recorded in this saga to other similar narratives and practices, it is possible to draw a number of conclusions. Firstly, that the partition agreement of 1208 demonstrates parallels with other partition agreements in the period 800–1250 in Scandinavia and Europe. Like those other agreements, it was based on the principles of possession, resources, and supporters, reflecting the military (neither side could 'win'), legal (possession really was nine-tenths of the law), and economic (equity sustained and rewarded leaders and their immediate followers) contexts. Secondly, that it provides the earliest evidence of an amnesty clause in any Scandinavian agreement or treaty. This evidence is important given the great debate

---

107 *Heimskringla* 3, p. 170.
108 *Heimskringla* 3, pp. 170–71.
109 *Bǫglunga sǫgur* II, p. 127; *Soga om baglarar og birkebeinar*, p. 345.

among Norwegian historians, in particular, over state formation in this period. However, the amnesty clause also reveals a dissimilarity with other partition agreements in that the denial of redress was not followed by a framework setting out how disputes between the factions or between the rulers might be resolved going forward. In other words, the agreement is depicted in the saga as resolving matters at the highest level and as providing redress in the form of the marriage to Filippus, but it made no provisions for the future or for supporters at the lower, community, level. This is further evident in the author's depiction of the circumstances in which the agreement was concluded, with few signs of those festivities that tended to accompany face-to-face meetings, and which were intended to foster peaceful, collaborative relations and collective action. Thirdly, that the author wrote in a moral and legal context, demonstrating significant familiarity with the European intellectual milieu and the development of canon and Roman law. Moreover, in its longer version at least, he wrote the saga from a retrospective vantage point. This authorial context significantly shapes what he tells us about this agreement and the transition, or not, from conflict to peace. It is evident, for instance, that his attempts to square the Christian unitary idea of kingship and his depiction of two factions — the Baglar and the Birkibeinar — with a tripartite division obfuscate the fact that, by its very existence, the agreement to divide the kingdom recognized the authority and jurisdiction of each ruler.[110]

The agreement of 1208 did not bring a lasting peace to Norway, if we conceive of peace as lasting forever and covering the whole of the kingdom. All the same, nor does the author state that the agreement broke down completely. Instead, he reveals that the agreement brought a peace that was interspersed with conflict, or threats of conflict, over particular issues and confined to specific areas. He further demonstrates how issues were resolved, highlighting that both the Church and secular rulers understood how to use and implement different practical instruments of law in various ways at different points to justify and to enforce action between different authorities or regions.[111] Such descriptions tally with what we know about the conceptualization of war and peace from other European agreements, in which specific areas or individuals could be in or outside the peace at specific times without breaking the overall agreement. Indeed, reprisals — whether perceived as raids and seizures to achieve redress, as threats of unilateral termination of agreement, as economic blockades or sanctions, as temporary occupation of territory, or as withholding

---

110 On recognition, see Benham, *International Law in Europe*, pp. 21–22.
111 As an example, see the dispute over Hakon's attempt to assume a royal title, which resulted in a settlement between Inge and Hakon that each would inherit the other's share of the kingdom in the event of death. *Bǫglunga sǫgur* II, pp. 124–25; *Soga om baglarar og birkebeinar*, pp. 340–42.

performance of obligations — demonstrate that the medieval peace was modular and that not every hostile act was a renewal of war.[112] Piecing this together is immensely tricky to do with only a single primary source available, and requires the evidence to be read against the grain, using a comparative approach, and a clear understanding of what to look for. Exploring the evidence from a perspective of how peace and agreements were perceived and practised in Europe, then, can offer alternative interpretations on the well-known history of the Nordic civil wars and beyond.

---

112 Benham, *International Law in Europe*, pp. 157–58, 235–36.

Works Cited

Primary Sources

Annales Bertiniani, ed. by G. Waitz, MGH SRG, 5 (Hannover, 1883)
Annales Fuldenses, ed. by Friedrich Kurze, MGH SRG, 7 (Hannover, 1891)
Annales Ryenses. in *Annales Danici medii ævi*, ed. by Ellen Jørgensen (Copenhagen: Selskabet for udgivelse af kilder til Dansk historie, 1920)
The Annals of St-Bertin, trans. by Janet L. Nelson (Manchester: Manchester University Press, 1991)
Bǫglunga sǫgur, 2 vols, ed. by Hallvard Magerøy (Oslo: Solum Forlag, 1988)
The Chronicle of John of Worcester, 3 vols, ed. by R. R. Darlington and P. McGurk (Oxford: Clarendon Press, 1995–1998)
Chronique d'Ernoul et de Bernard le Trésorier, ed. by M. L. de Mas Latrie (Paris, 1871)
Danakonunga sögur, Skjoldunga saga, Knýtlinga saga, Ágrip af sögu danakonunga, ed. by Bjarni Guðnason, Íslenzk fornrit, 35 (Reykjavík: Hið íslenzka fornritafélag, 1982)
The Digest of Justinian, 4 vols, ed. by Theodore Mommsen and trans. by Alan Watson (Philadelphia: University of Pennsylvania Press, 1985)
DD = *Diplomatarium Danicum*, ed. by Herluf Nielsen and others (Copenhagen: Munksgaard, 1938–)
Diplomatic Documents Preserved in the Public Record Office, 1101–1279, ed. by Pierre Chaplais (London: H.M. Stationery Office, 1964)
Die Gesetze der Angelsachsen, 3 vols, ed. by Felix Liebermann (Halle, 1903–1916)
The Five Books of Histories, in *Rodulfus Glaber Opera*, ed. and trans. by John France, Niethard Bulst, and Paul Reynolds (Oxford: Oxford University Press, 1989)
GD = Saxo Grammaticus, *Gesta Danorum: The History of the Danes*, ed. by Peter Fisher and Karsten Friis-Jensen (Oxford: Oxford University Press, 2015)
Hákonar saga Hákonarsonar, ed. by Albert Kjær (Oslo: Kjeldeskriftfondet, 1985)
Heimskringla I–III ed. by Bjarni Aðalbjarnarson (Reykjavík: Hið íslenzka fornritafélag, 1941–1951)
Heimskringla 1–3, ed. by Alison Finlay and Anthony Faulkes (London: Viking Society for Northern Research, 2011–2015)
Helmold von Bosau Slawenchronik, ed. by Bernhard Schmeidler, revised by Heinz Stoob (Darmstadt: Wissenschaftliche Buchgesellschaft, 1973)
Henry, Archdeacon of Huntingdon, *Historia Anglorum* trans. by Diana Greenway (Oxford: Oxford University Press, 1996)
Knytlingasaga: The History of the Kings of Denmark, trans. by Hermann Pálsson and Paul Edwards (Odense: Odense University Press, 1986)
Le Liber Censuum de l'eglise romaine, 3 vols, ed. by Paul Fabre and L. Duchesne (Paris, 1910)
'Nithard's Histories', in *Carolingian Chronicles*, trans. by Bernhard Walter Scholz (Ann Arbor: University of Michigan Press, 1972)

Nithard, *Histoire des fils de Louis le Pieux*, trans. by Philippe Lauer (Paris, 1926)

Norske middelalderdokumenter, ed. by Sverre Bagge, Synnøve Holstad Smedsdal, and Knut Helle (Bergen: Universitetsforlaget, 1973)

Radulphi Nigri Chronica. The Chronicles of Ralph Niger, ed. by Robert Anstruther (London, 1851)

'Saga of Magnus Erlingsson', in *Heimskringla. History of the Kings of Norway*, trans. with introduction by Lee M. Hollander (Austin: University of Texas Press, 2011)

Snorri Sturluson. *Heimskringla, Volume III*, trans. by Alison Finlay and Anthony Faulkes (London: Viking Society for Northern Research, 2015)

Soga om baglarar og birkebeinar. in *Noregs kongesoger*, vol. 3, ed. by Halvdan Koht and Gunnar Pedersen (Oslo: Det Norske Samlaget, 1979)

Soga om Håkon Håkonsson. in *Noregs Kongesoger*, vol. 4, ed. by Kristian Audne and Hallvard Magerøy (Oslo: Det Norske Samlaget, 1979)

'The Stateman's Book of John of Salisbury, Being the Fourth, Fifth and Sixth Books, and Selections from the Seventh and Eighth Books', of the *Policraticus*, trans. by John Dickinson (New York: Alfred A. Knopf, 1927)

The Treatise on the Laws and Customs of the Realm of England Commonly Called Glanvill, ed. and trans. by G. D. G. Hall (Oxford: Oxford University Press, 1993)

'Treaty of Meerssen (870)', in *MGH Capit. II*, ed. by A. Boretius and V. Krause (Hannover, 1897), pp. 193–95

Die Urkunden Friedrichs I, 4 vol., ed. by Heinrich Appelt (Hannover: Hahn, 1975–1990) 'Canons of the Third Lateran Council 1179', at <http://www.papalencyclicals.net/Councils/ecum11.htm> [accessed 10 October 2017]

William of Newburgh, *The History of English Affairs, Book II*, ed. by Peter G. Walsh and M. J. Kennedy (Oxford: Liverpool University Press, 2007)

Secondary Studies

Althoff, Gerd, 'Das Privileg der deditio. Formen gütlicher Konfliktbeendigung in der mittelalterlichen Adelsgesellschaft', in *Spielregeln der Politik im Mittelalter: Kommunikation in Frieden und Fehde*, ed. by Gerd Althoff (Darmstadt: Primus, 1997), pp. 99–125

——, 'Satisfaction: Amicable Settlement of Conflicts in the Middle Ages', in *Ordering Medieval Society. Perspectives on Intellectual and Practical Modes of Shaping Social Relations*, ed. by Bernhard Jussen and trans. by Pamela Selwyn (Philadelphia: University of Philadelphia Press, 2001), pp. 273–79

——, 'The Variability of Rituals in the Middle Ages', in *Medieval Concepts of the Past: Ritual, Memory, Historiography*, ed. by Gerd Althoff, Johannes Fried, and Patrick J. Geary (Cambridge: Cambridge University Press, 2002), pp. 71–88

Bagge, Sverre, *From Gang Leader to the Lord's Anointed: Kingship in Sverris saga and Hákonar saga Hákonarsonar* (Odense: Odense University Press, 1996)

——, *From Viking Stronghold to Christian Kingdom: State Formation in Norway, c. 900–1350* (Copenhagen: Museum Tusculanum Press, 2010)

——, 'Samkongedømme og enekongedømme', *Historisk Tidsskrift* (N), 54 (1975), 239–74

Benham, Jenny, 'Battle-Writing and Commemoration: The Transition from Conflict to Peace', in *Writing Battles: New Perspectives on Warfare and Memory in Medieval Europe*, ed. by Máire Ní Mhaonaigh, Rory Naismith, and Elizabeth Ashman Rowe (London: Bloomsbury Press, 2020), pp. 27–38

——, *International Law in Europe, 700–1200* (Manchester: Manchester University Press, 2021)

——, *Peacemaking in the Middle Ages: Principles and Practice* (Manchester: Manchester University Press, 2011)

——. 'Peace, Security and Deterrence', in *A Cultural History of Peace in the Medieval Age 800–1450*, ed. by Walter P. Simons (London: Bloomsbury Press, 2020), pp. 119–34

——, 'The Treaty of Verdun, 843', in *Encyclopedia of Diplomacy*, ed. by Gordon Martel (London: Wiley-Blackwell, 2018)

——, 'Walter Map and Ralph Glaber: Intertextuality and the Construction of Memories of Peacemaking', in *Citation, Intertextuality and Memory in the Middle Ages and Renaissance, 2: Cross-Disciplinary Perspectives on Medieval Culture*, ed. by Giuliano di Bacco and Yolanda Plumley (Liverpool: University of Liverpool Press, 2013), pp. 6–17

——, 'Writing Peace, Writing War: Roger of Howden and Saxo Grammaticus Compared', in *History and Intellectual Culture in the Long Twelfth Century: The Scandinavian Connection*, ed. by Sigbjørn Sønnesyn, Mia Münster-Swendsen, and Thomas Heebøll-Holm (Turnhout: Brepols, 2017), pp. 272–95

Bjørgo, Narve, 'Samkongedøme og einekongedøme', *Historisk Tidsskrift* (N), 49 (1970), 1–33

Bullough, Donald A., *Friends, Neighbours and Fellow-Drinkers: Aspects of Community and Conflict in the Early Medieval West*, H. M. Chadwick Memorial Lectures, 1 (Cambridge: Department of Anglo-Saxon, Norse, and Celtic, 1991)

Cox, Rory, 'The Ethics of War up to Thomas Aquinas', in *The Oxford Handbook of Ethics of War*, ed. by Seth Lazar and Helen Frowe (Oxford: Oxford University Press, 2018), pp. 99–121

Dalton, Paul, 'Sites and Occasions of Peacemaking in England and Normandy, c. 900–c. 1150', *Haskins Society Journal*, 16 (2005), 12–26

DeVries, Kelly, 'Medieval Mercenaries: Methodology, Definitions and Problems', in *Mercenaries and Paid Men: The Mercenary Identity in the Middle Ages*, ed. by John France (Leiden: Brill, 2008), pp. 43–56

Diggelmann, Lindsay, 'Marriage as Tactical Response: Henry II and the Royal Wedding of 1160', *English Historical Review*, 119 (2004), 954–64

——, 'Marriage, Peace, and Enmity in the Twelfth Century', *Common Knowledge*, 22 (2016), 237–55

Ekrem, Inger, and Lars Boje Mortensen, *Historia Norwegie*, ed. and translated by Peter Fisher (Copenhagen: Museum Tusculanum Press, 2006)

Ganshof, F, L., 'The Genesis and Significance of the Treaty of Verdun (843)', in *The Carolingians and the Frankish Monarchy*, trans. by J. Sondheimer (London: Longman, 1971), pp. 289–302

——, *The Middle Ages: A History of International Relations* (London: Harper & Row, 1971)

Géraud, Hercule, 'Les routiers au douzième siècle', *Bibliothèque de l'école des chartes*, 3 (1842), 125–47

Haltern, Ulrich, *Was bedeutet Souveränität?* (Tübingen: Niermeyer, 2007)

Helle, Knut, *Norge blir en stat 1130–1319*, 2nd edn (Bergen: Universitetsforlaget, 1974)

Hermanson, Lars, 'How to Legitimate Rebellion and Condemn Usurpation of the Crown: Discourses of Fidelity and Treason in the *Gesta Danorum* of Saxo Grammaticus', in *Disputing Strategies in Medieval Scandinavia*, ed. by Kim Esmark, Lars Hermanson, Hans Jacob Orning, and Helle Vogt (Leiden: Brill, 2013), pp. 107–40

Jón Viðar Sigurðsson and Anne Irene Riisøy, *Norsk historie 800–1536* (Oslo: Det norske samlaget, 2011)

Kjær, Lars, 'Feasting with Traitors: Royal Banquets as Rituals and Texts in High Medieval Scandinavia', in *Rituals, Performatives, and Political Order in Northern Europe, c. 650–1350*, ed. by Wojtek Jezierski, Lars Hermanson, Hans Jacob Orning, and Thomas Småberg (Turnhout: Brepols, 2015), pp. 269–94

Kolb, Werner, *Herrscherbegegnungen im Mittelalter* (Frankfurt: Herbert and Cie Lang AG, Buchhandlung Antiquariat, 1988)

Koziol, Geoffrey, *Begging Pardon and Favor: Ritual and Political Order in Early Medieval France* (Ithaca, NY: Cornell University Press, 1992)

Lunden, Kåre, *Norge under Sverreætten*, Norges historie, vol. 3 (Drammen: J. W. Cappelens forlag, 1993)

——, *Økonomi og samfunn: Synspunkt på økonomisk historie* (Oslo: Universitetsforlaget, 1972)

Lyons, Scott W., 'Ineffective Amnesty: The Legal Impact on Negotiating the End to Conflict', *Wake Forest Law Review*, 47 (2013), 799–842

Magerøy, Hallvard, 'Bǫglunga sǫgur', in *Medieval Scandinavia: an Encyclopaedia*, ed. by Phillip Pulsiano (New York: Taylor & Francis, 1993), pp. 60–61

——. 'Føreord til Soga om baglarar og birkebeinar', in *Norges kongesagaer* 3, trans. by Dag Gundersen and Finn Hødnebø (Oslo: Gyldendal, 1979), pp. 269–70

Magnou-Nortier, Elisabeth, 'The Enemies of the Peace: Reflections on a Vocabulary, 500–1100', in *The Peace of God: Social Violence and Religious Response in France around the Year 1000*, ed. by Thomas Head and Richard Landes (Ithaca, NY: Cornell University Press, 1992), pp. 58–80

Malmros, Rikke, 'Blodgildet i Roskilde historiografiskt belyst', *Scandia*, 45 (1979), 43–66

Mansfield, Mary C., *The Humiliation of Sinners: Public Penance in Thirteenth-Century France* (Ithaca, NY: Cornell University Press, 2005)

McEvoy, Kieran and Louise Mallinder, 'Amnesties in Transition: Punishment, Restoration, and the Governance of Mercy', *Journal of Law and Society*, 39 (2012), 410–40

Orning, Hans Jacob, 'Conflict and Social (Dis)order in Norway, c. 1030–1160', in *Disputing Strategies in Medieval Scandinavia*, ed. by Kim Esmark, Lars Hermanson, Hans Jacob Orning, and Helle Vogt (Leiden: Brill, 2013), pp. 45-82

——, *Unpredictability and Presence: Norwegian Kingship in the High Middle Ages*, trans. by Alan Crozier (Leiden: Brill, 2008)

Power, Daniel J., *The Norman Frontier in the Twelfth and Early Thirteenth Centuries* (Cambridge: Cambridge University Press, 2004)

Russell, Frederick H., *The Just War in the Middle Ages* (Cambridge: Cambridge University Press, 1975)

Scharf, Michael P., 'From the eXile Files: An Essay on Trading Justice for Peace', *Washington and Lee Law Review*, 63 (2006), 339–76

Schneider, Reinhard, 'Mittelalterliche Verträge auf Brücken und Flüssen (und zur Problematik von Grenzgewässern)', *Archiv für Diplomatik*, 23 (1977), 1–24

Steiger, Heinhard, 'Peace Treaties from Paris to Versailles', in *International Law in European History. From the Late Middle Ages to World War One*, ed. by Randall Lesaffer (Cambridge: Cambridge University Press, 2004), pp. 59–102

Taylor, Louisa, 'Bishops, War, and Canon Law. The Military Activities of Prelates in High Medieval Norway', *Scandinavian Journal of History*, 45 (2020), 263–85

Tollefsen, Thomas Malo, 'Scandinavian Kingship Transformed: Succession, Acquisition and Consolidation in the Twelfth and Thirteenth Centuries' (Unpublished Doctoral Thesis, University of Cardiff, 2020)

Voss, Ingrid, *Herrschertreffen im frühen und hohen Mittelalter* (Cologne: Böhlau, 1987)

Watkins, John, *After Lavinia: A Literary History of Pre-Modern Marriage Diplomacy* (Ithaca, NY: Cornell University Press, 2017)

Winroth, Anders, 'Decretum Gratiani and Eystein's *Canones Nidrosienses*', in *Archbishop Eystein as Legislator: The European Connection*, ed. by Tore Iversen (Trondheim: Tapir Academic Press, 2011), pp. 73–85

Wærdahl, Randi Bjørshol, *Incorporation and Integration of the King's Tributary Lands into the Norwegian Realm c. 1195–1397* (Leiden: Brill, 2011)

Ødegaard, Marie, 'State Formation, Administrative Areas, and Thing Sites in the Borgarthing Law Province, Southeast Norway', *Journal of the North Atlantic*, 5 (2013), 42–63

PART III

European Comparisons

GERD ALTHOFF, WARREN C. BROWN, AND
STEPHEN D. WHITE

Introduction to Part Three

Finally, Part Three of this book positions the Scandinavian 'civil war' experience in a broader comparative context by discussing the role of network politics and the complex, perspectival nature of internal war and conflict as it played out in other European realms with an evidently much richer and more differentiated landscape of historical sources. The chapters in this section are all written by expert non-Scandinavian scholars of medieval conflict, whose earlier works have fuelled our thinking about socio-political competition and internal war in the Nordic world.

In Chapter 8 Gerd Althoff looks at networks in action by discussing the mostly unwritten norms and customs that served to regulate behaviour in conflict and cooperation within the aristocratic warrior society of the Holy Roman Empire. Among other things, Althoff analyses the role of so-called *coniurationes*: sworn associations established for the purpose of specific political goals, which could be directed against even kings and emperors. Such oath-bound *ad hoc* formations contributed to escalating conflicts by binding men tighter together and adding a secret dimension to politics, but they also functioned as a balance to the dominance of rulers. In a detailed review of ritual procedures related to public peacemaking in Germany, Althoff sheds light back on events discussed in Parts One and Two of this volume. That goes, for instance, for the role of mediators and the free, unmolested withdrawal granted to surrendering forces, which are described in both German and Norwegian sources. Likewise, the specific meaning of Danish rulers' ceremonial surrender to German kings and emperors, discussed in Chapter 3, is clarified by Althoff's explication of the uses and symbolic language of this ritual among the German nobles. The main conclusions of this chapter — that conflict and violence was contained by norms and did not undermine the stability of aristocratic society, and that kings' ability to dominate and punish members of the ruling class was limited as well — seem indeed to find an echo in the Scandinavian case.

In Chapter 9, Stephen D. White offers a novel reading of the so-called 'rebellions' in twelfth- and early thirteenth-century England, further developing Robert Bartlett's 'revisionist model' of rebellions not as violations to be punished by kings, but as part of legitimate opposition and the political struggles of the day. Clerical Latin authors of the time evidently sought to impose a Christian-royalist ideology of kingship on contemporaries, by systematically representing armed opposition to English kings as treacherous rebellion. Here the parallels to Scandinavian Latin chroniclers are striking. In verse and prose histories written in the vernacular (Anglo-Norman or Old French) from the same period, however, most such conflicts were simply termed 'war' and constituted means by which elites — kings and magnates alike — pursued and fought over perfectly justifiable issues of vengeance and lawful redress. White's chapter thus brilliantly summarizes the main argument of this book: that war, civil war, rebellion, succession dispute, etc. should not automatically be seen as challenging or indeed undermining the socio-political order, but rather be conceived of as the very vehicles through which the polycentric order of medieval polities and politics played out.

In the concluding Chapter 10, Warren C. Brown takes a sweeping comparative view of the book's contributions as a whole. Reading the seven chapters on Norway, Denmark, and Sweden along with the two on Germany and England/Normandy in a panoramic context of European history from the Carolingians to the High and Late Middle Ages, Brown discusses the fundamental question: from the specific perspective of the book's problematic about power, networks, socio-political competition, and internal war, does the Nordic realm belong in the general history of medieval Europe? Reflecting critically on commonalities as well as differences between Scandinavia and the European world farther south, Brown's answer is clearly in the affirmative. However, in course of the discussion, Brown also points out new research problems that should engage historians in the coming years — problems about how far the Scandinavian cultural and political 'interior' extended into the surrounding regions; about the perceptions and practices of 'violence' in a society where political stability presumably required a certain amount of tension and potential use of force; and about the complicated relation between the norms of a network-driven society and those of an incipient king-centred order. As for the latter — the king-centred idea of order — it obviously arrived later in the north than in regions sharing the direct legacy of Rome and the Carolingians. Yet, even in the Scandinavian game of thrones, driven (according to the studies presented in this volume) by network dynamics and constant crisis, such an idea could — and would — increasingly be mobilized by players in the power field to legitimize centralized rule and monopolization of force.

GERD ALTHOFF

8. Political Networks in Conflict

A German Perspective

The new approach of understanding the civil wars in Norway from 1130 to 1240 mainly as a result of political networks in action, needs, wants, and deserves comparison with other societies separated in time and/or space. This comparison must concentrate on similarities as well as on differences. Such an approach promises deeper insights into long-lasting, widespread phenomena and their impact on societal developments. But even short-term, unique behaviour is of interest because it hints at an exceptional situation which causes extreme solutions. To concentrate such a comparison on societies in conflict makes sense, specifically because in conflict most of the elements which make a society function become visible. One must look at escalating activities, institutions, and rules, as well as at de-escalating ones.

Every observation in this field must take into account that behaviour in the medieval period was guided by patterns and customs which were mostly not fixed in writing but nevertheless had a strong normative quality, because societies were used to following such *consuetudines*. These were fixed only in the minds of people, and had to be developed and agreed upon at special gatherings. Gathering, counselling, and decision-making face to face seem to have been an omnipresent and extremely important practice in medieval societies. It is especially necessary to understand the rules of this power game, by which one means the strategies and tactics which led to success in these procedures. To reconstruct the observed or even violated rules with the help of descriptions and judgements about behaviour is not an easy business today. One must look for situations in which a behaviour can be observed, which is praised or condemned by authors as right or wrong. If one finds similar examples of the same behaviour on a larger scale, the conclusion is justified that this behaviour was guided by rules. It is self-evident that such rules were also broken,

Gerd Althoff (althofg@uni-muenster.de) is professor emeritus of medieval history in the Cluster of Excellence 'Religion and Politics', Universität Münster.

just as modern laws are infringed. Nevertheless, they existed and gave communication and interaction its necessary frame.

This chapter intends to describe such rules of power games in the German realm of the high Middle Ages, which, to some degree, has a more differentiated landscape of sources than Scandinavia in the same period.[1] At different times various scholars have produced historiographies with descriptions of and judgements about the same events. The different perspectives they explicitly and implicitly employ allow for a glance at underlying rules and customs. That means we are able to see problems from different points of view, which is made possible by source criticism and multiple perspectives. In most works the perspective of a king is the predominant one; nevertheless, ecclesiastical voices, voices of noble families or even of political networks are also audible and bring their perspectives to bear. Therefore we are able to describe the German noble warrior society from different angles, focusing on their behaviour in conflicts. These descriptions may offer possibilities for comparison with Scandinavian examples in order to learn from the similarities as well as the differences. To give my comparison a structure I will concentrate on questions about socio-political networks: norms, rules, and customs; escalation and de-escalation strategies; and peacemaking rituals.

Which Types of Networks Became Active in Germany in the Case of a Conflict?

I use the term network to characterize a loosely structured group of persons who work together and support each other in various fields and opportunities, without a higher developed organization and exactly formulated rights and duties. Medieval warrior society was mostly structured by personal bonds which established kin-groups, friendships, sworn associations, and feudal relations between lord and man. All these groups and a combination of them can also be understood as networks, but the term lacks a precise definition for the Middle Ages. The personal bonds in all these associations or networks include the fundamental obligation to support the other participants in all their concerns. Medieval societies in many fields were satisfied with such unspecified norms: details and exceptions

---

1 When writing this chapter, I simultaneously translated some of my former German articles concerned with the role of rules and rituals for the functioning of order in the German realm. This collection of articles and book-chapters has now been published in English as *Rules and Rituals in Medieval Power Games: A German Perspective*. The book offers several perspectives and many references to examples regarding the wide field of societies in conflict, which are partly discussed here as well. This article tries to give a summarizing overview of this field, using some guiding questions which are also answered in the book in a broader frame.

remained unsettled and open questions. Through gatherings of a single group and seeking advice from counsellors, one tried to establish consent on what to do in an individual case, only when it became necessary. It seems to be a characteristic of mostly oral societies to live with such general norms, while modern societies are aware that the devil is in the detail and therefore try to establish norms and rules which also provide details and to fix them in writing.

Apart from this, an exact hierarchy of the bonds mentioned is contested. Private bonds like kinship and friendship were often valued more highly than feudal relations even with a king.[2] On the one hand, kings demanded prerogatives for their relations with their followers. All this had a great impact on the behaviour of all players, if in case of conflict people requested support from those to whom they were bound. Furthermore, this made conflicts dangerous and damaging because the groups involved became very large.

On the other hand, conflicts brought problems for many people because they had bonds to all parties in the conflict. Without exaggeration, one can say that conflicts produced a strong insecurity with respect to social bonds, because the old order could be deeply disturbed by new enmities. In other words, everybody had to think about a new order of their friends and enemies if some of them became embroiled in conflicts. This situation entailed special consequences, and indeed we find some of these consequences in many descriptions of conflicts.

The best examples can be found in conflicts with kings, because sources report very often that participants in the king's court-diets separated when decisions in the royal assemblies became controversial. This behaviour was a strong sign that a severe conflict had arisen. In such cases, the authors use three terms to describe the following activities of the disappearing nobles: *conventicula* (secret gatherings), *conspiratio* (planning by conspiring), and *coniuratio* (a sworn association with a specific goal). In secret gatherings members of the noble elites planned future activities, especially, but not only, against the king. What made their doing so dangerous was that they became united by oath to a specific goal and this new bond was perceived as stronger than any other bonds the participants had from earlier times.[3] It is worth briefly characterizing the different characteristics of this network in respect to networks of relatives, friends, and followers which gave their members much more freedom to be inactive, neutral, or involved in the ending of the conflict in question.

The sworn association strongly bound its members by oath to a concrete goal of the highest priority. The sworn bond claimed a leading

---

2 Cf. Althoff, *Family, Friends and Followers*, pp. 65–101.
3 For the importance of sworn associations for the functioning of medieval societies, see the selected articles of Oexle, 'Die Wirklichkeit und das Wissen'.

quality in comparison with all other duties their members had from prior obligations. While the mentioned bonds of kinship, friendship, and feudal relations left open the question of hierarchy and remained ambiguous in this respect, the bond of a *coniuratio* demanded the whole person with all their abilities. This quality made it possible for *coniurationes* to practise special forms of political contact even with their royal opponents: they negotiated through representatives with the king's own representatives or with the king himself. In these negotiations they used a completely different approach to the one that advisers of kings were allowed to use. They were able to confront a king with his misdeeds, mistakes, and even crimes.

I will give one of the many possible examples from the reign of the Salian King Henry IV, against whom sworn associations in Saxony made especially successful opposition. When King Henry refused to hold council with a delegation of Saxon bishops and nobles and made them wait a whole day outside his palace at Goslar, they took this as an unbearable offence, met on the same night in a church and united in a *coniuratio*.[4] As a next step they convened a gathering of the entire Saxon political community. Most of the participants knew in advance that they would come together to deliberate the misdeeds and even crimes of the king. Duke Otto of Northeim, who had had especially bad experiences with King Henry, is said to have explicitly admonished all participants in an inauguration speech to tell the others openly what injustice the king had inflicted on them. So one after the other — archbishops and bishops, dukes, counts, nobles, and even free men — stood up and complained about the king's misdeeds, relating their personal experiences. When the Saxons had finished their accusations, according to the sources, they expanded their *coniuratio* considerably and promised each other to resist the king until death and to force him to change his behaviour.[5]

They went even further, by sending messengers to him in order to fling the accusations about his lifestyle and politics into the king's face. The sources underline the open and aggressive speech of these messengers. 'He should destroy the castles he had built everywhere in Saxony to annihilate the Saxons; he should give satisfaction to the princes, whose possessions he had confiscated without a judgement of a law court; he should leave Saxony for a period of time, where he had lived since childhood in idleness and laziness, and visit other parts of his realm. He should drive away the mob, by whose advice he had disturbed the whole country, from the court and he should leave the business to the princes, to whom it belonged.

---

4 This example is taken from Althoff, 'Conventiculum, conspiratio, coniuratio'; for the quoted source see Schmale, *Brunos Buch vom Sachsenkrieg*, pp. 220–23; Lampert von Hersfeld, 'Annales', pp. 1–304; a. 1073, pp. 148–49.
5 Schmale, *Brunos Buch vom Sachsenkrieg*, pp. 222–27.

And he should dismiss the crowd of concubines, with whom he cohabited without blushing'.

This is an extreme example of how representatives of a *coniuratio* could speak with a king. This way, they achieved a climbdown from the king and optimized the conditions for peace. A *coniuratio* was the most effective form of protecting one's interests. It worked as a network and as a group of people with the same goals and the same responsibilities, despite the fact that not all participants were of equal status and rank. It was a cooperative association which united people from the highest rank with many others by oath in order to realize a concrete goal. The sources mention several cases in which kings tried to convince leading figures to leave a *coniuratio* and in this way to save their positions and to sacrifice their co-*coniuratores*. But this never worked. We will later see that these *coniurationes* were also responsible for the peaceful ending of most of the conflicts which avoided a harsher punishment of the former enemies.

I will continue to try and elucidate the first question with the help of concrete stories taken from the sources. The *Historia Welforum*, the history of the famous noble dynasty of the Welfs, written by an unknown cleric in the 1170s, gives a detailed insight into the many conflicts the Welfs were involved in. Several times the author starts his narrative of a conflict by mentioning the same procedure: 'Duke Welf gathered his friends, relatives and followers and told them about the injury he had suffered. And he got the promise from all of them to support him intensively (*cum optima voluntate*) in the future feud'.[6]

The information contained in this short statement is of special interest for us: in case of conflict the duke had the possibility and even the obligation to gather his relatives, friends, and people who had a feudal relationship with him. But this did not mean that all these people supported him blindly in the subsequent conflict. He had to explain the injury he had suffered and convince the participants that a feud was justified. It seems that the gathered people decided which support had to be given or even that no support should be given. And, of course, it could happen that the participants came to different decisions about their participation, having reflected on the entirety of their obligations. This was obviously the case in this conflict, despite the fact that the author does not mention it.

---

6 *Historia Welforum*, cap. 30: 'Gwelfo enim illatam sibi iniuriam amicis, cognatis et fidelibus suis exponens omnium animos in adiutorium sui cum optima voluntate ascivit'; cf. the same procedure cap. 22: 'Episcopus enim, per totam quadragesimam cognatos et amicos suos conveniens, hoc agebat, ut ducem de finibus suis, si amplius eos hostiliter invaderet, ignominiose fugaret'; and cap. 25: 'Heinricus ergo dux Saxoniam ingressus, cum casum et miserias suas fidelibus et amicis exponeret, ad rebellandum eos imperatori et Alberto excitavit'.

Indeed, the author continues to report in detail who joined the later army which seemed to be ready to fight: he names three bishops of the region, another duke, several margraves, and a lot of counts; in total there were apparently 2200 warriors. This seems to be a powerful network, which became active because they had decided to take vengeance. But the opposite is the case.

The opponent was Welf's enemy, Count Palatine Hugo of Tübingen. He was supported by the Staufen Duke Frederick and other noble families in the region. In consequence, we can find many people on each side who had relatives, friends, and followers on the other. Therefore, it is especially interesting that we are informed about an unbelievable outcome of an unforeseen battle against Hugo's men: 900 of Welf's warriors gave up early and were captured. Only one person on either side was killed. Welf escaped with three of his supporters, which damaged his honour enormously.

This hints at very different opinions in Welf's network about the necessity of the feud and especially of a battle at this early stage. It shows a great variety of behaviour which was possible in such situations. If we take this into account, we will better understand some other statements about this conflict: the *Historia Welforum* states that in the night before the battle 'many had tried with sorrow to find an adequate satisfaction and a compromise'. Burchard of Ursberg, another source, gives a similar account, 'that some incautious individuals had opened the battle, while many of the nobles and princes were very eager to secure *concordia* and *pax*'.[7] I think it is justified to explain the surprising behaviour of the 900 captured warriors with their unwillingness to fight a battle before all possibilities for ending the conflict peacefully had been exhausted. Indeed, all these prisoners in the later part of the conflict were released without the payment of a ransom.

This small case-study yields several results. In every conflict, various groups were potential supporters of the leading figures, but these supporters had to be informed and convinced beforehand that in the case in question violence was justified. Gatherings were responsible for obtaining consent about what to do in that particular case. And violence was the last option, not the first. Duke Welf had to explain what happened, but the others decided on the right answer.

In the case quoted, all seemed to be convinced that participation in an armed conflict was justified and they seemed to have promised to take part in it. But the outcome shows that many warriors were united in the opinion that at that time a battle was not justified. We are not informed by the biased source of the Welfs why 900 warriors chose the drastic

---

7 *Historia Welforum*, cap. 30: 'totaque illa nocte alii orationi incumbebant, alii de satisfactione et compositione anxie tractabant'; cf. Burchard von Ursperg, *Chronicon*, a. 1164, 47.

option to let themselves be captured without fighting. But it is very likely that they wanted a different solution to the case than battle. It is not surprising that the *Historia Welforum* does not tell us the reasons why these warriors had refused to take part in the battle. In any case, they found an unconventional but impressive way to express their opinion which for unknown reasons had not succeeded in the preceding assembly. We will return to the development of this conflict at a later point in order to learn about peacemaking rituals.

There are other cases which witness similar decision-making processes. In the eleventh century two counts told Duke Ernst of Schwaben that they were not willing to help him in his feud against King Conrad II because of their relationship with the king — Ernst had to accept it.[8] Furthermore, we are informed several times that in the case of conflict people who had close relations to both sides saw themselves in the role of a mediator — and not as activists in one party. These are the exceptions, however. In the early Middle Ages and until the twelfth century, the problem of having relationships with both parties in conflicts and the consequences resulting from it is not present in the sources. Multiple possibilities of avoiding unintentional consequences of relationships with different people only became visible when, in the twelfth century, people began to enter into written treaties which regulated their future obligations in a much more detailed manner. This will be the topic of the next question.

Is it Possible to Notice Changes to the Norms, Rules, and Customs that Guided Behaviour in Conflicts?

It is a sign of change — and in a manner of speaking a learning process — that in various fields from the end of the eleventh century medieval people began to fix conventional agreements, treaties, and other arrangements of a normative character in writing.[9] In earlier times, people had been content with general agreements concluded in an oral or ritual manner. As an example one may call to mind that people who entered into a friendship or a feudal relation swore the same oath: 'I swear from now on to behave to my friend (lord) rightfully as a friend (man) shall behave to a friend (lord).'[10] This terminology took for granted that everybody knew exactly how to behave to a friend or a lord in any situation. Nobles who accepted a new king and promised him loyalty and service did this by kneeling and

---

8 Wipo, *Gesta Chuonradi II. Imperatoris*, cap. 20, 39–40.
9 For the general impact of literacy on the society and politics from the eleventh century onwards see the classical studies of Stock, *The Implication of Literacy*; Clanchy, *From Memory to Written Record*; Keller, 'Vom heilgen Buch zur Buchführung'.
10 Althoff, *Family, Friends and Followers*, pp. 74–101 with further information.

laying their hands in his (*Handgang*): oaths and ritual actions seemed clear enough to secure the future relations with all its rights and duties.

Much experience was necessary to notice the weaknesses of such a general und unspecified basis for public order. But written treaties in the case of marriage, inheritance, feudal contracts, or statutes of associations, and the written fixing of customs and many other products of a normative nature witness the triumphal march of literacy starting in the twelfth century.

Claudia Garnier has emphasized this phenomenon with respect to the treaties between the archbishops of Cologne, Mainz, and Trier and their followers in the thirteenth century.[11] She stated that the written treaties restricted the obligation to intervene in a conflict enormously, by fixing a specifically demarcated circle of persons and a strict geographical space, through which they determined exactly who could claim assistance and when it had to be given. An obligation to support a party was determined and restricted to the named persons and areas.

Another differentiation was achieved by 'positive' and 'negative' characterizations: there was the possibility of specifically naming people against whom such obligations should not be directed. Or the circle could be fixed for whom the obligations should be relevant. Other dispositions tried to ensure that the obligations would only be valid for a conflict over a specific problem and would end when that conflict ceased. Exceptions could also be an integral part of such treaties by which, for example, relatives and friends were explicitly exempted from any obligation. We find a series of treaties with several partners which in total enabled a person to be neutral in particular conflicts. It is very likely that these treaties have to be seen as the consequences of experience which was gained in earlier conflicts, when the overlapping networks produced many contradictory obligations, because many members of this warrior society had established relationships with parties who became enemies. They tried to solve this problem with this new form of explicit and unambiguous appointments.

New ways to guard against the breaking of such treaties were even invented: the oath was a well-known means of doing so, but it also became common to give bail and other sureties as well. These *fideiussores* promised to gather at a special place (*Einlager*) and to stay there till the parties had fulfilled their promises. These hostage-sureties were usually recruited from the circle of relatives and friends of one party to the treaty. This circle promised that they would sever their contact with that party, if that party did not implement the treaty.

The conclusions that people in the thirteenth century drew from earlier experiences hint at difficulties that had been produced by the overlapping

---

11 Garnier, *Amicus amicis – inimicus inimicis*, pp. 184–225.

networks of relatives, friends, and followers in the case of conflicts in which the numerous general obligations which most of the people had entered into came in conflict with each other. We do not have much source evidence that tells us how they had managed these problems in earlier times. But what we see with the help of these treaties is that people tried to reduce their obligations in violent conflicts. They were much more inclined to offer protection to people in distress than to help in offensive attacks. This is why we have to think carefully when we talk about the 'violent Middle Ages'.

Which Strategies Escalated Conflicts?

As in other fields of public behaviour in the Middle Ages, even in case of conflicts people were accustomed to use patterns of behaviour which were well known, and therefore allowed for a controlled escalation of a conflict. By using these patterns, the parties won time for negotiations and other de-escalating activities, because experienced people on both sides were able to see which stage of the conflict was signalled through the patterns used. This allowed for adequate and controlled reactions. On the other hand, such controlled escalation through accepted patterns sent a message to the opposing party about how decisive and impatient the other side was. This then helped to show how ready they were to settle the conflict through compromise and satisfaction. Considering the widespread image of the Middle Ages as a time of much, unrestricted violence, one has to emphasize that, especially inside Christian warrior society itself, it is unquestionable that there were many armed conflicts; however, the vast majority of them were ended peacefully through compromises and without much bloodshed. Bloody battles in feuds are exceptions to the norm in the German realm, because initiatives to end the conflict usually succeeded.[12]

The most damaging and cruel escalating activities in medieval feuds were marked by attacks on the opponent's properties and people, especially farms, fields, cattle, trees, vineyards, or even farmers, servants, or bondmen. These attacks were meant to force the opponent to give in and to give satisfaction for the actions that had caused the feud. It is worth underlining that these actions did not affect their instigators or their warriors in the first instance, but rather less-involved innocent people, who, as sources sometimes note, 'were slaughtered like cattle'. The basic

---

12 I have set out to underline this aspect in several articles: Althoff, 'Schranken der Gewalt'. For a very different position cf. Kortüm, *Krieg und Krieger. 50c–1500*, pp. 32–34. More on peacemaking and peace treaties in Chapter 6 of this volume.

idea behind this was to force the opponent to give in and to surrender because he was not able to protect his people and his property.

The next stage of escalation began with the summoning of an army of warriors and the besieging of the opponent's castle. Such sieges might have varying degrees of intensity. Traffic in and out of the castle might not necessarily be interrupted at all. In some cases, the siege began with the presence of the army as a warning sign and nothing else. But the other side could be sure that further steps would follow if they did not begin peace negotiations.

Making access to every entrance to the castle impossible, and interrupting the provision of food and other essential items demonstrated the obduracy of the besieged. Nevertheless, most sieges did not end with the taking of the castle by assault, but through negotiations which guaranteed the garrison of the castle free withdrawal and the license for the besiegers to destroy the castle. Such conditions depended on how much damage the former conflict had caused and how much blood had been shed. This gave every garrison the choice to surrender early on good terms and with an unhindered withdrawal, which only forbade them from taking any further part in the feud. The omnipresent knowledge about these rules is mirrored in the story of the so-called 'Weiber von Weinsberg' (Women of Weinsberg), who negotiated their unhindered withdrawal and the license to take with them all that they could carry. So they carried their husbands on their backs and saved them in this way. This anecdote, which very likely has no basis in reality, is repeated frequently by contemporary sources in reference to more than thirty different castles.[13]

Thietmar of Merseburg, who reports in detail about the feud of his relative, Count Henry of Schweinfurt, against King Henry II in 1003, gives another example and insight into this line of reasoning, when a garrison of a castle of Count Henry deliberated on what to do as the king had begun to besiege their castle and Count Henry had turned tail:

> Count Bukko (the brother of Count Henry), full of deep sorrow because of the flight of his brother, counselled with his companions about future steps. They had different opinions. Some, because of the faith they had promised their lord and in order to escape a lasting reproach of cowardliness, declared that they would prefer to die before handing over the castle with such pledges (meaning the wife and the children of Count Henry) to the king. As long as their lord was still alive, one could hope for relief. Others, reasonable people, stated that it would be dangerous to resist torrential water and a powerful man. The loser would seldom or never find grace. They also argued that now,

---

13 Bernhardi, *Konrad III*, p. 192, note 17.

free from losses and wounds, they could effect from the king a free withdrawal with their ladies, with other property and the whole crew.[14]

Count Bukko reached an agreement for the free withdrawal of the castle garrison, and the king had the castle destroyed 'with consideration', so that most of the buildings remained standing.

A seemingly totally different story is told by French historiographers of the fourteenth century, when in the year 1347 the English king Edward III besieged the city of Calais for a long time, during which his army suffered severe casualties. This damage to his honour induced the king to take appropriate vengeance. He demanded, as French historians record, that six citizens of Calais had to be decapitated as satisfaction for the English losses. Voluntarily six citizens declared themselves willing to sacrifice themselves for the city. It was only at the last moment that the English queen reminded her husband to show mercy and King Edward followed her admonition. If we survey the long history of conflicts in medieval Europe, the execution of volunteers would be a unique example; a long tradition on the other hand, has a ritual of surrender which signals the opposing party through verbal and non-verbal signs that one is prepared to die and that is witnessed by many examples in different countries. Therefore, in this case we can also assume that this dramatic occurrence was not as dramatic as it appeared. Prearrangements made it possible to create a situation of great tension but the outcome through the intervention of the queen was part of a choreography which had never intended the actual deaths of the volunteers.[15]

Nevertheless, in some parts of Europe, such merciful ways of dealing with enemies at the end of a conflict, as we have seen in the high medieval German realm, were not always utilized. This can be underlined by the example of Norman Sicily where the commanders who gave up their castle in return for the free withdrawal of the garrison were punished by their lords with blinding.[16] This approach to ensure that the garrison was willing to fight until the last drop of blood indicates how the standards of behaviour varied according to custom.

---

14 Thietmar von Merseburg, *Chronik*, p. v, 35: 'Tunc audita senioris sua fuga Bucco comes gravi dolore con cutitur ac, quid sibi tunc foret faciendum, socios consulit. A quibus diversa percepit responsa. Quidam dixerunt ob fidem seniori suimet promissam ac ignaviam perpetuo eis inputandam mori malle, quam urbem cum tali pignore regi umquam dare; superstite adhuc seniore suo auxilium semper sperare profuturum. Alii autem, qui plus sapiebant, aque torrenti et homini potenti arduum esse testabantur resistere; devictos raro aut numquam promereri veniam, incolomes et nullo se tunc vulnere tardatos cum domina suimet caeterisque bonis ac hospitibus abeundi licentiam apud regem imploraturos affirmabant'.

15 See Moeglin, 'Von der richtigen Art zu kapitulieren'.

16 Broekmann, *Rigor iustitiae, Herrschaft, Recht und Terror*, pp. 184–85.

Which Strategies Served Especially to De-escalate Conflicts?

A seemingly pan-European phenomenon aimed at de-escalation and at settling conflicts peacefully is the institution of mediation, which is well known and used in different medieval societies which we can now survey. It became famous among medievalists especially through studies of the free-state society of Iceland, which showed the practice, peculiarities, and impact of this institution especially in the process of settling conflicts in this special (kingless) society.[17] Studies which focused on the practices of mediation in other European societies have followed and added to our knowledge about this institution.[18] Through a series of studies, the functions, rights, duties, and limits of mediators in the German realm have also become well known. It does not seem necessary to describe the German experiences and insights in detail, because they do not differ much in comparison with other examples.

But the special character and essence of the mediator's work in the Middle Ages should be underlined, because this will elucidate the general principles of dealing with conflicts: mediators had no right to make and enforce decisions. They were responsible for opening and sustaining the communication and negotiations between the parties involved in the conflict. Mediators made proposals for amicable solutions and needed the agreement of the parties. This testifies that people in the Middle Ages were not eager to relinquish control over questions of peace, and only accepted decisions they had voluntarily agreed upon. If such a solution had been accepted by all the parties, the mediators supervised and guaranteed that everybody would behave according to the arrangements agreed upon. This meant that mediators were especially responsible for the performance of peace-making rituals. From the tenth century onwards, sources written in the east-Frankish-German realm offer many examples which elucidate this peculiarity of mediation.

Such a scope of duties needed virtues which candidates had to possess. In Germany, therefore, mediators were generally chosen from the highest ranks in society or from the circles of learned clerics. Kings, dukes, counts, archbishops, bishops, and abbots were considered to be suitable mediators based on their positions and offices. Additionally, the parties involved in conflict, who had the right to choose the mediators, placed a high value on the relationship that they already had to a candidate. It seems that they

---

17 Miller, *Bloodtaking and Peacemaking*; Byock, *Feud in the Icelandic Saga*; Jón Viðar Sigurðsson, 'The Role of Arbitration'.
18 Kamp, *Friedensstifter und Vermittler*, pp. 4–6 with an overview of international research in this field; for the pope as mediator see especially Maleczeck, 'Das friedenstiftende Papsttum im 12. und 13. Jahrhundert'.

preferred mediators who had close relationships with both parties. The sources record that a proposed mediator who only had a relationship with one party made a treaty of friendship with the other so as to compensate for any potential bias.[19]

Of course, one must take into account that it made a difference when a mediator had armed power at his disposal. Hermann Kamp used this observation to differentiate between authoritative and cooperative forms of mediation, and reserved the former for mediations conducted by kings. But the German sources do not confirm the idea that mediation was first and foremost the business of kings.

In this context it is worth noting that sometimes it was difficult to convince kings who were in a conflict with noble opponents to accept the independent position of mediators. A case in point is Archbishop Frederick of Mainz who had trouble with Otto the Great for decades because the king apparently expected that Frederick's mediation would favour him and not his opponents.[20] This seems to have changed as King Otto, according to the *vita* of his brother Bruno, conceded some years later in a long speech to his brother the independence of mediators. At that later point in time he is said to have admitted to his brother explicitly that the mediator could become active while being completely independent from the king's expectations and he, the king, would accept every proposal the mediator would make: 'Do everything, God-devoted man, do everything, I beseech you, with your influence, by which you are capable of so much, according to the circumstances in space and time — not as quick as possible but as effective as possible — either to prevent conflicts or to settle them by any kind of treaty. Even when I appear to be far away from you, you will be wherever I am, my pleasure, your circumspection and soberness will find my thankful approval. I will rule as justified, what you will do, may you also rule for justified what I will do'.[21]

Another impressive example of a tense relationship between kings and mediators is apparent in the conflicts between King Henry IV and the Saxons in the 1070s. The narratives of Lampert von Hersfeld, which are especially detailed on this point, ought to bring to light the treacherous and malicious activities of Henry, who made promises to mediators only to break them later. A negative aspect of this was the ritual of surrender which the ecclesiastical and noble elites of Saxony performed at Spier after cruel battles in 1075. Mediators had been very successful in obliging the king to give strong guarantees of life, honour, freedom, as well as fiefs and

---

19 Althoff, 'Compositio'; Althoff, 'Genugtuung (satisfactio)'.
20 Kamp, *Friedenstifter und Vermittler*, pp. 174–75.
21 Ruotger, *Ruotgeri Vita Sancti Brunonis*, cap. 20.

possessions of all participants of the *deditio*, but King Henry broke all of his guarantees and promises and kept the Saxon elites in prison.[22]

Even more interesting than the many single cases in which the similar activities of mediators are described seem to be those attempts to expand the possibilities and rights of mediators. In other words, the move from mediation to arbitration (*Schiedgerichtsbarkeit*), which, in Germany, can already be traced in its first steps from the eleventh century onwards. In the course of the reign of King Henry IV and its many, severe conflicts, especially with most princes of the realm, we find several attempts to install committees which were proportionally balanced from both parties, whose representatives had to agree upon one decision which then was decisive for the case in question. In this way they tried to make the agreement of the parties involved in conflict superfluous.

As a variant version of these attempts, we find early efforts of Pope Gregory VII to lead such a committee and to make the final judgement as highest arbiter. In this position, he tried to create a precedent by deciding whether Henry IV could remain in office as king or not. It seems that this remained Gregory's most important goal during the period between 1076 and 1080, when he, at last, came to the realization that King Henry had played a malicious game with him.

Subsequent popes, such as Innocent III, also exerted much energy attempting to reserve the act of arbitration, especially about the affairs of kings and emperors, to the papacy. This was part and consequence of the idea of *plenitudo potestatis* (full power in the church and the world) which the popes tried to reserve for themselves, without complete success.[23] Instead, in the thirteenth century arbitration became common on many levels of society in the German realm.[24] This seems to be a reaction to the weaknesses of mediation: the inability of mediators to make independent and final decisions, which was what the institution of arbitration tried to achieve.

Which Rituals Helped to End Conflicts?

Apart from the institution of mediation, there were other rituals in the German realm which also provided amicable ways to end conflicts and create peace. This is not surprising, because medieval society established order, not least, through the performance of rituals: rituals of investiture

---

22 Lampert von Hersfeld, 'Annales', a. 1075, pp. 234–39 with a long report on all negotiations of this ritual.
23 Kempf, *Papsttum und Kaisertum bei Innocenz III*.
24 For the origins of arbitration in the German Realm see Garnier, *Amicus amicis – inimicus inimicis*, pp. 231–94.

and the inauguration of officials such as kings, dukes, bishops, and abbots; rituals of meetings; rituals of (first) entrances into cities; rituals of performing a rank-order via processions; rituals of greeting and farewell; and, last but not least, rituals for ending conflicts and peace-making were essential acts to establish order. By performing and agreeing on symbolic acts in rituals, actors and other participants promised to take the behaviour they performed and to accept it as their obligation or right in the future. With these symbolic acts, a general order was created, although it only regulated and framed relations in a basic way, and not in detail. A coronation ritual turned a king into a king; it did not specify all his individual rights and duties. It has already been mentioned that such an order increasingly needed support through written specifications. This learning process became increasingly visible from the twelfth century onwards, as people began to add written peace-treaties to their rituals. Nevertheless, these rituals did not disappear in the field of political order; they were only supplemented by written confirmation.

There were two particular rituals which were used in the German realm — though not in every other realm in Europe — to bring about an end to conflicts. The first is the already mentioned *deditio*, a ritual of surrender, which was not used in every country and in some countries had different forms. It seems to have been invented during the crises of Louis the Pious in the 830s, where the ritual marked the amicable end of the conflict between Emperor Louis and his eldest son Lothar.[25] For some time it remained a privilege for ending conflicts inside the royal family of the Carolingians, but soon nobles, too, used the advantages of this ritual, which recognized remorse and self-humiliation, clemency and forgiveness as acts of satisfaction for the earlier material and immaterial damage the conflict had caused. Such acts of satisfaction were performed by one party wearing penitential clothes and falling to the feet of the former enemy, giving verbal statements of remorse and a change of mind. They were answered by the other with acts of satisfaction like mercy and forgiveness, lifting the 'penitent' from the ground and giving a kiss of peace. All this made the end of the conflict possible through the re-establishment of the old order. This was the general pattern of the ritual, which can be found regularly from the ninth to the sixteenth century.[26]

The fundamental idea of this ritual remained unchanged for centuries, even though many details hint at new elements, which point in different directions. We find strong tendencies to increase the humiliation and the acts of satisfaction of the party surrendering, as well as special possibilities, provided by particular cases, for the surrendering party to obtain more honourable conditions than usual. The variability and flexibility of all

---

25 Althoff, 'Das Privileg der deditio', pp. 116–19.
26 Althoff, *Die Macht der Rituale*, pp. 119–21; 145–47; Stollberg-Rilinger, *Rituale*, pp. 154–56.

details of the performance makes it very clear that the parties felt that these details were necessary and important in order to save face even when surrendering.

Despite the fact that the sources very seldom reveal the prearrangements and agreements the parties had made with the help of mediators, so as to guarantee the satisfying conduct of the ritual, we can be sure that every single act reflected aspects of the former conflict: the rank of both parties; the damage and bloodshed in the conflict; the intervention of friends and relatives in support of one party. Such a performance is not manageable without making prearrangements, and obligating the parties to behave in accordance with these agreements. The fundamental idea of satisfaction could only be realized in action in this way.

Some examples of exceptional acts in these rituals of surrender may allow us to uncover the deeper sense of such peculiarities. In the year 1158, when the Milanese had to surrender to Emperor Frederick Barbarossa for the first time, they offered him 5000 marks of silver, a very large sum, if they were allowed to perform the *deditio* with shoes on their feet; as, for the king's honour, it was obligatory that former opponents had to come barefoot to such a ritual, Barbarossa therefore refused the money.[27]

When the Milanese re-opened the conflict with the emperor some years later in 1162, the rules — for good reasons — did not allow for a second amicable solution. Therefore, the ritual of surrender was performed three times, but Barbarossa sent all the representatives of the Milanese back to the city without mercy every time: 'his face remained unmoved like a stone', while all others wept and begged Barbarossa for a pardon. At the end of this procedure, Barbarossa and his warriors began the complete destruction of the city and forced the Milanese to settle in a set of neighbouring villages. This reflected exactly the Milanese misdeed in re-opening the conflict, which had previously been ended with mercy and forgiveness.

In other cases, we hear about much better conditions that were given to the party surrendering. Danish kings and dukes or kings of the eastern neighbours of the German realm performed rituals to end conflicts with German kings and emperors several times. They mostly received entirely different conditions than other performers. They never came barefoot, and they almost never performed footfalls by throwing themselves at the feet of their former enemies. As illustrated by the supplication, discussed in Chapter 3, of Magnus, son of King Niels of Denmark, before Emperor Lothar in 1134, they were allowed to demonstrate their readiness for peace, subordination, and feudal service by carrying the sword of the

---

27 Cf. Vincent von Prag, *Annales*, p. 675: 'licet enim plurimam afferent pecuniam quod eis calciatis hanc satisfactionem facere liceret, nullomodo tamen obtinere potuerunt'.

emperor when he publicly walked to church with a procession of his loyal nobles, especially at Easter or Pentecost.[28]

Members of the German elites, and especially relatives of kings, were sometimes even exempted from going barefoot and making a footfall at the end of a conflict with a king. Instead, they could be allowed to serve at the king's table during a banquet. This was the case twice, in Frankfurt and in Quedlinburg, when Duke Henry the Quarrelsome gave up his attempts to usurp the child Otto III's throne. In the peace-ritual, he served with other dukes *humiliter* at the table of the young king, and by this showed his readiness and obligated himself to serve the king in the future. The promissory character of such symbolic actions must be taken into account.

The prearrangements of such rituals of surrender also included the behaviour of the spectators and supporters of the parties. In a conflict between an archbishop of Salzburg and a duke in the middle of the twelfth century, it was agreed that the supporters should silently follow the conduct of the ritual. It seems that crying and blaming the person surrendering was the more common behaviour. What is interesting is that they agreed to be silent after having refused earlier to participate without weapons, which had been the first condition of the other side. Here, we can see the signs of prior negotiation.[29]

Most characteristics of this ritual of surrender reflected the general tension concerning whether the humiliation of the one or the clemency of the other party should dominate the performance. The different solutions which were found in various cases cannot be explained primarily by the chronological developments. Two other factors were more responsible for such peculiarities.

To make this clear, it is helpful to come back to the conflict of Dukes Welf VI and Welf VII with the Count Palatine Hugo of Tübingen and the 900 captured warriors. It is undoubtedly the case that this event badly damaged the Welfs' honour. One can say that the Count Palatine was the triumphant winner of the feud. Frederick Barbarossa himself came to mediate the peace, and it was performed through a ritual of surrender at Ulm in the presence of the Emperor. For the inexperienced, what the sources tell us about what happened next might perhaps be surprising. Count Palatine Hugo came and had to repeat his footfall twice because the Welfs refused the first two. Even this did not seem to be enough satisfaction: Hugo was placed in chains and taken to prison by the Welfs. He remained there until the death of Welf VII three years later.[30] The inner logic of the ritual becomes very clear here: the very badly damaged honour of the Welfs needed more, special, satisfaction; therefore, Hugo had to be

---

28 Cf. Althoff and Witthöft, 'Les services symboliques entre dignité et contrainte'.
29 Althoff, *Die Macht der Rituale*, pp. 189–94.
30 Althoff, *Spielregeln der Politik*, pp. 70–71.

dishonoured in the ritual act in an especially extreme manner so as to re-establish the old order.

The fact that the old order had to be re-established through ritual activities every single time is also attested to by another case from the twelfth century. King Lothar of Supplingenburg had in 1126 conducted a feud with a Bohemian duke and had invaded his territory. In the dead of winter Lothar's army got into severe trouble, was defeated, and forced to agree to an unhindered withdrawal with many dead warriors. The duke had defended his position with great success. Nevertheless, in the following peace-making ritual, the Duke of Bohemia had to surrender by performing a footfall and was then rewarded with the mercy of the king. This outcome was required due to their respective rank order, which could not be changed by success in feuds.

Therefore, we can summarize that there were two principles responsible for the variability of this ritual of surrender. First of all, the ritual performance was oriented to the rank order: the higher the rank of the actors the more privileges, exceptions, and special acts they could expect and claim. 'Quod licet Iovi non licet bovi' (What is permitted to Jupiter is not permitted to an ox) seems to be the guiding principle here. The other principle is the idea of satisfaction: it was not success or defeat which primarily influenced the ritual performances that ended a conflict. On the contrary, the more success the lower-ranking party had had, the more satisfaction was necessary later on, because the old order had to be re-established. This gave the higher-ranking party enormous protection in a conflict, and rituals of surrender had a very conservative impact.

The other peacemaking ritual of the Middle Ages was the communal meal and drinking, which in Latin sources is usually called *convivium*. Such a ritual of eating and drinking together was not just used for peace-making. It had a place in almost every procedure for establishing associations: when people became relatives or friends, when they initiated a *coniuratio*, when monks or canons became members of ecclesiastical convents, when members of guilds met and counselled. All such associations celebrated their connection by eating and (especially) by drinking in *convivia* and usually repeated this at regular intervals. Parties who made peace did the same. *Convivium et munera* is a formula which describes this event. Gift-giving was an integral part of such symbolic acts which strengthened the coherence of the group.

As with the ritual of surrender, in the case of peace-making the *convivium* demanded a specific behaviour of all participants; such long-lasting *convivia* were characterized by intense communication, sometimes over days, modest joking, and an amicable atmosphere, which demonstratively showed the former enemies' change in attitude and readiness for an amicable relationship in the future. Sources from St Gall, where such peace-making *convivia* were initiated by King Conrad I in the beginning of the tenth century, show in detail how difficult such gatherings became if not everyone was willing to support a peaceful atmosphere through adequate behaviour.

Ekkehard of St Gall tells us in great detail how Salomo, bishop of Constance and abbot of St Gall, provoked his former enemies and new friends, the counts Erchanger and Berthold, who were brothers-in-law of the king, during such peace-*convivia* with bad jokes at their expense: he deceived the counts and let his serfs, whose unfree status he hid, offer rich gifts.[31] Accordingly, the counts rose to their feet and bowed to the seemingly noble men. The better-informed participants at the gathering repaid this with laughter which made the counts look like fools. The king had to intervene with the argument that he had to protect such harmless jokes and secure the peace. But the counts did not forget this affront and took vengeance on the bishop later on.

King Conrad himself had tried to lighten the atmosphere with other jokes which seemed more fitting for a peaceful atmosphere: during the liturgical performance of a chorus of young monks, Conrad had his men throw apples at the feet of the boys to disrupt their concentration. But he failed because none of the young ones took notice, as Ekkehard proudly records. Conrad later intensified his efforts to create a friendly atmosphere by offering rich meals with music and clowns which resulted in the elder monks disapproving of this obvious breaking of the Rule of St Benedict. Ekkehard comments on this with a biblical quotation: 'love cannot do injustice'.[32]

It is worth noting that in times of conflict such peace-making *convivia* were convoked even with pagans, for example in the Viking Age or at the Eastern border with Slavic chieftains and princes. But such attempts were often made with the malicious intention of killing the former enemies when they were drunk. Both the Carolingian and the Ottonian sources provide examples of this. When in the middle of the tenth century Margrave Gero invited thirty princes of the Slavs to such a *convivium* and had them killed in the night, Widukind of Corvey defended this with the argument that it would have been very likely that the pagans had had the same plan in mind.[33] But there are also reports of successful *convivia* with Christian Scandinavian princes, for example in the case of Archbishop Adalbert of Bremen who celebrated a *convivium* with a Danish chieftain

---

31 Ekkehard, *Casus St Galli*, cap. 15, 42–43.
32 Ekkehard, *Casus St Galli*, cap. 16, 44: 'Caritas, que non agit perperam, licenter sprevit disciplinam'.
33 Widukind von Corvey, *Sachsengeschichte*, 3–183, lib. 2, cap. 20, 106–07.

which lasted for eight days. As Adam of Bremen says, they changed the role of host several times and tried to outdo each other in the richness of their gifts.[34]

Conclusion

This compressed attempt to look at the ruling elites in the German realm as networks in action and at how they functioned in conflicts has stressed some aspects which may be relevant for the comparison with other societies in the following respects: Which bonds in society could people use for protection, help, and a successful conduct of conflicts? Which norms, rules, and customs existed and were observed for guiding and ending conflicts? Which institutions and strategies could claim validity for hindering the escalation and promoting the de-escalation of conflicts? Answering these questions produces a differentiated profile of a warrior society, which is open for comparison.

Firstly, I described the bonds inside warrior society which created groups and associations that guaranteed or promised its members support in conflicts. Apart from the common bonds of kinship, friendship, and feudal relations in the German realm, the sworn association (*coniuratio*) provided an especially powerful connection which was often used in feuds even against kings. The oath seems to have created a very strong bond and a reliable means of securing unanimity and coherence. It was difficult to break up such *coniurationes*; attempts to forbid them failed, they spoke with one voice and pursued a concrete goal. This strength did not exclude reaching their goals through the amicable ending of conflicts as well. Overall, it seems that a *coniuratio* was more reliable than feudal bonds, and even than the bonds of kinship and friendship, for these allowed for too many exceptions because of relationships with all the parties of the conflict. This often-used institution of a sworn association functioned as a balance to the dominance of kings, and as a means to an effective representation of interests. It seems fruitful to ask whether and to what extent this strategy was used in other societies.

Moreover, it is very significant that in the early Middle Ages bonds were secured mostly by very general promises. Several types of oaths use the formula: I will behave as one should behave '*per rectum*'. It seems that people had great trust in the fact that everybody knew how to behave in the right manner towards his kin, friends, or lords. This trust seemingly

---

34 Cf. Adam von Bremen, *Hamburgische Kirchengeschichte*, lib. III, cap. 18, 350: 'Ubi facile notus et reconciliatus superbo regi muneribus atque conviviis certavit archiepiscopalem potentiam regalibus anteferre divitiis. Denique, sicut mos est inter barbaros, ad confirmandum pactum federis opulentum convivium habetur vicissim per VIII dies'.

dissolved from the twelfth century onwards, and written treaties began to define the rights and duties of all parties in more and more detail. A strong trend to avoid general obligations, and especially to reduce obligations which involved unlimited military help, is noticeable here.

If we look at the normal conduct of feuds in this warrior society, it is striking, first and foremost, that most violent acts were directed not at the warriors on the other side but at innocent people like farmers and serfs of the other party, and at their possessions, farms, fields, and cattle. With this damage, one tried to make clear one's own determination to escalate the conflict until the other party gave in. Another often-used escalation tactic was the besieging of castles. But these activities were usually ended by negotiation with the result that the garrison surrendered the castle and was rewarded with a free withdrawal. These techniques must be taken into account when judging the character of such feuds. It is well known that in other warrior societies extremely different customs ruled.[35] In the German realm such a peaceable solution enjoyed much popularity and hindered the escalation of violence.

Such peaceable solutions, such as free and unmolested withdrawal, also known from the Norwegian wars analysed in Chapter 4, were due to an institution which was primarily dedicated to the peaceful ending of conflicts: the mediator. This institution enjoyed great prestige in the German realm. People of the highest rank, like kings, bishops, dukes, abbots, and counts, are mentioned in the sources as acting as mediators. For a long time, this was the only institution that successfully worked towards ending conflicts and establishing peace. Its possibilities were, however, restricted because the mediators themselves could not make a decision. They made proposals and had to convince the parties involved to agree to them. Attempts to change such mediation into arbitration were quite successful at the lower levels of society, but were seldom used when the nobility was involved. In the German realm, as in other European societies, mediation remained the only institution responsible for peace-making, and it is still relevant to this day as an institution that eases justice in national and international affairs.[36] Every comparison between different societies serves a good purpose if it looks intensively at the role and efficacy of mediators.

Rituals were the preferred means of ending conflicts, not only in the German realm, because people were generally used to making promises for one's future behaviour through symbolically condensed actions. The binding force of these actions resulted from the public, theatrical, and solemn performance which followed well-known patterns. Two rituals in particular were used to end conflicts: the ritual of surrender (*deditio*) and

---

35 Broekmann, *Rigor iustitiae, Herrschaft, Recht und Terror*, pp. 184–85.
36 For mediation in modern times cf. Breidenbach, *Mediation. Struktur, Chancen und Risiken*; Princen, *Intermediaries in International Conflict*.

the communal meal of the former enemies (*convivium*). The first fulfilled the function of giving satisfaction for the material and immaterial damage caused during the conflict. It is significant that in every case the party of lower rank had to give this satisfaction. The more damage there had been, the more satisfaction was necessary. Satisfaction could be given by verbal and non-verbal actions: penitents' clothing, going barefoot, verbal self-accusation, or footfall were often-used means of such satisfaction. They were rewarded by the opponents with clemency, forgiveness, kisses, and other signs of peace. But the opponent could also express the fact that further satisfaction was necessary. In such cases the party surrendering was taken prisoner for a certain amount of time.

The communal meal of the former opponents sometimes followed on directly after the ritual of surrender, sometimes it was performed later. Its main function was to create trust in the new relationship by showing friendly sentiments and thus also promising these sentiments for the future. Therefore, these *convivia* lasted for a very long time; the parties provided a friendly and peaceable atmosphere through intensive communication, harmless jokes, lots of drinking, and the exchange of gifts, which symbolized the new relationship as well. Sometimes things went wrong and the conflict broke out again during the *convivium*. Sometimes this was even planned in a treacherous manner.

This short overview of bonds and networks, customs, strategies, and rituals describes the interactions of the ruling classes in conflicts and their frequently used institutions and rituals. One of my main concerns was to weaken the idea of the unrestricted use of violence in the Middle Ages. There were rules and customs for conducting and ending violent conflicts without and before bloodshed amongst the ruling classes of the German realm. Medieval society knew and used ways of settling peace which especially protected the higher ranks and made giving-in more attractive. The ability of kings to punish members of the ruling classes was evidently limited. This limitation undoubtedly contributed to the stability of this realm.

Works Cited

Primary Sources

Adam von Bremen, *Hamburgische Kirchengeschichte*, ed. by Werner Trillmich, Ausgewählte Quellen zur deutschen Geschichte des Mittelalters. Freiherr vom Stein Gedächtnisausgabe 11 (Darmstadt: de Gruyter, 1973)

Burchard von Ursperg, *Chronicon*, ed. by Oswald Holder-Egger and Bernhard Simson, MGH SS rer. Germ. 16 (Hannover-Leipzig, 1916)

Ekkehard, *Casus St Galli*, ed. by Hans F. Haefele, Ausgewählte Quellen zur deutschen Geschichte des Mittelalters. Freiherr vom Stein Gedächtnisausgabe, 10 (Darmstadt: de Gruyter, 1980)

Historia Welforum, ed. by Erich König, Schwäbische Chroniken der Stauferzeit, 1 (Sigmaringen: Sage, 1978)

Lampert von Hersfeld, 'Annales', in *Lamperti monachi Hersfeldensis, Opera*, ed. by Oswald Holder-Egger, MGH SS rer. Germ. in us. schol. (Hannover, 1894), pp. 1–304

Ruotger, *Ruotgeri Vita Sancti Brunonis*, MGH SS rer. Germ. N.S X (Cologne, 1951)

Schmale, Franz-Josef, *Quellen zur Geschichte Kaiser Heinrichs IV. Ausgewählte Quellen zur Deutschen Geschichte des Mittelalters*, ed. by Brunos Buch vom Sachsenkrieg, Freiherr vom Stein-Gedächtnisausgabe, 12 (Darmstadt: de Gruyter, 1974)

Thietmar von Merseburg, *Chronik, V, 35*, ed. by Werner Trillmich, Freiherr vom Stein Gedächtnisausgabe, 9 (Darmstadt: de Gruyter, 1957)

Vincent von Prag, *Annales*, ed. by Wilhelm Wattenbach, MGH SS, 17 (Hannover, 1861)

Widukind von Corvey, *Sachsengeschichte*, ed. by Albert Bauer and Reinhold Rau, Quellen zur Geschichte der sächsischen Kaiserzeit. Freiherr vom Stein Gedächtnisausgabe, 8 (Darmstadt: de Gruyter, 1971)

Wipo, *Gesta Chuonradi II. Imperatoris*, ed. by Harry Bresslau, MGH SS rer. Germ., 61 (Hannover-Leipzig, 1915)

Secondary Studies

Althoff, Gerd, 'Compositio. Wiederherstellung verletzter Ehre im Rahmen gütlicher Konfliktbeilegung im Mittelalter', in *Verletzte Ehre. Ehrkonflikte in Gesellschaften des Mittelalters und der frühen Neuzeit*, ed. by Klaus Schreiner and Gerd Schwerhoff (Cologne: Böhlau Verlag, 1995), pp. 63–76

——, 'Conventiculum, conspiratio, coniuratio. The Political Power of Sworn Associations in Tenth and Eleventh Century Germany', in *Le Sacré et la parole. Le serment au Moyen Âge*, ed. by Jaume Aurell, Martin Aurell, and Montserrat Herrero (Paris: Classiq Garnier, 2018), pp. 57–66

———, *Family, Friends and Followers. Political and Social Bonds in Early Medieval Europe* (Cambridge: Cambridge University Press, 2004)

———, 'Genugtuung (satisfactio). Zur Eigenart gütlicher Konfliktbeilegung im Mittelalter', in *Modernes Mittelalter*, ed. by Joachim Heinzle (Frankfurt/M.: Insel, 1994), pp. 247–65

———, *Die Macht der Rituale. Symbolik und Herrschaft im Mittelalter* (Darmstadt: de Gruyter, 2003)

———, 'Das Privileg der deditio', in *Spielregeln der Politik im Mittelalter. Kommunikation in Frieden und Fehde*, ed. by Gerd Althoff (Berlin: de Gruyter, 1997), pp. 99–125

———, *Rules and Rituals in Medieval Power Games. A German Perspective* (Leiden: Brill, 2020)

———, 'Schranken der Gewalt. Wie gewalttätig war das "finstere Mittelalter"?', in *Der Krieg in Mittelalter und in der Frühen Neuzeit. Gründe, Begründungen, Bilder, Bräuche, Recht*, ed. by Horst Brunner (Wiesbaden: Wiesbaden Reichert, 1999), pp. 1–23

———, and Christiane Witthöft, 'Les services symboliques entre dignite et contrainte', *Annales*, 58 (2003), 1293–320

———, *Spielregeln der Politik im Mittelalter. Kommunikation in Frieden und Fehde* (Darmstadt: Primus-Verlag, 1997)

Bernhardi, Wilhelm, *Konrad III*, Jahrbücher der Deutschen Geschichte (Leipzig, 1883)

Breidenbach, Stefan, *Mediation. Struktur, Chancen und Risiken von Vermittlung im Konflikt* (Cologne: Verlag Dr Otto Schmidt KG, 1995)

Broekmann, Theo, *Rigor iustitiae, Herrschaft, Recht und Terror im Normannisch-Staufischen Süden (1050–1250)* (Darmstadt: de Gruyter, 2005)

Byock, Jesse, *Feud in the Icelandic Saga* (Berkeley: University of California Press, 1983)

Clanchy, Michael, *From Memory to Written Record. England 1066–1307* (London: John Wiley & Sons, 1979)

Garnier, Claudia, *Amicus amicis – inimicus inimicis. Politische Freundschaft und fürstliche Netzwerke im 13. Jahrhundert. Monographien zur Geschichte des Mittelalters 46* (Stuttgart: Anton Hiersemann, 2000)

Jón Viðar Sigurðsson, 'The Role of Arbitration in the Settlement of Disputes in Iceland c. 1000–1300', in *Law and Disputing in the Middle Ages*, ed. by Per Andersen, Kirsi Salonen, Helle Møller Sigh, and Helle Vogt, Proceedings of the Ninth Carlsberg Academy Conference on Medieval Legal History 2012 (Copenhagen: DJØF Publishing, 2014), pp. 123–35

Kamp, Hermann, *Friedensstifter und Vermittler im Mittelalter* (Darmstadt: de Gruyter, 2001)

Keller, Hagen, 'Vom heiligen Buch zur Buchführung. Lebensfunktionen der Schrift im Mittelalter', *Frühmittelalterliche Studien*, 26 (1992), 1–31

Kempf, Friedrich, *Papsttum und Kaisertum bei Innocenz III* (Rome: Pontificia Universita gregoriana, 1954)

Kortüm, Henning, *Krieg und Krieger. 500–1500* (Stuttgart: de Gruyter Oldenbourg, 2010)

Maleczeck, Werner, 'Das friedenstiftende Papsttum im 12. und 13. Jahrhundert', in *Träger und Instrumentarien des Friedens im hohen und späten Mittelalter*, ed. by Johannes Fried (Sigmaringen: de Gruyter, 1996), pp. 249–332

Miller, William I., *Bloodtaking and Peacemaking. Feud, Law and Society in Saga Iceland* (Chicago: University of Chicago Press, 1990)

Moeglin, Jean Marie. 'Von der richtigen Art zu kapitulieren. Die sechs Bürger von Calais (1347)', in *Krieg im Mittelalter*, ed. by Hans-Henning Kortüm (Berlin: de Gruyter, 2001), pp. 141–65

Oexle, Otto Gerhard, 'Die Wirklichkeit und das Wissen', in *Mittelalterforschung – Historische Kulturwissenschaft – Geschichte und Theorie der Historischen Erkenntnis*, ed. by Andrea von Hülsen-Esch, Bernhard Jussen, and Frank Rexroth (Göttingen: Verlag Vandenhoeck & Ruprecht, 2011), pp. 496–635

Princen, Thomas, *Intermediaries in International Conflict* (Princeton: Princeton University Press, 1992)

Stock, Brian, *The Implication of Literacy. Written Language and Models of Interpretation in the Eleventh and Twelfth Centuries* (Princeton: Princeton University Press, 1983)

Stollberg-Rilinger, Barbara, *Rituale* (Frankfurt/M: Campus Verlag GmbH, 2003)

STEPHEN D. WHITE

9. War Stories

Re-Thinking Rebellion in Anglo-Norman and Angevin England, 1066 to 1217

> '[R]ebellions and wars are fought on quasi-legal principles'.[1]

Rebellion

According to a discussion of 'Rebellion, Treason and the Punishment of Revolt' in England from 1066 to 1217,

> Hostilities arising from baronial insurrection accounted for a high proportion of the warfare waged in England, Normandy and other continental possessions of the Norman and Angevin kings. In England itself, for example, the king or his representatives were forced to fight major campaigns against discontented factions of the aristocracy or rebellious royal cadets in 1075, 1078–9, 1088, 1095, 1101, 1102, 1155, 1173–4, 1183, 1194, 1215–17, to list but the more prominent conflicts, while during Stephen's reign [1135–54] a combination of civil war and baronial insurgency demanded constant military action from the king.[2]

During the same period, the English king's lands on the continent were disrupted not only by the previously noted rebellions in England of 1088, 1101, 1102, 1155, 1173–1174, and 1183, but also by armed conflicts lim-

---

1 Pollock and Maitland, *The History of English Law*, vol. 1, p. 303.
2 Strickland, *War and Chivalry*, p. 230. Rebellions in England also included the ones that took place in 1068, 1082, 1083, 1091, 1094.

Stephen D. White (stephen.dwhite@gmail.com) is Asa G. Candler professor emeritus of medieval history in the Department of History, University of Emory.

New Perspectives on the 'Civil Wars' in Medieval Scandinavia, ed. by Hans Jacob Orning, Kim Esmark, and Jón Viðar Sigurðsson, Comparative Perspectives on Medieval History, 1 (Turnhout: Brepols, 2024), pp. 371–412
BREPOLS PUBLISHERS   10.1484/M.CPMH-EB.5.137266

ited mainly to individual territories on the continent such as Normandy, Maine, and Poitou.[3]

By pejoratively characterizing almost all armed conflicts between the king and his barons between 1066 and 1217 as rebellions, revolts, risings, insurgencies, or insurrections and using the term 'civil war' for the lengthy rebellion against King Stephen between 1138 and 1153,[4] the same analysis anticipates the broader argument that a rebellion against the English king marked a radical break in the established political order; and that because it was a heinous felony, an act of perjury, a violation of homage and sworn fidelity to the king, and a sacrilegious attack on 'the Lord's anointed' (as kings of England were sometimes called at this time),[5] it was also a form of treason and thus the greatest of all crimes long before 1352, when a parliamentary statute in French declared that levying 'war' — that is, *guerre* — against the king in his own realm was 'great treason'.[6] At the same time, the designation of the king's adversaries in these conflicts as 'rebellious royal cadets', 'discontented' aristocrats, and 'rebellious vassals' who merited 'severe chastisement', and the characterization of their armed opposition to the king as 'internal unrest' that 'demanded military action' from the king, presupposes not only that the legitimacy of every crowned king was indisputable, but also that a rebellion against an English king should generally be interpreted as an *ad hoc* aristocratic reaction against the progressive centralization of royal power that aimed to restore 'an earlier period of political centrifugality'.[7] In the same way, the dismissal of the rebels' reasons for rebelling against the king as a cloak for violently pursuing their own individual interests — and not as justifications for legitimately asserting what they saw as their own rights — implies that rebellion was not an integral part of the structure of English politics at this time;[8] and that the many rebellions of this period should not be interpreted as signs of built-in tensions and contradictions in Anglo-Norman and Angevin elite politics. Instead, this view of rebellion presupposes that each individual armed conflict of this kind should ordinarily be seen as an almost mindlessly destructive, but ephemeral political side-show, in

---

3 Strickland, *War and Chivalry*, p. 230. On rebellions against Henry II, see Hollister, *Henry I*, pp. 46–48, 108–49. On John's rebellion of 1194 against Richard I, see Gillingham, *Richard I*, pp. 236, 239–40, 243–44, 269–70.
4 On the so-called civil war of Stephen's reign as a lengthy rebellion, see Bartlett, *England under the Norman and Angevin Kings*, p. 52.
5 Strickland, *War and Chivalry*, pp. 232–40. According to Gillingham, '1066 and the Introduction of Chivalry into England', pp. 31–55 at p. 47, 'rebellion was always treason'.
6 Statute of 1352. For a critique of the view that rebellion was always treason, see White, 'Peace or Punishment'.
7 Strickland, *War and Chivalry*, pp. 230, 238, 240.
8 On the dismissal by historians of 'baronial viewpoints and justifications [for violence], which often conflicted with royal ones' see Valente, *The Theory and Practice of Revolt*, p. 4.

which traitors fought loyalists in a way that violently but only briefly interrupted the progress of state-building in medieval England. As a result, the many baronial rebellions taking place in England during a period of more than a century have not been explained by positing a structural connection between them and the political régime against which barons rebelled, as Marc Bloch, for example, did when postulating that medieval agrarian revolts were 'inseparable' from the seigneurial regime against which peasants revolted.[9] Instead, such rebellions have been explained with reference to the turbulent emotional dispositions and power-seeking impulses of individual rebel leaders and their rebellious followers. A king's deployment of military force against aristocratic rebels can thus be seen as a means not just of suppressing revolt, but of re-establishing central power and restoring law and order. According to the same view of rebellion, moreover, kings were indisputably justified legally in punishing aristocratic rebel leaders in England for the crime of treason by imprisoning or exiling them, disinheriting them of their landed property, and even putting them to death as traitors, though the last of these punishments was not imposed on a single English rebel leader before 1321.[10]

With only minor disagreements on such questions as when English rebel leaders could legally be executed as traitors, recent historians have generally accepted what this chapter calls the conventional model of rebellion in England from 1066 to 1217. A noteworthy exception, however, is Robert Bartlett, whose revisionist model of rebellion abandons assumptions that are built into the conventional one and resemble some of the presuppositions about medieval states and state-building that are contested in the present volume on 'civil wars' in medieval Scandinavia.[11] In *England under the Norman and Angevin Kings, 1075–1225*, Bartlett deviates from the conventional way of viewing rebellion from an exclusively royal, if not royalist, perspective and its presupposition of the existence of a single hegemonic legal order that English kings had imposed on their aristocratic subjects and members of the clerical elite in the Anglo-Norman era, if not earlier. By viewing rebellion partly from the perspective of aristocratic rebels themselves and examining their reasons for rebelling, Bartlett also rejected the unsubstantiated premise of the conventional model that these rebels were merely discontented, turbulent, rebellious, perjured aristocrats who disloyally, lawlessly, and violently acted to remedy their own private grievances by fighting against a king and the loyal nobles who faithfully observed their 'feudal' obligations to him. In addition, by suggesting,

---

9 Bloch, *Les caractères originaux de l'histoire rurale française*, p. 197, 'Aux yeux de l'historien [...] la révolte agraire apparait aussi inséparable du régime seigneurial que, par exemple, de la grande entreprise capitaliste, la grève'.
10 Strickland, *War and Chivalry*, pp. 232, 233, 240.
11 See Chapter 1.

in passing, that the violence rebels used against the king and his loyal supporters was less severe than the violence he used against them and their lands and dependants, Bartlett undermined the tendency of previous historians to see the royal suppression of aristocratic rebellions and the punishment of their leaders simply as a way of punishing wrong-doing and restoring law and order.

In formulating a revisionist model of rebellion to replace the conventional one,[12] Bartlett began by showing that between 1066 to 1217, when 'violent opposition to the king was recurrent' and not simply incidental,[13] every rebellion but one fell into one of two significantly different types. The single exception, discussed in detail below (pp. 397–407), was the rebellion of 1215–1217, which constituted a third type in which elements of the first two types were combined with a new element found in later rebellions during the reigns of Henry III and Edward II.[14] Bartlett illustrated Type 1 rebellions by citing Baldwin de Redvers' revolt of 1136 against King Stephen. This, because it was triggered by a 'personal grievance' in the form of the king's refusal to give Baldwin a great estate he wanted, can be interpreted as being emblematic of an individual lord's violent reaction to 'real or supposed infringements' on his rights or 'threats' to them by a royal government,[15] which Bartlett aptly describes as practising a kind of 'predatory and punitive rule' that often treated subjects as 'enemies'.[16] If this type of rebellion is slightly reconfigured so as to include revolts by small groups of nobles as well as individuals protesting against alleged infringements on their rights, Type 1 rebellions can be identified with those noted above in 1075, 1078–1079, 1088, and 1095, and in rebellions soon after 1066, including one in 1070–1071 to be discussed below.[17]

Significantly different from rebellions of the first type are Type 2 rebellions, which Bartlett describes as aristocratic political movements 'headed by, or in support of, members of the ruling dynasty' who had legitimate claims to replace the reigning king as the previous king's heir and who, if successful, could then reward their own noble supporters. However, in cases where aristocratic rebels supported a rival ruler by fighting against

---

12 Although I have tried to summarize Bartlett's argument accurately and to identify key assumptions that I believe to be essential to it, he himself bears no responsibility, of course, for my own interpretation of his illuminating analysis of Norman and Angevin rebellions.
13 Bartlett, *England under the Norman and Angevin Kings*, p. 51.
14 Bartlett, *England under the Norman and Angevin Kings*, pp. 51–67. On the rebellion of 1215–1217 as the first one 'to impose and defend a specific program of law and government', see Valente, *Theory and Practice of Revolt*, p. 10.
15 Bartlett, *England under the Norman and Angevin Kings*, p. 51.
16 Bartlett, *England under the Norman and Angevin Kings*, pp. 48, 49, 62. For an even darker assessment of how Angevin kings treated nobles, see Jolliffe, *Angevin Kinship*.
17 On the rebellions of 1075 and 1078–1079, see Bates, *William the Conqueror*, pp. 370–88 and 396–404, respectively. On the rebellion of 1095, see Barlow, *William Rufus*, pp. 346–59.

a reigning king who had alienated them by infringing on their rights, one can see how Type 2 and Type 1 rebellions could overlap. To demonstrate the frequency of Type 2 rebellions, Bartlett notes that 'between 1086 and 1215, there was virtually no decade [without] armed struggle between members of the ruling dynasty'.[18] These conflicts included several between brothers: in 1088, when Duke Robert of Normandy rebelled against William II; in 1101, when the same duke rebelled against Henry I; and in 1194, when the future king John rebelled against Richard I. There was one Type 2 rebellion by a nephew against his uncle in 1120, when William Clito, Duke Robert's son, rebelled against Henry I; two Type 2 rebellions by a son against his father in 1173–1174 and 1183, when King Henry the Young participated in revolts against Henry II; and, finally, the lengthy — and ultimately successful — rebellion between 1139 and 1153 against King Stephen by his cousin Matilda.[19] According to Bartlett, rebellions of the second type broke out so often partly because 'recurrent divisions within the ruling family meant that there was usually a focus for [aristocratic] opposition, in the person of the king's [close kinsman or, in one case, kinswoman]'.[20] Moreover, he argues,

> because high politics was dynastic politics ..., the structure of political life at its highest level was the same as that of family life. The great crises and turning points of both were birth, marriage, and death. Sibling rivalry and intergenerational tensions within the ruling house determined such fundamental issues as the level of public order, the shape of aristocratic faction, and the pattern of international alliances.[21]

In the absence of any precise and generally accepted rules of succession, the same forces also determined the kinds of claims that members of the royal house might make upon the 'inheritance' of the reigning king or his predecessor.

In a third type of rebellion illustrated by the one that began in May 1215 under King John and ended in September 1217 during the minority of his son Henry III, the distinguishing feature was a program of reform that was supported by the king's aristocratic adversaries, along with high-ranking clerics, and was partially embodied in three successive versions

---

18 Bartlett, *England under the Norman and Angevin Kings*, pp. 5–6.
19 Bartlett, *England under the Norman and Angevin Kings*, pp. 4–5.
20 Bartlett, *England under the Norman and Angevin Kings*, p. 52, which continues, 'Rebels could thus enjoy a semi-legitimacy in their opposition and envisage a future in which a new regime would be headed by their own leader. The civil war of Stephen's reign was simply a situation of this type that, because of military deadlock, became extended over years rather than months'.
21 Bartlett, *England under the Norman and Angevin Kings*, p. 6.

of Magna Carta in 1215, 1216, and 1217.[22] However, Bartlett maintains, because many rebels in 1215 had their own individual grievances against John, their rebellion had one feature in common with Type 1 rebellions from the very start.[23] Later on, the rebellion (sometimes called a 'civil war') shared another feature with Type 2 rebellions, when the rebels tried to replace John as king by offering the English crown to Prince Louis of France, the eldest son of Philip II (and the future Louis VIII).

Even though Bartlett applies the term 'rebellion' to all three of these overlapping types of armed opposition to the king and applies the term 'rebels' to nobles who engaged in any one of them, his model of rebellion differs significantly from the conventional one. First and foremost, instead of either dismissing justifications for fighting against the king as purely self-interested and legally spurious or postulating that 'rebellion was always treason', Bartlett comes close to adopting Frederic William Maitland's view that 'rebellions and wars [were] fought on quasi-legal principles'[24] by showing that from the perspective of nobles, there were legal grounds for contesting royal infringements on their rights in Type 1 rebellions and, in Type 2 rebellions, for supporting the replacement of the reigning king by a close kinsman or kinswoman who had a good claim to the throne and a disposition to reward his or her supporters.[25] There may even have been legal grounds for engaging in a Type 3 rebellion against a king who made a practice of disinheriting individual nobles, otherwise violated their rights, and/or refused to do them justice or grant them their liberties. Moreover, by implicitly rejecting the dubious presupposition that Anglo-Norman and Angevin kings had both the political power and the legal authority to treat any use of armed force against themselves as intrinsically illegitimate, Bartlett expressly undercuts the assumption underlying the conventional model of rebellion that nobles who openly led or participated in an armed conflict against the king were, almost by definition, perjurers, infidels, lawbreakers, and rebels.[26]

Indeed, Bartlett suggests that their conduct may well have been seen by some as fully legitimate, since 'the practice of "defiance" (*diffidatio*), whereby those about to rebel publicly renounced their allegiance to their lord, [implies that] bonds of subordination and obedience to the Crown

---

22 Bartlett, *England under the Norman and Angevin Kings*, p. 52. In this respect, the rebellion of 1215–1217 and several subsequent rebellions in England differ from Scandinavian rebellions discussed elsewhere in this volume.
23 Bartlett, *England under the Norman and Angevin Kings*, pp. 64, 63.
24 Pollock and Maitland, *History of English Law*, vol. 1, p. 303.
25 Bartlett, *England under the Norman and Angevin Kings*, p. 52. In a Type 2 rebellion, according to Bartlett, 'rebels could enjoy a semi-legitimacy [and imagine] a new regime ... headed by their own leader'.
26 Similar arguments are developed further in White, 'Alternative Constructions of Treason' and 'Peace or Punishment'.

were not irrevocable or innate, [and] if a man had good cause, he could proclaim that his lord was no longer his lord and then fight against him honourably'.[27] Moreover,

> The right of aristocrats to use force in the course of their quarrels was simply a given in most parts of medieval Europe. In England, the tradition of a powerful monarchy inhibiting such private warfare was strong, but, after 1066, the top ranks of the English aristocracy came from Normandy and continued to hold lands there. They thought as Norman lords, as well as subjects of the king of the English, and in Normandy the norms governing violent disputing were different and more lax.[28]

Furthermore, any norms limiting the use of armed force by English kings against their own barons were even more lax and allowed them to do far more than chastise rebels and restore law and order, as Bartlett makes clear by noting that 'John's campaigns [against his baronial enemies] in the winter of 1215–16 [became] notorious for the burning of houses and other buildings, the kidnapping and torture of men to extract ransoms, the cutting down of orchards, and the seizure of booty'.[29] In addition, as we shall see below, John's campaigns in England in late 1215 and 1216 could easily be understood by contemporaries as royal vengeance for the shame the king suffered when his barons compelled him to grant Magna Carta and tried to subject him to the rule of the twenty-five barons appointed to enforce the Charter.[30] Finally, because Bartlett argues persuasively that the tradition of 'justified aristocratic violence could invest resistance to the [English] king with a kind of acceptability', if not legitimacy,[31] it is easy to understand why, between the late eleventh and the mid-thirteenth century, English aristocratic rebel leaders were rarely 'dispossessed' permanently and 'scarcely ever maimed or killed in cold blood'.[32] In fact, it was only in 1321 that kings initiated the practice of putting English rebel leaders on trial for treason and then executing them as traitors.[33]

Although Bartlett's revisionist model of rebellion is a major advance on the conventional one, his argument that armed opposition to the king was legitimate under certain circumstances is hard to reconcile with the classification of such opposition as 'rebellion' and calling the nobles who en-

---

27 Bartlett, *England under the Norman and Angevin Kings*, p. 61. For a different view of *diffidatio*, see Strickland, *War and Chivalry*, pp. 231–32.
28 Bartlett, *England under the Norman and Angevin Kings*, p. 61.
29 Bartlett, *England under the Norman and Angevin Kings*, p. 255.
30 See below, p. 401.
31 Bartlett, *England under the Norman and Angevin Kings*, p. 61.
32 Bartlett, *England under the Norman and Angevin Kings*, p. 60.
33 See White, 'Peace or Punishment'.

gaged in it 'rebels'.[34] Indeed, the main reason for retaining this terminology appears to be that it was routinely employed by highly esteemed Anglo-Norman Latin authors such as John of Worcester, William of Malmesbury, Henry of Huntingdon, and, above all, Orderic Vitalis, who characterized nobles who engaged in armed resistance to their king as *rebelles*, *seditiosi*, and *proditores* and provided modern scholars with their best examples of the horrors of rebellion.[35] Even more highly charged denunciations of rebellion and rebels are found in the writings of Angevin Latin authors such as Peter of Blois, Roger of Howden, William of Newburgh, Richard of Devizes, and Ralph of Dis, the last of whom treated the rebellions of King Henry the Young against his father Henry II as the most recent in a long line of similar rebellions going back to the time of King David and Absalom.[36] Nevertheless, however important the study of textual images of rebellion and rebels may be for understanding how an ideology of Christian kingship was used to impose a royalist view of politics and law on contemporary political practice in England (if not on the narratives of modern political historians), the conventionalized historiographical practice of treating over-dramatized accounts of rebellions and pejoratively hyperbolic descriptions of treacherous rebels by clerical and monastic authors as transparent descriptions of political practice has sometimes impeded the study of so-called 'rebellions' in medieval England.

As the remainder of this chapter shows, the armed conflicts that Anglo-Norman and Angevin Latin authors called rebellions (or *seditiones* or *turbationes*) were consistently identified by the more neutral term 'war' (*guerre*) in twelfth- and early thirteenth-century verse- and prose-histories in Anglo-Norman or Old French, whose authors seem to have used the French word for rebellion (*revel*) only in connection with revolts by non-nobles.[37] These same authors also used the word 'war' for armed conflicts that modern historians ordinarily distinguish from rebellions and from one another by calling them 'foreign wars' and either 'private wars',

---

34 According to Valente, *Theory and Practice of Revolt*, p. 3, the use of the words 'rebellion' and 'revolt' reflects a failure to question 'the royal view of the illegitimacy of using force against the king'.
35 On the customs and rhetoric of rebellion, see Bartlett, *England under the Norman and Angevin Kings*, pp. 60–62.
36 See Staunton, *The Historians of Angevin England*, pp. 187–215; and Strickland, *Henry the Young King, 1155–1183*, pp. 4–9.
37 *La chanson de Roland* used the verb form in connection with an uprising by the Saxons and other subject peoples against the Emperor Charlemagne. The Anonymous of Béthune's *Histoire des ducs de Normandie et des rois d'Angleterre*, p. 111 uses the same verb when referring, for example, to the Irish 'rebelling' against King John.

'seigneurial wars', or 'feuds'.[38] In historical texts written in the language used by members of a francophone nobility in both England and continental territories — a nobility to which kings of England themselves belonged — all of these armed conflicts were called 'wars', seemingly without regard to whether one or both of the main antagonists were kings, dukes, counts, or lesser lords.[39]

Rebellion as War

To be sure, the fact that Geffrei Gaimar's *Estoire des Engleis* (c. 1136–1137),[40] Wace's *Roman de Rou* (mid-1170s),[41] Jordan Fantosme's *Chronicle* (1174–1175),[42] and *L'Histoire des ducs de Normandie and des rois d'Angleterre* by the Anonymous of Béthune [henceforth AB] (1220 or shortly thereafter)[43] all applied the word 'war' routinely and without qualification to all the armed conflicts just mentioned does not imply that their medieval authors saw no differences among them or that these texts should be privileged over Latin ones as transparent descriptions of political practice. But as I explain below, despite their many flagrant inaccuracies, anachronisms, and oversimplifications in describing the armed conflicts considered here, these texts represented virtually all 'wars' — including the ones historians now call 'rebellions' — as sharing certain key characteristics. This finding does more than show that in principle, their authors saw nothing intrinsically wrong or unlawful about English nobles making war on their own king, provided that they could justify doing so in one or more ways. It also provides further corroboration for Bartlett's revisionist model of rebellion, raises additional doubts about

---

38 *Anglo-Norman Dictionary (AND Online Edition)*, s.v., 'guerre', accessed 29 March 2023, <https://anglo-norman.net/entry/guerre>; *Anglo-Norman Dictionary (AND Online Edition)*, s.v., 'guerreier²', accessed 29 March 2023, <https://anglo-norman.net/entry/guerreier_2>.
39 Although Anglo-Norman and Angevin Latin narratives, too, used the word 'war' in Latinized form for armed conflict, they generally did so only selectively.
40 Gaimar, *Estoire des Engleis / History of the English*. When English translations of Gaimar's text and of the texts cited below are in quotation marks, they follow the translations I cite and sometimes include, in brackets, the original text for the sake of clarification.
41 Wace, *The Roman de Rou*.
42 Jordan Fantosme, *Jordan Fantosme's Chronicle*.
43 The Anonymous of Béthune [henceforth AB], *Histoire des ducs de Normandie et des rois d'Angleterre* [henceforth AB, *Histoire*]. For an English translation, see AB, *History of the Dukes of Normandy and Kings of England* [henceforth AB, *History*]. For another English translation of AB, *Histoire*, pp. 90–208, see Short, 'King John: A Flemish Perspective'. On the date of the text, see Spiegel, *Romancing the Past*, p. 231; and Webster's, 'Introduction', pp. 1–2. AB, *Histoire* overlaps with AB, *Chronique des rois de France*, which is partially published as AB, 'Extrait d'une chronique française'.

the conventional one, and calls into question assumptions built into the conventional approaches to the study of medieval 'civil wars' that are contested in this volume.[44]

The first of these key characteristics of 'war' was that every armed conflict of this kind could ordinarily be justified by nobles (including kings) *either* as a legitimate way of claiming a rightful inheritance — including a kingdom — that his adversary had wrongfully taken from him or had unjustly withheld from him, *or* as a legitimate means of defending his own inheritance — including a kingdom — against an enemy seeking to take it away from him unjustly by claiming it, for example, as an inheritance. For this reason, like other forms of violence, according to William Ian Miller, war was perspectival, in the sense that both the party initiating a war and the party against whom the war was initiated could have legal grounds for claiming to be waging war justly.[45] At the same time, in French historical texts as well as in *chansons de geste*, war could also be justified as a legitimate means of avenging the anger, grief, and shame that a noble (including a king) suffered when his enemy took away his rightful inheritance or withheld it from him or sought to disinherit him by wrongfully waging war on him.[46] Moreover, because war was also a vehicle for avenging injuries and dishonour in its double sense of shame and disinheritance, it was ordinarily represented in medieval French historical narratives as a kind of feud, in which each leader angrily retaliated against the other by seeking to shame and dishonour his enemy, sometimes capturing his castles and, even more commonly, by pillaging and plundering — that is, by ravaging — his lands and dependants.[47] If so, then the more claims to inheritances a noble lord or a king could make, the more easily he could accumulate grounds for making war and taking vengeance against enemies who had

---

44 See Chapter 1.
45 Miller, 'Getting a Fix on Violence'.
46 White, 'The Politics of Anger in Medieval France'; and 'Un imaginaire faidal'.
47 Ravaging has been aptly defined in general terms as 'an assault on the material and psychological basis of an opponent's lordship, achieved by the seizure or destruction of the central component of his landed wealth — his chattels, crops, livestock and peasants' by members of 'a professional warrior élite directing much of its attention in war against a largely defenceless peasantry or against the inhabitants of towns' (Strickland, *War and Chivalry*, p. 239). However, because ravaging was only loosely limited by recognized norms, could be carried out with varying degrees of intensity, and served different purposes and functions, including rewarding soldiers by giving them opportunities to take plunder, the role that it played in any given war depended on such variables as the size of the forces and the objectives of the opposing leaders. As a result, ravaging in war could be difficult to distinguish from what English legal historians call 'distraint'. Finally, to make the study of ravaging (or distraint) even trickier, the violence of ravaging was a matter of perspective, so that an enemy's ravaging always appeared to be worse than a friend's, while one's own either went unmentioned or, in a king's case, was euphemized as distraint and/or disseisin at his command.

disinherited him. Finally, because vindictive ravaging was evidently carried out by the English king's soldiers even more destructively than it was by his aristocratic opponents, and sometimes led to the latter's disinheritance and the granting of their lands to the king's supporters, the wars that kings waged against baronial enemies should be seen not so much as a means of defeating them militarily, suppressing their rebellion, re-establishing central authority, and/or restoring law and order, but rather as a way of taking revenge on them by disinheriting them and plundering their lands and providing the king's soldiers (including mercenaries and loyal barons) with opportunities to enrich themselves by pillaging and plundering.

As is clear from studies of so-called 'just war theory' in medieval Europe, the three justifications for waging war that medieval French historical writings explicitly mention or implicitly invoke closely resemble the ones considered to be valid ways of legitimating a war by Cicero, St Augustine, Isadore of Seville, Gratian, and later authors, who regarded wars as just if waged to recover lost goods seized unjustly, to repel an enemy attack, or to avenge injuries.[48] However, in contrast to the 'just war' theorists who insisted that great nobles lacked the requisite legal authority to wage war justly against their king, twelfth- and early thirteenth-century French historians rarely if ever questioned the right of nobles to do so for the purpose of recovering a rightful inheritance that had been unjustly withheld or taken away from them, even in cases where the inheritance they claimed was the kingdom of England and the claimant a close kinsman or kinswoman from the ruling dynasty. Nor did these authors suggest that it was sacrilegious or even wrong for nobles make war on kings of England, whom they, unlike monastic and clerical authors of histories and chronicles, did not represent as being endowed with sacral power or religious authority of any kind.

To show in greater detail how the study of these vernacular texts can facilitate the re-thinking of rebellion as 'war', the next section considers as an example of what I call, adapting Bartlett's classificatory schema, a Type 1 war, the one waged in 1068 by an Anglo-Saxon nobleman called Hereward against William I, as related by Geffrei Gaimar in his *Estoire des Engles*. To show how several Type 2 wars were narrated, I then examine, in chronological order: Robert Wace's accounts in his *Roman de Rou* of the war of 1088 between King William II and his brother, Duke Robert of Normandy and the war of 1101 between the same Duke Robert and his other brother King Henry I (1100–1135); and the story told in AB's *L'histoire des ducs de Normandie et les rois d'Angleterre* about the war that the Empress Matilda waged successfully between 1139 and 1153 against King Stephen. Finally, I analyse AB's lengthy account of the Type 3 war

---

48 See Russell, *The Just War in the Middle Ages*, pp. 60–68.

of 1215–1217, which, as noted above, includes elements of Type 1 and Type 2 wars. The Conclusion, on war and vengeance or 'payback' ends the chapter.

The Wars of 1070–1071, 1088, 1101, 1139–1153, and 1215–1217

Hereward v. King William I (1070–1071): Gaimar, L'Estoire des Engleis

In discussing armed resistance to King William I by nobles in eastern and northern England during the late 1060s and early 1070s, historians invariably cite the prominent role played in it by an English nobleman called Hereward. But they have largely ignored a lengthy passage about him in Gaimar's *Estoire des Engleis*, either because it is 'so grossly error-ridden as to be altogether unreliable' or because it was written more than sixty years after the events it describes 'for an Anglo-Norman audience that could celebrate its English antecedents'.[49] The entry on Hereward in the *Oxford Dictionary of National Biography* situates him in what is easily recognizable as the conventional model of rebellion by calling him a 'rebel' and associating him with earls Edwin and Morcar of Northumbria, who 'rebelled against Norman rule' in 1071, after 'a Danish fleet [of King Svend Estridsen had] arrived in the Humber and roused the country to revolt against the Normans' in the previous year. When the two earls 'retreated into the fenland with various discontented Englishmen', including Hereward, King William 'dispatched a fleet and land force and besieged the Isle of Ely. The rebels were forced to submit' except for 'Hereward alone and those who could escape with him and he led them out valiantly'. According to another source, the same biographical entry adds, 'Hereward led an assault on Peterborough Abbey as the leader of the abbey's tenants who resented the appointment of the Norman Turold to the house. Hereward at this time seems to have been in alliance with the Danes, and Peterborough tradition saw the action as one motivated by pure greed'.[50]

In his *Estoire des Engleis*, however, Gaimar represents Hereward not as a 'rebel' against William I, much less as an avaricious plunderer of monks, but rather as a nobleman who, though an outlaw, engaged rightfully in a war of revenge against his enemies, including William I, the king's Norman, French, and English followers, and his local supporters, such as the

---

49 Hollister, *Henry I*, p. 103, cited in Short, 'Introduction', in Gaimar, *Estoire des Engleis*, p. xiv; for other disparaging comments on Gaimar as an historical source, see p. xiv, n. 20.
50 Roffe, 'Hereward'. For a more complex view of Hereward, see, e.g., Bates, *William the Conqueror*, pp. 300, 332–33, 346–48, and the literature cited in p. 360, n. 60.

townsmen of Peterborough and Stamford.[51] Writing under the patronage of minor nobles of Lincolnshire — a region with which Hereward was closely connected — Gaimar wrote a history of England in Anglo-Norman French that provides, John Gillingham writes, 'unparalleled insight into the thought-world of the secular aristocracy of the early 12th c.'[52] Unlike other accounts of wars ordinarily identified by modern historians as rebellions against Norman or Angevin kings, this one recounts the war mainly from the perspective of a king's noble enemies, not the king.

As background to his story of Hereward's war with the Normans, Gaimar explains that after defeating the English army in a battle where Harold and his two brothers were killed, 'Count William had the land [païs] ... and remained the lord [il sire] of it for twenty-two years' (5344ff). Next, without mentioning William's coronation, Gaimar then writes that after he had briefly 'reigned' (regné) and had thoroughly 'pacified the country' (le païs bien apeisé) (5347–48), he went north with his barons and a large army. At Northampton he sent a message to the people of York, asking that 'all the barons of York and surrounding districts should come before [him]' and announcing that 'everyone who was willing to recognize him as their lord would duly receive back from him the inheritance [heritez] that their fathers, and their ancestors before them, had held, and that to such people he would grant his peace and safe-conduct'. William also declared that 'anyone wishing to part company with him, [should] simply return home in safety and without any sort of impediment' (5387–96). Upon arriving at York, however, William 'fortified a stronghold within the city', where he imprisoned all the English barons who answered his summons and 'made their lands over to the French. He then set off towards the south, plundering and leaving many towns in flames' (5397–5404).

Several years later, in 1071, Gaimar continues, Earl Morcar joined with Bishop Aethelwine of Durham and Siward Bearn, and as 'outlaws against king William, they attacked the English at Upwell [in Norfolk]' (5457–64). Using the term 'outlaw' with minimal, if any, pejorative connotations, Gaimar goes on to say that these 'outlaws' allied themselves with other outlaws, whose lord was Hereward, whom the Normans had 'disinherited' (5471); and that Count Morcar and his barons, Hereward and his followers, and the bishop with his men all 'plundered a large part of the country that the Normans had occupied' (5475–76), apparently for the purpose, on Hereward's part, of avenging his disinheritance. Without fearing their Norman 'enemies' (5478), the entire group proceeded to Ely to spend the

---

51 In the text and notes, Arabic numerals in parentheses refer to line numbers in Gaimar, *Estoire des Engleis*, which, according to Short, 'Introduction', p. xlvii, depicts Hereward as 'a heroic freedom fighter against Norman oppression'.
52 Short, 'Introduction', p. ix; Gillingham, 'Kingship, Chivalry and Love', p. 233.

winter. When King William learned of their whereabouts, he sent many soldiers and naval forces to surround Ely and threatened to kill everyone there. They all sought William's mercy, except Hereward, who escaped along with seven of his men. Later, Gaimar writes, Hereward and his small band of followers surprised William's soldiers while they were eating, killed twenty-six Normans and twelve Englishmen, stole their horses, and rode away, all without the author even hinting that Hereward's conduct was unlawful or even blameworthy. After recruiting about 700 men who were faithful to him, Hereward led them in an attack on the fortified town of Peterborough, where they took plenty of gold, silver, and other booty, while taking care to protect the property of the monks of Peterborough. When Hereward's army moved on to Stamford, they plundered it as well. To make clear that Hereward and his men not only did no wrong in plundering Stamford and Peterborough but were fully justified in taking vengeance on both towns, Gaimar wrote:

> The spoils they seize [at Stamford] are legitimate [*ne funt tort*], for its citizens had connived in Hereward being sent into exile [*fu dechacé*]: unfairly and without any justification they had been instrumental in his incurring the king's displeasure. In seeking vengeance against the inhabitants of Peterborough and Stamford, Hereward was, therefore, not acting in the least unlawfully [*S'il s'en vengat, ne fu mie tort*] (5564–70).

For several more years, according to Gaimar, Hereward 'held out against the Normans', as he and his noble companions 'waged war [*guerreierent*] against the French' (5577).[53] At least from this point in his narrative onwards, Gaimar contributed to the mythologizing of Hereward by describing how his extraordinary strength and bravery enabled him to survive repeated attacks by his enemies, until 'the Normans' finally killed him. But before they did so, Hereward clearly enunciated his own right to retaliate against them and marked his own killing as shameful and unlawful by telling them: 'The king has granted me a truce, but here you are threatening violence, stealing my property and butchering my men. You have taken me by surprise in the middle of my meal, but, treacherous curs that you are, I'll make you pay for this' (5636–40). Which Hereward did, according to Gaimar, by killing seven or more of his attackers before one of the survivors cut off his head, thereby marking his death as a vengeance killing, though not an honourable one (5641–5700).

The designation of Hereward as a 'rebel' makes him fit perfectly into the conventional model of rebellion, in which nobles, even when disinherited by their own king, have no right to make war on him, much less to

---

53 Here and elsewhere, Gaimar appears to use the words 'French' and 'Norman' interchangeably.

ambush and kill his soldiers and plunder lands and towns in his kingdom. However, the war that Gaimar's Hereward waged against King William can be classified as a Type 1 war in which a nobleman avenged his own disinheritance by warring against the king who had disinherited him and against the townspeople who had made sure that he would incur William's displeasure. Granted, Hereward could be portrayed as a heroic figure partly because Gaimar, for whatever reason, filled his story about him with historical inaccuracies and anachronisms. But what mainly differentiates his narrative from canonical stories of Hereward as a 'rebel' against King William is the perspective from which Gaimar tells it.

By representing the larger war against William from the perspective of the nobles who waged it, Gaimar shows that what triggered it was not the nobles' rebelliousness, their imagined if not imaginary grievances, or any unlawful act on their part that could have justified King William in disinheriting and/or making war on them. Instead, as Gaimar tells the story, the grounds for war are initially provided by the evil deeds of the felonious, treacherous King William, who, far from justifiably retaliating against Northern barons for their treacherous misdeeds, has shamelessly used evil trickery to imprison them, take away their ancestral inheritances, and use their lands to reward his own Norman followers, who secure further rewards for themselves when William grants them another form of patronage by sending them out to ravage the English countryside. Although there is no way of reconstructing the exact sequence of events in Hereward's war, this conflict, like the larger war in which it was embedded, cannot be attributed to his rebelliousness, his disaffection from King William, or his desire for gain. Instead, it was apparently triggered, according to Gaimar, by Hereward wrongfully incurring King William's displeasure (5567) and being disinherited by the Normans (5471) and exiled (*dechacé*) as well (5555). Gaimar's Hereward responds not by rebelling unlawfully against his king, much less against the Lord's anointed, but in the customary way by waging a war against his enemies. Although Hereward's war against William is not represented as a vehicle for asserting a claim to his lost inheritance, it serves to avenge that wrong, along with others he has suffered. Allying himself with Earl Morcar and the other magnates who are enemies of King William and his Normans, he joins with them to take vengeance by plundering the lands the Normans have taken over, presumably from the English, possibly when William gave the Normans the 'inheritances' of the English magnates. Moreover, Hereward joins in attacking and rightfully plundering Peterborough and Stamford to take vengeance (5569) on the people of both towns, who have 'connived' in putting him in conflict with the king who deprived him of his main estates (5567–68). Hereward's later killings of King William's men can also be interpreted as justifiable acts of vengeance.

Although Hereward's enemies, according to Gaimar, included Normans, Frenchmen, and Englishmen, his principal enemy was William himself, whom Gaimar represents, without even mentioning his coronation, as a bad, treacherous, and dishonourable king, who inspires fear, but no respect and conspicuously lacks the religious aura that clerical and monastic authors of Latin narratives seemed to attribute to him automatically. Indeed, Gaimar's William can hardly be distinguished from a very powerful nobleman who rewards the barons and knights who follow him by giving them the inheritances he has seized from others. As for the followers of Hereward — who is lauded as 'uns gentilz hom' and 'un des meillurs del region' (5468, 5470) — we can think of them as belonging to his personal social network, which includes 'a hundred fully armed men who recognized [him] as their liege lord [and] owed him fealty and were his men' (5549–51; see also 5468). To wage war against King William and his Normans, Hereward was also linked, Gaimar indicates, to a more loosely constituted network of allies, which includes: Earl Morcar of Northumberland and Bishop Aelfwine (54722–25) and their men; unspecified Norsemen; and Danes, including a brother and three sons of the Danish king Svend Estridsen (5431–50).[54] Although later sources for Hereward's life 'all agree that he was reconciled with William [I] and regained his patrimony', there is no reason to think that their reconciliation brought enduring peace even to the region where the two men had been at war.[55] Instead, all the signs are that the first half-decade of William I's reign in England was marked by major and minor Type 1 wars and Type 2 wars to replace William I as king, if not by 'constant crisis'. During the rest of his reign, wars of both types continued, including two so-called 'quarrels' with his eldest son Robert 'Curthose', who engaged in one small-scale armed conflict with his father in 1078–1080 (396–404) and another during the years preceding William's death on 9 September of 1087.[56] This was soon followed by a Type 2 war between William I's second son William II (known as Rufus), who quickly succeeded his father as king of England when he was crowned on 26 September of the same year, and his elder brother Robert, their father's heir and successor as Duke of Normandy.

---

54 On the importance of 'social networks' in Scandinavian civil wars, see Chapters 1 and 2.
55 Roffe, 'Hereward'.
56 Bates, *William the Conqueror*, pp. 171, 396–404, 455–57, 484–90.

Duke Robert of Normandy v. King William II (1088): Wace, Roman de Rou

In a short account of this war in Wace's *Roman de Rou*, which he wrote during the 1160s and early 1170s,[57] the author deviated radically from older narratives of the same conflict by Latin historians, including Orderic Vitalis, William of Malmesbury, John of Worcester, and Henry of Huntingdon. Viewing the conflict from a perspective that was largely favourable to William II's legitimacy as king, each of these authors tended to depict it as a horrifically violent rebellion against a legitimate king by rebels, perjurers, and conspirators in both England and Normandy, who, as John of Worcester put it, 'stirred up fire and sword, plundering and death over the whole country' in a rebellion that set 'fathers against sons, brothers against brothers, friends against their kinsmen, strangers against strangers'.[58] Around the time of William I's death, according to Orderic, 'a great revolution [*nimia rerum mutatio*] took place in Normandy', where 'the magnates ... expelled [William II's] garrisons from their castles and, plundering each other's lands with their own men at arms, they stripped the rich country of its wealth'.[59] Later, 'these magnates crossed to England, fortified and provisioned their castles, and had soon roused a considerable part of the kingdom against [William II]'. When the king realized that his own subjects 'were planning treason [*contra se pessima cogitare*] and going from bad to worse in their lawless acts [he] resolved to crush the rebellion [*rebellium*]', which Orderic blamed on unnamed '*perturbatores pacis*', '*perfidos proditores*', '*rebelles*', '*seditiosi*', and a '*cohors superba rebellium*'.[60]

In Wace's *Roman de Rou*, however, this violent, destructive rebellion against William II in Normandy and England by proud, perfidious traitors from both regions appears in a more favourable light as a war waged by Duke Robert of Normandy and his Norman followers to claim the kingdom of England as his rightful inheritance from his brother, King William II, who had the full support of the English nobles. Moreover, although he wrote his verse-history of the Norman dukes initially under the patronage of King Henry II and Queen Eleanor of Aquitaine during the 1160s and early 1170s, Wace — who had spent his life in Normandy — does not privilege the political perspectives of the two Norman kings of England, William II and Henry I, over that of their brother, Robert Duke of Normandy; nor does he state or imply that England should be united

---

57 On this war and local revolts associated with it, see Barlow, *William Rufus*, pp. 68–93; on the treaty of February 1091 that ended the war between William II and Duke Robert, p. 91.
58 John of Worcester, *Chronicle*, pp. 48–49.
59 Orderic, *Ecclesiastical History*, vol. 4, pp. 112–13.
60 Orderic, *Ecclesiastical History*, vol. 5, pp. 124–29.

with Normandy into an empire under the king of England's authority.[61] Instead, Wace treats this war as the product of what Bartlett calls 'sibling rivalry ... within the ruling house' combined with conflicting loyalties of magnates holding lands in both England and Normandy.[62]

Accordingly, by using language appropriate to a lawsuit between two brothers in an aristocratic lineage over an inheritance to which each has a legitimate claim, Wace represents the war of 1101 as an inheritance dispute between two brothers about which of them had the right to hold the kingdom of England after their father's death. At the same time, Wace clearly misrepresents the war by minimizing the conflicts of loyalty it created for nobles with ties to both William II and Robert and ignoring the cases of treason and side-switching highlighted by Orderic and other Latin authors. According to Wace, support for Robert came exclusively from his aristocratic Norman followers, while William II's supporters were all English nobles. Strangely, Wace's war involves virtually no armed violence, only the threat of it; and it ends in a peace agreement that resembles the ones reached in inheritance disputes between noble kinsmen, leaving William with his kingdom but still honouring Robert by according him an annual payment of 5000 pounds. A payment of this magnitude could only have been construed as a public acknowledgement that although Robert was peacefully surrendering any claim to hold England as an inheritance, the claim itself was not a spurious one, as one can see from the fact that according to Wace, Robert revived it in exactly the same form after William II's death in 1099 and their brother Henry's accession to the English throne in 1100.

The origin of the war of 1088, according to Wace, could be found in the gifts of England, Normandy, and Maine that William I made to his three grown sons on his deathbed in Normandy, 'so that after his death', the author notes ironically, 'there would be no quarrelling' (9101–03).[63] In a highly abbreviated version of Orderic's story about the same occasion, Wace writes that after summoning all his barons to Rouen, the king announced that he was giving to his eldest son Robert (who was absent) the duchy of Normandy, which, the king said, was his own inheritance (*mon heritage*), where 'most of his lineage' lived (9105–07). William I had previously granted the duchy to Robert in *c.* 1063 before becoming king of England, and he now gave him Le Mans in addition (9108–11). Next,

---

61 On Wace's poem, see 'Introduction', in Wace, *Roman de Rou*, pp. xiii–xxxviii; and van Houts, 'Wace as Historian', pp. xxxv–xl. According to Le Patourel, *The Norman Empire*, William I created a 'cross-channel empire'; for criticism of this view, see, e.g., Barlow, *William Rufus*, pp. 42–43 and p. 42, n. 174.
62 Bartlett, *England under the Norman and Angevin Kings*, p. 6.
63 For conflicting interpretations of William I's deathbed gifts to his sons, see Barlow, *William Rufus*, pp. 40–52; Bates, *William the Conqueror*, pp. 483–89.

William declared that although he wished 'to advance the cause of William my son, who is here and [who] desires England for himself and wants to become king of it', he himself could not do this, because he had conquered England 'wrongfully' and ought not to give to his son William 'what I stole wrongfully and had no right to'. Instead, the king said he would send William to England, where he was to 'beg the archbishop [Lanfranc] to grant him the crown, if he can do so by right. If he can do this by reason, I beg that he should give him this gift' (9133–54). Finally, the king gave his youngest son Henry 5000 pounds and ordered that William and Robert should each, in his own lordship, make Henry richer and wealthier than any other man.[64]

After King William I's death, according to Wace, his son William followed his father's instructions on how he should seek to become king of England. '[He] crossed the sea [to England]. In his father's name, he had a sealed letter taken to Lanfranc, Archbishop of Canterbury, [who] had the letter read out. Because of [Rufus's] father's goodness, [Lanfranc] held the son dear and crowned him in Westminster, on Michaelmas Day' (9349–57). However, 'Robert, who was in Normandy, was very envious of his brother [William, who] had been raised to the rank of a king, although he had been born after [Robert]'. Robert was therefore 'distressed' (*marriz*) and 'upset' (9375–79) — a clear sign of the shame he felt at being passed over. Robert raised some money from his brother Henry and gave him the Cotentin — a part of Normandy — as a pledge for it, because, Wace explained,

> he did not want to wait any longer before crossing to England to obtain what was rightfully his [*son dreit conquerre*] from King Rufus, who was acting wrongfully and shamefully with regard to him [*qui tort e honte li faiseit*] and who was younger than he and king. (9386–90)

Robert then 'sought knights and a fleet and crossed the sea with a very large army' (9423–27).

When Rufus 'heard that his brother was coming to attack him and ... wanted to take possession of England' (*Engleterre aveir voleit*), he summoned his men from the entire county and soon 'gathered together a very large army, for he preferred to die on the battlefield than to abandon England to the duke' (*Engleterre al duc guerpir*) (9428–34). However, before there was any fighting, the king's barons and the bishops advised him to make peace by giving his brother some of his wealth. William therefore agreed to 'give Robert each year from then onwards, as long as he lived, five thousand pounds in money' — the exact amount that William I

---

[64] For a lengthy account of how William I made deathbed gifts to his three sons, see Orderic, *Ecclesiastical History*, vol. 4, pp. 80–100.

had given to Henry. 'Robert agreed to this willingly [and] returned to Normandy with his barons' (9435–48).

Nevertheless, although the war of 1088 between Duke Robert and King William II ended in a peace agreement between them, it did not resolve the 'family tensions' that were built into dynastic politics, according to Bartlett; instead, it marked the beginning of a prolonged period of war among members of the royal dynasty established by William I about which of them would rule England as king and/or the continental territories he held at the time of his death in 1087.[65] Not surprisingly, William II's death in 1100, followed by the coronation of William I's third son Henry led to a kind of replay of the war of 1088, with Henry I assuming the role of his deceased brother Rufus.

Duke Robert of Normandy v. King Henry I (1101): Wace, Roman de Rou

In describing this war — which Robert initiated a year after Henry had succeeded their brother William Rufus as king of England and been crowned at Westminster — Wace again deviates radically from earlier accounts of it by Latin authors such as Orderic Vitalis, whose story substantiates the conventional model of rebellion in several ways. First, Orderic characterizes the conflict in pejorative terms as 'a great revolt [*ingens turbatio*] in England and Normandy'. According to Orderic, it was the work of the 'incorrigible plunderer of the country', Ranulph Flambard, 'the chief instigator of [the] mad plot' to make Robert king of England, and was brought about by countless acts of treason (*proditio*), faithlessness (*infida*), and sedition (*seditio*).[66] Orderic also denounces Duke Robert's followers as rebels (*rebelles*), troth-breakers (*perfidos*), seditionists (*seditiosi*), and 'traitors' (*proditores*), and describes the 'reckless' (*imprudens*) duke himself as 'damnably sunken into sloth, softness — that is, effeminacy — [*Socordia nempe mollicieque*]', and 'cowardice [*ignavia*]', adding that the duke was surrounded by 'treacherous magnates' (*seditiosi ... proceres*) and by 'harlots and rascals who ... knew his weakness [*lenitatem*]'.[67] Even though Orderic represents Robert as saying that 'I entered the kingdom of my father [and] demand the right due to me as the eldest son [*iure primogenitorum*]', the author has already shown asserted that it was only 'out of greed for the kingdom which his abler brother possessed' that the duke followed the 'plan of revolt [*decretum proditionis*]' concocted by evil counsellors to prepare a fleet for an invasion of England.[68]

---

65 Bartlett, *England under the Norman and Angevin Kings*, pp. 5–6.
66 Orderic, *Ecclesiastical History*, vol. 5, pp. 306–07, 310–11.
67 Orderic, *Ecclesiastical History*, vol. 5, pp. 300–01, 312–13, 306–07, 308–09.
68 Orderic, *Ecclesiastical History*, vol. 5, pp. 318–19, 308–09.

On the other hand, Orderic depicts King Henry's supporters as an honourable group of men, including Archbishop Anselm and all the bishops, abbots, and clergy, who 'preserved unshaken loyalty [to the king and] offered ceaseless prayers to the Lord of Hosts', and the king's 'loyal and provident barons [who] followed [him] faithfully and supplied him with counsel and military support' and 'protected their king'.[69] Meanwhile, 'all the English, who did not recognize the rights of the other prince, persisted in their loyalty to their king and were ready to go into battle to prove it'. Good counsel was provided to the king by Count Robert of Meulan, who declared that he and his fellow knights 'have been entrusted by God to provide for the common good and ought to keep a sharp lookout to preserve the safety of the realm and of the Church of God'.[70] To the nobles and knights who had failed to observe their obligations to King Henry, Count Robert declared:

> There is no doubt that anyone who chooses to desert his lord in an hour of deadly danger and seek another lord for greed of gain, or insists on payment for the military service that he ought to offer freely to his king for the defense of the realm, and attempts to deprive him of his own demesnes will be a judged a traitor [*proditor*] by a just and equitable judgment, and will rightly be deprived of his inheritance [*hereditariis rebus*] and forced to flee the country.[71]

In telling the story of Robert's rebellion against Henry I, Orderic first notes that in August of 1100, when William II's death became known in Normandy, 'the passions of the unruly Normans broke out in civil war, [as many] who had been nursing anger and hatred, but had not dared to avenge themselves openly because of the strict justice maintained by the prince, fell upon each other without restraint, now that control was relaxed, and by their mutual slaughter and pillaging devastated the unhappy province which was without a ruler'.[72] When Duke Robert returned to Normandy from crusade, nothing changed, because he was 'an object of contempt to the restless and lawless Normans. Theft and rapine were daily occurrences, and brutalities increased everywhere to the ruin of the whole country'.[73] Later, in 1101, 'a great revolt broke out in England and Normandy. Turbulent magnates ... began to hold treacherous conferences with one another [to plot against the king] and advised the duke to prepare a fleet and cross at the earliest opportunity'.[74] There were many

---

69 Orderic, *Ecclesiastical History*, vol. 5, pp. 310–11, 314–15.
70 Orderic, *Ecclesiastical History*, vol. 5, pp. 316–17.
71 Orderic, *Ecclesiastical History*, vol. 5, pp. 316–17.
72 Orderic, *Ecclesiastical History*, vol. 5, pp. 300–01.
73 Orderic, *Ecclesiastical History*, vol. 5, pp. 300–03.
74 Orderic, *Ecclesiastical History*, vol. 5, pp. 306–09.

'who approved the plan of revolt and helped the adherents of the duke, [who] did not give good government to his own dominions, but foolishly neglected them out of greed for the kingdom which his abler brother possessed'.[75] Ultimately, Ranulf Flambard, whom Henry I had imprisoned for plundering England during William II's reign, escaped to Normandy, where he 'urged the duke to a trial of strength with his brother, and stirred up hostility against the king by every means in his power. He advised the duke on how he might best secure the kingdom of England and promised him his help in all that he did'.[76] In the autumn of 1101, 'Duke Robert sailed across to England and, after being received as king by the distinguished and wealthy men who had formed a conspiracy and were expecting him, he prepared for war [...]. Urged on by the rebels, he challenged his brother to meet him in battle unless he was prepared to renounce the crown'.[77]

However, Orderic writes, even before Henry I went to meet Robert's army of rebels with a huge army of loyal soldiers, the king had been determined to seek peace with his brother, after Count Robert of Meulan advised him that 'our chief care [should] be to triumph peacefully by God's grace and win a victory without shedding Christian blood, so that our loyal people may enjoy the security of peace'.[78] Recognizing that the noble envoys going back and forth between him and his brother Robert were 'sow[ing] the seeds of dispute rather than concord between [them]', Henry spoke to Robert 'face to face', and they then 'embraced one another [and] were reconciled without a mediator' in the following way:

> Robert renounced in favour of his brother the claim he had made to the realm of England, and out of respect for his royal dignity released him from the homage which he had previous done him. King Henry promised to pay the duke a sum of three thousand pounds sterling every year and relinquished in his favour the whole Cotentin and everything that he possessed in Normandy except [the castle of] Domfront.[79]

After peace was made, 'The realm of England lay basking in the glow of peace'.[80]

Although Wace ends his account of this war between Robert and Henry as Orderic does, by describing the amicable compromise made between the two brothers, he presents a radically different picture of how

---

75 Orderic, *Ecclesiastical History*, vol. 5, pp. 308–09.
76 Orderic, *Ecclesiastical History*, vol. 5, pp. 312–15.
77 Orderic, *Ecclesiastical History*, vol. 5, pp. 314–15.
78 Orderic, *Ecclesiastical History*, vol. 5, pp. 316–17.
79 Orderic, *Ecclesiastical History*, vol. 5, pp. 318–19.
80 Orderic, *Ecclesiastical History*, vol. 5, pp. 320–21.

the agreement was reached; he also gives a totally different explanation of how and why the war began. He does so partly by explaining at the outset Robert's reason for contesting Henry I's claim to be king of England and partly by omitting all reference to treason by Henry's supporters or the Normans' violence and rebelliousness. As a result, Wace portrays the war of 1101 in the same terms as he uses in depicting the war of 1088, as an ordinary dispute over a father's inheritance between two brothers who both had legitimate claims to it. After the death of King William II in 1100, his 'younger brother' Henry 'established himself in the kingdom', Wace writes, though without indicating by what right. 'No one', he adds, 'had waited for Robert, but he did come very quickly; he returned from Jerusalem' (10297–10301) to Normandy, and 'took possession of [it] and had it fully under his power'. However, just as the duke had been angered in 1088 by the news that his younger brother Rufus had become king of England, 'he was [now] exceedingly distressed and exceedingly angered by Henry, his younger brother, who was king against his wishes; he himself should have been king, he said, through seniority of birth' (10319–30). After summoning his barons and knights, Robert crossed the sea with them, landed at Portchester, headed toward London, and entered Alton Wood, where he was advised 'not to advance rashly, for [King Henry, who had learned of Robert's arrival in England] was intending to surprise him as he came out of the wood'. Each army 'remained like this for a long time and feared each other for a long time, each afraid of entering the wood and no one wanting to go back' (10364–68).

Whereas Orderic represents the peace soon made between King Henry and Duke Robert as the product of bilateral negotiations between them, Wace attributes it to the barons of the two enemies, who were mindful of the kinship ties between both sides and the common interests of the barons who held land from both Henry and Robert. Because 'On both sides there were sons and fathers, uncles, nephews, cousins or brothers, and no one dared advance for fear of killing his relatives' (10369–72), 'The barons [knew] that relative would be killing relative, cousin cousin and brother brother, and a son his father'. So, they all decided to 'act quite differently and bring about peace between the brothers and never fight for them'. A group of magnates, including ones 'who held lands from both the king and the duke and owed service to both of them, undertook to bring about the peace, because of their fear of battle' (10387–10408). After the barons 'went back and forth from the king to the duke [and] sought to achieve peace and spoke of harmony [*la concorde*]' (1409–12), Robert and Henry 'each submitted to the judgement of the barons on their side. Through their advice they were reconciled and accepted their judgement' (10445–48). On the one hand, Robert had already refrained on his barons' advice from seeking 'from the king something that he should not do, or which could not be done, for after he had been crowned he ought not to be deposed' (10413–19). On the other, 'it was established by covenant that from that time onward, each year as long as he lived, the king would give Duke Robert three thousand marks of silver to keep the peace and repress all anger [*por tote ire remeneir*]'. Why repress his anger? Because Robert — who had been 'exceedingly distressed and exceedingly angered [when Henry had become] king against his wishes' (10325–28) — had to put aside his own anger to end his feud-like war against his brother.

The Empress Matilda v. King Stephen (1139–1153): The Anonymous of Béthune, Histoire des ducs de Normandie et des rois d'Angleterre (post 1220)[81]

The protracted armed conflict from 1139 to 1153 between Henry I's nephew King Stephen and his daughter, the Empress Matilda, was fought to determine which of them was the king's legitimate successor after his death on 1 December 1135. Because Stephen was merely the younger son of the count of Blois and Henry I's sister, Adela of Blois, his insubstantial claim to succeed Henry as king of England could only be articulated in a document purporting to show that after his coronation on 25 December, the king had made a deathbed 'gift' of Stephen, his count and kinsman, to unnamed English magnates.

> While King Henry sickened unto death, a great number of powerful people gathered about him, [...] increasingly concerned about what disposition he would make about himself and the kingdom. To them at the last he indicated what ought to happen. 'To you', he said, 'great and wise men, I give as king the worthy knight Stephen, my count, my most dear kinsman, a virtuous nobleman, yet firm in his faith in the Lord, for you to receive from me by right of inheritance, and you are all to be witnesses of this'. Immediately afterwards, the king breathed his last.[82]

After learning of his deathbed designation as king by Henry I, the document continues,

> The count took up this commission, and having gathered together a large body of knights, he hastened to England and came before the Londoners. Since he was a renowned count and a valiant knight, of proven integrity and greatly loved, and was descended from the stock of [unspecified] kings, and with the great men and the citizens won over by rewards and promises and the clergy fearing great disorder

---

81 In the text of this section, Arabic numerals in parentheses ( ) refer to page numbers in AB, *History*; and Arabic numerals in brackets [ ] to page numbers in AB, *Histoire*.
82 King, *King Stephen*, p. 48, citing *Liber Eliensis*, p. 285.

should he be turned away, he was received by the English as king of England.[83]

To establish Stephen as Henry I's legitimate successor, his supporters also needed to undermine the claim of Henry's daughter, the Empress Matilda, who, after the death of her first husband, Emperor Henry V of Germany in 1125, had married Count Geoffrey of Anjou in 1128 and then had three children with him: Geoffrey, Henry (the future Henry II), and William. It was common knowledge that in 1127, King Henry had arranged for his leading men, including Stephen of Blois, to swear 'fealty to the empress Matilda, Henry's daughter, and [swear] to help her secure all England and Normandy against all men after her father's death',[84] though it remained uncertain whether Henry's heir was Matilda or Henry, her son by Count Geoffrey of Anjou.[85] Therefore, King Stephen's supporters needed to stress that King Henry's barons had sworn this oath reluctantly, if not unwillingly, or even that Henry had known that they had sworn unwillingly and did not expect them to observe their oath to support Matilda.

However, in narrating the war between Stephen and Matilda, AB's *Histoire* tells a very different story from the one that justified Stephen's claim to the throne — one which simultaneously validates Matilda's claim to be Henry I's heir and undercuts Stephen's. It runs as follows: when Henry Emperor of Germany died, King Henry of England sent for his daughter Matilda, the deceased emperor's widow. He arranged for the barons of England and Normandy to swear fealty and do homage to her, and then gave her in marriage to Count Geoffrey Martel of Anjou, son of Count Fulk (83) [69]. Later, when King Henry died, he lacked 'a son by a faithful wife, but Geoffrey, count of Anjou, a cruel and violent man, had married the king's daughter Matilda, formerly empress of Germany, and she was [Henry's] true heir [*ses drois hoirs*]' (86) [71]. After King Henry's death, AB continues, the barons of England wrote to Matilda in Anjou that if she would come to England without her lord, the count of Anjou, 'they would receive her as lady and give her the crown, but her lord the count, they would not receive ..., because he was too violent and cruel [*fel et crueus*], so they were not willing to put themselves under his rule (86) [71]'. Matilda responded that she would not come to England and would never be queen if her lord the count was not king (86) [71]. When Matilda's 'nephew' Stephen heard that his grandfather King Henry was dead and his 'aunt' the empress would not go to England without her

---

83 King, *King Stephen*, pp. 48–49, 301–02; on Stephen's accession, see King, *King Stephen*, pp. 41–51, 301–02.
84 King, *King Stephen*, p. 30, citing John of Salisbury, *Historia Pontificalis: Memoirs of the Papal Court*, ed. and trans. by Marjorie Chibnall (London, 1956), pp. 82–83.
85 King, *King Stephen*, pp. 325–28.

husband Count Geoffrey, whom the barons refused to accept as their lord, Stephen went to Wissant, where, 'partly at the wish of the English and at their request', he took a ship to Dover.[86] Entering England, Stephen 'took seisin of the land and had himself crowned king through the power of his own brother [*par la force de son frere*], [Henry of Blois], the bishop of Winchester, and at the wish of the barons'. They 'granted him the crown on condition [*par tel couvent*] that he would observe for them the charters that his grandfather King Henry had given them and renew them (86) [71–72]'.

While the Empress Matilda, 'England's rightful heir [*drois hoirs*]', was in Anjou with her husband Count Geoffrey, she heard that after her father's death, her nephew Count Stephen had 'seized' [*saisi*] the realm of England. She thereupon went to Normandy and later made great gifts of land to Count Hoel of Maine, in return for his aid in conquering 'her inheritance [*son hiretage*]'. Meanwhile, after Count Geoffrey's death, according to AB's *Histoire* — which mistakenly implies that Geoffrey died soon after Henry I[87] — Geoffrey's son Henry did homage to King Louis of France for the lands that had been his father's. Though grief-stricken at her husband's death, Matilda did not delay 'in going to war and making every effort to regain her inheritance [*reconquerre son hiretage*]' (87) [73]. Upon hearing that his aunt was making war on him in Normandy, Stephen 'gathered a large army and crossed the sea, bringing such a strong force into Normandy, both Englishmen and others, that his enemies did not dare wait for him in the field' (87) [73]. However, after a dispute with his Norman supporters, who 'did great harm' to the Boulonnais following Stephen, the Normans decided to 'leave the king's service' and repented of having shamefully and sinfully supported him against their 'lawful lady the empress' (88) [74]. Fearing that the Normans would 'hand him over to the empress, his aunt, who hated him', Stephen prepared to leave Normandy (88–89) [75–76], where Matilda soon 'received the homage of all the barons of the land [*les barons de la tierre*] and of all the feudatories [*les fievés*]' (89) [76].

Once Stephen was back in England, Matilda's uncle, King David of Scotland, and the earl of Leicester invited her to come to England and undertook to help her secure the crown, which was 'her right' (*ki ses drois estoit*) [76]. After making her son Henry duke of Normandy and having him again 'do homage to Louis, king of France', who agreed to allow his men 'go with her to England and help her regain her inheritance' (89–90) [76–77], Matilda sailed with her Norman and Angevin supporters to England, where she was met by King David, the earl of Leicester, and

---

[86] As Matilda was the daughter of Stephen's mother's brother, they were first cousins by our reckoning.
[87] Count Geoffrey died in 1151, see AB, *History*, p. 87 note 374.

many other barons, all of whom did homage and swore oaths to her (90) [77]. She then 'warred against her nephew King Stephen' (*guerroia moult durement le roi Estievenon*), who was eventually defeated and imprisoned (90) [77]. After Stephen was released, the conflict recommenced, as Matilda warred bitterly against him. When she saw how long the war was lasting, she granted all her right in the land of England to her son Henry, who received the homage of all the men who supported her (91–92) [79–80]. The war continued. But finally, a concord was made between the two cousins: it provided that Stephen would be king for the rest of his life, and that Henry would then have the kingdom and be his heir after him (92) [80]. Like the Type 2 wars between brothers in 1088 and in 1101, as narrated by Wace, this intrafamilial war between a king's daughter, supported by her son, and the son of the king's sister to determine who was the king's rightful heir ended in an agreement which, in this case, led ultimately to the dead king's grandson and heir succeeding him as king of England.

The War of 1215–1217: The Anonymous of Béthune, Histoire des ducs de Normandie et des rois d'Angleterre *(post 1220)*[88]

Modern historians have been virtually unanimous in applying the term 'rebellion' to the armed conflict fought out in England between May of 1215 and 20 September of 1217 in three stages, first by King John and later by the regents of John's son Henry III, against various 'rebels'.[89] In the first stage, the main antagonists were King John and a faction of English barons, many, if not all, of whom had their own individual grievances against the king, but who joined together to support what Bartlett calls 'a reform program' that was embodied in mid-June of 1215 in a 'peace' between John and his barons that later became known as Magna Carta (1215).[90] After Innocent III annulled Magna Carta on 24 August and English bishops as well as the pope excommunicated the barons' leaders in early September, the second stage of the conflict began in October when John renewed

---

88 In this section of the chapter, Arabic numerals in parentheses ( ) refer to page numbers in Shirley, *History*; Arabic numerals in brackets [ ] refer to page numbers in AB, *Histoire*. I have also made use of the English translation of portions of AB, *Histoire* in Short, 'King John: a Flemish Perspective'.
89 For references to rebellion and rebels, see, e.g., Carpenter, *Struggle for Mastery*, p. 288; Holt, *Magna Carta*, pp. 174, 204, 208, 211; Warren, *King John*, pp. 227, 230, 231, 243, 246, 246, 256; Turner, *King John*, pp. 225, 234, 236, 249; Church, *King John*, pp. 207, 212; Carpenter, *Magna Carta*, pp. 299, 300; Carpenter, *The Struggle for Mastery*, pp. 6, 7, 10.
90 Other versions of Magna Carta were issued in 1216 and 1217 (Carpenter, *Magna Carta*, pp. 406–18; Church, *King John*, 242); the so-called final version was issued in 1225 (Carpenter, *Magna Carta*, pp. 417–29).

the conflict against the same group of English barons.[91] Meanwhile, they secured support against the king by offering the English crown to Prince Louis of France, the son of Philip II and husband of Blanche of Castile, daughter of Eleanor, daughter of Henry II and sister of King John.[92] In this way, the barons' armed conflict against John was transformed into a kind of succession dispute between rival claimants to the kingdom of England, while retaining their support for a reform program. The prince's first invasion of England in December of 1215 marked a continuation of the second stage of the conflict, which ended with John's death on 19 October 1216. In its third and final stage, the conflict was fought out between a shifting alliance of English baronial royalists led by Henry III's two Regents, William Marshal and the papal legate Guala, and an unstable coalition of English and French barons led by Prince Louis, who made peace with the Regents and withdrew from England in September of 1217.[93]

In contrast to modern historians, AB consistently describes each stage of this entire conflict as a war, while reserving the verb 'to rebel' for a rising in Ireland against John (120) [111] and a revolt by the people of York against him (156) [163]. Accordingly, AB never refers to the barons who waged war against John or against the regents of Henry III as 'rebels' but simply calls them the king's 'enemies', just as he would have done if the armed conflict had been between two magnates.[94] In presenting an extended narrative of the war of 1215–1217 and events leading up to it — which constituted a major part of his 'original account' of John's reign from 1199 to 1216 and the reign of Henry III down to 1220 — AB was writing from a perspective very different from the one adopted in the *Histoire*'s highly favourable account of how the Empress Matilda and her son Henry recovered their lost inheritance by waging war on King Stephen.[95] Although AB is considered to be 'an eye-witness' to some of the events he described and a source of 'extremely accurate information' about them,[96] how he regarded and evaluated King John and the entire war

---

91 See Carpenter, *Magna Carta*, pp. 395–98.
92 On the weakness of Prince Louis' hereditary claim to the English crown, see Carpenter, *Magna Carta*, p. 399.
93 On the war see McGlynn, *Blood Cries Afar*, pp. 133–241; on Prince Louis' invasion, see Hanley, *Louis: The French Prince Who Invaded England*, pp. 85–177.
94 In a future paper I will show that the same conflict was identified as a '*gwerra*' in several Latin chronicles and in royal records such as the *Close Rolls*, where barons who 'went against' King John were frequently called his 'enemies'.
95 On the relationship between this segment of AB's *Histoire* and the same author's text published as 'Extrait d'une chronique française des rois de France par anonyme de Béthune', see Spiegel, *Romancing the Past*, pp. 232–36; and Webster, 'Introduction', in AB, *History*, pp. 5–9.
96 Spiegel, *Romancing the Past*, pp. 225–28; see also Gillingham, 'The Anonymous of Béthune', pp. 28–34.

of 1215–1217 is difficult to determine. In gauging his attitude toward the conflict, one should keep in mind that since the 1180s, he had belonged to the retinue of an associate of the counts of Flanders, Robert VII of Béthune, who inherited his father's lands in England in 1214 and received large money payments from John in return for fighting in England against the king's enemies, including not only English barons, but Prince Louis and the French magnates and knights who followed the prince to England. After John's death, Robert fought for Henry III's Regents against the same group of enemies, though for how long is uncertain.[97]

Certain passages in AB's history have been read as indicating that while overall he regarded John favourably, as he had a strong interest in doing when the king treated his lord Robert well, he condemned John not only when he mistreated Robert and Robert's Flemish companions in England but when he later failed to aggressively prosecute his war in England against Prince Louis. Other passages suggest that AB regarded John's baronial enemies with 'distaste'[98] and considered Magna Carta 'overall a wretched document'.[99] Still, to focus on these issues alone is to overlook how AB's narrative of John's entire reign gives at least qualified support for the legitimacy of the hybrid Type 3/Type 1 war that the king's baronial enemies waged against him during the first stage of the conflict of 1215–1217. In AB's narrative of John's reign prior to 1214, he sets the stage for favourably representing the barons' war against John, by explaining in general terms and illustrating anecdotally how he incurred the hatred of English magnates by violating ordinary norms of aristocratic conduct; by behaving in a way that was neither kingly nor courtly, but shameful and unlawful; by quarrelling with great nobles who generally behaved more honourably than he did; and by practising what might be called anti-social networking.

According to AB,

> A very bad man was King John, crueller than any other, he was too covetous of beautiful women and so brought shame to many of the great men of the land, which made him much hated. Never did he speak his true mind. He set his barons against each other as much as he could and was delighted when he saw hatred between them. Out of envy he hated all good valiant men and greatly disliked to see anyone doing well. He was too full of faults (116) [105].

To illustrate John's 'many evil deeds' [*molt des maus*] in England [109], which included humiliating a generous archbishop, extorting large sums from both the aristocratic widow of a great magnate and the king's own

---

97 See Gillingham, 'The Anonymous of Béthune', pp. 31–44.
98 Gillingham, 'The Anonymous of Béthune', pp. 35, 42.
99 Gillingham, 'The Anonymous of Béthune', p. 42.

justiciar, disinheriting great nobles, imprisoning or exiling them without judgement, and otherwise interfering in the dynastic practices of his barons,[100] AB relates a series of damning anecdotes about the king. John, he writes, was so envious of the lavish hospitality maintained by Hubert Walter, 'the good archbishop of Canterbury, who was very generous and valiant and active in important matters' (116) [105], that the king threatened him, saying, 'You are so generous, so valiant and you spend so lavishly that no one can equal you, all the pomp and pride in England must be yours alone. But thank God I have now so dealt with you that you will never be able to support yourself, you will never have anything to eat' (117) [106–07]. Because John was 'greatly displeased' by Master Stephen Langton's election as archbishop of Canterbury, AB wrote, he 'took the archbishopric into his own hand, seized the monks' whole territory and drove them all out of the land'. To this, Pope Innocent III responded by placing England 'under an interdict which lasted five years' (119–20) [110–11].

Moreover, John's quarrel with William de Briouse, another great English magnate, led the king, first, to attack William and his formidable wife Maud and seize their lands, then to force William to flee to France, where he later died of grief, and, finally, to capture and then imprison Maud and their son in Corfe castle, where they died horrifying deaths from starvation (120–21, 122) [111–12, 114–15]. John also compelled the Countess Hawise, the widow of Baldwin of Béthune, count of Aumale, to give him 5000 pounds so that he would not marry her off against her will (123) [115] and 'exact[ed] a payment of 10,000 marks from the justiciar, [Geoffrey fitz Peter,] so that he hated [the king] bitterly and often afterwards did him harm' (124) [115–16]. After Geoffrey de Mandeville killed the leader of the [sergeants] of King John's favourite William Brewer, who had all attacked Geoffrey's [serjeants], Geoffrey 'felt afraid of the king, who hated him because his father [Geoffrey fitz Peter] loved him'. So he and his men fled. 'And when William Brewer heard that his servant had been killed', he complained to King John, who was 'very angry and swore by God's teeth that [...] he would hang [Geoffrey]'. Upon learning of the king's threat, Geoffrey's father-in-law, Robert fitz Walter, asked John to have mercy on his daughter's husband; and when the king still said he would hang Geoffrey, according to AB, Robert told him, 'By the body of God, you will not! No, you will see two thousand laced helms in your land if the man who has my daughter is hanged'. When Robert and his son-in-law appeared in John's court, according to AB, the former 'brought with him at least 500 knights, armed' (124–25) [116–18]. When John realized that he could do no harm to Robert (whom the king also

---

100 See Church, *King John*, p. 8.

disinherited and drove into exile (127) [121] or to Geoffrey, he was 'very angry' and found another way of harming Robert by telling citizens of London that 'if they valued his goodwill they should demolish Robert's castle in London'. After writing that the Londoners did so, AB concludes: 'This evil deed did King John do, and many more did he do all his life long'. (125) [118–19]. Finally, when John saw that 'everyone in his land hated him' (*il veoit que tout chil de sa tierre le haoient*) and that 'the king of France was coming to attack him' with such a strong force that 'he would not be able to defend himself' (128) [123], he made an agreement with Innocent III that on the one hand, he would take the cross by May of 1213 and hold England and Ireland from the pope in return for an annual tribute of 900 marks and, on the other, the pope would end the interdict (128–29) [123–24].

When, against this background, AB discusses 'How the barons of England formed an alliance against King John' (*Comment li baron d'Angletierre s'aloierent encontre le roi Jehan*), probably in November of 1214,[101] and explains 'the cause of the war in which King John died, [disinherited] of the greater part of England [*l'ocoison de la guerre dont li rois Jehans moru dehiretés de la plus grant partie d'Engletierre*]' (143) [145], he has already illustrated some of the grievances that several barons held against John. He now shows how their individual grievances against him and, in particular, disinheritance, became collectivized and transformed into justifications for these barons to make war on him. From this point in AB's narrative onward, disinheritance in the broad sense of unjustly taking away or withholding an inheritance, the right to inherit, or rights generally becomes thematized, along with revenge for disinheritance, in all three stages of the war of 1215–1217. Soon after King John's return to England in the fall of 1214, AB writes, a group of barons came together in a '*parlement*'. He then names eight of the most important of them, two of whom his readers have already met: Robert fitz Walter (whom John had previously disinherited); Saer de Quincy, earl of Winchester; Gilbert son of the earl of Clare; Geoffrey de Mandeville, earl of Essex (another enemy of the king's); and four 'Northerners' called Robert de Ros, Eustace de Vesci, Richard de Percy, and William Mowbray [126] (145). All eight of these men were later appointed to the group of barons sometimes called the Twenty-Five, who were charged to enforce Magna Carta's provisions against John, if necessary, by 'distressing and distraining' him in ways that would have amounted to making war on him. Later still, several of them did homage to Prince Louis of France (163) [171], while members of an overlapping group were captured and imprisoned after the battle of Lincoln in 1217 (181) [194].

---

101 For possible dates of the meeting, see Church, *King John*, p. 206 and note; and AB, *History*, p. 144 n. 624, citing Carpenter, *Magna Carta*, pp. 290–92.

Without foreshadowing these later events, AB relates that at the November meeting, the barons

> decided to ask the king to keep faith with them by upholding for them the charters which King Henry [I], [John's] father's grandfather, had given to their ancestors and which King Stephen had confirmed to them [*que il lor tenist les chartres que li rois Henris ... avoit donnés à lors ancissours and que li rois Estievenes lor avoit confremées*].[102] If he refused to do this, they would all of them together defy him and make war on him until he was forced to do it [*il le desfieroient tout ensemble et le guerroierent tant que il par force le feroit*]. Then they had some holy relics brought and together took oath on the matter, and so they all rose against the king [*s'emprisent tout encounter le roi*] (143–44) [145–46].

AB goes on to say that when John heard what the barons had done from a messenger, who 'repeat[ed] all that they had charged them to say' he was 'furiously angry' [*durement s'aira le roi*] and 'refused to give [the messenger] any fair reply'; and all the way through April, the king deferred meetings with the barons, who came to at least one of them 'so well equipped with weapons, horses and strong forces that the king cancelled [it]' (145) [146]. Finally, the barons met King John at a *parlement*. Here they 'could not reach a settlement [*pais*]' with him, so 'they went away because of the evil in him [*se partirent par mal de lui*]' (145) [146]. War soon followed, after the barons, as we know from other texts, defied the king on 5 May, at which point John quickly ordered 'the seizure' of the estates of his 'enemies'.[103] Finally, after Archbishop Stephen Langton had conferred with John about 'peace between him and the barons', the king agreed that 'he and the barons would meet for discussions at Staines', where he 'had to make the peace the barons wanted' (146–47) [149].

Whether AB assumed that the audience for his *Histoire* would be familiar with the events just described or was himself reluctant, unwilling or unable to write about them very clearly, he did not explain the barons' reasons for swearing to make war on the king if he would not uphold Henry I's charters or John's reasons for angrily refusing to do so. AB's account of the barons' meeting in November of 1214 was apparently meant to imply that the barons regarded whatever Henry I had originally

---

[102] The precise meaning of this passage is obscure. But in writing that the barons demanded that the king 'lor tenist' the charters that King Henry 'avoit données à lor ancissours' and that King Stephen 'lor avoit confrémées' (144) [146], AB evidently wished to distinguish Henry's initial act of 'giving' the charters to the barons' ancestors from Stephen's later act of 'confirming' Henry I's charters and from the act of upholding to the barons the charters that the barons now wanted John to take with respect to the same charters; but AB also indicated that the first act of giving was made by Henry I in relation to their ancestors and that the third act — 'holding' or 'observing' — was to be made to them.

[103] Holt, *Magna Carta*, p. 208; see also Church, *King John*, p. 212.

given to their ancestors by these charters as constituting their own inheritances and rights that came to them by birth and not, by implication, through the king's gift. If so, then they had grounds for regarding John's refusal to observe or hold to Henry I's charters to them as tantamount to disinheriting them, in which case the barons — as we have seen in earlier sections of this chapter — could claim the right not only to make war on the king to recover their lost inheritances — whatever those inheritances were — but also to take vengeance on him for disinheriting them. On the other hand, King John clearly had good reasons for refusing to confirm Henry I's charters to the barons, in order to maintain the principle that the barons had no right to their own inheritances or to whatever else Henry I's charters might have given to their ancestors.[104]

That the barons who, according to AB, swore the oath about Henry I's charters in the fall of 1214 may well have contested King John's claims is evident in Roger of Wendover's account of what is evidently the same meeting, which he locates at the abbey of Bury St Edmunds. There, Wendover writes, the barons wanted King John to confirm 'liberties and laws' that Henry I's charter granted to the nobles as well as to the church. After 'the earls and barons of England [had] placed before them the charter of king Henry the First, [which] contained certain liberties and laws granted to the holy church as well as to the nobles of the kingdom', these magnates 'swore on the great altar that, if the king refused to grant these liberties and laws, they themselves would withdraw from their allegiance to him, and make war [*guerram*] on him, till he should by a charter under his own seal, confirm to them everything they required'.[105] This oath, as represented by Wendover and AB, resembles other oaths that were sworn, according to David Carpenter, by English barons (and, sometimes, by others) before and after the fall of 1214. In November 1213, according to Ralph of Coggeshall, 'nearly all the barons of England confederated together to protect the liberty of the church and all the kingdom'.[106] In 1215, the Welsh author of *The Chronicle of the Princes*, wrote:

> All the leading men of England and all the princes of Wales made a pact together against the king that not one of them without his fellow would have from the king either peace or alliance or truce until he restored to

---

104 On the importance of this principle, see Church, *King John*, pp. xix, 8, 162.
105 Roger of Wendover, *Flowers of History*, vol. 2, part 1, pp. 303–04; Roger of Wendover, *Chronica sive Flores Historiarum*, vol. 3, pp. 293–94. Finally, the barons 'unanimously agreed [to go] to the king and demand the confirmation of the aforesaid liberties to them, and … in the meantime [to] provide themselves with horses and arms, so that if the king should endeavour to depart from his oath, they might by taking his castles, compel him to satisfy their demands'.
106 Carpenter, *Magna Carta*, pp. 289–90, citing *Radulphi de Coggeshall Chronicon Anglicanum*, p. 167.

the churches their laws and their rights which he or his ancestors had before that taken from them, and also until he restored to the leading men of England and Wales the lands and the castles which he had taken from them at his pleasure without either justice or law.[107]

Three additional arguments support the hypothesis that King John's past or prospective disinheritance of English barons, his past or prospective denial of their heirs' rights to inherit from them, and the right of barons to wage war to recover their inheritances and take vengeance on the king gave legitimacy to the barons' upcoming war against John in May and early June of 1215 and to the peace made between the barons and the king in Magna Carta. First, according to Henry I's charter, the king 'took away' from the kingdom of England 'all the bad customs [*malas consuetudines*] by which it had been unjustly burdened', including one concerning the inheritance of the land of the king's barons.[108] Here, the king's charter provided that: 'If any of my barons, whether earls or others who hold of me, shall have died, his heir shall not redeem his land [*redimet suum terram*] as he used to do in my brother's time [i.e. when William II was king], but shall relieve it with a lawful and just relief [*sed legitima et iusta relevatione relevabit eam*]'. This provision of Henry I's charter, which according to AB the barons who swore the oath on 20 November 1214 demanded that John observe as it pertained to them, was clearly a model for an important clause included in Magna Carta (1215).[109] As AB explains the provision, because 'the [amount of money for] the buying back of lands [of fathers or other ancestors by their heirs from the king] was too high, the king agreed to set it at such a price [for the buyback] as the barons demanded'.[110]

Second, although AB strongly disapproved of other provisions of Magna Carta and could hardly have condemned John for waging a war against his enemies in which AB's own lord Robert actively participated on the king's side, he never states or suggests that it was wrong for the barons to make war on the king. Instead, his narrative of the conflict implies that John and his baronial enemies justly waged war against each other to recover or defend their own inheritances and take vengeance on each

---

107 Carpenter, *Magna Carta*, 289–90, citing *Brut Y Tywysogon or The Chronicle of the Princes: Red Book of Hergest Version*, p. 201. For an undertaking by a confederacy, see Holt, *Magna Carta*, p. 200, citing *Memoriale fratris Walteri de Coventria*, ed. by W. Stubbs, 2 vols (Rolls Series, 1872–1873), II, pp. 217–18.
108 Holt, *Magna Carta*, p. 350. See Sharpe, 'Liberties, Treaties, and Letters'.
109 Another clause in Magna Carta to which AB did not object was also related to a provision in Henry I's charter providing that John 'was forced to undertake never to arrange a marriage that would result in the woman being disparaged'.
110 My own translation of the following passage: 'Les rachas des tierres, qui trop grant estoient, li couvint metre à tel fuer comme il vaurrent deviser' [p. 150]. For a different translation, see AB, *History*, p. 147. For the corresponding clause in Magna Carta (1215), clause 2, see Holt, *Magna Carta*, pp. 378–81.

other, as did Henry III's Regents, along with their baronial supporters, and Prince Louis, along with the English and French barons supporting him.[111] Only in this way could AB have made sense of the back-and-forth, two-sided armed conflict that was fought out during the three stages of the war of 1215–1217. While the war between the barons and John was understood from the barons' perspective, first, as a vehicle for asserting their rights to their inheritances and to the rights and liberties on which those inheritance claims were based and, secondly, as a means of avenging the wrongs the king had done to them through the customary methods of seizing their castles and ravaging their lands, the same war took on totally different meanings from the perspective of King John, for whom it was a means of defending royal rights that the barons taking or trying to take from him and avenging the shame they inflicted on him: initially, by warring against him and, then, by using force to compel him to make a humiliating peace with his baronial enemies by granting Magna Carta.[112] Third and finally, the crucial role of King John's disinheritance of his barons in the first phase of the war of 1215–1217 is clear from several clauses included in June of 1215 in Magna Carta. Although the many clauses intended to constrain royal action in the future have understandably received the most attention from historians, one of the few designed to remedy unlawful royal acts in the past provides additional evidence of the importance that the barons attached to past royal acts of disinheritance. According to clause 52, 'If anyone has been disseised or dispossessed by us, without lawful judgement of his peers, of lands, castles, liberties or his right [i.e. royal acts that were all perceived as "disinheritance"], we will restore these to him immediately'.[113]

The importance of vengeance for both sides in the war between King John and his barons becomes even clearer in AB's narrative when we consider how he represents the relationship between the king and the Twenty-Five barons who were appointed, according to Magna Carta (1215), clause 61 to 'distress and distrain the king' in every way they could, if he or his subordinates offended against any of the charter's provisions without later providing redress.[114] Whatever AB may have thought about most of Magna Carta's provisions, the one he objected to most strongly

---

111 The fact that so many English barons switched sides at least once during the war of 1215–1217 and made war on their former royal lords in order to recover their own lost inheritances confirms, rather than undercuts, the argument about war made in this chapter.
112 A fuller study would consider the perspectives on the war of John's English baronial supporters, the Flemings who supported John and/or Prince Louis, and the mercenaries who fought for John.
113 Carpenter, *Magna Carta*, p. 57 and, on the importance of this clause, p. 227.
114 See Holt, *Magna Carta*, clause 61 at pp. 395–97. These barons are identified by name from the text quoted in Holt, *Magna Carta*, Appendix 8, 'The Twenty-Five Barons of Magna Carta', pp. 402–04.

was the provision establishing this committee of twenty-five and granting it extensive powers. However, because AB represents this provision in such a way as to greatly exaggerate those powers and because, as we shall see, he goes on to represent the committee as exercising power for the purpose of shaming and humiliating King John, he apparently believed that the Twenty-Five used their power to take vengeance on the king, thereby giving him further grounds for taking vengeance on them.

Indeed, every member of this group already had scores to settle with the king, since they had all fought in the war against him. Moreover, as we have already seen, eight of them had joined other barons in swearing the oath of 20 November 1214; and one of them — Robert fitz Walter — had led the barons' army.[115] For this reason, when AB explains how the twenty-five barons (whom he never names) humiliated King John, he must have realized that they had their own reasons for doing so and would be obvious targets for vengeance, if John regained the power to avenge the shame and humiliation that inflicted on him by his baronial enemies. In describing the powers of the Twenty-Five, AB emphasizes how humiliating the arrangement was for King John by exaggerating the committee's powers and taking the royalist position that Magna Carta was imposed on King John by force. 'Their principal requirement was that [the king] would deal with [all matters] according to [their] judgment. All the changes they might put forward to him, or he to them, should be done through them' (147) [150]. At the same time, AB asserts, they wanted that 'the king should never be able to appoint a bailiff in his land except through these 25' (147) [150]. 'All this', AB continues, 'the king was compelled by force to grant. He gave his charter to the barons, guaranteeing to keep this settlement, as one who had no better choice' (147) [150]. The Twenty-Five required John to 'keep exactly to the agreement he had made [with them], but they had no intention of honouring any agreement they themselves had made with their own vassals' (147) [151]. To illustrate their arrogance and their exalted sense of their own rights, AB describes an occasion when 'the 25 barons were in the king's court to give judgment' and refused, when John told them he was too ill to come to them, to 'come to his bed-chamber to deliver judgement', because to do so 'would be against their lawful rights'. When John 'had himself carried to the 25, in the place where they were, [...] they did not rise to greet him as he came in, for, they said, if they [had done so], this would have been contrary to their rights'. According to AB, 'Such pride and such insolence did they use towards him in large measure' (148) [151].

In response, 'Shame and anger at his [men's] arrogance [and the outrages they committed] filled [John's] heart, and he began to think about

---

115 Turner, *King John*, pp. 234–35.

vengeance [against them]' (148) [151]. Because he 'saw clearly that he could never [avenge himself for their treatment of him] except through the power of the pope' (148) [151], he sent messengers to Rome to tell 'the pope, as his lord he should for God's sake have mercy on him ..., for his [men] had forced such a peace on him as he could see in [John's letter to him] and as his envoys would fully inform him' (148) [151–52]. In response, Innocent III not only told John that 'he must not uphold this settlement, because it was not good'; he also took his own kind of vengeance on John's enemies by 'excommunicat[ing] all who should support the [settlement]' and ordered the barons 'to allow the king to hold his land in the same condition and manner that his father King Henry and his brother King Richard had held it, and as he himself held it [when] he took the cross and received his land from Rome' (148) [152]. Upon hearing what the pope had decided, the barons were angry [irié] and sought to take vengeance on John by 'doing evil to him [mal faire]' (149) [152]. With King John and his baronial enemies both determined to take vengeance on the other, the war resumed and continued beyond the time of John's death in October of 1216.

Conclusion

In closing, it is important to point out that like the authors of the other Anglo-Norman or Old French war stories considered in this chapter, AB constructed a narrative of an armed conflict between an English king and a faction of his own nobles that differs significantly from modern accounts of the conflict. As previously noted, these modern accounts represent the conflict, not as a war between a king supported by one faction of his barons against another, but as a rebellion initiated by 'rebel' barons against a king who sought to suppress the rebellion with support from 'loyalist' barons and restore law and order, rather than avenging himself on his baronial enemies. At the same time, by highlighting the anger, ill-will, and hatred that John expressed for his enemies well before he and they waged open war with each other, and by depicting these emotions as driving the king to take vengeance upon them, AB created an image of King John that sharply contrasts with the one of John as an administrator-king that has long been dominant in the historiography of medieval England.[116] As John Gillingham explained in 1999, 'In his "Good and Bad Kings in Medieval English History", published in 1945, V. H. Galbraith suggested that "a new

---

116 On King John's expressions of anger, hatred and/or desire for vengeance, see, e.g., AB (111) [99], (115) [104], (116) (105], (117) [107], (118) [108], (124) [116], (125) [117], (125) [118], (127) [122], (128) [123], (142) [144], (145) [146], (146) [148], (148) [151], (156) [163–64], (157) [164], (171) [180].

approach to the problem of John's character" would probably [lead to] the notion of a king capable of a consistent policy of state-building [...] in the true line of Henry II'. The 'new approach', Gillingham explains, 'was to be based on the systematic use of record evidence'. In other words, the foundation of the new way of understanding John's character and, by implication, the motivation of the king's political actions would be the systematic study of royal records of his reign and not Latin chronicles or vernacular histories such as AB's *Histoire*. 'Galbraith's observations', Gillingham concludes, 'were to be the harbinger of a new orthodoxy [...] that has lasted [...] to the present day'.[117]

However, Galbraith's 'new approach' rested on several highly debatable assumptions: first, that a 'state' was being built during the reigns of Henry II and John; second, that the latter, like his father, intended to build it by following 'a consistent policy of state-building'; and third, that definitive evidence of John's 'state-building' was transparently encoded by royal clerks in the *Close Rolls*, the *Patent Rolls*, the *Curia Regis Rolls*, and the other royal records. By itself, AB's story of the war between John and a faction of his barons in May and early June of 1215 and his account of John's reign before the war broke out obviously provides insufficient evidence to undermine these three assumptions. But it certainly provides grounds for questioning the second, by suggesting that King John's political behaviour was determined, not by consistent policy of state-building, but by irrepressible emotional impulses to promote his own honour and avenge his own shame. To propose this hypothesis about John is not to return to the Victorian view of him as a monstrous tyrant or to J. E. A. Jolliffe's claim that he 'rule[d] by his passions more than by his kingship'.[118] It is simply to see John, along with other kings of this era, as fully participating in the honour-based political culture (or *habitus*) of the high nobility of the twelfth and early thirteenth century.

---

117 Gillingham, 'Historians Without Hindsight', p. 1.
118 Jolliffe, *Angevin Kingship*, p. 87.

Works Cited

Primary Sources

The Anonymous of Béthune, 'Extrait d'une chronique française des rois de France par un Anonyme de Béthune', in *Recueil des historiens des Gaules et de la France*, ed. by Léopold Delisle, vol. 24 (1904), pp. 750–75
——, *Histoire des ducs de Normandie et des rois d'Angleterre*, ed. by Francisque Michel (Paris, 1840)
——, *History of the Dukes of Normandy and the Kings of England by the Anonymous of Béthune*, trans. by Janet Shirley with historical notes by Paul Webster (London: Routledge, 2021)
Geffrei Gaimar, *Estoire des Engleis / History of the English*, ed. and trans. by Ian Short (Oxford: Oxford University Press, 2009)
Holden, Anthony J., *The Roman de Rou*. Translated by Glyn S. Burgess (St Helier, Jersey: Société Jersiaise, 2002)
Innocent III, *Selected Letters of Pope Innocent III concerning England (1198–1216)*, ed. by C. R. Cheney and W. H. Semple (London: Cambridge University Press, 1953)
John of Worcester, *The Chronicle of John of Worcester*, ed. and trans. by Patrick McGurk, vol. 3, *The Annals from 1067 to 1140 with the Gloucester Interpolations and the Continuation to 1141* (Oxford: Oxford University Press, 1998)
Jordan Fantosme, *Jordan Fantosme's Chronicle*, ed. and trans. by Ronald Carlyle Johnston (Oxford: Oxford University Press, 1981)
La chanson de Roland, ed. and trans. by Ian Short (Paris: Livre de Poche, 1990)
Orderic Vitalis, *The Ecclesiastical History of Orderic Vitalis*, ed. and translated by Marjorie Chibnall, 6 vols (Oxford: Oxford University Press, 1968–1980)
Roger of Wendover, *Chronica sive Flores Historiarum*, ed. by Henricus Coxe, 5 vols (London: Sumptibus Societatis, 1841–1844)
Roger of Wendover, *Flowers of History*, trans. by J. A. Giles (1849. Reprinted Felinfach, 1995)

Secondary Studies

Algazi, Gadi, 'The Social Uses of Private War', *Tel Aviver Jahrbuch für deutsche Geschichte*, 22 (1993), 253–74
Anglo-Norman Dictionary (AND Online Edition). <https://anglo-norman.net/entry/guerre> [accessed 21 December 2020]
Aurell, Martin, 'Révolte nobiliaire et lutte dynastique dans l'empire angevin (1154–1224)', *Anglo-Norman Studies*, 24 (2002), 25–42
Barlow, Frank, *William Rufus* (Berkeley: University of California Press, 1983)
Bartlett, Robert, *England under the Norman and Angevin Kings, 1073–1225* (Oxford: Oxford University Press, 2000)

Bates, David, *William the Conqueror* (New Haven: Yale University Press, 2016)
Bloch, Marc, *Les caractères originaux de l'histoire rurale française* (Paris: Société d'édition, 1931)
Carpenter, David, *Magna Carta* (London: Penguin, 2015)
——, *The Struggle for Mastery: Britain, 1066–1284* (Oxford: Oxford University Press, 2003)
Church, Stephen, *King John and the Road to Magna Carta* (London: Basic Books, 2015)
Crouch, David, *The Reign of King Stephen, 1135–1154* (Edinburgh: Longman, 2000)
English Historical Documents, 1327–1485, ed. by A. R. Myers (London: Routledge, 1969)
Galbraith, Vivian Hunter, 'Good Kings and Bad Kings in Medieval English History', *History*, n.s. 30 (1945), 119–32
Gillingham, John, '1066 and the Introduction of Chivalry into England', in *Law and Government in Medieval England and Normandy: Essays in Honour of Sir James Holt*, ed. by George Garnett and John Hudson (Cambridge: Cambridge University Press, 1994), pp. 31–55
——, 'The Anonymous of Béthune, King John and Magna Carta', in *Magna Carta and the England of King John*, ed. by Janet S. Loengard (Woodbridge: Boydell Press, 2015), pp. 27–44
——, 'Historians Without Hindsight: Coggeshall, Diceto and Howden on the Early Years of John's Reign', in *King John: New Interpretations*, ed. by Stephen D. Church (Woodbridge: Boydell Press, 2003), pp. 1–26
——, 'Kingship, Chivalry and Love. Political and Cultural Values in the Earliest History Written in French: Geoffrey Gaimar's *Estoire Des Engleis*', in *The English in the Twelfth Century: Imperialism, National Identity, and Political Values*, ed. by John Gillingham (Rochester: Boydell Press, 2000), pp. 233–58
——, *Richard I* (New Haven: Yale University Press, 2002)
Hanley, Catherine, *Louis: The French Prince Who Invaded England* (New Haven: Yale University Press, 2016)
Hollister, Warren, *Henry I* (New Haven: Yale University Press, 2001)
Holt, J. C., *Magna Carta*, 3rd edn (Cambridge: Cambridge University Press, 2015)
Jolliffe, J. E. A., *Angevin Kinship*, 2nd edn (London: A & C Black Publishers Ltd, 1963)
King, Edmund, *King Stephen* (New Haven: Yale University Press, 2010)
Le Patourel, John, *The Norman Empire* (Oxford: Oxford University Press, 1976)
McGlynn, Sean, *Blood Cries Afar: The Forgotten Invasion of England, 1216* (Cheltenham: The History Press, 2013)
Meyers, Alec R., *English Historical Documents, 1327–1485* (London: Eyre & Spottiswoode, 1969)
Miller, William Ian, 'Getting a Fix on Violence', in *Humiliation*, ed. by William Ian Miller (Ithaca: Cornell University Press, 1993), pp. 53–92

Pollock, Sir Frederick, and Frederic William Maitland, *The History of English Law before the Time of Edward I*, 2nd edn, 2 vols (Cambridge: Cambridge University Press, 1898)

Power, Daniel, '"La rage méchante des traîtres prit feu": Le discours sur la révolte sous les rois Plantagenêt (1144–1224)', in *La trahison au moyen âge: De la monstruosité au crime politique (V^e-XVe siècle)*, ed. by Myriam Soria and Maïté Billoré (Rennes: Presses Universitaires de Rennes, 2010), pp. 53–65

Roffe, David, 'Hereward [called Hereward the Wake] (fl. 1070–1071), rebel', *Oxford Dictionary of National Biography* (2004) <https://www.oxforddnb.com/view/10.1093/ref:odnb/9780198614128.001.0001/odnb-9780198614128-e-13074> [Accessed 30 March 2023]

Russell, Frederick H., *The Just War in the Middle Ages* (Cambridge: Cambridge University Press, 1975)

Short, Ian, 'King John: A Flemish Perspective by the Anonyme de Béthune', An English translation of AB's narrative from 1199 to 1220. Anglo-Norman Text Society <http://www.anglo-norman-texts.net/?p=259> [Accessed 30 March 2023]

Spiegel, Gabrielle M., *Romancing the Past: The Rise of Vernacular Prose Historiography in Thirteenth-Century France* (Berkeley, 1993) <http://ark.cdlib.org/ark:/13030/ft209nbonm/> [Accessed 30 March 2023]

Staunton, Michael, *The Historians of Angevin England* (Oxford: Oxford University Press, 2017)

Strickland, Matthew, *Henry the Young King, 1155–1183* (New Haven: Yale University Press, 2016)

——, 'Reconciliation ou humiliation? La suppression de la rébellion aristocratique dans les royaumes anglo-normand et angevin', in *La contestation du pouvoir en Normandie (X^e-XVe siècles)*, ed. by Catherine Bougy and Sophie Poirey (Caen: PU CAEN, 2007), pp. 65–77

——, *War and Chivalry: The Conduct and Perception of War in England and Normandy, 1066–1217* (Cambridge: Cambridge University Press, 1996)

Sunderland, Luke, *Rebel Barons: Resisting Royal Power in Medieval Culture* (Oxford: Oxford University Press, 2017)

Turner, Ralph V., *King John* (London: Longman, 1994)

Valente, Claire, *The Theory and Practice of Revolt in Medieval England* (Aldershot: Ashgate, 2003)

van Houts, Elisabeth, 'Wace as Historian', in *The History of the Norman People: Wace's Roman de Rou*, trans. by Glyn Burgess (Woodbridge: The Boydell Press, 2004), pp. xxxv–lii

Vincent, Nicholas, 'Dating the Outbreak of Civil War, April-May 1215', *The Magna Carta Project*. <https://magnacartaresearch.org> [Website a work in progress. Accessed 30 March 2023]

——, '"Our barons who are against us", 3 May 1215–9 May, 1215', *Magna Carta Project*. <https://magnacartaresearch.org> [Website a work in progress. Accessed 30 March 2023]

Warren, W. L., *King John*, new edn (New Haven: Yale University Press, 1997)

White, Stephen D., 'Alternative Constructions of Treason in the Angevin Political World: *Traïson* in the *History of William Marshal*', *e-Spania*, 4, December 2007, pp. 1–47 [online]. <http://e-spania.revues.org/document2233.html> [Accessed 30 March 2023]

——, 'Un imaginaire faidal: La représentation de la guerre dans quelques chansons de geste', in *La vengeance, 400–1200*, ed. by Dominique Barthélemy and others (Rome: Ecole française de Rome, 2006), pp. 175–98

——, 'Peace or Punishment in Medieval England: 1215 to 1322', in *Peacemaking and the Restraint of Violence in Medieval Europe*, ed. by Simon Pierre Louis Lebouteiller and Louisa Taylor (London: Routledge, 2023), pp. 36–64

——, 'The Politics of Anger in Medieval France', in *Anger's Past: The Social Uses of an Emotion in the Middle Ages*, ed. by Barbara H. Rosenwein (Ithaca: Cornell University Press, 1998), pp. 127–52

WARREN C. BROWN

10. Scandinavia in Medieval Europe

According to its title, this volume deals with civil war in high medieval Scandinavia. But as I began to read it, I quickly concluded that it is really about much more. On its face, the volume asks whether the conflicts that spread throughout the region in the twelfth and thirteenth centuries can be properly understood — or even understood at all — through the lens of 'civil war', given all of the assumptions about states and national boundaries that underlie the concept. To answer this question, however, the contributors are forced, each from his or her own perspective, to confront others that are larger and more fundamental: How did Scandinavians in this period understand violence and order? What resources, both physical and conceptual did they have available to them to justify and carry out their competition for power?

At the same time, the volume implicitly raises another important question, by focusing on Scandinavia but including two essays on regions beyond it: Does Scandinavia belong to the mainstream of medieval history? Is the long historiographical tradition, that has consigned the regions we now call Denmark, Norway, and Sweden to a separate arena, occupied mainly by scholars from those regions themselves or outsiders interested in the Vikings or Iceland, justified, or should it be challenged?

It is this latter question I would like to tackle here, from the particular perspective of the volume's subject and the issues the contributors raise as they explore it. I do so from the perspective of an outsider: a social historian of the early Middle Ages as they played out on the grounds of what became the Carolingian Empire, who has nevertheless followed the attitudes towards violence, order, and power of people who lived there across the first millennium into the high and late Middle Ages and a bit

Warren C. Brown (wcb@hss.caltech.edu) is professor of history in the Division of the Humanities and Social Sciences, California Institute of Technology.

New Perspectives on the 'Civil Wars' in Medieval Scandinavia, ed. by Hans Jacob Orning, Kim Esmark, and Jón Viðar Sigurðsson, Comparative Perspectives on Medieval History, 1 (Turnhout: Brepols, 2024), pp. 413–428
BREPOLS PUBLISHERS   10.1484/M.CPMH-EB.5.137267

beyond.[1] The answer I will argue for is unequivocal: yes, Scandinavia belongs in the history of medieval Europe. Its cultures of power share much in common with those visible farther south, and those cultures undergo some of the same changes over time. The changes do appear to happen more quickly and in a more concentrated span of time than in the rest of Europe, and they often seem to overlap. As I worked through each of the essays, I sometimes felt that I was in the early Middle Ages, sometimes in the high or late Middle Ages; sometimes I heard echoes of Carolingian or even Merovingian Francia, sometimes medieval Germany, sometimes France. I also noticed other differences that reflect Scandinavia's particular geographical place with respect to the rest of Europe. Nevertheless, both the commonalities and the differences anchor Scandinavia firmly in European medieval history and help us to understand that history a little better.

Much of the action, and the discussion, in this volume is driven by networks of personal ties. These are entirely familiar: they connect family and kin, friends, lords and followers, and members of warbands. As I and others have noted for early medieval Europe, and Gerd Althoff (in this volume and elsewhere) and others for the high and later Middle Ages, power flowed along these channels as much or more than they did along ties that connected governing and governed.[2] This remains true even in times and places, such as Carolingian Europe, where central power appears to peak. The *flokkr*, too: this warband, composed of men whose sworn bond to their leaders and their leaders' goals transcended their personal ties to others, appears here as a destabilizing novelty. Yet it likewise has its analogues farther south. Patrick J. Geary, pulling together the results of a range of earlier work, was pointing out already in the late 1980s how the Germanic warband (called by Tacitus the *comitatus*) cut across lines of kin, clan, and tribe in ways that could threaten relationships and the balance of power among tribal groups.[3] Althoff, in his essay for this volume, points out echoes of the *flokkr* in the *coniurationes* of high medieval Germany. Stephen D. White does the same when he talks about the armed following of the English nobleman Hereward in the 1060s and 70s, who were sworn to him personally as their liege lord and thus owed him their primary fealty. And we need look no farther than Charlemagne to see a ruler, who wanted to erect a king-centred polity, trying to squash the threat posed

---

1 See e.g. Brown, *Unjust Seizure*, and *Beyond the Monastery Walls*, as well as Brown, Costambeys, Innes, and Kosto (eds), *Documentary Culture and the Laity*; on violence and order see *Violence*, 'The Pre-History of Terrorism', 'Terrorism, History, and Periodization', as well as the forthcoming Brown, Cox, and Jahner (eds), *Violence and Order: Past and Present*.
2 See Brown, *Beyond the Monastery Walls*, pp. 252–83; Le Jan, *Famille et pouvoir*; Gilsdorf, *The Favor of Friends*; Koziol, *Begging Pardon and Favor*; Althoff in this volume and the literature that he cites, esp. *Family, Friends and Followers*; Garnier, *Die Kultur der Bitte*.
3 Geary, *Before France and Germany*, pp. 56–57.

by such groups by banning all sworn and armed associations that did not include him.[4]

The degree to which power and political competition in Scandinavia flowed along such personal networks raises a question that lies at the heart of this volume, and is also central for understanding medieval societies farther south: is it wise, or even possible, to use state, nation, or ethnic 'people' labels to identify groups and understand what motivates them to act? The contributors to this volume pose this question repeatedly and very effectively; I found myself asking over and over again as I read: do constructs like 'Denmark', 'Norway', or 'Sweden' even apply to what's going on here — and getting the answer 'no'. The contributors also highlight how problematic it is to use the categories 'public' and 'private' to understand such network-driven societies. As in high medieval Scandinavia, so too farther south, in the early and high Middle Ages in particular (and in some regions even later), kings played the game of power by the same rules as everybody else.[5] Hermanson further undermines the distinction between 'public' and 'private' by showing the crucial role women played in high medieval Scandinavia in creating, maintaining, and activating the ties along which power and competition flowed. For me this evokes in particular the political world of seventh-century Francia, where queens and female saints in the Merovingian kingdoms built up networks of marriage and patronage that enabled and motivated political action — Queen/Saint Balthild comes especially strongly to mind.[6]

And yet: if Charlemagne could create an image of a quasi-public order by claiming to protect entire social groups (e.g. the clergy, widows, orphans, etc.) and trying rein in all uses of force that he had not authorized; if the earliest Peace of God councils of the late tenth and early eleventh centuries could exempt royal wars from the limits on violence that their participants swore to respect; if princes in high medieval France, Flanders, Normandy, and England — and later Germany — could use such Peace oaths to insert themselves into the process of maintaining certain kinds of order; if in twelfth and thirteenth-century England a concept of 'crime' could evolve that reserved jurisdiction over individual acts of force to royal courts:[7] all of this suggests a glimmering notion of a public order, or at least of a royal sphere of authority. With these and other examples in mind, I found Jón Viðar Sigurðsson's discussion of the *leiðangr* — a military force under the direct command of the king that could only be used in

---

4 Capitulare Haristallense a. 779, c. 14: *de truste faciendo nemo praesumat*; MGH Capit I, 50.
5 See e.g. Brown, *Violence*, pp. 33–67, 195–220; Hyams, *Rancor and Reconciliation*; Lambert, *Law and Order*.
6 Fouracre and Gerberding, *Late Merovingian France*; on Balthild see pp. 97–132.
7 Brown, *Violence*, pp. 69–96, 116–24, 169–70, 200, 223–25, 228–32, 256–58, and 'The Criminalization of Violence'.

the kingdom's defence or to attack other realms — extremely interesting. It too suggests that for all that Scandinavian societies in the twelfth and thirteenth centuries were organized and driven by personal networks, here too there was nevertheless an idea of a 'public' good or sphere of action that kings could draw on to legitimate action.

All of the contributors, but most notably Orning,[8] argue that network-driven societies tend to produce stable orders marked by what we might call extra-legal (rather than 'informal' — they could be quite formal) mechanisms for processing conflict and limiting violence. Nevertheless, the societies described in this volume were not entirely 'peaceful', if one defines 'peace', say, as the complete absence of homicide. I was struck by how much actual killing the contributors report; what they describe is often far from 'peace in the feud'.[9] These orders depended in fact on a steady level of sometimes violent conflict. Orning, for example, notes that armed followers had an interest in keeping disputes among their lords going in order to continue extracting resources from others. Benham suggests the same when she points out that armed reprisals within the context of an agreed peace did not necessarily violate agreements; she argues that agreements incorporated and depended on both the threat and the occasional reality of such reprisals. Similar orders can also be observed to the south, e.g. in Althoff's Germany, or in White's England, where he presents us with a (more or less) stable order that incorporated legitimate rebellion. And one need in my opinion look only to the world remembered or imagined in *Beowulf* (a work which has feet in both Scandinavia and Anglo-Saxon England) to find a society whose stability depended on its (male) members constantly displaying their willingness and ability to wield force to avenge injury or insult. They did so not only to bring in wealth and honour, but also to display their fitness for power and to ward off threats to their groups from the outside. When the charismatic leader who embodied this willingness and ability disappeared, as Beowulf did when he was slain by the dragon, the group was threatened with extinction.[10]

Orning argues that the biggest threat to the stability of such societies was not conflict itself, but rather the possibility that one party to a conflict would try to dominate the others — in other words, that that one party would try to really win. Both in Scandinavia and farther south, it appears that violence aimed at really winning — and by this I mean either exterminating or imposing complete control over the other parties — required the

---

8 See also Orning, 'Violence, Conflict and Order in Medieval Norway'.
9 Gluckman, 'The Peace in the Feud'; Brown, *Violence*, pp. 16–18, where he observes that the 'merciful customs' visible in high medieval Germany did not necessarily apply, say, in Norman Sicily.
10 *Beowulf*; cf. Hill, *The Cultural World in Beowulf*.

targets to be placed on the other side of some line that marked them as fundamentally different (referred to in Chapter 1 of this volume as 'radical othering').[11] In the 'mainstream' Middle Ages, the First Crusade comes to mind, involving as it did religious 'othering' and the wholesale massacre of populations. I am also reminded of the warrior aristocratic society of the fourteenth century so vibrantly celebrated by Jean Froissart. Inside the line that bounded this society — but that nevertheless transcended emerging 'national' boundaries — a constant level of conflict on the battlefield and tournament ground anchored and advertised its members' inclusion in the club. The club's internal rules usually (though not always) protected its members from serious danger. Yet when faced with the revolt against their depredations by the peasants, townspeople, and lesser gentry of northern France now known as the Jacquerie — in other words, by people outside the line — these same aristocrats mowed rebels (or people they thought had been rebels) down like the cattle they plainly thought they were.[12]

What surprised me as I read through this volume was how far 'inside' extended geographically, and how little 'Scandinavia' seemed to matter to the boundaries; competitors in Scandinavia's 'game of thrones' extended their networks well outside the bounds of Scandinavia itself. As Esmark tells us, Knud Lavard was perfectly capable of working with German networks; he became the friend of the German king and emperor Lothar of Supplinburg. Lavard's cousin Magnus had Lothar knight him and crown him king of the Danes. The German king, in other words, was not only a source of material support that could be accessed through the same kinds of networks that applied in Scandinavia; he was a recognized and valuable source of legitimacy to players inside Scandinavia. Althoff takes this observation one step farther when he observes how often Danish kings or dukes ended conflicts with German kings and emperors by participating in German-style rituals. They never, however, approached the German king barefoot and never performed footfalls, as was customary for Germans performing their ritual surrender before the king. Magnus, for example, displayed his readiness to peace instead by carrying the king's sword in procession. Apparently, Scandinavians understood the Germans' ritual language and knew how to demand that they be 'spoken' of in the ways that they wanted to be. Germany thus lay 'inside' the Scandinavian cultural world; nationality, and ethnicity, had nothing to do with the game of power. In this respect too, then, Scandinavia was thoroughly integrated into the rest of Europe.

The observation that 'constant crisis' underlay stable orders in Scandinavia (and elsewhere), prompts another question: what is 'violence' when

---

11 See Chapter 1.
12 Brown, *Violence*, pp. 261–71; on the Jacquerie see most recently Firnhaber-Baker, *The Jacquerie of 1358*.

a constant level of it, or a constant threat of it, is required for political stability? 'Violence' as an English word derives from the Latin *violentia*, which focused more on violations of norms or boundaries than it did on acts of physical force, though it could include them. The word is now used in English to capture more or less all uses of force. Nevertheless, it still has a whiff of the illegitimate about it, particularly given that in most of the English-speaking world, acts of force not sanctioned by the state are defined as criminal.[13] In the Scandinavia covered in this volume, in contrast, as in much of the rest of medieval Europe, we are dealing with societies in which many uses of force that we would consider criminal were legitimate, even necessary. This is a point that I have made elsewhere, when dealing with the question of whether Europe in the Middle Ages was a more violent world than our own. I have argued that medieval Europe was not more violent, but rather differently violent, because its inhabitants regarded many uses of force as licit that to us are not.[14] This point is also made in different ways in this volume, most forcefully by White when he argues against approaching medieval English rebellion armed with modern state- or king-centred ideas about legitimacy. It would be worth the effort, I think, to explore the words that medieval Scandinavians used to describe the use of force in different contexts. It may be just as dangerous to try to understand them with the word 'violence' in mind as it is with the rubric 'civil war'. The same applies to the putative opposite of 'violence', which in the modern west is 'peace'. In her essay, Benham casts 'peace' not as the absence of violence, but rather as a subjectively understood collection of rights and obligations that could include outbreaks of violent conflict, when she argues that peaceful relations depended on parties being able to redress wrongs by force. Her observations resemble those made by others about the meaning of 'peace' farther south.[15]

The stability of 'constant conflict' in high medieval Scandinavia appears to have been disrupted by a renewed or increased tension between the norms of a network-driven society and those of an order centred on the king. This tension runs right through the history of the rest of medieval Europe. Charlemagne derived from his position as an anointed king an image of a Christian kingship with the right and responsibility to protect God's people and to regulate uses of force of which he had not approved. As Orning notes, kings who tried to make such an image real sought to make 'the bonds linking other men to them more binding than bonds based on kinship, friendship and patronage [linking them to people other] than themselves'.[16] The fate of this image, its rise, fall, and renewed rise in

---

13 Brown, 'The Criminalization of Violence'.
14 Brown, *Violence*, p. 5.
15 Cf. Malegam, *The Sleep of Behemoth*.
16 See Chapter 4, p. 190.

different times and places, amid larger developments in Europe's economy and society that either buried or promoted it, is a story central to understanding how European political society evolved.[17] The tension between king-centred and network-driven views of proper order persisted in much of Europe even into the late Middle Ages, as adherents to the international culture of chivalry, for example, held stubbornly to their rights to wage war on their own behalf and for their own reasons, and contested the ambitions and claims of kings.[18]

Observing this tension highlights the fact that in order to understand violence, power, and order, both in Scandinavia and throughout medieval Europe, we need to understand legitimacy, and especially the resources that competitors could draw on to claim it. Everybody involved in this volume agrees that in order to get people to support you, it was vitally important to get your story right. Esmark discusses the 'officializing stories', justifying war as an act of revenge, that leaders told to legitimize their claims in terms that potential supporters would recognize. Orning points out that enmity was contextual, not absolute; the crucial issue in any conflict was how to define a situation. Benham argues that agreements ending conflicts were often an expression of the right to determine what was legal and just in both war and peace. Althoff too stresses how important it was in his high medieval Germany, if you wanted to justify violence, to nail down your story and persuade everybody involved that it was the right one. White's entire essay — which leads off with an observation by Pollock and Maitland that rebellions and wars were fought on quasi-legal principles — is devoted to uncovering an alternative set of norms (i.e., alternative to a state-based view of kingship as *per se* the source of legitimacy) that were current in high medieval England and that barons could reach for to justify rebellion against the king. The arrival in Scandinavia of a king-centred idea of order offered an alternative legitimating resource that players in the Scandinavian power game could use to justify monopolizing power, and to assert their solitary rule over increasingly geographically defined areas.

This reveals, I think, one major difference between Scandinavia and much if not most of Europe farther south: if I read the essays right, this king-centred image appears to have been imported into Scandinavia from the south, starting in the eleventh century. In the rest of Europe, in contrast, it had been there much longer. This difference in turn reflects a much deeper difference, perhaps the most significant one, in fact: Scandinavia lay outside of the regions that shared the direct legacy of Rome. The rest of Europe, to varying degrees, and excepting large areas of north-central and north-eastern Europe, were built on and continued to be influenced by their Roman heritage. The Romans had a language of civil war, or *bellum*

---

17 Brown, *Violence*.
18 Brown, *Violence*, pp. 280–81; Kaeuper, *Chivalry and Violence*.

civile. This language was transmitted in the medieval West by (among others) Isidore of Seville in his *Etymologies*. According to Isidore, civil war occurs when factions arise among fellow citizens and hostilities are stirred up, causing leaders of these factions to wage *bellum civile* against each other within one nation (*in una gente*) — precisely the understanding of civil war that the contributors to this volume argue does not apply to high medieval Scandinavia. Isidore takes one step farther, however, when he states that there is such a thing as a 'more than civil war' (*plus quam civile bellum*): this is when not only fellow-citizens, but also kinsfolk fight.[19] This latter image, of a 'more than civil war', is the one projected by the Frankish warrior Angelbert in his poem on the battle that pitted the three Carolingians Lothar, Charles the Bald, and Louis the German against each other at Fontenoy in 841, a battle in which Angelbert himself participated. Frank, says Angelbert, spilled the blood of Frank and Christian of Christian. Far worse, however: brothers spilled the blood of brothers, uncles of nephews, and sons of fathers.[20] From Angelbert's perspective, in other words, the ambitions and claims of kings turned the members of an 'inside' group against each other and ripped apart the normal bonds of kinship networks. Contrast this with the situation in the twelfth century Norway described by Jón Viðar Sigurðsson, where these networks were so intertwined that the risk of killing brother, relative, or friend served as a brake on conflict, and kings had as yet no language to justify tearing them apart. It may therefore be safer to include 'civil war' among the possible conceptual frameworks for understanding violent political conflict in western Europe, given that the notion was in circulation and could be used by political actors and observers to process what they were doing and seeing.

The chief institutional manifestation of the Roman legacy in Europe was the Roman Church. It appears that the arrival of the Roman Church in Scandinavia provided a major catalyst for change. As Esmark notes, when a permanent diocesan structure was implanted in Scandinavia in the second half of the eleventh century, for the first time high ecclesiastical offices, distributed by the king, became attractive prizes for members of the elites. This was already an age-old phenomenon in the rest of Europe; kings, and in some regions lesser lords, had been happily distributing church offices or control of monasteries to attract and reward followers for centuries. The serious conflicts that erupted after the Gregorian church reforms of the later part of the eleventh century, when Roman reformers tried to assert the church's independence, tells us how important a tool rulers thought this was.[21] In Scandinavia, we get to see what happened when this tool

---

19 *Isidori Hispalensis Episcopi Etymologiarum sive Originum Libri XX*, vol. 2, XVIII, i; *Etymologies of Isidore of Seville*, p. 359.
20 Godman, *Poetry of the Carolingian Renaissance*, pp. 262–65.
21 Blumenthal, *The Investiture Controversy*; Vollrath, 'The Western Empire'.

became available more or less all at once. The results seem to have been dramatic; by giving the kings, or people who wanted to be kings, a new way to legitimate their claims to power, and a new set of stories to tell, it distorted the old networks and redefined kingship. Benham points to Norwegian churchmen pushing a more southern, that is, Christian, ideal of kingship in order to limit or eliminate competition over the crown. Such efforts struck at the roots of an older order that, as these essays have shown us, depended on that competition for its stability. Jón Viðar Sigurðsson echoes this observation when he argues that the new *flokkr* essentially broke the system and promoted in its place a southern-style ideology of a unitary kingship. As the players in the Scandinavian power game adapted their tactics in the new environment, we see more things that look (to this 'mainstream' medievalist at any rate) thoroughly and typically medieval. Members of the political class turned to founding monasteries and carrying out other acts of religious devotion in order to promote family identities and family traditions, or to create other kinds of communities, and with them new networks. Erik the Unforgettable sought to recast the assassination of Knud Lavard as a holy martyrdom by reorganizing and newly endowing Knud's burial place at the priory of Ringsted — thus participating in what Esmark calls a new 'politicizing of monasticism'. Harald Gille tried to draw St Olav into his own friendship network by building him a church in Bergen. In doing so, he was mapping his understanding of the political world onto the Christian universe and trying to access divine power in a way that he understood.

Another catalyst for change in eleventh- and twelfth-century Scandinavia looks to me to have been economic development, and the social and political transformations that accompanied it. Economic change from the Viking period onwards, combined with cultural and political influence from the south, reshaped the landscape of power and offered new opportunities and ammunition for elites to legitimate their claims to power and the use of force. As both Esmark and Poulsen point out, towns became sites where economic, religious, and political power came together, and therefore a new focus for conflict. Serving both as economic centres and as anchors for the developing diocesan structure of the Church, towns offered geographically fixed nodes of power, tied to Christian cult centres, which kings (or those who wanted to be kings) fought over, where they wanted to live, and from which they could build more geographically defined realms. As one consequence of a new style of political competition, that depended less on projecting power by ships and more on control of fixed sites and territories, Scandinavians began to adopt (or add into the mix) southern ways of fighting: with knights on horseback, and from fortified defensive positions — i.e., castles.

The development of towns as sites of political competition is not something that was pushed into Scandinavia from the south, but rather something that Scandinavia shared in this historical moment with the south. As I read this volume, I was repeatedly and forcibly reminded of the explosion that took place to the southwest of Scandinavia, in Flanders, in 1127–1128, after the murder in St Donatian's church in Bruges of Count Charles 'the Good'. There is of course a direct link between this incident and Scandinavia: Charles himself was born in Denmark, to King Knud the Saint and Adela of Flanders. As such, he was understood in Scandinavia from the perspective and within the framework of Scandinavian conflict; as Esmark tells us, the annals of Lund attribute his assassination at the hands of the Flemish Erembald clan to 'the advice of Magnus, son of King Niels'.[22] Looked at from the perspective of Flemish accounts, most notably that of Galbert of Bruges, the murder of Charles and the war over the countship that followed can be understood as the result of a collision between old-style network competition led by the Erembald clan and its allies, and a style of rule based on the centralized authority of the count being pushed by Charles and celebrated by at least one ecclesiastical advocate (Galbert). But the outcome of the conflict (which Galbert calls a *bellum civile*)[23] was influenced, warped, and ultimately determined by the armed citizens of the newly powerful Flemish towns, who were able to turn their economic, political, and military power to assert their own rights and interests as political actors, and ultimately to control who became count of Flanders. Here too, then, the collision of old and new ways of understanding order, and the appearance of new resources, produced conflict.[24]

There were differences, of course. The growth of towns in Scandinavia appears to have been provoked as much by the arrival of the Roman church with its geographical patterns of organization as by economic development. In the south, the church structure was already there, to provide a framework around which pre-existing towns could grow larger as trade and industry picked up in the eleventh and twelfth centuries. A second difference that struck me as I read was the persistence in Scandinavia of the local assembly as a geographically rooted locus of political power and interest, and the frequent location of assembly meeting sites in towns. I am not used to seeing the assembly discussed with any frequency among 'mainstream' medievalists beyond those who work on the Germanic societies of the very earliest Middle Ages, Anglo-Saxon England, or Iceland.[25] In the Scandinavia discussed in this volume, the frequent location of assembly meeting sites in towns attracted royal interest and power. As

---

22 Chapter 3, p. 112.
23 *Galbertus notarius Brugensis de multro*, pp. 121, 168. On Galbert and his text see Rider, *God's Scribe*.
24 Brown, *Violence*, pp. 167–92; cf. Rider, *God's Scribe*, pp. 50–76.
25 Cf. Beck and others, 'Ding'.

Paulsen notes, it was therefore vital for kings to control towns in order to get regional acclamation and followers. That kings or royal claimants in Scandinavia could hope to control towns was a consequence of the fact that, up through the first part of the twelfth century at least, the towns remained largely unfortified. The siege as a military action developed in Scandinavia only gradually, as stone castles replaced their motte and bailey predecessors. As a consequence, and in contrast to the walled towns of the south, Scandinavian towns were not independent political actors. They were sites of power and legitimacy that were fought over; they did not, as did their compatriots in Galbert's Flanders, fight for power and legitimacy themselves. In Flanders, kings and counts sought to gain the support of towns. They were not, despite their best efforts, able to control them.

Finally: I felt myself on familiar ground as I read that here too, the sources we use to do history were themselves parts of the history that we use them to learn about. The texts shown us by the contributors to this volume reflect the worldviews and assumptions of their authors and/or their authors' attempts to control memories of the past for present purposes. They thus warp the images that we see, much as their southern counterparts do.[26] Orning, for example, flags the two *flokkr* he deals with, the Birkibeinar and the Baglar, as 'constructs of a double order'.[27] On the one hand, we can understand them as groups designed to unify people with divergent interests by emphasizing their members' common bond to a leader and common cause against an enemy. On the other, we can see them as products of the kings' sagas. These were written as arguments in favour of a king-centred way of understanding politics; they therefore privileged conflicts between royally-led groups operating within national borders. Benham notes that the author of her primary source, the *Bǫglunga sǫgur*, was clearly familiar with intellectual and legal developments in Europe to the south. Looking back at the partition agreement of 1208, between three claimants to the Norwegian kingship, he tried to square a southern-style picture of two factions fighting for control of a unitary, Christian kingship with the tripartite division of the kingdom that was actually laid out in the agreement. In the process, he obscured the fact that by its very existence, the agreement recognized the authority and jurisdiction of each of the three parties.

Where Scandinavia differs from the south is in its patterns of source survival. Much of the work on power and order in medieval western and central Europe has been fuelled by charters. These have permitted us to learn a great deal about how local social and political actors — lesser

---

26 The literature on this issue among 'mainstream' medievalists is vast. To pick just one important example from my particular corner of the scholarly universe: Geary, *Phantoms of Remembrance*.
27 Chapter 4, p. 189.

as well as greater landowners, castellans as well as counts, priests and monks as well as abbots and bishops — competed with each other for power and resources.[28] As is pointed out in Chapter 1 and other chapters, however, surviving charters from high medieval Scandinavia are few and far between. When Hermanson discusses one of them, a charter from 1164–1167 that represents the oldest preserved charter from Sweden, what he shows us would look entirely typical farther south: a dispute between a woman and her son over a farm that the woman had donated to a monastery. This suggests to me that if we had more charters from the region, we would likely see more examples of Scandinavians acting, and thinking, in ways that would connect their history even more firmly to that of the rest of medieval Europe.

---

[28] e.g., for the early Middle Ages, Brown, *Beyond the Monastery Walls*, pp. 216–51. Examples from high medieval France: White, 'Feuding and Peace-Making'; McHaffie, 'Law and Violence'. See also Brown and Górecki (eds), *Conflict in Medieval Europe*.

Works Cited

Primary Sources

Beowulf, ed. by Michael Alexander (New York: Penguin, 1995)
Galbertus notarius Brugensis de multro, traditione, et occisione gloriosi Karoli comitis Flandriarum, ed. by Jeff Rider (Turnhout: Brepols, 1994)
Isidori Hispalensis Episcopi Etymologiarum sive Originum Libri XX, 2 vols, ed. by Wallace Martin Lindsay (Oxford: Clarendon Press, 1911)
Monumenta Germaniae Historica, Capitularia Regum Francorum I, ed. by Alfred Boretius (Hannover; Hahn, 1883)
The Etymologies of Isidore of Seville, trans. by Stephen A. Barney, W. J. Lewis, J. A. Beach, and Oliver Berghof (Cambridge: Cambridge University Press, 2006)

Secondary Studies

Althoff, Gerd, *Family, Friends and Followers: Political and Social Bonds in Early Medieval Europe*, trans. by Christopher Carroll (Cambridge: Cambridge University Press, 2004)
Beck, Heinrich, Reinhard Wenskus, Per Sveaas Andersen, Helmut Schledermann, Magnús Stefánsson and Göran Dahlbäck. 'Ding', *Reallexikon der germanischen Altertumskunde*, 2nd edn, Band 5: *Chronos – dona* (Berlin: de Gruyter, 1984), pp. 443–65
Blumenthal, Uta-Renate, *The Investiture Controversy: Church and Monarchy from the Ninth to the Twelfth Century* (Philadelphia: University of Pennsylvania Press, 1988)
Brown, Warren C., *Beyond the Monastery Walls: Lay Men and Women in Early Medieval Legal Formularies* (Cambridge: Cambridge University Press, 2023)
——, 'The Criminalization of Violence in the Medieval West', in *A Companion to Crime and Deviance in the Middle Ages*, ed. by Hannah Skoda (Leeds: Arc Humanities Press, 2023), pp. 226–41
——, 'The Pre-History of Terrorism', in *Oxford Handbook of Terrorism*, ed. by Andreas Gofas, Richard English, Stathis N. Kalyvas, and Erica Chenoweth (Oxford: Oxford University Press, 2019), pp. 87–100
——, 'Terrorism, History, and Periodization', in *The Cambridge History of Terrorism*, ed. by Richard English (Cambridge: Cambridge University Press, 2021), pp. 58–80
——, *Unjust Seizure: Conflict, Interest and Authority in an Early Medieval Society* (Ithaca, NY: Cornell University Library, 2001)
——, *Violence in Medieval Europe* (Harlow: Routledge, 2011)
——, and Piotr Górecki (eds), *Conflict in Medieval Europe: Changing Perspectives on Society and Culture* (Aldershot: Routledge, 2003)

———, Rory Cox, and Jennifer Jahner (eds), *Violence and Order: Past and Present*, special issue of the journal *Global Intellectual History* (in press, expected publication winter 2024)

———, Marios Costambeys, Matthew Innes, and Adam J. Kosto (eds), *Documentary Culture and the Laity in the Early Middle Ages* (Cambridge: Cambridge University Press, 2013)

Firnhaber-Baker, Justine, *The Jacquerie of 1358: A French Peasants' Revolt* (Oxford: Oxford University Press, 2022)

Fouracre, Paul, and Richard A. Gerberding, *Late Merovingian France: History and Hagiography, 640–720* (Manchester: Manchester University Press, 1996)

Garnier, Claudia, *Die Kultur der Bitte: Herrschaft und Kommunikation im mittelalterlichen Reich* (Darmstadt: Wissenschaftliche Buchgesellschaft, 2008)

Geary, Patrick J., *Before France and Germany: The Creation and Transformation of the Merovingian World* (Oxford: Oxford University Press, 1988)

———, *Phantoms of Remembrance: Memory and Oblivion at the End of the First Millennium* (Princeton: Princeton University Press, 1996)

Gilsdorf, Sean, *The Favor of Friends: Intercession and Aristocratic Politics in Carolingian and Ottonian Europe* (Leiden: Brill, 2014)

Gluckman, Max, 'The Peace in the Feud', *Past and Present*, 7 (1955), 1–14

Godman, Peter, *Poetry of the Carolingian Renaissance* (London: Gerald Duckworth & Co, 1985)

Hill, John M., *The Cultural World in Beowulf* (Toronto: University of Toronto Press, 1995)

Hyams, Paul R., *Rancor and Reconciliation in Medieval England* (Ithaca, NY: Cornell University Library, 2003)

Kaeuper, Richard, *Chivalry and Violence in Medieval Europe* (Oxford: Oxford University Press, 1999)

Koziol, Geoffrey, *Begging Pardon and Favor: Ritual and Political Order in Early Medieval France* (Ithaca, NY: Cornell University Library, 1992)

Lambert, Tom, *Law and Order in Anglo-Saxon England* (Oxford: Oxford University Press, 2017)

Le Jan, Régine, *Famille et pouvoir dans le monde franc (VIIe-Xe siècle). Essai d'anthropologie sociale* (Paris: Éditions de la Sorbonne, 1995)

Malegam, Jehangir Y., *The Sleep of Behemoth: Disputing Peace and Violence in Medieval Europe, 1000–1200* (Ithaca, NY: Cornell University Library, 2013)

McHaffie, Matthew W., 'Law and Violence in Eleventh-Century France', *Past and Present*, 238 (2018), 3–41

Orning, Hans Jacob, 'Violence, Conflict and Order in Medieval Norway', in *Violence and Order: Past and Present*, ed. by Warren C. Brown and others, special issue of the journal *Global Intellectual History* (in press, expected publication winter 2024)

Rider, Jeff, *God's Scribe: The Historiographical Art of Galbert of Bruges* (Washington, DC: The Catholic University of America Press, 2001)

Vollrath, Hannah, 'The Western Empire under the Salians', in *The New Cambridge Medieval History*, ed. by David Luscombe and Jonathan Riley-Smith, vol. IV *c*. 1024 – *c*. 1198, Part II (Cambridge: Cambridge University Press, 2004), pp. 38–71

White, Stephen D., 'Feuding and Peace-Making in the Touraine Around the Year 1100', *Traditio*, 42 (1986), 195–263

Index

Abbot: 291, 356, 359, 365, 391, 424
Abduction: 84, 297
Absalon, archbishop: 69, 103, 123, 222, 230–32, 244, 250–51, 253, 314
Accumulation point: 15, 106, 108, 154–55, 274, 277, 290, 300
Adam of Bremen, chronicler: 221, 225, 246, 364
Adela of Blois, princess of England: 394
Adela of Flanders, queen of Denmark: 110, 271, 422
Adelbero, archbishop: 145
Adelbjorn, bishop: 136, 147, 149
Adolf I, count: 133
Adolf II, count: 133
Afghanistan: 14, 26, 80
Agency: 14, 266, 282, 290, 295, 298–300
Agge, magnate: 137, 142
Ágrip: 44
Althoff, Gerd, historian: 329, 343, 414, 416–17, 419
Alvastra abbey: 292–93, 295–96
Ambush: 97, 172, 175, 183, 187, 192, 197, 385
Amendments: 48, 53
Amund Gyrdsson, magnate: 58, 60, 69, 70
Anacletus, pope: 145
Anderson, Benedict, political scientist: 292
Andersson, Catharina, historian: 291
Angelbert, Frankish warrior: 420

Anger: 117–18, 125–26, 380, 391, 394, 406–07
Anglo-Norman: 246, 344, 371–73, 376, 378, 382–83
Annales ryenses: 129
Annals of Erfurt: 131
Anonymous of Béthune, chronicler: 394, 397
Aquitaine: 313, 387
Aristocracy: 14, 238, 240, 245, 249, 282, 371–73, 377, 383, 417
Arnbjorn Jonsson, magnate: 187
Arne of Ståreim, magnate: 74, 75, 185, 278, 282
Arstad, Knut, historian: 253
Asmild: 138, 143
Assembly: 18, 41, 46, 58–59, 75, 79, 105–06, 118, 122, 124, 126–29, 146, 150, 153–54, 181–82, 215, 227–31, 237, 281, 311, 321, 329, 351, 422; *see also* thing
Asser, archbishop: 102, 105, 107, 109, 127, 134, 142, 145, 149–50, 152–53

Bagge, Sverre, historian: 25, 79, 203, 309, 317, 318
Baglar: 38, 82, 166–77, 180, 182–89, 192–94, 196–97, 199–203, 205–08, 216, 222, 225–26, 233, 235, 240, 253, 284, 309–10, 315, 319, 326–27, 329, 330, 333, 423
Balance of power: 38, 122, 136, 139, 145, 152, 155, 168, 169, 173–74, 205–06, 288, 414
Baldwin of Béthune, count: 400

Balthild, Merovingian queen and saint: 415
Baltic Sea: 60, 108, 114, 116
Bard Guttormsson, magnate: 179, 180
Baron: 73, 372–73, 377, 381, 383, 385–86, 388–91, 393, 395–408, 419
Bartlett, Robert, historian: 190, 343, 373–77, 379, 381, 388, 390, 397
Battle: 19–20, 41–42, 49–52, 55–56, 60, 71, 73–74, 78, 81–83, 126, 133, 136–37, 139, 147, 149, 154, 156, 170, 175, 187, 193–94, 196, 201, 203–04, 223, 225–26, 231–35, 244, 278, 280, 293, 296, 332, 350–51, 383, 391–93, 401, 408, 420
Battlefield: 82, 194, 215, 231, 293, 389, 417
Beata stirps: 292
Bellum civile: 420, 422
Benham, Jenny, historian: 169, 198, 216, 416, 418–19, 421, 423
Beowulf: 416
Bergen: 41, 48, 51, 54–58, 83, 169, 170–71, 180, 183–84, 186–88, 193–94, 196–97, 199–221, 223, 230, 233, 236–37, 240–41, 246–48, 251–52, 329–30, 421
Berwick: 407
Béthune, chronicler: 379, 394, 397, 407
Bias: 102, 166–67, 191, 198, 357
Bijsterveld, Arnoud-Jan, historian: 15
Bilateral kinship: 267, 271, 290
Birger Brosa, earl: 16, 63, 165, 284, 288
Birkibeinar: 17, 38, 82, 166–79, 182–89, 192–94, 196–97, 199–200, 203, 205–07, 216, 219, 222–23, 232–33, 235, 244, 423

Bishop: 15, 55, 56, 58, 79, 102, 105, 107–08, 123, 127, 135–36, 138, 145–47, 149, 152–53, 156, 180, 185, 222, 230–31, 235, 237, 239–40, 243, 245, 249, 250, 253, 284, 310, 318, 320, 327–29, 348, 350, 356, 359, 363, 365, 383, 389, 391, 396–97, 424
Bishopric: 14, 136, 149, 155
Bisson, Thomas, historian: 103
Bjarkøy: 69
Bjernede: 122
Bjorn Egilsson, magnate: 59, 60
Bjorn Ironside, magnate: 109, 115, 130, 137, 151, 272, 285
Bjälbo family: 288
Bodil Eriksdatter, queen of Denmark: 105, 112
Bodilsen family: 103
Bohuslän: 64, 224, 228, 236, 245
Boleslaw III, duke of Poland: 116, 286
Booty: 117, 191, 195–97, 200, 206, 224, 233, 377, 384
Borgarthing: 58, 227–28, 243
Borgundkaupangen: 247
Bornholm: 113, 250
Bouchard, Constance B., historian: 292
Bourdieu, Pierre, sociologist: 121, 202, 265–66, 298–300
Breengaard, Carsten, historian: 136
Bremen: 78, 107, 145, 363
Brigida Haraldsdatter, queen of Sweden: 60, 63, 284, 287, 288
Brown, Warren C., historian: 344, 413
Bruges: 110, 422
Buris Henriksson, magnate: 282, 283
Burning: 191, 377, 407
Bury St Edmunds: 403
Byzantine: 24, 272, 276

Bǫglunga sǫgur: 38, 166–67, 173, 184, 190, 193–94, 196, 199, 206–08, 224, 240, 244, 253, 310, 319, 322, 330, 332, 423

Canon law: 216, 333
Canones Nidrosienses: 79
Canterbury: 389, 400
Carolingians: 312, 344, 359, 363, 413–14, 420
Carpenter, David, historian: 403
Castells, Manuel, sociologist: 72, 73
Castle: 114, 137–39, 151, 170–71, 194, 196, 199–200, 215, 233, 238–39, 248, 249–53, 348, 354–55, 365, 380, 387, 392, 401, 404–05, 407–08, 421, 423
Cavalry: 252
Cecilia Sigurdsdatter, princess of Norway: 112, 179
Celestine III, pope: 297
Charlemagne, Frankish king and emperor: 414–15, 418
Charles the Bald, Frankish king and emperor: 312, 420
Charles the Good, count: 422
Charter: 19, 26–28, 98, 102, 110, 218, 238, 253, 275, 396, 402–03, 423–24
Chester: 407
Cheyette, Fredric L., historian: 26
Children: 61, 64–66, 68–69, 151, 202, 231, 278, 281, 286, 291, 354, 361, 395
Chivalry: 195, 200, 419
Christia, Fotini, political scientist: 26, 80
Christiern Svensen, magnate: 134, 136–37, 142, 149, 151, 153, 156
Christmas: 120, 142, 150, 178, 241
Chronicle of Roskilde: 241
Chronicle of the Princes: 403
Chronicle of the Slavs: 98, 312

Chronicle of Vitskøl abbey: 295
Civil war: 11–14, 16, 20, 22–23, 26, 37–38, 39, 41–43, 49–51, 76, 82–86, 97, 99, 165–66, 199, 205, 216, 300, 309, 328, 331, 334, 343–45, 371–73, 376, 380, 391, 413, 418–20
Church 14, 21, 42, 55–56, 78–79, 98–99, 102, 105, 107, 109, 114, 123, 138, 143, 145, 150, 157, 197–98, 200, 225, 235, 238–39, 242–46, 249, 251, 268–69, 271, 276, 287, 290, 292, 294, 299, 309, 319, 333, 348, 358, 361, 391, 403, 420, 421–22
Class: 19, 24, 57, 156, 191, 198, 199, 200, 343, 366, 421
Comaroff, John, anthropologist: 13
Community: 18, 38, 124, 198–201, 203, 205–08, 227, 248, 269, 290–94, 333 Conflict: 12–15, 19–26, 28, 37–39, 52, 76, 83, 85–86, 97–99, 120, 122–23, 126, 136–39, 142–43, 145, 150, 153, 155–57, 166, 168–69, 177–79, 181, 190, 192–93, 197–98, 203, 205, 215–16, 229–31, 252, 266, 284, 289, 309–10, 312–15, 319–24, 326, 328, 331–33, 343, 345–47, 349–66, 372, 376, 380, 385–87, 390, 394, 397–99, 404–05, 407, 416–22
Constant crisis: 22, 25–26, 37, 38, 153–54, 166, 168, 174–76, 183, 185–86, 189, 201, 203, 205–07, 215, 217, 344, 386, 417
Constantinople: 219
Conuiratio: 124
Coopétition: 24, 25, 154, 217
Corfe castle: 400
Coroban, Costel, historian: 73
Count: 348, 350–51, 356, 363, 365, 379, 399, 423–24

Coup: 37, 76, 78, 85–86
Court: 112, 114–15, 118–19, 129, 134, 140, 152, 178, 230, 240, 278, 288, 297, 312, 347, 348, 400, 406
Crime: 21, 122, 127, 231, 322, 348, 372–73, 415
Crisis: 23, 26, 42, 81, 103, 106, 117–19, 126, 155, 165, 177, 183, 205, 224, 249, 275
Crouch, David, historian: 53
Crown: 14, 16–17, 39, 46, 49, 118, 129, 216, 272, 280, 283, 294, 320, 376, 389, 392, 395–96, 417, 421
Crusade: 105, 235, 391
Cyprus: 105

Dagfinn Bonde, magnate: 193, 199
De antiquitate regum Norwagiensium: 83
De Bello civili: 20
Debt: 194, 267
Defiance (diffidatio) 376
Disinheritance: 380–81, 383, 385, 401, 404–05, 407
Divided leadership: 173, 183
Drink, drinking: 48, 204, 235, 240, 362, 366
Duke: 45, 348, 356, 359, 360–61, 365, 379, 387, 417

Earl: 15–16, 45, 53, 60, 107, 112, 115, 140–41, 150, 165, 174, 182, 188, 202, 284, 288, 296, 311, 315–16, 324, 326–27, 331, 382, 396, 401, 403–04, 407–08
Ebbe Sunesen, magnate: 17
Edmund Ironside, king of England: 328
Eider: 134
Eidsivathing: 227
Einar Kongsmag, magnate: 180, 183, 197, 200
Eirik Ivarsson, archbishop: 181, 182, 226

Eirik Oddsson, chronicler: 43
Election: 105, 114, 116, 130, 180–81, 184–86, 189, 311, 314, 320, 329, 400
Elite: 15, 19, 22, 24, 28, 39, 46, 53, 59, 71, 73, 75–76, 97, 100, 102–03, 107, 110, 112, 118, 128, 145, 148, 153, 179, 181, 185, 198, 199–201, 203, 205, 216, 266, 277, 278, 283–84, 289–91, 299–300, 309
Ellisif Jarizleifsdatter, queen of Norway: 63
Emanuelsson, Anders, historian: 292
Empire: 115–17, 145, 312, 388
  Holy Roman: 343
Enemy: 83, 85, 116, 137, 173, 176, 190, 231, 278, 280, 296, 322, 350, 359, 380–81, 386, 401, 407, 423
England: 12, 16, 75, 271, 322, 328, 330, 343–44, 371–73, 377–83, 386–97, 399, 401, 403–04, 407, 415–16, 419, 422
English crown: 376, 398
Enmity: 76, 190, 203–04, 268, 282, 320–21, 419
Erembald clan: 422
Erik Eriksson, king of Sweden: 296
Erik Jedvardsson, king of Sweden: 75, 208, 285, 287–88, 293, 295, 297
Erik Deacon Haraldsen: 151
Erik the Good, king of Denmark: 97, 102, 105–07, 109, 112–15, 121–22, 130, 142, 228, 249, 267
Erik the Lamb, king of Denmark: 148, 218, 232–33
Erik the Unforgettable, king of Denmark: 51–52, 60, 97–99, 106, 108, 115, 120–22, 126, 128–31, 134, 136–42, 144, 146–53, 156–57, 220, 223, 225, 231, 233, 239, 241, 251, 274, 278, 280, 293, 314, 421

Erik family: 284–85, 288–89, 295
Erling Skakke, magnate: 66, 74–79, 86, 175–76, 222, 224–25, 228, 230–31, 233, 235, 239, 242, 283, 311, 319
Erling Skjalgsson, magnate: 324
Erling Stonewall, Norwegian king: 170–72, 174, 184, 188, 197, 200, 226, 228, 233
Eskil, archbishop: 138, 149, 152–53, 250, 314
Esmark, Kim, historian: 11, 37, 177, 179, 417, 419, 420–22
Esrum Abbey: 293
Europe: 12–13, 24, 26, 39, 56, 64, 75, 103, 113, 195, 215, 248, 276, 290–92, 315, 324, 326, 332, 334, 344, 355, 359, 377, 381, 413–14, 417–20, 423
Execution: 151, 197, 355
Exile: 105, 127, 151, 215, 225, 297, 384, 401
Eyjarskeggjar: 167
Eyrathing: 171, 177, 181, 227–28, 243

Face-to-face meetings: 253, 333
Faction: 14–16, 18, 22–26, 28, 38, 79, 104, 106, 108, 128, 130, 136, 150–51, 155, 166, 168, 170, 179, 183, 186, 206, 208, 281–82, 284, 288, 309, 310, 315–16, 318–19, 323, 326, 333, 371, 375, 397, 420, 423
Fagrskinna: 43, 77, 286
Falster: 108, 112, 115, 120, 248
Family: 13, 15–16, 18–19, 22, 37, 41, 43–46, 52, 61, 63–66, 68–69, 71, 80–81, 85, 97, 101–09, 112–13, 115, 119–20, 123, 126, 137, 151–52, 154–55, 157, 179, 185, 192–93, 207, 218, 226, 265–72, 274, 277–86, 288–300, 314, 331, 346, 350, 359, 375, 390, 414, 421
Farm: 45, 48, 49, 53, 54, 60, 81, 231, 236, 353, 365
Faroes: 179
Feast: 117, 120, 170, 178, 239, 240–42, 315, 327, 329
Felony: 372
Feud: 50–51, 99, 126, 139, 148, 349, 350–51, 353–54, 361–62, 380, 394, 416
Fidelity: 149, 372
Filippus Simonsson, Norwegian king and earl: 171, 174, 182, 185–86, 188–89, 196, 199, 201–02, 284, 309, 320
Fimreite: 50, 81, 223
First Novgorod Chronicle: 272
Fjenneslev: 122
Flanders: 110, 399, 415, 422–23
Fleet: 48, 129, 137, 146, 170–71, 186, 200, 222–24, 233, 248, 382, 389–91
Flensburg: 247
Flokkr: 17, 37, 41, 43, 51, 54, 73–83, 85, 156, 172, 175–76, 185, 414, 421, 423; *see also* party
Folkungar: 288
Folkvid, lawman: 179, 182
Follower: 13, 15, 19, 23, 39, 76, 81, 117, 120, 123, 136, 139, 143, 146, 149, 151, 153–54, 182, 196, 197, 200, 203, 216, 242, 313, 316, 318, 321–23, 328, 332, 347, 349–50, 352, 353, 373, 382, 383–88, 390, 414, 416, 420, 423
Fontenoy, battle of: 420
Fortification: 137, 143, 175, 215, 234–36, 240, 244, 248–52
Fosterage, fosterer, fosterfather: 37, 43, 57, 63, 68–71, 85, 101–02, 112, 115, 120, 122–23, 180, 183,

216, 268, 270–71, 282, 323, 331, 333
Fotevig: 146, 149–51, 155, 157, 280, 293
Framlingham: 407
France: 13, 16–27, 275, 291–92, 324, 344, 355, 372, 376, 378, 380–84, 396, 398,-401, 405, 414–15, 417
Francia: 414–15
Franks: 24, 66, 325, 356, 420
Friend, friendship: 12–13, 15, 18–19, 24, 37–41, 43–49, 54–61, 64, 71–74, 76–77, 80–81, 83, 85–86, 97, 101, 112, 114, 117, 119–25, 130–31, 136, 140–42, 148–49, 151–54, 172, 178, 182, 185, 190–91, 198, 204–05, 222, 240, 270, 288, 311, 347–53, 357, 360, 362–64, 387, 414, 417–18, 420–21
Frisians: 112
Froissart, Jean, chronicler: 417
Funen: 124, 146, 227, 236, 238–39, 243, 250, 312
Fyrileiv: 20, 41, 48–51, 82, 231

Galbert of Bruges, chronicler: 422
Gammelnorsk homiliebok: 55
Geary, Patrick J., historian: 414
Geffrei Gaimar: 379, 381
Gender: 216, 265, 285, 289
Genealogical accidents: 23, 101, 272, 274, 278, 283, 298
Generosity: 44, 55, 57
Geoffrey de Mandeville, earl: 400–01
Germany: 12–13, 16–17, 27, 52, 75, 98–99, 112, 114, 118, 120, 131–34, 144, 147–48, 152, 155–56, 246, 275, 312, 325, 343–46, 353, 355–61, 364–66, 395, 414–17, 419
Gesta Danorum: 77, 218, 240, 244, 327; *see also* Saxo Grammaticus
Gift: 15, 46, 52, 150, 157, 291, 294, 389, 394, 403

Gilbert, earl: 401, 407–08
Gillingham, John, historian: 383
Gluckman, Max, anthropologist: 50
Grathe Moor: 20, 234, 245, 293
Gregorian reforms: 420
Gregorius Dagsson, magnate: 54, 74, 80, 230
Grenå: 247
Grid, *grið*: 82, 83, 194, 197, 200, 329
Grief: 380, 396, 400
Group identity: 82
Guerre: 372, 378, 401
Guerrilla: 60, 170–71, 173, 187, 206, 219
Guinea-Bissau: 14
Gulathing law: 49, 55, 61, 79, 81, 84, 227, 322–23
Gunhild, princess of Sweden: 271
Gunnar of Gimsar, magnate: 59, 60
Guttorm Asolfsson of Rein, magnate: 58
Guttorm Sigurdsson, king of Norway: 58, 169, 180–81, 329
Gyrd Law-Bersason, magnate: 58
Göta älv: 224, 248
Götaland: 60, 116, 127, 177, 208, 221, 224–26, 274, 286, 321
Götar: 112, 116, 140

Haderslev: 247
Hakon Broad-shouldered, king of Norway: 42, 71, 73–74, 77–79, 85, 175, 223, 232, 242
Hakon Galen, earl: 170–71, 173, 177–83, 187–88, 201–02, 208, 309, 324, 327
Hakon Hakonsson, king of Norway: 85, 166, 174, 311, 315–16
Hakon Haraldsson, king of Norway: 76
Hakon Magnusson, king of Norway: 63, 227

Hakon Sigurdsson, king of Norway: 228, 242
Hakon Sunnivasen, magnate: 112, 119, 122, 124–25, 148
Hakon Sverresson, king of Norway: 169, 172–73, 179, 181, 184, 198, 228
Hakon Ubbesen, magnate: 119
Halberstadt: 144–45
Halland: 51–52, 170, 225, 232
Halldor Sigurdsson, magnate: 59–60, 66
Hallkell Huk, magnate: 41, 63, 64, 74
Hamar: 74, 247
Hamburg: 78, 107, 145
Hamburg-Bremen: 107, 145
Handgengnir menn: 45, 74, 80
Harald Finehair, king of Norway: 83
Harald Gille, king of Norway: 37, 41–43, 45–60, 63–65, 69, 70, 74, 82, 85, 120, 134, 141, 151, 179, 225, 228, 231–32, 236, 242, 278, 280–81, 284, 287, 310, 332, 421
Harald Gormsson, king of Denmark: 77, 311
Harald Hardruler, king of Norway: 52, 63, 224, 228–29, 239, 241, 246, 311, 326, 328, 331
Harald Hen, king of Denmark: 105, 245
Harald Kesja, magnate: 105–06, 109, 114–15, 126, 130, 135–37, 139, 143–44, 146–47, 149–51, 229, 231, 249, 251, 270, 272, 274
Haraldsborg: 114, 137–39, 249, 251
Haraldsted: 97–100, 102, 106, 110, 117, 120–23, 126, 131, 147, 154–55
Hardeknud, king of Denmark: 52
Hauck, Karl, historian: 292
Hauskloster: 18, 103, 152, 295, 296
Hebrides: 41, 197

Heimskringla: 43, 44, 47–48, 50, 54–60, 69–71, 74, 77, 83, 217, 282, 310, 327
Heklungar: 82, 167
Helena, queen of Sweden: 272, 274, 290–91, 293–95, 297
Helge, bishop: 238
Helgøya: 184
Helias, bishop: 249
Helle, Knut, historian: 166, 167
Helmold of Bosau, chronicler: 98, 112, 118–19, 121, 128, 131–33, 146, 156, 267, 275, 312
Helsingborg: 246–47, 249
Henrik Gottskalksen, magnate: 114
Henrik Skadelar, magnate: 106, 109, 115, 118–20, 146–47, 278
Henrik, bishop: 147
Henry I, king of England: 375, 381, 387, 390–96, 402–04
Henry II, king of England: 75, 325, 330, 354, 375, 378, 387, 395, 398
Henry III, king of England: 374–75, 397–99, 405, 408
Henry IV, king of England: 348, 357–58
Henry of Huntingdon, chronicler: 328, 378, 387
Henry the Young, king of England: 375, 378
Hereward, magnate: 381–86
Hermanson, Lars, historian: 70, 108, 216, 415, 424
Hertford castle: 408
Herward, magnate: 414
Hierarchy: 15, 17, 22, 25, 79, 104, 108, 291, 347, 348
Hirð, hirðmenn: 43, 45–47, 50, 58–59, 70–71, 80; *see also* retinue, retainers
Hjørring: 247
Holstein: 52, 114, 133, 155–56

Homage: 132, 328, 372, 392, 395–97, 401, 408
Honour: 19, 63–65, 106, 110, 117, 133, 178, 202, 280, 282, 291, 300, 320, 323, 328, 350, 355, 357, 360–61, 416
Horsens: 247
Hryggjarstykki: 43
Hubert Walter, archbishop: 400
Húskarlar: 74, 80
Hvide family: 102, 103, 151, 218, 250, 314
Hålogaland: 69
Haastrup, Ulla, art historian: 276

Iceland: 43, 55, 66, 73, 78, 80, 113, 310, 356, 413, 422
Illugo, bishop: 149
Imprisonment: 117, 140
Inge Bardsson Hunchback, king of Norway: 42, 54, 58–61, 70–71, 73–74, 85, 169, 180–82, 184–85, 223, 226, 228, 232, 244, 281, 283, 309, 315, 317–27, 329, 330–32
Inge Hallsteinsson, king of Sweden: 63
Inge Stenkilsson, king of Sweden: 109, 266–67, 272, 290–91, 293, 295
Inge the Younger, king of Sweden: 269, 272, 286
Ingeborg Magnusdatter, princess of Norway: 179, 181, 204
Ingeborg Mstislavsdatter, princess of Denmark: 109, 113, 115, 119, 134, 268, 277, 279, 284, 286, 291, 297
Ingegerd Knudsdatter, queen of Denmark: 63, 288, 294, 295
Ingham castle: 407, 408
Ingrid Ragvaldsdatter, queen of Norway and Denmark: 58, 70, 74, 109, 115, 185, 266, 277–78, 280–83, 287–88, 290, 293, 299–300
Ingrid Nielsdatter, princess of Denmark: 108
Inheritance: 23, 101, 109, 113, 115, 140, 267–68, 269–70, 272, 281, 285, 287, 289, 293, 315, 323, 352, 375, 380–81, 383, 385, 387–88, 391, 393–94, 396, 398, 401, 404–05
Innocent II, pope: 145
Innocent III, pope: 358, 397, 400–01, 407
Isidore of Seville, church father: 420
Isøre: 106, 129, 222, 228–29
Italy: 24

Jacquerie: 417
Jarnberaland: 219
Jean Bodin, theologian: 190
Jelling: 133
Jerusalem: 219, 228, 329, 393
Johan Sverkersson, king of Sweden: 294, 296
John de Lacy, baron: 407, 408
John of Salisbury, chronicler: 322
John of Worcester, chronicler: 328, 378, 387
John, king of England: 238, 375–76, 377, 397–408
Joint rule: 11, 37, 86, 175
Jon Hallkelsson, magnate: 63, 74
Jon Loptsson, magnate: 65
Jón Viðar Sigurðsson, historian: 11, 37, 175, 177, 179, 276, 415, 420–21
Jorgen Bodilsen, earl: 150
Jutland: 52, 77, 97, 102, 105, 110, 112, 115, 124, 127, 130–31, 133–34, 136–40, 142, 146, 149–50, 153, 156, 170, 221, 224–25, 227, 229, 234, 237–38, 243, 247, 311, 313–14

Kalmar: 116, 234
Kalundborg: 247, 250
Karl Eriksen, prince of Denmark: 296
Karl Sonason, earl: 60, 63, 284
Karl Sverkerson, king of Sweden: 16, 283, 288
Karl, count: 112
Katarina Ragvaldsdatter, princess of Sweden: 109, 115, 272, 285
Kattegat: 52, 222, 224, 226, 247, 253
Kings' saga: 55, 190, 192, 423
Kingship: 16–17, 28, 76, 97, 104–06, 108–10, 115, 118, 120, 126–27, 129–30, 134, 140, 143, 145, 150, 152, 189, 215, 239, 270, 288, 291, 311, 314, 319–22, 333, 343, 378, 418–19, 421, 423
Kinship: 12, 38, 50–51, 58, 61, 73, 76, 82, 85–86, 109, 190–91, 205, 267, 270–71, 282, 288–90, 298, 347–48, 364, 393, 418, 420; see also relative
Kinsmen: 15, 19, 65, 120, 126–27, 142, 148, 156, 268, 274, 297, 311, 387–88
Kjær, Lars, historian: 150
Knight: 148, 156, 386, 389, 391, 393–94, 399, 400, 421
Knud Lavard, duke: 20, 97–100, 102, 104, 106, 109, 112–20, 122, 123–31, 133–34, 136, 140–41, 143, 149–50, 155–56, 223, 230, 237–38, 240–41, 245, 267–68, 275, 278–79, 280–81, 297, 314, 417, 421
Knud Magnussen, king of Denmark: 225, 230, 294, 297
Knud Prislavson, magnate: 250
Knud the Great, king of Denmark, England and Norway: 52, 78, 227, 243

Knud the Saint, king of Denmark: 106, 110, 122, 241, 243–45, 288, 296
Knud Valdemarsson, king of Denmark: 165
Knut Eriksson, king of Sweden: 17, 288, 295, 297, 298
Knýtlinga saga: 51, 98, 105, 110, 113–15, 117, 120–22, 130, 142, 144, 151–54, 241
Kolding: 231, 247
Konghelle: 52–53, 74, 230, 232, 234, 236–37, 240–41, 244, 247, 250
Kristin Nikolasdatter, wife of Hakon Galen: 178–82, 208, 297
Kristin Sverresdatter, princess of Norway: 178, 201
Kristin Knudsdatter, princess of Denmark: 134–35, 140–41, 279, 285, 298
Kristina Ragvaldsdatter, queen of Kiev: 109, 113, 272
Kristina Bjornsdatter, queen of Sweden: 277, 284–85, 295, 296
Kræmmer, Michael, historian: 21
Kuflungar: 168, 194
Kvitingsøy: 169, 197, 200–01, 216, 309, 320, 323, 325, 328
Königsnähe: 103, 281

Leding: 47, 129, 146; see also *leiðangr*
Legend of Knud Lavard: 267, 274
Legitimacy: 16, 39, 82, 128–29, 154, 180, 184, 242, 281, 285, 291, 293, 320, 372, 377, 387, 399, 404, 417–19, 423
Leiðangr: 47, 73, 77, 85, 116, 146, 197, 415; see also leding
Lendr maðr: 41, 42, 45–47, 53, 58, 61, 74, 77, 232, 235, 240, 278, 283, 329
Letter: 59, 145–46, 177–78, 180, 192, 198–99, 253, 297, 315, 389, 407

L'Estoire des Engles: 379, 381–86
Liberties: 376, 403, 405
Lið 43, 47, 48, 53, 60, 80, 81
Lincoln: 401, 408
Lind, John, historian: 276
Lindesnes: 52
Little Belt: 221, 223
London: 328, 393, 401, 407
Lopt Sæmundarson, magnate: 66
Lord, lordship: 18, 44–47, 52–55, 60–61, 63, 64, 66, 69–72, 74–76, 78–81, 85, 101, 116, 133, 233, 241, 270, 355, 364, 377, 379, 389, 414, 416, 420
Lothar of Supplinburg, king and emperor: 112, 114, 131–33, 144–45, 152, 360, 362, 417
Lothar, emperor and king of Italy and Middle Francia: 312–13, 359, 420
Louis the German, king of East Francia: 312, 420
Louis the Pious, king of the Franks: 359
Louis, prince of France (Louis VIII, king of France): 376, 396, 398–99, 401, 405, 407–08
Lovén, Christian, art historian: 294
Loyalty: 19, 44, 49, 54, 63, 69, 75, 80, 82, 120, 122, 127, 147, 191, 194, 203, 268, 282, 351, 388, 391
Lund: 69, 78, 98, 101–02, 105, 107–10, 124, 142–43, 145, 147, 149–50, 153, 229–30, 233, 235, 237–39, 241, 243, 247–48, 251, 314, 422
Lund, Niels, historian: 136
Lunden, Kåre, historian: 199, 326
Lurö 293, 295
Luttwak, Edward N., author: 51
Lödöse: 225–26, 247

Magerøy, Halvard, philologist: 167, 330

Magna Carta: 376, 377, 397, 399, 401, 404–05
Magnate: 11, 14–18, 24, 28, 63, 101, 103, 104–05, 107–08, 112, 114, 118, 120, 123–25, 127, 130–31, 134, 136, 139, 148, 150, 152–53, 155, 180–82, 199, 201, 203, 207, 215, 238, 271, 278, 281–82, 288, 328, 344, 385, 387–88, 390–91, 393–94, 398–99, 403
Magnus Barefoot, king of Norway: 41–42, 57, 61, 63–66, 74, 76–77, 109, 115, 266, 270–72, 274, 276
Magnus Erlingsson, king of Norway: 37, 42, 65, 71, 75, 77–81, 83–84, 86, 170, 172, 179, 181, 184, 188, 192, 200, 204, 221, 223, 228, 232–33, 240, 242, 283
Magnus Henriksson, king of Sweden: 63, 282–84, 287–88, 293–95, 297
Magnus Nielsen, king of Denmark: 99–100, 104, 106, 109–10, 112, 114–17, 119–24, 126–29, 131–35, 138, 140–41, 144–46, 148, 151–53, 156–57, 223, 268, 281, 286, 297
Magnus Sigurdsson the Blind, king of Norway: 37, 41–43, 45, 47–51, 53–61, 69, 85, 120, 122, 134, 151, 225–26, 228, 231, 236, 242, 246, 251, 278–80, 310, 332
Magnus the Good, king of Norway and Denmark: 52, 64, 227, 228–29, 233, 246, 311, 326, 328, 331
Maine: 372, 388, 396
Maitland, Frederic William, legal historian: 376, 419
Malmfrid Mstislavsdatter, queen of Denmark and Norway: 109, 119, 134, 139–40, 277, 279, 283
Mann, Michael, sociologist: 71
Margrethe Eriksdatter, queen of Norway: 298

INDEX 439

Margrethe Stigsdatter, queen of Sweden: 286
Margrethe Ingesdatter Fredkulla, queen of Norway and Denmark: 66, 108–10, 112–13, 115, 119, 140, 155, 216, 265–72, 274–78, 281, 284–87, 290, 292, 297–98, 300
Margrethe Haraldsdatter, princess of Norway: 63
Maria Haraldsdatter: 63
Marriage: 12–13, 15, 18, 63, 81, 101, 109–10, 113, 115, 117, 134, 140–41, 155, 182, 215, 225, 233, 265, 268–72, 274, 276, 278, 280, 283, 285–87, 290, 296, 298, 320–21, 333, 352, 375, 395, 415
Matilda, empress and queen of England: 375, 381, 394–98
Mediator: 193, 198, 267, 351, 356–57, 365, 392
Mercenary: 19, 207, 318, 381
Mercy: 76, 82, 139, 144, 188, 193–94, 197, 200, 206, 234, 319, 329–30, 355, 359–60, 362, 384, 400, 407
Merovingians: 414–15
Miller, William Ian, legal historian: 380
Moldefjord: 170
Monarchy: 18, 99, 377
Monastery: 41, 56, 59, 218, 238, 243, 244–45, 275, 290–97, 420–21, 424
Morkinskinna: 43–44, 57
Mortal enmity: 190, 200, 203–04
Mstislav, prince of Novgorod: 109, 113, 272
Murmur: 182, 197
Målöw Church: 276

Negotiate: 18, 23, 76, 124, 127, 153, 155, 189, 206, 219, 227, 231, 236, 240, 243, 289, 325, 365

Network, networking: 11–16, 18–19, 22–24, 26–28, 37, 39, 43–47, 50, 54, 57, 59–61, 64, 68–73, 76, 85, 100–02, 104, 106–07, 110, 112, 114–15, 117, 119–21, 130–31, 133–34, 136, 139–40, 150–51, 153–57, 179, 185, 190, 205–07, 215–16, 219, 224–25, 227, 231, 246–48, 266, 272, 276–77, 300, 343–47, 349–50, 352–53, 364, 366, 386, 399, 414–22
Nidaros: 78, 169–71, 177, 180, 186–87, 192, 204, 226, 242, 244, 319, 324
Niels Svendsen, king of Denmark: 20, 97, 98, 100–02, 104–06, 108–10, 112–23, 126–30, 132–49, 151–54, 156–57, 222–33, 235, 237, 241, 245, 249, 267, 270–72, 274–76, 279–80, 285, 360, 422
Nikolas Arnesson, bishop: 184–85, 188, 284
Nikolas Skjaldvarsson, magnate: 74
Noble: 112, 119–20, 134, 147, 157, 343, 347–50, 359, 361, 373–74, 376–85, 387–88, 391, 399–400, 403, 408
Nordland: 222, 247
Norman rule: 382
Normandy: 324, 344, 371–72, 375, 377, 381, 386–93, 395–96, 415
Normans: 382, 383, 384, 385, 386, 391, 393, 396
Northampton: 383
Northeim: 348
Northumbria: 382
Nothold, chaplain and bishop: 102, 149
Nuer: 26
Nysether, Hilde A., historian: 82
Næstved: 102, 124, 152, 218, 247, 293

Oath: 41, 45, 79, 119, 124, 127, 145, 151, 156, 182, 194, 196–97, 200, 322, 347, 349, 351–52, 364, 395, 402–04, 406–08
Odense: 105, 109, 149, 236, 238–39, 243–45, 275, 292
Ogmund Dengir, magnate: 70
Ólafs saga helga: 54
Olav Haraldsson, king of Norway: 54–56, 64, 84, 236, 243, 244–46, 249, 324, 421
Olav Kyrre, king of Norway: 236, 241, 246
Olav Magnusson, king of Norway: 45, 64
Oluf Haraldsen, king of Denmark: 226, 229, 232–34
Oluf Hunger, king of Denmark: 63
Oppland: 59, 60, 169–71, 183–84, 310, 316
Ordeal: 41, 45, 57, 178, 185
Orderic Vitalis, chronicler: 246, 378, 387, 390
Orkneys: 223, 318
Orning, Hans Jacob, historian: 11, 38, 80, 224, 253, 416, 418–19, 423
Oslo: 45, 48, 60, 74, 83, 151, 177, 183, 185, 224–26, 228, 232–33, 237–38, 240–41, 246–47, 249, 320–21, 324
Ottar Birting, magnate: 58, 70, 278, 282
Oystein Haraldsson, king of Norway: 42, 70–71, 79, 85, 228, 232, 244
Oystein Magnusson, king of Norway: 45, 64, 74, 221, 242
Oystein Møyla, king of Norway: 167
Oystein, archbishop: 78–79, 236, 240, 249, 319

Pac, Grzegorz, historian: 292
Palace: 55, 59, 236, 239–40, 244, 251, 348

Pardon: 193, 197, 200, 207, 360
Party: 14, 18, 25, 37, 39, 61, 65, 120, 128, 130, 134, 153, 154–55, 157, 166–69, 173–75, 190, 194–95, 198–99, 205–06, 216, 222, 225, 231–32, 284, 289, 312–13, 315–17, 320–21, 325–26, 328–29, 331, 347, 351–53, 355–62, 364–66, 380, 416, 418, 423; see also *flokkr*
Patron: 15, 18, 53, 63, 120, 123, 190, 244, 291, 314, 383, 385, 387, 415, 418
Peace: 19–21, 22, 47, 50–51, 53, 66, 69, 71, 84, 85, 107, 109, 118–19, 146, 172–73, 193, 198–99, 201–04, 215–16, 268–69, 274, 276–77, 310, 318–19, 321–23, 325, 327–29, 331–34, 349, 354, 356, 358–63, 365–66, 383, 386, 388–90, 392–94, 397–98, 402–05, 407, 416–19
Peace of God councils: 415
Peacemaker, peacemaking: 14, 192, 199, 201, 269, 282, 310, 325–26, 328–32, 343, 346, 351, 356, 359, 362–63, 365
Peasant: 124, 172, 181–82, 184, 188, 195, 202, 208, 373, 417
Peder Bodilsen, magnate: 102, 124, 125, 149–50, 152, 218
Peder, bishop: 135, 136, 139
Perjury: 127, 372
Peter Sauda-Ulfsson, magnate: 58
Peter Stoype, magnate: 177–82, 200, 204, 297
Peterborough: 382–85
Philip Augustus, king of France: 291
Philip Halstensson, king of Sweden: 269
Philip II, king of France: 376, 398
Plunder: 19, 23, 49, 52, 53, 60, 83, 84, 115, 117, 141, 144, 156, 175, 193,

195, 197, 235, 270, 318, 319–81, 383–85, 387, 392
Poison: 178, 180
Poitou: 372
Political culture: 126, 166–67, 206
Pollock, Frederick, legal historian: 419
Pomerania: 114, 116, 232
Population: 48, 50, 73, 121, 172–73, 199, 230–31, 248, 249
Poulsen, Bjørn, historian: 49, 83, 215, 217, 421
Primogeniture: 79, 290, 320
Prince: 109, 113, 144, 232, 234, 241, 286, 376, 398–99, 401, 405, 407–08
Princess: 266, 271
Punishment: 227, 349, 374

Queen: 44, 58, 63, 70, 74, 119, 134, 177–78, 185, 208, 216, 268, 275, 278, 294, 355, 395

Ragnhild Eriksdatter, princess of Denmark: 112
Ragnhild Magnusdatter, princess of Norway: 64, 115, 270
Ragvald Ingesson: 272
Ragvald, earl: 282–84, 287–88, 293
Ragvald Roundhead: 285
Ralph of Coggeshall, chronicler: 403
Ralph of Dis, chronicler: 378
Ramløse: 231
Randers: 225–26, 234, 239, 247
Ratibor I, Slavic Prince: 232, 234
Ravaging: 195, 380–81, 405
Rebellion: 86, 97, 104, 110, 127–28, 134, 139, 147, 150, 155, 174, 202, 230, 237, 314, 331, 344, 372, 373–79, 381–85, 387, 390–91, 397, 398, 416, 418–19; *see also* revolt

Region: 17–18, 23, 26, 41, 48, 60, 70, 97, 100, 108, 116, 124, 127, 136, 138, 140, 155, 174–75, 194, 208, 215, 219, 221–24, 226–27, 231, 233, 243, 247, 249, 253, 310, 323, 333, 344, 350, 383, 386, 387, 413, 415, 419–20, 424
Reidar Sendemann, magnate: 183, 187, 189, 200, 204
Relative: 19–21, 37, 43, 50, 61, 63, 77, 85, 103, 110, 120, 172, 177–79, 185, 188, 193, 207, 245, 278–79, 283, 291–92, 294–95, 330, 347, 349–50, 352–54, 360–62, 393, 420; *see also* kinship
Retainer: 18, 81, 101, 104, 125, 144, 171, 184, 191, 198, 203, 206, 239; *see also* hirðmenn
Retinue: 43, 46, 113, 114, 130, 140, 142, 149, 153, 172, 177–78, 180, 182, 189, 232, 237, 399; *see also* hirð
Reuter, Timothy, historian: 17
Revenge: 37, 97, 102, 120–22, 125–26, 128, 130, 136, 141, 148, 151–52, 155, 157, 381–82, 401, 407, 419; *see also* vengeance
Revolt: 21, 121, 128, 130, 152–53, 373, 374, 382, 390–92, 398, 417; *see also* rebellion
Ribbungar: 174, 193
Ribe: 108, 109, 117–18, 126, 133, 147, 149, 238, 246, 249
Riber Ulf, magnate: 249
Richard I, king of England: 407
Richard of Devizes, chronicler: 378
Richiza, princess of Poland: 116–17, 286, 287, 297
Rights: 278, 280, 282, 287, 291, 293, 299–300, 312–13, 315, 318, 346, 352, 356, 358–59, 365, 372, 374–76, 391, 401, 403–06, 418–19, 422

Rike, bishop: 149
Ringkøbing: 247
Ringsted: 120, 123–24, 126–27, 150, 229–30, 237–38, 241, 243, 245, 247–48, 293, 421
Risk: 23, 25–26, 45, 56, 80, 123, 192, 203–04, 420
Ritual: 25, 330, 343, 351–52, 355, 357, 359–62, 365–66, 417
Robert de Vere, earl: 407–08
Robert fitz Walter, magnate: 400–01, 406, 408
Robert I, count: 110
Robert II, king of the Franks: 325
Robert of Ely, monk: 151
Robert of Wendover, chronicler: 403
Robert VII of Béthune, magnate: 399
Robert, duke: 375, 381, 387, 390–94
Roger le Bigod, earl: 407
Roger of Howden, chronicler: 330, 378
Roman law: 216, 322, 333
Rome: 105, 144–45, 219, 344, 407, 419
Roskilde: 98, 102, 108–09, 114, 120, 123, 127–28, 130–31, 135–37, 139–40, 142, 144, 146–49, 152, 224, 230–33, 235, 237, 239–41, 243, 245–49, 251, 315, 327, 329
Roskilde Chronicle: 98, 128, 130–31, 139, 140, 142–43, 146–47, 152, 243
Royal burials: 237, 244, 246
Royal manors: 215, 236, 239, 240
Rumour: 112, 125, 180
Rural: 11, 218, 230–31, 236–38, 240, 243, 245, 253
Rus: 113, 144, 297
Russia: 105
Rydjøkul: 231
Rügen: 152
Rygjarbit: 77, 310–11, 320
Rønbjerg: 137, 156

Sacrality: 219, 242, 244
Sada-Gyrd Bardsson, magnate: 58, 69–70
Saer de Quincy, earl: 401, 408
Sarpsborg: 55, 74, 229, 236, 240–43, 247, 249
Saxo Grammaticus, chronicler: 69, 77–78, 98, 103, 105, 109, 112–15, 117–19, 121–30, 132–37, 139, 141–43, 148–49, 151–53, 218, 220, 222–23, 225, 227–31, 235, 237–41, 243–45, 247–51, 253, 267–68, 269, 270, 274–77, 279–80, 296, 311–12, 314–15, 327–28
Saxon: 98, 118, 138–39, 348, 358, 381, 416, 422
Saxony: 112, 138, 348, 357
Scania: 52, 97, 105, 116, 124, 129–30, 139–40, 142–44, 146, 150–51, 153, 172, 220–21, 226–27, 229–30, 233, 239, 241, 245, 276, 311, 314
Scanians: 105, 129, 131, 139, 142–43, 146, 147–48, 314
Schlei river: 113, 137
Schleswig: 52, 108, 112, 118, 120, 133, 136, 138, 147, 149, 150, 151, 157, 232, 238, 239, 246, 247, 248, 314
Scotland: 42, 70
Segmentary opposition: 25, 166–67, 175
Seigneurial: 373
Sejrø: 137, 223
Self, bishop: 149
Seløyene: 232
Settlement: 15, 39, 78, 169, 174, 182, 196–97, 200, 201, 204, 222, 267, 292, 311, 315–17, 331, 402, 406–07
Shame: 19, 122, 135, 136, 377, 380, 389, 399, 405–06

INDEX   443

Ship: 58, 130, 140, 147, 171, 186–88, 204, 221–26, 253, 324, 396
Siege: 19, 133, 137–38, 156, 171, 175, 183, 193, 194, 196, 199, 215, 235, 251, 354, 423
Sigtuna: 147
Sigurd Haraldsson Mouth, king of Norway: 42, 58, 59, 61, 65, 69–71, 73, 76, 85, 179, 281
Sigurd Sigurdsson, magnate: 54
Sigurd Sigurdsson Markusfostre, Norwegian throne heir: 228
Sigurd Magnusson Slembe, heir to the Norwegian throne: 41–43, 57–61, 64–65, 85, 225
Sigurd Magnusson the Crusader, king of Norway: 20, 41–42, 44–47, 54, 56, 64, 71, 74–75, 83–84, 86, 109, 119, 134, 234, 236, 240, 244, 246, 250, 279, 283, 310
Sigurd Ugaeve, Norwegian throne heir: 225
Simon Skalp, magnate: 63
Skagerrak: 52
Skanør: 172, 226
Skien: 247
Skjalm, clan: 102, 124, 152
Skjalm Hvide, magnate: 102–03, 112
Skule Bardsson, earl and king of Norway: 20, 167, 174, 241, 315–16, 331
Slagelse: 238, 243, 247
Slangerup: 234, 238, 247
Småland: 116
Snorre Sturlason, magnate: 43, 156, 217, 219, 221, 224, 225, 227–29, 233–34, 236, 239–42, 244, 246–47, 279, 310–11, 317, 324, 326–28, 331–32
Sogn: 58, 81
Spatial practice: 218–19
Saint-Étienne abbey: 275
Stamford: 383–85

States: 48, 54–55, 84, 152, 172, 182, 196, 202–03, 241, 253, 265, 267–69, 274, 276, 279, 294, 310, 313, 326, 327, 331, 350, 373, 404, 413, 420
Stavanger: 56, 170, 183, 197, 247, 324
Stenkil family: 109, 274, 277, 279–80, 284–90, 293, 294
Stephan, archbishop: 293
Stephen Langton, archbishop: 400, 402
Stephen, king of England: 12, 75, 328, 371–72, 374–75, 381, 394–98, 402
Stiklestad: 49, 55
Store Heddinge: 247
Strickland, Matthew, historian: 191, 195
Stronghold: 137, 139, 168, 249, 383
Ståreim: 185
Succession: 11, 16, 18, 23, 68, 76, 79, 101, 103–04, 106, 110, 112, 118–20, 144, 146, 153, 155, 188, 216, 275, 278, 284, 289, 293, 296, 299, 320, 327, 344, 375, 398
Suetonius, chronicler: 125
Support: 15–16, 19, 44–47, 50–51, 53–54, 56, 59–61, 63–66, 68, 71–72, 77–78, 101, 104–05, 108, 110, 116–17, 121, 125, 128, 131, 133–34, 136, 139, 141–42, 145–46, 150, 152, 154, 156, 171–73, 175, 185–86, 188, 194, 207, 230, 244, 279, 282–83, 287–88, 290, 293, 311, 314–17, 327, 346–47, 349, 352, 359–60, 363–64, 374, 387–88, 391, 395, 397–400, 404, 407, 417, 419, 423
Surprise attack: 143, 146, 155, 186, 187, 194

Surrender: 133, 169, 196, 321, 329, 343, 354, 355, 357, 359–62, 365, 366, 417
Svealand: 116
Svend Aggesen, chronicler: 98, 102–03, 121, 129, 137, 152
Svend Alfivason, king of Norway: 49
Svend Estridsen, king of Denmark: 52, 75, 78, 104–07, 110, 122–23, 179, 222, 228, 233, 237, 239, 245, 271, 274, 276
Svend Grathe, king of Denmark: 249, 296
Svend, prince of Denmark: 106
Svend Tjugeskjegg, king of Denmark: 77
Svendborg: 250
Sverker the Elder, king of Sweden: 75, 280, 285, 293–96
Sverker the Younger, king of Sweden: 288
Sverker family: 284–85, 289, 295
Sverre Sigurdsson, king of Norway: 81, 83, 165–67, 169, 173, 181, 188, 195, 199, 203, 204, 223, 228, 232, 237, 244, 246, 250, 297, 309, 316, 320
Sverresborg: 250
Sverris saga: 83, 176, 183, 192, 221
Switching sides: 156, 194, 195, 200, 207
Sýslumaðr: 183, 185, 197, 200, 329
Søborg: 238, 247, 250–51
Søderup: 237
Sønderjylland: 237
Sørum: 231

Tacitus, chronicler: 414
Taylor, Louisa, historian: 82
Theodoricus Monachus, chronicler: 20, 83
Thing, thingmen: 18–19, 84, 121, 124, 127–28, 153, 227–31, 234, 237, 242–44, 323, 327–28; *see also* assembly
Thomas Hobbes, philosopher: 190
Thora, concubine: 270
Thord, bishop: 133, 147
Tittelsnes: 204
Tjostolv Alason, magnate: 58, 60, 70
Tommarp: 247
Tora Joansdatter, queen of Norway: 64
Tora Magnusdatter, princess of Norway: 64, 65
Tore Gudmundsson, archbishop: 182, 196, 198, 202, 324
Torgrim Torsteinsson, magnate: 66
Town: 15, 18–19, 23, 55, 74, 107–08, 112–14, 117, 123, 127, 133, 137–39, 142, 149, 155–56, 170, 187, 194, 215, 217–18, 223, 225, 229–51, 253, 319, 324, 383–85, 407, 421, 422, 423
Townsmen, townpeople: 15, 19, 45, 53, 58, 120, 123, 133, 149, 157, 196, 197, 230, 383, 385, 417
Transmitters of power: 265–66, 290, 292, 298–99
Treason: 137, 141, 230, 322, 372–73, 376–77, 387, 388, 390, 393
Trondheim: 48, 56, 65, 69–70, 77–78, 83, 184, 221–23, 226, 233, 235–36, 239, 240–41, 243–44, 246–49, 251, 310
Trugund family: 102–03, 105, 107
Trund family: 134, 151, 153
Trøndelag: 58–59, 70, 166, 169, 173, 179–80, 182–83, 202, 221, 227, 310, 324, 326, 331
Tyranny: 152, 189
Tønder: 247
Tønsberg: 41, 46, 74, 169, 177, 188, 224–25, 228–29, 232–33, 240–41, 246–47, 251, 316, 324, 326

Ubbe, prince of Denmark: 105
Ubbe, son-in-law of King Niels: 108, 115, 119, 141, 276
Ulkil, bishop: 149
Ulvhild Hakonsdatter, queen of Sweden and Denmark: 140–41, 281, 285–86, 293, 295
Uppland: 221
Uppsala: 238, 287
Urnehoved: 150

Valdemar the Great, king of Denmark: 52, 69, 77–79, 99, 134, 165, 185, 208, 222–23, 228–30, 234, 238–40, 244–45, 250, 253, 282–83, 293, 296, 311–12, 314–15, 327–28
Varde: 247
Varnhem abbey: 295, 296
Vartislav I, duke: 114
Vassal: 45, 372, 406
Veizlr: 48, 53, 65, 241
Vejle: 247
Vengeance: 25, 121, 122, 139, 193, 317, 344, 350, 355, 363, 377, 380, 382, 384, 385, 403–07; see also revenge
Vest-Agder: 52
Vestfold: 232
Vestlandet: 70, 77, 221, 240
Viborg: 105, 108–09, 124, 137–38, 149, 225, 227–30, 234–35, 238, 243, 245–47
Viby: 292
Victory: 25, 54–55, 57, 60, 81, 137, 149–50, 169, 173, 196, 204, 206–07, 280, 293–94, 392
Vidkun Jonsson, magnate: 69
Viken: 48, 51–54, 58, 64–65, 69, 70, 77, 166, 168–71, 173–74, 185–87, 221, 224, 226, 228–29, 231, 240, 310–11, 316, 324, 326

Violence: 19–20, 26, 50, 83–84, 86, 123, 154, 173, 190, 205, 217, 235–37, 280, 290, 318, 343–44, 350, 353, 365–66, 374, 377, 380, 384, 388, 393, 413, 415–19
Vitskøl abbey: 295
Volodar, prince of Minsk: 286
Vordingborg: 238, 250
Vreta abbey: 291
Vä: 247, 276
Vä Church: 276
Værebro: 139, 143, 225, 233
Värmland: 297, 321
Västergötland: 284–85, 289, 295, 321

Wace, chronicler: 379, 381, 387–90, 392–93, 397, 408
Wagrians: 114, 133
War: 11, 13–14, 17, 20–23, 25–26, 37, 38, 50–51, 73, 79, 85, 97–102, 108, 121–22, 131, 136–39, 142, 147, 149–51, 154–55, 157, 166, 168, 172, 174, 186, 191, 201, 204, 206, 208, 215, 221, 223–24, 226, 233, 236, 253, 280, 296, 310, 318, 322–23, 333–34, 343–44, 371–72, 378–88, 390, 392–99, 401–08, 419, 422
Warbands: 11, 156, 414
Wealth: 16, 23, 45, 54, 60, 81, 84, 101, 107, 114, 154, 157, 203, 234, 248, 268–70, 275–77, 294, 311, 317, 387, 389, 416
Weber, Max, sociologist: 16
Weiler, Björn, historian: 18
Wendish: 108, 113–14, 144, 152, 234, 248
Wends: 52
White, Stephen D., historian: 18, 121, 343, 371, 414
William de Briouse, magnate: 400
William de Mandeville, earl: 408

William I, king of England: 381–82, 386–90
William II, king of England: 375, 381, 386–88, 390–93, 404
William Marshal, regent: 398
William of Malmesbury, chronicler: 378, 387
William of Newburgh, chronicler: 204, 378
William the Conqueror, king of England: 75
William, abbot: 291
Women: 21, 61, 64, 84, 85, 106, 109, 216, 231, 265–66, 268, 274, 276–79, 284–85, 287–92, 294, 296–300, 329, 399, 415

York: 383, 398

Zealand: 52, 97, 102, 109, 112, 114, 115, 119, 120, 123, 124, 125, 126, 128, 129, 130, 135, 137, 138, 139, 140, 142, 143, 146, 149, 152, 153, 218, 226, 227, 229, 230, 231, 232, 233, 235, 241, 247, 248, 249, 250, 253, 312, 314, 315

Æilnoth of Canterbury, chronicler: 227

Øresund: 52, 143, 220, 226, 234, 247
Östergötland: 284–85, 289, 290, 293, 295

Åhus: 239
Aalborg: 60, 185, 225, 246, 247
Aarhus: 223, 233, 238, 246–47

Comparative Perspectives on Medieval History

All volumes in this series are evaluated by an Editorial Board, strictly on academic grounds, based on reports prepared by referees who have been commissioned by virtue of their specialism in the appropriate field. The Board ensures that the screening is done independently and without conflicts of interest. The definitive texts supplied by authors are also subject to review by the Board before being approved for publication. Further, the volumes are copyedited to conform to the publisher's stylebook and to the best international academic standards in the field.

Titles in Series

The Cult of Saints and Legitimization of Elite Power in East Central and Northern Europe up to 1300, ed. by Grzegorz Pac, Steffen Hope, and Jón Viðar Sigurðsson